Middle School Mathematics

Mathematical Reasoning™ products available in print or eBook form.

Beginning 1 • Beginning 2
Level A • Level B • Level C • Level D • Level E
Level F • Level G • Understanding Pre-Algebra
Understanding Algebra I • Understanding Geometry
Grades 2-4 Supplement • Grades 4-6 Supplement
Middle School Supplement (Grades 7-9)

Written by
Terri Husted

Edited by
Patricia Gray

THE CRITICAL THINKING CO.™
www.CriticalThinking.com
Phone: 800-458-4849 • Fax: 541-756-1758
1991 Sherman Ave., Suite 200 • North Bend • OR 97459
ISBN 978-1-60144-909-2

Printed in China by Imago (Feb. 2018)

Introduction

Understanding Pre-Algebra teaches and develops the math concepts and critical thinking skills necessary for success in Algebra I and future mathematics courses at the high school level. It was written with the premise that students cannot problem solve or take leaps of reasoning without understanding the concepts and elements that lead to discovery. My philosophy of math, after 35 years of teaching, is that understanding leads to confidence and confidence gives students the resolve to succeed in higher level mathematics rather than fear it.

This book is standards-based, but what makes this book different from other pre-algebra books is that it organizes concepts in a logical fashion, stressing practice and critical thinking. It avoids the mistakes—found in many other math books—of trying to teach new concepts before students receive the prerequisite skills and practice necessary for success. The concepts are presented clearly and in connection to other concepts. Math vocabulary is very important to success in higher mathematics. A glossary of important terms is provided.

Word problems are taught by using charts and tables, stressing the importance of translation. Students fail at word problems because they are not given strategies to solve them. Throwing a bunch of word problems together, as it's often done in many math classrooms, and letting students "think" through how to solve them is not teaching critical thinking. This sink or swim approach contributes to the common claim that "math is my worse subject."

The chapter on Polynomials only presents monomial work. Being a pre-algebra course, it's my strong belief that the more students understand the rules of exponents and work with monomials, the better prepared they will be to understand the polynomials chapter in *Understanding Algebra I*, which is so important for future courses. However, the chapters on Functions, Transformations, and Probability and Statistics do cover some topics that later appear in Algebra I. These chapters serve as foundation chapters to help the student truly understand the meaning of a "function," the difference between "permutations and combinations," and why some statistical graphs are different than others. Those concepts are often brushed over in high school and a preview of those concepts in this book are helpful to students.

I had a student my first year of teaching 8th grade who said: "I stopped liking math when I failed to understand division of fractions back in Grade 4." That remark taught me the importance of making topics clear and simple. *Understanding Pre-Algebra* will give students the keys to tackle higher level mathematics!

Dedications: For my grandson Paulo who is truly the math whiz in our family. Thank you to Bob Huckle for working out many problems and offering suggestions.

Table of Contents

Chapter 1

Family of Numbers

Numbers are the tools used for counting and doing operations, so it's important to know how different families of numbers are related. Let's get started with the numbers you first learned to count with, the Natural (Counting) numbers. These will be written in set notation using braces {}. Think of a set as a collection or family.

The Natural (Counting) numbers is the set: {1, 2, 3, 4, ...}.

If you add the number 0 to the counting numbers, you get the set of Whole numbers.

The Whole numbers is the set: {0, 1, 2, 3, 4, ...}.

Can you see that every member (or element) of the set of Natural numbers is in the set of Whole numbers? The set of Natural numbers is called a subset of the set of Whole numbers, since every member of the Natural numbers can also be found in the Whole number set.

Now, if you take the whole numbers and their "opposites," a new set called the Integers is created.

The Integers is the set: {..., −4, −3, −2, −1, 0, 1, 2, 3, 4, ...}.

Notice it's infinite in both directions. Also, there are no fractions or decimals in these sets.

The opposite of 0 is 0. And, it's also important to remember that 0 is NOT positive or negative. Zero is neutral.

There are additional families of numbers.

The Even numbers is the set: {0, 2, 4, 6, 8, ...}.

The Odd numbers is the set: {1, 3, 5, 7, 9, ...}.

Remember even numbers are numbers that when divided by 2 have no remainder (they are divisible by 2). A negative number, for example, −8, is technically even, since when −8 is divided by 2, there is no remainder.

Prime numbers are whole numbers that have only two factors, one and itself. Notice that the number 1 is not a prime. The first prime is 2.

The Prime numbers is the set: {2, 3, 5, 7, 11, 13, 17, etc.}.

Around 200 B.C., a Greek mathematician named Eratosthenes developed a method of finding prime numbers called the Sieve of Eratosthenes. You may have learned his method in elementary school. Mathematicians have been studying prime numbers since that time, raising questions such as: Is the set of prime numbers an infinite set? Are there infinite numbers of twin primes (two units apart)? Examples are 3 and 5, 5 and 7, and 11 and 13.

Some numbers such as 51 and 57 "look" like prime numbers but are not. Prime numbers are important because they will help you factor, which is an important tool in algebra. Review the divisibility rules on the next page to help you determine if a number might be prime or not.

Positive numbers that are not prime are called Composite numbers.

Important Divisibility Rules

A number is divisible by	IF
2	the number is even.
3	you add the digits and the sum is divisible by 3.
5	it ends in 5 or 0.
9	you add the digits and the sum is divisible by 9
10	it ends in 0.
4	the last two digits form a number that is divisible by 4.
8	the last three digits form a number that is divisible by 8.

Practice

1. Why is 0 an even number? (Show that when 0 is divided by 2 there is no remainder.)

2. Are the Even integers a subset of the Integers? Explain your thinking.

____

____

3. The integers −5 and 5 are called "opposites." Another term for "opposite" is additive inverse.

   a. What is the additive inverse of 10? ______

   b. What is the additive inverse of −100? ______

   c. If $-x + x = 0$, what can you say about x and $-x$? ________________

   ____

4. True or False?

   ______ a. The number 0 is a whole number.

   ______ b. The set of Natural numbers is a subset of the Integers.

   ______ c. The number 1 is NOT prime.

   ______ d. All the prime numbers are odd.

   ______ e. All even numbers are divisible by 2.

5. Show why 51 and 57 are not prime numbers. Explain your thinking.

   ____

   ____

6. Why does the set of Primes end in "etc." while the other infinite sets use "..."? Explain your thinking.

   ____

   ____

   ____

7. Determine if these numbers are divisible by 2, 3, 4, 5, 9, or 10.

   a. 300 ____________________

   b. 1,824 ____________________

   c. 97 ____________________

   d. 5,925 ____________________

   e. 10,911 ____________________

8. Joan said that 27 cannot be divided by 2. Is she right? Explain your thinking.

____

____

____

9. In mathematics there is a property called the fundamental theorem of arithmetic which states that any integer greater than 1 can be rewritten by a unique product of Prime numbers. A prime factorization rewrites the number using only prime factors.

Example:

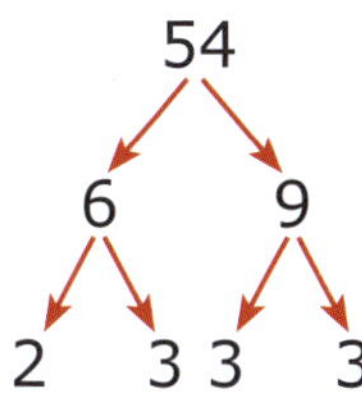

So $54 = 2 \bullet 3 \bullet 3 \bullet 3$
or $54 = 2 \bullet 3^3$

a. Find the prime factorization of ... 360.

____

b. Find the prime factorization of ... 1,000.

____

1 is not used when doing a prime factorization, because 1 is not prime.

10. List three sets of "twin primes."

____

____

____

The RATS!

When you take our set of Integers and add fractions and decimals (only the decimals that stop or repeat) you create a new very important set called the Rational numbers (RATS). Since it's impossible to list all the fractions and decimals in a set (as you would in a roster), you use a description (called a rule).

A rational number is any number that can be written as a fraction $\frac{p}{q}$ (p and q are integers), and where the denominator is not 0.

Every fraction can be written as a decimal that either stops (terminates) or repeats.

Be very careful when you use a calculator to divide two numbers. For example: 13 divided by 61 equals 0.21311475409; do not assume this decimal stops just because your calculator screen cannot display the rest of the numbers that follow. Also do NOT assume the answer has no pattern. This decimal will repeat because every fraction when changed to a decimal will terminate or repeat.

A very important set is the set of Perfect Squares. It is a subset of the Whole numbers.

The Perfect Squares is the set: {1, 4, 9, 16, 25, 36, 49, ...}

When you square a number, you are multiplying the number by itself. So 8 • 8 = 64. You can say the square root of 64 or = $\sqrt{64}$ = 8. Finding the square root of 64 is the same as asking: What number (singular) times itself is 64?

If someone asks you what number times itself is 5, you can only get an approximation for the answer. It's about 2.2360679775 (using a calculator). The answer does not end AND does not repeat. There are many decimals that do not terminate AND do not repeat. These numbers are called Irrational numbers. A number such as π (PI), which you've used to find the circumference and area of circles, is irrational. So is the square root of any number that is not a perfect square.

When you put together the set of Rational numbers and the set of Irrational numbers, you create the set of Real numbers. Real numbers are all the numbers you can find on the number line.

Practice

1. List the next four perfect squares after 64. _______ _______ _______ _______

2. Which of these numbers is NOT a member or element of the set of Rationals? Explain your thinking.

$$\frac{3}{5}, -3, .065, \sqrt{7}$$

____

____

____

3. Explain to a friend that the mixed fraction $3\frac{1}{2}$ fits the definition of a rational number. Explain your thinking.

____

____

4. Explain to a friend that a whole number, such as 8, fits the definition of a Rational number. Explain your thinking.

____

____

5. Which of the following graphs represent Real numbers? Explain your thinking.

a. 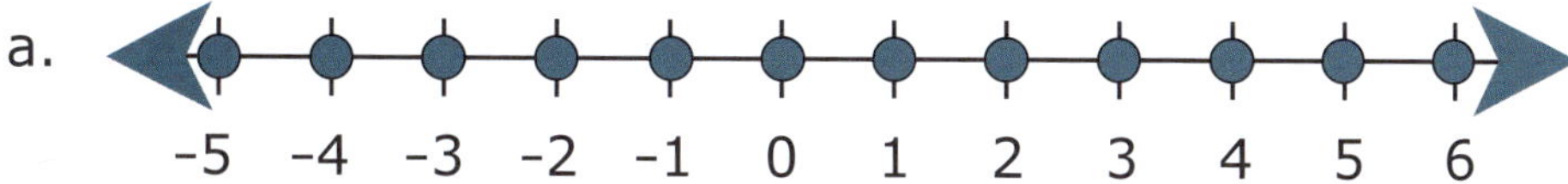

b. 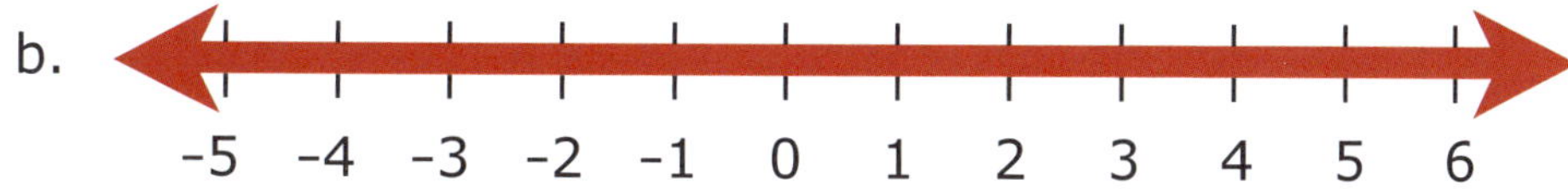

____

____

6. A student changed $\frac{22}{7}$ to a decimal on her calculator and got an answer of 3.14286. The student believed she had just proven that a fraction can actually be changed to an irrational number. Is the student's reasoning correct? Explain your thinking.

____

____

____

7. Which of the following words can be used to describe the number 0.

Odd, Even, Whole, Integer, Prime, Natural,

Perfect Square, Rational, Irrational, Real

____

____

____

____

8. Finish the following concept map.

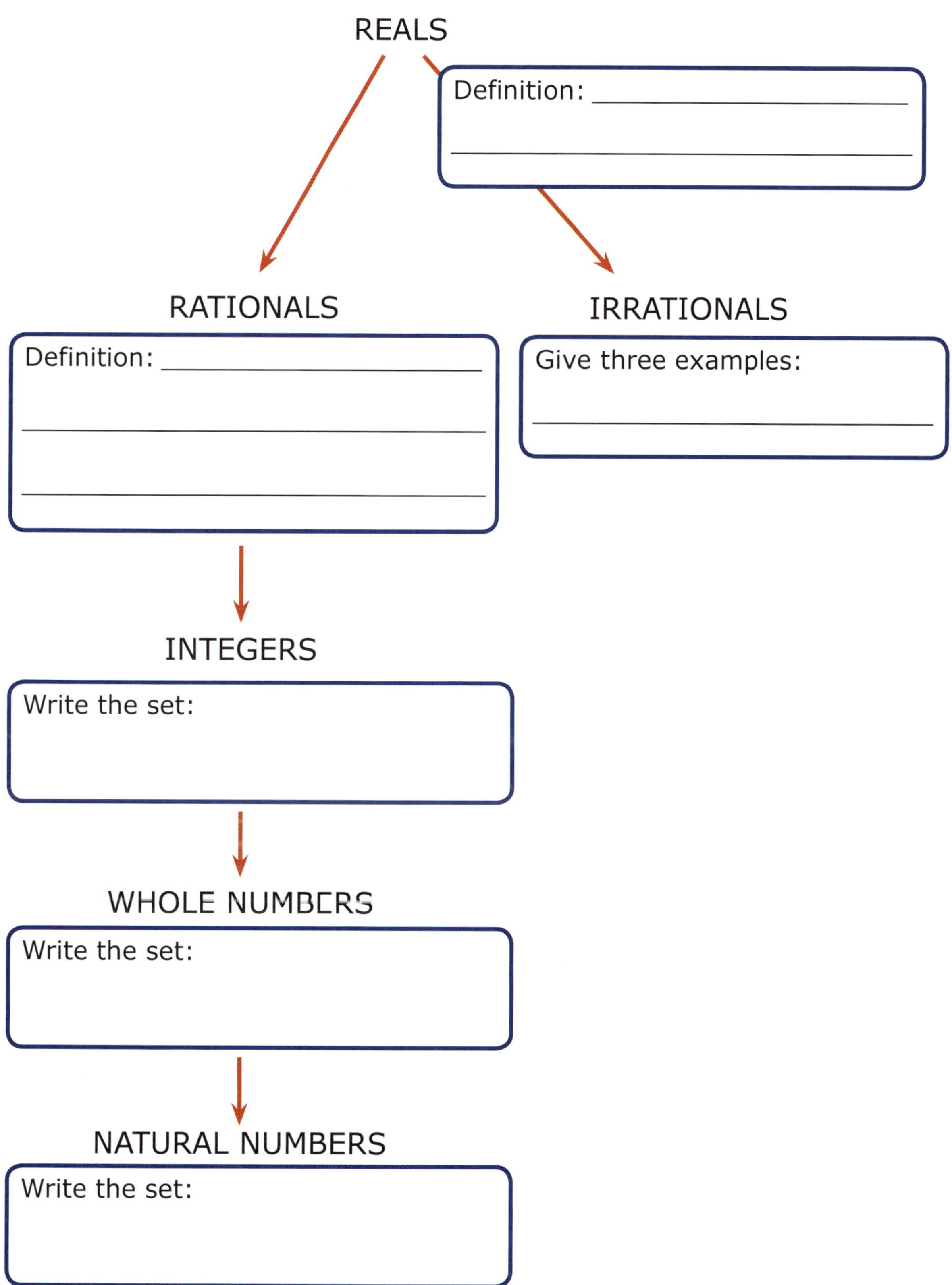

Important Factors

Problem-solving always involves critical thinking, but people cannot problem solve if they lack the basic facts. It's important to know your times tables. These additional factors are also handy to know. Those you can do in your head (such as 3 X 13 or 4 X 11) are not included. You can turn these into small flash cards and quiz your friends and family for fun! The • will be used for the "X" multiplication sign from now on.

Number	Factors	Number	Factors
32	2 • 16	**34**	2 • 17
36	2 • 18 3 • 12	**38**	2 • 19
42	3 • 14	**45**	3 • 15
48	3 • 16 4 • 12	**51**	3 • 17
52	2 • 26 4 • 13	**54**	2 • 27 3 • 18
56	2 • 28 4 • 14	**57**	3 • 19

58	2 • 29	**60**	4 • 15 5 • 12
64	4 • 16	**65**	5 • 13
68	4 • 17	**70**	2 • 35 5 • 14
72	2 • 36 3 • 24 4 • 18	**75**	3 • 25
76	2 • 38 4 • 19	**78**	2 • 39 6 • 13
80	5 • 16	**81**	3 • 27
84	3 • 28	**85**	5 • 17
87	3 • 29	**90**	2 • 45 5 • 18 6 • 15

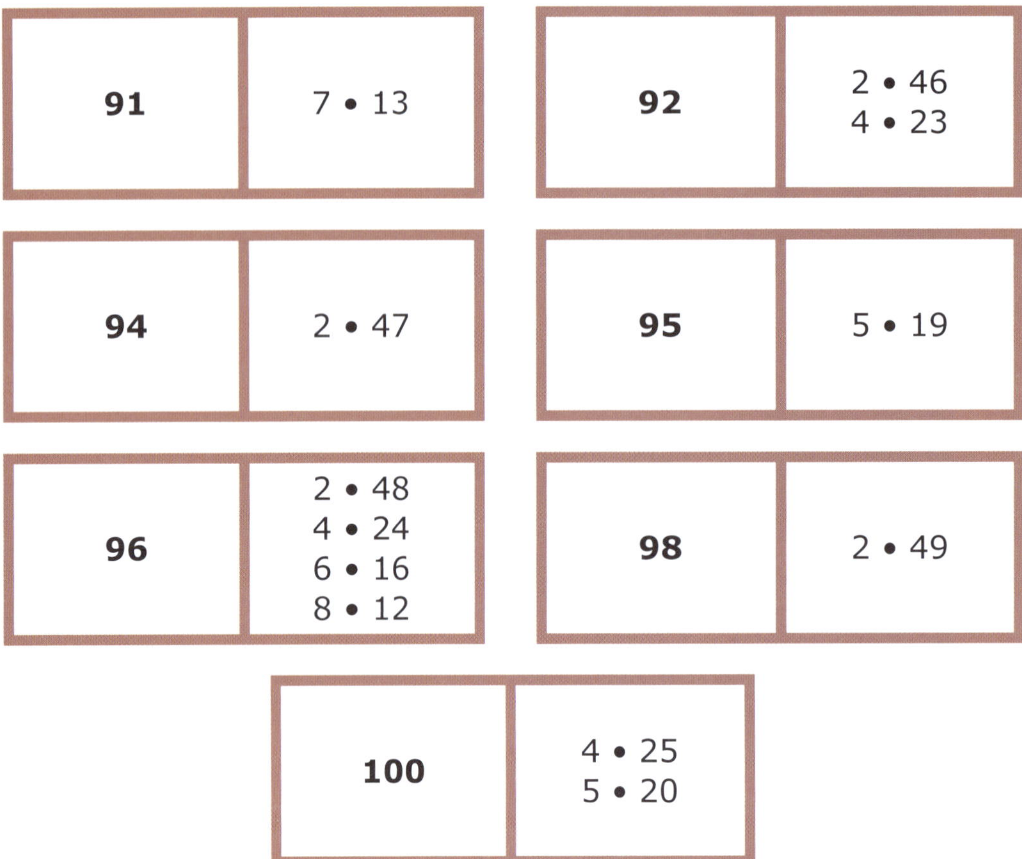

Number	Factors
91	7 • 13
92	2 • 46 4 • 23
94	2 • 47
95	5 • 19
96	2 • 48 4 • 24 6 • 16 8 • 12
98	2 • 49
100	4 • 25 5 • 20

While some people may tell you that using a calculator will solve all your problems, remember that the calculator is only as good as the user. Refer to the Important Factors when doing a prime factorization. In first-year algebra, many of the facts shown will become very useful when you learn factoring.

Never memorize anything you do not understand. And even though Einstein said: "Never memorize anything you can look up," basic math facts, especially knowing your multiplication tables, will help you spend more time doing critical thinking.

"Never memorize something that you can look up."

Albert Einstein

Chapter 1 Review

Choose the letter of the best words to describe these sets.

______	1. {0, 2, 4, 6, 8, ...}	a. Odd numbers
______	2. {0, 1, 2, 3, 4, 5, ...}	b. Integer numbers
______	3. {1, 3, 5, 7, 9, ...}	c. Whole numbers
______	4. {..., −3, −2, −1, 0, 1, 2, ...}	d. Perfect square numbers
______	5. {1, 4, 9, 16, 25, 36, ...}	e. Even numbers

6. Give three examples of real numbers from three different sets and state why the numbers you chose are real.

____

____

____

____

7. State what you think these numbers have in common (besides that they are odd numbers).

   169, 225, 289

____

____

8. Write the prime factorization of these numbers.

   a. 125 ______________________________

   b. 72 ______________________________

   c. 92 ______________________________

   d. 960 ______________________________

9. True or False?

______ a. All fractions and decimals are rational numbers.

______ b. Rationals and Irrationals make up the set of Real numbers.

______ c. All square roots are irrational numbers.

______ d. The fraction $\frac{9}{0}$ is an example of a rational number.

______ e. 1 is prime number.

______ f. 2 is a prime number.

______ g. 0 is an even number.

10. Are these numbers prime? If not, list two numbers that divide the number evenly.

a. 75 ________________________________

b. 91 ________________________________

c. 97 ________________________________

d. 111 ________________________________

e. 120 ________________________________

11. Are these numbers rational (RAT) or irrational (IRRAT)?

a. .7 ______________

b. −4.25 ______________

c. $\frac{5}{6}$ ______________

d. $.\overline{28}$ ______________

e. $\sqrt{16}$ ______________

f. $\sqrt{7}$ ______________

12. The divisibility rule for 6 states that if a number is divisible by 2 AND 3, then it's also divisible by 6. Pick a number that is divisible by 2 and 3 to show that the number is also divisible by 6.

Chapter 2

Working With Integers

You just learned that the set of Integers includes 0, the positive Whole numbers, and their additive inverses (or opposites). Here's the set of Integers written as a roster (or list): {..., −4, −3, −2, −1, 0, 1, 2, 3, ...}.

Study the graph of the set of Integers below. Notice that dots are used to graph the integers and dark arrows are drawn at each end of the number line to indicate that the set is infinite in both directions.

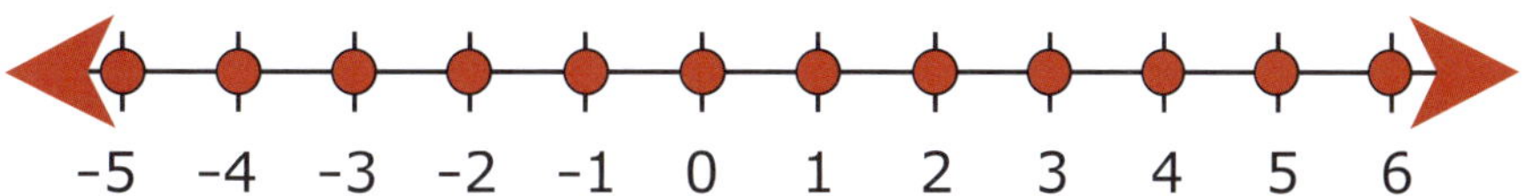

Addition of Integers

When you see the symbol **+** between two numbers, you will be "adding." But keep in mind that addition actually means putting together or combining two numbers.

You've been doing addition of positive integers for a long time. So when you add two positive numbers you will always get a positive number.

Example 1: Add 3 + 2

While you know the sum is 5. Let's see what is happening on the number line. Start at 0 and move to the right (positive direction) 3 units. Then move 2 units to the right (positive direction) to end at 5.

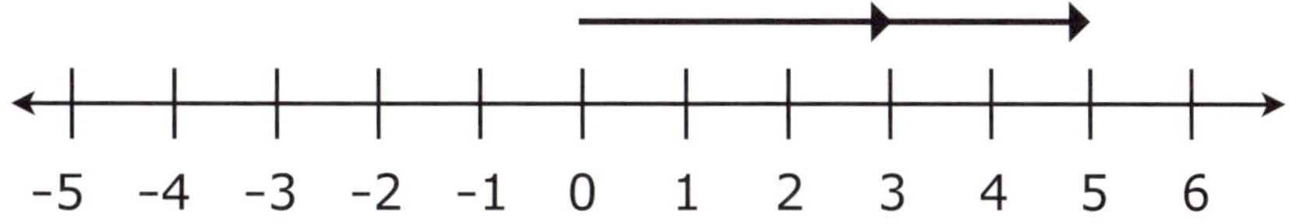

Example 2: Add –3 + (–2)

Parenthesis is used to make the negative number easier to read.

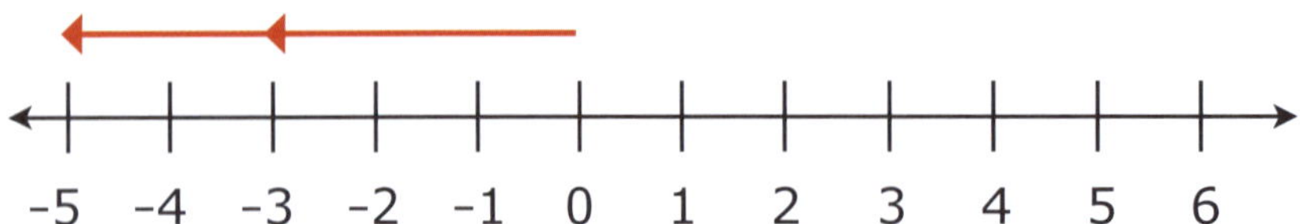

Start at 0. Move left (negative direction) 3 units and then move left again (negative direction) 2 units. The sum is –5.

Take an example that deals with money. If someone loses \$10 at a fair and then loses another \$5, then in total she or he has lost \$15. You can write the expression –\$10 + (–\$5). The sum is –\$15.

Take an example from the weather. If the temperature in Ithaca, NY, is –4º Fahrenheit and then drops another 7º Fahrenheit, you can write the expression –4 + (–7). The sum is –11ºF.

When the signs are the same, either both positive or both negative, add and keep the sign!

Absolute Value

The absolute value of a number is the <u>distance</u> a number is away from zero. The symbol for absolute value is | |. Whatever number is inside the absolute value symbol will be positive. Think of it as the digit without its sign!

Example 1: Find |6|. The absolute value of 6 is 6. The number 6 is 6 units away from 0.

Example 2: Find |–7|. The absolute value of –7 is 7. The number –7 is 7 units from 0.

Example 3: Find |0|. The absolute value of 0 is 0. Zero is 0 units away from itself!

Example 4: Find –|20|. Since the absolute value of –20 is 20, the outside negative sign remains where it is, so the answer is –20.

Even though a number such as –17 is smaller than 17, its distance from 0 is the same. If you understand this concept, then you understand absolute value!

Adding Positive and Negative Integers

Example 1: Add −5 + 8

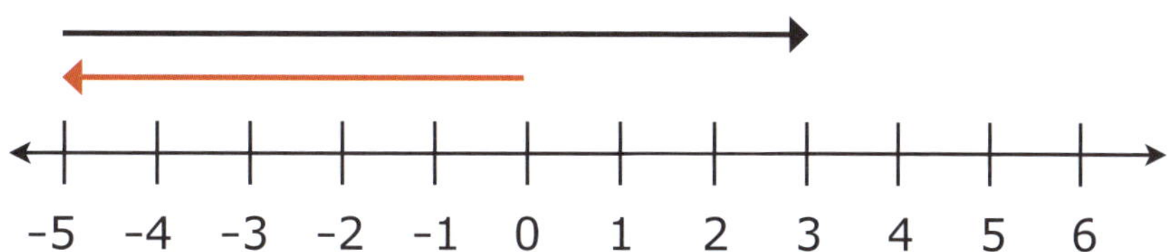

Start at 0. Move left (negative direction) 5 units and then move right (positive direction) 8 units. You end up at positive 3.

Example 2: Add 4 + (−7)

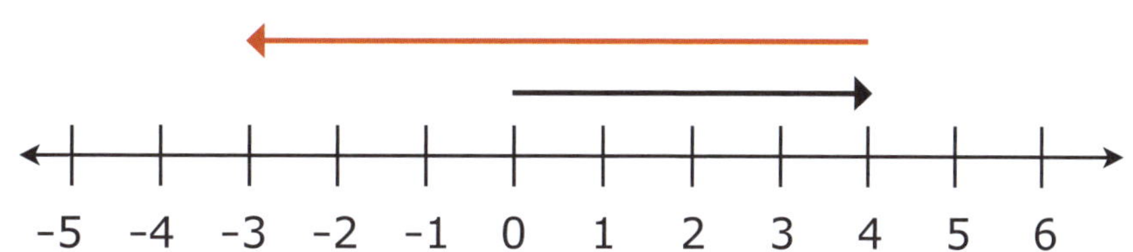

Start at 0. Move right (positive direction) 4 units and then move left (negative direction) 7 units. You end up at −3.

When you're adding and the signs are different, you subtract and take the sign of the larger absolute value. In other words, keep the sign of the larger "digit."

It helps to visualize the problem in another way. Add 4 + (−7), You have:

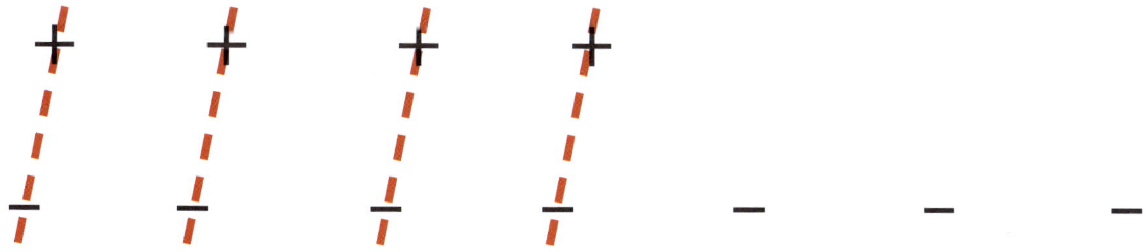

Can you see how you have three negative units left over? This also shows you that when you add 1 + (−1), or −6 + 6, or any number plus its additive inverse you get zero!

Example 3: Find the sum $(-12) + 9 + (-22) + 10$.

$$-34 + 19$$

$$-15$$

A good strategy is to combine the integers with the same sign together, and then find the sum.

Addition of Integers Rules

1. When the signs are the same, add and keep the sign.
2. When the signs different, subtract and keep the sign of the number with the larger absolute value.

Practice Adding Integers

Use a separate sheet of paper if needed.

1. $-90 + 90$
2. $10 + (-10)$
3. $-12 + (-12)$
4. $(-25) + (-25)$
5. $-8 + 10$
6. $0 + (-23)$
7. $(-18) + 9$
8. $(-3) + 83$
9. $|3| + (-83)$
10. $|17|$
11. $|-3|$
12. $-|45|$
13. $-9 + 3 + 5 + (-9)$
14. $10 + (-20) + (-2) + 12$
15. $9 + (-40) + 8 + |40|$
16. $|-4| + (-5) + (-7) + 8 + 2$
17. $|9| + |-9|$
18. $-|-2|$

19. A scuba diver went straight down 15 feet from sea level. Then she went straight up 8 feet from that location. How far down from sea level is she now? Which expression represents what is happening? Find the answer.

a. $15 + (-8)$

b. $-15 + (-8)$

c. $-15 + 8$

d. $15 + 8$

20. Seth was playing football, and on the first play he lost 20 yards. Then on the next play he lost another 5 yards. Write an expression to figure out how many total yards he lost the first two plays. Then find the answer.

____

____

21. The temperature in the village of Frost Hollow located in the state of New York was -19° F at 10 p.m. When Robert woke up at 8 a.m. he noticed that the temperature had dropped another 3°. What was the temperature at 8 a.m.?

____

Use the number line below to find the missing numbers.

22. _____ + 5 = 0

23. 3 + ______ = 0

24. −2 + ______ = −5

25. 5 + ______ = 1

26. −4 + ______ = 3

27. 6 + ______ = −5

28. 4 + ______ = −1

−5 −4 −3 −2 −1 0 1 2 3 4 5 6

Dice Game

Duplicate this page and cut out the templates to make two dice and create a game to practice adding integers.

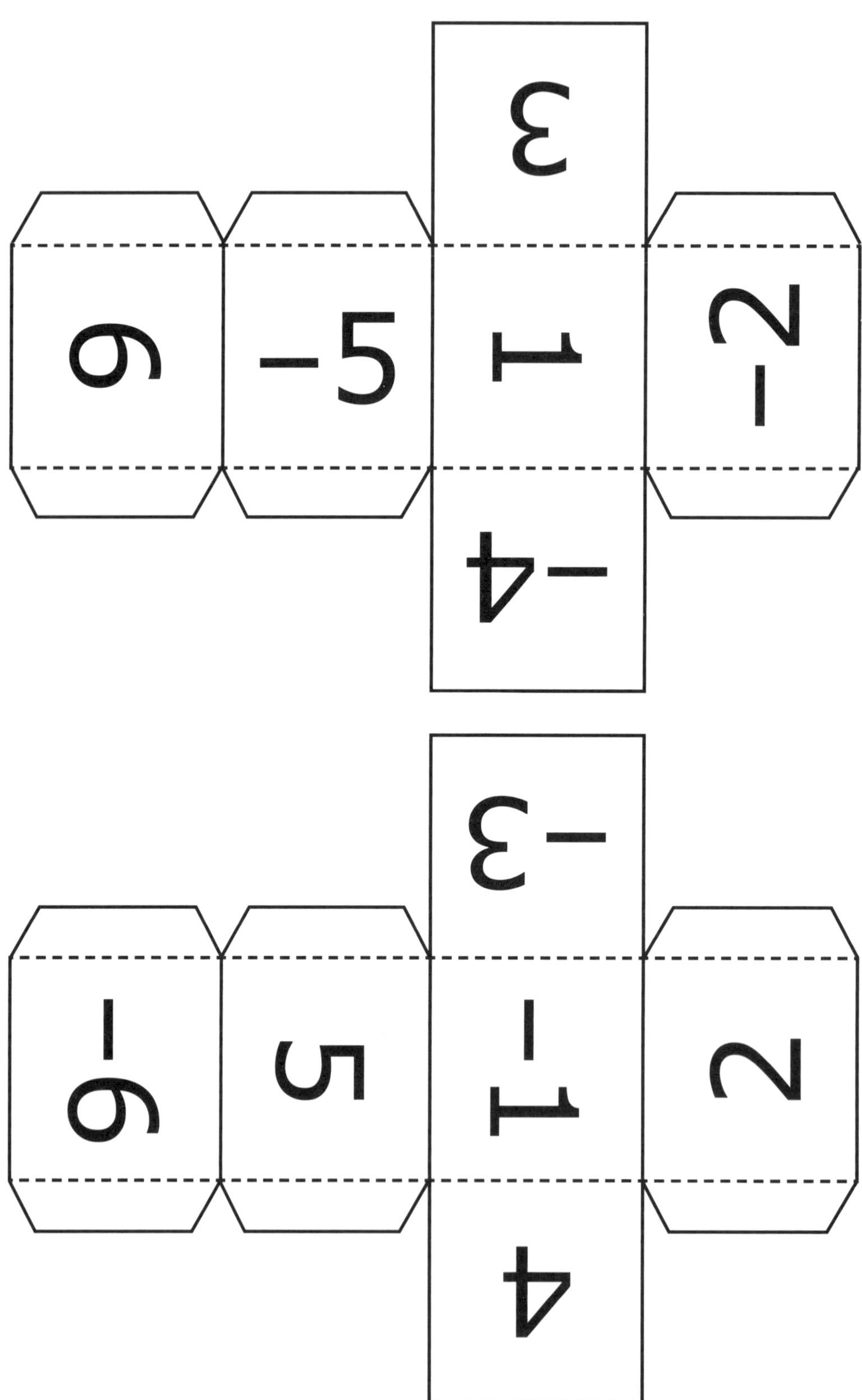

Subtraction of Integers

Subtraction with positive and negative numbers is the same as adding the additive inverse of the number you're subtracting. When you see the subtraction (–) symbol between two numbers, you need to make two changes to your problem. This will turn the problem into an "addition" problem.

Example 1: Subtract: 6 – 5

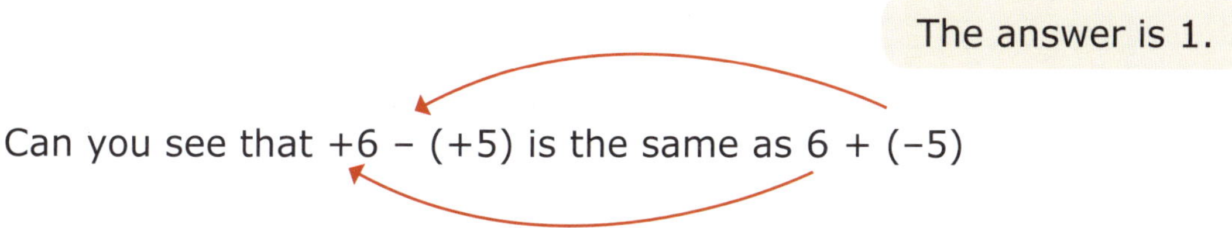

Change the subtraction sign to a plus sign AND then change the 5, which is to the right of the subtraction sign, to a –5. You will then follow the addition of integer rules.

Example 2: Subtract: –6 – (–8)

–6 + (+8)

Make two changes, but do not change the first number.

Change the subtraction sign to a plus sign and then change the (–8) to (+8). This becomes –6 + (+8) which is 2.

Example 3: Find the <u>difference</u>: –9 – 12

Make two changes.

This is the same as –9 + (–12) and the answer is –21.

Think of subtraction as "take away" or "opposite."

Example 4: What is –(–25)?

This can be read as the opposite of –25, so the answer is 25.

You can use the number line to do subtraction of integers, but it takes longer and it's not very efficient when the numbers are large. On the next page, you will see subtraction of integers on the number line to help you visualize what is taking place.

Example 5: Show on the number line why −5 − (−6) is 1.

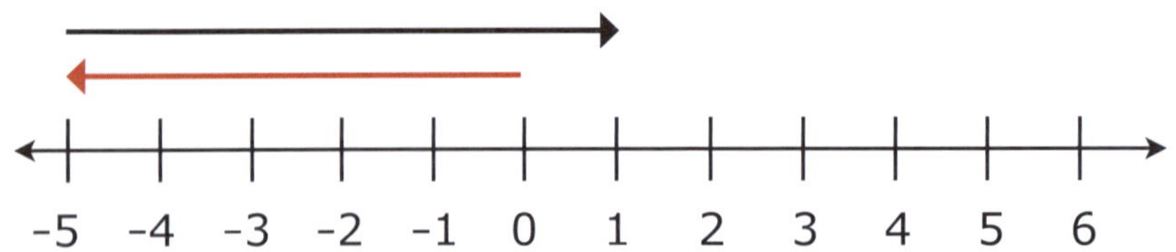

Start at 0 and go down to −5. So instead of adding −6, do the reverse or opposite. This means you will go to the right 6 units from −5 and end up at 1.

Subtraction of Integers Rules

1. Change the subtraction sign to an addition sign.
2. Change the number that follows the subtraction sign to its additive inverse (or opposite).
3. Follow the addition of integers rules.

Practice Subtracting Integers

Use a separate sheet of paper if needed.

1. −8 − (−9)
2. −8 − 9
3. 0 − (−19)
4. 5 − 12
5. −9 − 30
6. 1 − 99
7. −3 − 12
8. 0 − 15
9. 4 − 14
10. −3 − 20
11. 9 − 15
12. 16 − 7
13. −16 − 7
14. 1 − (−23)
15. 10 − (−3)
16. −7 − 7
17. 18 − 9
18. −20 − 24
19. 100 − 200
20. −34 − 34

Treasure Game

You're a pirate looking for treasure. Follow the pirate ship's path. If at the end you get a positive answer, then you win that many gold coins! If your answer is negative, then you are captured by other pirates!

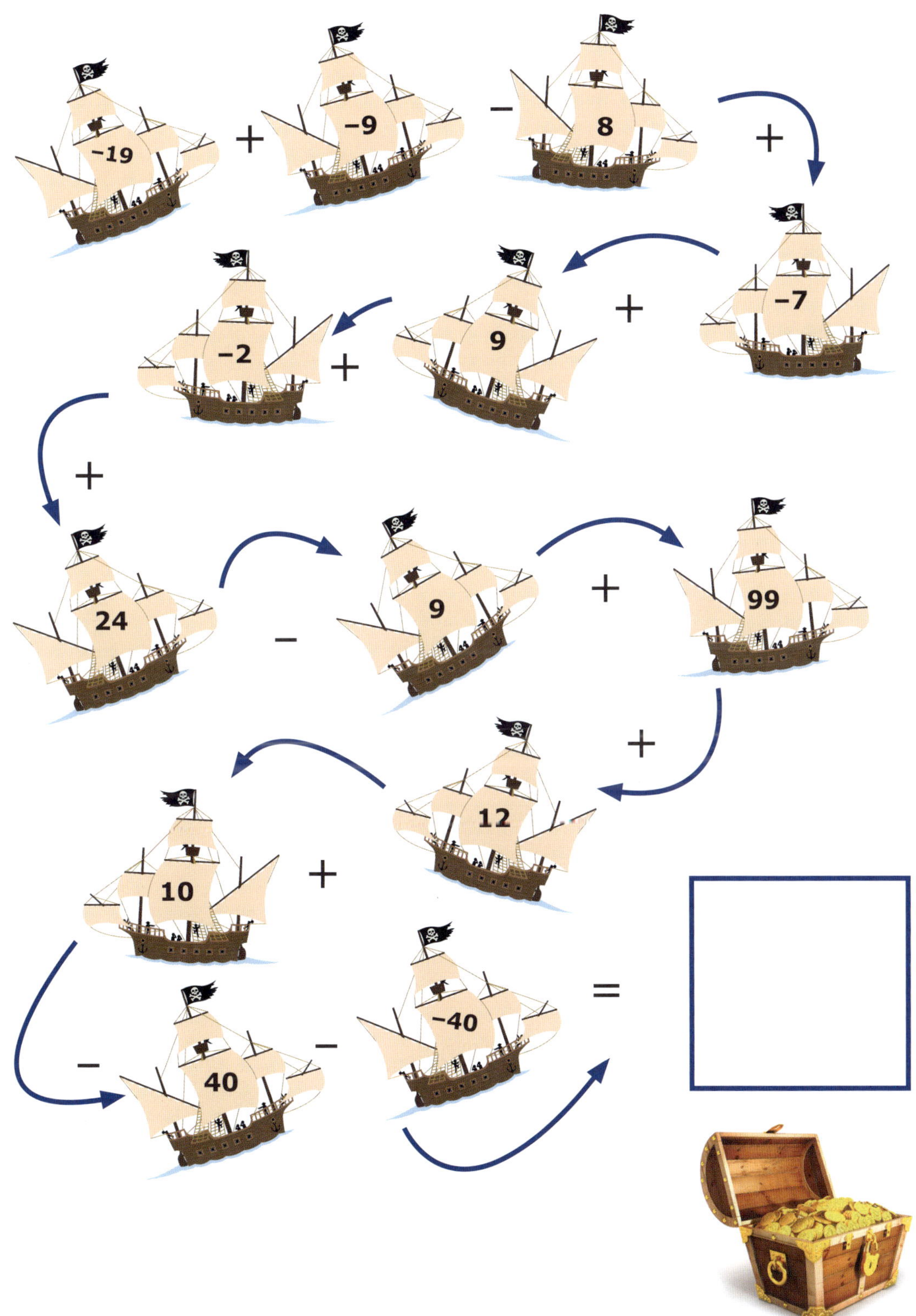

Practice Adding and Subtracting Integers

1. Robert and Paulo were playing a card game. They shuffled a deck of cards. The red cards represented negative numbers, and the black cards represented positive numbers. Robert picked out 5 cards without looking and added the numbers. Paulo picked out 5 cards without looking and added the numbers. Whoever gets the largest sum wins. Who won?

   Robert's cards:

   Paulo's cards:

   Explain your thinking.

   ____

   ____

2. The temperature was 47° F in the morning, and then overnight it went down to –10° F. Which expression represents how to find the difference between the two temperatures? Find the answer.

   a. 47 – 10 c. 47 – (–10)

   b. –10 – 47 d. 10 – 47

   ____

3. Latarsha and her friend, Roland, left school and went in opposite directions. Latarsha went north 10 blocks to her house, and Roland went south 13 blocks to his home. Which of these absolute value expressions represents the distance between their homes? Find the answer. ____________

   a. $10 - |13|$

   b. $13 - |10|$

   c. $|10| + |-13|$

   d. $|13| + (-10)$

4. Use a shorter way to find the answer to these problems. Use a separate sheet of paper if needed.

   a. $-10 + 200 + 10 + (-200)$ __________

   b. $34 + 199 + (-34) + (-199) + 5$ __________

   c. $-(-20) + (-40) + 20 + 40$ __________

   d. $|-14| + 5 - 14 - 5$ __________

   e. $-285 + 410 - 410 + 285 - 199$ __________

   Explain your strategy.

   ____

   ____

Use a separate sheet of paper if needed.

5. $-14 - (-5)$

6. $20 + (-3)$

7. $-23 - 40$

8. $-3 - (-3)$

9. $-10 + (-24)$

10. $-(-5) + (-12)$

11. $0 - (-34)$

12. $0 - 10$

13. $12 - 18$

14. $-2 - 4 - 5$

15. $9 - (-4) + 8$

16. $-80 + (-80)$

17. $56 - 67 + 40$

18. $-70 - (-70)$

Multiplication and Division of Integers

Multiplication is repeated addition. So when you add (−3) five times, (−3) + (−3) + (−3) + (−3) + (−3), it is the same as (−3) • 5. The answer is −15, because 3 • (−5) is (−5) + (−5) + (−5), which is also −15. You can conclude that a negative number times a positive number or a positive number times a negative number is always negative.

Now, look at a negative times a negative. Suppose you had to multiply −3 • −5, you can change the −3 to (−1) • 3 (as shown above), so you can rewrite −5 • −3 as (−1) • 3 • (−5)

(−1) • (−15)

This can read as the opposite of (−15), so the answer is positive 15.

A negative number times a negative number is always positive.

The division rules for dividing integers are the same as for multiplying integers. Let's see why. When you divide a positive number by a positive number the answer is always positive. You can always check your quotient (the answer to division) by multiplying your quotient by your divisor (denominator) to get your dividend (numerator).

$\frac{12}{3} = 4$ The answer is 4, because 4 • 3 = 12.

$\frac{-12}{3} = -4$ The answer is −4, because −4 • 3 = −12.

$\frac{12}{-3} = -4$ The answer is −4, because −4 • −3 = 12.

$\frac{-12}{-3} = 4$ The answer is 4, because 4 • −3 = −12.

Multiplication and Division of Integers Rules

1. When you multiply or divide two numbers with the same sign, the answer is always positive.
2. When you multiply or divide two numbers with different signs, the answer is always negative.

Multiplication can also be written with two parentheses. $(a)(b)$ means a times b.

Example 1: Find the product: $(-5)(6)$

The answer is -30, because a negative number times a positive is always negative.

Example 2: Find the product: $-4 \bullet 5 \bullet -3 \bullet 2 \bullet -1$

A good strategy is to multiply the positive numbers together, $5 \bullet 2 = 10$, then multiply the negative numbers together, $-4 \bullet -3 \bullet -1 = -12$, so $10 \bullet -12 = -120$.

Example 3: Find the quotient: $-100 \div -200$

This is the same as $\frac{-100}{-200}$. The answer will be positive.

Notice this is a proper fraction that reduces to $\frac{1}{2}$.

Example 4: Find the quotient: $\frac{0}{6}$.

The answer is 0. Notice how the answer checks. $\frac{0}{6} = 0$

The answer 0 times 6 (denominator) = 0 (the numerator)

Example 5: Find the quotient: $\frac{6}{0}$.

There is NO answer to this problem. Any answer you choose does not check by multiplication. Also $\frac{0}{0}$ has NO answer.

You cannot divide by zero. The answer is not 0. The answer is the empty set or Ø. There is NO answer.

Working With Exponents

Another way of writing 2 • 2 • 2 • 2 • 2 is to write 2^5. The number 2 is called the base and 5 is called the power or exponent. The exponent tells you how many times the base will be multiplied by itself.

Example 1: Find $(-4)^3$

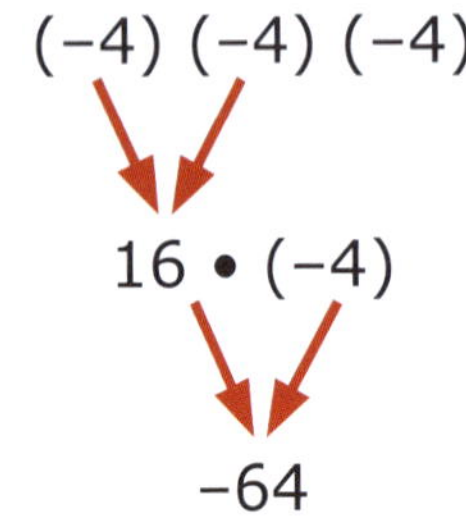

Example 2: Find $(-5)^4$

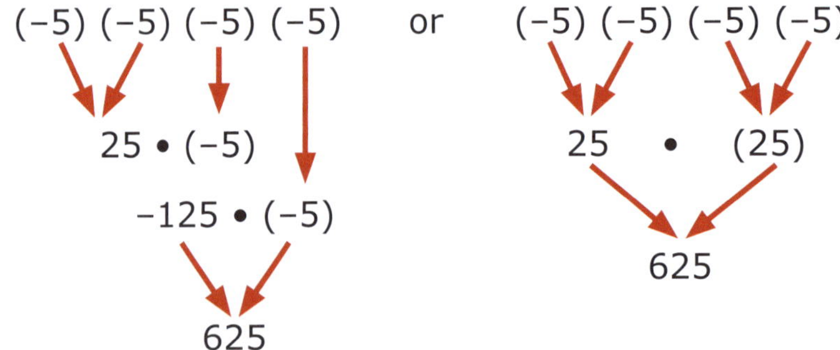

When the base is a negative number, and the exponent is odd, the answer will be negative. If the base is negative and the exponent is even, the answer will be positive.

Practice Multiplication and Division of Integers

Use a separate sheet of paper if needed.

1. $5 \bullet -12$
2. $(-3)(-15)$
3. $-10 \bullet 5 \bullet 10$
4. $(-3)^3$
5. $(-3)^4$
6. $\frac{-78}{2}$
7. $\frac{-57}{-3}$
8. $\frac{0}{9}$
9. $(-1)^{19}$
10. $(19)^1$
11. $-400 \div -100 \div 2$
12. $(-81) \div (-3)$
13. $(-4)^4$
14. $\frac{7}{0}$
15. $\frac{-64}{16}$
16. $(-1)^5$
17. $54 \div (-3)$
18. $(-10)^4$
19. 10^5
20. $\frac{-36}{12}$
21. Nadia thinks that $\frac{0}{0}$ has more than one answer. Explain by using multiplication what Nadia means. (Remember that when 0 is in the denominator, there is still NO answer and you should write Ø. Explain your thinking.

____

____

22. The average record low temperatures in Anchorage, Alaska, are -34°F, -26°F, and -24°F for the months of January, February, and March respectively. What is the average for those winter months? Hint: To find the average, add the quantities and divide by the number of quantities you have.

____

Chapter 2 Review

Use a separate sheet of paper if needed.

1. $9 + (-10)$
2. $10 - 12$
3. $-18 - 20$
4. $0 - 13$
5. $-10 + 3 + (-12)$
6. $-(-23)$
7. $|-9|$
8. $|9|$
9. $6 \bullet 13$
10. $-6 \bullet -13$
11. $72 \div -18$
12. $-72 \div -18$
13. $-2 \bullet 49 \bullet 10$
14. $(-2)^3$
15. $(-2)^4$
16. $(-6)(0)$
17. $\frac{0}{-12}$
18. $34 \div 0$
19. $-94 \div -47$
20. $-7 \bullet -13 \bullet 1{,}000$
21. $(-12)^2$
22. $(-13)^2$
23. $|0|$
24. $-2 \bullet -26$
25. 10^6
26. $(-1)^{20}$
27. Write $-3 \bullet -3 \bullet -3 \bullet -3 \bullet -3$ using an exponent. ______________
28. Write $(-3) + (-3) + (-3) + (-3) + (-3)$ using two factors. ______________
29. Use a good strategy to find the sum of these numbers: $-289 + 500 + (-678) + 289 + (-500)$. Explain your thinking.

____

____

30. Use a good strategy to find the product of these numbers: $(789)(-56)(-900)(435)(0)$. Explain your thinking.

____

____

The Cowboy Story

This is a cool story my college professor, Sr. Paul James, shared with me as a fun way to remember the rules for multiplying and dividing integers.

Cowboys were moving to the West settling new towns. Some were good cowboys (+) and some were bad (–).

Some cowboys came into a town (+), and some then left (–).

Here's the story:

When a good (+) cowboy comes into a town (+), it is good (+) for the town. + • + = +

When a bad (–) cowboy comes into a town (+), it is bad (–) for the town. – • + = –

When a good (+) cowboy leaves a town (–), it is bad (–) for the town. + • – = –

When a bad (–) cowboy leaves a town (–), it is good (+) for the town. – • – = +

Chapter 3

Working With Rational Numbers

The set of Rational numbers is the set of Integers, fractions, terminating decimals, and repeating decimals. The integer rules you just learned apply to the rational numbers, since the integers is a subset of the Rationals.

Adding and Subtracting Rational Numbers

Example 1: Add $-\frac{4}{5} + (-\frac{2}{5})$

Notice that the signs are the same so the answer will be negative. Add the fractions. The denominator is the same for each fraction so it stays the same.

You get $-\frac{6}{5}$ which simplifies to $-1\frac{1}{5}$.

Example 2: Subtract: $-\frac{6}{13} - (-\frac{3}{13})$

Remember subtraction is the same as adding the additive inverse.

First, make two changes. You get $-\frac{6}{13} + (+\frac{3}{13})$. The signs are different, subtract and you get $-\frac{3}{13}$.

When a fraction is negative, write the negative sign in the middle of the fraction. While the fraction $\frac{-3}{13}$ is the same as $\frac{3}{-13}$, the final answer is $-\frac{3}{13}$. Remember the fraction bar means divide. A negative divided by a positive, or a positive divided by a negative, gives a negative answer.

Example 3: Add: 1.06 + (−7.05)

Notice that the signs are different, so you subtract.

$$\begin{array}{r} 7.05 \\ -\ 1.06 \\ \hline 5.99 \end{array}$$

Larger absolute value number goes on top.

The answer is **−**5.99 because you keep the sign of the number with the greater absolute value.

Example 4: Subtract: .093 − 4

Make two changes. .093 + (−4)

$$\begin{array}{r} 4.000 \\ -\ \ .093 \\ \hline 3.907 \end{array}$$

← Larger absolute value number goes on top.

The answer is **−**3.907 because you keep the sign of the larger absolute value number.

Adding and Subtracting Fractions With Different Denominators

Even if you're familiar with adding and subtracting fractions with different denominators, below is a method from a South American student for finding the GCF (Greatest Common Factor) and the LCM (Least Common Multiple). The GCF will help you reduce fractions. The LCM will help you find the LCD, the least common denominator.

It's very important to remember that the LCM or LCD is always one of the numbers you start with or it must be greater.

Factors are numbers that multiply together to give a product. For example, 3 and 4 are factors of 12. The number 12 is divisible by 1, 2, 3, 4, 6 and 12.

Multiples are the numbers you get when you take a number and multiply it by the natural numbers 1, 2, 3, 4, ... For example, the multiples of 12 are: 12, 24, 36, 48, 60, ... When you see the word "multiple" think of the multiplication table.

Example 1: Find the GCF and LCM of 12 and 18.

Write 12 and 18 inside the dividing box below. Write any factor (except 1) that goes into both 12 and 18. For example: Use 2 as your first factor. Divide 12 by 2 and divide 18 by 2. Then keep finding more factors (except 1) until you're done.

$$\begin{array}{c|cc} 2 & 12 & 18 \\ \hline 3 & 6 & 9 \\ \hline & 2 & 3 \end{array}$$

Multiply the outside numbers (left side). 2 • 3 = 6 and that is your GCF.

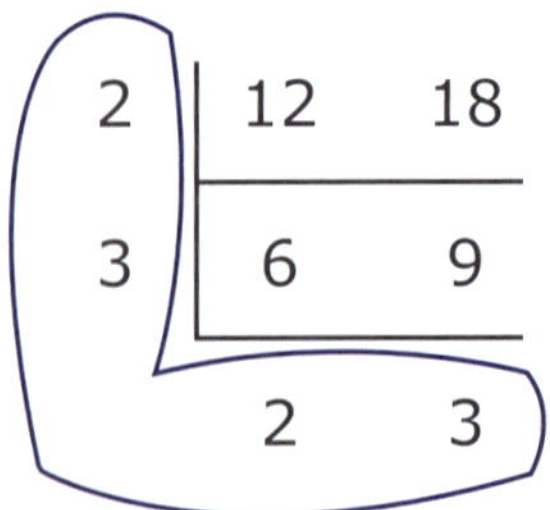

Look at the letter "L" for LCM!

Now multiply all the outside numbers (see L shape above). 2 • 3 • 2 • 3 = 36. That is your LCM.

Remember you can always find the GCF by factoring the two numbers and circling the common factors. To find the LCM of two numbers, list the multiples until you find the LEAST common multiple.

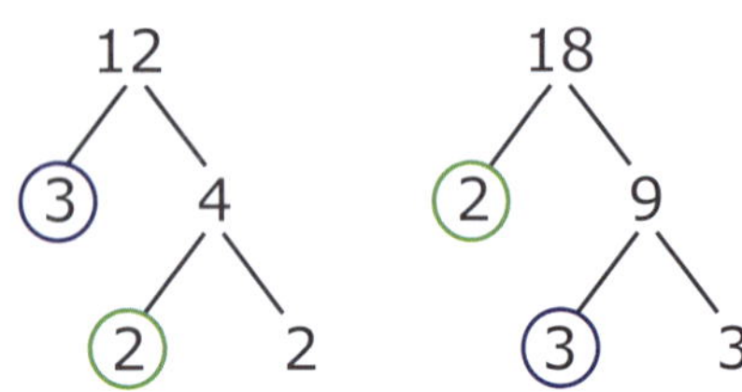

For every pair of factors that appear in both, write it down once. 2 appears in both, and 3 appears in both, so the GCF is 2 • 3 = 6.

Multiples of 12: 12, 24, 36, 48, ... Multiples of 18: 18, 36, 54, ... The LCM is 36.

Practice Adding and Subtracting Rationals

Simplify when possible. Simplify means to reduce and/or change any improper fractions to proper fractions. Use a separate sheet of paper if needed.

1. $-5.09 + (-.87)$
2. $-4 -(-2.98)$
3. $8 - 9.567$
4. $-12.5 + (-4.09)$
5. $-28.9 - 29.99$
6. $-\frac{5}{11} + (-\frac{6}{11})$
7. $-\frac{3}{4} + \frac{1}{4}$
8. $\frac{4}{5} - \frac{6}{5}$
9. $0 - 3\frac{5}{6}$
10. $18\frac{1}{10} - (-3\frac{4}{10})$
11. $-6 - 10\frac{1}{2}$
12. $-\frac{7}{12} + 9\frac{8}{12}$
13. $-5\frac{1}{8} + 9\frac{7}{8}$
14. $-3\frac{2}{5} - 5\frac{1}{5}$

Find the GCF and the LCM of these numbers. Use any method you wish. Use a separate sheet of paper if needed.

15. 3 and 8

    GCF _____ LCM ______

16. 5 and 9

    GCF _____ LCM ______

17. 7 and 28

    GCF _____ LCM ______

18. 18 and 24

    GCF _____ LCM _____

19. 12 and 36

    GCF _____ LCM _____

20. 15 and 35

    GCF _____ LCM _____

Working With Different Denominators

Now that you have practiced how to find the LCM, you're ready to work with negative and positive fractions that have different denominators. The trick is to take it one step at a time.

Example 1: Find the sum: $\frac{3}{4} + (-3\frac{1}{2})$

The LCD (least common denominator) is 4, so rewrite the problem with the same denominators.

$$\frac{3}{4} + (-3\frac{2}{4})$$

Do fractions up and down. Notice the signs are different, so you will subtract. Just as before, the larger absolute value number goes on top.

$$\begin{array}{rcr} 3\frac{2}{4} & = & 2\frac{6}{4} \\ -\ \frac{3}{4} & = & -\ \frac{3}{4} \\ \hline & & 2\frac{3}{4} \end{array}$$

You need to borrow.

Add $\frac{4}{4}$ or 1 whole.

Answer: $-2\frac{3}{4}$

Always go back to double check the sign of the answer!

The answer is negative, because the number with the greater absolute value has a negative sign.

Example 2: Find the difference: $-6\frac{1}{9} - 7\frac{2}{5}$

First, make two changes. The problem becomes $-6\frac{1}{9} + (-7\frac{2}{5})$. The signs are the same, so you will add and keep the sign. Rewrite the problem with the same denominators. The LCD is 45.

$$\begin{array}{rcr} 6\frac{1}{9} & = & 6\frac{5}{45} \\ +\ 7\frac{2}{5} & = & 7\frac{18}{45} \\ \hline & & 13\frac{23}{45} \end{array}$$

The answer is $-13\frac{23}{45}$.

Example 3: Solve the following word problem. Make a picture if necessary.

Ms. Stein had a 20″ piece of wood. She needed the piece to be $18\frac{3}{16}$″. How much should she cut off the piece of wood?

You need to subtract:

$$\begin{array}{r} \not{2}\not{0} \\ -\ 18\frac{3}{16} \\ \hline \end{array} \qquad \begin{array}{r} 19\frac{16}{16} \\ -\ 18\frac{3}{16} \\ \hline 1\frac{13}{16} \end{array}$$

She should cut off $1\frac{13}{16}$″.

Practice

Make sure to simplify your answers. Use a separate sheet of paper, if needed.

1. $9 - (-\frac{2}{9})$
2. $-\frac{5}{6} - (-\frac{2}{3})$
3. $-3\frac{1}{5} + (-6\frac{3}{4})$
4. $4\frac{7}{8} - 5$
5. $-\frac{1}{4} + (-\frac{1}{24})$
6. $-3\frac{1}{9} - (-\frac{1}{36})$
7. $-\frac{1}{4} + 5\frac{1}{16}$
8. $-5\frac{1}{7} + 9\frac{1}{6}$
9. Jessica went scuba diving. She went down $7\frac{1}{2}$ feet from sea level and then she went down another $5\frac{3}{4}$ feet. How far down from sea level is she now?
10. A student was asked to subtract $16\frac{3}{8}$ from $20\frac{1}{8}$. Is the student's work correct?

$$\begin{array}{r} 16\frac{3}{8} \\ -\ 20\frac{1}{8} \\ \hline -4\frac{2}{8} \end{array} = -4\frac{1}{4}$$

Explain your thinking. ______________________________

____

____

If the student's work is incorrect, show how you would correct it.

Multiplication and Division of Positive and Negative Rationals

Review the rules for multiplying and dividing integers. Remember when you don't see an operation symbol between parentheses it means to multiply. Always go back to the original problem to determine the answer.

Example 1: Find the product: $(3.5)(-6.2)$

The answer will be negative.

Multiply

$$\begin{array}{r} 3.5 \\ \times\ 6.2 \\ \hline 70 \\ 210 \\ \hline 21.70 \end{array}$$

The answer is −21.7

Example 2: Find the quotient: $-90 \div -4.5$

The answer will be positive.

Divide $4.5\overline{)90.0}$ = 20

$$\begin{array}{r} 20 \\ 4.5\overline{)90.0} \\ 90 \\ \hline 00\ 0 \end{array}$$

The answer is 20.

Example 3: Find the product: $-\frac{3}{8} \bullet \frac{7}{14}$

The answer will be negative.

Remember you can cancel any numerator with any denominator.

$$-\frac{3}{8} \bullet \frac{\cancel{7}^{\,1}}{\cancel{14}_{\,2}}$$

Now multiply across. The answer is $-\frac{3}{16}$.

Example 4: Find the product: $-3\frac{1}{2} \bullet -4\frac{1}{2}$

The answer will be positive.

Change each fraction to an improper fraction.

$$\frac{7}{2} \bullet \frac{9}{2} = \frac{63}{4}$$

This simplifies to $15\frac{3}{4}$.

Example 5: Find the quotient: $3\frac{1}{6} \div -1\frac{1}{3}$

The answer will be negative.

Follow these steps:

Step 1: Change each fraction to improper as you did for multiplication.

$$\frac{19}{6} \div \frac{4}{3}$$

Step 2: Change the division problem to multiplication by using the reciprocal of the second fraction and copy the problem over.

$$\frac{19}{6} \bullet \frac{3}{4}$$

Do not do this step in your head.

Step 3: Proceed as for multiplication.

$$\frac{19}{\cancel{6}_2} \bullet \frac{\cancel{3}^1}{4} = \frac{19}{8} = 2\frac{3}{8}$$

Step 4: Go back and write the sign of your final answer.

The final answer is $-2\frac{3}{8}$.

In many of the problems above, if you determine the sign of the answer ahead of time, and not carry the sign from step to step, it can make your work cleaner. It's very easy to lose a negative sign along the way.

However, you MUST NOT forget to go back and determine if the answer is positive or negative. Also always check if your answer makes sense.

Practice

Make sure to simplify your answer. Use a separate sheet of paper if needed.

1. $-600 \bullet (.02)$

2. $(-4.5)(4.5)$

3. $(-.8)^3$

4. $60 \div .3$

5. $-.25 \div -.5$

6. $(-\frac{2}{3})^2$

7. $-\frac{3}{4} \bullet \frac{4}{3}$

8. $-\frac{1}{2} \bullet \frac{8}{10}$

9. $-3\frac{1}{2} \bullet 1\frac{1}{4}$

10. $-\frac{3}{4} \div -\frac{9}{8}$

11. $-\frac{4}{5} \div -\frac{40}{10}$

12. $-2\frac{2}{7} \div -\frac{16}{21}$

13. $-2 \div 4\frac{1}{10}$

14. $-.006 \div .006$

15. Today's temperature is 5 times yesterday's temperature. If yesterday's temperature was -3.5°. What is today's temperature? ______________

16. After a bad snow storm, the snow started to melt at $\frac{1}{2}$ cm per hour. Which of these two expressions (a math statement or math phrase without an equal or inequality symbols) demonstrates how much snow has melted after 3 hours ?

a. $-3 \bullet \frac{1}{2}$ b. $3 \bullet -\frac{1}{2}$

17. A carpenter wanted to divide a 24″ board into $1\frac{1}{2}$″ pieces. How many pieces can she make?

18. Look at this student's work and correct any mistakes.

Problem: $-3\frac{1}{2} \div -2\frac{1}{4}$

Step 1: $-\frac{7}{2} \div -\frac{9}{4}$

Step 2: $-\frac{7}{2} \bullet \frac{4}{9}$

Step 3: $-\frac{11}{11} = -1$

Order of Operations

Now that you have practiced operations (+, –, •, and ÷) with Rational numbers, it's important to review the steps when a problem has more than one operation.

Step 1: Perform any operations that are in parentheses.

Step 2: Work with exponents, depending if the exponents are inside or outside the parentheses.

Step 3: Multiply or divide (or divide or multiply), which ever is first from left to right.

Step 4: Add or subtract (or subtract or add), which ever is first from left to right.

Example 1: Simplify $5 - 18 \div 3 \bullet 2$

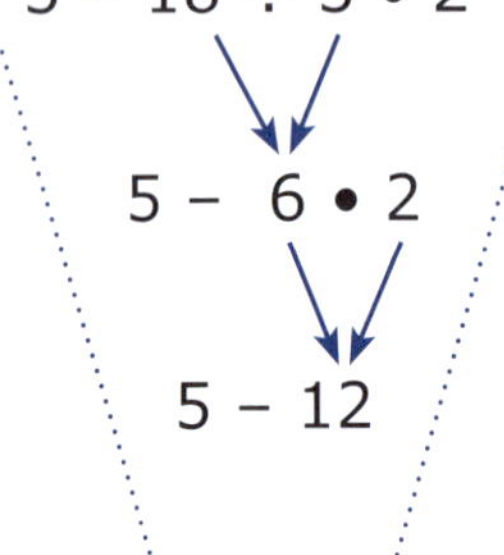

From left to right, divide first.

Multiply next.

Now subtract from left to right.

Work down showing each step. You should end up with your work looking like a funnel.

Example 2: $-3 - 5\frac{1}{2} \bullet -\frac{1}{11} + 2$

$3 + -\frac{11}{2} \bullet -\frac{1}{11} + 2$ From left to right, multiply first.

$3 + \frac{1}{2} + 2$ Notice two changes were made because of the subtraction sign.

$5\frac{1}{2}$ Add from left to right.

Example 3: $-8 - (2 + 5)^2 + 9$

$-8 - 7^2 + 9$ Do parentheses first.

$-8 - 49 + 9$ Then the exponent.

$-57 + 9$ Go left to right. $-8 - 49$ is the same as $-8 + -49$

-48

Example 4:

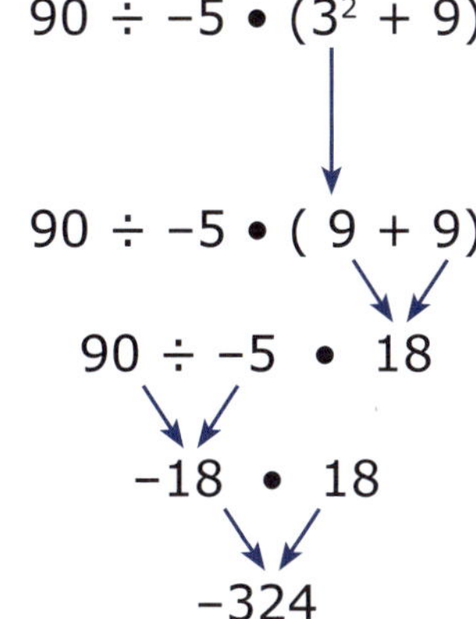

Do the exponent first since it's inside the parentheses.

Now, do the parentheses.

Go left to right.

Example 5: $\dfrac{6.59 + 11.02}{-1 + 4}$ ← This division line acts like parenthesis for the numerator and parentheses for the denominator.

$\dfrac{17.61}{-3}$ Simplify the numerator first. Simplify the denominator.

-5.87 Divide.

Practice

Simplify the following problems. Show the steps working down to your final answer.

1. $-45 + 6 \bullet 7$

2. $-7.3 \div 7.3 \bullet 3$

3. $(8 + 9) \bullet 2 - 34$

4. $8^2 - 2^3 + 4$

5. $-68.4 + 2 \div 2$

6. $-\frac{3}{4} - \frac{1}{4} + 8$

7. $90 \div \frac{3}{5} \bullet (-2)$

8. $\frac{4 + (3 - 5)^3}{-2 \bullet 3}$

9. $-3\frac{1}{3} \div \frac{3}{4} - \frac{5}{9}$

10. $25 - (2 + 7)^2 + 8$

11. $[(-4)^2 + 5]^2$

Brackets are inclusion symbols like parentheses.

12. $[(-4 + 5)^2 - 1]^2$

Understanding Why Order of Operations Is Important

Example: Maria made \$6.00 per hour babysitting. On Saturdays she gets \$3.00 added to her total for working on the weekend. If she babysat 3 hours during one weekday and 4 hours on a Saturday, write an expression that reflects her total earning.

One way to represent what is happening is to write (3 • \$6) + (4 • \$6 + \$3). You can also write 7 • \$6 + 3.

Practice

1. Hayley bikes to school 3 miles round trip each school day. On Saturdays and Sundays, she rides 5 miles round trip each day to her grandparents. Write an expression to represent the number of miles she rides per week.

2. Ritzoy bought 3 pairs of pants at \$20.00 and two sweatshirts for \$15.00 each. He got a discount of \$3.50 on each sweatshirt. Write an expression to represent what he spent. Do not worry about tax.

3. Which of the following expressions describes how to find the answer to this problem? How much money did Lucia have to spend after sharing with her friends? Lucia had \$20 to take to a carnival which she divided equally among herself and two friends. Her grandmother was so proud that Lucia shared her money that she gave Lucia an extra \$8.00 to spend but only for herself.

   a. (\$20 + 8) ÷ 3

   b. \$20 ÷ 3 + \$8

   c. (\$20 + 8) + 3

   d. \$20 • 3 + \$8

   ____

4. Use the order of operations and the integers −3, −2, −1, 0, 1, and 2 to create an expression that gives you a value of −18. You may use parentheses.

5. Use the order of operations and the integers –2, 1, 3, 4, and 5 to create an expression that gives you a value of –29. You may use parentheses.

6. The Famous "Another Day, Another Dollar" Problem

Three business women need to rent a car for one day. The cost is $30 so they each pay $10. As they approach their rental car, the owner at the counter says: "Wait, there's been a change. It's your lucky day. The fee is only $25. Here's $5 back." Since the women are in a hurry and do not want to split the $5, they give the owner a $2 tip and they keep the $3. So, each woman paid $10 – $1 (money they each got back) – $9 times 3 is $27. It you add the $2 tip, you get only $29! Wait! Where's the extra dollar? Show your work. Explain your thinking.

____

____

____

____

____

____

Chapter 3 Review

Simplify the following problems. Use a separate sheet of paper if needed.

1. $-\frac{4}{5} + (\frac{1}{5})$

2. $-\frac{3}{8} + (-\frac{2}{8})$

3. $5 + (-3\frac{1}{4})$

4. $-6.5 + (-8.5)$

5. $-9 + .08$

6. $-8\frac{3}{4} + (-7\frac{1}{8})$

7. $3\frac{6}{7} - 4\frac{1}{7}$

8. $(6.5)(-.03)$

9. $-\frac{3}{5} \bullet -3\frac{1}{3}$

10. $-4\frac{1}{8} \div -\frac{33}{8}$

11. $-60 \div (-.03)$

12. $(-4.5)^2$

13. $(5 - 8^2) + (5 - 8)^2$

14. $\dfrac{-3\frac{1}{5} \bullet \frac{5}{4}}{2 - 3}$

Answer the following questions.

15. Which of the following expressions has the answer 2?

   a. $-3 + 2 \div 2$

   b. $9 \div 9 + 2$

   c. $6 + 6 \div 6$

   d. $8 - 9 + 3$

16. Joan thinks that the answer to the problem below is −10, and Heidi thinks it is −160. Who is right and why? Explain your thinking.

Problem: $-80 \div 2 \bullet 4$

____

____

17. A school store sells pencils for $.35 each, erasers for $.20 each and 6″ rulers for $1.00 each. Neesa bought 6 pencils, 3 erasers, and 2 rulers. Write an expression for how much money she has left from $20. What is the answer? Do not worry about tax.

____

____

18. Emilia wanted to change a recipe that serves 24 people to one that serves 8 people. The original recipe called for $6\frac{1}{2}$ cups of flour.

a. How much flour does she need now? ____________________

b. How much less flour is she using compared to the original recipe?

____

Chapter 4

Ratio, Proportion, and Percent

Fractions, decimals, and percents are different ways of representing the same quantities. For some situations, you'll know whether it's better to represent a quantity by a fraction, a decimal, or a percent. Let's review how to change fractions to decimals and terminating decimals to fractions.

Remember from Chapter 1 that any fraction can be changed to a terminating (a decimal that stops) or to a repeating decimal.

Converting Fractions to Decimals and Terminating Decimals to Fractions

Example 1: Change $\frac{3}{8}$ to a decimal.

The fraction bar means "divide." You're dividing 3 by 8. You can think of the 3 sitting on a chair and falling into the box. Since 8 cannot go into 3, put a decimal point after the 3 and add a few zeros. Then start dividing and keep dividing until the decimal terminates or repeats.

$$\begin{array}{r} 0.375 \\ 8\overline{)3.000} \\ -\,24 \\ \hline 60 \\ -\,56 \\ \hline 40 \\ -\,40 \\ \hline 0 \end{array}$$

Example 2: Change .375 to a fraction.

The 5 sits on the thousandths place, so write 375 as the numerator and 1,000 as the denominator and reduce. Then divide the fraction by 5. If the GCF (which is 125) was found, the fraction could have been reduced in one step.

$$\frac{375}{1{,}000} = \frac{75}{200} = \frac{15}{40} = \frac{3}{8}$$

Example 3: Change $-5\frac{2}{3}$ to a decimal.

Since −5 is an integer, you just need to find out what $\frac{2}{3}$ is as a decimal. Again, drop the 2 into the box and divide.

```
     0.666...
3 ⟌ 2.000
  - 18
     20
   - 18
      20
    - 18
       0
```

You can see that the 6 will repeat, so the answer is $-5.\overline{6}$. The bar on top of the 6 indicates that the 6 repeats. And yes, you can write your answer as $-5.\overline{66}$.

Common Fractions/Decimals

You can always use the above methods to covert fractions to decimals and terminating decimals to fractions. However, there are 10 common fractions/decimals that appear in many real life situations, as well as in many standardized tests that you might take in the future. It is a great advantage to memorize these. Making flashcards may be useful. Make sure you do not memorize these unless you understand the concept.

$\frac{1}{2} = .5$	$\frac{3}{8} = .375$
$\frac{1}{4} = .25$	$\frac{5}{8} = .625$
$\frac{3}{4} = .75$	$\frac{7}{8} = .875$
$\frac{1}{5} = .2$	$\frac{1}{3} = .\overline{3}$
$\frac{1}{8} = .125$	$\frac{2}{3} = .\overline{6}$

$\frac{1}{5} = .2$. What are the decimals for $\frac{2}{5}$, $\frac{3}{5}$, and $\frac{4}{5}$. Why?

_______________ _______________ _______________

____

PLACE VALUE CHART

millions	hundred-thousands	ten-thousands	thousands	hundreds	tens	ones	.	tenths	hundredths	thousandths	ten-thousands	hundred-thousandths	millionths
							•	0	0	0	1	6	

Practice

Change the following decimals to fractions. Make sure to simplify each fraction. If you memorized the "Common Fractions/Decimals," you do not need to show work.

1. .08
2. .004
3. −5.025
4. .375
5. −9.875
6. .00016 (see chart)
7. −6.008
8. 26.75
9. −9.248
10. .00065

Change the following fractions to decimals. Remember to reduce the fraction first. If you memorized the "Common Fractions/Decimals," then you do not need to show work.

11. $\frac{7}{100}$

12. $\frac{3}{24}$

13. $\frac{2}{5}$

14. $\frac{5}{8}$

15. $-8\frac{3}{10{,}000}$

16. $\frac{3}{16}$

17. $-10\frac{1}{3}$

18. $-9\frac{27}{72}$

19. $\frac{125}{100}$

20. $\frac{18}{24}$

21. $-\frac{5}{32}$

22. $\frac{22}{7}$

23. a. Change $\frac{1}{9}$ to a decimal.

b. Change $\frac{2}{9}$ to a decimal.

Finish the pattern.

c. $\frac{3}{9}$ = ______, $\frac{4}{9}$ = ______, $\frac{5}{9}$ = ______, $\frac{6}{9}$ = ______, $\frac{7}{9}$ = ______, $\frac{8}{9}$ = ______

d. So $\frac{9}{9}$ = ______. But isn't $\frac{9}{9}$ the same as 1 whole?

Explain your thinking. ____

____

How to Tell if a Fraction Terminates or Repeats

When changing a fraction to a decimal, it helps to know ahead of time if the decimal will terminate or repeat. To figure this out, follow these steps.

Example 1: Does the fraction $\frac{6}{40}$ terminate or repeat when changed to decimal?

Step 1: Reduce the fraction first! It becomes $\frac{3}{20}$.

Step 2: Do a prime factorization of the denominator. Do not worry about the numerator.

The prime factorization of 20 is: $2 \bullet 2 \bullet 5$ or $2^2 \bullet 5$.

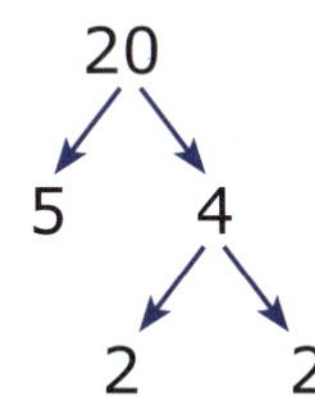

Step 3: If you have only factors of 2, or only factors of 5, or both, but no other primes such as 3, 7, 11, etc. in the prime factorization of the denominator, then the fraction will terminate when changed to a decimal.

Example 2: Does the fraction $\frac{3}{70}$ terminate or repeat when changed to a decimal?

The fraction is already reduced. The prime factorization of 70 is $2 \bullet 5 \bullet 7$. Therefore the prime number 7 will make this fraction repeat when changed to a decimal repeat.

Practice

1. Why do you think having only the primes 2 and/or 5 and no other primes will make the fraction terminate when changed to a decimal? Explain your thinking.

____

____

2. Do these fractions terminate (T) or repeat (R) when changed to a decimal? Use an extra sheet of paper if needed. Don't forget to reduce each fraction first.

a. $\frac{1}{20}$ = ______ b. $\frac{3}{30}$ = ______ c. $\frac{22}{14}$ = ______

d. $\frac{1}{64}$ = ______ e. $\frac{9}{54}$ = ______ f. $\frac{8}{41}$ = ______

Ratio, Rate, and Unit Rate

A ratio is the relationship between two quantities.

Example 1: In a classroom there are 15 girls to 7 boys. What is the ratio of girls to boys?

You can write the answer as 15 to 7, 15:7, or $\frac{15}{7}$.

Since the question reads "girls" to "boys," then the number that matches with girls goes first. If you write the ratio as a fraction, you can reduce.

Example 2: In the problem above, what is the ratio of boys to the total number of students in the classroom?

The answer is 7 to 22, 7:22, or $\frac{7}{22}$.

Example 3: At a dance the principal of a school wants to have the ratio of chaperones to students to be 2 chaperones for every 9 students. If the total number of chaperones plus students was 110, how many chaperones were there?

2 chaperones + 9 students = 11 people. $\frac{2}{11}$ is the ratio of chaperones to total people.

So $\frac{2}{11}$ of 110 must be chaperones. $\frac{2}{\cancel{11}} \bullet \overset{10}{\cancel{110}} = 20$. There are 20 chaperones.

Example 4: Dana drove 200 miles using 5 gallons of gas. Simplify the ratio of miles to gallons.

$\frac{200 \text{ miles}}{5 \text{ gallons}} = \frac{40 \text{ miles}}{1 \text{ gallon}}$ You can say Dana's car gets 40 miles per gallon or 40 mi/gal or 40 mpg (miles per gallon).

$\frac{200}{5}$ is called a rate (a special type of ratio used to compare measurements with different units) and $\frac{40}{1}$ is called a unit rate.

A unit rate is a rate with a denominator of 1.

Practice

Find the answer to these problems using these bathroom tiles. Be sure to reduce if possible. Use a separate sheet of paper if needed.

1. What is the ratio of yellow shapes to squares? ________________
2. What is the ratio of red triangles to total triangles? ________________
3. What is the ratio of green triangles to green squares? ________________
4. What is the ratio of triangles to squares? ________________
5. What is the ratio of triangles to total shapes? ________________
6. If the design above has to be repeated multiple times on a bathroom wall to make a border and the final design has 104 total shapes (squares plus triangles), how many triangles are there on the banner? Show your work.
7. Dan drove his car for 250 miles and used 10 gallons of gas. Elsie drove her truck for 300 miles and used 20 gallons of gas. DJ drove his motorcycle 120 miles and used up 3 gallons of gas. You can also use the abbreviation "mpg" for miles per gallon. Complete the table below.

Vehicle	Rate	Unit Rate
(car)		
(truck)		
(motorcycle)		

8. If gas costs $2.30 per gallon, how much did each trip in problem 7 cost? Show your work.

   a. Dan's trip ________

   b. Elsie's trip ________

   c. DJ's trip ________

9. A banana bread recipe calls for 1 cup of sugar for every 2 cups of flour. Finish the following table.

Flour (Cups)	Sugar(Cups	Flour and Sugar (Cups)
2	1	3
3		
6		
		12
	5	
		$16\frac{1}{2}$

10. The same recipe above calls for $\frac{1}{4}$ tsp of salt for every 2 cups of flour. If Mr. Baker used $1\frac{1}{2}$ tsp salt, how many cups of flour should he use? Show your work.

11. Find each unit rate.

a. The average human walks 9 miles in 3 hours.

b. Michael Phelps swims 3 miles in a $\frac{1}{2}$ hour.

c. Katie Ledecky swims 800 meters in about 8 minutes.

d. A gray wolf runs 70 miles in 2 hours.

e. Usain Bolt runs 55 miles in 2 hours.

f. A cheetah runs 245 miles in $3\frac{1}{2}$ hours.

12. Fill in the table below.

Two 8" pizza pies for $21.90.

Number of Pizza Pies	Cost
1	
2	$21.90
3	
16	

13. In problem 12, the dependent variable is the "cost" and the independent variable is the "number of pizzas." What do you think is meant by those terms? Explain your thinking. Hint: Think of independent as free to choose what you want. A variable is something that changes.

____

____

____

____

Proportions

A proportion is defined as two ratios that are equal. The following are examples of proportions.

$$\frac{3}{6} = \frac{5}{10} \qquad \frac{3}{4} = \frac{75}{100} \qquad \frac{3}{51} = \frac{1}{17}$$

You can check if two ratios or fractions are equal in several ways.

1. You can reduce both fractions and compare, or change them to the same denominator and compare.
2. You can divide each into decimals and compare.
3. You can also multiply going up (see below) and see if you get the same answer. This is called finding the cross product.

30 30

$$\frac{3}{6} = \frac{5}{10}$$

Let's look at a generic proportion.

$$\frac{a}{b} = \frac{c}{d}$$

a and *d* are called the extremes and *b* and *c* are called the means. In any proportion, the product of the means equals the product of the extremes.

Example 1: Every week Martha works 35 hours and gets paid \$525 weekly. Her sister thinks that if Martha works 80 hours she should make \$1,300. Is Martha's sister correct? Explain your thinking.

You can find out what Martha makes per hour and multiply that amount by 80 if you divide first.

You can also check if $\frac{35}{\$525}$ is equal to $\frac{80}{\$1,300}$.

45,500 *42,000*

$$\frac{35}{\$525} \quad \frac{80}{\$1,300}$$

If you put "hours" in the numerator of one fraction, then you must put "hours" in the numerator of the second fraction. If "money" is the numerator in one fraction then "money" must the numerator in the second fraction.

Martha's sister is incorrect. The ratios are not equal so her answer is not based on a proportion.

Example 2: Using proportions, how much would Martha make if she works 80 hours?

Set up a proportion $\frac{35}{525} = \frac{80}{n}$ and use cross products.

35 • n can be written as 35n

$35 \bullet n = 42{,}000$ (35 times n equals 42,000).

$\frac{35n}{35} = \frac{42{,}000}{35}$ Now divide each side by 35.

$n = 1{,}200$ So Martha makes $1,200 if she works 80 hours.

Example 3: During a sunny afternoon, a boy with a height of 4 feet casts a shadow that is 10 feet in length. At the same time, in the same location, someone measures the shadow of a tree to be 30 feet long. What is the height of the tree? Solve by using a proportion.

$\frac{4}{10} = \frac{n}{30}$ The height of the boy is to his shadow as the height of the tree is to the tree's shadow.

OR

$\frac{4}{n} = \frac{10}{30}$ This is another possibility. The height of the boy is to the height of the tree as the boy's shadow is to the tree's shadow.

$10n = 120$ Divide by 10

$n = 12$ The height of the tree is 12′.

Example 4: The following ingredients are needed to make 30 chocolate chip cookies.

$\frac{1}{2}$ cup unsalted butter

$\frac{3}{4}$ cup dark brown sugar

$\frac{3}{4}$ cup white sugar

1 tsp salt

1 tsp vanilla extract

2 large eggs

$2\frac{1}{4}$ cups flour

1 bag (12oz.) chocolate chips

$\frac{3}{4}$ tsp baking soda

Complete the table if the ingredients change as shown.

Recipe	Eggs	Flour	Brown Sugar	Unsalted Butter
1	4	_____	_____	_____
2	_____	_____	1 cup	_____

Recipe #1 was doubled since 2 eggs became 4 eggs. So multiplying each amount in the original recipe by 2 gives you $4\frac{1}{2}$ cups flour ($\frac{9}{4} \bullet 2 = \frac{9}{2}$). You also get $1\frac{1}{2}$ cups brown sugar ($\frac{3}{4} \bullet 2 = \frac{3}{2}$) and 1 cup unsalted butter. In recipe #2, brown sugar became 1 cup, and $\frac{3}{4}$ was multiplied by $\frac{4}{3}$ to get 1, so multiplying each amount by $\frac{4}{3}$ gives $2\frac{2}{3}$ eggs. You also get 3 cups flour ($\frac{9}{4} \bullet \frac{4}{3} = 3$) and $\frac{2}{3}$ cups of unsalted butter ($\frac{1}{2} \bullet \frac{4}{3} = \frac{2}{3}$).

Practice

Show your work. Use a separate sheet of paper if needed.

1. Using the chocolate chip cookie recipe on page 60, how much vanilla extract would you need if you used 8 eggs?

2. Using the chocolate chip cookie recipe on page 60, how much baking soda would you need if you used 9 cups of flour?

3. Using the chocolate chip cookie recipe on page 60, how much unsalted butter would you use if you used 1 cup white sugar?

4. Bill's car gets 84 miles for every 2 gallons. Answer the following questions.

   a. What is the unit rate? ________

   b. How many gallons does Bill use if he drives 336 miles? ________

   c. How many miles can Bill drive on a full tank of gas if his tank holds 11.9 gallons? ________

5. Louise types 90 words in 75 seconds. How many words can she type in 3 minutes? Hint: Make sure you use the same units.

   ____

6. Eva told her dad that she weighed 100 lbs at the doctors office. Her dad said: "On Jupiter, you would weigh 236 lbs which is what I weigh on Earth. Eva's little sister weighed 38 lbs at the doctors, which is what Eva would weigh on Mars. Answer the following questions. Round to the nearest pound. You may use a calculator.

   a. How much would her dad weigh on Jupiter? ______________

   b. How much would her dad weigh on Mars? ______________

   c. How much would Eva's little sister weigh on Jupiter? ______________

7. Twelve honeycrisp apples cost $4.50. At this rate, how many honeycrisp apples can be bought with $54.00? Show your work.

   ____

8. Rafael can read 24 pages in 20 minutes. How many minutes will it take him to read a 600 page novel? Show your work.

   ____

Scale Drawings

Scale drawings are used in many professions. Anyone who needs to build a bridge, a building, a machine, a new playground, etc., can do so on a smaller scale before building the real product. Even fashion designers use scale drawings before making a pattern. The smaller drawing must be in proportion to the final product. Every scale drawing has a legend that shows you the scale ratio or scale factor.

Example 1: Find the actual dimensions of the master bedroom and the bathroom shown on this scale drawing. Each square on the graph paper represents $\frac{1}{4}$ inch. Also, find the area of the master bedroom.

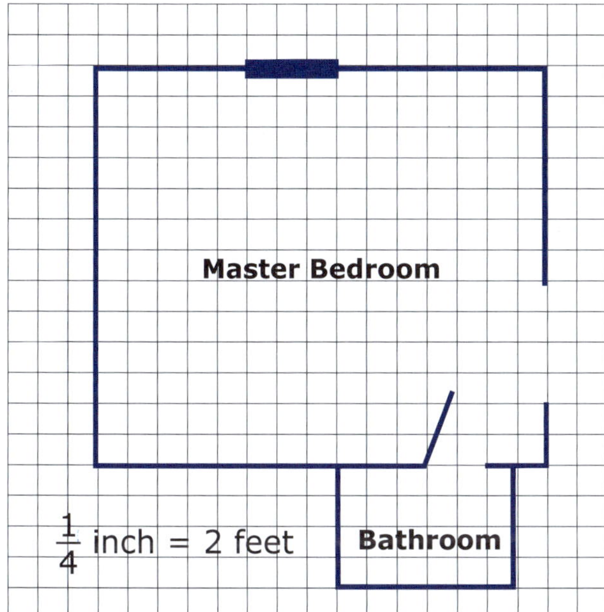

Answer: The master bedroom is 30 ft X 26 ft and the bathroom is 12 feet X 8 ft. Since each square in the grid is 2 feet, count the squares and multiply by 2.

The area is length X width, so the area of the master bedroom is 780 square feet.

Now, had you not been given the grid and only told that the dimensions of the living room on the scale drawing were $3\frac{3}{4}$ $(\frac{15}{4})$ inches by $3\frac{1}{4}$ $(\frac{13}{4})$ inches, and $\frac{1}{4}$ inch equaled 2 feet, you would set up two proportions.

inches, feet

$$\frac{\frac{1}{4}}{\frac{15}{4}} = \frac{2}{n}$$

← Use cross products. →

inches, feet

$$\frac{\frac{1}{4}}{\frac{13}{4}} = \frac{2}{n}$$

$$\frac{1}{4}n = \frac{30}{4}$$

so $n = 30$ feet

$$\frac{1}{4}n = \frac{26}{4}$$

so $n = 26$ feet

Example 2: On a map 2.5 cm equals 30 miles. If on a map Philadelphia, PA, is about 8 cm from New York City, about how far apart in miles is Philadelphia from New York City?

Set up a proportion.

cm miles

$$\frac{2.5}{8} = \frac{30}{n}$$

$2.5n = 240$ Use cross products.
Divide each side by 2.5

$n = 96$ So Philadelphia is about 96 miles from New York City.

Practice

Show your work. Use a separate sheet of paper if needed.

1. An architect is designing a rectangular park that is to be 200′ X 300′. What are the dimensions of the rectangular park on the architect's blueprint, if she's using the scale of $\frac{1}{8}$ in = 1 foot?

2. On a map 1.4 cm = 400 miles. Michelle measured the distance on her map between her home in Portland, Oregon, and where her best friend lives and found it to be 2.2 cm. About how far away in miles does her friend live? Use proportions to find the answer. Round to the nearest tenth of a mile.

3. A model plane is 24 cm in length. It represents a real plane that is 72 meters in length. What is the scale used?

4. Make a scale drawing of any room in your home. Make sure you use a title and state what scale you're using. You can add furniture and/or fixtures that are in the room if you want.

5. Roberta drew the following design on paper to make a rectangular quilt. Her design on paper is 10 cm X 15 cm. If the width of the actual quilt is 60″, what is the actual length of the quilt? Also, find the area of the actual quilt.

6. The scale on a map is $\frac{1}{4}$ in.: 20 mi. The airport is 200 miles from the beach. How far is the airport from the beach on the map?

7. A diagram of a wooden box in an instruction booklet uses a scale of 1:20. The diagram is 10 cm in height, 9.5 cm in width, and 8.4 cm in length. What are the actual dimensions of the box? If the volume of the box is lwh (length • width • height), find the volume of the actual box in meters.

8. A child in a photograph is 1.5 inches tall. His mom's height in the photograph is 2 inches tall. If his mom's real height is 65 inches, what is the child's actual height? Change your answer to feet and inches.

9. The following rectangles are in proportion.

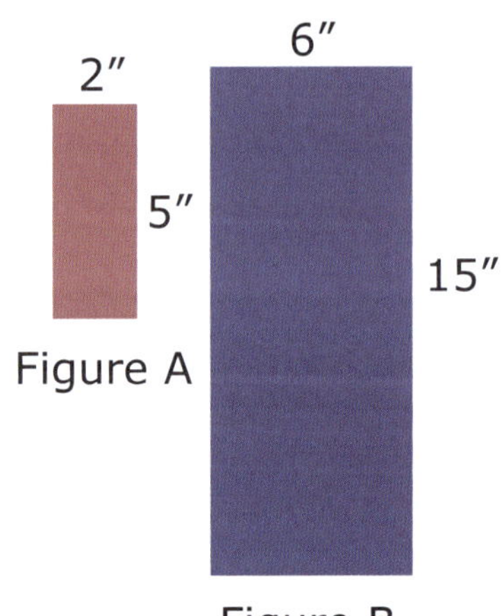

a. What is the scale factor? ________

b. Find the perimeter of each figure. (2l + 2w)
Fig. A _______, Fig. B _______

c. What is the ratio of their perimeters? ________

d. Find the area of each rectangle (l•w).
Fig. A _______ Fig. B ______

e. What is the ratio of their areas? _______

The ratio of the areas is the ratio of the perimeters squared (times itself).

Understanding Percent

A percent is the ratio of a number to 100. The word comes from the Latin term "per centum" which means per one-hundred. This means that when the denominator is 100 you can write the numerator with the percent symbol %. If you have $\frac{13}{100}$ you can write 13%. And when you see 13%, it means 13 is being divided by 100 or 13 parts out of 100 parts. You can change fractions to percents, percents to fractions, decimals to percent, and percent to decimals. Some comparisons are best done with fractions and decimals, but percents are used in many real life situations such as finding the tip at a restaurant, getting a loan or mortgage, figuring out salary increase or decrease, and taxes and discounts when you go shopping.

Changing Fractions to Percent and Percent to Fractions

Example 1: Change $\frac{4}{5}$ to a percent.

To change $\frac{4}{5}$ to a percent, you need to set the fraction equal to a fraction with a denominator of 100.

$\frac{4}{5} = \frac{n}{100}$ Can you see that 5 • 20 is 100? Therefore, 4 • 20 is 80.

$\frac{4}{5} = \frac{80}{100}$ So the answer is 80%.

You could have used cross products since $\frac{4}{5} = \frac{n}{100}$ is a proportion.

$5n = 400$ and dividing each side by 5 gives you $n = 80$. Since 80 is over 100, the answer is 80%.

Example 2: Change 35% to a fraction.

Write 35% as $\frac{35}{100}$ and simplify the fraction. The answer is $\frac{7}{20}$.

Example 3: Change $\frac{1}{2}$% to a fraction.

When you see $\frac{1}{2}$% it means $\frac{1}{2}$ of 1%. Since percent means "divided by 100" you need to divide $\frac{1}{2}$ by 100 or $\frac{1}{2} \div 100$. This becomes $\frac{1}{2} \bullet \frac{1}{100} = \frac{1}{200}$.

See the drawings on the next page.

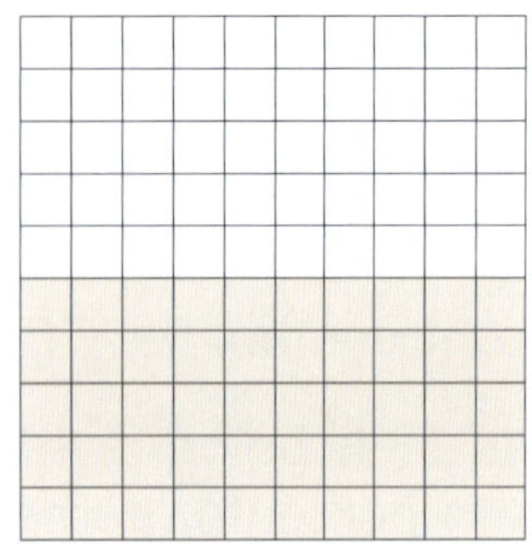

$50\% = \frac{1}{2}$

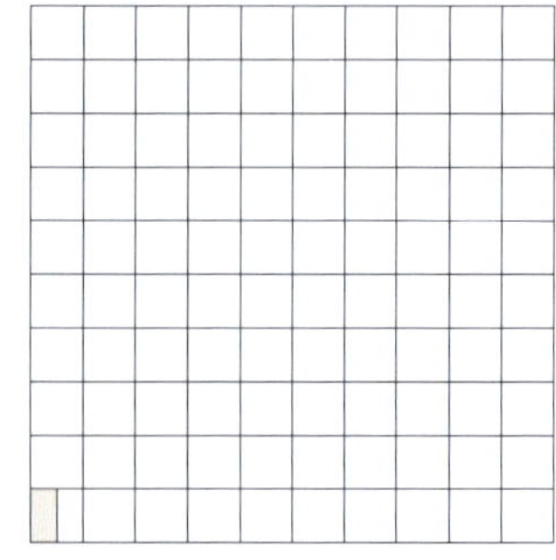

$\frac{1}{2}\% = \frac{1}{200}$

Changing Percent to Decimals and Decimals to Percent

Example 1: Change 8% to a decimal.

Since 8% is $\frac{8}{100}$ or 8 hundredths, then the answer is .08.

Since you're dividing by 100, you can move the decimal place to the left two places.

Example 2: Change 2.4% to a decimal.

Since 2.4 is being divided by 100, move the decimal place to the left two places. The answer is .024.

Example 3: Change 120.5 to a percent.

To change 120.5 to a percent, multiply it by 100 and then use the percent symbol. Move the decimal place now to the right two places. The answer is 12050%.

To change a percent to a decimal, move the decimal point twice to the left. PDL (Percent Decimal Left - Please Don't Laugh!)

To change a decimal to a percent, move the decimal point twice to the right. DPR (Decimal Percent Right - Don't Pick Roses!)

See Common Fractions/Decimals/Percent on page 70.

Practice

Simplify your answers. Use a separate sheet of paper if needed.

1. Change 25% to a fraction.
2. Change 200% to a fraction.
3. Change 2.5% to a fraction.
4. Change $\frac{1}{8}$ to a percent.
5. Change $\frac{2}{3}$ to a percent.
6. Change 125% to a decimal.
7. Change 15% to a decimal.
8. Change 62.5% to a fraction.
9. Change .09 to a percent.
10. Change .085 to a percent.
11. Change $\frac{1}{4}$% to a fraction.
12. Change $\frac{3}{125}$ to a percent.

Common Fractions/Decimals/Percent

$\frac{1}{2} = .5 = 50\%$	$\frac{3}{8} = .375 = 37.5\%$
$\frac{1}{4} = .25 = 25\%$	$\frac{5}{8} = .625 = 62.5\%$
$\frac{3}{4} = .75 = 75\%$	$\frac{7}{8} = .875 = 87.5\%$
$\frac{1}{5} = .20 = 20\%$	$\frac{1}{3} = .\overline{3} = 33.\overline{3}\%$
$\frac{1}{8} = .125 = 12.5\%$	$\frac{2}{3} = .\overline{6} = 66.\overline{6}\%$

Working With Percent

The rate is the percent amount. The base (whole) or total amount always follows the word "of" ("of" means to multiply). The percentage follows the word "is" ("is" means "equals"), so 8 is the percentage or answer to the problem. Here are the 3 cases of percent problems that will be solved on the next page.

Case 1: You know the rate and the base but you don't know the the percentage. 10% of 80 is what?

Case 2: You know the rate and the percentage but you don't know the base. 10% of what number is 8?

Case 3: You know the base and the percentage but you don't know the rate. What percent of 80 is 8?

In Case 1 you know the rate and the base so the quickest way to solve these problems is to change the rate either to a decimal or to a fraction and then multiply. Remember the word "of" tells you to multiply. Here's where knowing your Common Fraction/Decimal/Percent facts can really help you!

Example 1: Find 8% of $12.99.

Multiply .08 times 12.99

$$\begin{array}{r} 12.99 \\ \times\ .08 \\ \hline 1.0392 \end{array}$$

Since you're working with money, round to the nearest cent. The answer is $1.04.

Example 2: Find 12.5% of 240.

Remember that 12.5% is the fraction $\frac{1}{8}$, so $\frac{1}{8}$ times 240 is 30.

You could have also multiplied .125 times 240.

Remember that to change a percent to a decimal, move the decimal to the left two spaces.

In Cases 2 and 3, you can solve the problem by using a proportion.

Example 1: 20% of what number is 62. (Case 2)

Remember that whatever follows the word "of" is the base or the whole. Write 20% as a fraction. 20% is always $\frac{20}{100}$. The base n goes in the denominator .

$$\frac{20}{100} = \frac{62}{n}$$

What number follows "of?"

$20n = 6{,}200$ Now divide by 20.

$n = 310$

OR

$$\frac{1}{5} = \frac{62}{n}$$

$n = 310$

Example 2: 3% of what number is 900. (Case 2)

$$\frac{3}{100} = \frac{900}{n}$$

$3n = 90{,}000$ Now divide by 3.

$n = 30{,}000$

You can check the answer by multiplying .03 times 30,000.

Example 3: What percent of 20 is 5? (Case 3)

What percent means that you don't know the rate. Write "what percent" as $\frac{n}{100}$. Remember that 20 is after the word "of" so it's the whole or base. Here's the proportion.

$$\frac{n}{100} = \frac{5}{20}$$

$20n = 500$ Now divide by 20.

$n = 25$ The answer is 25%

Why is 25% of 20 equal to 5? It's because $\frac{1}{4}$ of 20 = 5.

Example 4: What percent of 8 is 7? (Case 3)

$$\frac{n}{100} = \frac{7}{8}$$

$8n = 700$ Now divide by 20.

$n = 87.5$ The answer is 87.5%

Did you recognize that $\frac{7}{8}$ is 87.5%?

Case 1 can also be solved by using a proportion although it's not as fast as multiplying the rate times the base.

Example 5: Find 18% of 360.

18% is $\frac{18}{100}$. The base or whole is 360 since it's after the word "of," so it goes in the denominator. Let n be the unknown. You're finding the percentage.

$$\frac{18}{100} = \frac{n}{360}$$

$100n = 6{,}480$

$n = 64.8$

Practice

Round your answers to the nearest hundredths. Use a separate sheet of paper if needed.

1. What is 10% of 20?
2. What is 7% of $200?
3. What is 8.5% of $5.99?
4. Find 7.5% of $650.
5. What is 37.5% of 80?
6. 20% of what number is 30?
7. 75% of what number is 16?
8. $33\frac{1}{3}$% of what number is 9?
9. $\frac{1}{2}$% of what number is 2?
10. 25% of what number is 8?
11. What percent of 8 is 4?
12. What percent of 45 is 9?
13. What percent of 68 is 17?
14. What percent of 200 is 35?
15. What is 100% of 9?
16. What is 300% of 45?

Chapter 4 Review

Solve the following problems. Reduce when possible. Use a separate sheet of paper if needed.

1. Change the following to a fraction, decimal or percent.

Fraction	Decimal	Percent
$\frac{3}{20}$		
		8%
	3.96	
$\frac{7}{8}$		
		140%

2. Use the following information to find the ratios below.

   DeWitt Middle School 8th grade has 14 girls, 22 boys, and 6 teachers.

   a. What is the ratio of boys to girls? ______________________

   b. What is the ratio of girls to boys? ______________________

   c. What is the ratio of teachers to students? ______________________

   d. What is the ratio of teachers to girls? ______________________

3. DeWitt Middle School's principal wants to keep the same ratio of teachers to students for the entire school. If the school has 180 students, how many teachers should there be? Show your work. ______________________

4. Do these fractions terminate (T) or repeat (R) when changed to a decimal?

a. $\frac{3}{75}$ ______ b. $\frac{11}{77}$ ______ c. $\frac{1}{28}$ ______ d. $\frac{7}{42}$ ______ e. $\frac{8}{200}$ ______

5. Jim drove 200 miles and used up 5.5 gallons of gas. Write this as a rate. Then write is as a unit rate.

6. If 10 lbs of potatoes cost $4.50. What is the unit rate?

7. Here's a list of some of the ingredients to make croissants.

$1\frac{1}{4}$ tsp yeast 3T warm water 2 tsp sugar $1\frac{3}{4}$ flour $\frac{2}{3}$c warm milk

If Mrs. Baker uses 7 cups of flour, how much of the ingredients listed above should she use?

______ yeast ______ warm water ______ sugar ______ warm milk

8. $\frac{8}{20} = \frac{2}{n}$

9. $\frac{1}{8} = \frac{n}{100}$

10. $\frac{4}{14} = \frac{n}{42}$

11. $\frac{n}{2} = \frac{46}{92}$

12. $\frac{18}{24} = \frac{n}{99}$

13. $\frac{2.5}{15} = \frac{n}{125}$

14. Ms. Jones can type 140 words per minute. At this rate, how many words can she type in $1\frac{1}{4}$ minutes? Round to the nearest hundredths.

15. On a map 2cm = 150 miles. How far are two towns that are 4.6 cm apart on the map? What is the scale ratio? Round to the nearest hundredths.

16. Two squares are in the ratio of 1:4. Draw your own squares with your choice of measurements using the given ratio. Find the ratio of the perimeters. Find the ratio of their areas. Round to the nearest hundredths.

17. What is 8.5% of 200?

18. What is 10% of 300?

19. What is 2% of $42.50?

20. What is 150% of 5?

21. What is $\frac{1}{4}$% of $600?

22. 75% of what number is 12?

23. 62.5% of what number is 40?

24. 12.5% of what number is 5?

25. 8% of what number is 32?

26. 125% of what number is 60?

27. What percent of 6 is 2?

28. What percent of 5 is 4?

29. What percent of 4 is 5?

30. What percent of 200 is 1?

Chapter 5

Percent Applications

Going Shopping - Tax and Tips

Example 1: Joel lives in Alabama and his state's sales tax is 4%. Joel has $30 to buy a sweater. If the price of the sweater is $28.95, does he have enough money to pay for the sweater, including tax?

Find 4% of $28.95. Multiply .04 times $28.95. The answer is $1.16 (rounded to the nearest cent). Now add $1.16 to $28.95 and that totals $30.11. He does not have enough to buy the sweater.

There's another way to do this. Joel will be paying the entire price (100%) plus the tax (4%). In other words, he will be paying 104% or 1.04. So if you multiply $28.95 by 1.04 you will get $30.108, which rounds to $30.11. This is the total amount Joel has to pay including tax.

Example 2: Jeanne wants to buy a bedspread for her parents. The bedspread is on sale for 25% off. If the bedspread was $90 before the discount, what's the new price?

Find 25% of $90. Multiply .25 times 90, or find $\frac{1}{4}$ of 90. The discount is $22.50.

SPECIAL 25% OFF

Now subtract $90 – $22.50. The new price $67.50.

Another way to do the problem is to find 75% of \$90 since Jeanne is paying 25% less than the original amount. Find .75 of 90 or $\frac{3}{4}$ of 90. That gives you \$67.50 in one step. See below.

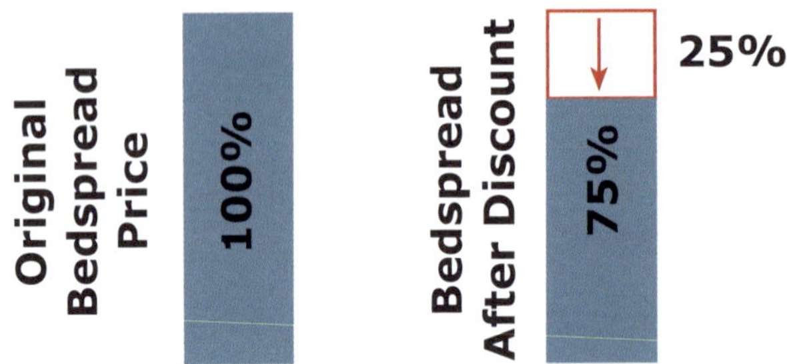

Example 3: Kate bought an antique car for \$25,000. In one year she found out her car increased in value a total of 15%. How much is her car worth after one year?

You can find 15% of \$25,000, or .15 times \$25,000, which is \$3,750. Then add \$3,750 to \$25,000 to get \$28,750.

You can also find the answer in one step by multiplying \$25,000 by 115%. Remember, 100% is the value of the car, which is \$25,000 and 15% is the increase in value. 115% is the original price she paid including the increase.

Example 4: Mason bought a video game for \$32.10. This included the tax at a rate of 7%. When his friend asked him how much was the video game without the tax, Mason did not know. Help Mason find the answer to his friend's question.

If Mason paid \$32.10 with an 7% tax, then \$32.10 is 107% and you need to find 100%, which would be the price without the tax.

Set up a proportion.

$$\frac{32.10}{107} = \frac{n}{100}$$

$107n = 3{,}210$ Divide by 107.

$n = 30$

So the cost of the video game before tax was \$30.00.

Example 5: Maria goes out to dinner with her family. The total bill is $82.00 including tax. Maria wants to leave a 20% tip. How much will her tip be?

You can find the answer by multiplying .20 times $82.

Hint: When you need to tip at 20%, you can find 10% of 82, which is $8.20 and then double that amount which would be $16.40 for the total tip.

Practice

Solve these real life percent problems. Show your work. Use a separate sheet of paper if needed.

1. Joaquín buys a shirt at the mall for $25.00. He has to pay tax at the rate of 6%. How much does he pay in tax? ____________________

2. Olga wants to buy a TV because it's on sale for 25% off the original price. If the original price was $350, how much is the TV now. ____________________

Trevor works on commission at a men's clothing store. His base salary is at $4,000 a month, but he gets 12% of what he sells in addition to his salary. If one month he sold $2,520 worth of clothing, how much was his salary that month? ____________________

3. Use one step to find how much you would pay in total if you bought $300 worth of house paint and had to pay a sales tax of 8%. ____________________

4. What is the sales tax rate if an item was $50.00 and then after adding tax it cost $53.00? ____________________

5. Mr. Huckle wants to put a 12.5% down payment on a house that is is selling for $240,000. After his down payment, how much will he still owe?

____

6. Hanna and Tanya each set up a proportion for the following problem. A sofa was \$250 before the holidays, and after the holidays it was marked up 40% (this means it went up in price 40%). What is the new price? Who set the problem right? Explain your thinking.

Hanna	Tanya
$\frac{250}{100} = \frac{n}{140}$	$\frac{250}{100} = \frac{n}{60}$

____

____

____

7. A shirt costs \$24.00. The sales tax is 7.5%. It is now on sale for 30% off. Is it the same to figure out the cost of the shirt plus the tax and then take 30% off or is better to take 30% off the shirt's price first and then add the tax? Explain your thinking.

____

____

____

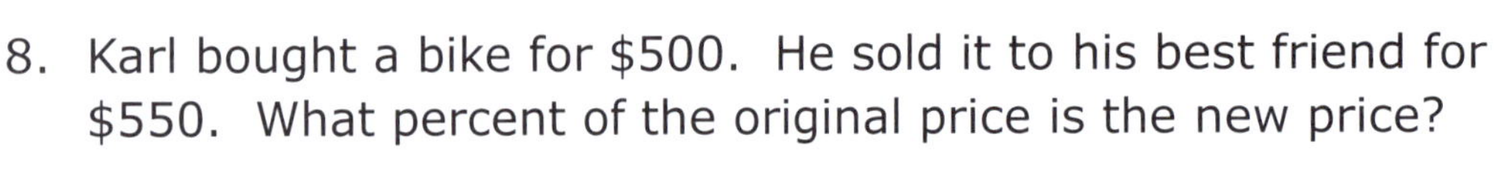

8. Karl bought a bike for \$500. He sold it to his best friend for \$550. What percent of the original price is the new price?

____

9. The original price of a dining room set is \$650. Next month, the price will go up by 5%. What will the new price be? Now if that price drops by 5% the month after that, will the price return to \$650? Why or why not? Explain your thinking.

____

____

____

Percent Increase and Decrease

You have worked with percent increase when you figured out what percent an item has gone up, and you've also done percent decrease when you found out the discount on an item. However, sometimes these problems are phrased differently and knowing a simple formula can help you.

Example 1: This is problem 9 from the previous section.

Karl bought a bike for $500. He sold it to his best friend for $550. What percent of the original price is the new price?

Hopefully, you set up this proportion. $\frac{550}{500} = \frac{n}{100}$ and found the answer to be 110%. What if you're asked, what is the percent increase? The increase is clearly 10%. Here's how you can find the percent increase in one step.

To find the percent of increase or decrease, find the absolute value of the difference between the two amounts, write that difference or change over the original amount. Then set that equal to $\frac{n}{100}$.

So the difference between 550 and 500 is 50. Set 50 over the original amount which is 500.

$$\frac{50}{500} = \frac{n}{100}$$

$500n = 5{,}000$ Divide now by 500.

$n = 10$ So the percent increase is 10%.

Example 2: The price of milk decreased from $3.50 to $3.15. Find the percent decrease.

The difference is $.35. Set up this proportion.

original amount

$$\frac{0.35}{3.50} = \frac{n}{100}$$

$3.50n = 35$(Divide 35 by 3.5)

$n = 10$ So the percent decrease is 10%.

Understanding Simple Interest vs Compound Interest

If you borrow money from a friend who decides to charge you simple interest, you will multiply the principal (amount you borrowed) times the rate (percent of interest) times the amount of time you will have the money until you pay it back.

Simple Interest: Principal • Rate • Time = Simple Interest

Example 1: Louisa borrowed $2,000 from her uncle to buy her college books. Her uncle told her she must pay the amount back in a year and a half at a rate of 10% a year. How much will Louisa owe her uncle after a year and a half?

Principal • Rate • Time = Simple Interest

$2,000 • .10 • 1.5 = $300

Louisa will owe the original $2,000 plus the interest which is $300 for a total of $2,300.

In compound interest, the interest is compounded. This means that you have to pay interest on the original amount, and then pay interest on a new principal that includes the previous interest and so on. Remember, this is why carrying a balance on a credit card can be so dangerous.

Example 2: Jon charged his new $500 stereo on his credit card. His credit card charges 12% a year on any balance not paid. If Jon were to not pay his credit card monthly, what would he owe after 3 years?

Year	Principal		Rate		Interest	New Amount Owed
1	$500	•	.12	=	$60	$560
2	$560	•	.12	=	$67.20	$627.20 ($560 + $67.20)
3	$627.20	•	.12	=	$75.26	$702.46 ($627.20 + $75.26)

He would owe $702.46! Later, you'll learn a formula that you can use with a calculator to make finding compound interest easier.

Practice

Show your work. Use a separate sheet of paper if needed.

1. A round trip flight to Rome, Italy, from New York City, is on sale for $1,200 if you go in February. Unfortunately, Ron has to go in March when he has time off from work, but the round trip flight in March is $4,200. What is the percent increase for the round trip from February to March?

   ____

2. A computer monitor used to be $240, and now it's on sale for $180. What is the percent decrease (percent of discount)?

   ____

3. The cost of a movie ticket in 2016 was $8.00 at the Ramada Mall. In the year 2000, the cost was $5.00. What is the percent of increase from 2000 to 2016?

   ____

4. Mr. Curtis explained to his daughter that inflation is the increase in the price you pay for goods. He also explained that when prices go up, people have less buying power. Using the example below, explain what Mr. Curtis meant by "inflation" and find the percent of increase.

   The cost of gluten free bread went up from $4.50 to $6.00 in one month.

   ____

   ____

   ____

   ____

5. John was hoping for a 5% increase in his salary this year. His current salary is $50,000 a year. He just found out that his new salary is $52,000. Did he get a 5% raise? Explain your thinking. If not, what was his percent of increase?

   ____

   ____

   ____

   ____

6. Magda borrowed $3,000 from her brother, and they agreed that she would pay it back in 4 years at 3% simple interest.

   a. How much interest will Magda owe her brother in 4 years? __________

   b. How much will she have to pay her brother in total? __________

7. Which of the following choices would allow Joanna to save more money?

Choice 1	Choice 2
Joanna borrows $5,000 at 6% simple interest yearly rate for 5 years from her dad.	Joanna borrows $5,000 at a compound yearly interest rate of 6% for 5 years from a bank.

   a. Choice 1:

   b. Choice 2: (You may use a calculator.)

Year	Principal	Rate	Interest	Principal + Interest
1	$5,000	.06	________	________
2	________	.06	________	________
3	________	.06	________	________
4	________	.06	________	________
5	________	.06	________	________

8. Dave thinks his new car depreciated (went down in value) 20% during the first year he drove it. He bought it for $36,000 and after a year it was worth $28,000. Is he correct? Explain your thinking.

____

____

____

____

Chapter 5 Review

Solve the following word problems. Show your work. Use a separate sheet of paper if needed.

1. Nadia bought a backpack when she was visiting her grandparents in Ohio. The sales tax rate she paid was 5.75%. How much in total did she pay (including tax), if the backpack was $30.00? Round to the nearest cent.

   ____

2. Lydia is a teacher and last year she made $50,000 a year. This year she got a new job making $55,000. What is the percent of increase?

   ____

3. Finally, the video game Roger has been wanting is on sale! The original price was $80, and now he can buy it for $30. What is the percent of discount? Nathan thinks his discount is 62.5%, and Tom thinks it's 37.5%. Who is right? Explain your thinking.

   ____

   ____

   ____

4. Ana bought a pair of shoes for $42.80 including sales tax. She could not remember the original price, but she knew the sales tax rate in her state was 7%. What was the cost of the shoes before the tax? Use a proportion to solve this problem.

   ____

5. Keene got 14 problems correct on a 15 question quiz. What was his percent score to the nearest percent?

   ____

6. A student answered 150 problems correctly on a math test and her score was 75%. If all the problems were worth the same number of points, how many problems were on the test?

   ____

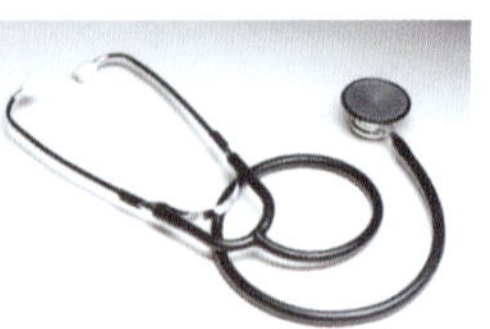

7. At a hospital, the nursing staff is made up of 12 women nurses. The rest are male nurses. If $66\frac{2}{3}\%$ of the nursing staff are women, how many nurses are male?

____

8. A computer cost $450 after a 20% discount. What was the original price of the computer?

____

9. What is the simple interest you would pay if you borrowed $10,000 at a yearly 5% rate for 4 years? What is the total that you would have to pay back.

____

10. Find the simple interest you would pay if you borrowed $500 at a monthly rate of 2% for 2 years.

____

11. Fill out the chart below to find the total you would owe if you borrowed $10,000 at a yearly rate of 5% for 4 years using compound interest. (You may use a calculator.)

Year	Principal	Rate	Interest	New Principal
1	$10,000	.05	______	______
2	______	.05	______	______
3	______	.05	______	______
4	______	.05	______	______

12. Now compare what you would owe in problem #11 with what you owe in problem #9. Explain the reason for the difference in the amounts.

____

____

____

____

Chapter 6

Algebraic Expressions

An algebraic expression is any mathematical statement that does not have an equal or an inequality sign. An equation always has an equal sign (=). Study the following to see the difference between an expression and an equation.

Expressions	Equations
$-15 + 2$	$-15 + 2 = -13$
$2n$	$2n + 5 = 11$
$7a + b$	$7a + b = b + 14$
90	$90 = (-2)(-45)$

Think of an expression as a "phrase" as opposed to a "sentence." An equation is a sentence, so it contains a <u>verb</u>. For example, −15 plus 2 <u>is</u> −13.

You can think of an equation as two expressions that are set equal to each other. An equation is asking you to find an answer. An expression such as "$n + 3$" is left alone until you know a value for the <u>variable</u> n. Once you know the value of the variable you can evaluate the expression. To evaluate an expression means to 1) substitute or plug in a value, and 2) simplify or find the final answer. When you evaluate an expression, try to work down instead of sideways and avoid using equal signs as you simplify.

Remember that $5a$ means 5 times the variable a. The expression 5 times −4 can be written as 5(−4), (5)(−4), or 5 • −4. Don't use an X for multiplication when you're working with variables as it can be easily confused with the variable x. When you see 54, it means fifty-four, but when you see ab it means a times b.

Evaluating Expressions

Example 1: If $a = -4$, $b = 3$ and $c = 2$, evaluate $5a - b + 4c$.

$5(-4) - 3 + 4(2)$ Substitute or plug in a value.

$-20 - 3 + 8$ Simplify using the order of operations.

$-23 + 8$

-15

Don't forget to work down!

Example 2: If $n = 3$ and $m = -2$, evaluate $4n^2 - m$.

$4(3)^2 - (-2)$ Substitute or plug in a value.

$4 \bullet 9 - (-2)$ Remember the order of operations.

$36 + 2$ Simplify.

38

Practice

1. Nathan thought that the variable n would be a positive number and that $-n$ would be a negative number. What is wrong with Nathan's thinking. Explain your thinking.

____

____

2. Explain how these two expressions are different.

Expression 1	Expression 2
$(x + 3)^3$	$(x + 3^3)$

____

____

3. Evaluate each of the expressions in #2, if $x = 0$ and then if $x = 1$.

   a. Expression 1 if $x = 0$ ______, Expression 2 if $x = 0$ ______

   b. Expression 1 if $x = 1$ ______, Expression 2 if $x = 1$ ______

4. As you learned in Chapter 2, you cannot divide by 0. When that happens the expression has NO answer. You can say the answer is the empty set and write Ø. You can also say the expression is undefined. State what value cannot exist for the variable because the expression would be undefined.

   a. $\frac{4}{x}$ ____________

   c. $\frac{1}{x - 9}$ ____________

   b. $\frac{-5}{x + 8}$ ____________

   d. $\frac{1}{2x - 6}$ ____________

Evaluate these expressions. Show substituting step, work, and final answer. Use a separate sheet of paper if needed. Let $n = 3$, $x = 6$, $y = -2$, and $r = 0$.

5. $-n + y$ ________

12. $\frac{20}{r}$ ________

6. $|\,y\,| + x - y$ ________

13. $\frac{18}{2 + y}$ ________

7. $19y + x$ ________

14. yn ________

8. $x^n + n^x$ ________

15. $nx^2 + (nx)^2$ ________

9. nxy ________

16. $5n + n$ ________

10. $5n + 4x + 2y + 8r$ ________

17. $6n$ ________

11. $(2x + y)^4$ ________

18. $xnyr$ ________

Translating Expressions

Translating expressions from words to math will help you solve word problems. The following is a list of words that mean the operations add, subtract, multiply, or divide.

+	−	•	÷
add	subtract	multiply	divide
plus	take away	times	split into
increase	minus	of	divide by
more	less	twice	break into
augment	less than	squared	half
(sum)	from	cubed	**quotient**
	decrease	by	
	diminish	**product**	
	(difference)		

Notice the words in bold. Sum is the answer to an addition problem. Difference is the answer to a subtraction problem. When you see the words "sum" or "difference," you must put parenthesis around those expressions as those words mean to find the answer first.

Product is the answer to multiplication. Quotient is the answer to a division problem. Since multiplication and division are done first (in the order of operations), they do not need parenthesis. Just follow these examples to help you.

In this book, n will be used as the variable anytime you see "a number." Later, you can use any variable you want.

Example 1: twice a number plus eight

Answer: $2n + 8$

It helps to read aloud what you just wrote.

Example 2: twice the sum of a number plus eight

Answer: $2(n + 8)$

Notice the word "sum."

Example 3: three times a number minus ten

Answer: $3n - 10$

Example 4: Three times the difference of a number minus ten.

Answer: $3(n - 10)$

Notice the word "difference."

Understanding "Less," "Less Than," and "From"

The word "less" is the same as the word "minus." However, the words "less than" or "from," mean you reverse the order.

Example 1: A number less seven: $n - 7$

Example 2: A number less than seven: $7 - n$

Example 3: A number from 7: $7 - n$

In both of these cases you're taking the number from 7.

Example 4: A number squared times eight.

$n^2 \bullet 8$ or $8n^2$

In the expression $8n$, the 8 or outside number is called the coefficient. Remember from chapter 2 that n, our variable in this case, can also be called the base and "2" is the exponent or power.

Practice

Translate the words into math.

1. twice a number increased by ten ______________
2. two more than the product of five and a number ______________
3. a number decreased by twenty ______________
4. the quotient of a number divided by three ______________
5. eleven from a number ______________
6. a number squared decreased by four ______________
7. seventeen less than a number ______________
8. twice the sum of a number plus eight ______________
9. twice a number plus eight ______________

10. half a number ____________

11. half the sum of a number augmented by one ____________

12. the product of a number with one-hundred ____________

13. four times the difference of a number less than twenty ____________

14. the square of a number less fifteen ____________

15. eighteen from a number ____________

$(n + 8)^2$ can be read as "the sum of a number plus eight quantity squared." It can also be read as the sum of a number plus eight squared, but the word "quantity" is more commonly used to express that you will square the entire quantity and not just the eight.

Translate the math into words.

16. $2(n + 9)$ ________________________

17. $18 - n$ ________________________

18. $(n - 4)^2$ ________________________

19. $\frac{2n + 3}{5}$ ________________________

20. $n^3 - 4$ ________________________

21. $2n - 5$ ________________________

22. $5 - 2n$ ________________________

23. $(3n)^3$ ________________________

24. $\frac{n}{9} + 1$ ________________________

Write the letter of the words that matches the math.

______ 25.	$2n + 5 = 20$	a. undefined if $n = 4$
______ 26.	$(2n)^3$	b. n plus eight quantity cubed
______ 27.	$2(n - 8)$	c. n increased by 10
______ 28.	$2n - 8$	d. example of an equation
______ 29.	$n - 8$	e. n diminished by 10
______ 30.	$8 - n$	f. product of 8 and n
______ 31.	$\frac{8}{n - 4}$	g. undefined if $n = -8$
______ 32.	$8n$	h. two times n plus 1
______ 33.	$2n^3$	i. n less than 8
______ 34.	$(n + 8)^3$	j. undefined if $n = 0$
______ 35.	$\frac{-8}{n}$	k. cube the product of two times a number
______ 36.	$\frac{8}{n + 8}$	l. 8 from n
______ 37.	$2n + 1$	m. twice the difference of n less eight
______ 38.	$2(n + 1)$	n. twice a number cubed
______ 39.	$n - 10$	o. twice the sum of n plus one
______ 40.	$n + 10$	p. twice n minus 8

Polynomials

The word polynomial is another word for an expression. "Poly" means many and "nomial" has to do with numbers. Polynomials can contain numbers only, variables only, or variables and numbers. They are classified according to the number of terms. A term is a unit that is separated by the operations + or –. Any polynomial that has more than 3 terms is just called "polynomial."

Monomials	Binomials	Trinomials
$3n$	$3n + 4$	$2n^2 + 5n - 8$
$3x^3y^2z$	$x^3 - 7$	$5x + 2y + 9z$
-10	$\frac{x}{2} + 4$	$15ab + c + 4d$

A polynomial CANNOT have a variable with a negative exponent. It cannot have a variable in the denominator or have a variable inside a square root symbol. So these are not polynomials: $5n^{-3}$, $\frac{5}{n}$, $\sqrt{x}$.

Terms are separated by the operations of addition and subtraction. That is why $3x^3y^2z$ is one term.

Polynomials are the tools of algebra. Algebra is used to solve problems without having to do trial and error. You will learn the basics of how to add, subtract, multiply, and divide polynomials, and how to manipulate them to solve equations. At first, you may not see how any of this relates to real life situations, but later on you will! Sometimes in math, as in other subjects, you have to hang in there before it dawns on you how what you're learning relates to something real and important.

Understanding "Like Terms"

The Roberts family was having a reunion at a local park. They made signs and t-shirts. The Robertson family was also having a reunion at the same park. Their last names were so similar that the lady at the park gate started to get confused as to which pavilion to send each family member. Yet, just because the last names sound so similar it's clear that the ending of the last names are different. The same is true of polynomial terms like xy and xy^2. They look very similar, but they are not like terms.

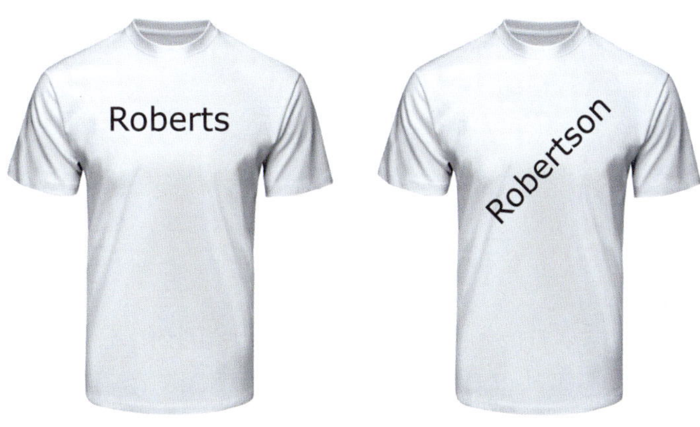

Look at these pairs of like terms:

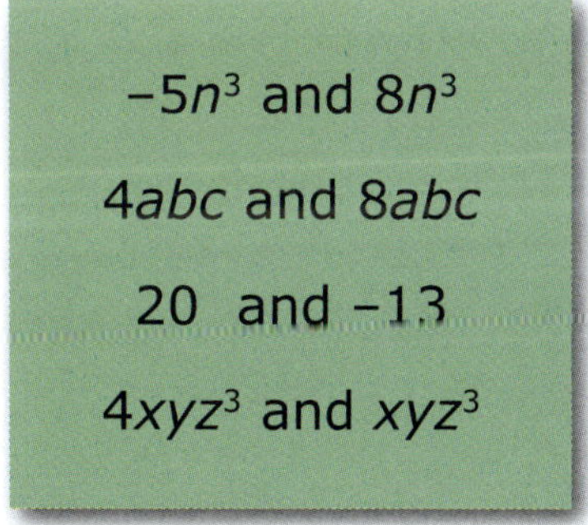

$-5n^3$ and $8n^3$

$4abc$ and $8abc$

20 and -13

$4xyz^3$ and xyz^3

Like terms can have different coefficients but their variable component (what follows the coefficient) must be identical. This means the variables must be the same and the exponent must be the same. All constants are considered like terms.

Adding or Combining Like Terms

You can ONLY add and subtract like terms by adding or subtracting their coefficients and then keeping the like term as it was when you started.

A subtraction sign in front of a term is the same as a negative sign. Every term carries the sign in front of it.

Example 1: Add: $3x^2 + 5x + 3 + 8 - 8x + x^2$

$3x^2 + 5x + 3 + 8 - 8x + 1x^2$ The coefficient here is 1.

Answer: $4x^2 - 3x + 11$

The endings stay the same. It's like adding 3 bananas plus 2 bananas. You get 5 bananas, not 5 bananas bananas!

Example 2: Simplify: $-abc + ab + ab + 4abc + 2c$

$3abc + 2ab + 2c$

Words such as "simplify" and "combine" are often used when adding. Parenthesis are sometimes used as a grouping symbol to help with reading.

Example 3: Simplify: $(3x^3 + 4x + 3) + (-4x^3 - 6x - 9)$

Answer: $-x^3 - 2x - 6$

Practice

Circle which terms are like terms.

Remember: Same Ending!

1. $5a$, 7, $-6a$, $8x$, $8z$
2. $6b$, $8n$, $-8n$, 10
3. $20n^3$, $10n$, $8y$, $-4n$
4. $5xy$, $3x^2$, $3x^3$, $-10xy$, xy
5. $3ab$, $4b$, $4a$, $-9ab$, $8ab$

Simplify the following by combining like terms. Tell if the result is a monomial, a binomial, or a trinomial.

Avoid double signs. $4a - 4b$ is better than: $4a + -4b$.

Type of Polynomial

Example: $(3a + 2b) + (a - 6b)$

$4a - 4b$ ________ binomial ________

When you write your answer, try to keep the highest exponents first, constants at the end, and keep alphabetical order. This makes it easier for more than one person to check answers with each other or with the answer key.

6. $-9x + 5x + 3 - 10$ Type of Polynomial

________ ________

7. $-15 + 7n + 15 - 7n$

________ ________

8. $9n^2 + 7n^3 + 10n - 10n^3$

________ ________

9. $-5a + 6b + 7c + 9b - 8c$

________ ________

10. $-7 + 7p + 7 + 10p + 8r$

________ ________

11. $(n + 3) + (n - 9) + (n + 10)$

________ ________

12. $(x + 8) + (-x + 9) + (3x + 2)$

________ ________

13. $\frac{n}{2} + 5 + \frac{n}{2} - 5$

________________ ________________

14. $-7abcd + 15abcd$

________________ ________________

15. $-7w + 9w - 10w + w + w + 3$

________________ ________________

Answer the following.

16. If $x = 3$, show why $8x + 2x$ is the same as $10x$ and NOT $10x^2$.

____

17. If $a = -2$, $b = 3$, show why $5ab + ab = 6ab$.

____

18. Show why $5x + 6x^2 \neq 11x^3$ by letting x equal a number other than 0 or 1.

____

Find the missing term.

19. $(10a + b) + (\_\_\_ + 5b)$

$-12a + 6b$

____

20. $(3x^2 + 9) + (\_\_\_ - 9)$

$-x^2$

____

Subtracting Polynomials

To subtract polynomials you need to remember that subtracting is the same as adding the inverse.

Example 1: Subtract $(6x + 7) - (-8x + 9)$.

Notice the subtraction sign!

Change the subtraction to + and change the signs of the terms that follow the subtraction sign inside the parenthesis. You get:

$6x + 7 + 8x - 9$

Answer: $14x - 2$

How would the answer differ if the problem had been

$(6x + 7) - (8x + 9)$?

Here the $8x$ is positive and changes to $-8x$.

$6x + 7 - 8x - 9$

Answer: $-2x - 2$

Example 2: Subtract $(9a + b)$ from $(10a - 3b)$.

Notice the word "from."

Rewrite the problem: $(10a - 3b) - (9a + b)$

$10a - 3b - 9a - b$

Answer: $a - 4b$

Example 3: Simplify $(4x^2 + 8x + 3)$ less than $(9 - 2x + 7x^2)$.

Notice the word "less than."

Rewrite the problem: $(9 - 2x + 7x^2) - (4x^2 + 8x + 3)$

$9 - 2x + 7x^2 - 4x^2 - 8x - 3$

$3x^2 - 10x + 6$

Practice

Use a separate sheet of paper if needed.

1. $(3x + 5) - (-4x + 8)$ ____________

2. From $(2n + 8)$ subtract $(3n - 9)$. That's the subtraction sign!

____

3. $(3ab + 2b + c) - (2b + c)$ ____________

4. $(5Q + 3)$ less than $(8Q + 4)$ ____________

5. $(11n^2 - 6n + 4) - (11n^2 - 7n + 8)$ ____________

6. From $(2a + b)$ take away $(2a + 2b)$. That's the subtraction sign!

____

7. $(-4n - 7r + 8f + 2w) - (-3w + 8r + 5n - 2f)$ ____________

8. $(5xy + 2)$ decreased by $(2xy + 3)$ ____________

9. $(3x + y) + (-8x + 2y) + (4y + x)$ ____________

10. $(-7b + 2b) + (2 + 8b - 4)$ ____________

11. Subtract -18 from $(2x + 19)$. Hint: This means $(2x + 19) - (-18)$

____

12. Subtract $2x$ from $(5x + 3)$. ____________

13. $(3x^2 + 5x - 7) + (-3x^2 - 5x + 7)$ ____________

14. $(x + 2y) - (2x + 3y) + (8x - 9y)$ ____________

Multiplication of Monomials - Exploring Exponent Rules

Addition and subtraction of polynomials is very strict. You can only add or subtract like terms. However, when you multiply and divide monomials the rules are different.

Example 1: Multiply $a^4 \bullet a^5$

$a \bullet a \bullet a \bullet a \;\bullet\; a \bullet a \bullet a \bullet a \bullet a$

Answer: a^9

You're NOT adding the *a*'s. You're adding how many factors of *a*'s you have.

Since the base (a) is the same for both you can put the base down and add the exponents.

Example 2: Find the product of $(-3n)(4n^4)$.

The exponent of the n is 1.

This is the same as $-3 \bullet n \bullet 4 \bullet n \bullet n \bullet n \bullet n$

Multiply the coefficients $(-3)(4)$, which is -12. Put the base (n) down and add the exponents.

Answer: $-12n^5$

Example 3: Find the product of $(3n^5w)(-7n^3w^2)$.

This means $3 \bullet n \bullet n \bullet n \bullet n \bullet n \bullet w \bullet -7 \bullet n \bullet n \bullet n \bullet w \bullet w$

Answer: $-21n^8w^3$

To multiply monomials, <u>multiply</u> the coefficients, put any base that is the same down, and <u>add</u> their corresponding exponents.

Thinking More About Monomials

Look at how these expressions are different.

Expression 1: $a + a + a + a + a$

You are adding a five times. So if $a = 2$, you are adding $2 + 2 + 2 + 2 + 2$, which is the same as $5 \bullet 2$ or 10. Don't forget multiplication is repeated addition. Answer: $5a$.

Expression 2: $a \bullet a \bullet a \bullet a \bullet a$

You are multiplying a by itself five times. So if $a = 2$, you are multiplying $2 \bullet 2 \bullet 2 \bullet 2 \bullet 2$, which is 32 (not 10). A shorter notation is to write 2^5. Answer: a^5

Expression 3: $n + n + n + w + w + w + w$

You have $3n + 4w$, and you cannot do any more adding as you don't know the value of n or the value of w. Once you know the values of n and w, you would evaluate and then simplify using the order of operations.

Expression 4: $n \bullet n \bullet n \bullet w \bullet w \bullet w \bullet w$

You have n^3w^4. If you knew the value of n, you would multiply it by itself 3 times, and if you knew the value of w you would multiply it by itself 4 times. Once you had both products, then you'd multiply those as well.

Practice

1. Show by letting $x = 4$ that $x + x + x + x + x + x$ is the same as $6x$.

____

2. Show by letting $x = 4$ that $x \bullet x \bullet x \bullet x \bullet x \bullet x$ is NOT $6x$.

____

Multiply these monomials.

3. $h^4 \bullet h^5 \bullet h^6$ ____________________

4. $(3x)(9x^3)$ ____________________

5. $-5y \bullet -6y$ ______________________

6. $(12w)(-4w)$ ______________________

7. $(17n^5)(-2n^6)$ ______________________

8. $(-8xy^5)(-x^5y)$ ______________________

9. $(9w^5)(9w^5)$ ______________________

10. $-n \bullet -n \bullet -n \bullet -n \bullet -n$ ______________________

11. $(11w^4y)(-11w^9y^5)$ ______________________

12. $(-18abc)(-3abc)$ ______________________

13. $12m \bullet 12m \bullet m$ ______________________

Fill in the term that is missing.

14. $v^4 \bullet$ _______ $= v^8$

15. _______ $\bullet\ 3a = 51a^5$

16. $(-16w^5) \bullet$ _______ $= 48w^7$

17. _______ $\bullet\ 34x^7 = 17x^8$

18. $(3n^5y) \bullet$ _______ $= 54n^8y^8$

19. $5x \bullet$ _______ $= 90x^4$

20. _______ $\bullet\ 100n^8 = 75n^8$

21. $5x \bullet 2x \bullet$ _______ $= 100x^7$

22. $13n^5 \bullet 13n^3 \bullet$ _______ $= -169n^8$

Powers

As you know from the order of operations, $5n^2$ and $(5n)^2$ will give you different answers (unless n is 0). Remember that $5n^2$ is the same as $5 \bullet n \bullet n$, while $(5n)^2$ is $5 \bullet n \bullet 5 \bullet n$ or $25n^2$. When you take an entire term to a power (or exponent), it helps to write out the term as many times as the power tells you to do.

Example 1: Simplify: $(-3n^5)^2$

Write it out: $(-3n^5)(-3n^5)$

Answer: $9n^{10}$

Write the term in the parenthesis as many times as the exponent tells you.

Example 2: Simplify: $(10n^4)^3$

Write it out: $(10n^4)(10n^4)(10n^4)$

Answer: $1{,}000n^{12}$

Practice

Simplify the following.

1. $(9x)^2$
2. $(-4m^6)^2$
3. $(-8w^3)^2$
4. $(2h^6)^3$
5. $(-10n^5)^3$
6. $(-10n^5)^4$
7. $(9x^4)^2$
8. $(15x)^2$
9. $(-15x)^2$
10. $(3ab)^3$

Answer the following.

11. Do you see a shortcut for the problems above that would help so you do not have to write the problem out every time? For example, is there a shortcut to doing the problem below? Explain your thinking.

$(10n^3y^6)^7$

____

____

____

12. In the expression $6n^3$, 6 is defined as the coefficient, n as the base (which happens to be a variable), and 3 as the power or exponent. Also, when $6n^3 \bullet 6n^3$, the answer is $36n^6$, because the coefficients are multiplied, the base (n) is put down, and the exponents are added. Explain that the answer to the problem below is 10^6 and NOT 100^6?

$10^3 \bullet 10^3 = 10^6$

____

____

____

____

13. Fill in the answers to the following powers of 10.

	Number		**Written Out**		**10 to a Power**
a.	1,000,000	=	10 • 10 • 10 • 10 • 10 • 10	=	10^6
b.	100,000	=	10 • 10 • 10 • 10 • 10	=	________
c.	10,000	=	____________________	=	________
d.	1,000	=	____________________	=	________
e.	100	=	____________________	=	________
f.	10	=	____________________	=	________
g.	1	=	→	=	________

Division of Monomials

In problem 13, on the previous page, the powers of ten kept losing a zero, so there was one less factor of 10. This was because it was divided by 10 each time.

So 1,000,000 became 100,000 because 1,000,000 was divided by 10, and then 100,000, became 10,000 because it was divided by 10. On the right hand side of the chart, the exponent was decreasing by 1 each time. So why is 10^0 the same as 1? Because any base (except a base of 0) to the 0 power is also 1.

Example 1: Divide $\frac{n^5}{n^2}$.

This means $\frac{n \bullet n \bullet n \bullet n \bullet n}{n \bullet n}$. Since you're dividing, you can cancel.

$\frac{n \bullet n \bullet n \bullet \cancel{n} \bullet \cancel{n}}{\cancel{n} \bullet \cancel{n}}$ and you get n^3.

Can you see that you would get the same answer by putting n down and subtracting the exponents?

Example 2: Find the quotient $\frac{n^6}{n^6}$.

Again this means $\frac{\cancel{n} \bullet \cancel{n} \bullet \cancel{n} \bullet \cancel{n} \bullet \cancel{n} \bullet \cancel{n}}{\cancel{n} \bullet \cancel{n} \bullet \cancel{n} \bullet \cancel{n} \bullet \cancel{n} \bullet \cancel{n}}$ because you can cancel.

You are dividing, so the answer is NOT 0. The answer is 1.

If you put the base down and subtract the exponents, you would get n^0 which is the same as 1.

> To divide monomials, divide the coefficients. Put any base that is the same down and subtract their corresponding exponents.
>
> Any base to the zero power is 1 (except a base of 0).

Example 3: Divide $\frac{15x^{10}}{-3x}$.

Divide the coefficients. You get -5. Put the x down and subtract the exponents. Remember x in the denominator has an exponent of 1.

Answer: $-5x^9$

Example 4: Divide $\frac{4a^3}{16a^2}$.

Remember to reduce. It's 4 divided by 16.

Answer: $\frac{1a}{4}$ or $\frac{a}{4}$

Example 5: Find the quotient $\frac{45a^7b^4}{-15a^3}$.

Notice how b^4 carries to the answer.

Answer: $-3a^4b^4$

Simplify the following. Assume none of the variables in the denominator are zero.

1. $\frac{h^6}{h^3}$

6. $\frac{87n^8}{3n^5}$

2. $\frac{h^6}{h^6}$

7. $\frac{-18w^6}{-36w^2}$

3. $\frac{-32n^8}{8n^4}$

8. $\frac{-4p^6}{-48p^6}$

4. $\frac{-84a^7}{-3a}$

9. $\frac{-90ab}{-90ab}$

5. $\frac{-200a^7}{-8a^6}$

10. Divide $20x$ by 40.

Understanding Negative Powers

Using negative exponents is a way of representing terms that end up in the denominator.

Example 1: What is $\frac{10^3}{10^4}$?

This is the same as $\frac{1{,}000}{10{,}000}$ or $\frac{10 \bullet 10 \bullet 10}{10 \bullet 10 \bullet 10 \bullet 10}$.

You can cancel $\frac{\cancel{10} \bullet \cancel{10} \bullet \cancel{10}}{\cancel{10} \bullet \cancel{10} \bullet \cancel{10} \bullet 10}$ and this leaves $\frac{1}{10}$.

If you use the rules for dividing, you put the base (which is 10) down and subtract the exponents. Therefore the following is true.

$$\frac{1}{10} = 10^{-1}$$

Go back to the powers of 10 problem #13 to see how if you keep dividing 1 by 10, you will get $\frac{1}{10}$ = .1 which is 10^{-1}. Then dividing $\frac{1}{10}$ by 10 again you will get $\frac{1}{100}$ = .01 which is 10^{-2}, etc.

Example 2: Find the quotient $\frac{-54a^3}{9a^5}$.

You can write your answer in two ways $\frac{-6}{a^2}$ leaving the extra a factors in the denominator or you can write your answer as $-6a^{-2}$.

A negative exponent indicates a reciprocal.

Example 3: Write b^{-5} as a fraction with a positive exponent.

Write $\frac{b^{-5}}{1}$. Remember that the −5 exponent indicates that five b factors were left in the denominator. You can use the reciprocal (flip the fraction upside down), but then change the exponent to a positive exponent.

Answer: $\frac{1}{b^5}$

Practice

Simplify the following problems. If you end up with a negative exponent, write your answer two ways (see Example 2). Assume none of the variables in the denominator are zero.

1. $\frac{-10a}{-5a}$ ________________

7. $\frac{-88mn^8}{-11m^9n}$ ________________

2. $\frac{40c^4}{2c^9}$ ________________

8. $\frac{-50w}{-75w^3}$ ________________

3. $\frac{-26a^6}{13a^7}$ ________________

9. $\frac{-50}{-25w}$ ________________

4. $\frac{2a^6}{200a^8}$ ________________

10. $\frac{-34x}{-68x^9}$ ________________

5. $\frac{-90x^8}{-90x^9}$ ________________

11. $\frac{80}{-40x^9}$ ________________

6. $\frac{18m^6n}{-9m^2n8}$ ________________

12. $\frac{3^3}{3^4}$ ________________

Scientific Notation

Scientific Notation is a shortcut for writing long numbers, especially numbers in science that are very large or very small in quantity. Scientific notation uses positive and negative exponents with powers of ten.

To write a number in scientific notation, write the first digit followed by the decimal point. Keep any significant digits (those are non-zero digits unless there's a zero between two non-zero digits), get rid of the rest of the zeros and multiply the number by a power of 10. Use the X symbol for multiplication.

Example 1: Write 5,870,000,000,000 in scientific notation.

Answer: 5.87×10^{12}

The length of a light year is about 5,870,000,000,000 miles!

Remember when you multiply a number by a 10 that is raised to a positive power, you move the decimal point to the right as many times as the exponent indicates. When you multiply a number by a 10 that is raised to a negative power, you move the decimal point to the left as many times as the exponent indicates. That's because 10 to a negative power is the same as dividing by a power of 10.

Example 2: A red blood cell is about .000008 meters long. Write this number in scientific notation.

Answer 8×10^{-6}

Remember that the 8 has the decimal point after it. Now, you're going to multiply the 8 by 10^{-6} which is the same as multiplying it by this fraction $\frac{1}{1,000,000}$ (or dividing by 1,000,000). Since you're dividing by a power of 10, move the decimal point to the left 6 places to check your answer.

Example 3: Write 403,000,000 in scientific notation.

Here, the first zero between the 4 and the 3 must be kept as it's between two significant digits.

Answer 4.03×10^{8}

Always remember to check your answer.

Practice

Write the following in scientific notation. Be sure to check your answers. Fill in the missing exponent in some problems.

1. The distance from Earth to Jupiter is about 588,000,000 km.

   _______________ X $10^{\square}$

2. A nanometer is one billionth (.000000001) of a meter. 1 X $10^{\square}$.

3. The population of Earth is about 7 billion. 7 X ______

4. A micrometer is one millionth (.000001) of a meter. 1 X $10^{\square}$.

5. A strand of hair is about .000003 of a meter. __________________

6. Scientists estimate that there about 10 billion observable galaxies in the universe. __________________

7. The U.S. population is about 324,000,000 people. __________________

8. A flu virus is about .00000013 meters long. __________________

Write the following as a decimal number.

9. The population of China is about 1.387 X 10^{9} __________________

10. The radius of a hydrogen atom is about 2.5 X 10^{-11} m. __________________

11. Light travels about 1.86 X 10^{5} miles per second. __________________

12. The moon is 2.389 X 10^{5} miles from Earth. __________________

Using Scientific Notation to Simplify

Scientific notation can help you find the answer to multiplication and division of very long numbers.

Example 1: Divide 9,000,000,000 by 30,000,000.

You can write the division problem like this:

Divide 9 ÷ 3 $\frac{9 \text{ X } 10^9}{3 \text{ X } 10^7}$

Same base! Put the base down and subtract the powers.

The answer is: 3 X 10^2 or 300.

Example 2: Multiply 4,000,000 X 5,000,000,000,000.

Rewrite the problem as (4 X 10^6)(5 X 10^{12}).

The answer is 20 X 10^{18}.

In scientific notation this is the same as 2 X 10^{19}. Do you know how to read the number 20,000,000,000,000,000,000? It's 20 quintillion!

Practice

Use scientific notation and the rules for multiplying and dividing with exponents to simplify these problems without a calculator. Write your final answer in scientific notation.

1. 3,000,000 X 2,500,000

____

3. $\frac{4{,}000{,}000{,}000}{2{,}000{,}000}$

____

2. (4.5 X 10^6)(2 X 10^5)

____

4. (3.52 X 10^6)(4 X 10^7)

____

5. $\dfrac{4.5 \text{ X } 10^5}{9 \text{ X } 10^5}$

____

6. $(6 \text{ X } 10^6)(1.5 \text{ X } 10^3)$

____

7. $(3 \text{ X } 10^9)(6.5 \text{ X } 10^3)$

____

8. 120,000,000 ÷ 6,000

____

9. $\dfrac{1.8 \text{ X } 10^2}{3 \text{ X } 10^8}$

____

10. 5,000 X 5,000,000

____

It's important to know that when you type long numbers in the calculators, you may get answers that look like this, 6 E 9 or 6 E –9. An answer of 6 E 9 means $6 \text{ X } 10^9$ and 6 E –9 means $6 \text{ X } 10^{-9}$.

Chapter 6 Review

1. Which of the following is the same as the expression –4 times n?

   a. $-4n$ b. $(-4)(n)$ c. $-4 \bullet n$ d. all of the above

2. Which of the following is the same as -3^2?

   a. 6 b. –9 c. 9 d. –6

3. If $a = -3$, $b = 5$ then the answer to $2a + 4b$ is

   a. 14 b. –14 c. 26 d. 3

4. Which of the following is UNDEFINED?

   a. $5 \div -5$ b. $0 \div 5$ c. $5 \div 0$ d. none of these

5. In this expression, $\frac{3}{n - 4}$, which value for n would make the expression undefined?

   a. $n = 0$ b. $n = -4$ c. $n = 4$ d. $n = -3$

6. If $x = -8$, and $y = 2$, evaluate x^y.

   a. –64 b. 16 c. –16 d. 64

7. If $n = 9$, $w = 6$ and $z = -3$, evaluate $|w| + 5n - z$.

   a. 54 b. 48 c. 39 d. 42

8. Which of the following is the translation of "twelve less than a number n"?

   a. $12 - n$ b. $n - 12$ c. $12n$ d. $n + 12$

9. Which of the following is the translation of "eighty from ten"?

   a. 10 – 80 b. 10 + 80 c. 70 d. 80 – 10

10. Which of the following is the translation of "three times the sum of a number n plus seven"?

    a. $3(n + 7)$ b. $3n + 7$ c. $3n - 7$ d. $7 - 3n$

11. Which of the following is the translation of "twice the difference of a number w less fifteen"?

a. $2w - 15$ b. $2(15 - w)$ c. $30w$ d. $2(w - 15)$

12. Which of the following is the translation of "the square of the quantity n less than ten"?

a. $2(10 - n)$ b. $(n - 10)^2$ c. $(n^2 - 10)$ d. $(10 - n)^2$

13. Which of these is not a polynomial?

a. $-10m$ b. $\frac{5}{n}$ c. $3n^2 - 2n$ d. $\frac{n}{5}$

14. Which of these is a monomial?

a. $2xy^3z$ b. $x + 5$ c. $2x + y^3 + z$ d. $2x + y$

15. Which of the following is a "like term" that can be combined with $-10n^3y^4$?

a. $-10a^3b^4$ b. $30ny$ c. $9n^4y^3$ d. $5n^3y^4$

Simplify the following.

16. Add $(4n^3 - n + 5) + (8 - 4n + 10n^3)$

____

17. Subtract $(a - b)$ from $(-3a + b)$

____

18. What is $(3w^4 - 7w + 6)$ less than $(3w^4 - 8w)$?

____

19. Multiply $(9ab)(-9ab)$

____

20. Find the product $(-3n^6)^3$

____

21. Divide $\frac{-9n^5}{-3n}$

____

22. What is 10^6?

____

23. What is 10^{-5}?

____

24. What is n^0? (assume $n \neq 0$)

____

25. Find the quotient: $\frac{6nm^7}{12nm^9}$. Write your answer two ways.

____

26. Write 8,300,000 in scientific notation.

____

27. Write .000068 in scientific notation.

____

28. Multiply $(2 \text{ X } 10^6) \text{ X } (6 \text{ X } 10^7)$ and write the answer in scientific notation.

____

29. Divide $(8 \text{ X } 10^8) \div (2 \text{ X } 10^3)$ and write the answer in scientific notation.

____

30. Write $21 \text{ X } 10^7$ in scientific notation.

____

Chapter 7

Equations and Solving Word Problems

In this chapter you will learn how to solve equations with one variable and use equations to solve problems that otherwise would take lots of "trial and error" time. But first, review the properties of real numbers and the properties of equality as these are the rules used to solve equations.

Properties of Real Numbers (Part 1)

Property	Example	Using Words
Addition Property of 0	$5 + 0 = 5$	Any number added to 0 stays the same. 0 is called the identity for addition.
Multiplication Property of 1	$-8 \bullet 1 = -8$	Any number times 1 stays the same. 1 is called the identity for multiplication.
Commutative Property of Addition	$9 + 2 = 2 + 9$	The order in which you add does not change the answer.
Commutative Property of Multiplication	$-8 \bullet -3 = -3 \bullet -8$	The order in which you multiply does not change the answer.
Associative Property of Addition	$(3 + 4)+ 8 = 3 +(4 + 8)$	Regrouping does not change the answer when you add.
Associative Property of Multiplication	$(-2 \bullet 3) \bullet 5 = -2 \bullet (3 \bullet 5)$	Regrouping does not change the answer when you multiply.

It's sometimes easy to confuse the associative property with the commutative property, so this illustration might help you!

Number People Sitting on a Sofa

In the drawing above, people 5, 7, and 9 are sitting in the same order on both sofas. In other words, 5 is to the right of 7, 7 is in the middle both times, and 9 is to the left of 7. What is different is that 5 and 7 are sitting closer to each other on one sofa, and later 7 moved closer to 9 on the other sofa. This illustrates the associative property. The way the number people are associating or grouping with each other has changed but not the order.

In this second drawing, even though there are grouping symbols, the order of the number people has changed. The 7 moved or commuted from one end of the sofa to the other end, and 9 and 5 are still grouped together. This illustrates the commutative property.

Remember that both properties *only* work for addition and multiplication.

Example: What property is being shown? $(-2 + 3) + 6 = 6 + (-2 + 3)$

The group $(-2 + 3)$ has remained the same, so this is not the associative property. Remember that the "commutative" property has to do with "commuting" or moving. The 6 is now in a different order. So the property shown is the commutative property.

Practice

1. Show how the associative property works for addition using this example. Work down as you simplify each side of the equation.
   $(-90 + 10) + 12 = -90 + (10 + 12)$

2. Show how the associative property works for multiplication using this example. Work down as you simplify each side of the equation.
   $7 \bullet (20 \bullet -2) = (7 \bullet 20) \bullet -2$

3. Show why the commutative property does not work for subtraction. Use this example. $30 - 20 = 20 - 30$

4. Show why the commutative property does not work for division. Use this example. $-28 \div 4 = 4 \div -28$

5. Show why the associative property does not work for subtraction. Use this example. Work down on each side of the equation. $(-4 - 6) - 8 = -4 - (6 - 8)$

6. Create your own example to show why the associative property does not work for division.

Properties of Real Numbers (Part 2)

Property	Example	Using Words
Additive Inverse Property	$-9 + 9 = 0$	Two opposite numbers always add to 0.
Multiplicative Inverse Property	$\frac{3}{4} \bullet \frac{4}{3}$	A number and its reciprocal always multiply to 1.
Distributive Property of Multiplication over Addition or Subtraction	$3(5 + 2) = 15 + 6$ $4(6 - 3) = 24 - 12$	You can multiply a number by each term inside a parenthesis as long as you have + or – inside the parenthesis.

Two real numbers that add to zero (the identity for addition) are called additive inverses or opposites. Two real numbers that multiply to 1 (the identity for multiplication) are called multiplicative inverses or reciprocals.

The additive inverse of 0 is 0. But 0 does NOT have a reciprocal.

The distributive property allows us to simplify an expression in two ways. Remember that when you distribute, you must multiply the outside number by each term inside the parenthesis.

Example 1: Show that $3(5 + 2) = 15 + 6$

$$3 \bullet 7 = 21$$

When you have numbers inside the parentheses, you can use the order of operations to add the numbers inside the parenthesis and then multiply. However, the distributive property is very useful for getting rid of parenthesis when you have a variable in the problem.

Example 2: Use the distributive property to simplify this expression.

$$3(x + 2)$$

Answer: $3x + 6$

Example 3: Use the distributive property to simplify this expression.

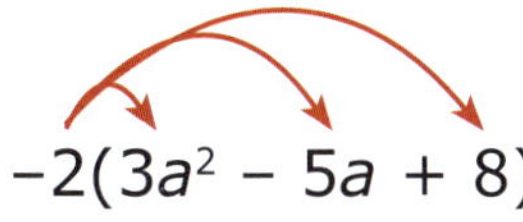

$$-2(3a^2 - 5a + 8)$$

Answer: $-6a^2 + 10a - 16$

Notice how the middle term turned positive. You're done, since you cannot combine like terms.

Practice

1. What is the additive inverse of –3? Explain your thinking.

2. What is the multiplicative inverse of –5? Explain your thinking.

3. What is the additive inverse of $2a$? Explain your thinking.

4. What is the multiplicative inverse of $\frac{5}{6}$? Explain your thinking.

5. What is the multiplicative inverse of $-\frac{5}{6}$? Explain your thinking.

6. Explain why 0 has no reciprocal. Explain your thinking.

7. What is the additive inverse of $-20n$? Explain your thinking.

8. What is wrong with this problem? Explain your thinking.

$$40 \div (10 + 5) = 4 + 8$$

9. Explain why $6(5 - 8)$ is the same as $(5 - 8)6$. Then distribute both expressions.

10. Distribute the following expressions and simplify if possible.

a. $-7(8 + 2)$

b. $(9 + y)10$

c. $-2(n - 1)$

d. $(-9 + 5 - 4)3$

e. $4(8x^2 - 4x - 1)$

f. $2.5(10 + 4)$

g. $50(3 - 5)$

h. $-4(4 + 1)$

i. $4(a + b + c)$

j. $-3(a + b - c)$

k. $5(x - y)$

l. $-1(k + w)$

11. Why is $-(3 + 5 - 7)$ is the same as $-1(3 + 5 - 7)$? Explain your thinking.

____

____

12. Is there something wrong with this student's work? Explain your thinking.

Distribute: $-2(n + 6) + 8$

$-2n - 12 - 16$

____

____

Properties of Equality

There are more properties that govern equations. These will seem like common sense, but they are important to discuss.

Property	Example	Using Words
Reflexive (or Identity)	$10 = 10$	A number always equals itself.
Symmetric Property of Equality	If $x = 10$ then $10 = x$	Quantities that are equal can be read both ways.
Transitive Property of Equality	If $2 \bullet 3 = 6$ and $6 = 5 + 1$, then $2 \bullet 3 = 5 + 1$	If two quantities are equal to the same quantity then they are equal to each other.

Working With Equations

An equation is a balance. To balance an equation each side of the equation must stand for an equal quantity. The equation below states that $6 = 5 + 1$.

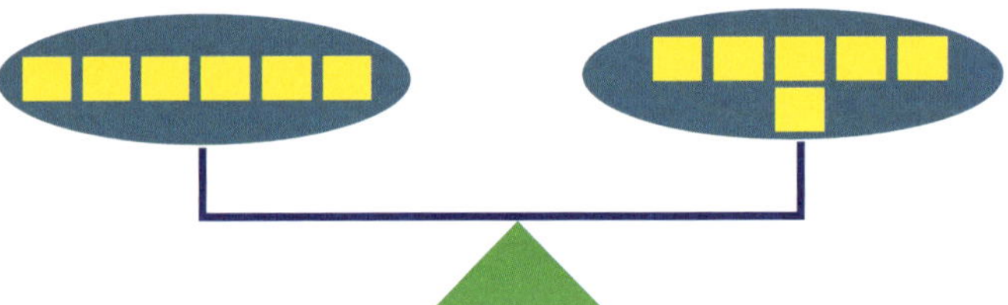

If you added two more blocks to the left side, you would have to add two of the same blocks to the right side to keep the balance.

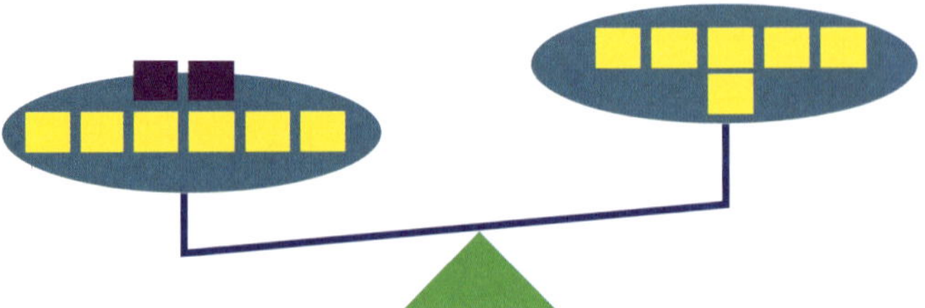

The above illustrates the addition property of equality. In any equation, if you add one quantity to one side of the equation, you must add the same quantity to the *other* side in order to preserve the balance.

Practice

1. The subtraction property of equality states that if you subtract one quantity from one side of an equation, you must subtract the same quantity from the other side of the equation to preserve the balance. Complete this example.

$$x + 20 = 40$$

$$x + 20 - 20 = \_\_\_\_\_\_\_\_$$

2. The multiplication property of equality states that if you multiply one quantity to one side of an equation, you must multiply the same quantity to the other side of the equation to preserve the balance. Complete this example.

$$x = 12$$

$$3 \bullet x = \_\_\_\_\_\_\_\_$$

3. The division property of equality states that if you divide a quantity from one side of an equation, you must divide the same quantity from the other side of the equation in order to preserve the balance.

$$4 \bullet x = 48$$

$$\frac{4 \bullet x}{4} = \_\_\_\_\_\_\_\_$$

4. Is there something wrong with this student's work? Explain your thinking.

$$n + 10 = 30$$

$$n + 10 - 10 = 30 + 10$$

____

____

____

Solving Algebra Equations

To solve equations, reverse the order of operations using the steps outlined below.

Solving Equations Steps

Step 1: **Distribute** (if needed).

Step 2: **Combine** like terms on each side.

Step 3: **Move** variable terms to the same side.

Step 4: **Undo** + and – operations (additive inverses).

Step 5: **Undo** • and ÷ operations (multiplicative inverses/reciprocals).

You will learn steps 4 and 5 first. You may be tempted to guess the answer but follow the steps so that when the equations become more complicated (and you can no longer guess an answer), you'll be able to quickly solve them. That's the beauty of algebra - no more guessing or trial and error!

Step 4: Solving Equations by Using the Additive Inverse

Solve for *n*. The goal is to isolate the variable on one side of the equation.

Example 1: $n - 23 = 42$

$\quad +23 \quad +23$

$n + 0 = 65$

$n = 65$

Start on the side that has the variable. Undo subtraction by adding 23 on each side. 23 is the additive inverse of −23. Remember that "minus 23" is the same as −23.

65 <u>satisfies</u> the equation.

To check your answer, substitute 65 for the variable.
65 – 23 = 42? Yes!

Example 2: $10 = n + 16$

$-16 \quad -16$

$-6 = n$

Start on the side that has the variable. Undo the 16 by adding −16 (or subtracting 16). You can cancel the 16 with the −16. It's okay not to write 0.

−6 <u>satisfies</u> the equation.

To check your answer: 10 = −6 + 16? Yes!

Practice

1. What property of equality allows you to write $10 = n + 16$ as $n + 16 = 10$? (See Example 2.) Explain your thinking.

____

____

2. What property allows you to say that $-23 + 23$ equals 0? (See Example 1.) Explain your thinking.

____

____

3. What property allows you to say that $n = 65$ when $n + 0 = 65$? (See Example 1.) Explain your thinking.

____

____

Solve for n. Show the steps. Use a separate sheet of paper if needed.

4. $n + 4 = 1$ __________

5. $-10 + n = 6$ __________

6. $0 = n - 3.5$ __________

7. $n - 2 = 8.5$ __________

8. $\frac{3}{4} + n = 6$ __________

9. $n + 6 = 0$ __________

10. $-5.5 = n + 5$ __________

11. $5\frac{1}{6} + n = -1\frac{5}{6}$ __________

12. $19 + n = -30$ __________

13. $-12 = n - 12$ __________

Step 5: Solving Equations Using the Multiplicative Inverse

Solve for n. Remember you're trying to get $1n$ or n on one side of the equation.

Example 1:

$$\frac{n}{3} = 27$$

Start on the side that has the variable and undo the division by multiplying by 3 on each side.

$$(3)\frac{n}{3} = 27\,(3)$$

This is the same as multiplying by $\frac{3}{1}$. You're trying to get $1n$ or n alone.

$$1n = 81$$

$$n = 81$$

Example 2:

$$-4n = 96$$

Start on the side that has the variable and undo the multiplication by dividing by −4 on each side.

$$\frac{-4n}{4} = \frac{96}{4}$$

$$1n = -24$$

$$n = -24$$

Example 3:

$$40 = -\frac{4}{5}n$$

Start on the side that has the variable and use the multiplicative inverse of $-\frac{4}{5}$ to get $1n$.

$$(-\frac{5}{4})40 = (-\frac{5}{4})(-\frac{4}{5})n$$

The reciprocal of $-\frac{4}{5}$ is $-\frac{5}{4}$.

$$(-\frac{4}{5}) \bullet \frac{40}{1} = -50$$

(with 40 and 5 cancelled to 10)

$$-50 = 1n$$

$$n = -50$$

Example 4:

$$-n = 200$$

Start on the side that has the variable. Remember that $-n$ means $-1n$. Divide each side by −1.

$$\frac{-1n}{-1} = \frac{200}{-1}$$

$$1n = -200$$

You can skip this step if you wish.

$$n = -200$$

Practice

1. What property allows you to write $1n$ as n? Explain your thinking.

____

____

2. Why is $-\frac{3}{4}$ the multiplicative inverse of $-\frac{4}{3}$? Explain your thinking.

____

____

3. What is wrong with the work below even though the answer is correct? Explain your thinking.

$$\frac{w}{4} = -1$$
$$4 \bullet \frac{w}{4} = -1 \bullet 4$$
$$w = -4$$

____

____

4. Peter thinks the answer to this equation $\frac{1}{6}n = 36$ is 6. Joanna used the reciprocal of $\frac{1}{6}$, which is 6, and she multiplied both sides by 6. Her answer is 216. Who is right? Explain your thinking.

____

____

5. Show a check for Peter's and Joanna's answers below.

Peter	Joanna
$\frac{1}{6}n = 36$	$\frac{1}{6}n = 36$

Solve the following equations using the additive inverse or the multiplicative inverse.

6. $5n = -125$ __________

7. $-5 + n = 125$ __________

8. $-100 = -4n$ __________

9. $0 = 3 + n$ __________

10. $\frac{n}{7} = 1$ __________

11. $\frac{n}{8} = 24$ __________

12. $\frac{4}{3}n = -60$ __________

13. $-\frac{1}{3}n = 5$ __________

14. $\frac{2}{3}n = -60$ __________

15. $9.5 + n = 18.7$ __________

16. $50 = \frac{2}{5}n$ __________

17. $-n = -28$ __________

18. $-18 = n - 11$ __________

19. $-25 = \frac{n}{5}$ __________

Solving Two Step Equations

Solving two step equations involves using Steps 4 and 5 in that order. First, undo the addition and subtraction operations (using the additive inverse) and only then, undo the multiplication and division operations, including reciprocals (using the multiplicative inverse). Then solve for the variable.

Example 1: $-5n + 8 = 48$

$\quad +8 \quad -8$ Go to the side that has the variable. Undo addition by subtracting 8 from each side.

$\frac{-5n}{-5} = \frac{40}{-5}$ Now undo multiplication by dividing each side by −5.

$n = -8$

It always helps to check your answer. This is a proper check:

$-5n + 8 =$	48	Always copy the equation over.
$-5(-8) + 8 =$	$48?$	Substitute the answer in the variable.
$40 + 8 =$	$48?$	
$48 =$	48 Yes!	

Example 2: $0 = 9 - \frac{n}{6}$

$-9 \quad -9$ Go to the side that has the variable. Undo the 9 (it's a positive 9) by subtracting 9 from each side.

$-9 = -\frac{n}{6}$

$(-6)(-9) = -\frac{n}{6}(-6)$ Now undo division by multiplying each side by −6. Remember you want a positive n.

$54 = n$ or

$n = 54$ Symmetric Property of Equality

Practice

1. Do a check for Example 2 below.

Solve for the variable.

2. $5w + 9 = 19$ ________

3. $-2x - 10 = 34$ ________

4. $18 = 3p - 18$ ________

5. $0 = -4n - 24$ ________

6. $\frac{2}{3}c - 10 = 26$ ________

7. $-50 = \frac{k}{4} - 6$ ________

8. $40 - n = -67$ ________

9. $-8x - 2 = -26$ ________

10. $\frac{1}{3}y - 15 = -45$ ________

11. $24x - 9.9 = 2.1$ ________

12. $-18 - 5n = 22$ ________

13. $80 - \frac{n}{5} = -60$ ________

14. $-10y - 8 = -202$ ________

15. $-\frac{y}{6} + \frac{1}{2} = \frac{1}{4}$ ________

Solving Word Problems Using Equations

Before you start this section, please review the translating section in Chapter 6 that starts on page 90. These words translate as the equal sign.

=
is equals gives is the same as yields totals

Example 1: Mary's age less than 20 is the same as −52. Find Mary's age.

To start you need to identify the variable. Use a let statement so that anyone looking at your work knows what it is you're looking for.

Let n = Mary's age

Now, translate the words into an equation.

$$20 - n = -52$$

Notice the words "less than."

Then solve!

$$\begin{array}{rcl} 20 - n &=& -52 \\ -20 & & -20 \\ \hline -n &=& -72 \end{array}$$

Now divide by −1.

$$n = 72$$

When you have $-n$ as your last step, you can divide each side by −1, or multiply each side by −1 in your head and not show work. You can automatically change the signs on each side of the equation as a short-cut. For example, if $-n = 10$, then $n = -10$. If $-n = -10$, then $n = 10$.

Example 2: Twice a number plus eleven yields twenty. Find the number.

Let n = the number

Equation:

$$\begin{aligned} 2n + 11 &= 20 \\ -11 \quad & \quad -11 \\ \hline \frac{2n}{2} &= \frac{9}{2} \\ n &= 4.5 \text{ or } 4\tfrac{1}{2} \end{aligned}$$

The number is 4.5.

Practice

Translate and solve each equation. Use a let statement.

1. Half a number plus eight gives you eleven. Find the number.

____

2. Three times a number is the same as –300. Find the number.

____

3. One-half a number added to fifty yields one-hundred. Find the number.

____

4. The opposite of a number gives 3. Find the number.

____

5. The number 0 is the same as a –4 times some missing number less eight. What's the missing number?

____

Steps 3, 4, and 5: Moving Variable Terms to the Same Side

Sometimes you have variables on both sides of the equation. Your job is to get the variable terms on the same side and the constant terms on the opposite side. To move variable terms you must undo the entire variable term. You can choose the side you want to move to, but in many of these examples, the variable terms will move to the left side and constants to the right side.

Solve for n:

Example 1:

$$4n + 6 = -2n + 18$$
$$+2n \qquad +2n$$

To move $-2n$ to the left side, add $2n$ to each side. Remember you can only add $2n$ once per side to keep the balance.

$$6n + 6 = 18$$
$$-6 \qquad -6$$

Undo addition (Step 4).

$$\frac{6n}{6} = \frac{12}{6}$$

Undo multiplication (Step 5).

$$n = 2$$

Example 2:

$$-7n + 8 = 6n - 44$$
$$-6n \qquad -6n$$

To move $6n$ to the left side, subtract 6n from each side.

$$-13n + 8 = -44$$
$$-8 \qquad -8$$

Undo addition (Step 4).

$$\frac{-13n}{-13} = \frac{-52}{-13}$$

Undo multiplication (Step 5)

$$n = 4$$

Practice

Solve the following equations.

1. $9n + 3 = 4n - 17$ __________
2. $y - 8 = -y + 12$ __________
3. $7m - 42 = -7m$ __________
4. $46 + w = -w + 1$ __________

5. $92 + p = -4p - 3$ __________

6. $46 - 5m = m - 2$ __________

7. $\frac{3}{4} - 6y = -5y + 3\frac{1}{2}$ __________

8. $18.7 + n = -3.2 + 4n$ __________

Answer the following.

9. In the equation $3n + 9 = 3n + 9$, a student solved the equation this way.

$$\begin{array}{rcl} 3n + 9 & = & 3n + 9 \\ -3n & & -3n \\ \hline 9 & = & 9 \end{array}$$

This equation is called an identity equation. Since $9 = 9$ is a true statement, or if 9 is moved to one side, you get $0 = 0$, which is also true, so all values for n will work in this equation. Try several values in the equation to check if indeed all values work for n.

10. Solve the equation $3n + 9 = 3n + 10$. Are there any solutions for n that satisfy the equation (make the equation true)? Explain your thinking.

____

____

____

____

Steps 2 – 5: Combining Like Terms on Each Side

Often equations have many like terms on each side. You should combine the like terms on each side BEFORE you move the variable terms to the same side. If you don't, you will end up doing more work.

Solve for n:

Example 1:

$7 + 3n + 3n - 8$	$=$	$4n + 3 + 3n$	Combine on each side (Step 2).
$-1 + 6n$	$=$	$7n + 3$	Move variable terms to the same side. Undo $7n$ from each side (Step 3).
$-7n$		$-7n$	
$-1 - n$	$=$	3	Undo -1 by adding 1 to each side (Step 4).
$+1$		$+1$	
$-n$	$=$	4	Divide by -1 (Step 5).
n	$=$	-4	

Remember to combine like terms on each side. However, to move terms <u>across</u> the equal sign, you must UNDO the operation in front of the term you are moving.

Example 2:

$-9 + n + 9 + 6n + 3$	$=$	$6n - 5n$	Combine on each side (Step 2).
$7n + 3$	$=$	n	Move variable terms to the same side (step 3).
$-n$		$-n$	
$6n + 3$	$=$	0	Undo addition (Step 4).
-3		-3	
$\frac{6n}{6}$	$=$	$\frac{-3}{6}$	Undo multiplication (Step 5).
n	$=$	$-\frac{1}{2}$	

Practice

Solve the following equations.

1. $6w + 4 - 10 = 30$

____

5. $-8n + 2n + 2 + 10 = -60$

____

2. $3y + 2y + 50 = -125$

____

6. $n + n + n + n - 56 = 104$

____

3. $-19 + 3y + 3 = y + y + 2$

____

7. $w - w + 4 + 11 = -30w$

____

4. $5.6 + x + 2.4 = 28$

____

8. $8y + 9 - 9y + 1 = 10 + 4$

____

Translate and solve. Use a let statement. Use a separate sheet of paper if needed.

9. When twelve is added to Mary's age you get the same answer as twice Mary's age plus eleven. What is her age? ______________________

10. Zero is the same as Paulo's locker number divided by 5 less one-hundred thirteen. What is Paulo's locker number? ______________________

11. A number plus twice the same number plus eight is the same as the number. Find the missing number. ______________________

12. Three times a number minus the same number yields nine plus five times the number. Find the missing number. ______________________

Steps 1-5: Using All the Steps to Solve Equations

Now you're ready to add Step 1. You don't always have to distribute, but if you see a number multiplying a quantity, you should distribute first, then follow the steps in order. Review the steps below.

Solving Equations Steps

Step 1: **Distribute** (if needed).

Step 2: **Combine** like terms on each side.

Step 3: **Move** variable terms to the same side.

Step 4: **Undo** + and – operations (additive inverses).

Step 5: **Undo** • and ÷ operations (multiplicative inverses/reciprocals).

Example 1:

$3(n + 5) + 3 = 40 + 8$ Distribute (Step 1). It's okay to add 40 + 8, too.

$3n + 15 + 3 = 48$

$3n + 18 = 48$ Combine like terms (Step 2).

$-18 \quad -18$ There is no step 3, so do Step 4.

$\frac{3n}{3} = \frac{30}{3}$ Do step 5.

$n = 10$

Example 2:

$20 - (6n - 3) = n + 2$ Distribute (Step 1).

$20 - 1(6n - 3) = n + 2$ Careful with the negative! (It helps to multiply by −1.)

$20 - 6n + 3 = n + 2$ Combine like terms (Step 2).

$23 - 6n = n + 2$ Move variables to the same side (Step 3).

$-n \quad -n$

$23 - 7n = 2$ Do Step 4.

$-23 \quad -23$

$\frac{-7n}{-7} = \frac{-21}{-7}$ Do Step 5.

$n = 3$

Practice

Solve the following equations. Follow Steps 1-5 in order as you do each equation. Soon the steps will become automatic. Use a separate sheet of paper if needed. The correct answers are below, but not in order.

1. $10n + n = -121$
2. $-\frac{3}{4}n = 48$
3. $4(w + 2) = -12$
4. $2(3x - 8) = 2$
5. $-60 = \frac{x}{2}$
6. $3 + 3(n - 1) = 5n - 8$
7. $8y - 3y = 2y - 39$
8. $-18 + 4n = 7 - 4 + n$
9. $-250 = 5(x + 10)$
10. $9 + 2w - 8 = 10$
11. $10 + n = \frac{1}{3}(6n - 3)$
12. $\frac{x}{5} + 3 - 2 = -8$
13. $5x - 8 = 4x - 2$
14. $-4(n - 1) = 4$
15. $7n + 6 = 7n + 5$
16. $2(5w + 20) = -32 + w$

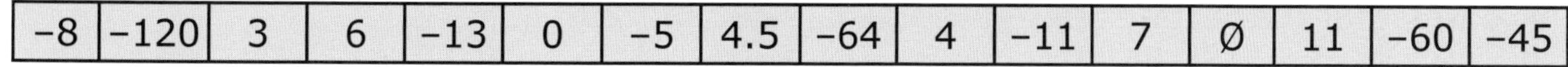

-8	-120	3	6	-13	0	-5	4.5	-64	4	-11	7	Ø	11	-60	-45

Solving a Calendar Problem

Jeff was trying to play a magic trick with his friends. He asked them to choose 4 days that form a square on any calendar. He told them: "If you tell me the sum of the four days, I will tell you which days you picked." His friends secretly looked at the December 2016 calendar and told him the sum was 100. Jeff used his knowledge of algebra and guessed the days. How did he do it?

2016 DECEMBER

SUN	MON	TUE	WED	THU	FRI	SAT
				1	2	3
4	5	6	7	8	9	10
11	12	13	14	15	16	17
18	19	20	21	22	23	24
25	26	27	28	29	30	31

Let n = the first number date.

Then $n + 1$ must be the next number date (the day after), $n + 7$ must be the date seven days after n, and $n + 8$ must be seven days after $n + 1$.

Equation: $n + n + 1 + n + 7 + n + 8 = 100$

$$4n + 16 = 100$$

$$-16 \quad -16$$

$$\frac{4n}{4} = \frac{84}{4}$$

$$n = 21$$

Try this with another month. Play this trick with your friends!

The dates that make the square are 21, 22, 28, and 29.

Check: Does the sum of 21 + 22 + 28 + 29 = 100? Yes!

Consecutive Integer Problems

Consecutive integer problems are meant to be fun, and they show you that knowing algebra avoids unnecessary guessing. Remember that the word consecutive means to go in order. On the number line below, consecutive integers increase by 1 unit as you go from one integer to the next one (to the right). If your first integer is n, then the next consecutive integer is $n + 1$, and then $n + 2$, etc. These are integers (no decimal or fraction answers).

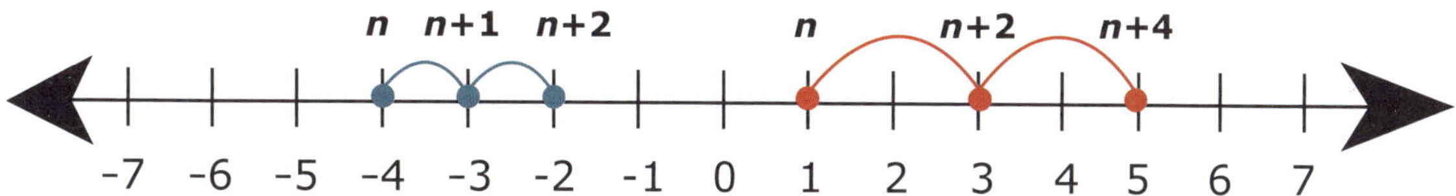

If n is an even integer, then $n + 2$ is your next consecutive even integer and the next one is $n + 4$. The same is true if n is your first odd integer. Your next odd integer is $n + 2$, then $n + 4$, etc, as you go to the right.

Consecutive Integers	**Consecutive Even/Odd Integers**
Let n = 1st cons. integer	Let n = 1st cons. even/odd integer
$n + 1$ = 2nd cons. integer	$n + 2$ = 2nd cons. even/odd integer
$n + 2$ = 3rd cons. integer	$n + 4$ = 3rd cons. even/odd integer

Example 1: Find three consecutive integers whose sum is 138.

Let n = 1st cons. integer
$n + 1$ = 2nd cons. integer
$n + 2$ = 3rd cons. integer

Equation:
$$n + n + 1 + n + 2 = 138$$
$$3n + 3 = 138$$
$$-3 \quad -3$$
$$\frac{3n}{3} = \frac{135}{3}$$
$$n = 45$$

The consecutive integers are 45, 46, and 47. Check the answer.

Example 2: Find two consecutive odd integers whose sum is –52.

Let n = 1st cons. integer
$n + 2$ = 2nd cons. integer

Equation:

$$n + n + 2 = -52$$
$$2n + 2 = -52$$
$$-2 \quad -2$$
$$\frac{2n}{2} = \frac{-54}{2}$$
$$n = -27$$

The two consecutive odd integers are –27 and $n + 2 = -25$.
Check the answer. Remember –25 is to the right of –27.

Practice

Solve the following problems. Use a let statement and show your equation and work. Use a separate sheet of paper if needed.

1. Find four consecutive integers whose sum is 494.

   __________ __________ __________

2. Find three consecutive integers whose sum is 171.

   __________ __________ __________

3. Find three consecutive even integers whose sum is 72.

   __________ __________ __________

4. Find three consecutive odd integers whose sum is 429.

   __________ __________ __________

5. Find three consecutive integers whose sum is –27.

   __________ __________ __________

6. Find two consecutive odd integers whose sum is –4.

   __________ __________ __________

7. Find four consecutive even integers whose sum is 60.

__________ __________ __________ __________

8. Find three consecutive integers such that the first integer and the third has a sum of 32.

__________ __________ __________

9. Find three consecutive integers such that twice the first plus the third integer adds to 62.

__________ __________ __________

10. Find three consecutive odd integers such that three times the first plus twice the second plus the third has the sum of 62.

__________ __________ __________

11. Check the answer to #8.

12. Check the answer to #9.

13. Check the answer to #10.

14. Write your own consecutive integer problem and solve it.

15. If $n + 2$ is an odd integer, how would you represent the next even integer after $n + 2$? Explain your thinking.

____

____

Thinking More About Equations

Before leaving this chapter, it's important to revisit the concept that an equation is a balance. Look at a different way of solving the equation $3(n + 4) = 15$.

$$\frac{3(n + 4)}{3} = \frac{15}{3}$$

$$n + 4 = 5$$

$$\underline{\quad -4 \quad -4}$$

$$n = 1$$

Why is this step legal even though you're starting with Step 5? The reason is that $3(n + 4)$ is one term. Remember terms are "tied" by multiplication or division signs. If you distributed the 3, then $3n$ and 12 are separate terms. So as long as you do division once per term on every term of the equation, you won't change the answer to the equation. You can also think of it this way:

$$3(n + 4) = 3 \bullet 5$$

Therefore, $n + 4$ must equal 5.

In the equation $3(n + 4) + 9 = 15$, the following is NOT legal. Can you see why?

$$\frac{3(n + 4)}{3} + 9 = \frac{15}{3}$$

$$n + 4 + 9 = 5$$

$$n + 13 = 5$$

$$\underline{\quad -13 \quad -13}$$

$$n = -8$$

This is NOT the answer as it won't check!

Check: $3(-8 + 4) + 9 = 15?$

$3(-4) + 9 = 15?$

$-12 + 9 = 15?$ NO!

So, if you can divide first, make sure you undo division on each term of the equation. This would be legal:

$$\frac{3(n + 4)}{3} + \frac{9}{3} = \frac{15}{3}$$

$$n + 4 + 3 = 5$$

$$n + 7 = 5$$

$$\underline{\quad -7 \quad -7}$$

$$n = -2$$

Check: $3(-2 + 4) + 9 = 15$?

$3(2) + 9 = 15$?

$6 + 9 = 15$? Yes!

Chapter 7 Review

Write the letter of the property which is shown.

______ 1. $-4 + 0 = -4$		a. Associative property of +
______ 2. $5 \bullet 1 = 5$		b. Associative property of •
______ 3. $3 \bullet 4 = 4 \bullet 3$		c. Commutative property of +
______ 4. $(-8 + 1) + 2 = 2 + (-8 + 1)$		d. Commutative property of •
______ 5. $(9 \bullet 2) \bullet 5 = 9 \bullet (2 \bullet 5)$		e. Addition property of 0
______ 6. $1 + (-4 + 2) = (1 + -4) + 2$		f. Multiplication property of 1

Answer the questions. Explain your thinking.

7. Why is $15 = 3n$ the same as $3n = 15$? ______________________________

____

8. Why is $-\frac{7}{8}$ the multiplicative inverse of $-\frac{8}{7}$? ______________________________

____

____

9. What is the additive inverse of the term $-6a$ and why?

____

____

10. Why does 0 not have a reciprocal? ______________________________

____

11. What is wrong with this student's work? $3(n^2 + 2n - 1) = 3n^2 + 6n - 1$

____

____

Solve the following equations. Use a separate sheet of paper if needed.

12. $-5n = -65$ __________

13. $\frac{w}{5} = -1$ __________

14. $-y = -90$ __________

15. $x + x + 2 = -14$ __________

16. $3r + 1 = -120$ __________

17. $-2(n - 1) = 40$ __________

18. $\frac{2}{3}x = -12$ __________

19. $-12 = -\frac{2}{3}x$ __________

20. $\frac{2}{5}w + 10 = 50$ __________

21. $a + a + 5 + 2a = -30 + 10$ __________

22. $-4(n + 5) = 2(n + 2)$ __________

23. $2 + 3(x + 5) = -13$ __________

24. $11 = -11w + 11$ __________

25. $-9(y + 2) + 1 = 10$ __________

26. $3n - 1 = 2n$ __________

27. $5.6x + 1.4 = 18.2$ __________

28. $30 + n = 30 + n$ __________

29. $18 + 2n = 2n + 17$ __________

Choose the correct equation that can solve the problem. Let n = missing information.

30. John gets $20 from his dad as an allowance, plus his dad pays him $5.00 an hour when he babysits his little sister. One week John made $100 in total, including his allowance. How many hours did he babysit?

 a. $20 + 5n = 100$

 b. $20n = 100$

 c. $5n = 120$

 d. $5(n + 20) = 100$

31. Five times the sum of a number plus eight is the same as 140. Find the number.

 a. $5n + 8 = 140$

 b. $5n = 148$

 c. $5(n + 8) = 140$

 d. $5 \bullet 8 + n = 140$

32. The sum of three consecutive odd integers is 75. What are the integers?

    a. $n + n + 1 + n + 2 = 75$

    b. $n + n + 2 + n + 4 = 75$

    c. $n + n + 1 + n + 3 = 75$

    d. $n + n + 2 = 75$

33. The sum of two consecutive even integers is –38. Find the integers.

    a. $n + n + 2 = -38$

    b. $n + n + 1 = -38$

    c. $n + n + 2 + n + 4 = -38$

    d. $n + n + 1 + n + 2 = -38$

34. Find three consecutive integers such that twice the first plus two times the third equals 164.

    a. $2n + 2(n + 1) = 164$

    b. $n + 2n + 2 = 164$

    c. $2n + 2n + 2 = 164$

    d. $2n + 2(n + 2) = 164$

Solve the following word problems. Show a let statement and an equation. Use a separate sheet of paper if needed.

35. Lucia gets $40 a week for mowing her aunt's lawn, plus $2 an hour for taking care of her pets. If one week she made $52, how many hours did she take care of her aunt's pets? ____________________

36. Twice the difference of a number minus ten is the same as the number plus 20. Find the missing number. ____________________

37. When you add a number to three times its additive inverse you get ten. What is the number? What is its additive inverse? ____________________

38. Today's date and seven days from now has a sum of 23. What is tomorrow's date? ____________________

39. The sum of three consecutive integers is 87. Find the integers.

__________ __________ __________

40. The sum of two consecutive odd integers is −280. Find the integers.

__________ __________

41. Solve this equation by dividing each term by 10.

$10(y - 2) + 20 = 30$

42. Check your answer to the problem above.

43. Luke solved this equation by moving terms as shown. Are his steps legal? Explain your thinking.

$$-n + 20 = 3n - 40$$
$$+n \qquad\qquad +n$$
$$20 = 4n - 40$$
$$+40 \qquad\qquad +40$$
$$\frac{60}{4} = \frac{4n}{4}$$
$$15 = n$$

44. Check the answer to Luke's equation.

45. If $a = b$ and $b = c$, what property allows you to say $a = c$?

Chapter 8

Inequalities and Applications

Many real life problems involve situations that have more than one answer. That is the reason to study inequalities. Inequalities have the following symbols.

- $>$ is greater than ○
- $\geq$ is greater than or equal ●
- $<$ is less than ○
- $\leq$ is less than or equal ●
- $\neq$ is not equal ○

Graphing Inequalities

Example 1: Graph $n > -2$; $\{n \mid n \in \text{Real Numbers}\}$

This reads: The set of all n such that n is an element or member of the Real Numbers.

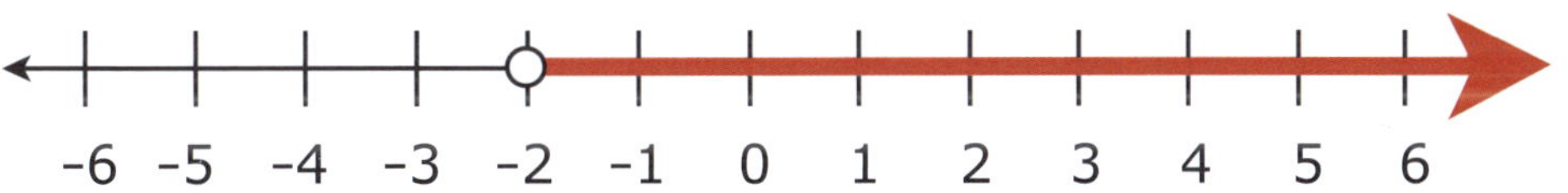

Use an open circle at −2 since you do not want to include −2. The bar indicates you want all real numbers and the arrow head is darker at the right to indicate that the answers continue infinitely to the right.

Example 2: Graph $n \leq 3.5$; $\{n \mid n \in \text{Real Numbers}\}$

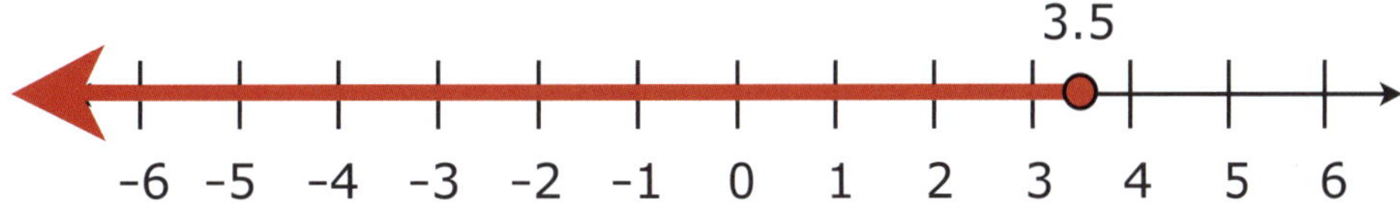

Use a dark circle at 3.5 to indicate that you do want to include 3.5. Again, darken the arrow head at the left side of the graph to show that the answers continue infinitely to the left.

Example 3: Graph $n > -1$; $\{n \mid n \in \text{Integers}\}$

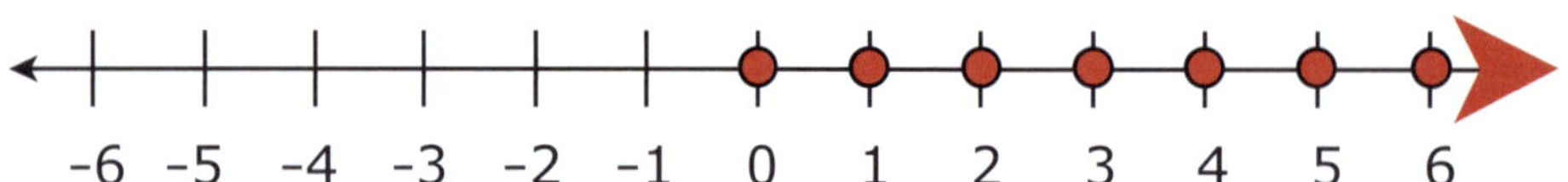

This time only the integers greater than −1 were graphed. The arrow head is darker on the right to indicate the graph keeps on going.

Practice

1. What does this notation mean? $\{x \mid x \in \text{Real Numbers}\}$

____

____

2. Use set notation to write "The set of all *n* such that *n* is an element or member of the Integers."

____

____

Write the letter of the inequality that matches the graph. See the choices on the next page.

______ 3. 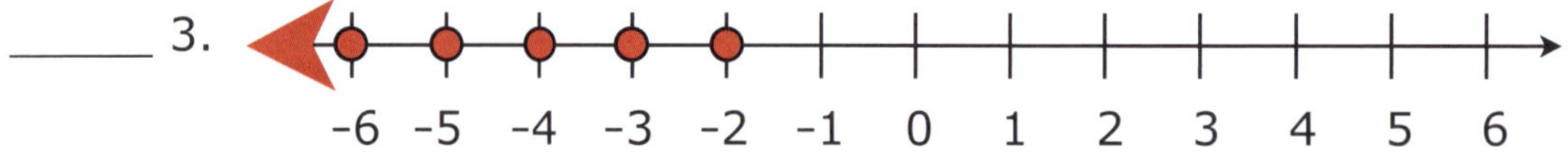

______ 4. 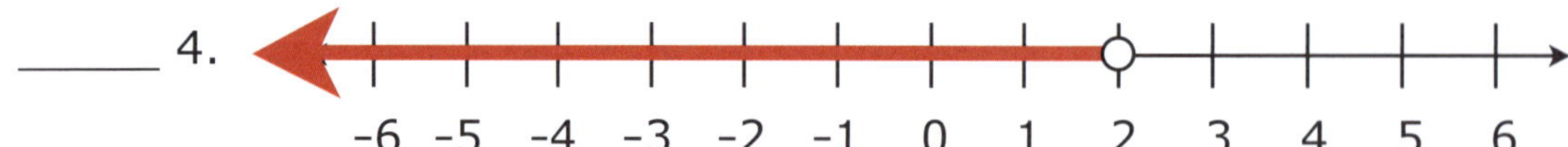

______ 5. 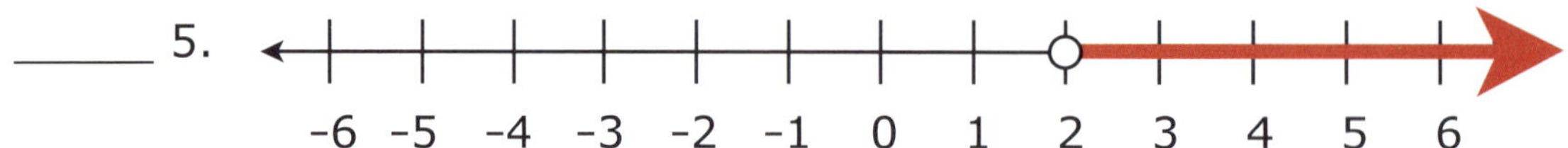

______ 6. 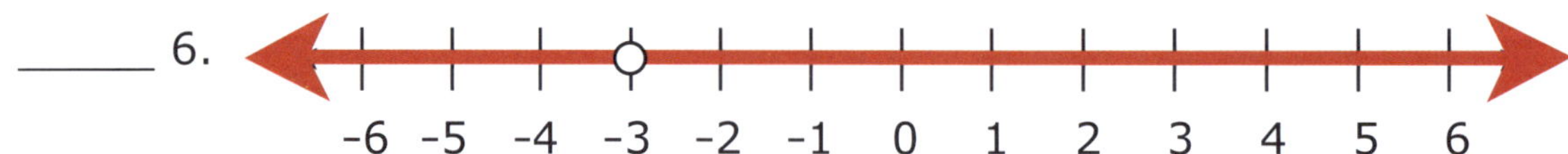

______ 7. 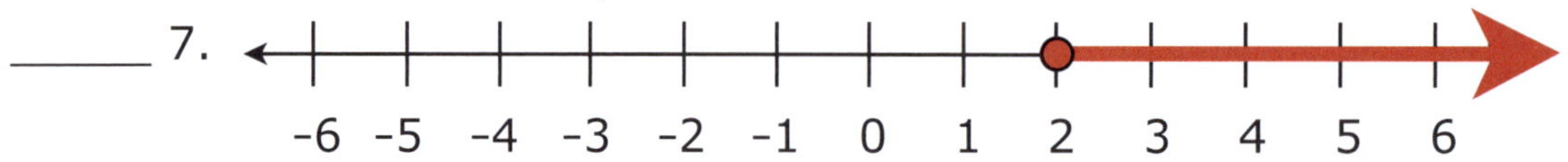

a. $x \geq 2$; $\{x \mid x \in \text{Reals}\}$

b. $x \leq -2$; $\{x \mid x \in \text{Integers}\}$

c. $x \neq -3$; $\{x \mid x \in \text{Reals}\}$

d. $x < 2$; $\{x \mid x \in \text{Reals}\}$

e. $x > 2$; $\{x \mid x \in \text{Reals}\}$

Graph the following inequalities.

8. $n > -4$; $\{n \mid n \in \text{Reals}\}$

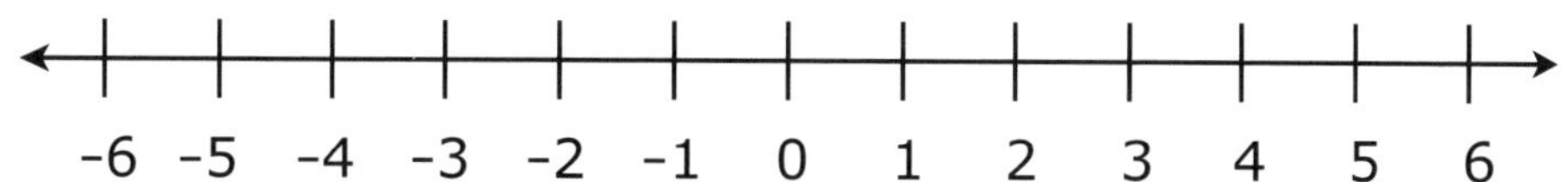

9. $n \leq -1$; $\{n \mid n \in \text{Reals}\}$

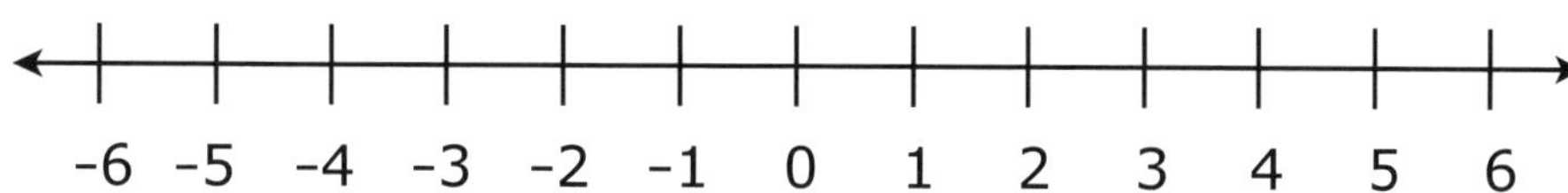

10. $n > 0$; $\{n \mid n \in \text{Integers}\}$

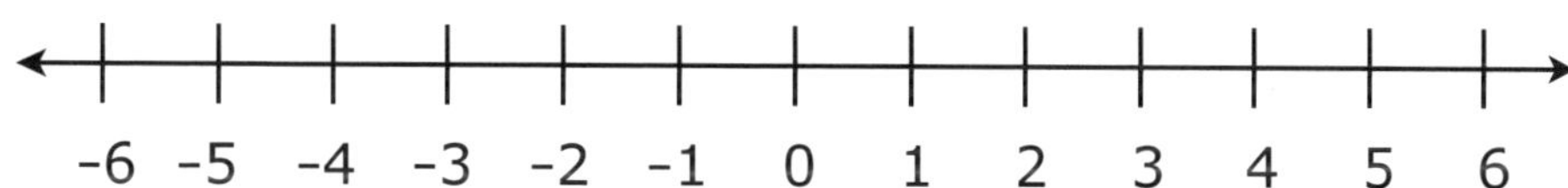

11. $n \geq -1.5$ $\{n \mid n \in \text{Reals}\}$

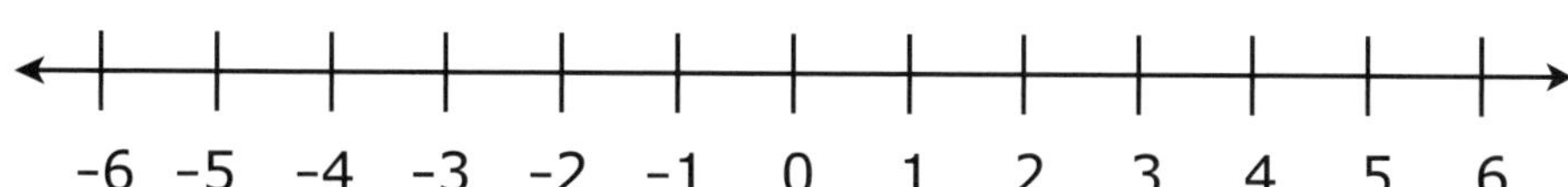

12. $n > 25$ $\{n \mid n \in \text{Reals}\}$

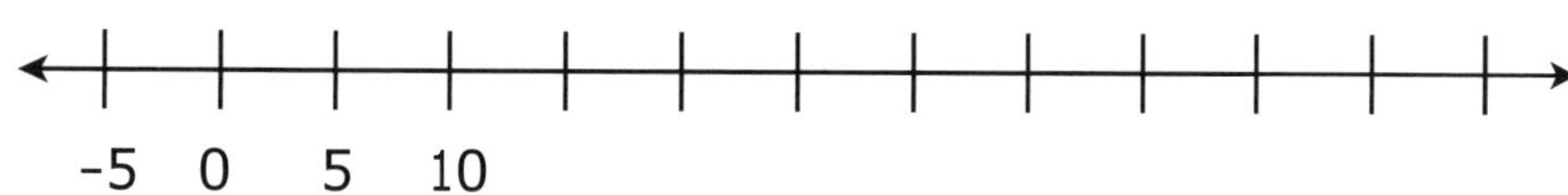

When you graph, always show 0 on the number line, even when you change your scale.

Answer the questions.

13. If $5 < 6$, you can also say $6 > 5$. What is another way of writing $5 < n$?

____

14. What is another way of writing $-6 \geq n$?

____

15. What's another way of writing $0 > -3n$?

____

16. What's another way of writing $0 > 3n + 18$?

____

Solving Inequalities

Inequalities are solved just like equations except for some exceptions below.

Start with a true statement: $10 < 20$

This is the original statement.

Add a positive number to each side. Add 5 to each side of the original inequality. Does it remain a true statement?

$$15 < 25$$

Yes, it's still a true statement.

Add a negative number to each side of the original statement. Suppose you add −3 to each side of the original inequality. This is the same as subtracting 3 as you know. Does it remain a true statement?

$$7 < 17$$

Yes, it's still a true statement.

Multiply the original statement by a positive number on each side. Multiply each side of the original inequality by 8. Does it remain a true statement?

$$80 < 160$$

Yes, it's still a true statement.

Multiply the original statement by a negative number on each side. Multiply each side of the original inequality by −3. Does it remain a true statement?

$$-30 < -60$$

No, this is now a false statement because −30 is greater than −60.

Divide the original statement by a positive number on each side. Divide each side of the original inequality by 5. Does it remain a true statement?

$$2 < 4$$

Yes, it's still a true statement.

Divide the original statement by a negative number on each side. Divide each side of the original inequality by −2. Does it remain a true statement?

$$-5 < -10$$

No, this is now a false statement because −5 is greater than −10.

These examples show that multiplying and dividing by a negative number changes the inequality from a true statement to a false statement.

When solving an inequality, every time you multiply or divide by a negative number, you must reverse the inequality symbol.

Example 1: Solve and graph the following inequality over the set of reals.

$-2(n - 3) \geq 8$ Distribute. Watch the negative sign!

$-2n + 6 \geq 8$

$\quad -6 \quad -6$

$\dfrac{-2n}{-2} \geq \dfrac{2}{-2}$ You're dividing by a negative.

$n \leq -1$ Notice the reversal of the inequality.

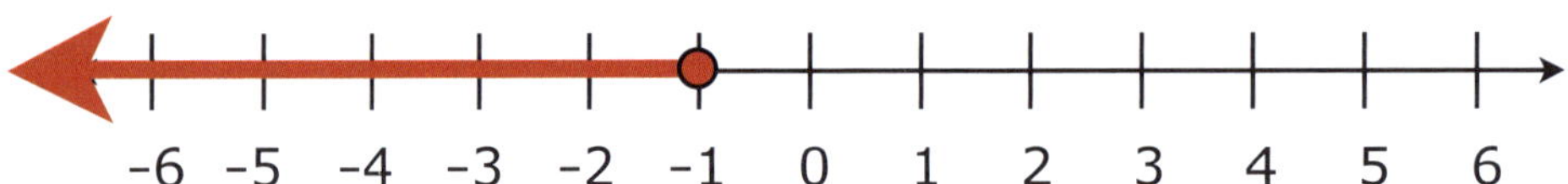

To check, pick a number in the solution set and plug it in! Try −4.

$-2(n - 3) \geq 8$ Write the original inequality.

$-2(-4 - 3) \geq 8?$

$-2(-7) \geq 8?$

$14 \geq 8?$ Yes!

Example 2: Solve the following inequality. Do not graph.

$18 - x > -30$

$-18 \quad -18$ Move the constants to the right side.

$-x > -48$ Divide by −1.

$x < 48$ Notice the reversal of the inequality.

To check, pick a number in the solution set. An easy number would be 0 since 0 is less than 48.

$$18 - x > -30$$

$$18 - 0 > -30?$$

$$18 > -30? \text{ Yes!}$$

Practice

Solve the following inequalities. Do not graph.

1. $11n + 1 > -120$

2. $-12n > -144$

3. $3(y - 1) \leq 2(y - 5)$

4. $18 - w < 3w - 2$

5. $7n - n + 3 - 8 \geq 13$

6. $-n > 300$

7. $\frac{3}{4}x < -120$

8. $-\frac{3}{4}y > -120$

9. $0 > 3n + 18$

10. Show a check for #9

Solve and graph over the set of reals.

11. $5n - 20 < -25$

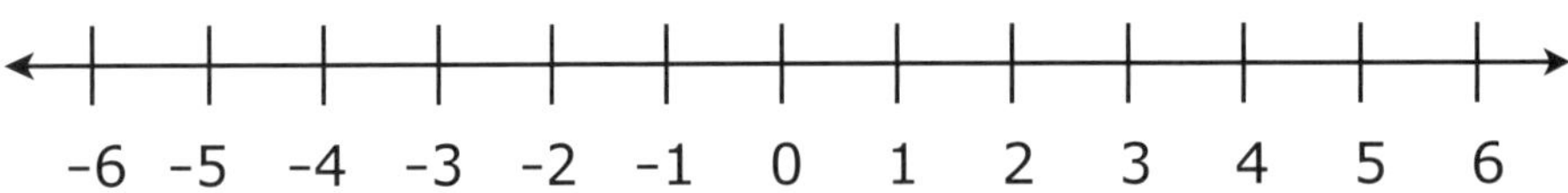

12. $0 \geq -3n$

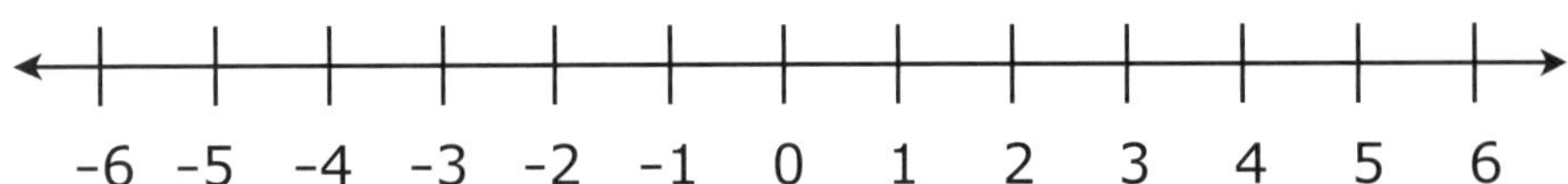

How to Tell an Equation From an Inequality in Word Problems

To be an inequality, you must have the three words: is less than or is greater than together. The words must be touching. The same is true for is less than or equal OR is greater than or equal.

Example 1: Twice a number less than ten is the same as twenty four.

The words "less than" and "is" are not together. They are separated by the word "ten." Therefore, this is NOT an inequality. This translates to:

$$10 - 2n = 24$$

Example 2: Twice a number is less than twenty four.

The words "is less than" are together, all three words are next to each other. This is an inequality. This translates to:

$$2n < 24$$

Example 3: Three times the sum of a number plus eleven is greater than or equal fifteen.

The five words "is greater than or equal" are together. All five words are touching each other, so this is an inequality. This translates to:

$$3(n + 11) \geq 15$$

As you work with word problems now and in the future, underline the words: less, less than, is less than, is greater than, is less than or equal, or is greater than or equal. When those words are not immediately next to each other, you are not working with inequalities. Be a careful reader!

Another set of words that could be confusing are the words "at least" and "at most."

Example 1: Brett's brother was at least 12 years old. Write an inequality using the variable B as the brother's age.

Answer: $B \geq 12$.

So "at least" means greater than or equal to. Use the greater than or equal symbol.

Example 2: The maximum speed of the Viper ride at the Darien Lake Amusement park near Rochester, NY, has a speed of at most 50 mph. Write an inequality using the variable S to describe the speed of the ride.

Answer: $S \leq 50$.

So "at most" means less than or equal to. Use the less than or equal symbol.

Practice

Translate the following into an equation or an inequality. Use n for your variable. Do not solve.

1. A number less than twenty is the same as three times the number.

____

2. The sum of three consecutive integers is at most 60.

____

3. Ten added to five times a number is greater than –50.

____

4. If Joanna gets cable TV her bill will definitely be at least $125.

____

5. Three times the difference of a number less four is less than forty.

____

6. When a number is divided by ten, the result is less than or equal to five.

7. A child who wants to ride the Viper at the Darien Lake Amusement Park must be at least 4 feet in height.

8. Sylvia's monthly salary added to her holiday bonus of $100 is less than $500.

9. The elevator at Maria's apartment complex has a weight limit of 2 tons.

10. When eleven is added to twice a number, the result is five less than the same number.

11. John's mother told him that the movie was rated for children 13 and up.

12. The musical should last at most 2 hours including intermission.

13. The sum of three consecutive odd integers is less than or equal to 75.

14. The missing number is greater than one-thousand.

15. Andrew rents a bike from Bikes Galore. He gets charged $4 per hour plus a one time $15 fee. His total is less than $39.

Solve the following inequalities. Use a let statement and show your inequality and all steps.

16. A school bake sale needs to make at least $225. Each baked good will sell for $0.75. How many baked goods must be sold to reach school's goal?

17. Victoria wants to buy a $10 binder and five notebooks. The amount she has to spend must less than or equal to $40. What is the most she spent on each notebook?

18. The sum of three consecutive integers is less than or equal to 57. What are the largest possible integers that fit this situation?

19. At a park the entry fee is $8.00. To rent a row boat at this park costs $12 per hour. If you go over one minute, you still have to pay for the entire hour. What is the most hours you can rent a boat if you want to spend is less than $45?

20. Robert makes $80 a day and $12 per hour for overtime. In a 5 day week he earned at least $520. What is the minimum number of hours of overtime he worked that week?

Understanding Compound Inequalities

A compound inequality is a sentence with two inequality statements that are joined by the words "and" or "or." There are many situations in life where compound inequalities are used.

Example 1: The ages of the children invited to the party were between 10 and 13 years old.

Instead of writing $x > 10$ and $x < 13$. You can write $10 < x < 13$. This is read as: 10 is less than x and x is less than 13 where x represents the age of each child. In $10 < x < 13$, the inequality symbols are facing in the same direction.

You can also write: $13 > x > 10$. This is read as 13 is greater than x and x is greater than 10. Again, make sure the inequality symbols both face in the same direction.

The above is an AND statement, meaning that the answers must fit both situations. So if a child is 11, he or she is between 10 and 13 at the same time.

Example 2: The students who scored more than 95 on a math test or those who scored less than or equal to 65 were asked to take a note home. Let's hope the notes were different!

You can write $n > 95$ or $n \leq 65$. This is an OR compound inequality.

A score that meets one criteria does not meet the other criteria.

Example 3: Write the compound inequality that matches this graph.

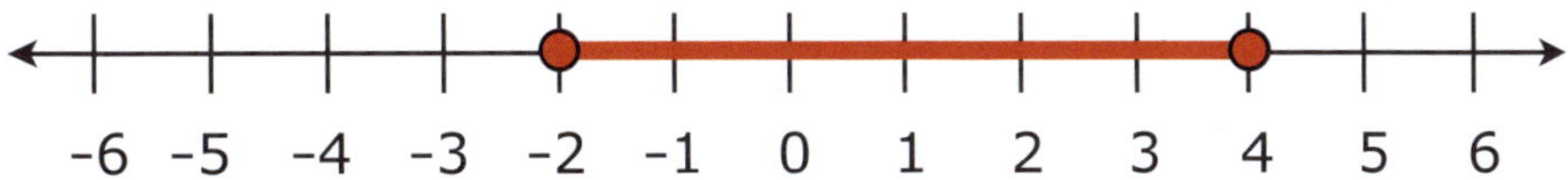

Answer: $-2 \leq n \leq 4$ {Reals}

You can also write $4 \geq n \geq -2$ $\{n \mid n \in \text{Real Numbers}\}$

Graphing Compound Inequalities

Example 1: Graph $-3 < n \leq 5$; $\{n \mid n \in \text{Reals}\}$

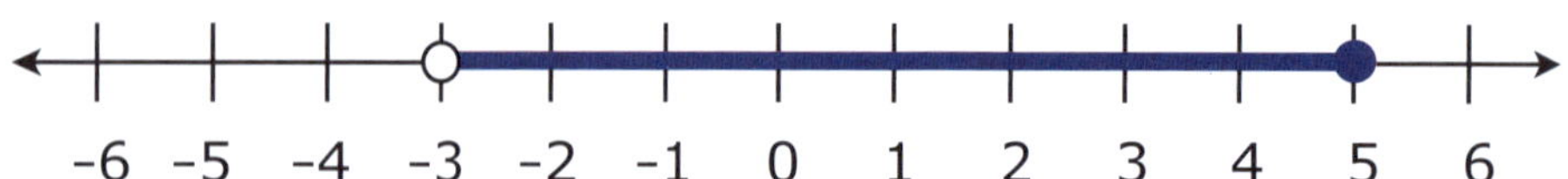

You want all the real numbers less than or equal to 5 AND greater than –3. Any number in the blue fits both conditions.

You can also read the graph as all the reals numbers between 3 and 5, including 5.

Example 2: Graph $n > 2$ or $n < -4$; $\{n \mid n \in \text{Reals}\}$

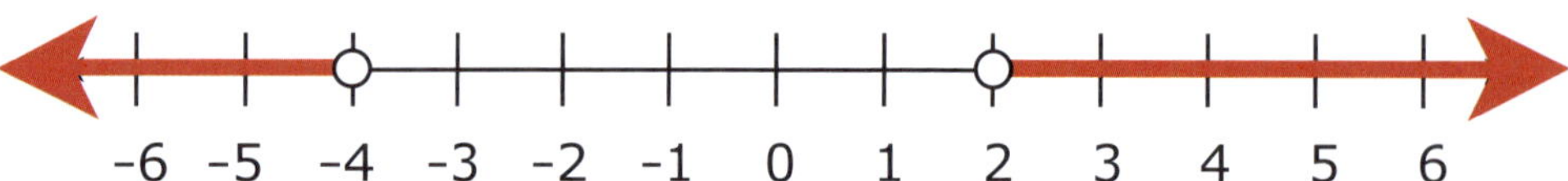

Can you see that a number such as –5 works for $n \leq -4$, but not for $n > 2$?

Example 3: What are all the integer solutions to this compound inequality?

$-7 \leq n < 2$ $\{n \mid n \in \text{Integers}\}$

Answer: –7, –6, –5, –4, –3, –2, –1, 0, and 1.

Example 4: How would you write a compound inequality for this graph?

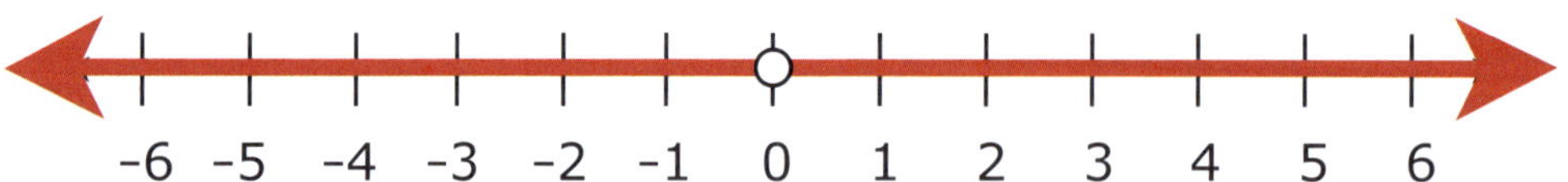

Answer: $n < 0$ or $n > 0$ $\{n \mid n \in \text{Reals}\}$

Practice

Write a compound inequality for each of the following. Use *x* for your variable.

1. I estimate that Joan is at least 90 pounds but less than 120 pounds.

2. Either you buy that video game for less than $50, or go to the other store and spend more than $80.

3. The most comfortable temperature in the den is between 72° and 78° F.

4. You can only park in front of the store between 1 p.m. and 6 p.m.

5. Either your number is less than or equal to –4, or it must be greater than 10.

6. Water will become non-liquid if it's less than or equal to 32° F, or at least 212° F.

Write a compound inequality for these graphs over the set of Reals.

7. 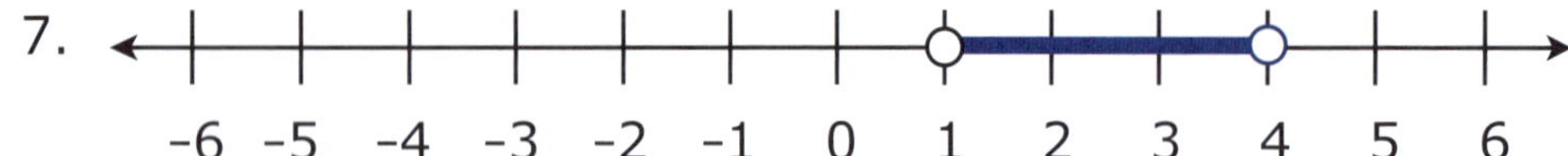

____

8. 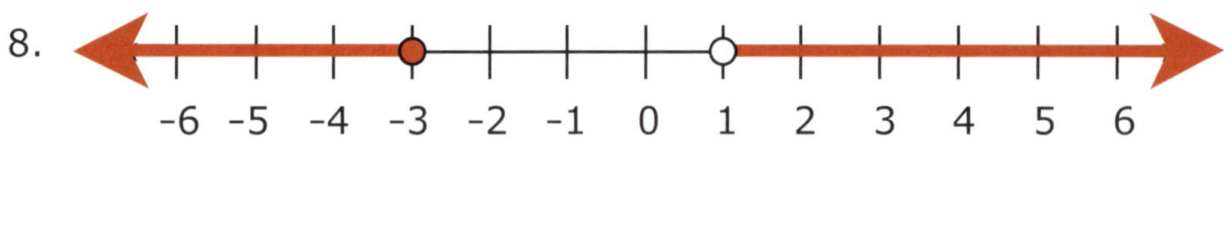

____

9.

4.5

-6 -5 -4 -3 -2 -1 0 1 2 3 4 5 6

____

10. 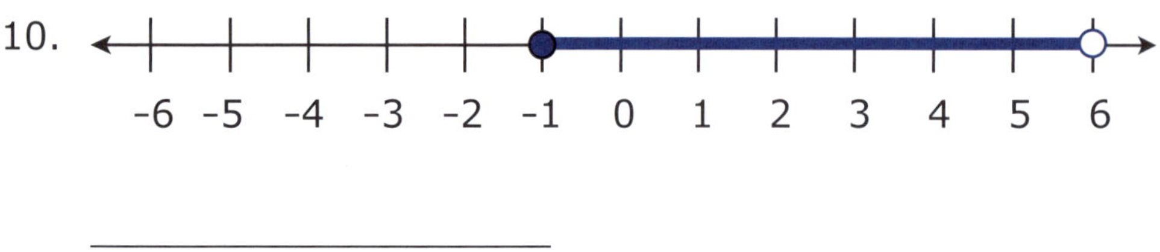

____

Chapter 8 Review

Graph the following inequalities over the set of Reals.

1. $n > 5$

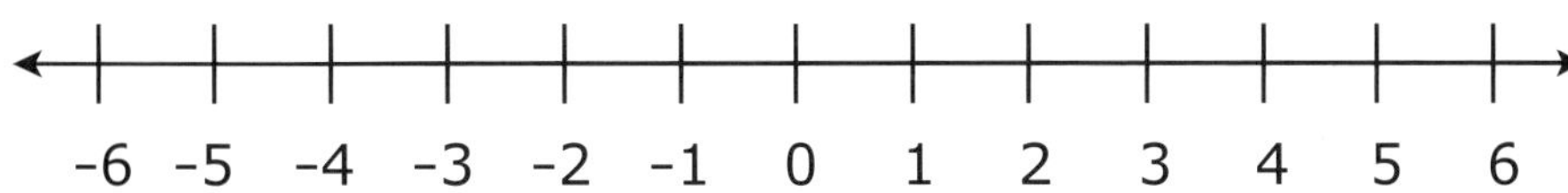

2. $n \leq -1.5$

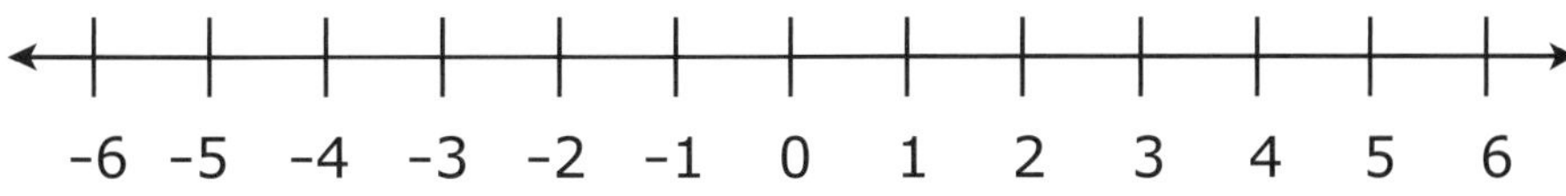

3. $n < 0$

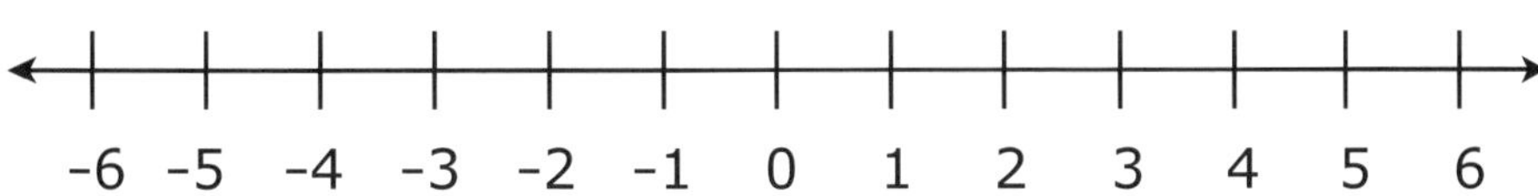

4. $-2 < n < 4$

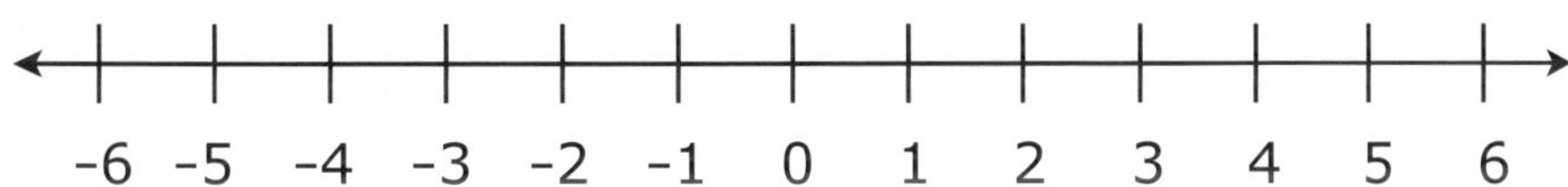

5. $-1 < n \leq 3$

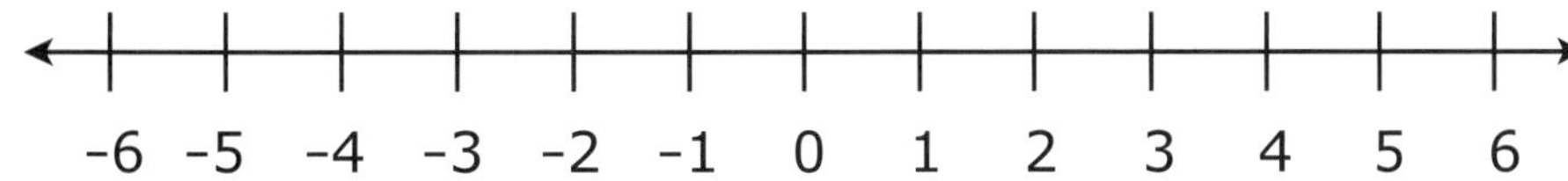

6. $n \leq 0$ or $n > 2$

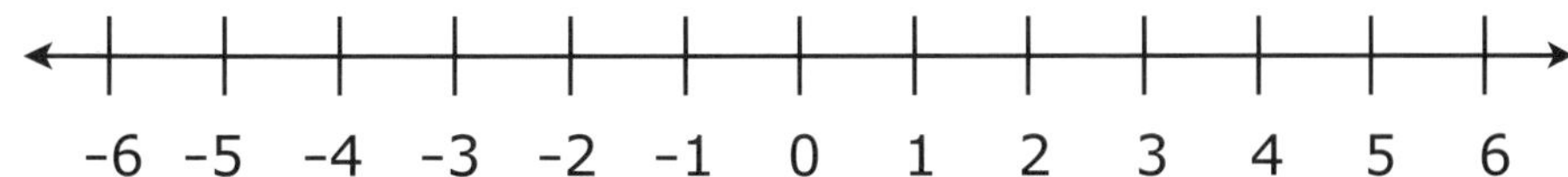

Solve the following word problems. Some are equations and some are inequalities. Show a let statement and show your equation or inequality and all steps.

7. José earns $400 a week and $15 an hour for or overtime. One week he made $520. How many hours of overtime did he work?

____

8. The sum of three consecutive even integers is less than 102. What are the largest consecutive even integers whose sum is less than 102.

____

9. Marta wants to save more than $500 to buy her mother a new TV. Her older brother gave her $120 to start. Each month she wants to save $40. How many months will she have to save to reach her goal?

____

10. Andrew wants to raise money for his hockey team. He has to sell chocolate bars at $2.50 a bar. How many chocolate bars must he sell to make at least $180?

____

11. Eleven less than a number is the same as twenty-four. Find the missing number.

____

12. In this rectangle, the length is twice the width. If the perimeter is 120 feet, what are the dimensions of the rectangle? Hint: The perimeter is the entire distance around a shape. ______________________

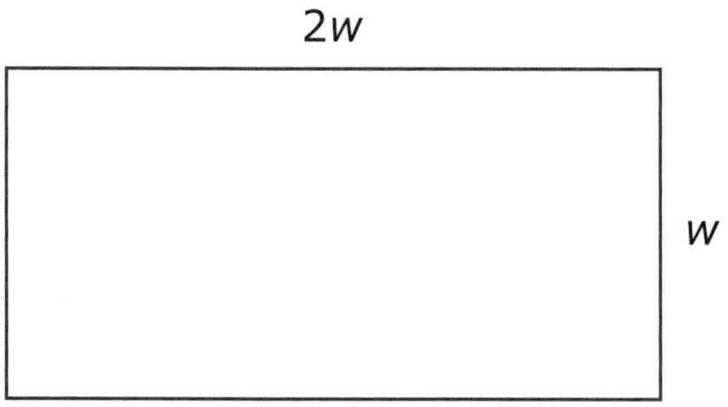

$2w$

w

13. In this rectangle, the length is twice the width. What are the biggest integer dimensions possible if the rectangle has to have a perimeter that is less than 120 feet? ______________________

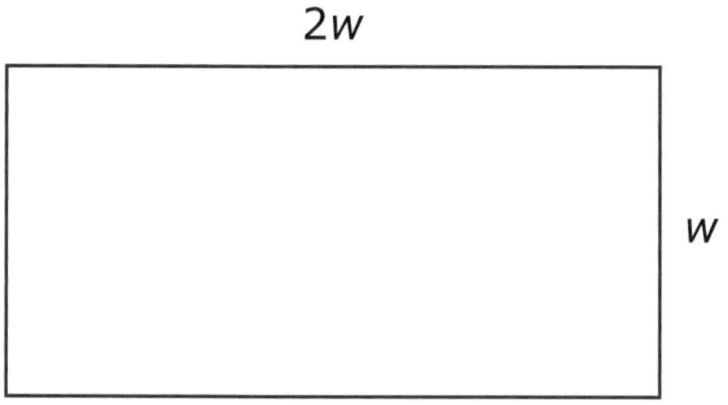

$2w$

w

14. Maria ate three times as many cookies as Tom. Emily ate 5 cookies. Altogether Maria, Tom, and Emily ate 21 cookies. How many cookies did Maria and Tom eat?

____

15. One-half a number plus three times the same number is greater than fourteen. Find the smallest integer that fits this situation.

____

Chapter 9

Understanding Square Roots and Irrational Numbers

Irrational numbers are numbers that cannot be written as a fraction of the form $\frac{p}{q}$ where p and q are integers, and $q \neq 0$. You learned in Chapter 1 that all fractions can be written as a decimal that either repeats or terminates. Therefore, irrational numbers are decimals that never repeat AND never terminate. A number such as π (PI) and the square roots of non-perfect square numbers are also irrational.

Repeating Decimals Cannot Be Irrational Numbers

You now have the algebra tools to prove that any repeating decimal can be turned to a fraction.

Example 1: Change $.\overline{6}$ to a fraction.

Let $n = .66666...$ Write it with a long tail.

$10n = 6.6666...$

You're multiplying by 10 since only one digit repeats. This moves the decimal point to the right one place.

Now write $10n$ on top of n:

$$10n = 6.6666...$$

$$n = .6666...$$ Line up the tails. Subtract the equations.

$$\frac{9n}{9} = \frac{6}{9}$$ The tails fall off!

Solve the equation and reduce.

$$n = \frac{2}{3}$$

So $.\overline{6}$ is the fraction $\frac{2}{3}$.

Using this method, you can change any repeating decimal to a fraction. The number of repeating digits tells you what power of ten to multiply by, since the goal is to get rid of the "tail" of repeating decimals.

Example 2: Change $.\overline{123}$ to a fraction.

Let n = .123123... Now set up the two equations.

$$\begin{aligned} 1{,}000n &= 123.123123... \\ n &= .123123... \\ \hline \frac{999n}{999} &= \frac{123}{999} \end{aligned}$$

So the repeating decimal $.\overline{123}$ is the same as the fraction $\frac{123}{999}$.

Practice

Change the following repeating decimals to fractions using the method above. Use a separate sheet of paper if needed.

1. $.\overline{3}$ __________

2. $.\overline{1}$ __________

3. $.\overline{4}$ __________

4. $.\overline{09}$ __________

5. $.\overline{45}$ __________

6. $.\overline{126}$ __________

7. $.\overline{034}$ __________

8. Using the method you just learned, prove that $.\overline{9}$ is the same as 1.

Squaring and Square Roots

As you know, addition and subtraction are inverse operations, just like multiplication and division are inverse operations. When you square a number, which means multiplying the number times itself, the inverse operation of squaring a number is taking the square root of that number.

For example, 5 • 5 = 25, you can say that the square root of 25 is 5.

The symbol for square root is $\sqrt{\ }$. This symbol is called "the radical," so $\sqrt{25} = 5$. It's incorrect to say that $\sqrt{25} = 5 \bullet 5$, so be careful. You're being asked for one root (or one answer), what is called the principal square root, a positive real answer. So even though $-5 \bullet -5 = 25$, to get a negative answer, you would see this: $-\sqrt{25}$ which is –5.

The set of perfect squares is infinite.

Set of Perfect Squares

{1, 4, 9, 16, 25, 36, 49, 64, 81, 100, 121, 144, 169, 196, 225, 256, 289, 324, 361, 400, 441, 484, 529, 576, 625, etc}

The square root of any perfect square is rational, NOT irrational.

Practice

Simplify the following. You may use a calculator with a square root key, or use the square root table on page 374.

1. 12^2 __________
2. $\sqrt{144}$ __________
3. $-\sqrt{49}$ __________
4. 20^2 __________
5. $\sqrt{81}$ __________
6. $\sqrt{400}$ __________
7. 25^2 __________
8. 13^2 __________
9. $\sqrt{361}$ __________
10. $\sqrt{100}$ __________
11. 40^2 __________
12. 100^2 __________

13. $\sqrt{121}$ ________

14. $\sqrt{225}$ ________

15. $-\sqrt{289}$ ________

16. $\sqrt{529}$ ________

17. 19^2 ________

18. 70^2 ________

19. 1^5 ________

20. 11^2 ________

21. 17^2 ________

22. $\sqrt{169}$ ________

23. $\sqrt{1,600}$ ________

24. $\sqrt{10,000}$ ________

When you find the square root of a non-perfect square, the answer is a non-terminating and non-repeating decimal. The answer needs to be rounded. You can use your calculator with a square root key, or use the table on page 374, which has rounded the answer to three decimal places.

Practice

Simplify the following. Make sure to round your answer to the nearest thousandths.

1. $\sqrt{5}$ ________

2. $\sqrt{10}$ ________

3. $\sqrt{79}$ ________

4. $\sqrt{2}$ ________

5. $\sqrt{63}$ ________

6. $\sqrt{20}$ ________

7. $\sqrt{3}$ ________

8. $\sqrt{26}$ ________

9. $\sqrt{101}$ ________

10. $-\sqrt{11}$ __________ 13. $\sqrt{60}$ __________ 16. $\sqrt{15}$ __________

11. $-\sqrt{8}$ __________ 14. $-\sqrt{24}$ __________ 17. $\sqrt{50}$ __________

12. $-\sqrt{39}$ __________ 15. $-\sqrt{7}$ __________ 18. $\sqrt{35}$ __________

Answer the following.

19. Celeste did not have a calculator but she was able to estimate that the $\sqrt{50}$ had to be a little larger than 7 and not that close to 8. How was she able to determine that? Explain your thinking.

____

____

____

____

20. Without using a calculator or a table of values, what would be your best estimate for these problems? Round your estimate to the nearest tenth. Then check your answer.

	Your Estimate	Correct Answer (nearest tenth)
a. $\sqrt{35}$	__________	__________
b. $\sqrt{102}$	__________	__________
c. $\sqrt{119}$	__________	__________

Cube Roots and Other Roots

When you cube a number (multiply a number by itself three times), you can reverse the process by taking the cube root of the number.

Example 1: Simplify 2^3. Then take the cube root of the answer.

$2 \bullet 2 \bullet 2 = 8$

You can now find the cube root of 8 which is written $\sqrt[3]{8}$.
The answer to the cube root of 8 is 2.

Example 2: Simplify 2^4. Then take the 4th root of the answer.

$2 \bullet 2 \bullet 2 \bullet 2 = 16$

You can then find the fourth root of 16, which is written $\sqrt[4]{16}$.
The answer to the fourth root of 16 is 2.

If you have a scientific calculator, you can find the "*n*th root" of a number.

The same is true if you have a graphing calculator. The next set of exercises does not require you to have either type of calculator, but in case you do, here's how to figure out different roots besides the square root.

Another way of writing the $\sqrt{49}$ is to write 49 to the one-half power or $49^{\frac{1}{2}}$.

In the same way, the cube root of 8 can be written as $8^{\frac{1}{3}}$.

On a scientific calculator, while there might be an x^y key, another simple way to type the cube root of 8 is by entering 8 ^ 1/3. Look for the caret key (^) which indicates an exponent.

In a graphing calculator (TI 84), you can do the same or go to the key that says MATH, scroll down to row 4 for cube root or to row 5 for $\sqrt[x]{y}$ and type in what you need.

Practice

Answer the following.

1. $16^{\frac{1}{2}}$ ________

2. 2^5 ________

3. $\sqrt[5]{32}$ ________

Have you ever seen the joke above on a math t-shirt? You would need to understand that you cannot find the square root of a negative number. In fact, $\sqrt{-1}$ is defined as *i* which stands for "imaginary."

4. 10^3 ____________

5. $\sqrt[4]{10{,}000}$ ____________

6. 4^3 ____________

7. $\sqrt[3]{64}$ ____________

8. Why isn't it possible to have real number answer to $\sqrt{-1}$? Explain your thinking.

____

____

____

9. What is the cube root of 64,000? How does knowing the cube root of 64 and the cube root of 1,000 help you? Explain your thinking.

____

____

____

10. Look at the drawings below. Explain how knowing square roots and cube roots help you find the side of each of these shapes.

a. 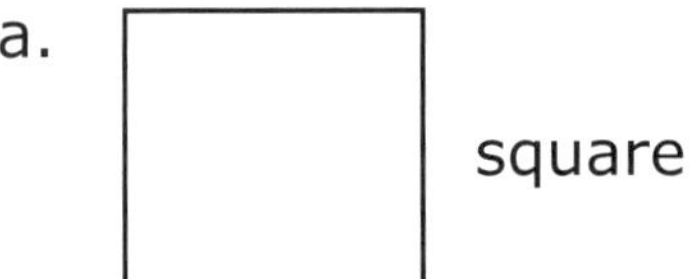

square

Area: 961 square units

b. 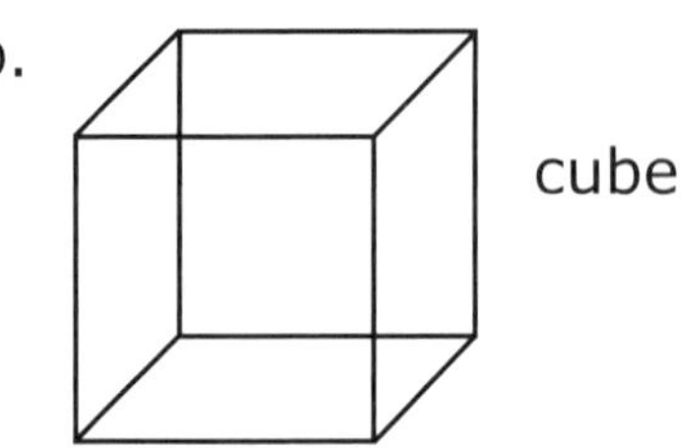

cube

Volume: 1,000 cubic units

____

____

____

Simplifying Square Roots

You can leave the answer in radical form as long as the radical is simplified.

Example 1: Simplify $6\sqrt{49}$.

The 6 has no symbol between it and the radical so this indicates you need to multiply the 6 by the answer to the square root of 49. Since $\sqrt{49} = 7$, the answer is $6 \bullet 7$ which simplifies to 42.

Example 2: Simplify $-3\sqrt{16} + 7\sqrt{81} - \sqrt{4}$.

$-3 \bullet 4 + 7 \bullet 9 - 2$ Follow the order of operations.

$-12 + 63 - 2$

Answer: 49

Example 3: Simplify $\sqrt{50}$.

There's a perfect square that is a factor of 50. Break up 50 into $25 \bullet 2$

$\sqrt{25 \bullet 2}$

$\sqrt{25} \bullet \sqrt{2}$

$\sqrt{ab} = \sqrt{a} \bullet \sqrt{b}$

Answer: $5\sqrt{2}$

Example 4: Simplify $\sqrt{300}$.

There's a perfect square as a factor of 300.

$\sqrt{100 \bullet 3}$

Make sure to use the biggest perfect square that is a factor of the number.

Answer: $10\sqrt{3}$

Remember the factors you learned in Chapter 1 such as $16 \bullet 2 = 32$, $16 \bullet 3 = 48$, $36 \bullet 2 = 72$, and $49 \bullet 2 = 98$. If you pull out a perfect square factor that is not the biggest perfect square factor of a number, you will just have to do more steps, but the answer should still be correct.

Practice

1. Maddy and April simplified $\sqrt{32}$ below.

April's Work	Maddy's Work
$\sqrt{32}$	$\sqrt{32}$
$\sqrt{4 \bullet 8}$	$\sqrt{16 \bullet 2}$
$2\sqrt{8}$	$4\sqrt{2}$

Who is correct and why? Explain your thinking. ______________________

____

____

____

____

2. Which of the following is correct and why? Explain your thinking.

a. $\sqrt{4 + 9}$

$2 + 3$

5

b. $\sqrt{4 \bullet 9}$

$2 \bullet 3$

6

____

____

____

____

Simplify the following square roots. Use a separate sheet of paper if needed.

3. $\sqrt{500}$ ______

10. $\sqrt{98}$ ______

4. $\sqrt{25} + \sqrt{121}$ ______

11. $10\sqrt{400}$ ______

5. $-9\sqrt{81}$ ______

12. $-8\sqrt{625}$ ______

6. $\sqrt{144} - \sqrt{49}$ ______

13. $\sqrt{48}$ ______

7. $\sqrt{12}$ ______

14. $\sqrt{125}$ ______

8. $\sqrt{75}$ ______

15. $(\sqrt{25})^2$ ______

9. $-5\sqrt{64} - 6\sqrt{64}$ ______

16. $(\sqrt{36})^2$ ______

A Look at Irrational PI

PI π is probably the most well known irrational number. PI is the ratio of the circumference of a circle to its diameter. This ratio has been known for thousands of years. The Babylonians used 3 as an approximation for PI and sometimes 3.12 which is even more accurate.

$$\pi = \frac{Circumference}{Diameter}$$

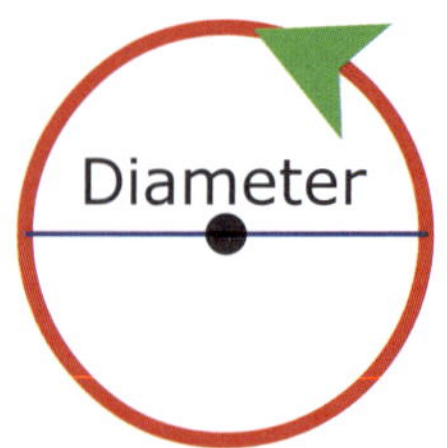

Circumference - distance around the circle

Archimedes of Syracuse, a famous Greek mathematician (287-212 B.C.), approximated the area of a circle by <u>inscribing</u> regular polygons and <u>circumscribing</u> them, then finding the areas of each. He did this for polygons of many sides. He was then able to approximate PI to be the following: $3\frac{10}{71} < \pi < 3\frac{1}{7}$.

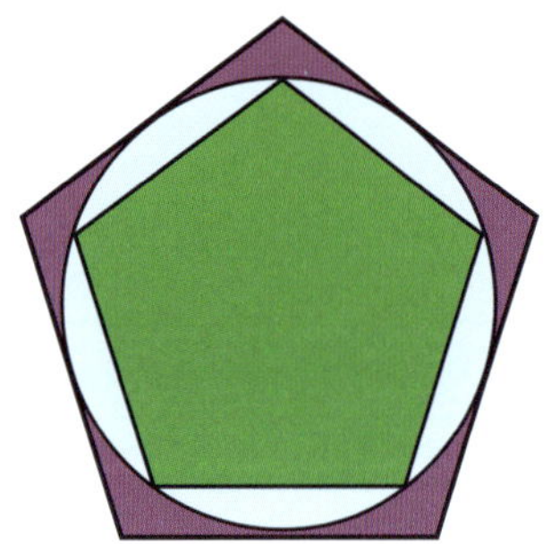

The green pentagon is inscribed, and the purple one is circumscribed around the circle. The inscribed and circumscribed polygons touch the circle.

However, it wasn't until 1761 that a mathematician by the name of Lambert proved that PI was irrational.

Before the age of calculators, many students used $\frac{22}{7}$ as a good approximation of PI. $\frac{355}{113}$ is an even better approximation.

You will do more with PI when you work with circumference and areas of circles, but to have a sense for the randomness of PI on the next page is a list of its first 1,000 digits. Remember PI is infinite!

π

3.1415926535 8979323846 2643383279 5028841971
6939937510 5820974944 5923078164 0628620899
8628034825 3421170679 8214808651 3282306647
0938446095 5058223172 5359408128 4811174502
8410270193 8521105559 6446229489 5493038196
4428810975 6659334461 2847564823 3786783165
2712019091 4564856692 3460348610 4543266482
1339360726 0249141273 7245870066 0631558817
4881520920 9628292540 9171536436 7892590360
0113305305 4882046652 1384146951 9415116094
3305727036 5759591953 0921861173 8193261179
3105118548 0744623799 6274956735 1885752724
8912279381 8301194912 9833673362 4406566430
8602139494 6395224737 1907021798 6094370277
0539217176 2931767523 8467481846 7669405132
0005681271 4526356082 7785771342 7577896091
7363717872 1468440901 2249534301 4654958537
1050792279 6892589235 4201995611 2129021960
8640344181 5981362977 4771309960 5187072113
4999999837 2978049951 0597317328 1609631859
5024459455 3469083026 4252230825 3344685035
2619311881 7101000313 7838752886 5875332083
8142061717 7669147303 5982534904 2875546873
1159562863 8823537875 9375195778 1857780532
1712268066 1300192787 6611195909 2164201989

Practice

1. Why is the rational number $\frac{22}{7}$ a good approximation of PI? Explain your thinking.

2. Why is the rational number $\frac{355}{113}$ an even better approximation to PI? Explain your thinking.

3. How do you know that both $\frac{22}{7}$ and $\frac{355}{113}$ are rational numbers? Explain your thinking.

The Pythagorean Theorem

In every right triangle (a triangle with a 90º angle) the following is always true: The longest side squared, is always equal to the sum of the squares of the other two sides. The longest side is across from the right angle and it's called the hypotenuse.

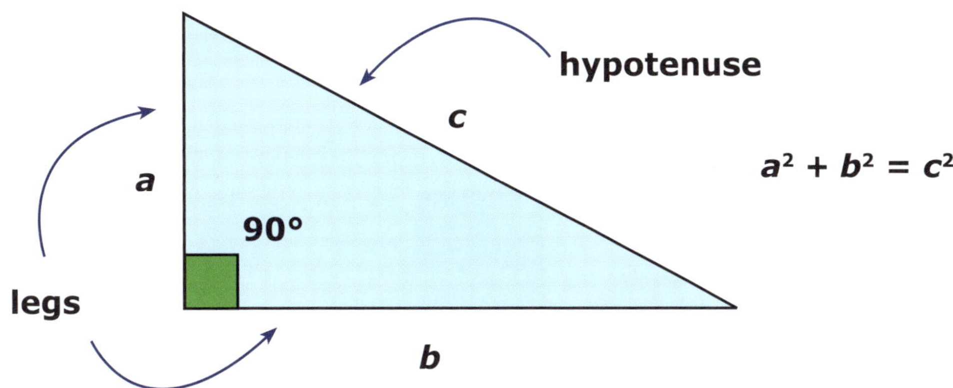

A famous Greek mathematician named Pythagoras (569-500 B.C.E) gets credit for the Pythagorean Theorem as it's thought that he was one of the first to offer a proof. A theorem is a property that can be proven. The numbers that satisfy the Pythagorean Theorem are called Pythagorean Triples. The most famous of all Pythagorean triples is 3,4,5.

Look at the triangle below whose measurements are 3, 4, and 5 units.

$$3^2 + 4^2 = 5^2$$

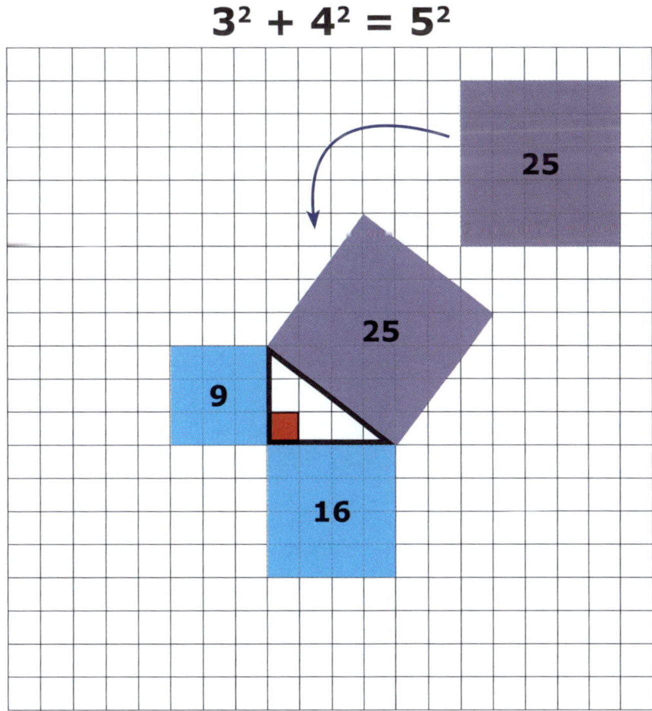

If you need to know that a triangle is a right triangle, remember that if the sides satisfy the Pythagorean Theorem, then the triangle is automatically a right triangle.

Example 1: Could 6", 8", and 10" be the sides of a right triangle?

Plug in those numbers into the Pythagorean Theorem.

$$a^2 + b^2 = c^2$$

It doesn't matter whether you choose 6 or 8 (the legs of the triangle) for *a* or *b*, but you must choose 10 for *c*, the longest side.

$$6^2 + 8^2 = 10^2?$$

$$36 + 64 = 100? \text{ Yes!}$$

The sides satisfy the Pythagorean Theorem, a triangle with those sides must be a right triangle.

Example 2: Find the missing side of this right triangle.

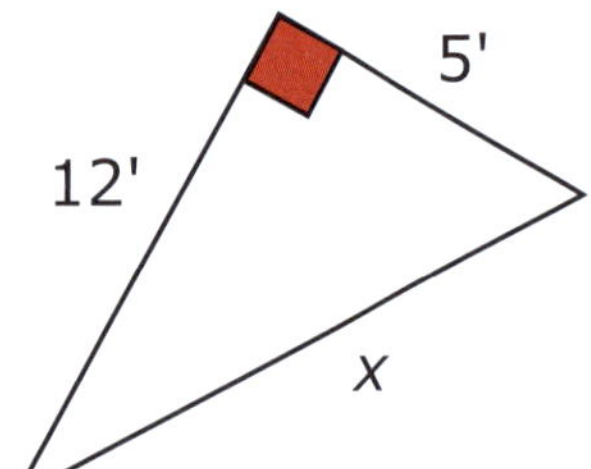

$$a^2 + b^2 = c^2$$

$$5^2 + 12^2 = x^2$$

$$25 + 144 = x^2$$

$$169 = x^2$$

You know $\sqrt{169} = 13$, the principal square root. However, when solving an equation such as $x^2 = 169$, there are actually two possible answers, 13 (since $13 \bullet 13 = 169$) and -13 (since $-13 \bullet -13 = 169$). Because a side of a triangle cannot be a negative number, the correct answer is 13'.

Example 3: Find the missing side of this right triangle.

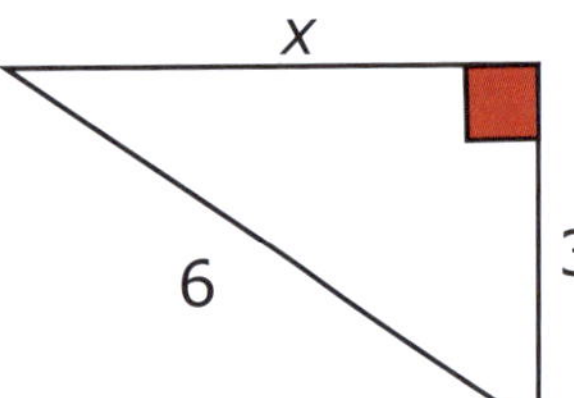

$$a^2 + b^2 = c^2$$

$$3^2 + x^2 = 6^2$$

$$9 + x^2 = 36$$

$$-9 \qquad -9$$

$$x^2 = 27$$

Simplify.

$$x = \sqrt{27} \text{ or } 3\sqrt{3} \text{ units}$$

The hypotenuse is known, but one of the legs is missing.

Practice

1. Is this a right triangle (don't rely on the picture)? Use the Pythagorean Theorem to determine your answer. Explain your thinking.

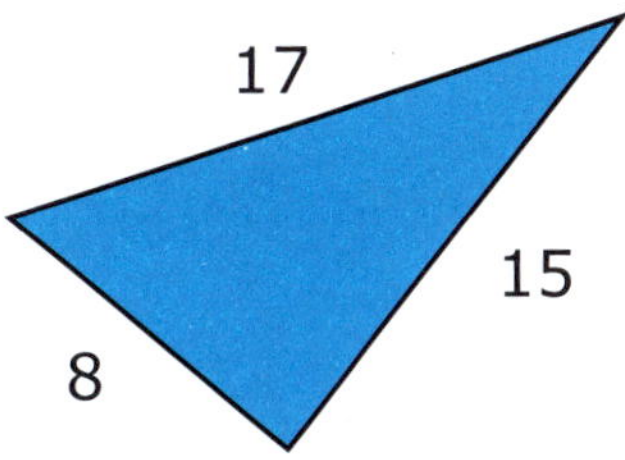

____

____

2. Is 12, 37, and 35 a Pythagorean triple? Explain your thinking. You may use a calculator. Remember that the longest side has to be tested as the possible hypotenuse.

____

____

Find the missing side of these right triangles. Show your work. You can leave your answer as a radical but make sure to simplify. You may use a calculator.

3. 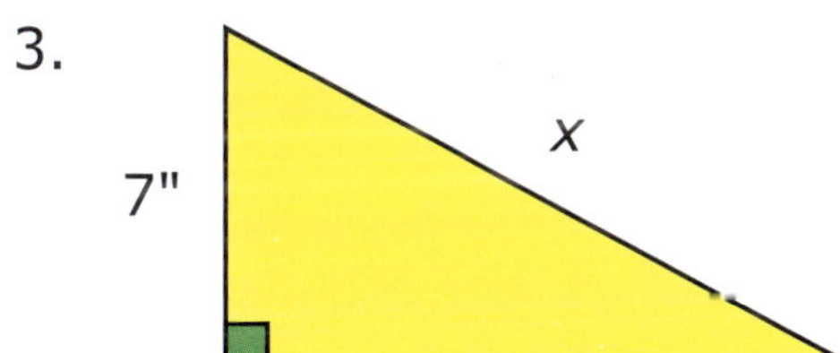

____

4. 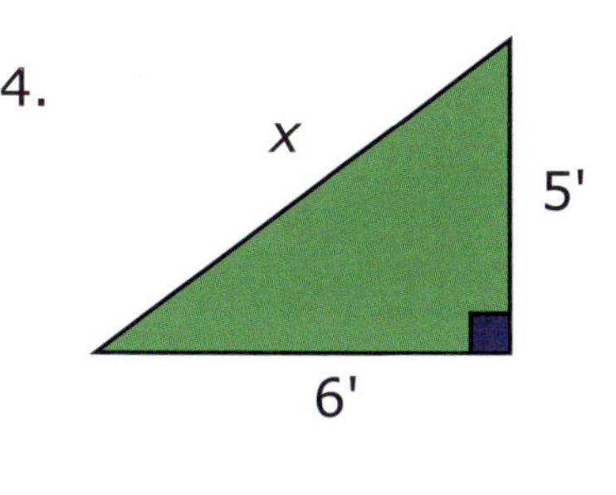

____

5.

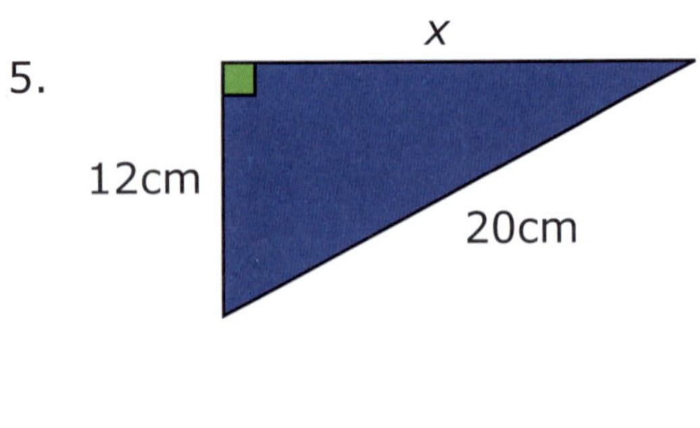

____

6.

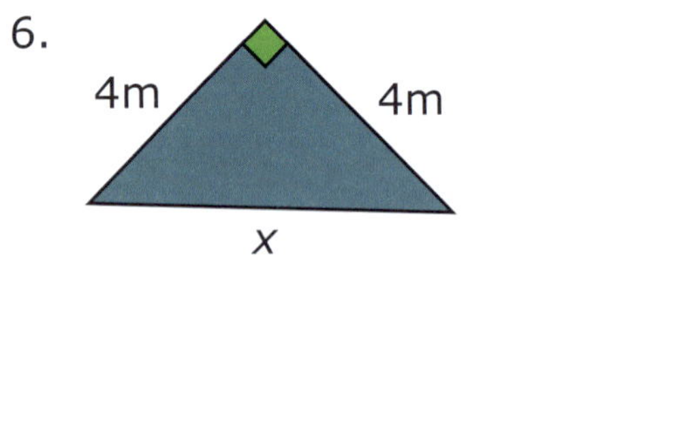

____

7.

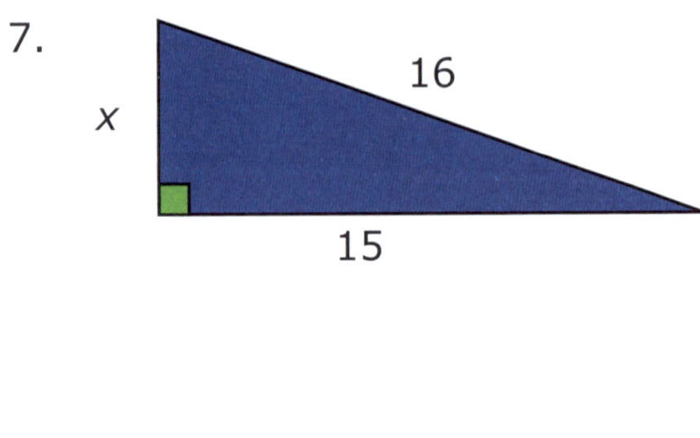

____

8.

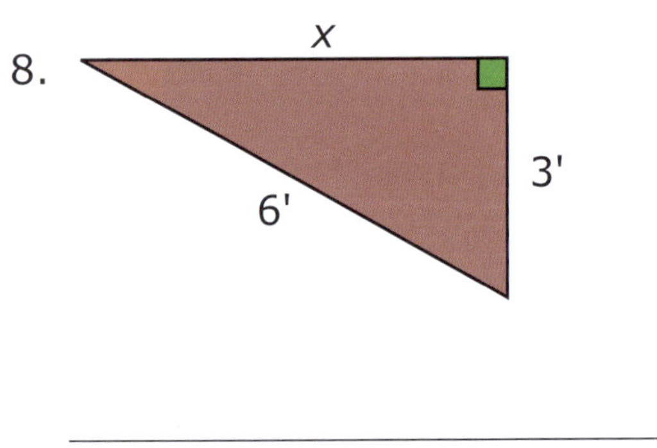

____

Solve these real problems using the Pythagorean Theorem. Use a calculator to round your answer to the nearest tenth.

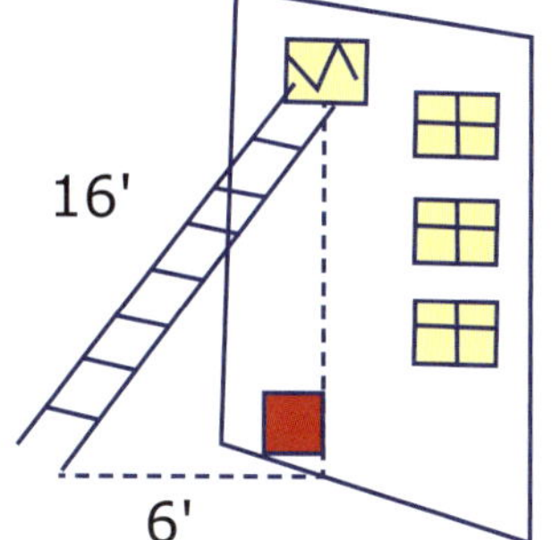

9. A 16' ladder leans against a house. The base of the ladder is 6' from the bottom of the house. How high is the window that needs fixing? ______________________

10. A baseball diamond is actually a square 90' on each side. How far is second base from home plate? Round to the nearest tenth.

____

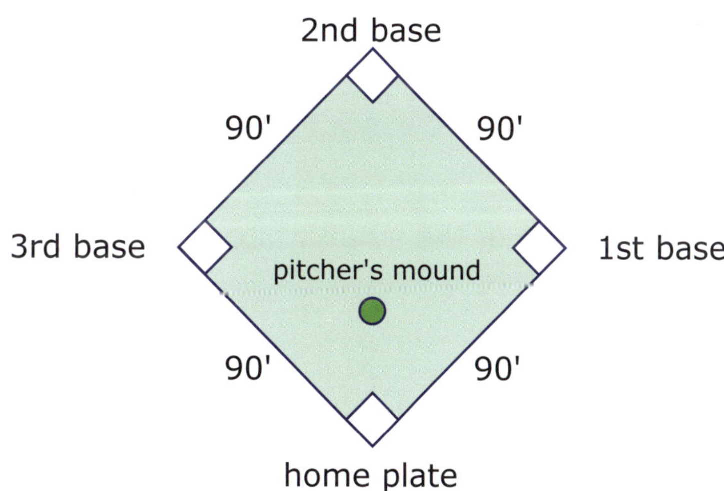

Chinese Proof of the Pythagorean Theorem

The following proof from China dates back to about 40 A.D. Look at these two identical squares, each having lengths $a + b$. Each are divided into 4 congruent (identical) triangles.

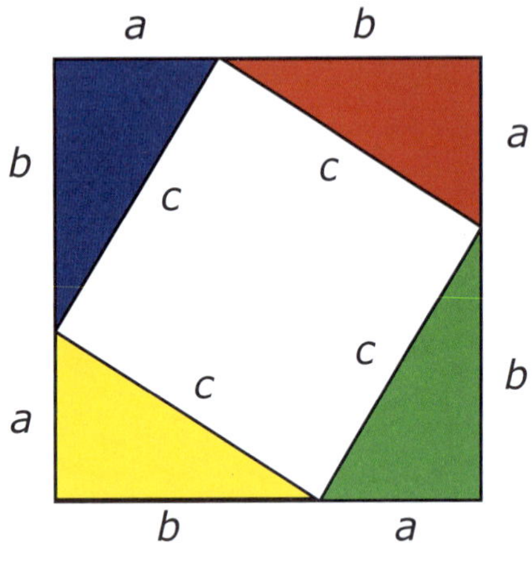

Figure 1

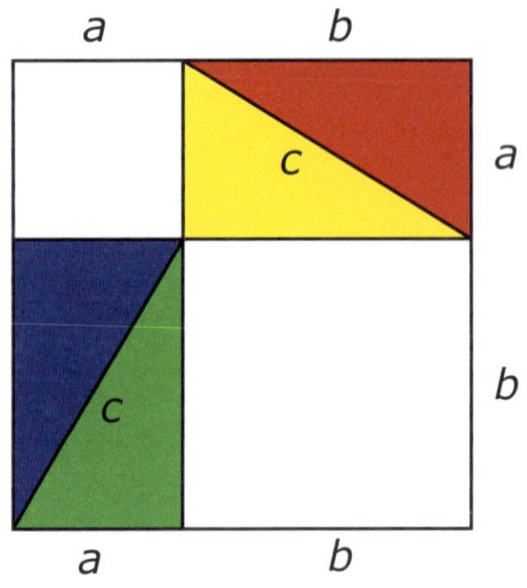

Figure 2

Practice

Remember that the area of a square is side • side.

1. In Figure 1, what is the area of the white square? ___________

2. In Figure 2, what is the area of the small white square? ___________

3. In Figure 2, what is the area of the bigger white square? ___________

4. Since each figure has the same 4 congruent triangles, what can you say about c^2, when you compare the white squares from both figures? ___________

Chapter 9 Review

Change the following repeating decimals to fractions.

1. $.\overline{7}$ __________

2. $.\overline{54}$ __________

3. $.\overline{055}$ __________

Find the answer to the following. Use a calculator (if needed) and round to the nearest thousandths, or use the table on page 374.

4. 18^2 __________

5. 100^2 __________

6. $\sqrt{169}$ __________

7. $-\sqrt{49}$ __________

8. $\sqrt{41}$ __________

9. $\sqrt{67}$ __________

10. $-\sqrt{92}$ __________

11. $\sqrt[3]{125}$ __________

Fill in the blanks.

12. If $n^2 = 81$, then n = ______ or ______. This is true because you're solving an equation. However, $\sqrt{81}$ = ______ and $-\sqrt{81}$ = ______.

13. If the area of a square is 100 square feet, then one side is the square root of ______, which equals ______.

14. If the volume of a cube is 64 square meters, then one side is the cube root of ______, which equals ______.

Answer the following.

15. A student thinks that the square root of odd numbers are always irrational and the square root of even numbers are rational. Is the student correct? Give at least 5 examples of why or why not.

____

____

____

____

____

Simplify the following square roots. When the answer is not rational, make sure to leave your answer in simplest radical form.

16. $\sqrt{8}$ ________

21. $5\sqrt{49}$ ________

17. $\sqrt{128}$ ________

22. $-\sqrt{242}$ ________

18. $\sqrt{200}$ ________

23. $6\sqrt{16} - \sqrt{64}$ ________

19. $\sqrt{45}$ ________

24. $-2\sqrt{9} - 3\sqrt{9}$ ________

20. $\sqrt{625}$ ________

25. $(\sqrt{4})^2$ ________

Solve the following problems using the Pythagorean Theorem. Leave your answers in simplest radical form. Use a separate sheet of paper if needed.

26.

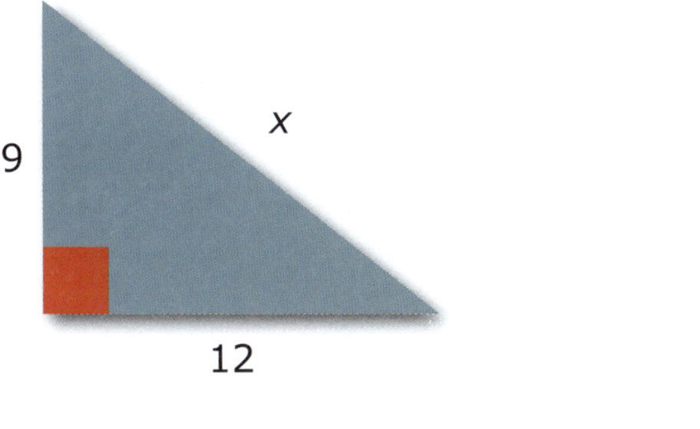

____

27.

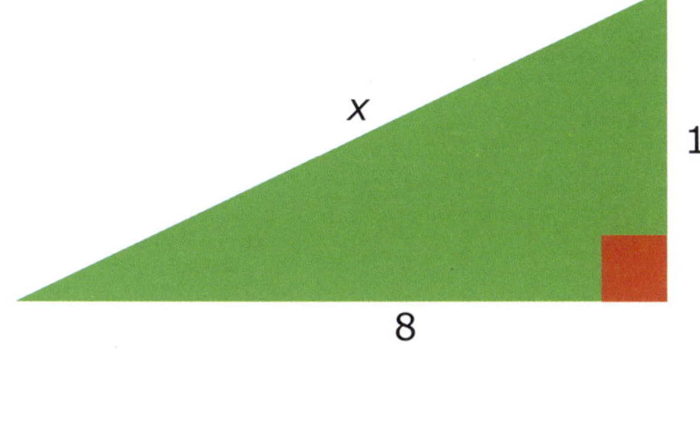

____

28.

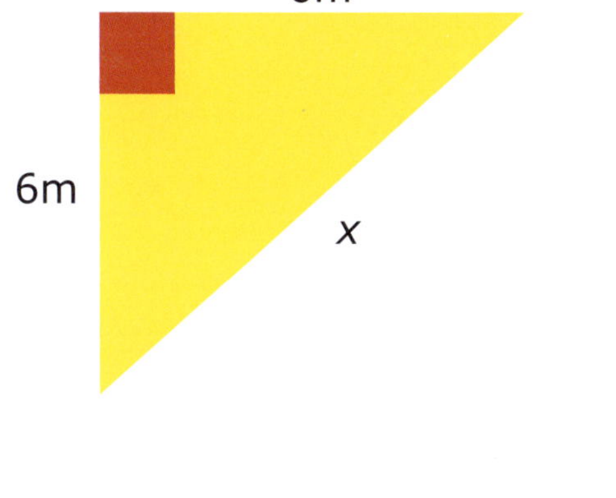

____

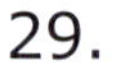

29.

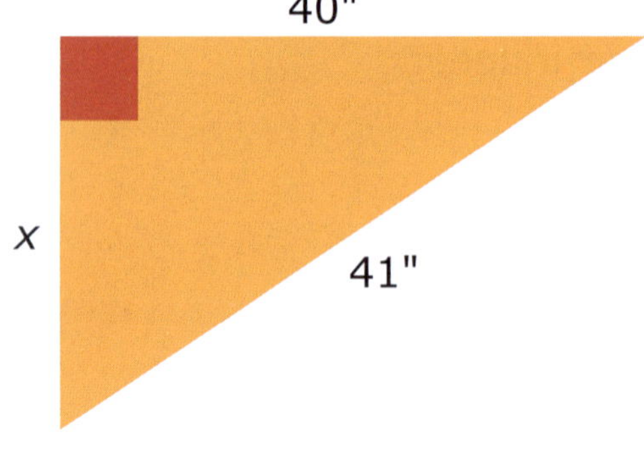

____

30.

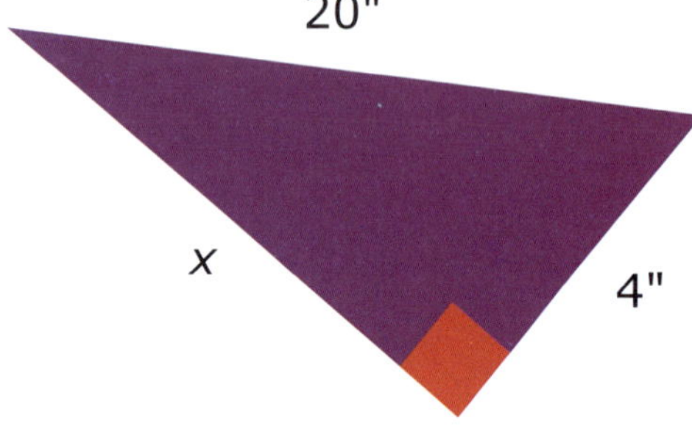

____

31.

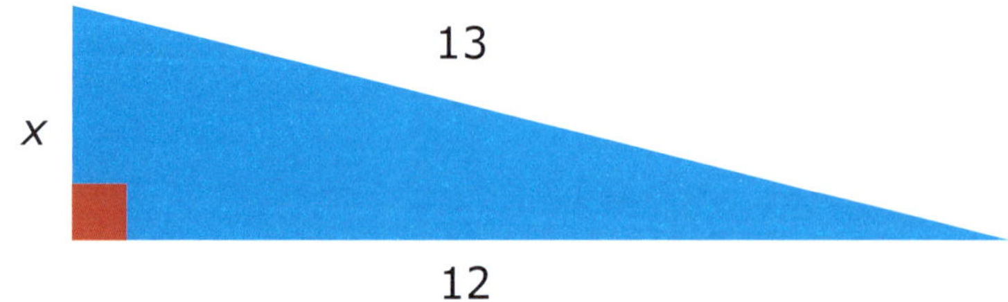

____

Solve the following problems using the Pythagorean Theorem.

32. A boat goes east 8 miles and then turns north and goes 6 miles. How far is the boat from the dock? ______________________

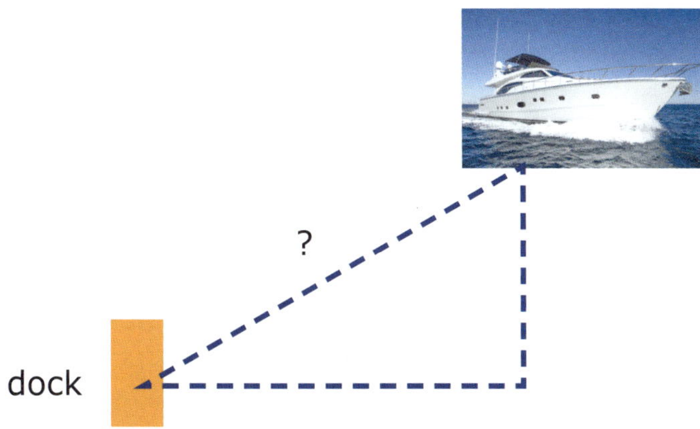

33. A rectangle has a length of 21 feet and a width of 20 feet. How long is its diagonal? ______________________

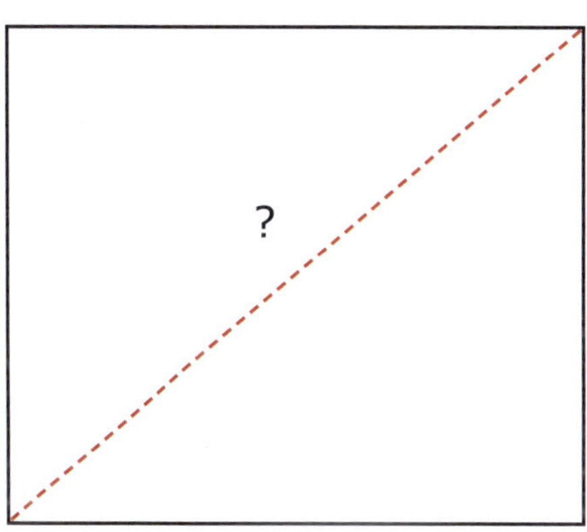

34. A ladder 12 feet in length is placed 5 feet from a building. How far above the ground does the ladder touch the building? Draw a picture. Round your answer to the nearest foot. ______________________

Chapter 10

Two Dimensional Geometry

In this chapter you will review geometry concepts you may already know and also learn how to use algebra to solve many geometry problems.

Naming Angles

An angle is the union of two rays with a common endpoint (or vertex). The angle shaded below is $\angle ACD$ or $\angle DCA$. Capital letters are used to indicate the points on the angle, and the vertex is in the middle. You cannot call it $\angle C$ since there is another angle with vertex C in the picture.

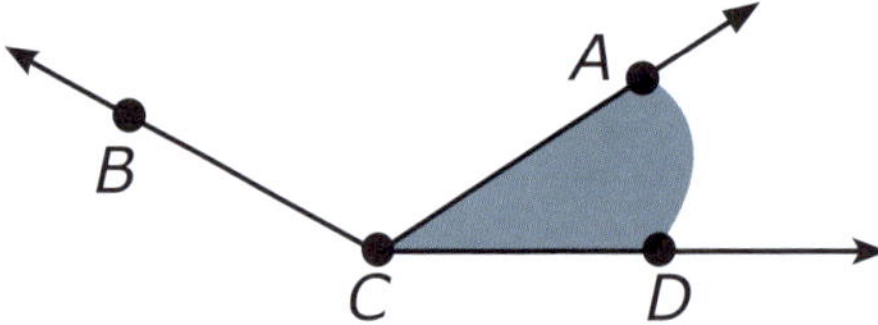

$\angle BCA$ and $\angle ACD$ are adjacent angles. Adjacent angles are coplanar (angles on the same plane) that share a vertex and a side.

You might have learned that two segments, rays, or lines that make a right angle (90º) are called perpendicular (⊥). Two angles that form a 90º angle are called complementary, and two angles that form a line (180º) are called supplementary.

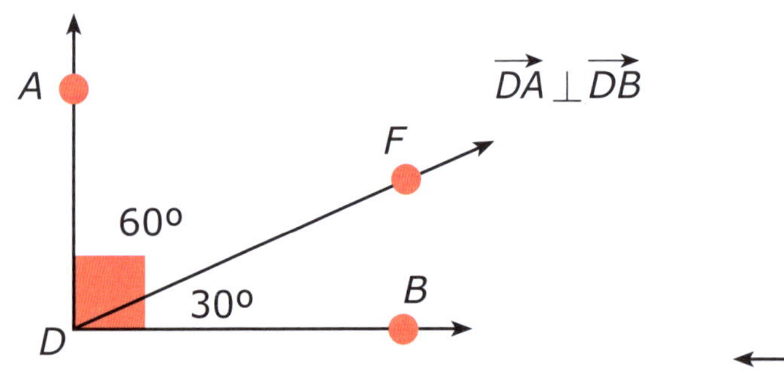

Complementary Angles
(60º and 30º)

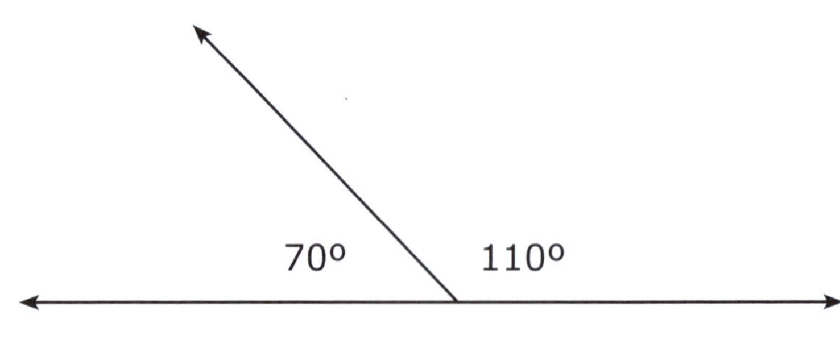

Supplementary Angles
(70º and 110º)

Another set of very important angles is vertical angles. Vertical angles have nothing to do with being "vertical." Vertical angles are the opposite angles created when two lines intersect (or meet).

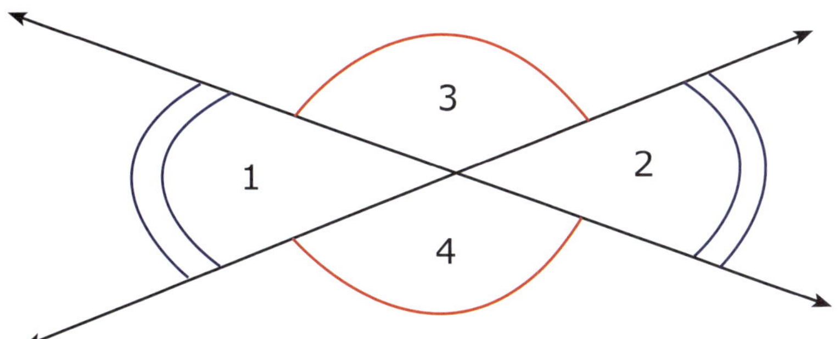

$\angle 1$ and $\angle 2$ are vertical angles.

$\angle 3$ and $\angle 4$ are vertical angles.

Vertical angles are always congruent.

Example 1: What is the complement and the supplement of an angle that is 79º?

The complement of 79º is the angle whose measure with 79º adds to 90º. The supplement of 79º is the angle whose measure with 79º adds to 180º degrees.

Answer: The complement of 79º is 11º, and the supplement of 79º is 101º.

Example 2: The picture below shows two angles that are complementary. Find the value of n. Find the measure of each angle.

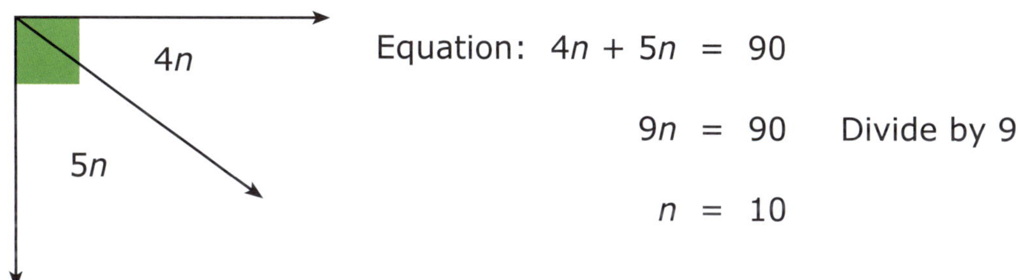

Equation: $4n + 5n = 90$

$9n = 90$ Divide by 9.

$n = 10$

Answer: $n = 10$. One angle is 40º, and the other angle is 50º.

Example 3: Find the value of x and find the measure of $\angle ABC$ and $\angle DBE$.

Since the angles shown are vertical and vertical angles are congruent, then you can set up an equation:

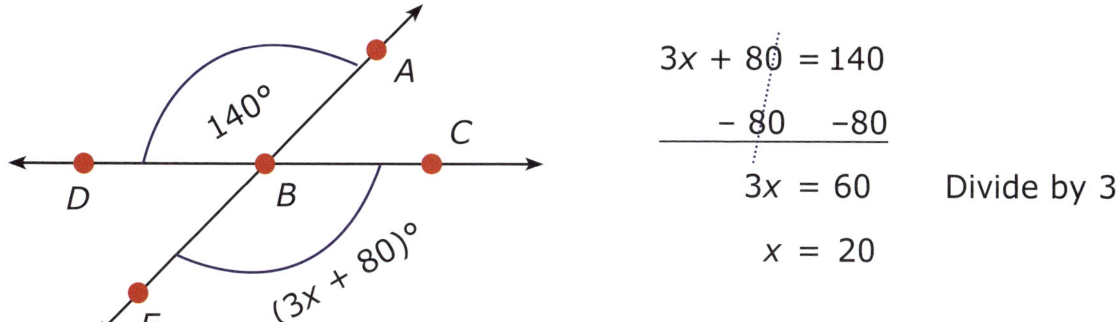

$3x + 80 = 140$

$-80 \quad -80$

$3x = 60$ Divide by 3.

$x = 20$

Answer: $x = 20$. $\angle ABC$ is supplementary with 140º so the measure of $\angle ABC$ is 40º. The measure of $\angle DBE$ is 40º as it's also supplementary with 140º and vertical with $\angle ABC$.

Use m to signify "measurement" which is a number, so $m\angle ABC$ means the measure of $\angle ABC$. When comparing measurements, use the equal sign (=) since numbers are being compared. When angles or other shapes are compared to each other without using their measurement, use the word "congruent." So if two angles $\angle ABC$ and $\angle DBE$ are congruent (identical in size and shape) you can say: $\angle ABC \cong \angle DBE$ or $m\angle ABC = m\angle DBE$.

Practice

Use a separate sheet of paper to show your work.

1. These two red segments are perpendicular. They meet to form a 90º angle. Find the missing angle x. The figures are not to scale.

a. 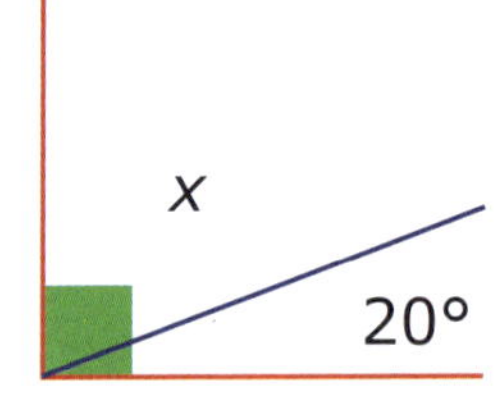

b. 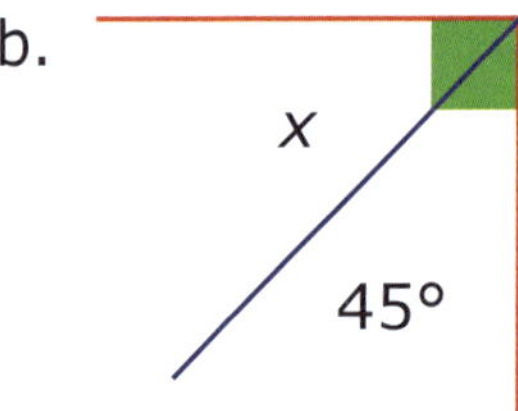

c. 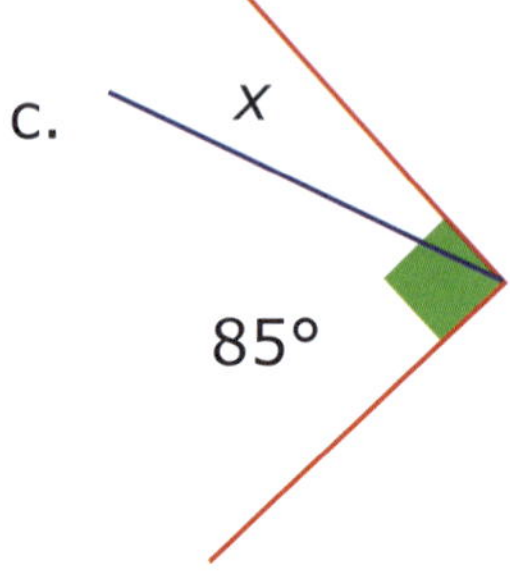

____________ ____________ ____________

Remember, two <u>angles</u> that add up to 90º are called <u>complementary</u>. Two <u>lines</u> or <u>segments</u> that create a right angle are called <u>perpendicular</u>.

Use algebra to find the missing value of x. The figures are not to scale.

2. 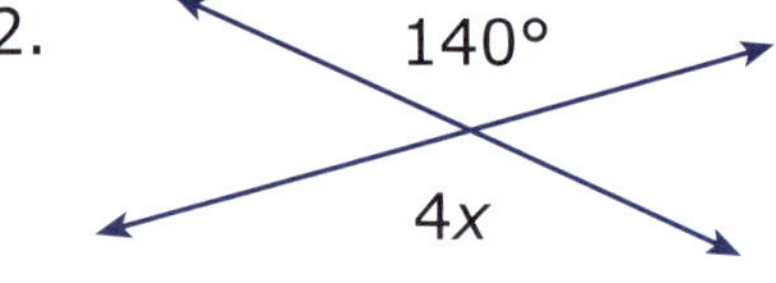

3. 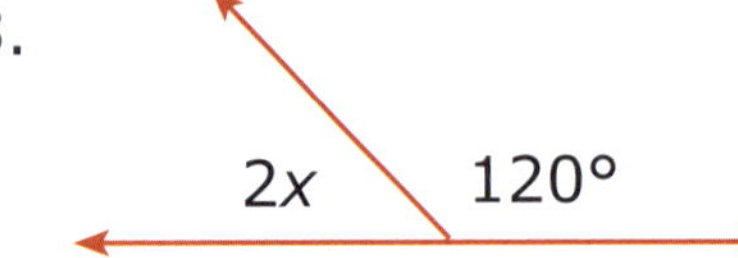

____________ ____________

4. 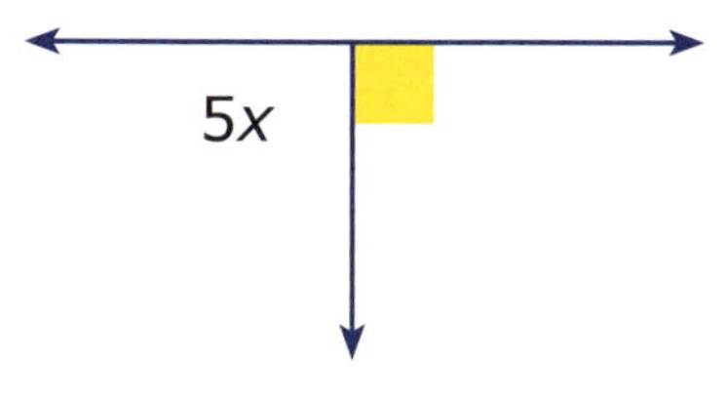

______

8. 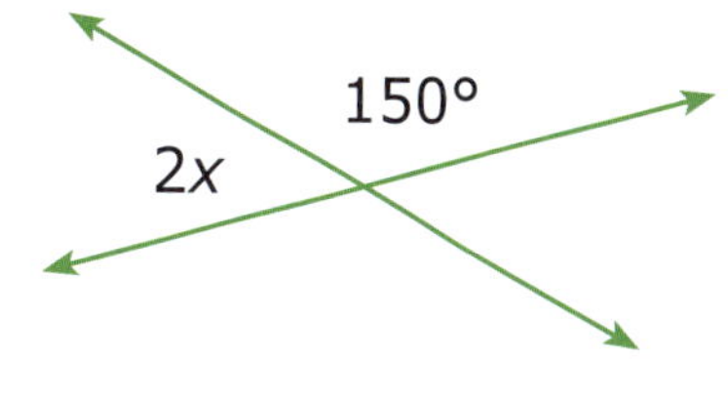

______

5. 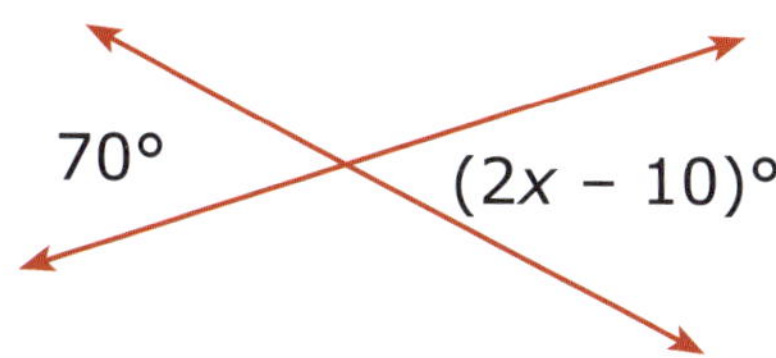

______

9. 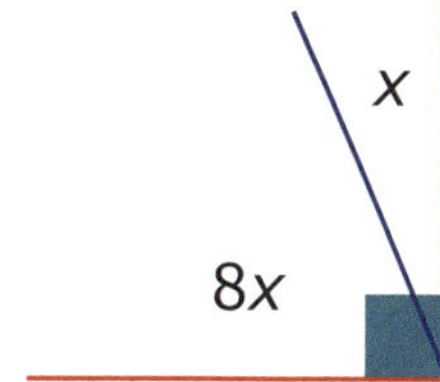

______

6. 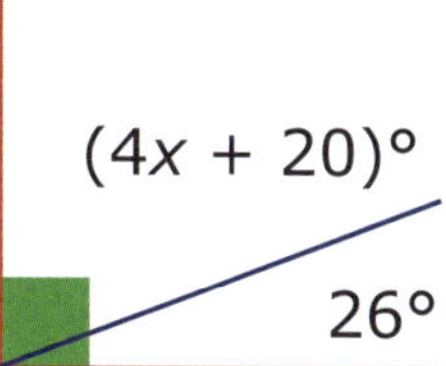

______

10. 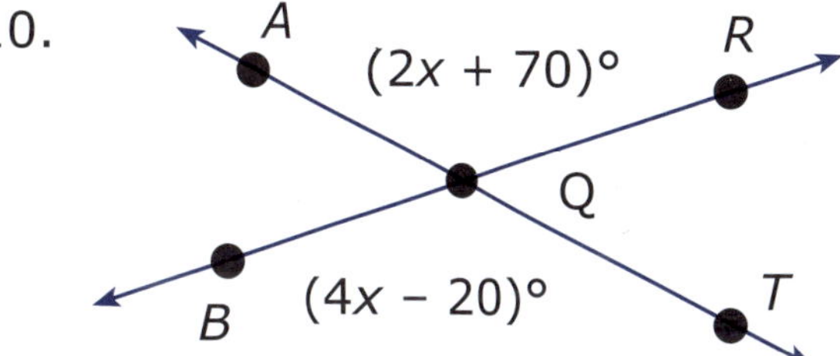

a. $x =$ ______

b. Find $m\angle AQR$ ______

c. Find $m\angle AQB$ ______

7. 5x 3x

______

Parallel Lines and Transversals

A line that intersects (cuts through) two or more lines is called a transversal.

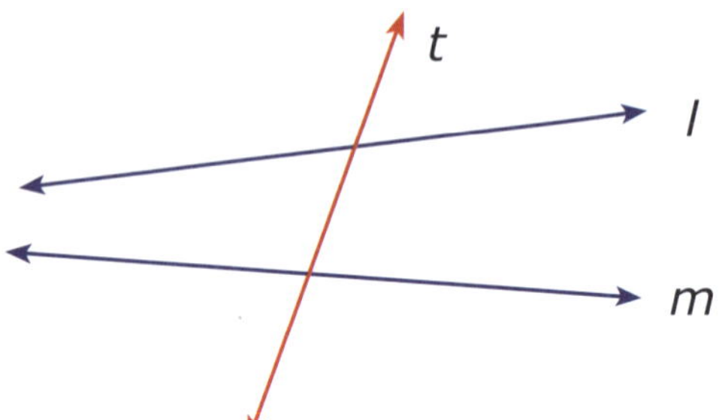

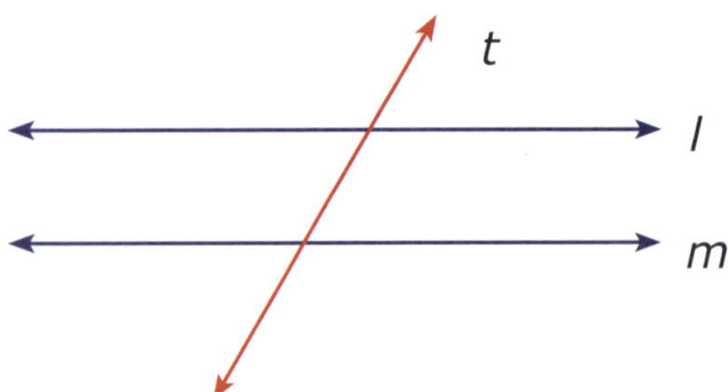

A transversal intersecting two lines.

A transversal intersecting two parallel lines.

Line *l* || *m*.

symbol for parallel

When a transversal intersects two or more lines many angles are formed.

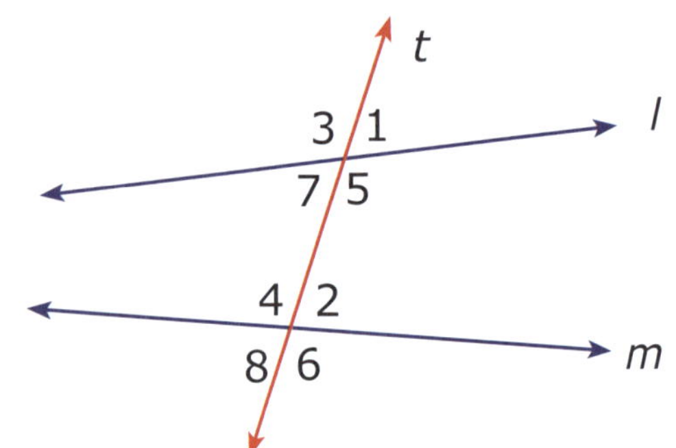

The following pairs are called corresponding angles.

$\angle 1$ and $\angle 2$ $\angle 5$ and $\angle 6$

$\angle 3$ and $\angle 4$ $\angle 7$ and $\angle 8$

When parallel lines are intersected by a transversal, the corresponding angles are congruent. The converse is true: When corresponding angles are congruent, then the lines are parallel.

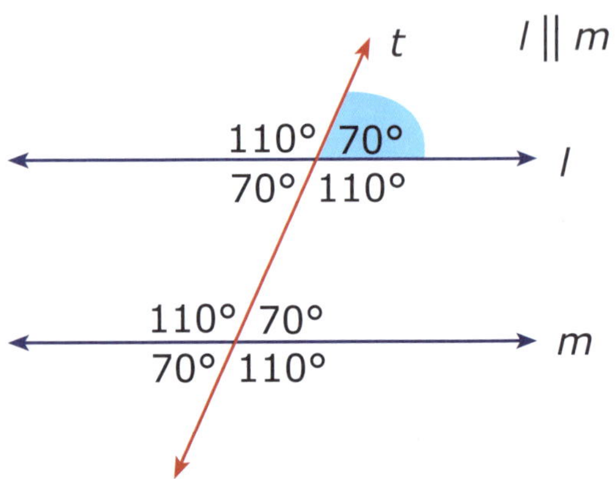

Assume $\angle 1$ is 70° (angle shaded in blue), since the lines are given to be parallel, you would automatically know the rest of the angles.

Practice

The drawings are not to scale.

1. Name the following shaded angles.

a. 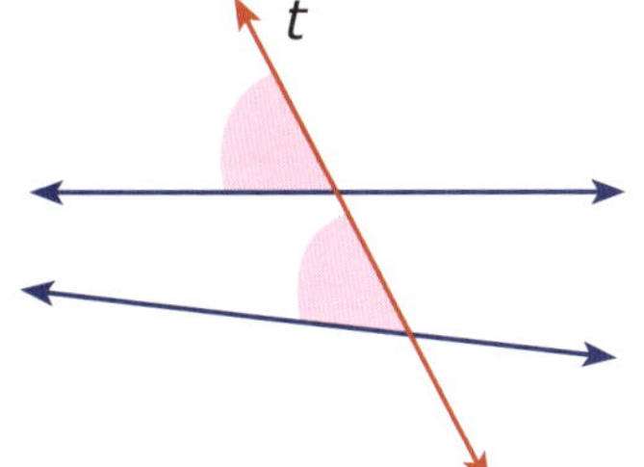

b. 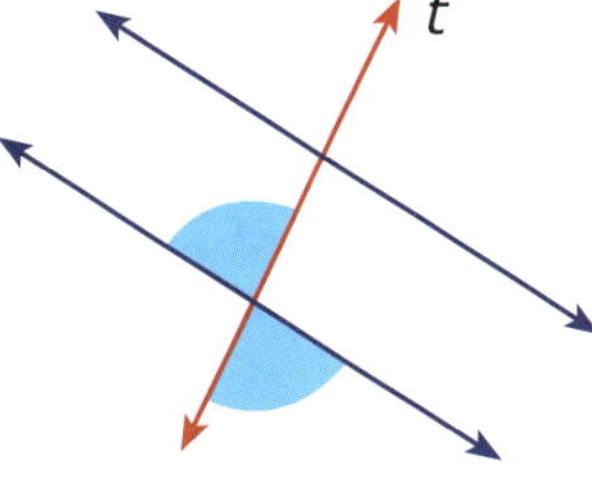

c. 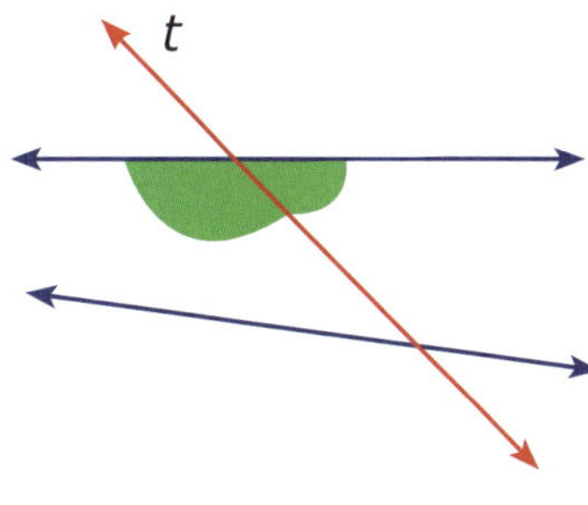

__________ __________ __________

2. Find the missing angles x and y in the drawings below. Lines m and n are parallel. Explain the reason for each of your answers.

a. 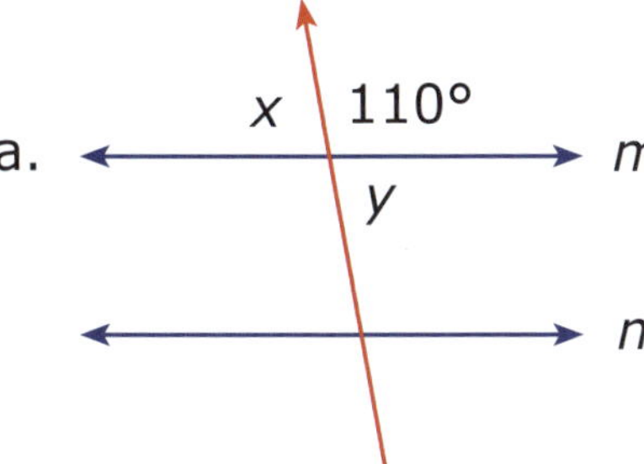

b. 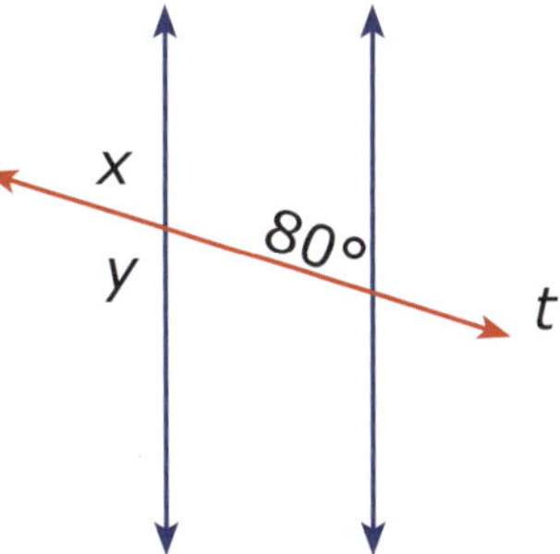

c. 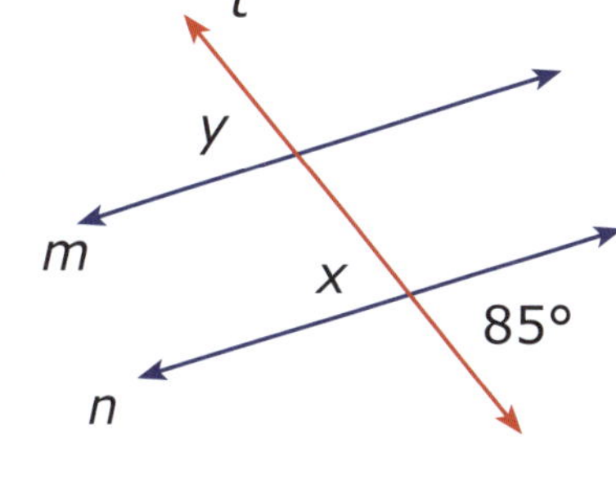

a. $m\angle x$ = _______ Why? ____________________

$m\angle y$ = _______ Why? ____________________

b. $m\angle x$ = _______ Why? ____________________

$m\angle y$ = _______ Why? ____________________

c. $m\angle x$ = _______ Why? ____________________

$m\angle y$ = _______ Why? ____________________

3. Find all the missing angles in this picture. Lines p and q are parallel.

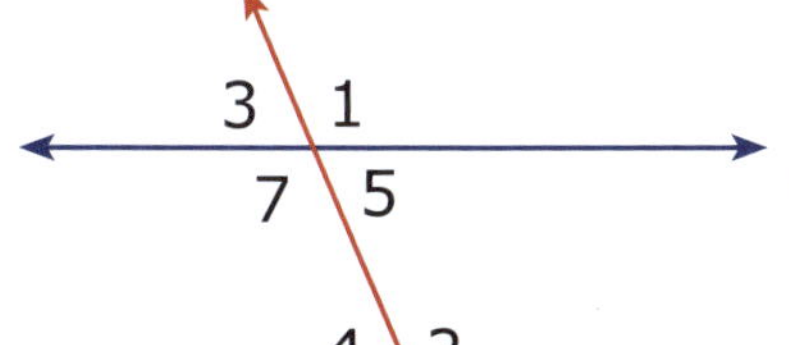

$m\angle 1$ = _______, $m\angle 2$ = _______, $m\angle 3$ = _______

$m\angle 4$ = _______, $m\angle 5$ = _______, $m\angle 6$ = _______

$m\angle 7$ = _______.

The drawing shows another pair of angles created by a transversal called interior angles.

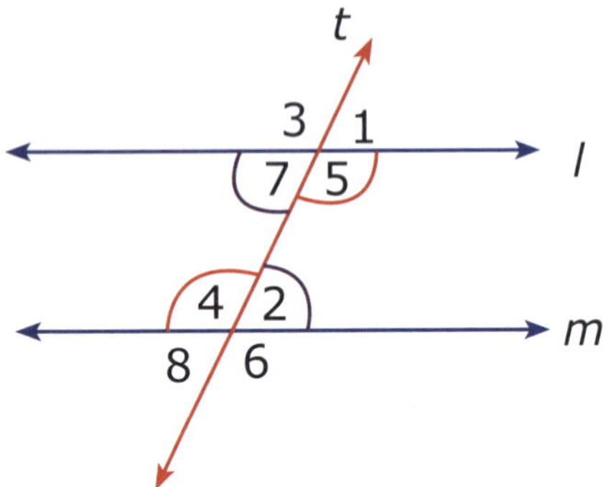

The following pairs are called alternate interior angles: ∠5 and ∠4 and ∠7 and ∠2.

"Alternate" refers to being on opposite sides of the transversal, and "interior" refers to being on the inside area between the two lines.

When parallel lines are intersected by a transversal, the alternate interior angles are congruent. The converse is true: When alternate interior angles are congruent, then the lines are parallel.

In the drawing above, ∠1 and ∠8 are called alternate exterior angles. So are ∠3 and ∠6.

Practice

1. Are alternate exterior angles congruent if the lines are parallel? Explain your thinking.

____

____

____

2. What can you say about the lines shown below? Explain your thinking:

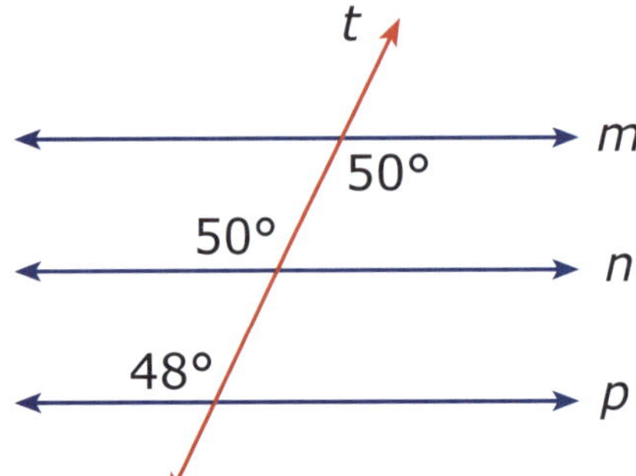

____

____

____

____

Find the missing angles. Lines *p* and *q* are parallel. The figures are not to scale. Use a separate sheet of paper if needed.

3.

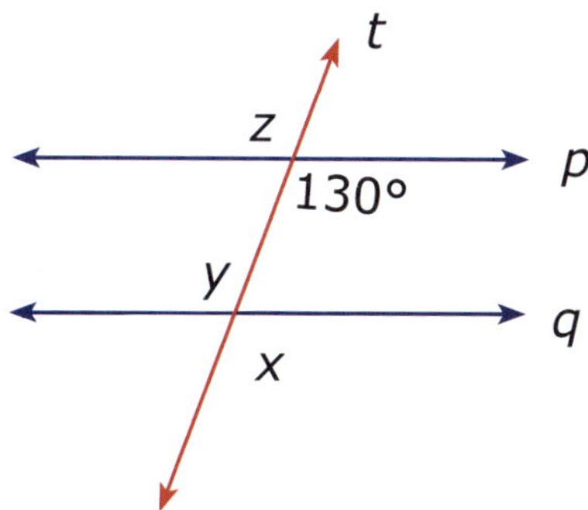

4.

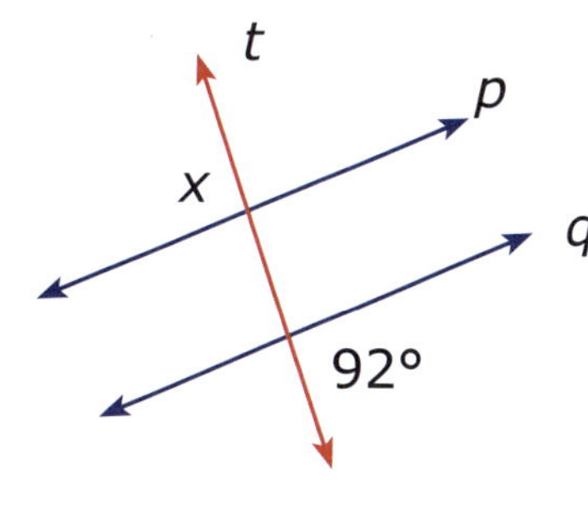

5.

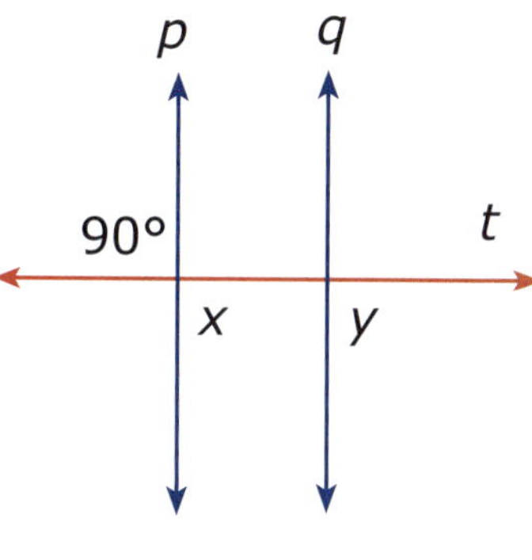

6.

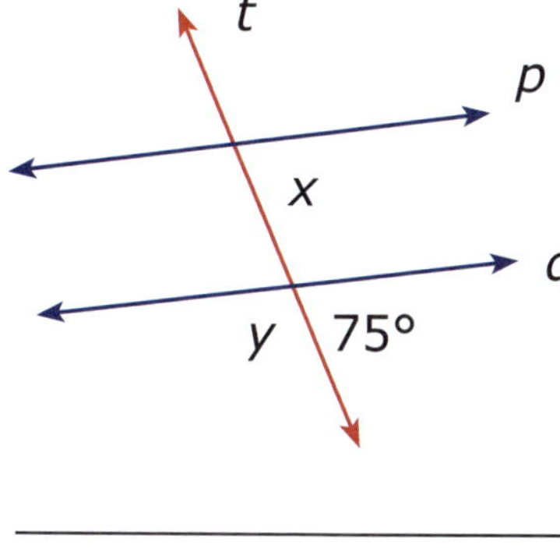

7.

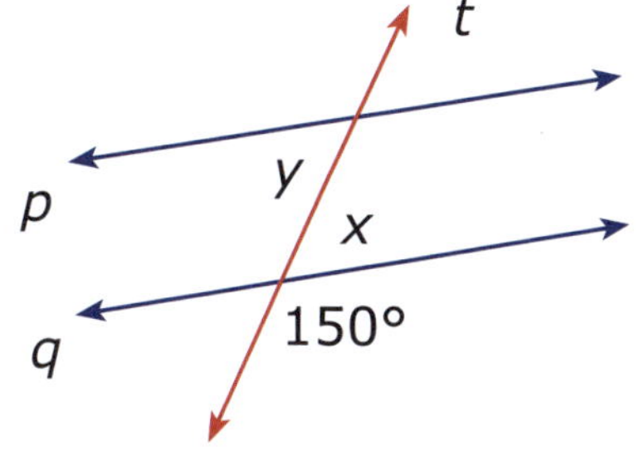

8.

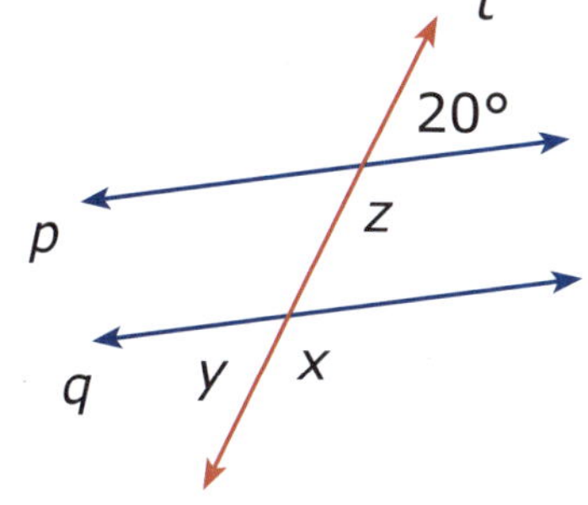

Find the value of *x* in the following problems. Line *l* || *m*. The figures are not to scale. Use algebra and explain below how to set up your equation.

9.

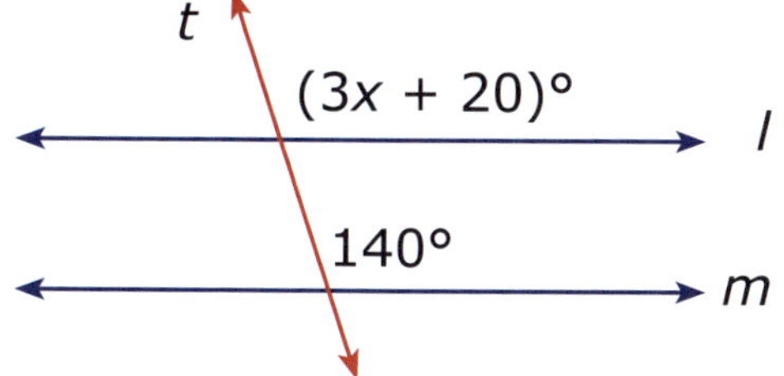

$x =$ ________

Explain your thinking.

10. 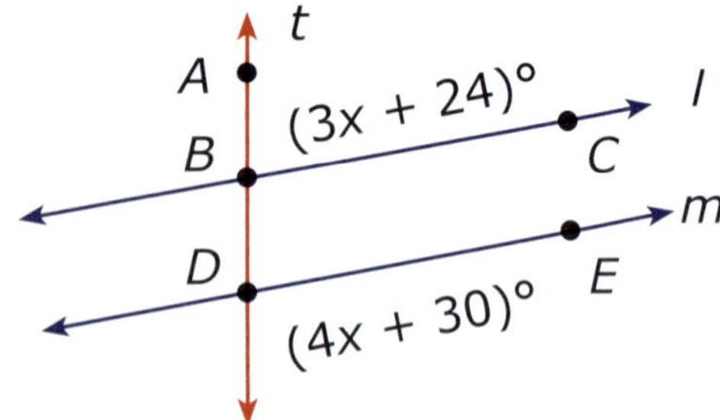

a. x = ________

b. $m\angle ABC$ = ________

c. $m\angle BDE$ = ________

Explain your thinking. Hint: Are the angles congruent or supplementary?

____

____

____

____

____

Perimeter

The perimeter of a two-dimensional shape is the distance around the entire shape.

Example 1: The perimeter of a rectangle is 58 inches. The width is one unit less than the length. Find the dimensions of the rectangle.

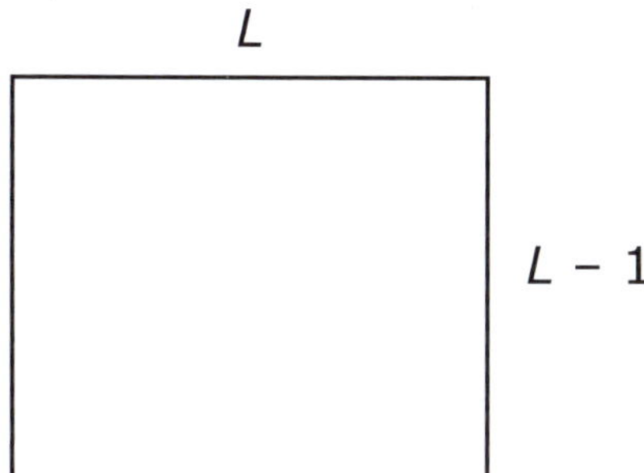

You can also use w for the width and let the length be $w + 1$. Now add all sides of the rectangle.

Equation: $L + L - 1 + L + L - 1 = 58$ OR $2L + 2(L - 1) = 58$

$$\begin{aligned} 4L - 2 &= 58 \\ +2 \quad &\quad +2 \\ \hline 4L &= 60 \quad \text{divide by 4} \\ L &= 15 \end{aligned}$$

So the length is 15″ and the width is 14″. Check: $2(15) + 2(14) = 58$? Yes!

You can also solve it this way:

Equation: $w + 1 + w + 1 + w + w = 58$

$$\begin{aligned} 4w + 2 &= 58 \\ -2 \quad &\quad -2 \\ \hline 4w &= 56 \quad \text{divide by 4} \\ w &= 14 \end{aligned}$$

So the width is 14", and the length is 15".

Polygons

A polygon is a closed two-dimensional shape with straight sides.

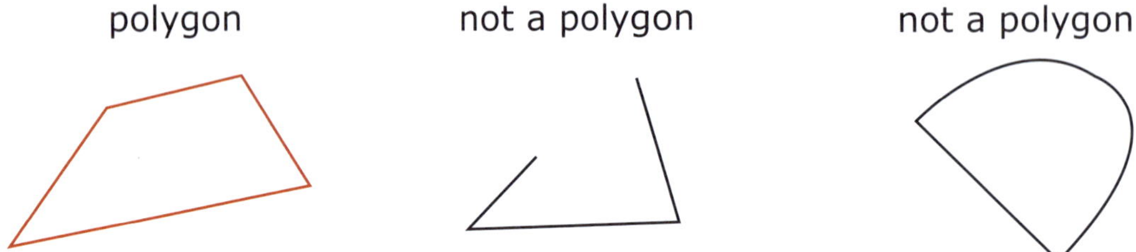

Poly means "many" and gon means "angle." A polygon can be "regular" or "irregular." A regular polygon has congruent sides and congruent angles.

Names of Polygons

Polygon	Sides	Polygon	Sides
Triangle	3	Octagon	8
Quadrilateral	4	Nonagon	9
Pentagon	5	Decagon	10
Hexagon	6	Undecagon	11
Heptagon (Septagon)	7	Dodecagon	12

Example 2: The Pentagon building in Washington D.C. is a regular pentagon with a perimeter of about 4,605 feet. Write an algebra equation to represent one side. Use x for one side.

Answer: $5x = 4605$ or $\frac{4{,}605}{5} = x$

One side is about 921 feet.

Example 3: In the quadrilateral below (which happens to be an isosceles trapezoid) the perimeter is 52 units. Find one of the two congruent sides.

10

x x

30

Equation: $x + x + 10 + 30 = 52$

$$2x + 40 = 52$$

$$-40 \quad -40$$

$$2x = 12 \text{ (divide by 2)}$$

$$x = 6$$

Answer: One of the two congruent sides is 6 units.

Practice

1. Why is this shape NOT a polygon? Explain your thinking.

Name the regular polygons below and find their perimeters. One side is given. Make sure to label.

2.

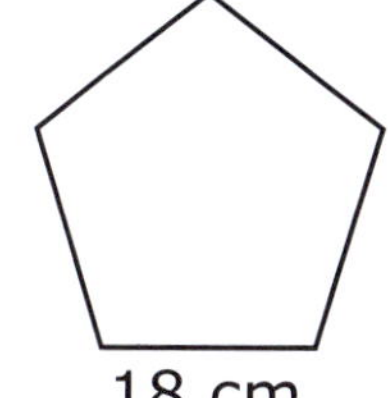

Name ______________

Perimeter ___________

3.

Name ______________

Perimeter ___________

4. 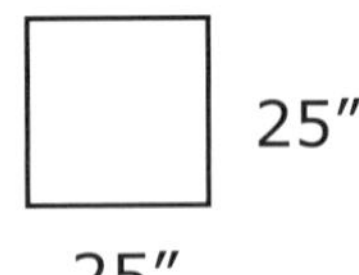

Name ______________

Perimeter __________

6. 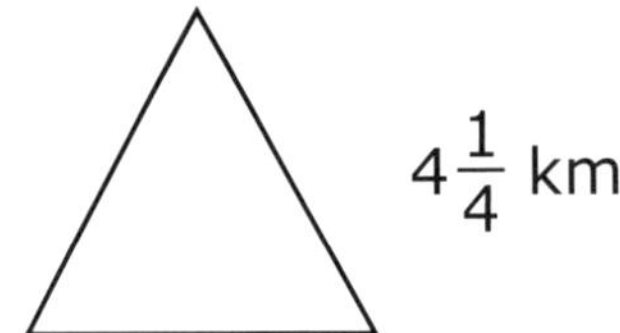

Name ______________

Perimeter __________

5. 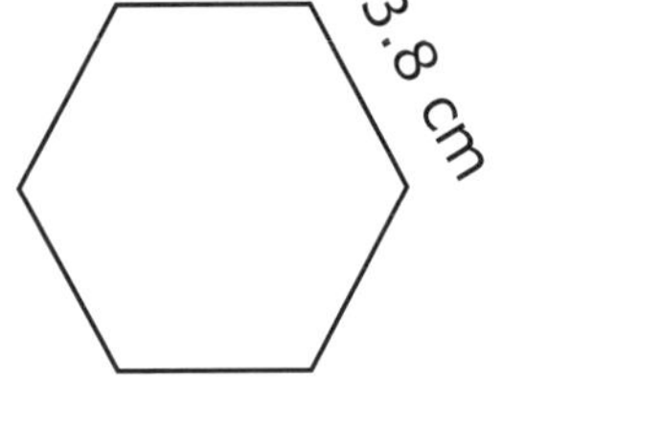

Name ______________

Perimeter __________

7. 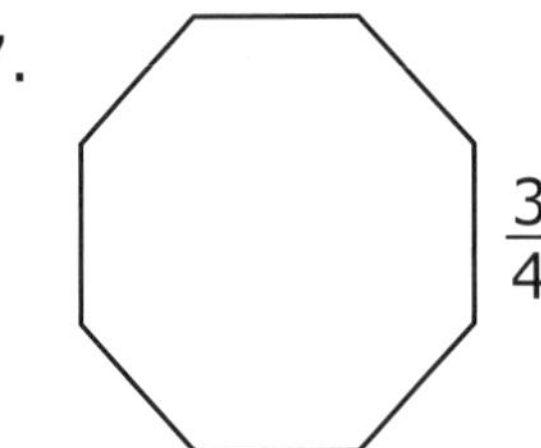

Name ______________

Perimeter __________

Solve the following problems using algebra. Draw a picture or show a let statement.

8. An Olympic size swimming pool has a length of that is twice its width. If the perimeter is 150 meters, find the length of the pool.

9. In a regular octagon each side is $5n$.

   a. Write an expression to represent its perimeter. __________

   b. Find n if the perimeter is 160 meters __________

10. Find the length of the sides of this parallelogram if its perimeter is 70 units

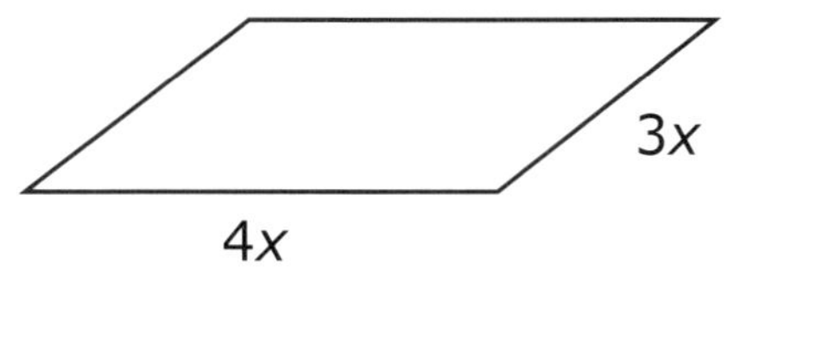

____

11. In a rhombus (a quadrilateral with equal sides but not necessarily equal angles) each side is $3x - 2$. If the perimeter is 40, find the value of x.

____

12. If an equilateral triangle has a perimeter of $51x$, write an expression for one side.

____

Angles of Triangles and Polygons

In any triangle, the sum of the angles always measures 180º. The sum of the angles measure 360º in any quadrilateral.

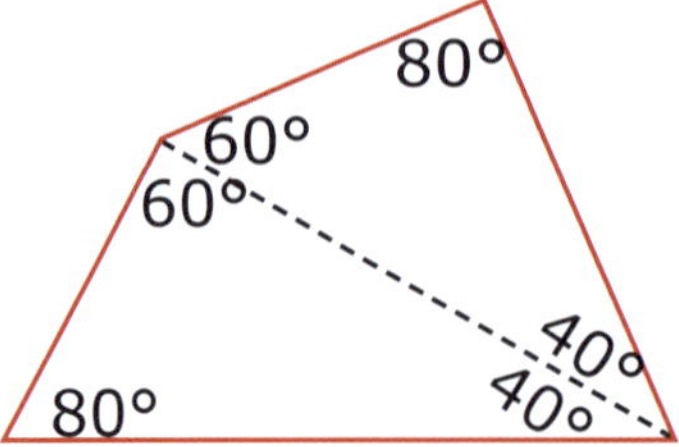

You can find the sum of the angles of any polygon (regular or irregular) by drawing diagonals from only one vertex and then counting how many triangles are in the polygon.

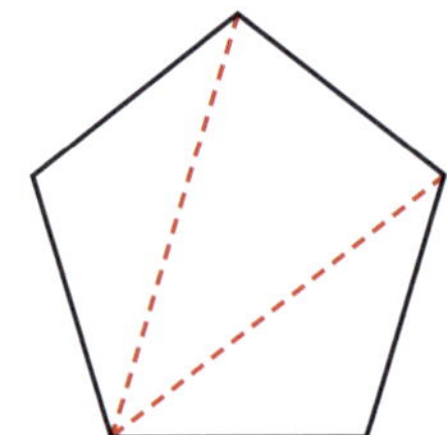

Sum of degrees: 180(3) = 540º

Practice

Name the polygons and find the sum of the angles.

1. 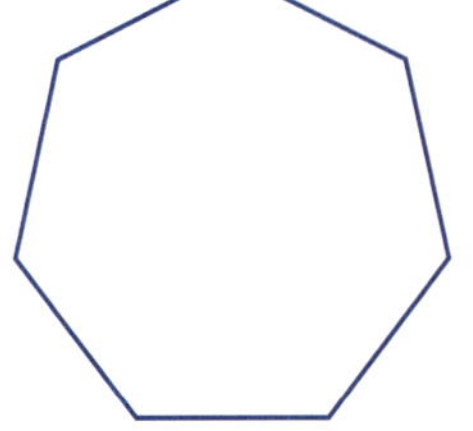 ______________

Sum ________

3. 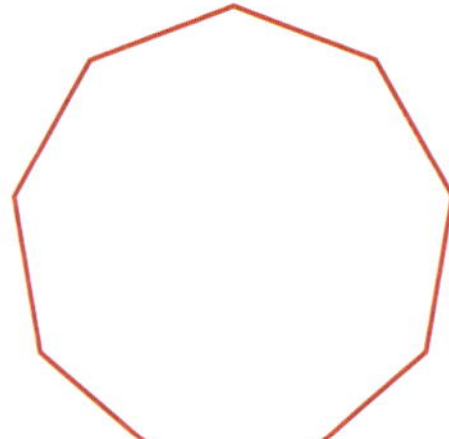 ______________

Sum ________

2. 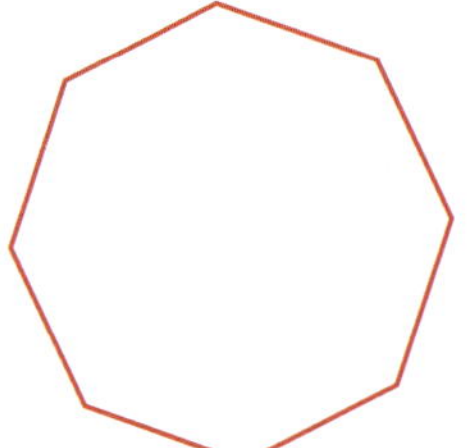 ______________

Sum ________

4. 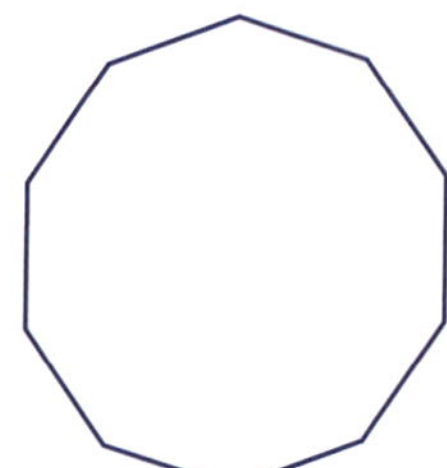 ______________

Sum ________

Find the measure of the missing angle in these triangles.

5. 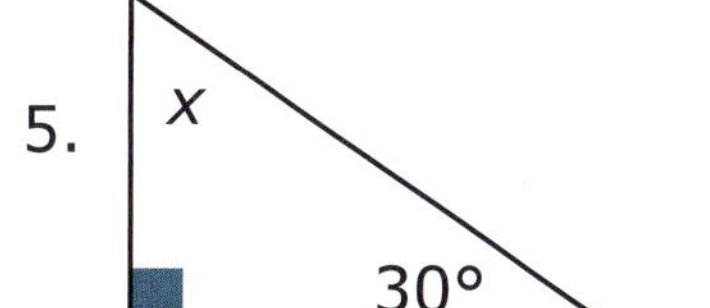

____

6. 70° 45° x

____

7. 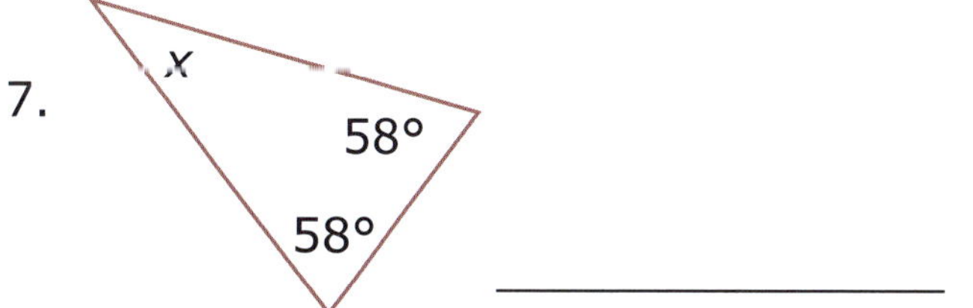

____

8. 89° 30° x

____

9. 24° x 78°

____

10. 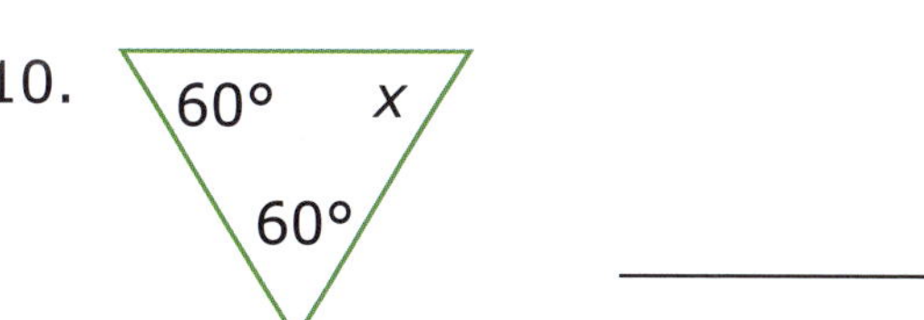

____

Find x using algebra and find all the missing angles in each triangle. Show your equation. Use a separate sheet of paper if needed.

11. 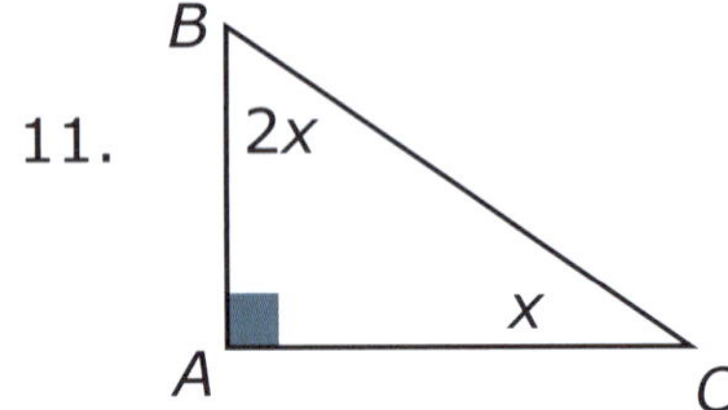

$m\angle A$ = ________ ; $m\angle B$ = ________ ; $m\angle C$ = ________

12. D E F; x, $2x$, $5x$

$m\angle D$ = ________ ; $m\angle E$ = ________ ; $m\angle F$ = ________

13. 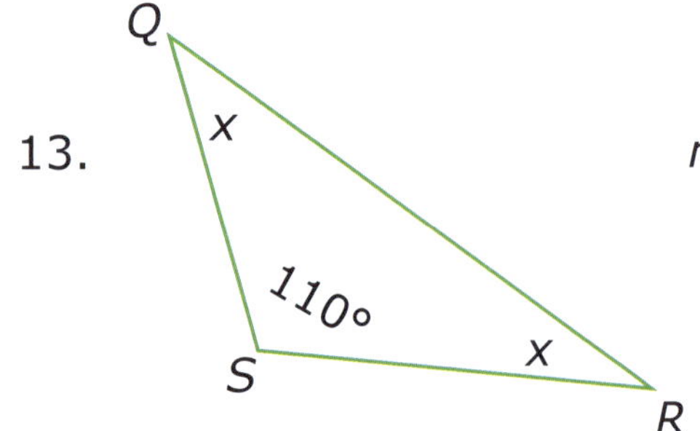

$m\angle Q$ = ________ ; $m\angle R$ = ________

Types of Triangles

Right Triangle One of the angles is a right angle (90°).	**Equilateral Triangle** All three sides are congruent (same size).
Isosceles Triangle Two sides are congruent (same size).	**Scalene Triangle** No sides are congruent (same size).

Practice

1. Can a right triangle be isosceles, equilateral, or scalene? Explain your thinking.

2. How do you know that this is an isosceles triangle? Rely on the given information and not the picture.

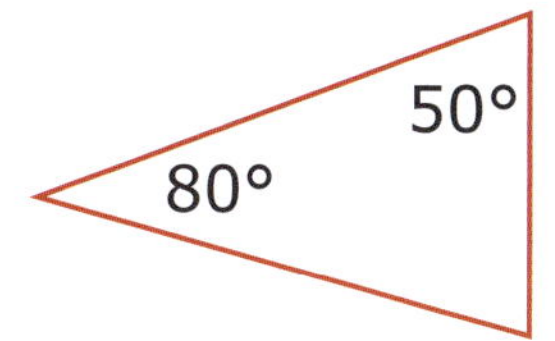

3. Both of these triangles are equilateral. Are the triangles congruent? What do they have in common? Explain your thinking.

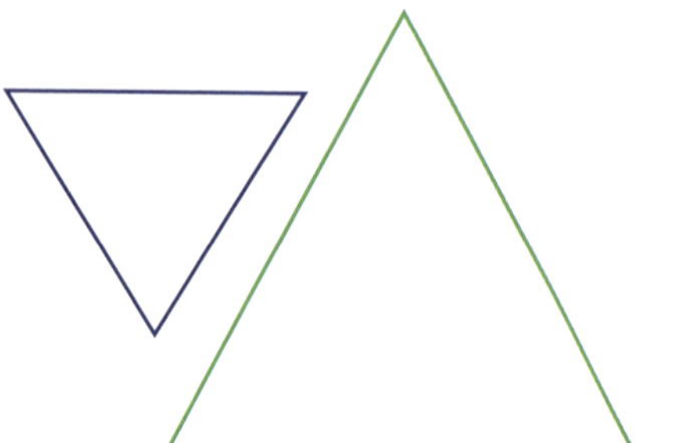

4. Find the measure of exterior angle x. Do you think there a connection between the measure of angle x and and $\angle B$ and $\angle A$. Explain your thinking.

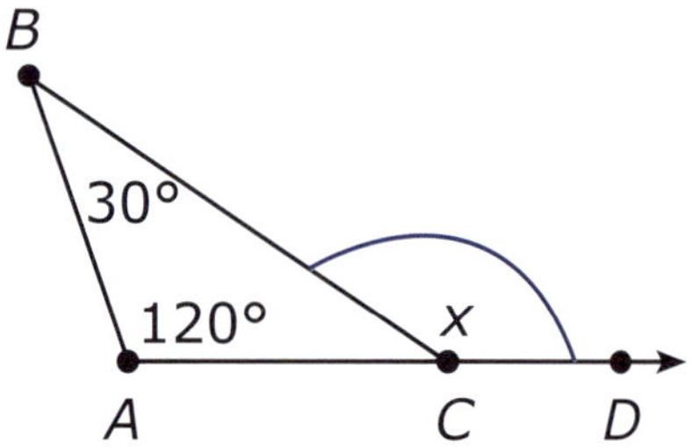

Find the measure of the missing angle in these triangles. The figures are not to scale.

5.

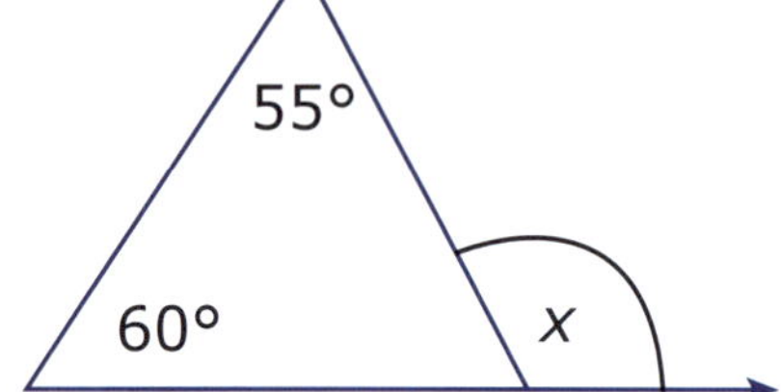

6.

20°
130°
x

7. 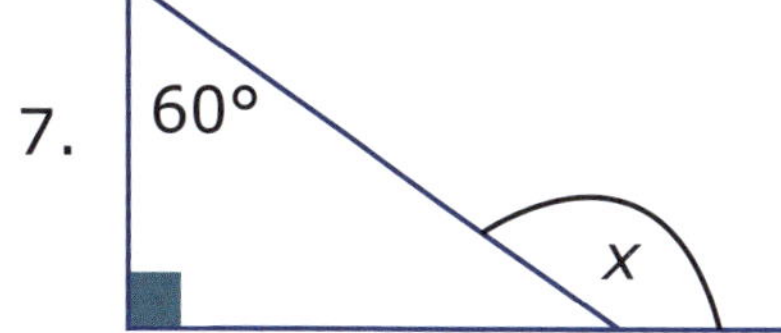

____

8. 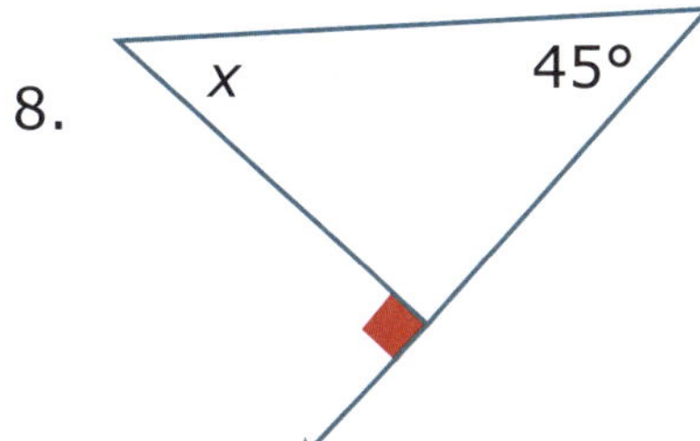

____

Are you ready to conclude the following?

In any triangle, the measure of an exterior angle is always equal to the sum of the measures of the two remote interior angles.

$m\angle a + m\angle b = m\angle x$

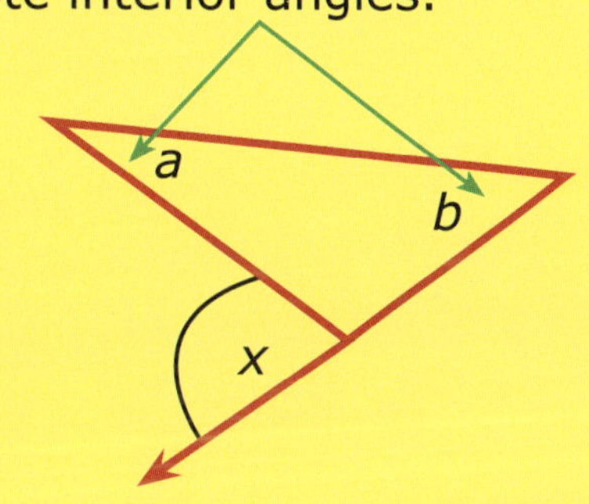

9. Find the measure of the missing angles below. Line $n \| m$. Use a separate sheet of paper if needed.

a. $m\angle 1 =$ ________

b. $m\angle 2 =$ ________

c. $m\angle 3 =$ ________

d. $m\angle 4 =$ ________

e. $m\angle 5 =$ ________

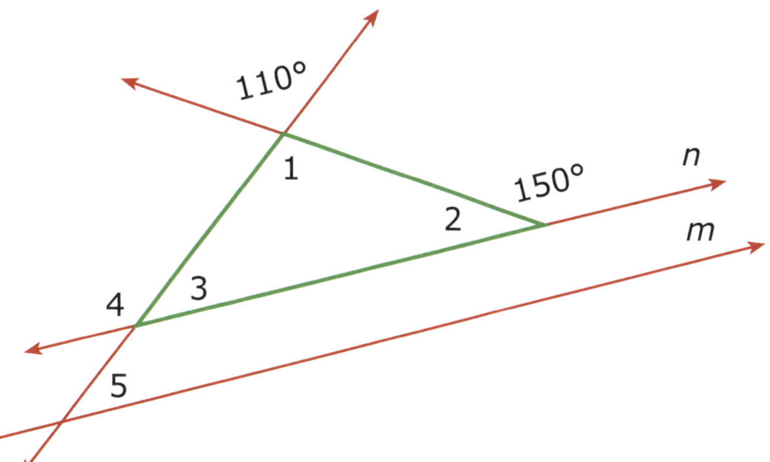

Areas of Parallelograms, Triangles, and Trapezoids

Parallelograms and trapezoids belong to the quadrilateral family.

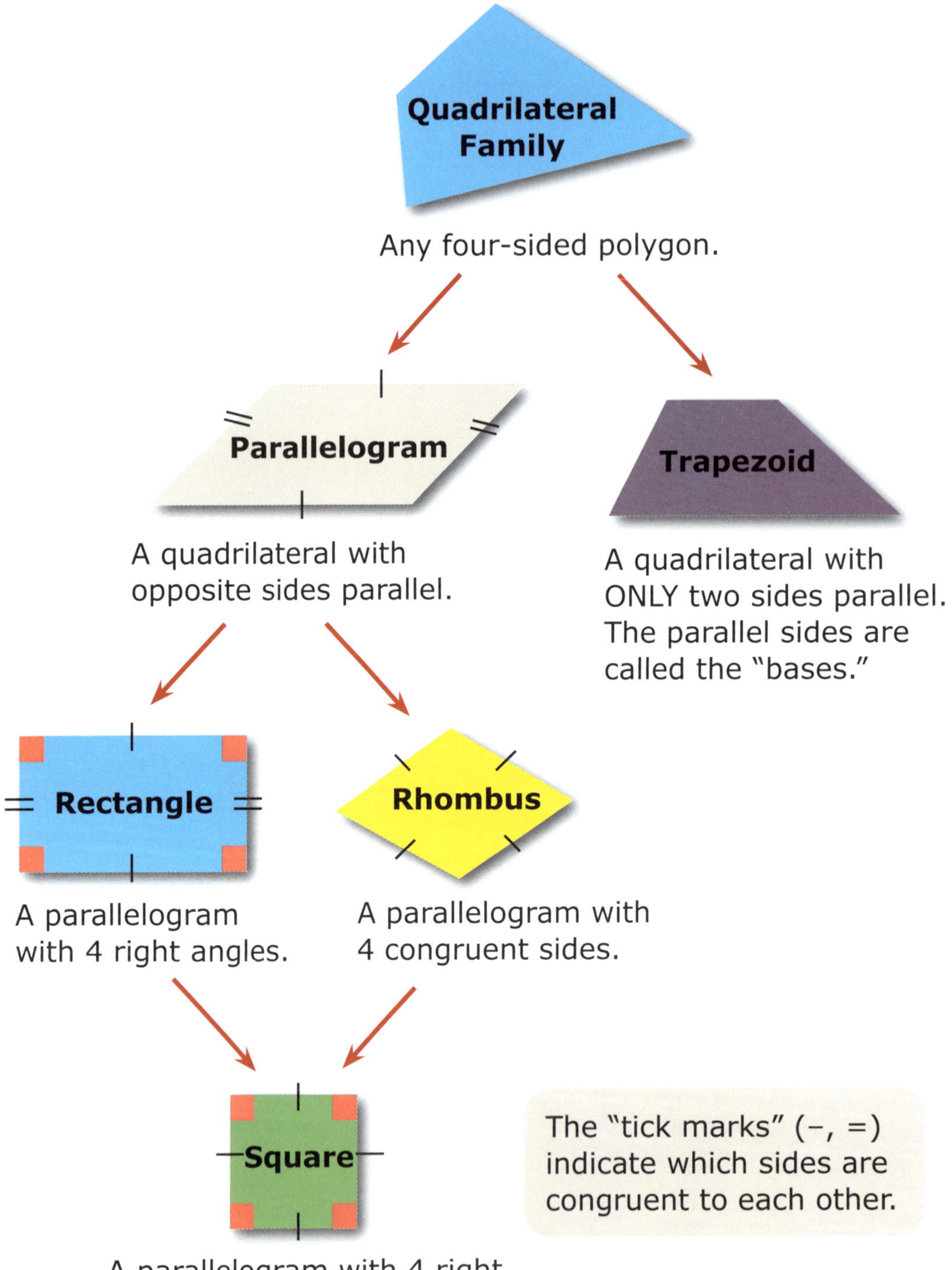

The "tick marks" (–, =) indicate which sides are congruent to each other.

Practice

Tell if these statements are true or false based on the Quadrilateral Family diagram on the previous page.

______ 1. A trapezoid is a type of parallelogram.

______ 2. All parallelograms have opposite sides parallel.

______ 3. A square is a rectangle but a rectangle is not always a square.

______ 4. A rhombus is a type of square.

______ 5. Opposite sides of any parallelogram are congruent.

______ 6. A square can be called a regular quadrilateral.

______ 7. An equilateral triangle is a regular triangle.

______ 8. A pentagon is part of the quadrilateral family.

______ 9. Every rhombus is a square.

______ 10. An isosceles trapezoid has two congruent sides.

______ 11. Every isosceles triangle has two congruent angles.

______ 12. A right triangle can be equilateral.

Area of Parallelograms

To find the area of any parallelogram multiply base times height.

$A = bh$

Example:

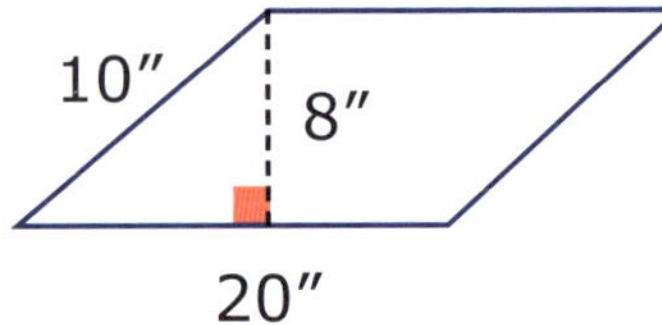

The height is always perpendicular to the base.

$A = bh$

$A = 20 \bullet 8$

$A = 160$ square inches (sq. in or in^2)

Practice

Find the area of these parallelograms. Use a separate sheet of paper if needed. Make sure you label your answer.

1. 4″ 5″ Rhombus $A =$ ____________

4. 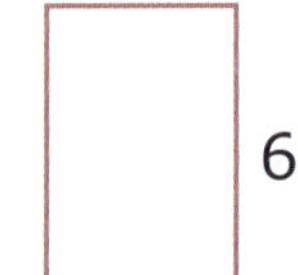 6.8 cm 3 cm $A =$ ____________

2. 4′ 25′ $A =$ ____________

5. 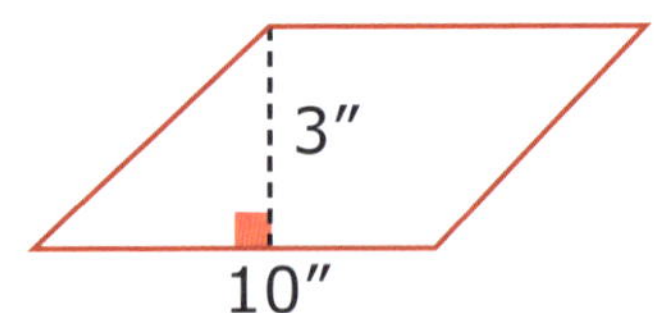

$A =$ ____________

3. 13 m Square $A =$ ____________

6.  Square with perimeter of 36″ $A =$ ____________

Area of Triangles

To find the area of any triangle multiply base times height and divide by 2.

$$A = \frac{1}{2}bh$$

A triangle is half of a parallelogram. The height is always perpendicular to the base.

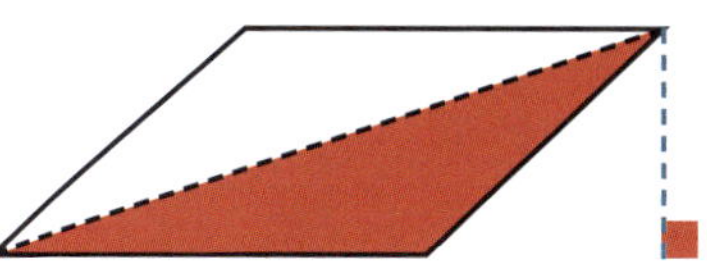

Practice

Find the area of the following. Make sure to label your answer.

1. 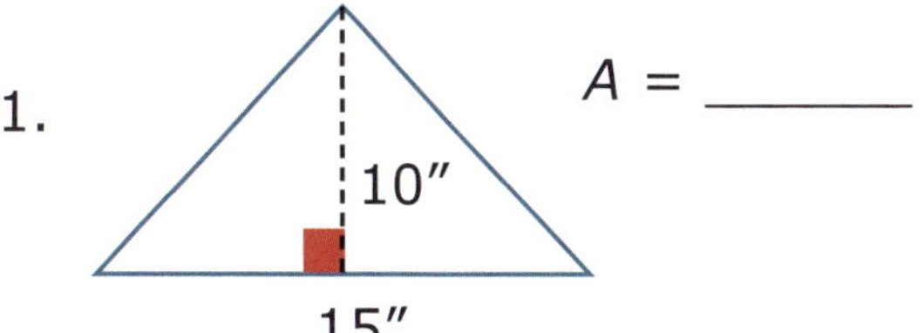

$A =$ ______

4. 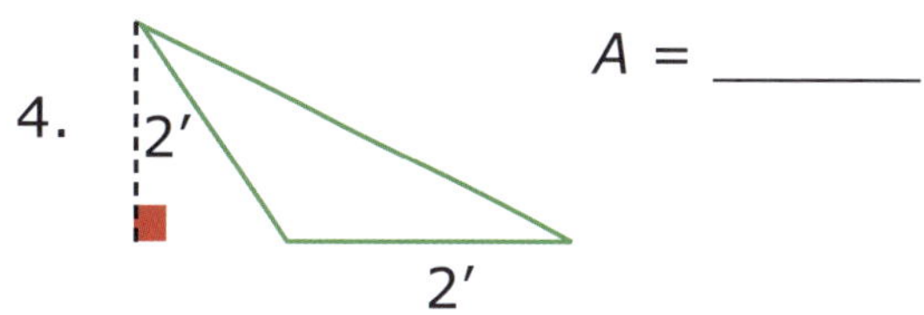

$A =$ ______

2. 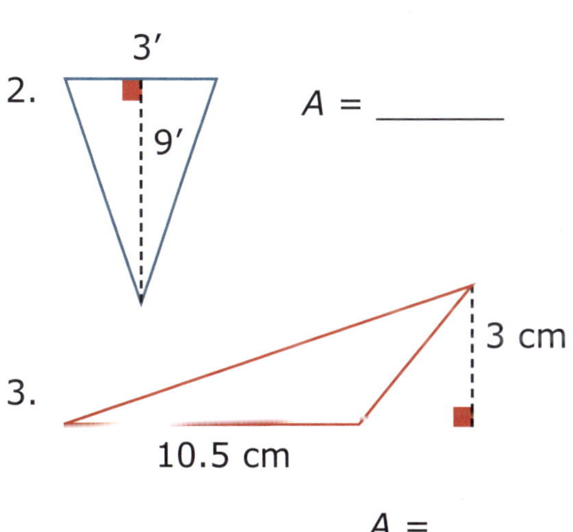

$A =$ ______

3. 3 cm
10.5 cm
$A =$ ______

5. 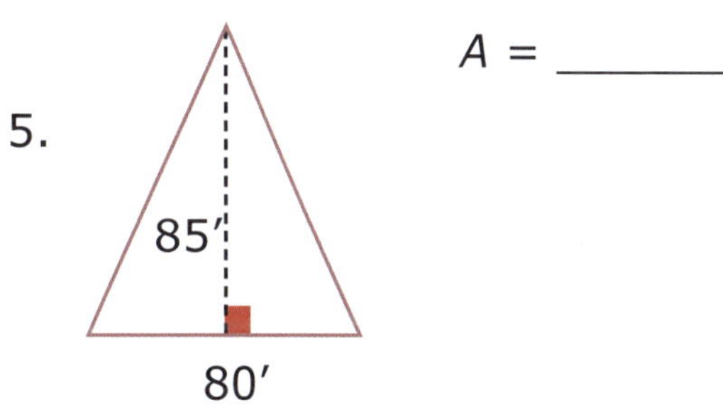

$A =$ ______

6. 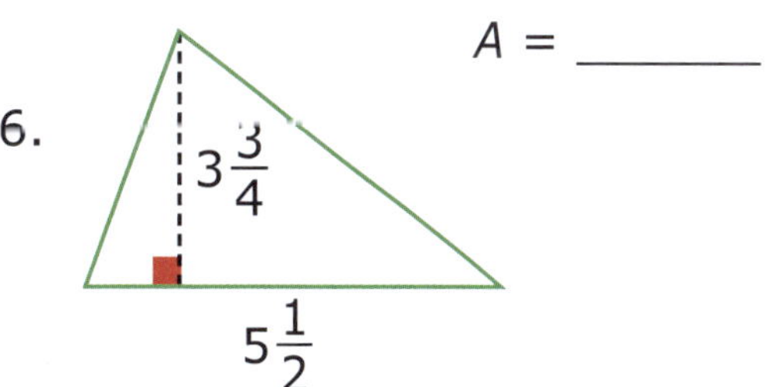

$A =$ ______

Find the area shaded in green. A triangle is inscribed inside a rectangle. Show your work.

7. 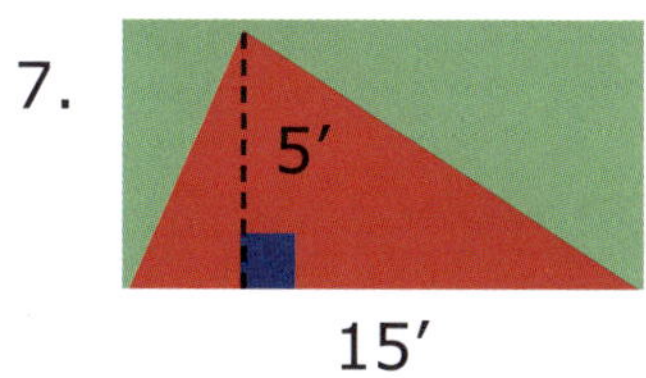

$A =$ ______

8. 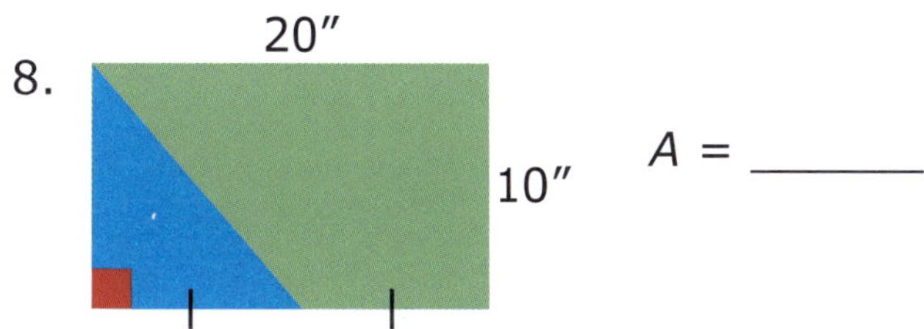

$A =$ ______

Area of Trapezoids

To find the area of a trapezoid, add the two bases (sides that are parallel), multiply by the height, and divide by 2.

$$A = \frac{1}{2}h(b + B)$$

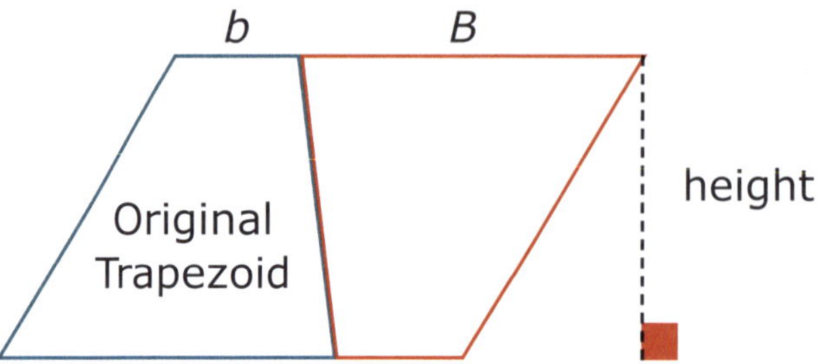

When you duplicate a trapezoid, flip it horizontally and vertically and place them together creating a parallelogram. The small base (b) and the longer base (B) are shown above.

The area of the parallelogram is $(b + B) \bullet h$. But our original trapezoid is half of that area, so that explains the formula.

These two trapezoids are special. Remember their names.

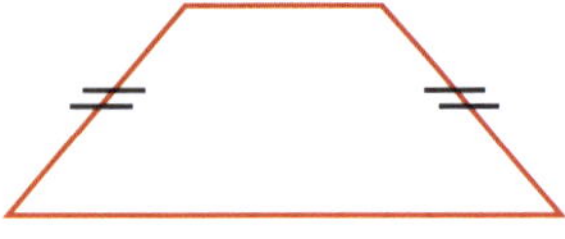
Isoceles Trapezoid

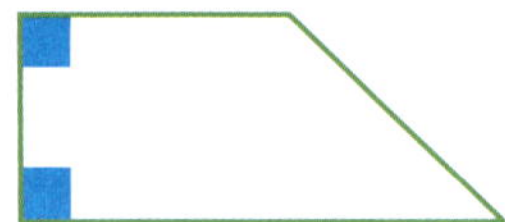
Right Trapezoid

Example: Find the area of this trapezoid.

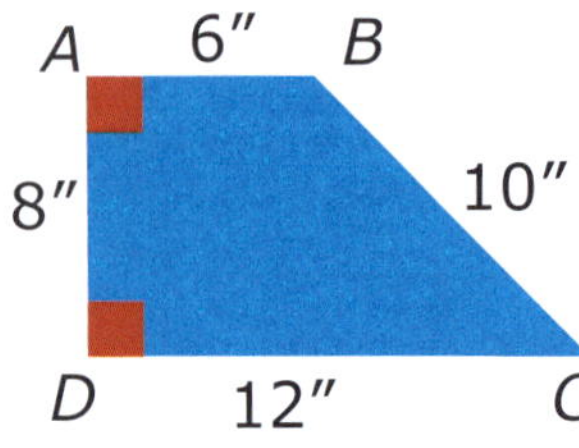

This is a right trapezoid. It has two right angles which guarantees that $\overline{AB} \parallel \overline{DC}$. The parallel sides are the bases.

$A = (6 + 12) \bullet 8 \div 2$
$A = 18 \bullet 8 \div 2$
$A = 72$ sq in.

Practice

Find the area of these trapezoids. Label your answer.

1. 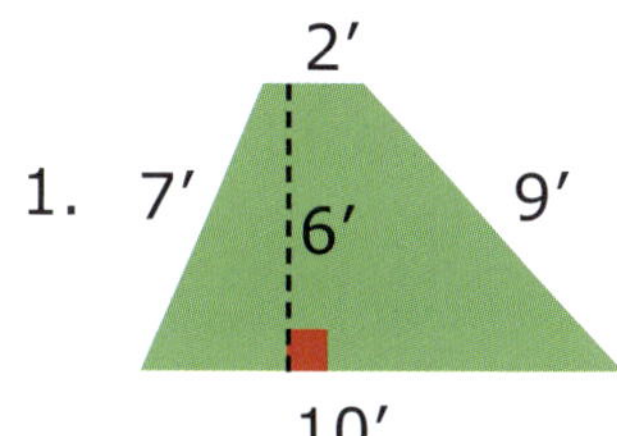

$A =$ ________

4. 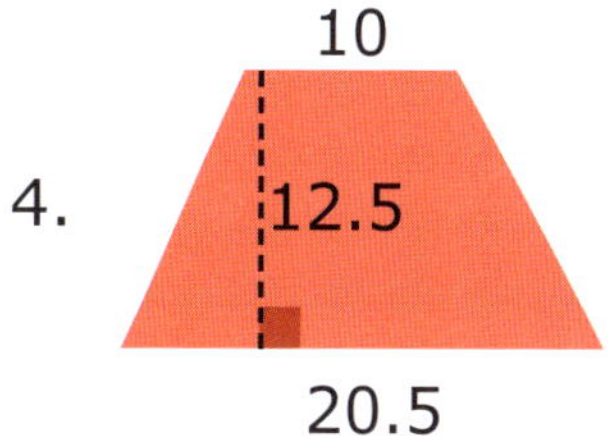

$A =$ ________

2. 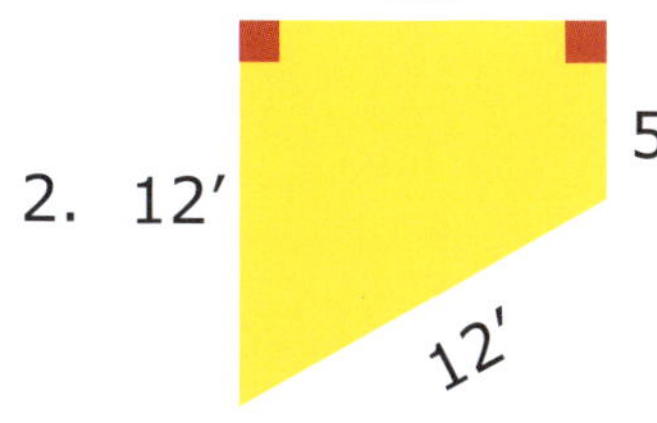

$A =$ ________

5. 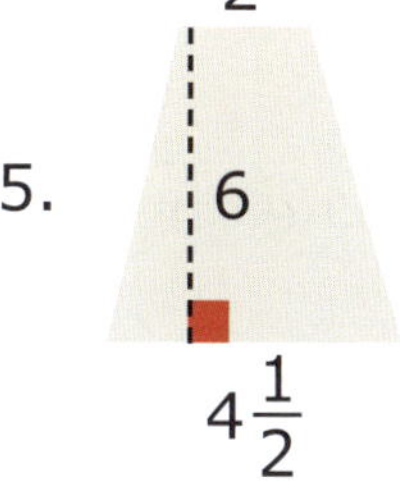

$A =$ ________

3. 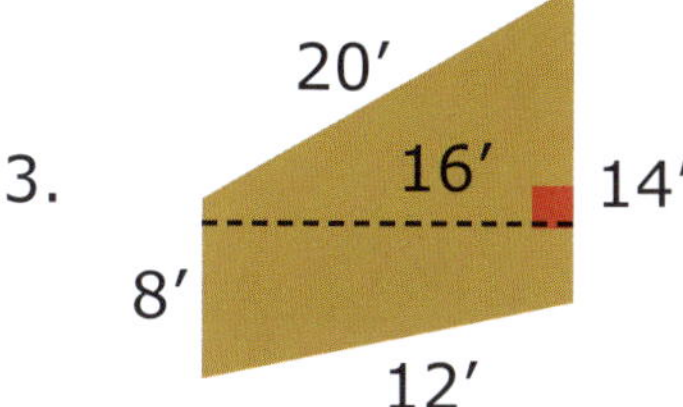

$A =$ ________

6. 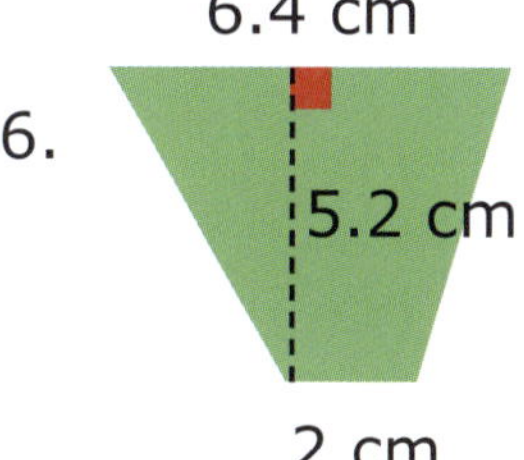

$A =$ ________

7. A student found the area of the blue parallelogram by doing following.

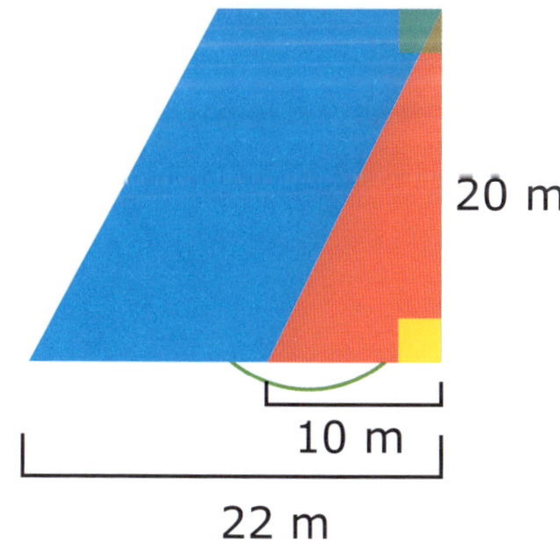

a. Area of the right trapezoid ________

WORK:

b. Area of the right triangle ________

WORK:

c. Parallelogram ________
(trapezoid – triangle)

WORK:

8. What is an easier way to find the area of the shaded blue parallelogram? Explain your thinking.

____

____

Using Algebra to Solve Geometry Problems

Example 1: A triangle has base of 20 inches and an area of 60 square inches. Find the height of the triangle.

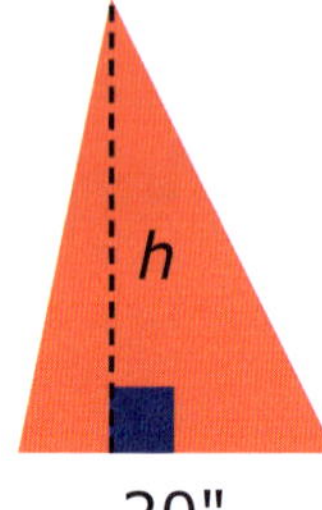

Draw a picture (don't worry if it's not to scale).
Write the formula:

$\frac{1}{2}bh = A$

$\frac{1}{2} \bullet 20 \bullet h = 60$ Substitute.

$10h = 60$ Divide by 10 on each side.

$h = 30$

Answer: The height is 30″.

Example 2: A trapezoid has a height of 6′ and a small base of 10′. Its area area is 72 square feet. Find the larger base.

$\frac{1}{2}(b + B) \bullet h = A$

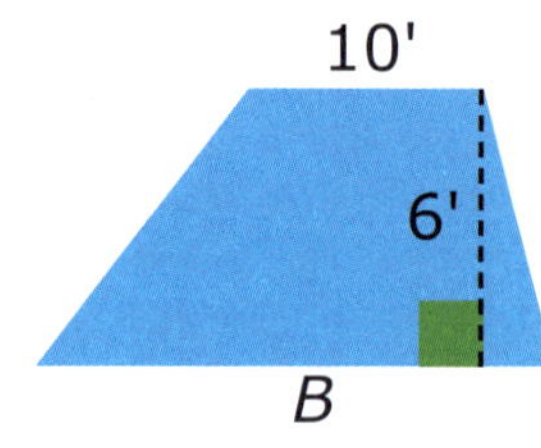

$\frac{1}{2}(10 + B) \bullet 6 = 72$ Substitute and distribute.

$(5 + \frac{B}{2}) \bullet 6 = 72$ Divide by 6 on each side, or you could distribute again.

$5 + \frac{B}{2} = 12$ Subtract 5 from each side.

$\frac{B}{2} = 7,$ Multiply each side by 2.

So, $B = 14$

Answer: The larger base is 14′.

Practice

Solve the following problems using algebra. Start by writing down the area formula.

1. A triangle has an area of 600 square meters and a base of 300 meters. Find its height. ____________________

2. A triangle has a height 4 inches and an area of 10 square inches. Find the base of the triangle. ______________________

3. A trapezoid has a small base of 5 cm and a larger base of 12 cm. If the area of the trapezoid is 34 square centimeters, find the height.

____

4. Huck bought a land lot in the shape of a trapezoid with an area of 125,000 square feet. The smaller base is 400′ and the height is 250′. Find the larger base. ______________________

Finding the Circumference and Area of a Circle

A circle is the set of points that is equidistant from a given point called the center. Think of a circle as a ring. When you measure the distance around that ring you are finding the circumference (perimeter of the circle). When you find the area of a circle, you are finding the area enclosed by that ring.

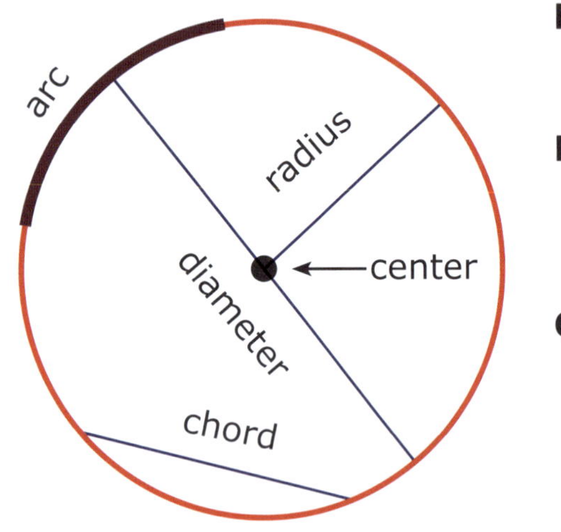

Radius - The distance from the center of the circle to a point on the circle.

Diameter - The distance from one point on the circle to another point on the circle going through the center.

Chord - A segment connecting one point of the circle to any other point on the circle. The largest chord in a circle is its diameter.

Arc - A piece of the circle.

To find the circumference of a circle, multiply the diameter times PI.

$$C = \pi d$$

You can always estimate the circumference of a circle. It's a little over 3 times the diameter and the diameter is twice the radius.

Practice

Find the circumference of these circles. Use PI as 3.14. Label your answer.

1. 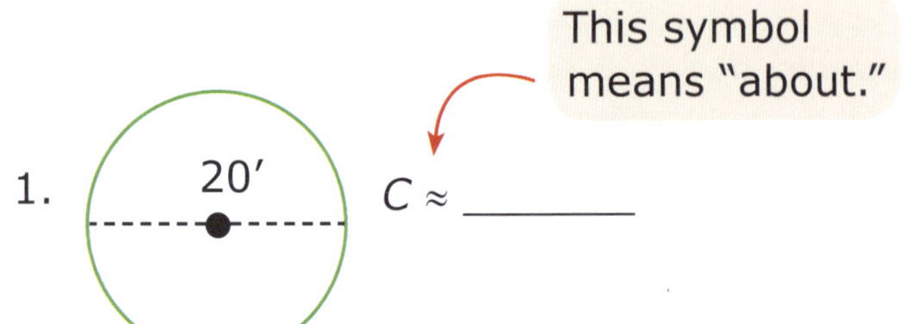

$C \approx$ ________

2. 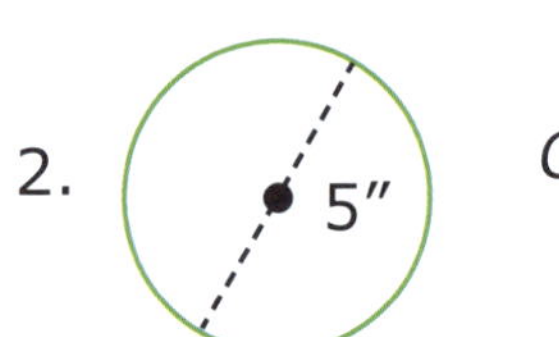

$C \approx$ ________

3. 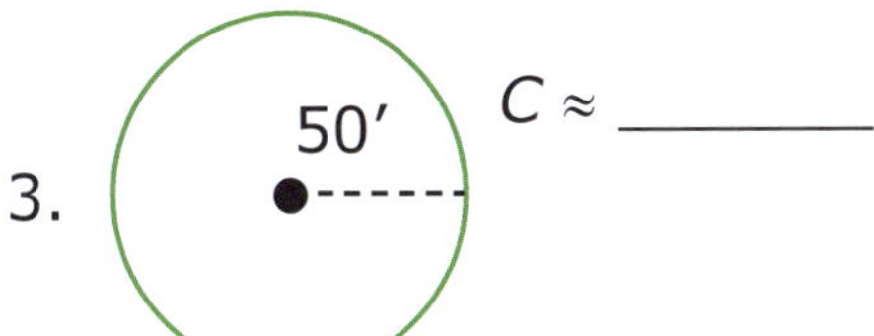

$C \approx$ ________

5. 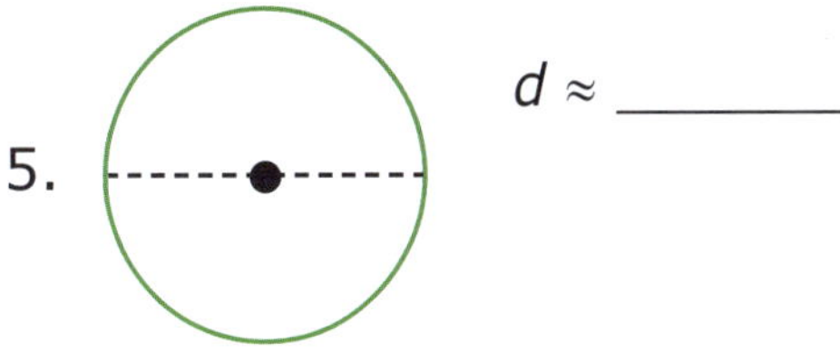

$d \approx$ ________

The circumference is 78.5 units.

4. 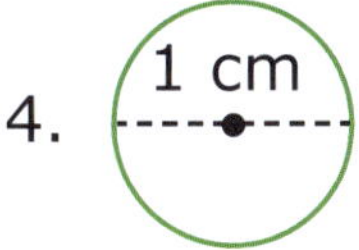

$C \approx$ ________

6. Find the radius in problem #5.

____

To find the area of a circle multiply PI by the square of the radius.

$$A = \pi r^2$$

Example: Find the area of the circle and leave your answer in terms of PI.

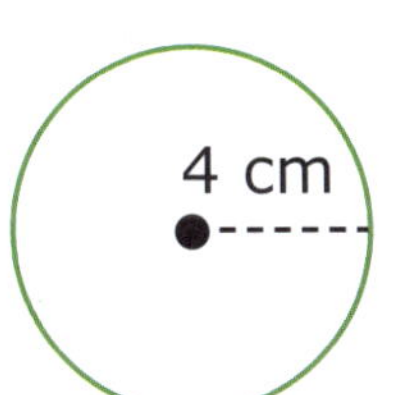

Write the formula:

$A = \pi r^2$

Multiply the radius times itself (r^2).

Answer: 16π sq cm

This is what is meant to leave your answer in terms of PI.

Find the area of these circles. Leave your answer in terms of PI. Label your answers.

1. 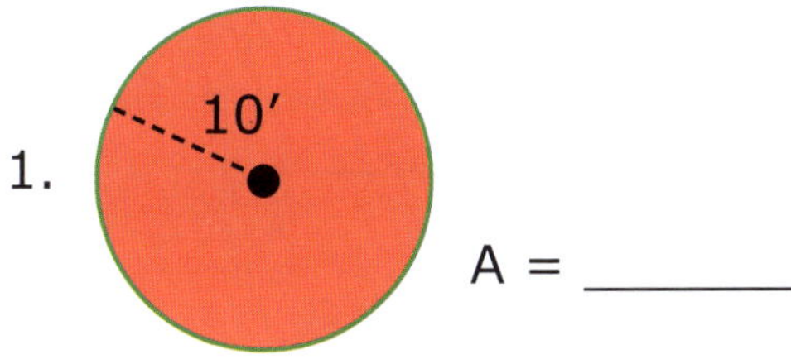

A = ________

2. 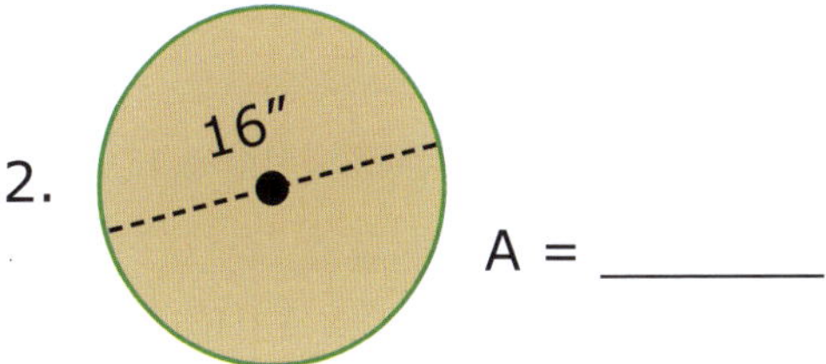

A = ________

3. 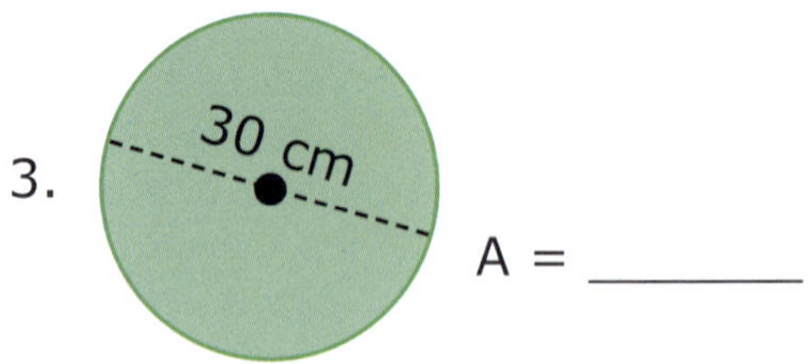

A = ________

5. 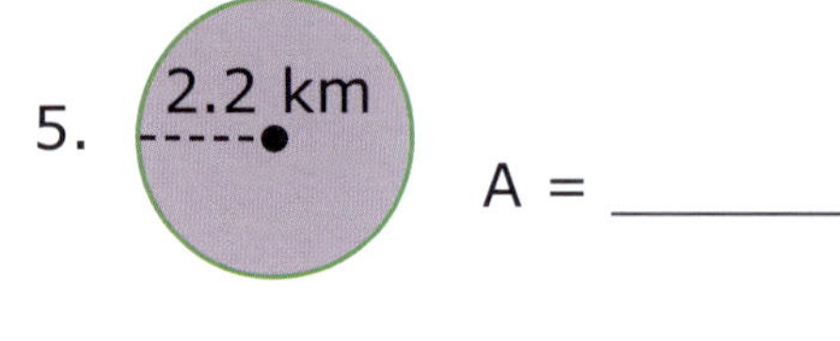

A = ________

4. 

A = ________

6. 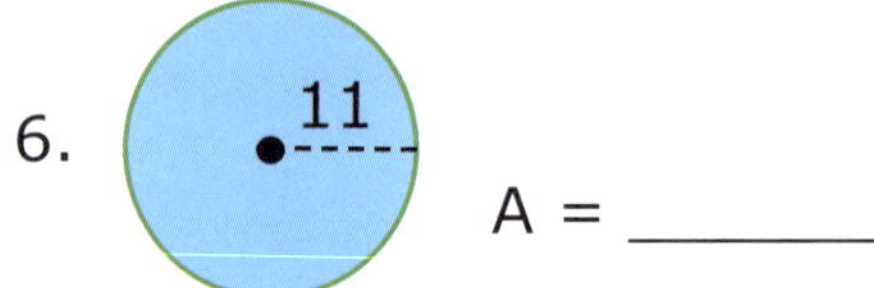

A = ________

Answer the following. Use a calculator if needed.

7. If a circle has an area of 153.86 meters, find the radius and the diameter. Use PI as 3.14.

   radius ______________

   diameter ______________

8. A circle is inscribed inside a square. If the square has an area of 49 square feet, find the area shaded in red. Use PI as 3.14.

   a. Find one side of the square. ______________

   b. Find the radius of the circle. ______________
   (Hint: It's half one side of the square.)

   c. Find the area of the circle. ______________

   d. Find the shaded area in red. ______________

9. A triangle is inscribed inside a semicircle with a diameter of 10 meters. Find the area shaded in orange. Use PI as 3.14. Make sure you label your answer.

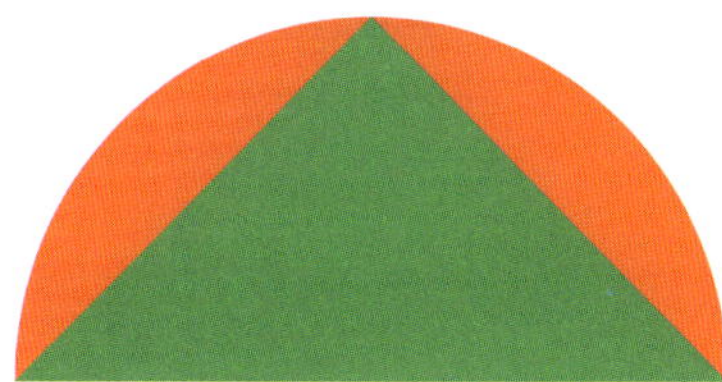

a. Find the base of the triangle. ____________

b. Find the radius of the circle. ____________

c. Find the height of the triangle. ____________

d. Find the area of the triangle. ____________

e. Find the area of the semicircle. ____________

f. Find the area shaded in red. ____________

10. A circle is inscribed in a semicircle. Find the area shaded in orange. Use PI as 3.14. Make sure you label your answer.

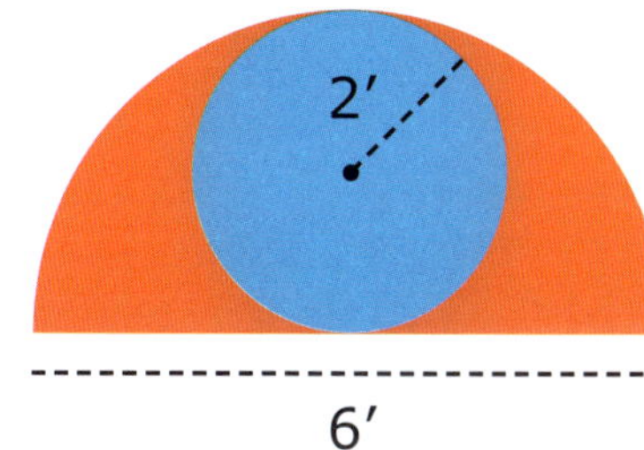

a. Find the area of the semicircle. ____________

b. Find the area of the small circle. ____________

c. Find the area shaded in orange. ____________

Chapter 10 Review

Find the missing ∠*ABC* in each of these drawings if ∠*DBC* is 70°. The figures are not to scale.

1. 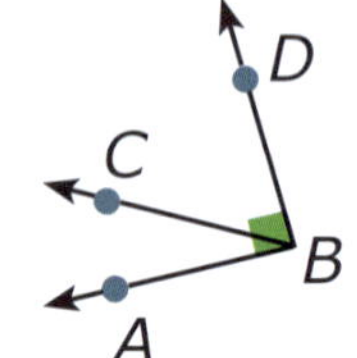

____

2. 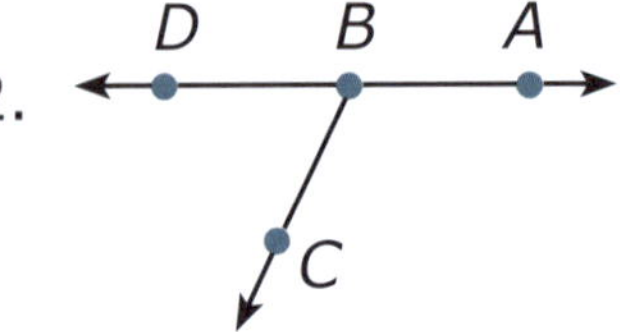

____

3. 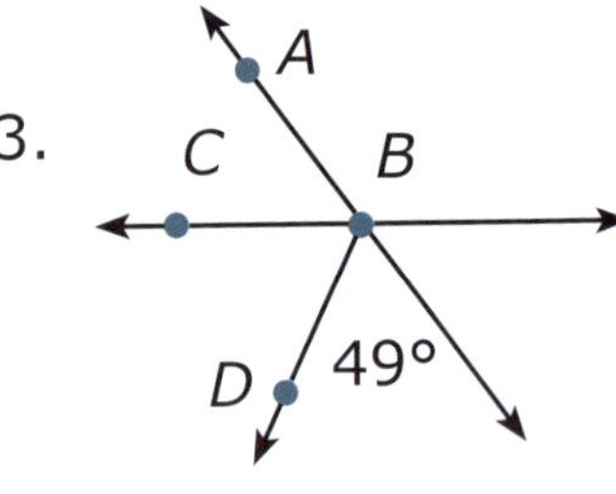

____

4. Which of the following words can you use to describe ∠*ABC* and ∠*DBC* in the above drawings? Choose: complementary, supplementary, adjacent.

   a. Problem #1 ______________________________

   b. Problem #2 ______________________________

Find the missing x in the figures below. The figures are not to scale.

5. 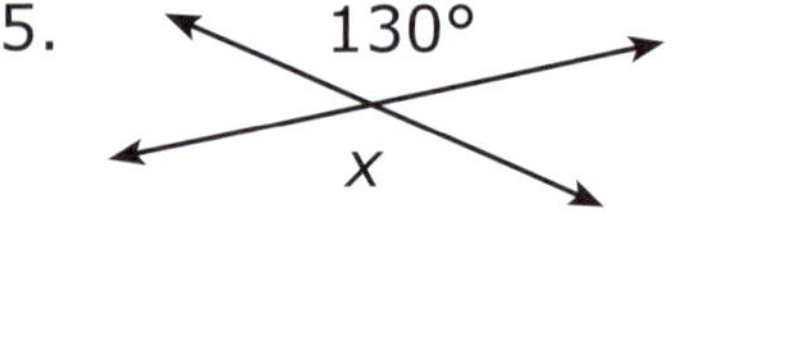

____

8. 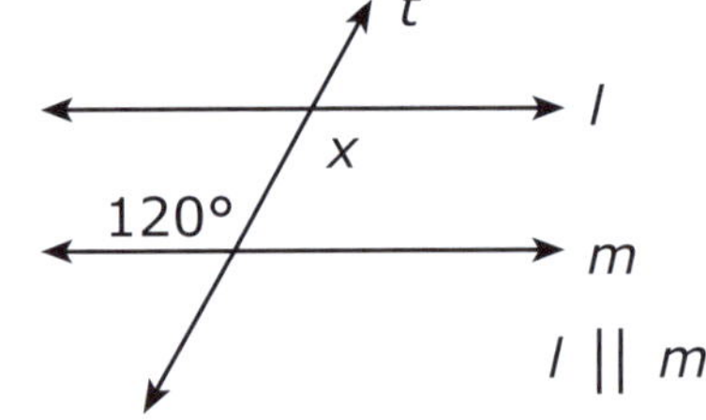

____

6. 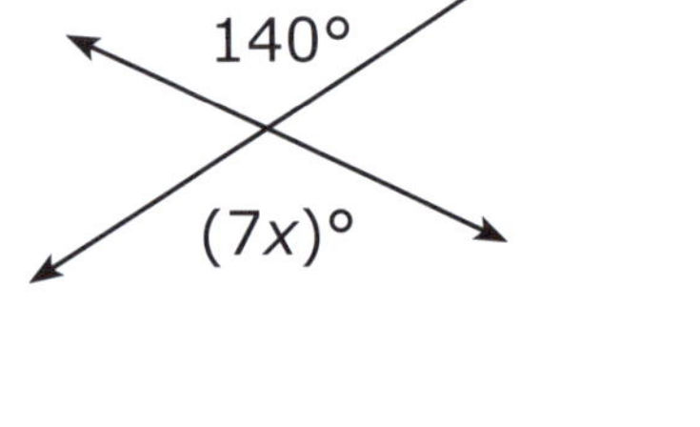

____

9. 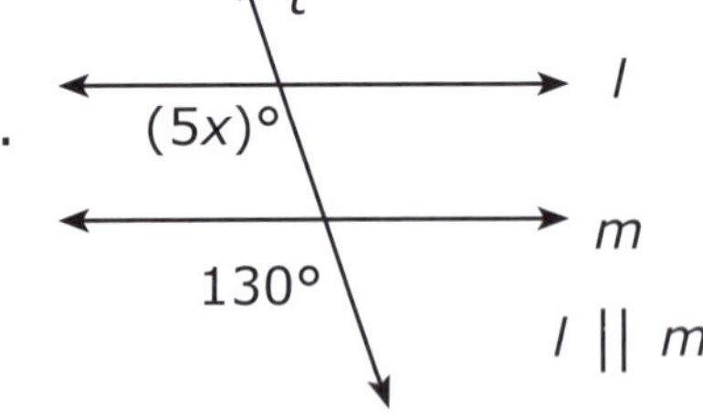

____

7. 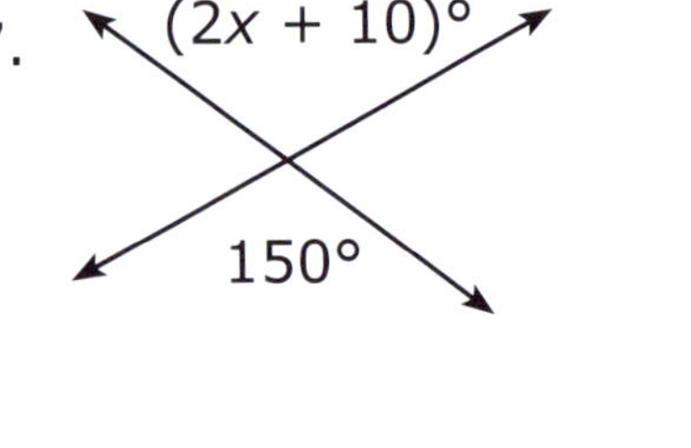

____

10. 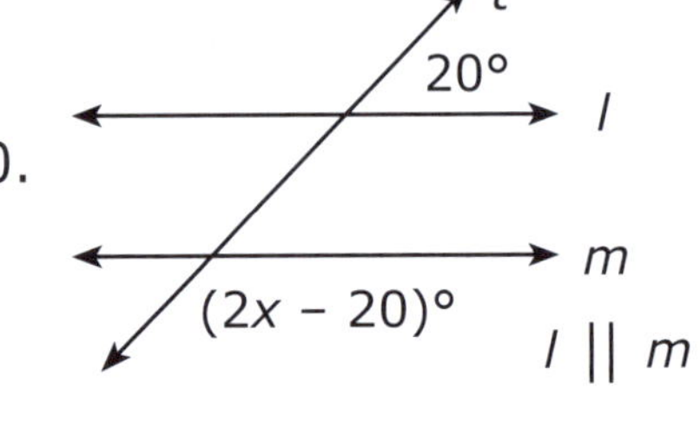

____

Write the letter of the drawing below that matches the description.

_____ 11. Alternate interior angles

_____ 12. Corresponding angles

_____ 13. Vertical angles

_____ 14. Perpendicular lines

_____ 15. Complementary angles

_____ 16. Supplementary angles

a. 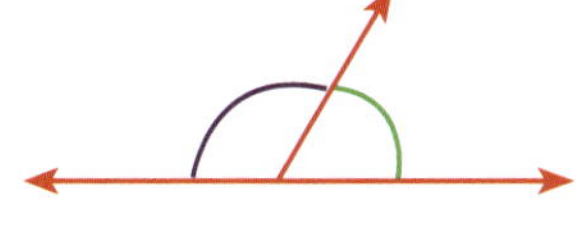

b. 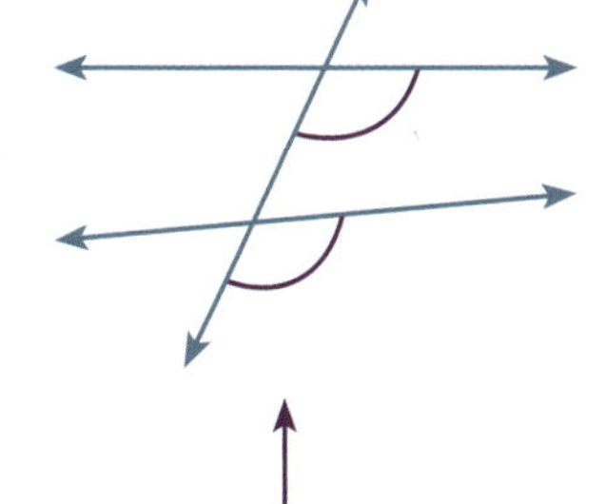

c.

d. 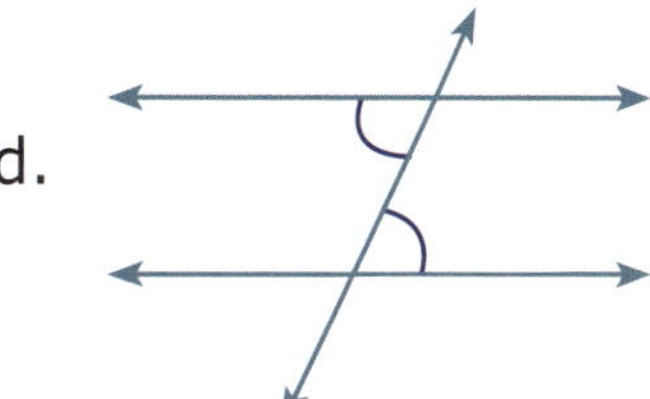

e. 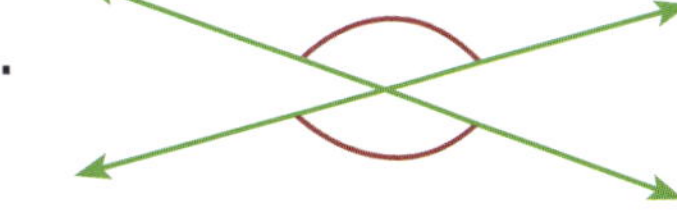

f. 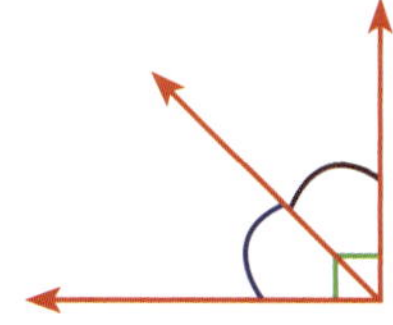

Find the missing x in the following triangles. Then answer the questions.

17. 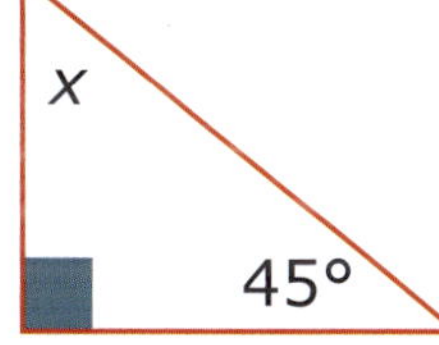

$m\angle x =$ _______ What type of triangle is it?

Explain your thinking.

____

____

18. 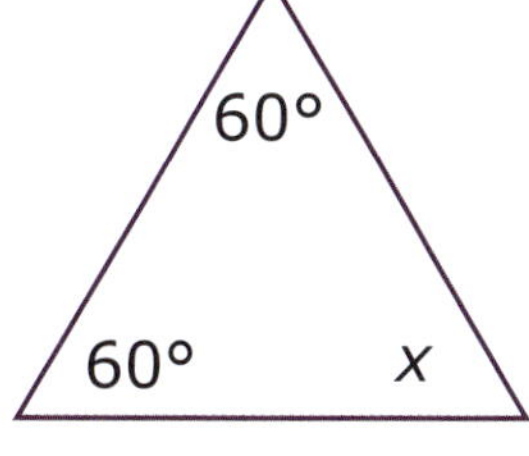

$m\angle x =$ _______ What type of triangle is it?

Explain your thinking.

____

____

Use algebra solve the following problems. The figures are not to scale. Use a separate sheet of paper if needed.

19. 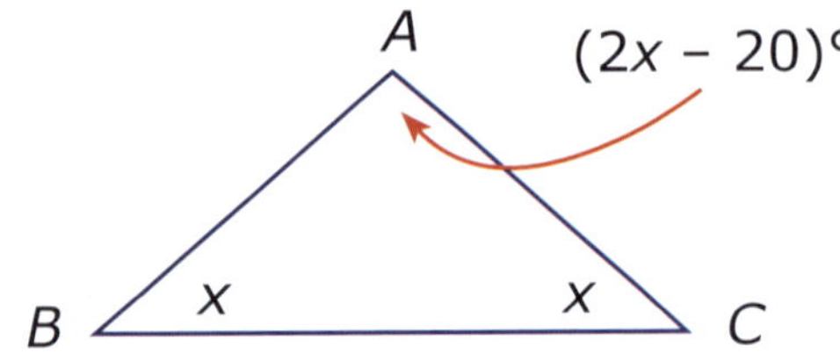

$m\angle x =$ __________, $m\angle A =$ __________ What type of triangle is it? Explain your thinking. ______________________________

____

20. A rectangle has a width that is half of its length. If the perimeter is 78 meters, find the width, length, and area.

21. Find the sum total degrees of the following regular polygon and then find the value of x.

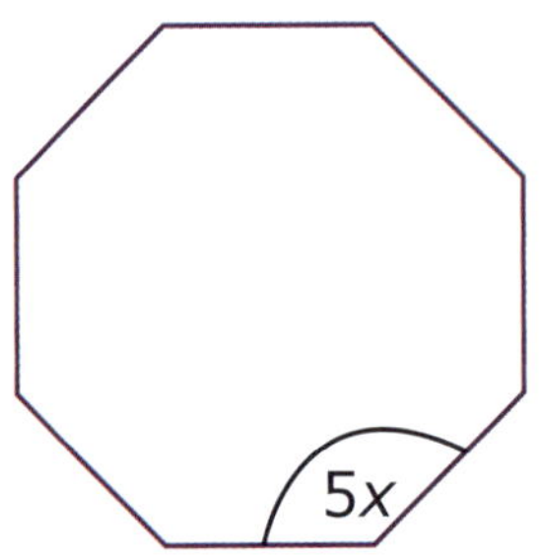

a. Name of the polygon __________

b. Sum total of degrees __________

c. One of its angles __________

d. $x =$ __________

22. Find the value of x.

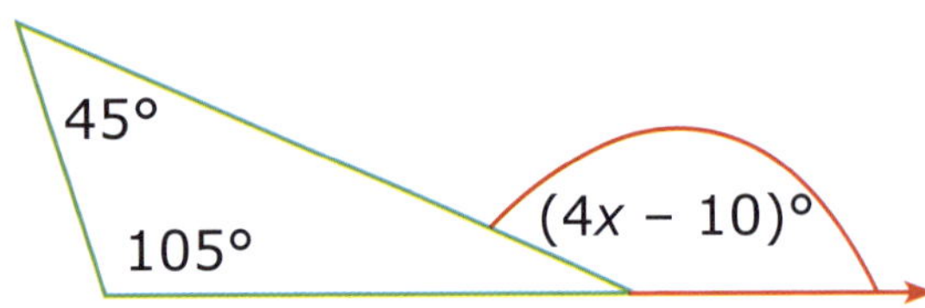

a. $x =$ __________

b. In every triangle the __________ angle always equals the sum of the measures of the two __________ interior angles.

Find the perimeter and the area of the following shapes. Don't forget to label.

23.

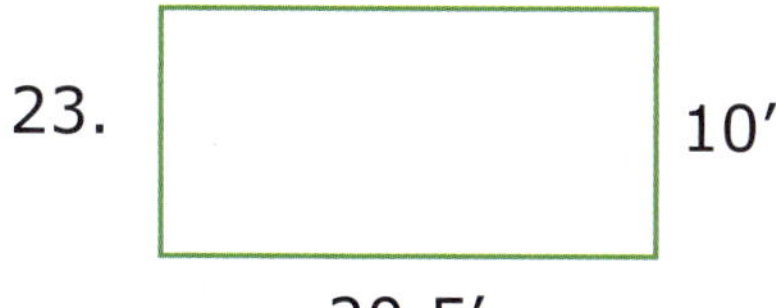

20.5′

$P =$ __________

$A =$ __________

24.

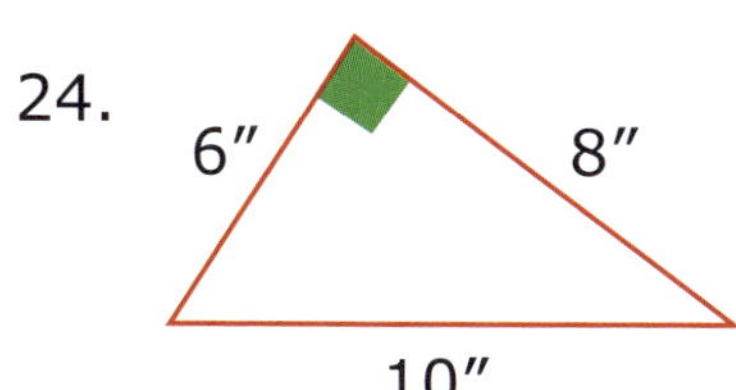

$P =$ __________

$A =$ __________

25.

6 cm

4 cm

4 cm

15 cm

$P =$ __________

$A =$ __________

26.

10′ rhombus 8′

$P =$ __________

$A =$ __________

Find the circumference and area of these circles. Leave your answer in terms of PI.

27.

$C =$ __________

$A =$ __________

28.

11'

$C =$ __________

$A =$ __________

Find the shaded area.

29. 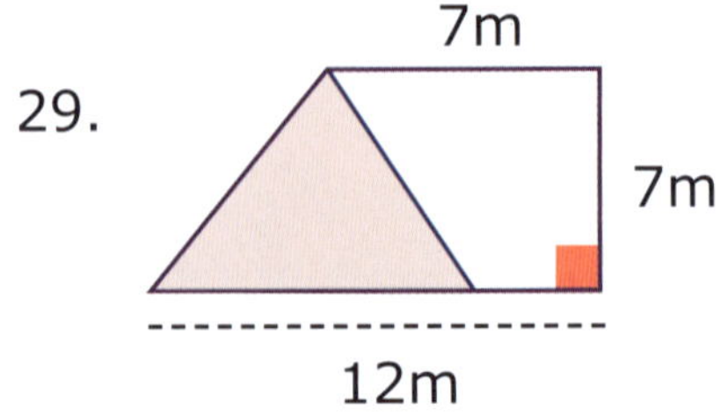

$A =$ ________

30. 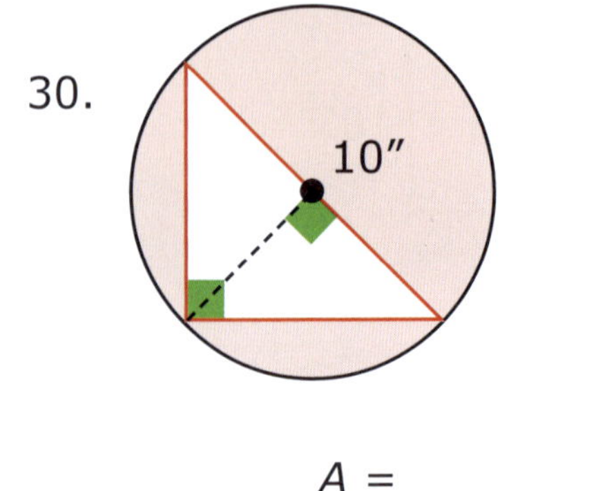

$A =$ ________

A right triangle is inscribed inside a circle with diameter of 10″. Use 3.14 for PI.

31. Finding the Sum of the Measures of the Angles in a Triangle

a. Take a sheet of paper and trace the following triangle or make your own triangle with a ruler. Make sure you also darken the vertices as below.

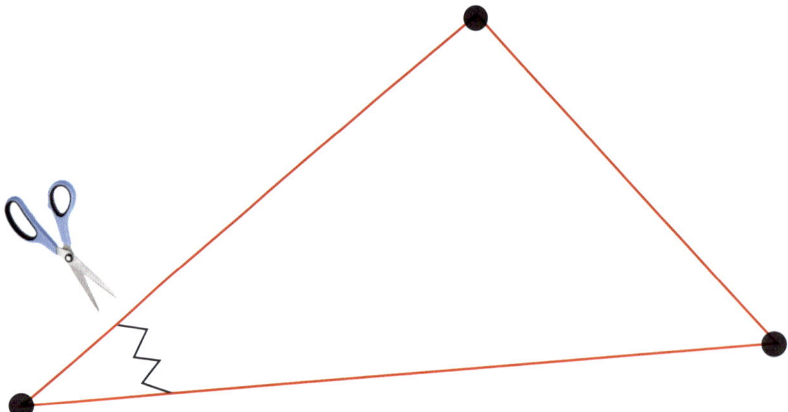

b. Cut out the triangle and cut out the angles, making sure you know where the vertices are located after you cut the angles.

c. Place all the angles together on the line below. The angles should line up on the line (make sure you put the vertices together) demonstrating that the angle measures of a triangle have a sum of 180°.

32. Sum of All Angles in a Polygon

Fill in the blanks. Find an algebraic expression that can be used to determine the sum of all the angle measures in a polygon.

Polygon	No. of Sides	Total Measure of all Angles
a. Triangle	3	180º
b. Quadrilateral	4	________
c. ________	5	540º
d. Hexagon	________	720º
e. ________	7	________
f. Octagon	________	1,080º
g. *n*-sided polygon	*n*	Formula: ________

33. Total Number of Diagonals in a Polygon

Fill out the following by drawing diagonals.

Polygon	Draw Diagonals	No. of Diagonals
a. Triangle		0
b. Parallelogram		2
c. Pentagon		________
d. Hexagon		________
e. Heptagon		________

Answer these questions to help you find the formula.

f. How many vertices are in the heptagon? __________

g. How many diagonals did you draw from just the first vertex? __________

h. If the number of vertices is n, the number of the diagonals from that one vertex is __________.

i. Now multiply the answer to h by the number of vertices in the polygon (n). This new expression is _________.

j. Why is the formula for the total number of diagonals, $\frac{n(n-3)}{2}$?

Explain your thinking. ____

____

____

____

Chapter 11

Understanding Volume and Surface Area

Volume of Prisms

Polygons are two dimensional shapes. Prisms belong to the polyhedra family, solids with many polygon faces. A prism is a three dimensional shape with two bases that are congruent and parallel. The other faces of a right prism are parallelograms. A prism is named by its type of polygon base.

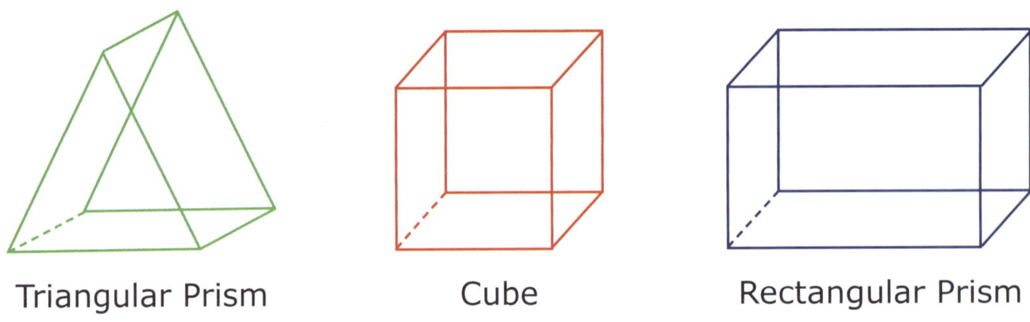

A cube is a type of rectangular prism whose faces are all squares.

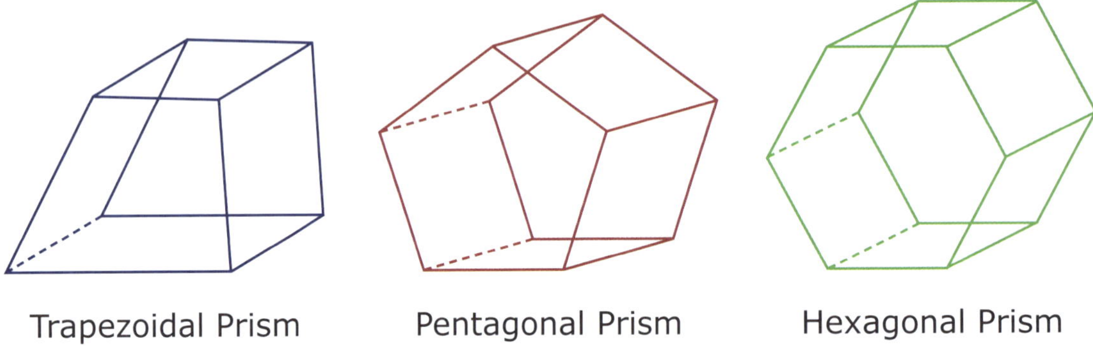

The volume of a three dimensional shape is the amount of space inside the shape. Find the area of one BASE and think of multiple layers (cross sections) of that BASE as shown on the picture on the next page.

> To find the volume of a prism, find the area of one BASE and multiply by the HEIGHT of the prism (in the picture, it's the depth of the shape because the BASE is not facing down).
>
> $$V = BH$$

Example: Find the volume of this triangular prism.

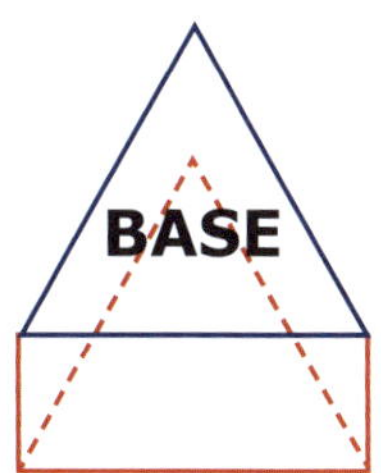

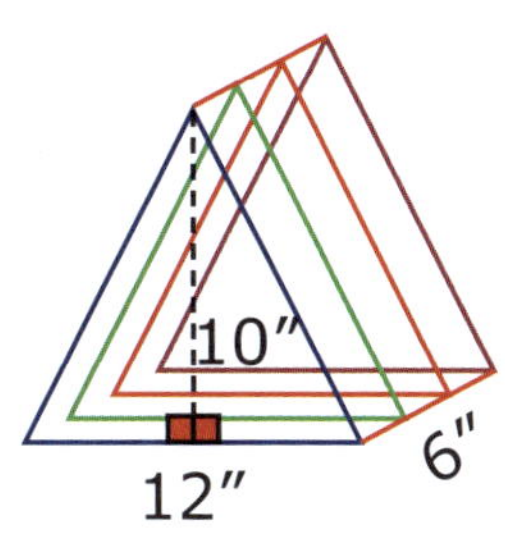

$V = BH$

$V =$ Area of the triangle • HEIGHT

$V = (\frac{1}{2} \bullet 12 \bullet 10) \bullet 6$

$V = 60 \bullet 6$

$V = 360$ cubic inches

Practice

Find the volume of the following prisms. Use a separate sheet of paper if needed. Make sure to label your answer.

1.

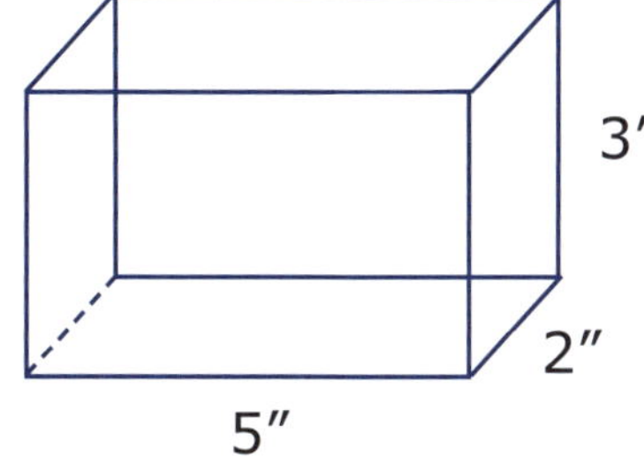

In rectangular prisms, use $V = lwh$ (length • width • height). That's the same as the area of the entire BASE times the HEIGHT.

____

2.

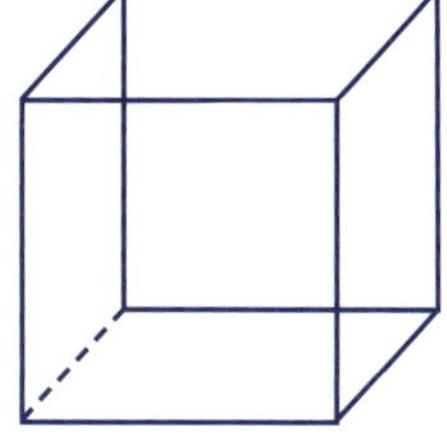

Cube, one side is 8 cm.

____

3.

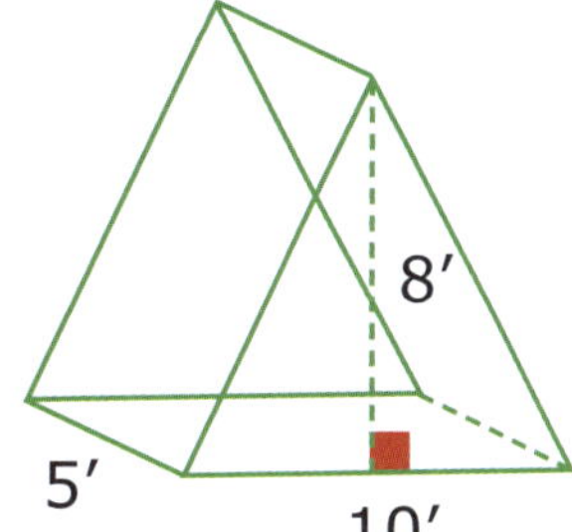

____

4.

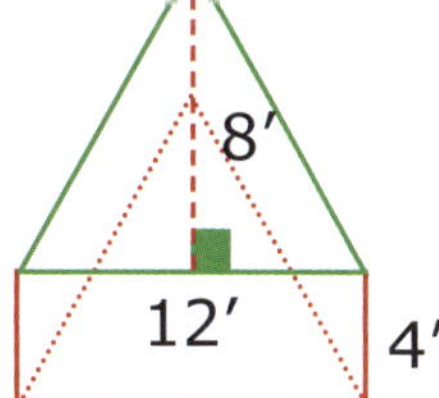

____

5.

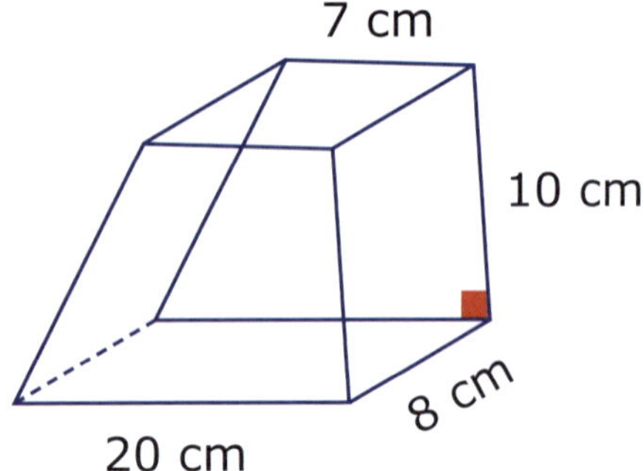

____

6.

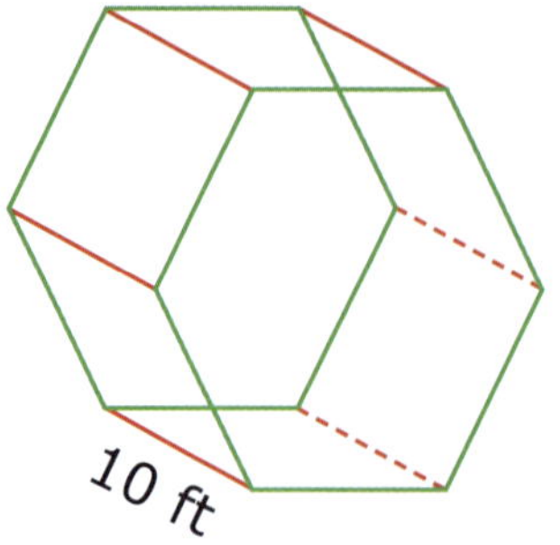

Area of the hexagon is 300 ft^2

____

7.

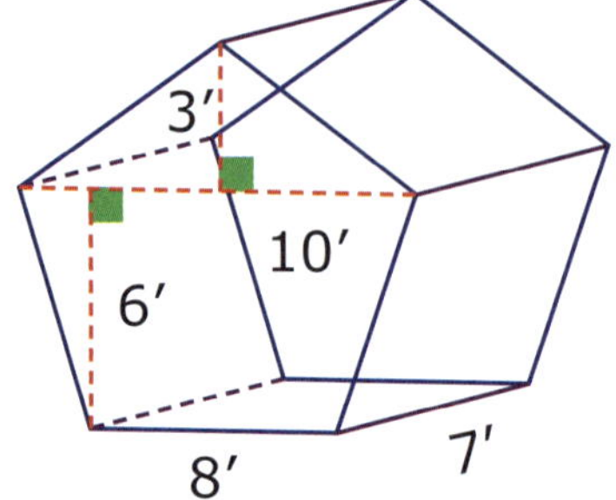

The area of the BASE (pentagon) is the area of the triangle plus the trapezoid.

____

Answer the following.

8. Find one side of this cube if the volume is $\frac{1}{8}$ cubic inches.

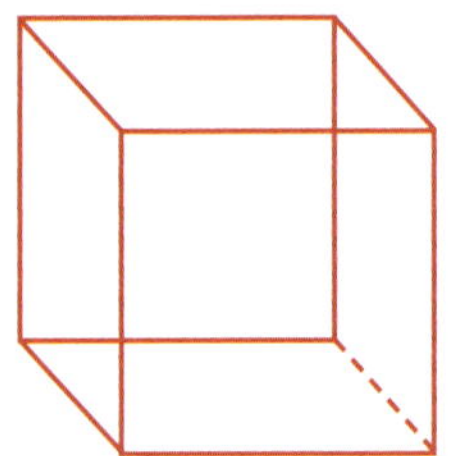

9. Find one side of this cube if its volume is 216 cubic feet.

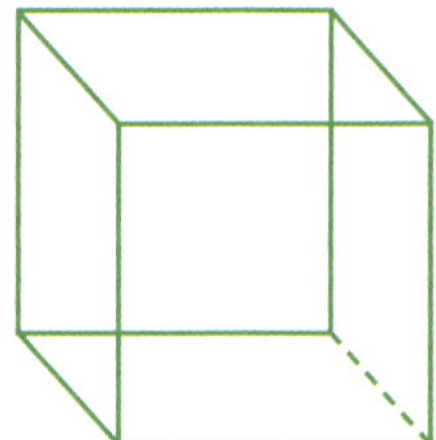

10. Find the height if the volume is 516 cubic centimeters.

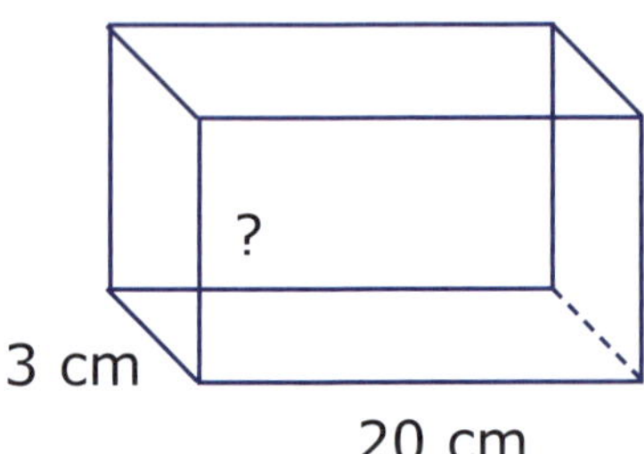

Volume of Pyramids

A pyramid is a polyhedra with a polygon base with three or more triangles which meet to form the top, called the apex.

To find the volume of a pyramid, find the area of the BASE, multiply by the HEIGHT, and then divide by 3.

$$V = \frac{1}{3}BH$$

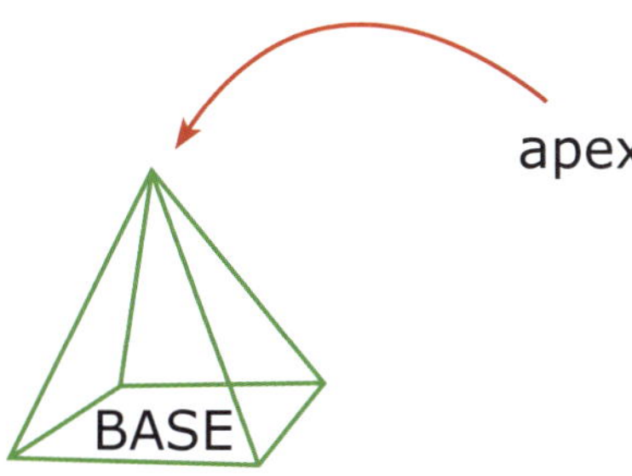

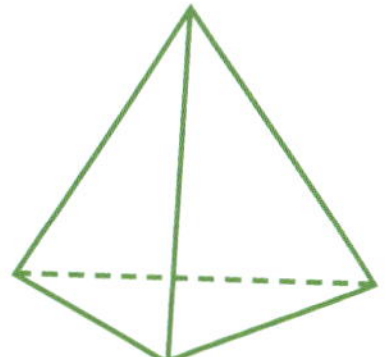

Tetrahedron

A tetrahedron is a pyramid with four congruent triangular faces.

The formula shows that if you inscribe a pyramid inside a prism with the same base and height, the volume taken up by the pyramid is one-third of that of the prism.

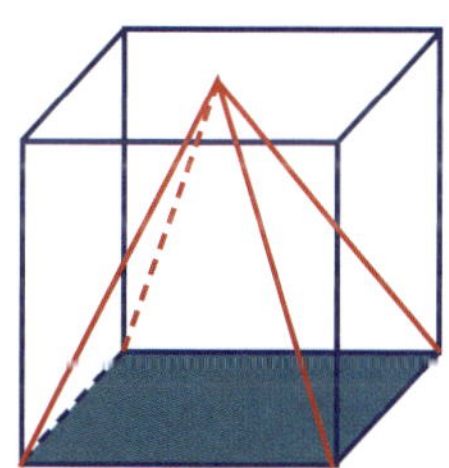

Example: Find the volume of the pyramid.

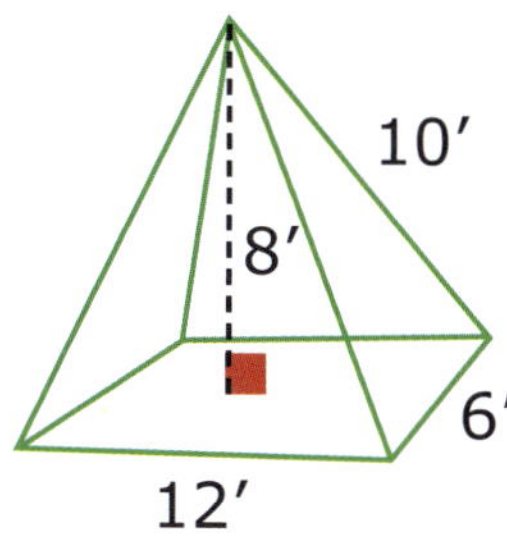

$$V = \frac{1}{3}BH$$

$$V = (12 \bullet 6) \bullet 8 \div 3$$

$$V = 192 \text{ ft}^3$$

Area of pyramid equals the BASE times HEIGHT divided by 3.

Another word for HEIGHT is ALTITUDE. Just remember that the HEIGHT is always perpendicular to the BASE. You can also take one-third of 72, then multiply by 8, or take a third of 6 times 12, and multiply by 8.

Practice

Find the volume of the following pyramids. Make sure to label your answer.

1.

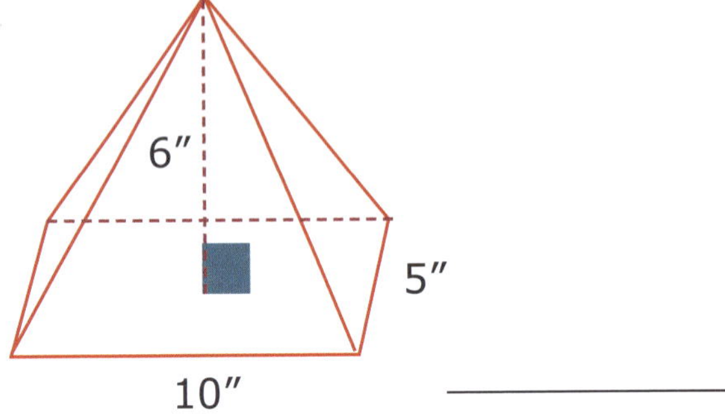

Rectangular pyramid with a height of 6″.

____

2.

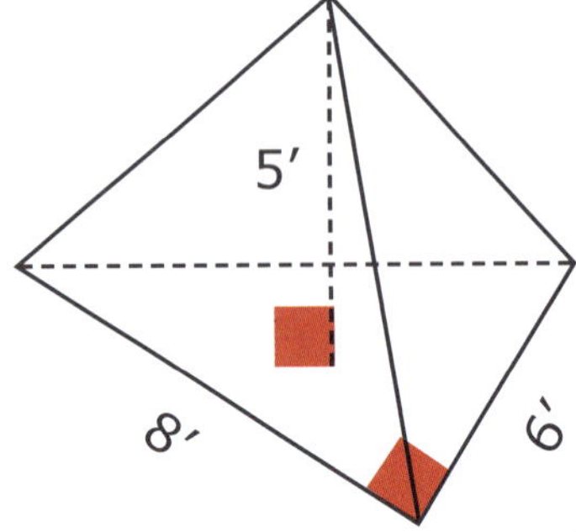

Triangular pyramid with height of 5′.

____

3.

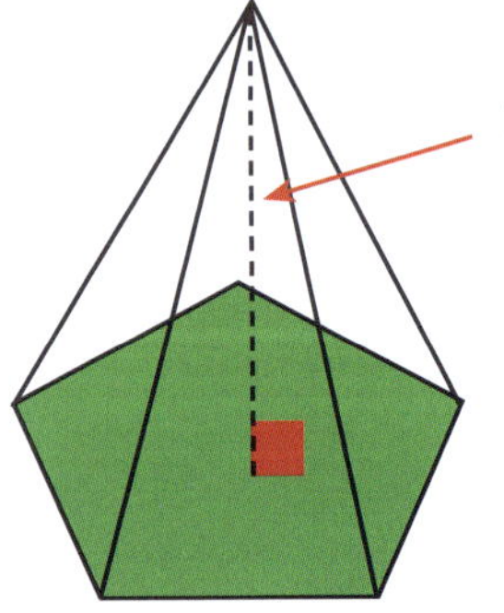

The area of the pentagon is 200 ft^2 with a height of 12′.

____

4.

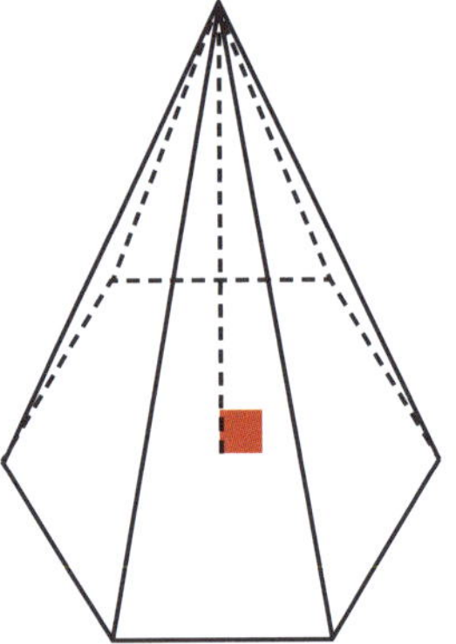

Area of the regular hexagon is 120 ft^2. Pyramid with a height of 20 feet.

____

5.

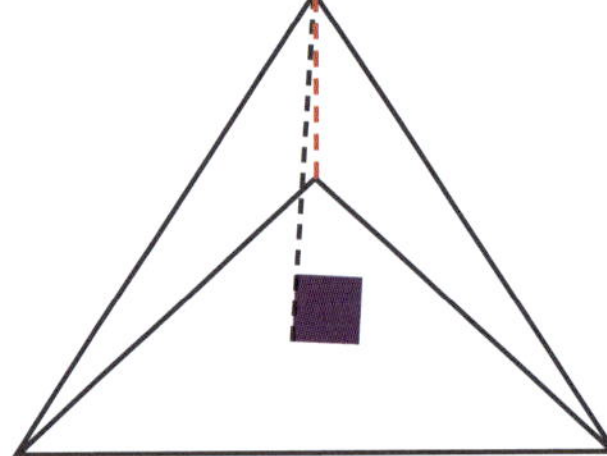

Tetrahedron with a height of 8.16 ft. Base is an equilateral triangle with an area of 43.3 ft.

____

Answer the following.

6. The volume of the great pyramid of Giza in Egypt is 2,592,100 cubic meters. If its base is a square that is 230 meters on each side, find its height.

Volume of Cylinders and Cones

A cylinder is a three dimensional figure with two parallel circular bases. Cylinders are NOT prisms.

To find the volume of a cylinder, find the area of the BASE (which is a circle) and multiply it by its HEIGHT.

$$V = \pi r^2 H$$

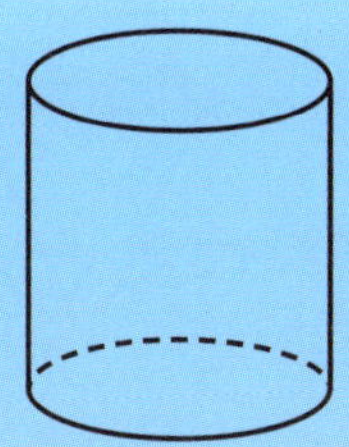

To find the volume of a cone, find the area of its BASE (which is a circle), multiply it by its HEIGHT, and divide it by 3.

$$V = \frac{1}{3}\pi r^2 H$$

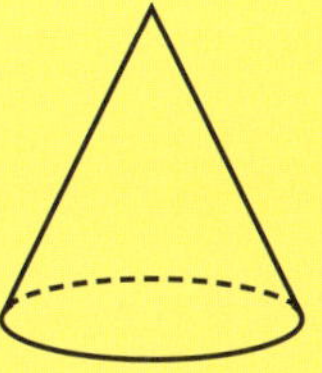

A cone inscribed in a cylinder with the same BASE and HEIGHT takes up one-third of the cylinder's volume.

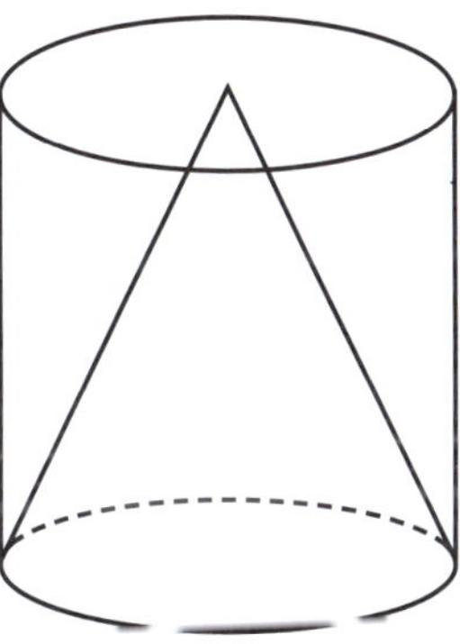

Example 1: Find the volume of the cylinder. Leave your answer in terms of PI. Make sure to label your answer.

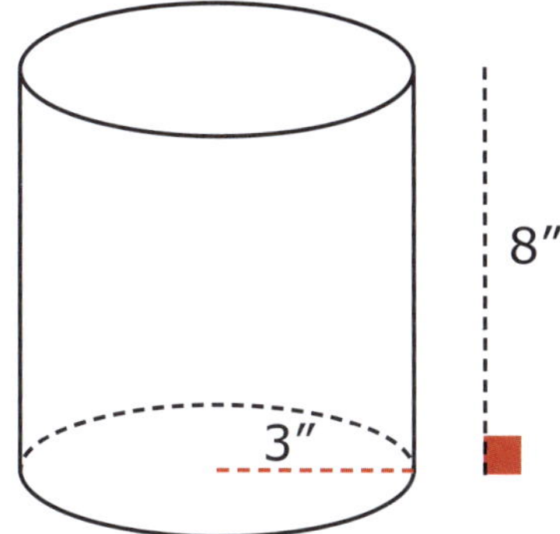

$$V = \pi r^2 H$$

$$V = 3 \bullet 3 \bullet 8 \bullet \pi$$

$$V = 72\pi \text{ cubic inches}$$

Example 2: Find the volume of the cone. Use PI as 3.14. Make sure to label your answer.

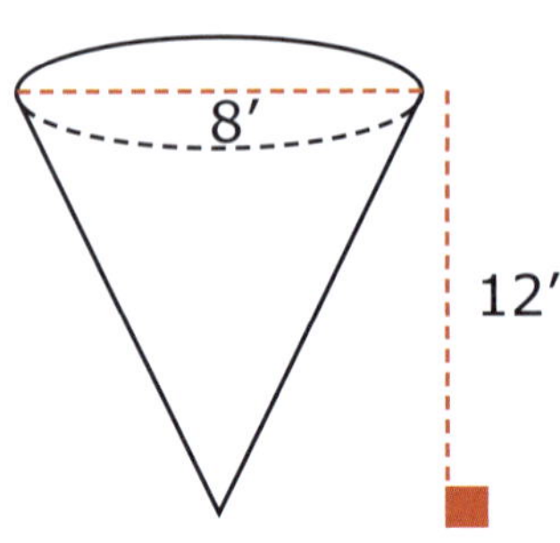

$V = \frac{1}{3}\pi r^2 H$

$V = \pi r^2 H$

$V = 4 \bullet 4 \bullet (3.14) \bullet 12 \div 3$

$V = 200.96 \text{ ft}^3$

The diameter is 8′, so the radius is 4′.

Practice

Find the volume of the following cylinders and cones. Leave your answer in terms of PI. Make sure to label your answer.

1.

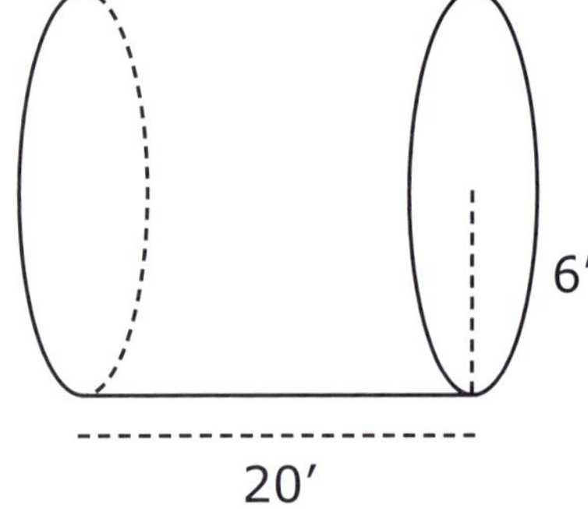

____

3.

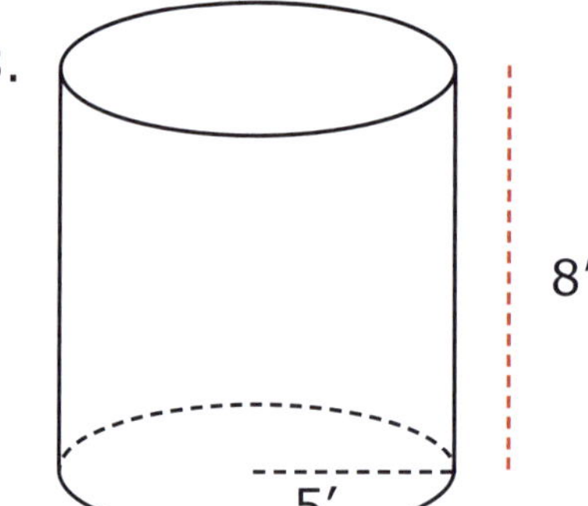

____

2.

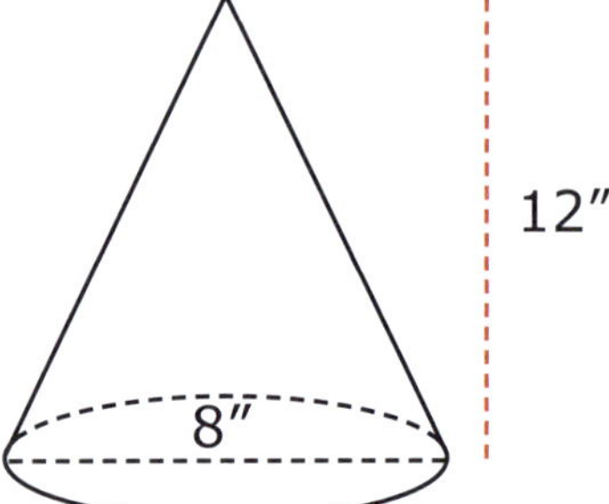

____

4.

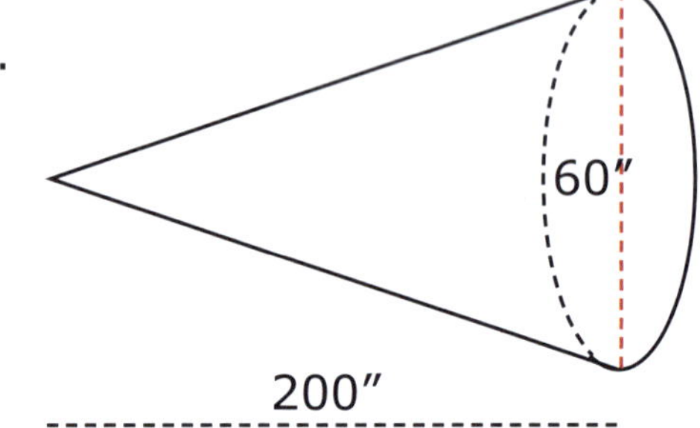

____

5.

6 cm

Diameter: 8 cm

____

6.

9′

6′

____

7.

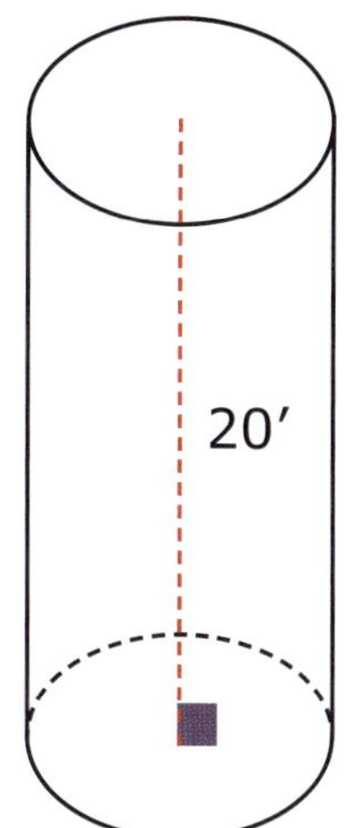

Diameter: 2.5′

____

Surface Area

The surface area of a three dimensional object is the sum of the areas of every face on that object.

Example 1: Find the surface area of this rectangular prism.

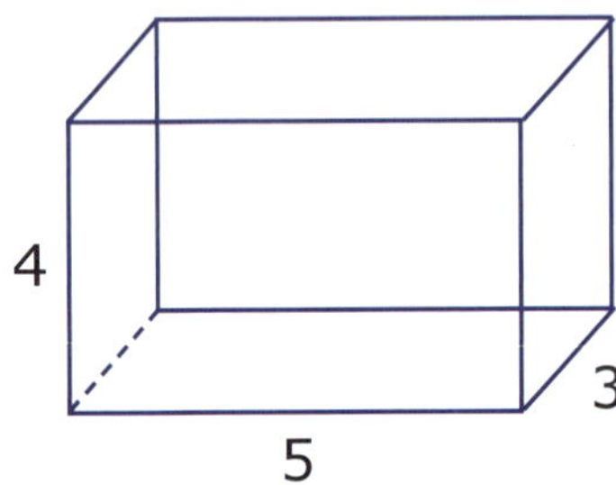

Area of the front and back faces:	2(5 • 4)	=	40
Area of top and bottom faces:	2(5 • 3)	=	30
Area of right and left faces:	2(4 • 3)	=	24
Total sum of all areas:			94

Answer: 94 square units

Example 2: Find the surface area of this cylinder.

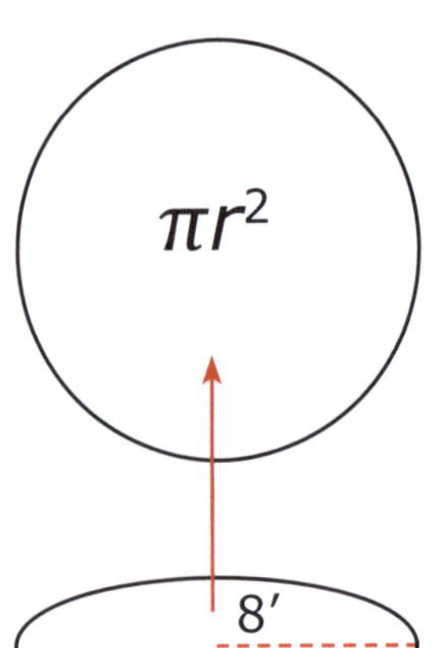

You have two circles.

If you open the sides of the cylinder (think of taking out the label from a can), you get a rectangle. The dimensions of the rectangle are the circumference of the circle times its height.

$$SA = 2\pi rh + 2\pi r^2$$

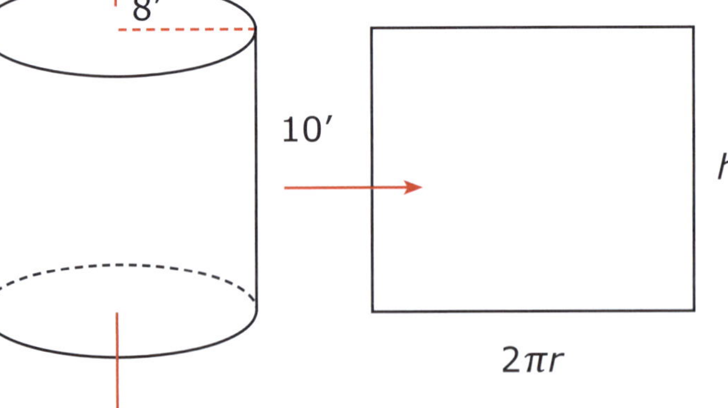

πr^2

Surface Area (SA) = $2 \bullet \pi \bullet 8 \bullet 10 \;+\; 2\pi 8^2$

$160\pi \;+\; 128\pi$

So the surface area is 288π square feet.

Example 3: Find the surface area of the following square pyramid.

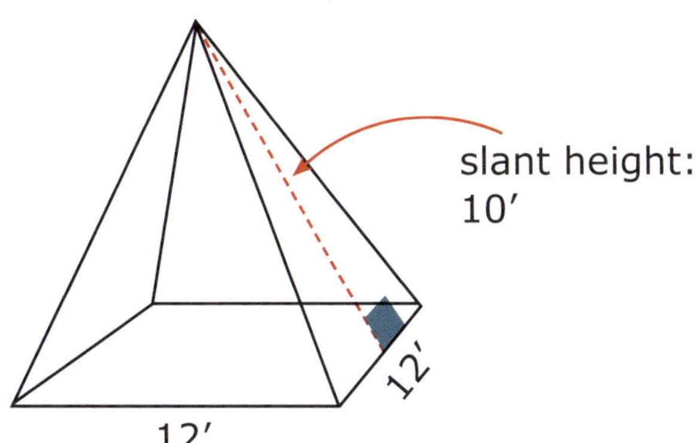

The base is a square so its area is 144 ft^2 (12 • 12).

Each triangle has an area of 60 ft^2 (12 • 10 ÷ 2).

All four triangles: 240 ft^2

Total surface area: 384 ft^2 (144 + 240)

Practice

Find the surface area and label. Use a separate sheet of paper if needed.

1.

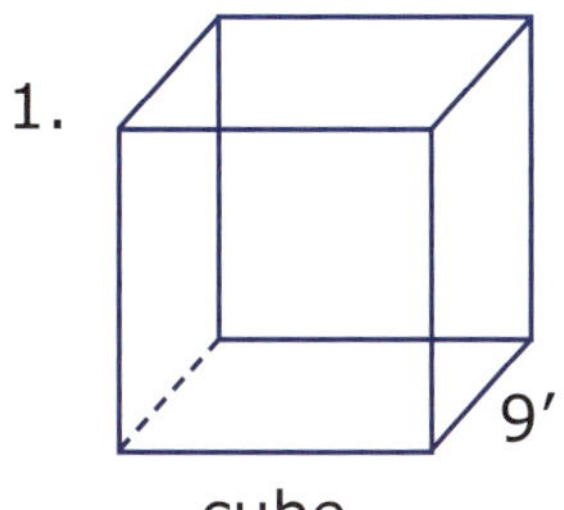

____

3.

13″

12″

8″

10″

____

2.

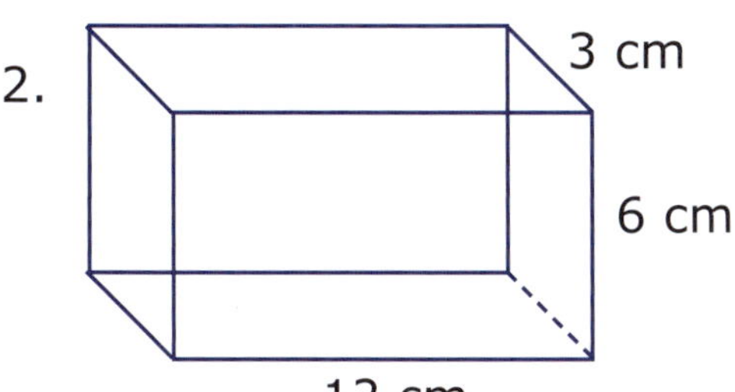

____

4.

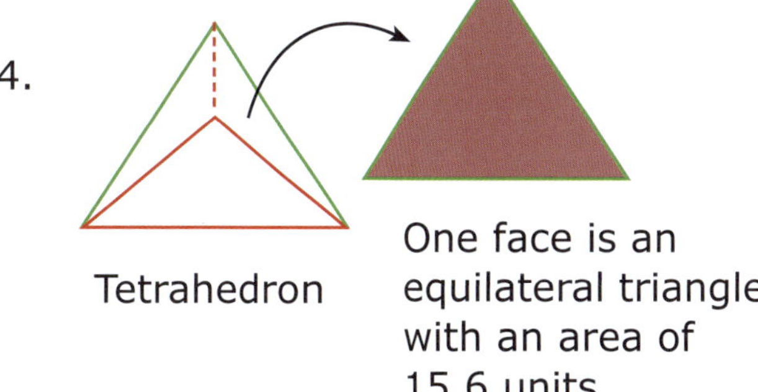

One face is an equilateral triangle with an area of 15.6 units.

____

5.

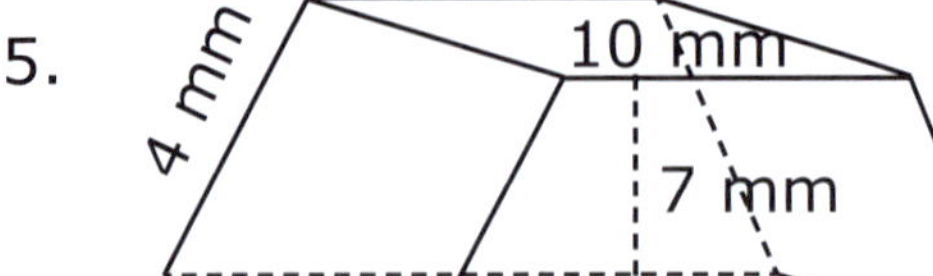

____

6.

10″

16″

Leave your answer in terms of PI.

____

7.

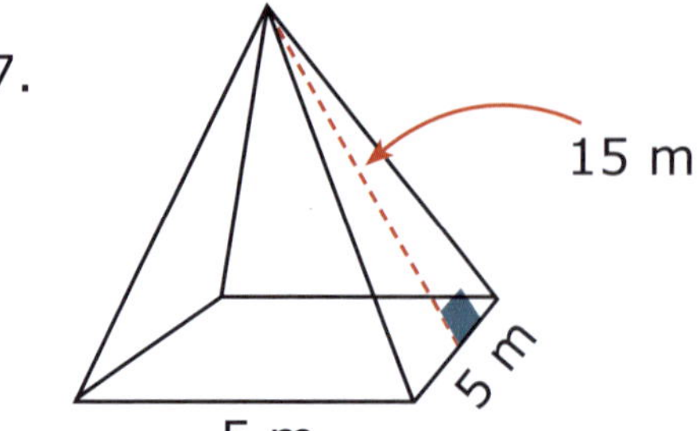

Square Pyramid

____

Surface Area of a Cone

To find the surface area of cone you need to use the formula below.

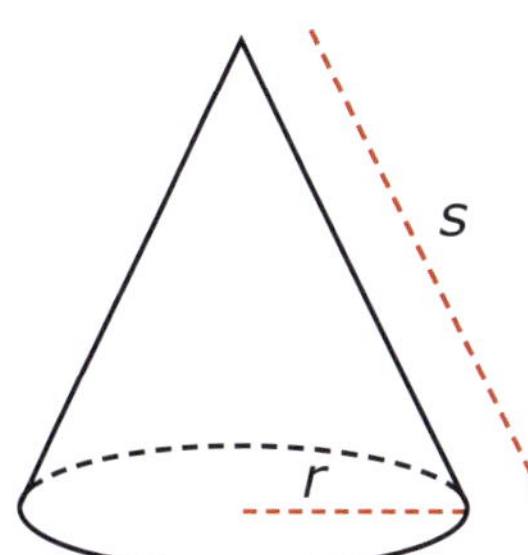

$SA = \pi rs + \pi r^2$ ← area of the circle base

s = slant height
r = radius

To find the slant height, use the Pythagorean Theorem if you know the radius and the HEIGHT of the cone.

Example: Find the surface area of the cone below.

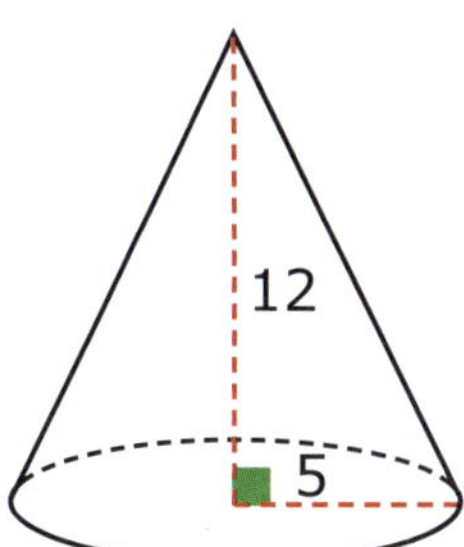

In order to find the slant height, we need to use the Pythagorean Theorem, $a^2 + b^2 = c^2$.
So $5^2 + 12^2 = c^2$ and $25 + 144 = c^2$.
Therefore, $c^2 = 169$ and $c = 13$. The height is 13.

$SA = \pi \bullet 5 \bullet 13 + \pi \bullet 25 = 90\pi$ square units

Practice

Find the surface area of these cones. Leave your answer in terms of PI.

1. 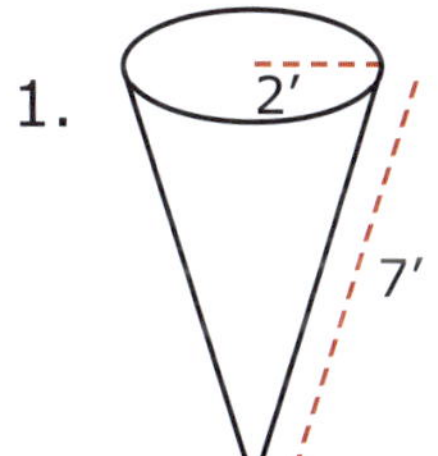

____

4. 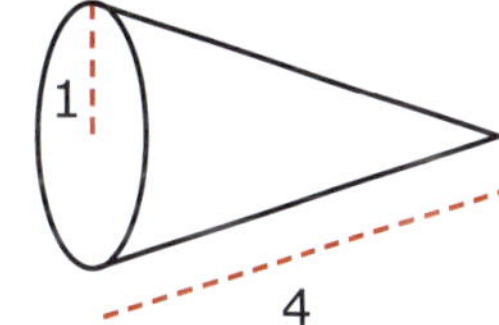

____

2. 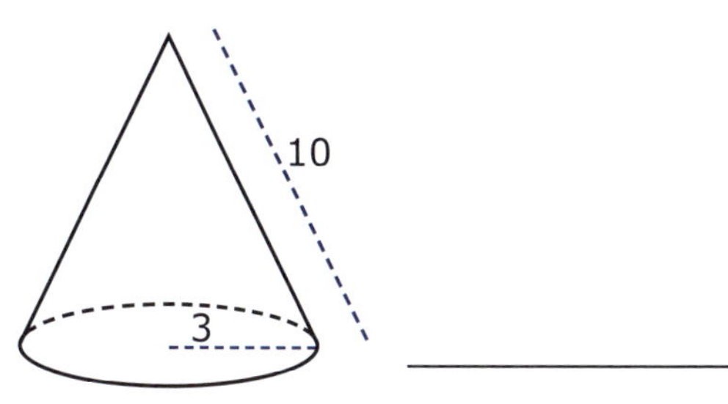

____

5. 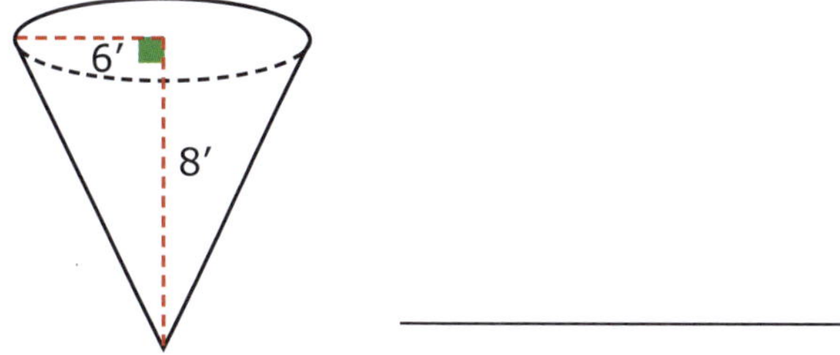

____

3. 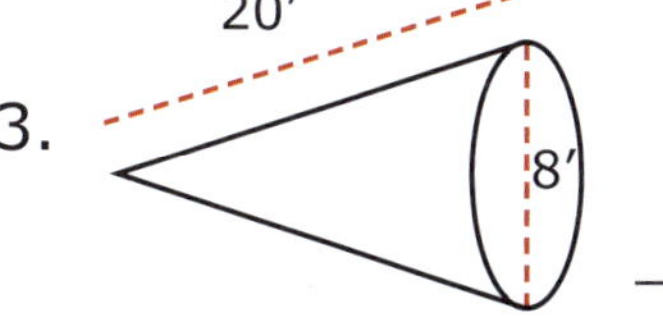

____

6. 24, 7

____

Volume and Surface Area of a Sphere

To find the volume and surface area of a sphere, use the two formulas below.

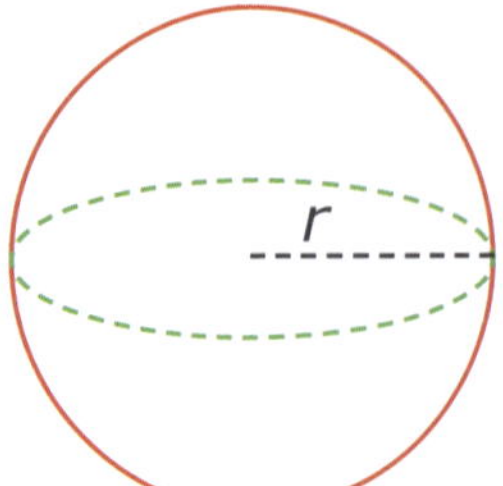

Volume $= \frac{4}{3}\pi r^3$

$SA = 4\pi r^2$

Example: Find the volume and the surface area of this sphere. Keep your answer in terms of PI. Label your answer.

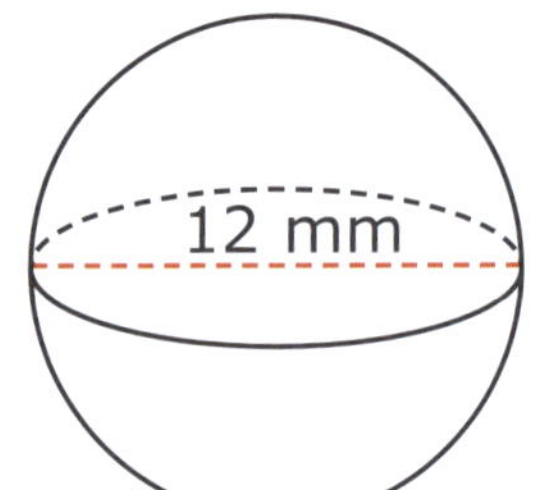

The diameter is 12 mm so the radius is 6 mm.

$V = \frac{4}{3} \bullet \pi \bullet r^3 = \frac{4}{3} \bullet \pi \bullet 6^3 = \frac{4}{3} \bullet \pi \bullet 216 = 288\pi \text{ mm}^3$

$SA = 4 \bullet \pi \bullet r^2 = 4 \bullet \pi \bullet 36 = 144\pi \text{ mm}^2$

Practice

Find the volume and surface area of the following spheres. Leave your answer in terms of PI. Use a separate sheet of paper to show your work.

1. 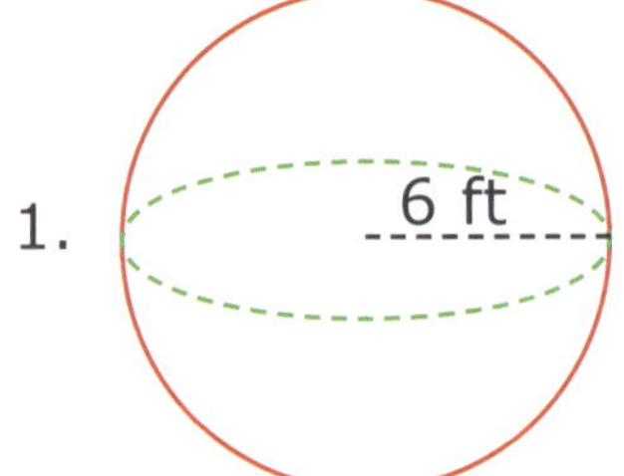

V = __________

SA = __________

2. 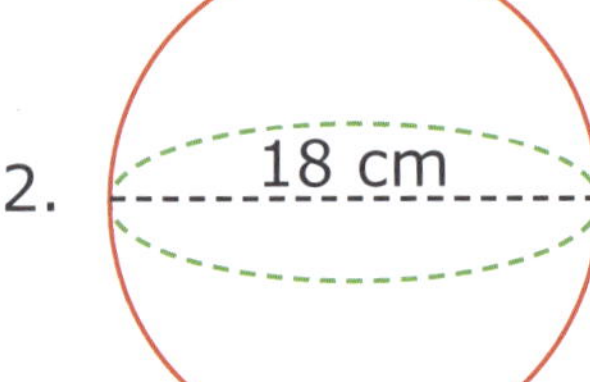

V = __________

SA = __________

3. 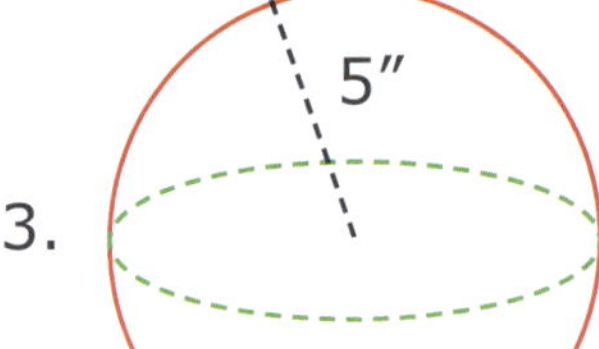

V = __________

SA = __________

4. 

V = __________

SA = __________

Diameter is 9.5″. Round your answer to the nearest tenth. Use PI as 3.14.

Answer the following.

5. If the surface area of a sphere is 144π square units, find its volume in terms of PI.

Chapter 11 Review

Find the volume and the surface area of the following prisms. Make sure to label your answer.

1. 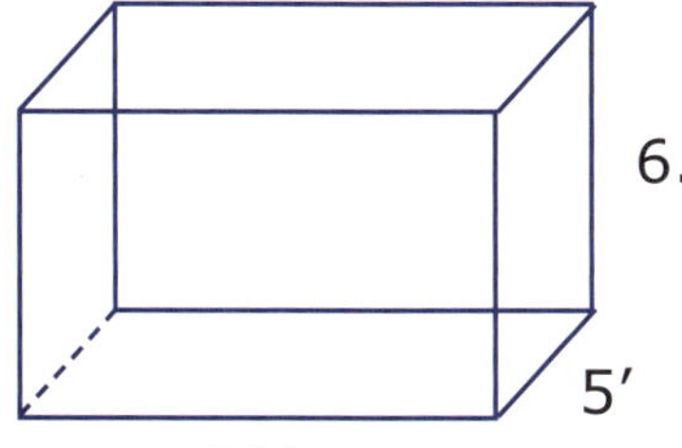

V = ________

SA = ________

2. 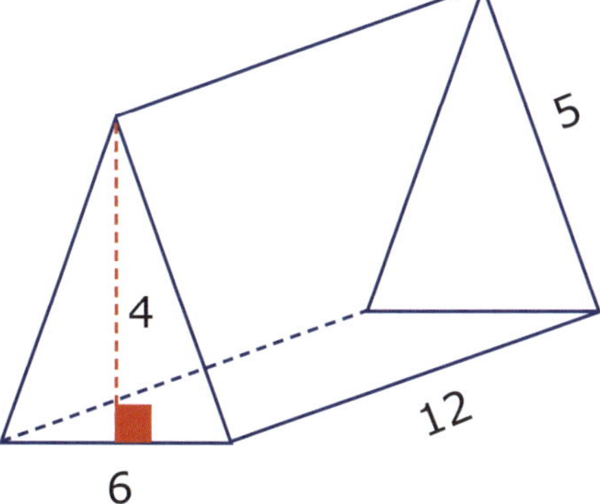

V = ________

SA = ________

Find the volume of the following objects. Make sure to label your answer. Leave your answer in terms of PI.

3. 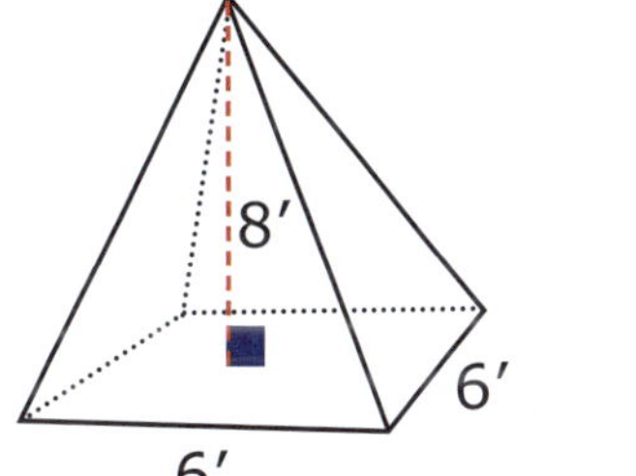

____

4. 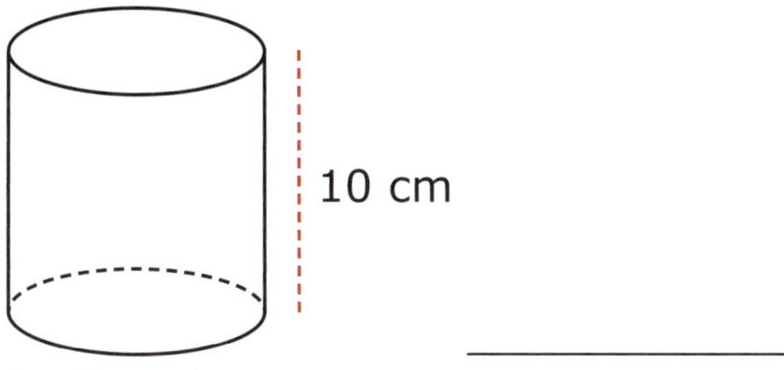

Radius: 8 cm

____

5. 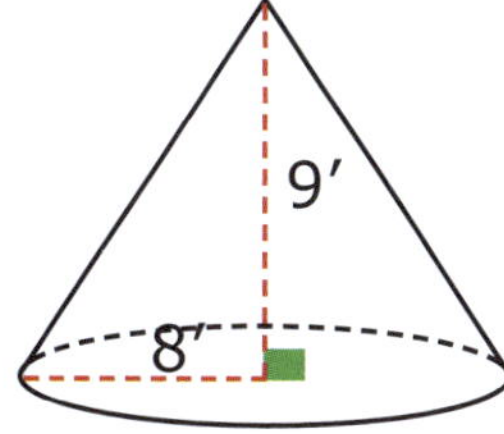

____

6. 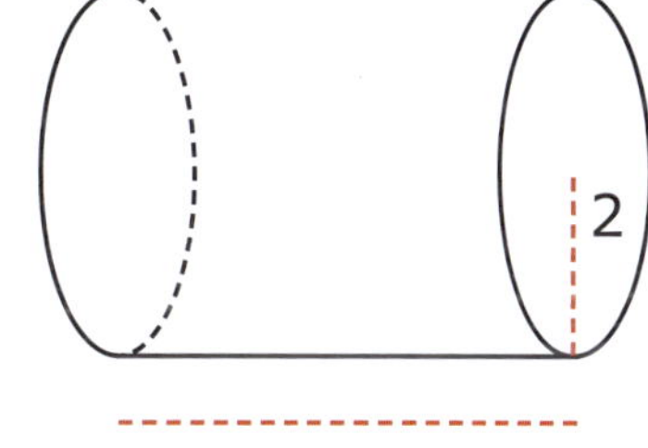

____

7. 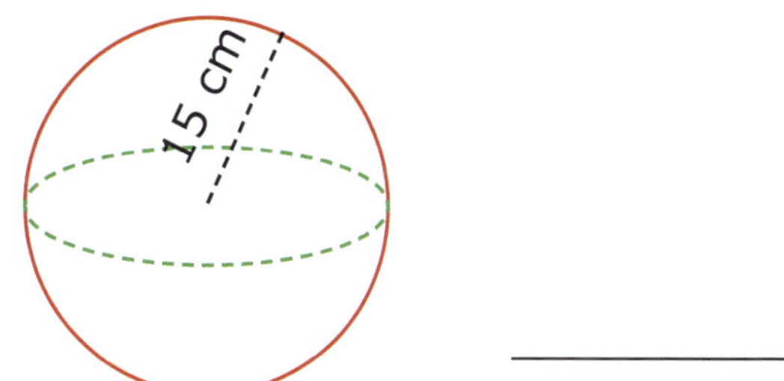

____

8. 18 mm

____

Find the surface area of the following cylinders. Leave your answer in terms of PI.

9. 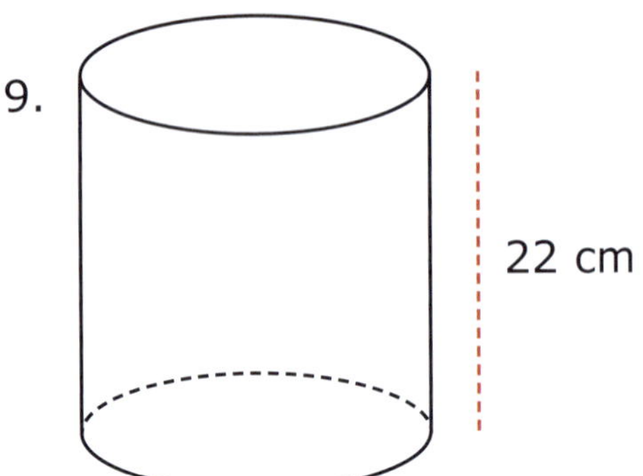

Diameter: 10 mm

____

10. 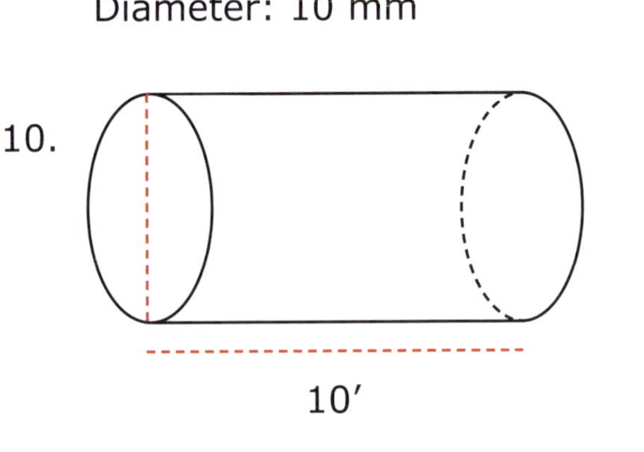

Diameter: 2′

____

Answer the following.

11. a. What is the name of the prism below? Why? Explain your thinking.

____

____

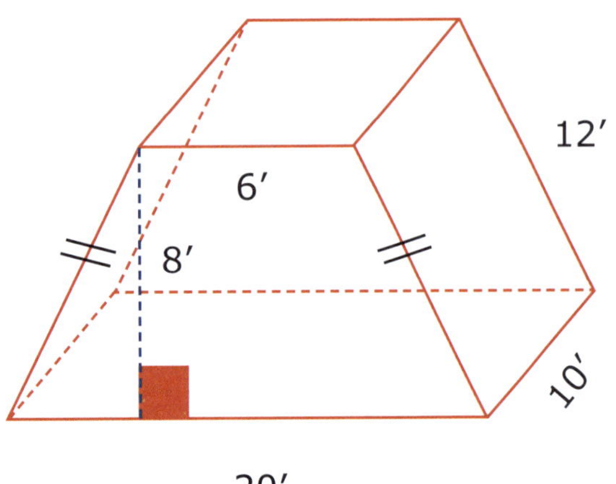

b. Find the volume of the prism and label.

____

c. Find the surface area and label.

____

12. A cylinder with the same height as problem 11 and the same diameter as the small base of the trapezoid is inserted as shown. Find the difference between the two volumes. Use 3.14 for PI and round your answer to the nearest hundredths.

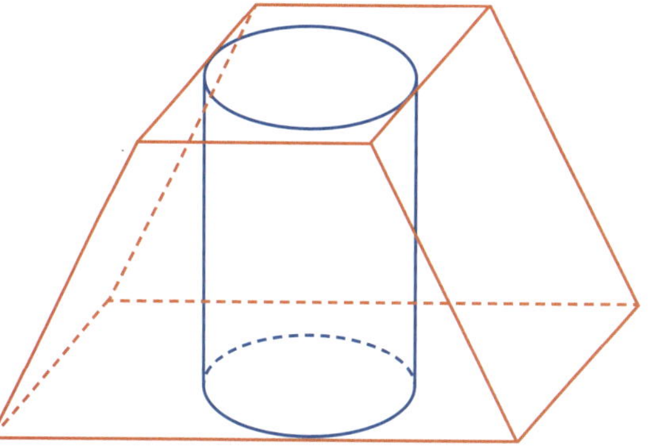

13. A water tower is made up of a hemisphere, a cylinder and a cone with the dimensions shown below. Find the total volume of the cone, cylinder and hemisphere. Keep your answer in terms of PI.

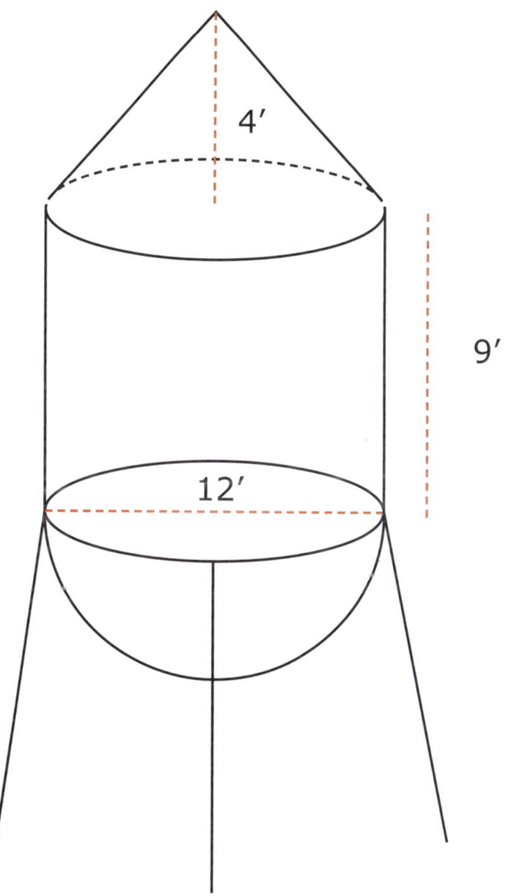

a. Volume of the cone: ____________

b. Volume of the cylinder: ____________

c. Volume of the hemisphere: ____________

d. Total volume of the water tower: ____________

Chapter 12

Graphing on the Coordinate Plane

The coordinate plane is also known as the Cartesian plane in honor of French mathematician Renè Descartes (1596-1650). Descartes, who was also a philosopher and scientist, developed the coordinate plane to graph geometric lines and curves by using algebraic equations. Notice that the quadrants are labeled.

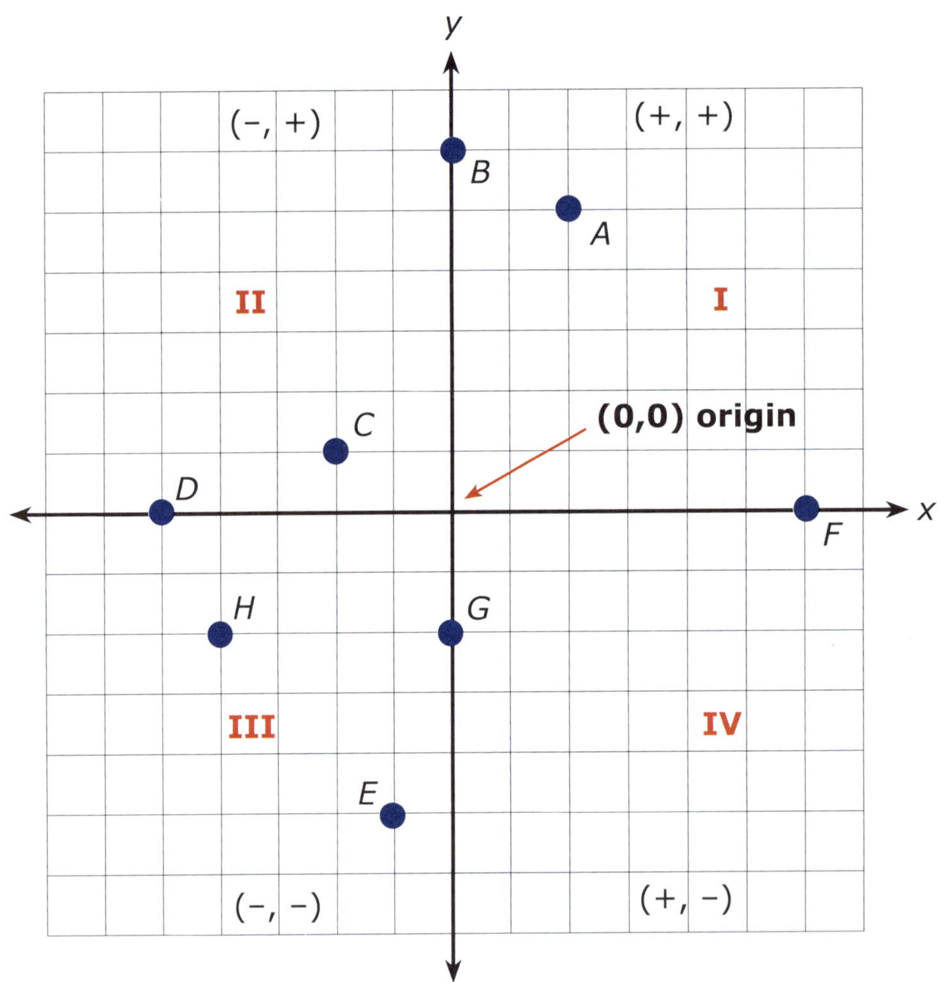

Practice

Write the ordered pairs that match the points above.

1. Point *A* (1, 4)
2. Point *B* ________
3. Point *C* ________
4. Point *D* ________
5. Point *E* ________
6. Point *F* ________
7. Point *G* ________
8. Point *H* ________

Graphing Linear Equations

A linear equation is an equation that creates a line when graphed.

Example: Graph the equation $y = 2x + 1$ using the table of values below. Substitute or plug in the values given for x to find the y values.

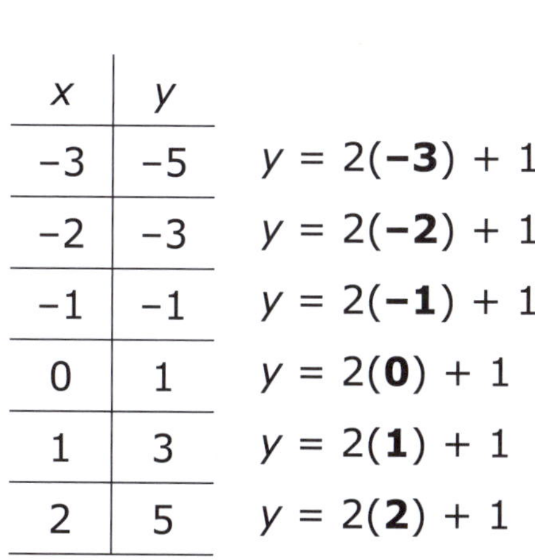

x	y	
−3	−5	$y = 2(\mathbf{-3}) + 1$
−2	−3	$y = 2(\mathbf{-2}) + 1$
−1	−1	$y = 2(\mathbf{-1}) + 1$
0	1	$y = 2(\mathbf{0}) + 1$
1	3	$y = 2(\mathbf{1}) + 1$
2	5	$y = 2(\mathbf{2}) + 1$

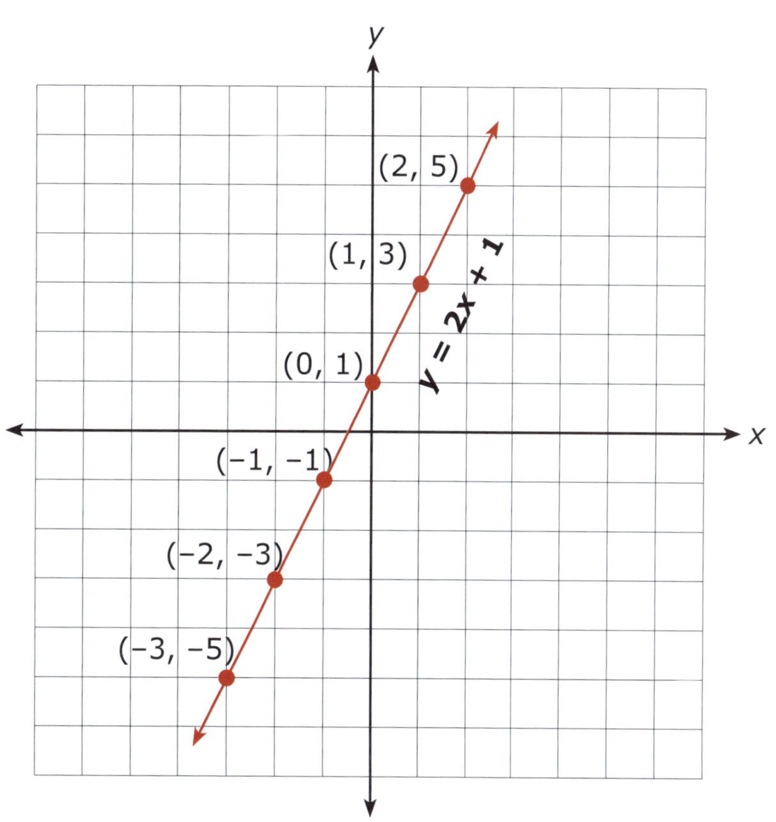

Always use arrow heads on your line to indicate that the line is infinite and write the equation on the line.

The x values on the table are called the independent values. You are "independently" free to choose values for x that are integers, fractions, or decimals. You should always use some negative values, 0, and some positive values. The y values are called the dependent values since the y values depend on what you choose for x. The x values are called <u>domain</u>, and the y values are called the <u>range</u>.

Practice

Graph the following equations using the table of values. Use your own graph paper.

1. $y = 3x$
2. $y = -3x$
3. $y = 2x$
4. $y = \frac{1}{2}x$
5. $y = 2x - 5$
6. $y = 2x + 3$
7. $y = 4x - 5$
8. $y = x$
9. $y = -x$

Special Graphs

Suppose you are asked to graph $y = 3$, or $x = -5$. How do you make a table of values? How do you graph these equations that are each missing a variable? Look at $y = 3$. If you wanted to make a table of values, it would look like the table below. No matter what x value you choose, the y value is always 3. Your graph is the horizontal line that crosses the y axis at 3.

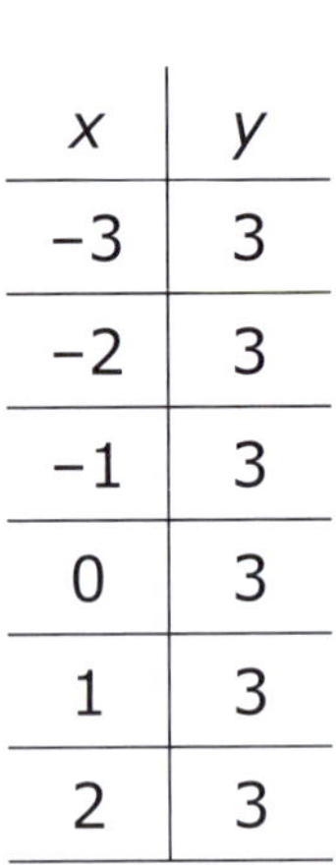

x	y
−3	3
−2	3
−1	3
0	3
1	3
2	3

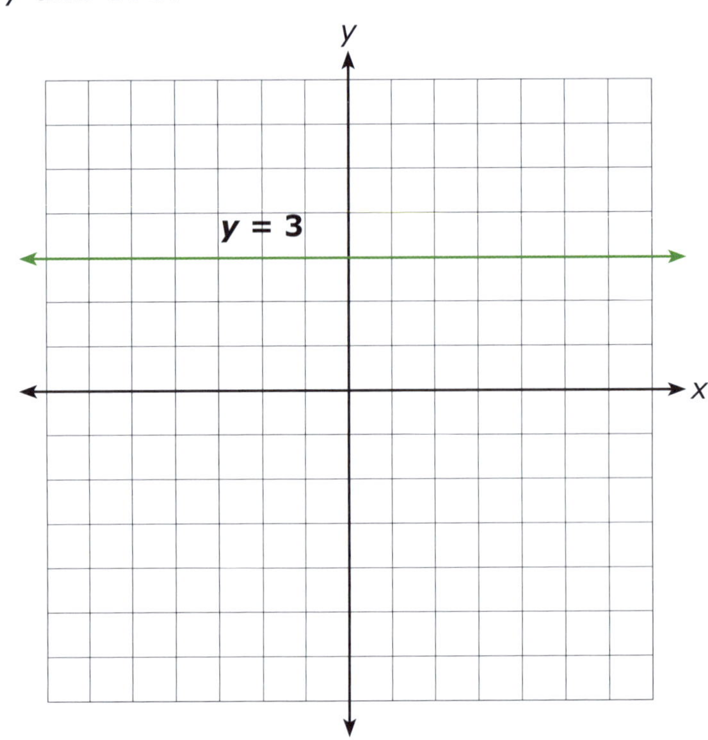

Now look at $x = -5$. Can you see that in this case all the values of x would be −5? The graph is the vertical line that crosses the x-axis at −5 shown below.

x	y
−5	−4
−5	−3
−5	−2
−5	−1
−5	0
−5	1

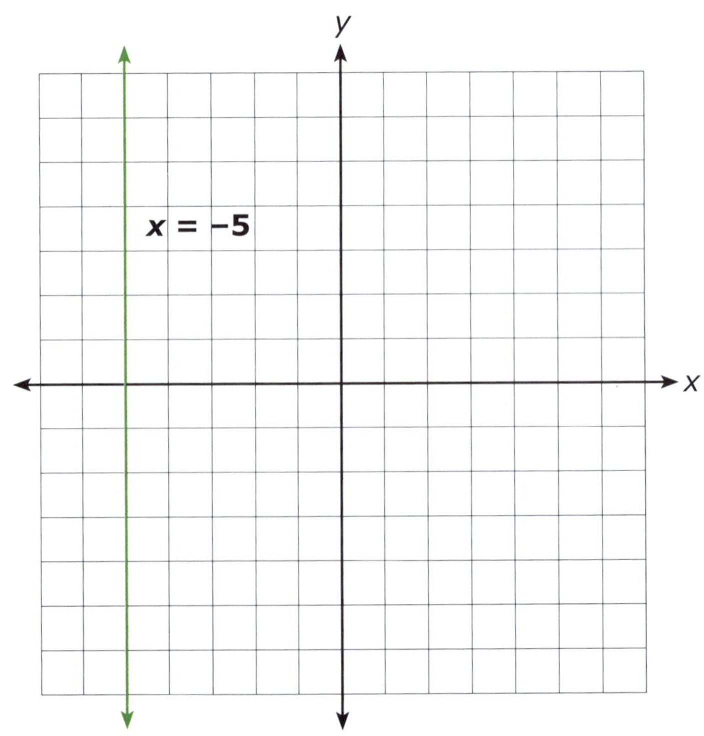

Practice

Write the letter of the graph that matches the equation.

______ 1. $y = 4$	______ 3. $y = -4$	______ 5. $y = 0$
______ 2. $x = -3$	______ 4. $x = 0$	______ 6. $y = x$

A.

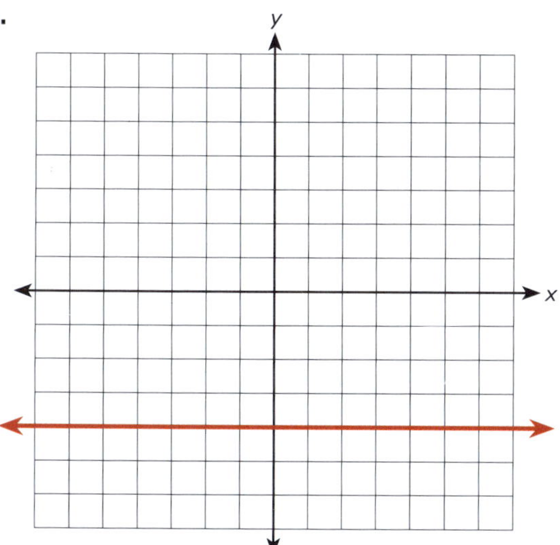

D.

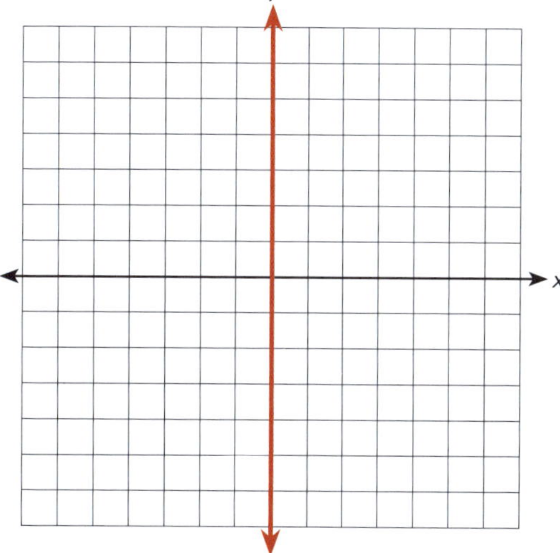

B.

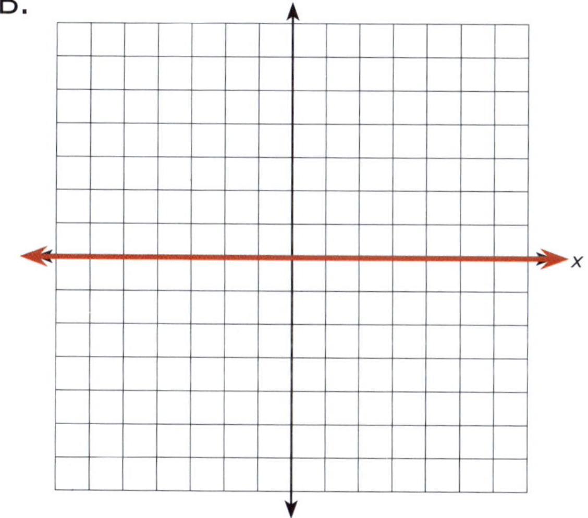

E.

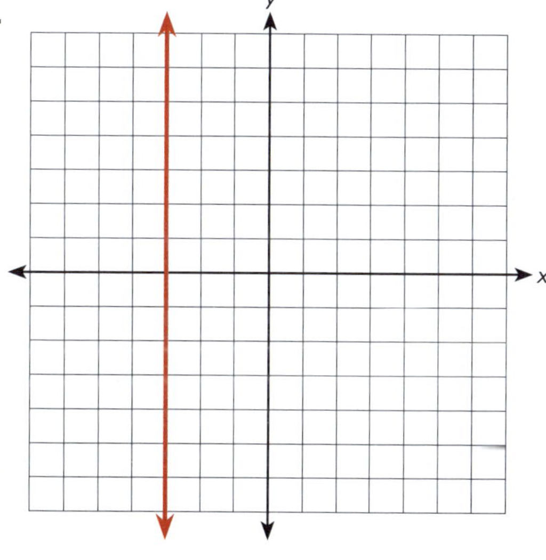

C.

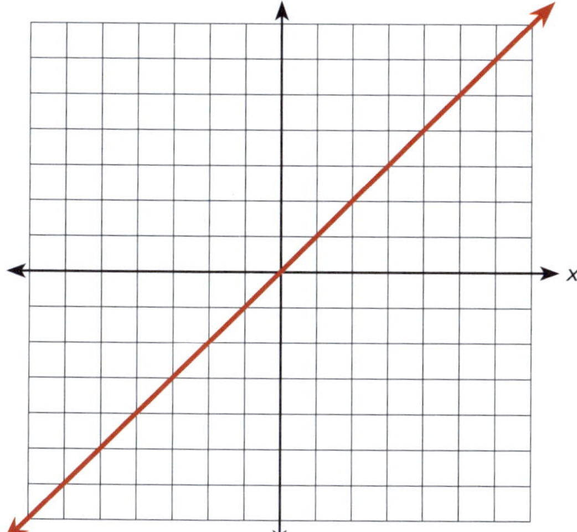

F.

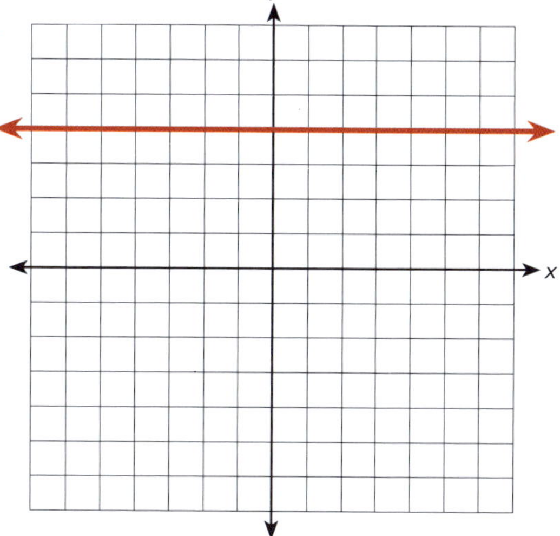

Using Slope and *Y*-Intercept to Graph Linear Equations

Equations 5, $y = 2x - 5$, and 6, $y = 2x + 3$, on page 253, are similar but different.

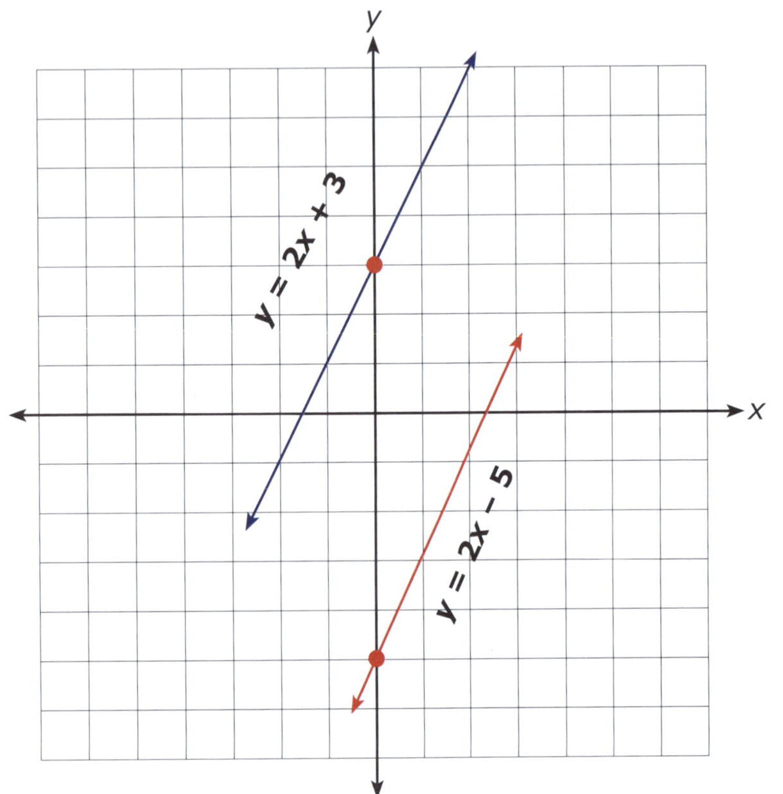

The equations are similar in that they both have the same slant or slope. In fact, they are parallel to each other.

They are different in that the graph of $y = 2x + 3$ crosses the y-axis at (0, 3) and the graph of $y = 2x - 5$ crosses the y-axis at (0, –5).

When an equation is written in the form of $y = mx + b$, the coefficient in front of the x variable is called the slope (the slant or inclination of the line), and the constant b is called the *y*-intercept (where the line crosses the y-axis).

> The slope of a line is defined as $\frac{\Delta y}{\Delta x}$ (delta y divided by delta x), or the change in y divided by the change in x.

In the case of the equations above, the slope is 2 or $\frac{2}{1}$. The points on the line are moving up 2 and over 1.

The y-intercept of $y = 2x + 3$ is 3, and the y-intercept of $y = 2x - 5$ is –5.

The format $y = mx + b$, is called the slope/intercept form of an equation. When a linear equation is not in that format, you can solve for y to make it easier to graph without a table.

Example 1: Graph $-3x + y = -2$ on the coordinate plane below.

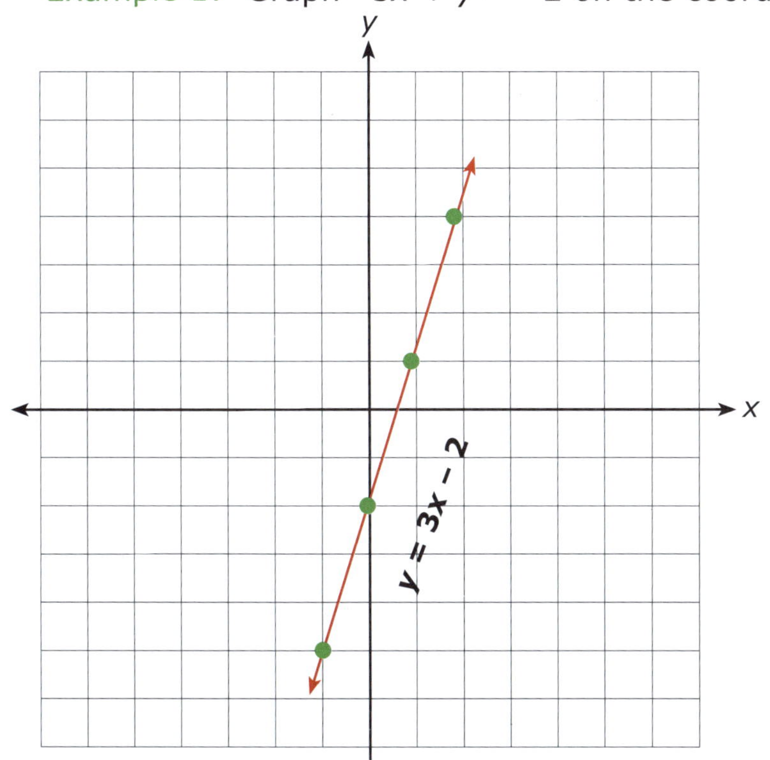

Solve for y first: $y = 3x - 2$

Add $3x$ on each side.

Graph the y-intercept $(0, -2)$

Starting at $(0, -2)$, use the slope $\frac{3}{1}$ to find the next point. Go up three units and over one unit to the right, OR go down three units and to the left one unit. Remember $\frac{3}{1} = \frac{-3}{-1}$. Make sure to graph at least 3 to 4 points.

Example 2: Graph $-\frac{2}{3}x - y = 1$ on the coordinate below below.

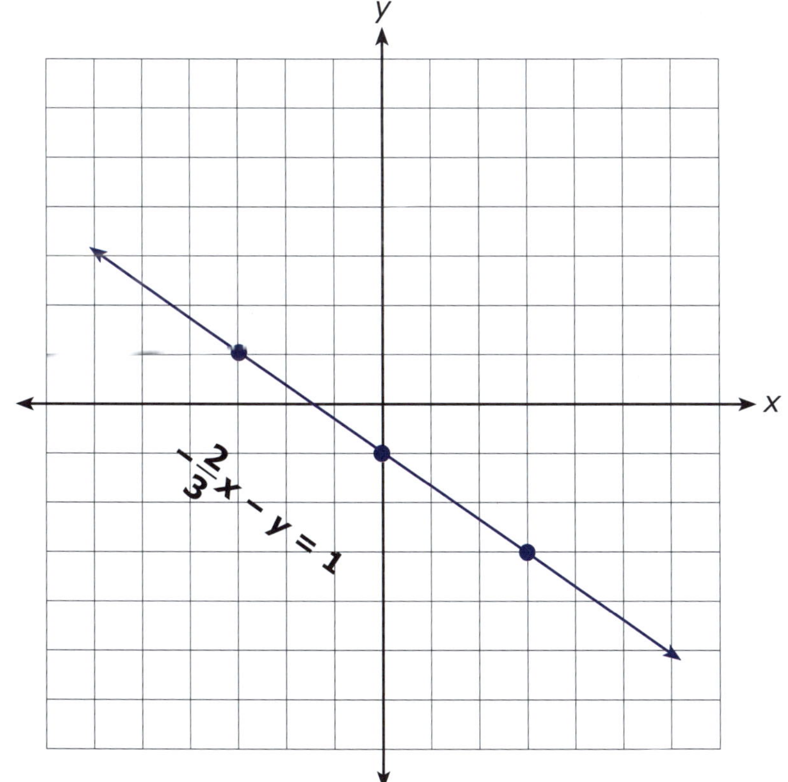

Solve for y: $-\frac{2}{3}x - y = 1$

$$-y = \frac{2}{3}x + 1$$

Add $\frac{2}{3}x$ on each side.

$$y = -\frac{2}{3}x - 1$$

Multiply each term by -1.

Start at $(0, -1)$. The slope is $-\frac{2}{3}$.

$-\frac{2}{3} = \frac{-2}{3} = \frac{2}{-3}$ Go down two units and to the right 3 units, OR go up to units and to the left 3 units.

A line with a negative slope rises toward the left.

Types of Slopes

A.

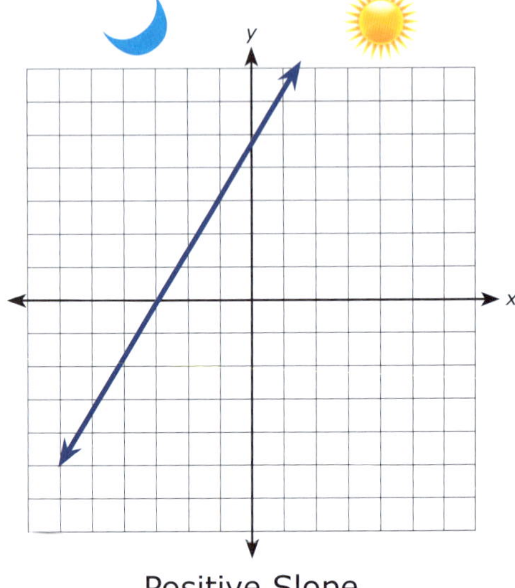

Positive Slope

C.

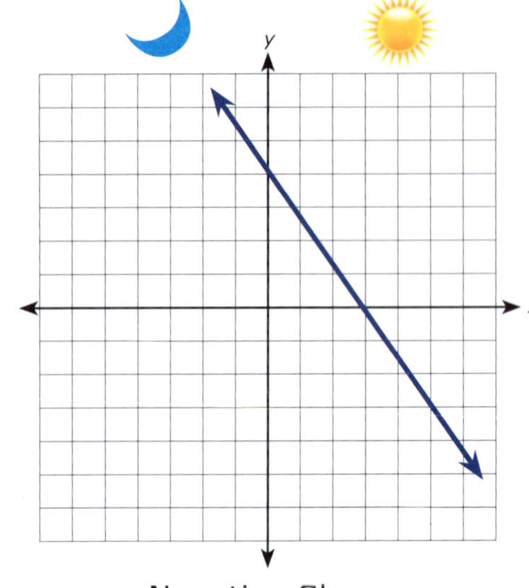

Negative Slope

B.

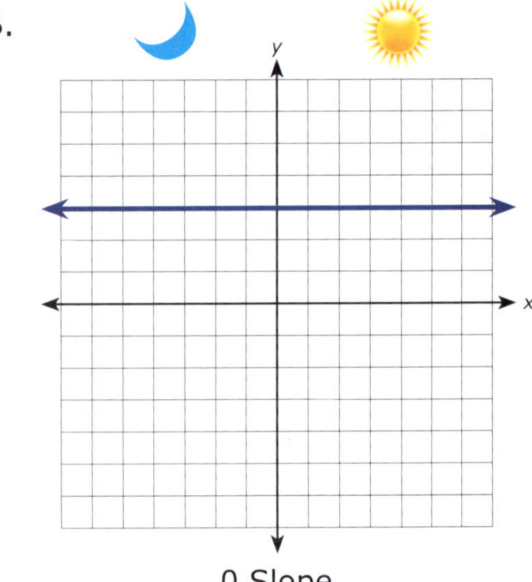

0 Slope

D.

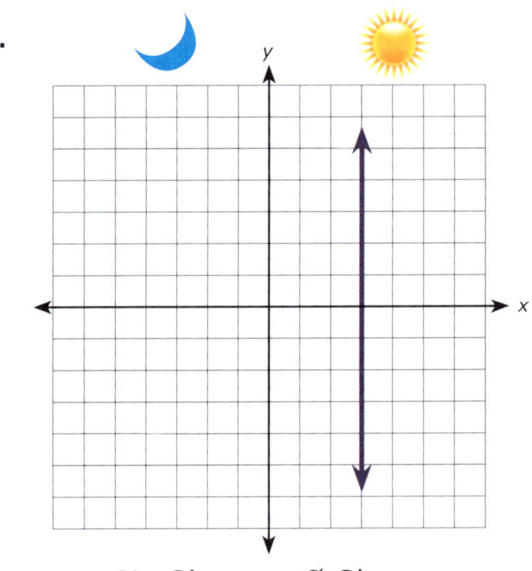

No Slope or Ø Slope

If a line points toward the right (sun), then its slope is positive. If a line points toward the left (moon), then its slope is negative.

Practice

Which of these equations match the graphs above? Explain your thinking.

______ 1. $y = 3$ ______________________________

______ 2. $x = 3$ ______________________________

______ 3. $y = \frac{5}{3}x + 5$ ______________________________

______ 4. $y = -\frac{4}{3}x + 4$ ______________________________

5. Write $y = 3$ in slope/intercept form. ______________

6. Which of the following slopes, $\frac{0}{5}$ or $\frac{5}{0}$ would indicate a vertical line?

   Why? ____

Solve the following equations for *y*. Write your answer in slope/intercept form. Then state the slope *m* and the *y*-intercept *b*.

7. $2y = 4x - 4$

   $m =$ ____ , $b =$ ____

8. $-y = 3x - 2$

   $m =$ ____ , $b =$ ____

9. $3y = -9$

   $m =$ ____ , $b =$ ____

10. $-x + y = 2$

   $m =$ ____ , $b =$ ____

11. $4y + 8x = -12$

   $m =$ ____ , $b =$ ____

12. $0 = 6x + y$

   $m =$ ____ , $b =$ ____

13. $-3y + 21 = -9x$

   $m =$ ____ , $b =$ ____

14. $4x + 5y = 20$

   $m =$ ____ , $b =$ ____

15. $-\frac{4}{5}x + 4y = 16$

   $m =$ ____ , $b =$ ____

16. $\frac{2}{3}y = -20$

   $m =$ ____ , $b =$ ____

Graph the following equations using your own graph paper. Use the slope/y-intercept method of graphing. Please graph #17 and #22 on the same coordinate plane. Also graph #18 and #20 together on a separate coordinate plane.

17. $y = 2x - 4$
18. $-y = -\frac{2}{3}x + 5$
19. $x = 2.5$
20. $y = -\frac{3}{2}x + 2$
21. $3x - y = 2$
22. $4y = 8x - 4$
23. $y = -x + 2$
24. $\frac{1}{3}y = x + 1$
25. $10x + 5y = -10$

Answer the following.

26. Compare the slopes of equation #17 and equation #22. What do you notice?

____

Now compare their graphs. What do you notice?

____

27. When two equations that have the same slope then the lines are

____________________.

28. Compare the slopes of equation #18 and equation #22. What do you notice?

____________________.

Now compare their graphs. What do you notice?

____

29. When two equations have negative reciprocal slopes then the lines are

____________________.

30. What can you say about the graphs of equation #21 and #24? How can you be sure? Explain your thinking.

____

Finding Slope Given Two Points

Slope is defined as the change in *y* divided by the change in *x*. If you are given two points, you can find the slope by counting how to get from one point to another point.

Example: Find the slope of the line that connects (−3, −2) to (1, 3).

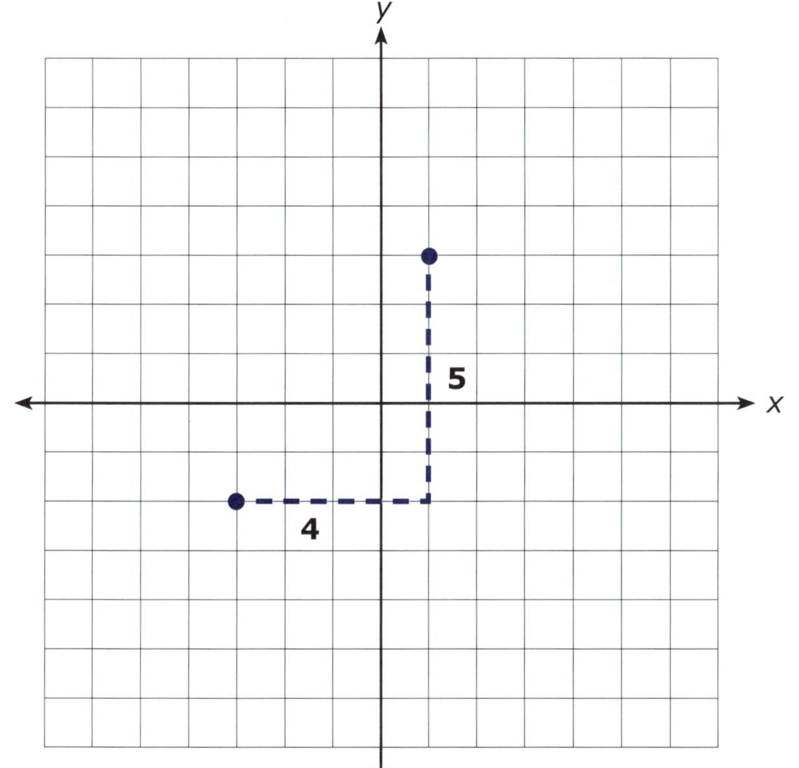

The slope is $\frac{5}{4}$.

m is used to represent slope.

Another way of finding slope is to use the slope formula below.

$$m = \frac{y^2 - y^1}{x_2 - x_1}$$

Take (−3, −2) and (1, 3). Take either *y* value to begin, but make sure you start with the *x* value that matches the *y* value you started with.

$$m = \frac{3 - (-2)}{1 - (-3)} = \frac{5}{4}$$

Using the slope formula will help you find the slope between two points that might be far away from each other or points that contain larger numbers too hard to count on your coordinate plane.

Practice

Find the slope of the line that connects these points using the slope formula.

Using parentheses really helps.

$\frac{(\ ) - (\ )}{(\ ) - (\ )}$ $\frac{\text{Change in } y}{\text{Change in } x}$

1. (0, 5) and (–4, 8)

6. (5, 0) and (–5, 2)

2. (–2, –5) and (0, 1)

7. (0, –24) and (–7, –23)

3. $(\frac{1}{2}, 4)$ and $(3\frac{1}{2}, 8)$

8. $(-2, 8\frac{1}{2})$ and $(-3, 7\frac{3}{4})$

4. (4, 5) and (3, 5)

9. (7, 1) and (8, 6)

5. (–2, 8) and (–2, 9)

10. (–3, –7) and (–4, –8)

Writing an Equation Given Two Points

Now that you know how to find the slope of a line given two points, you can write an equation.

Example: Write an equation for the line that connects (−2, −5) and (0, 1).

The slope of the line is $\frac{(1) - (-5)}{(0) - (-2)} = \frac{6}{2} = 3$

You have this equation $y = 3x + b$. How can you find b, the y-intercept? Since the line passes through (−2, −5) and (0, 1) if you plug in either one of those points, you will find b. Substitute (0, 1) in $y = 3x + b$.

$1 = 3(0) + b$

Solve for b: $1 = 0 + b$

$1 = b$ The equation $y = 3x + 1$.

Notice that if you had substituted (−2, −5), you would also get a y-intercept of 1.

$y = 3x + b$

$-5 = 3(-2) + b$

$-5 = -6 + b$

$1 = b$ (adding 6 to each side)

Practice

Given the information below, write the equation on the line. Use a separate sheet of paper to do your work.

1. $m = 4$ and $b = -5$ ____________________

2. $m = -3$ and $b = 0$ ____________________

3. $m = 0$ and $b = -2.5$ ____________________

4. $m = -2$ and passes through (0, 3) ____________________

5. $m = 3$ and passes through (1, 2) ______________________

6. passes through (–3, 5) and (–2, 7) ______________________

7. passes through (0, 4) and (–2, 8) ______________________

8. passes through (–2, 5) and (3, 5) ______________________

9. Graph #4 below.

10. Graph #8 below.

#4

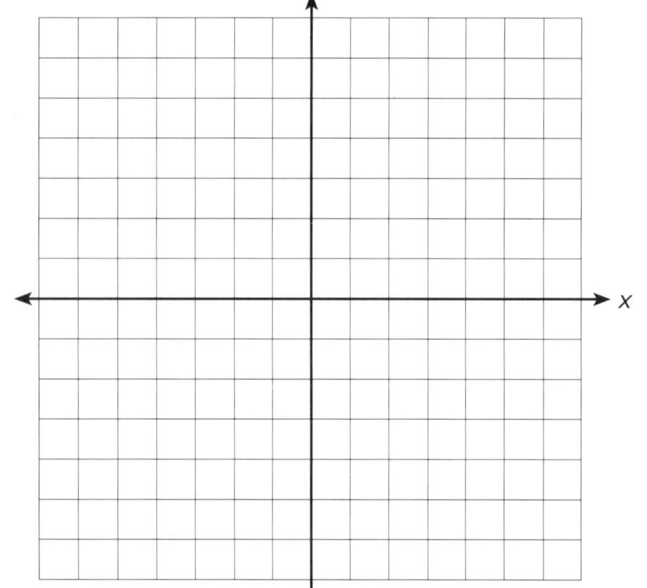

#8

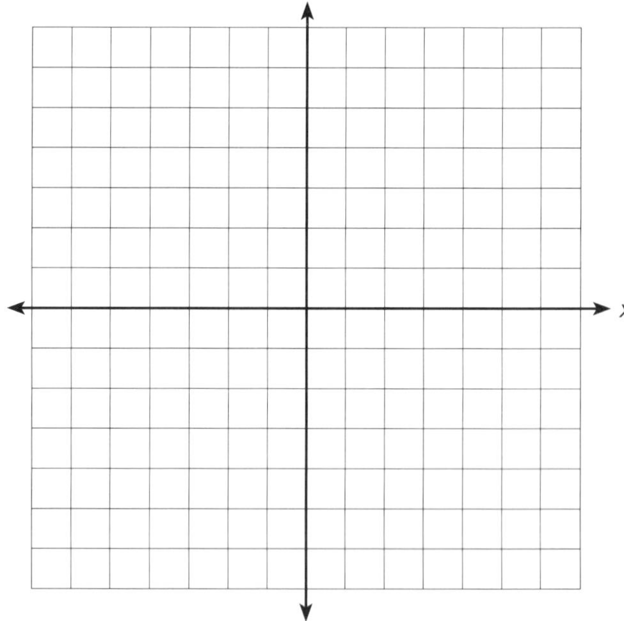

Graphs of Proportional Relationships

Graphs visually help us find information, show us growth or decline, and help us determine trends and predict answers. They even show us when a set of data has no pattern. Graphs of proportional relationships (like those you learned in Chapter 4) are unique. All proportional relationships have the equation $y = kx$ (or $y = mx$) where k (or m) is called the constant of proportionality. The y-intercept is 0.

Example 1: Around Valentine's Day a rose costs $2.00. Let r = rose and c = cost and graph this relationship. What is the equation? What is the constant of proportionality?

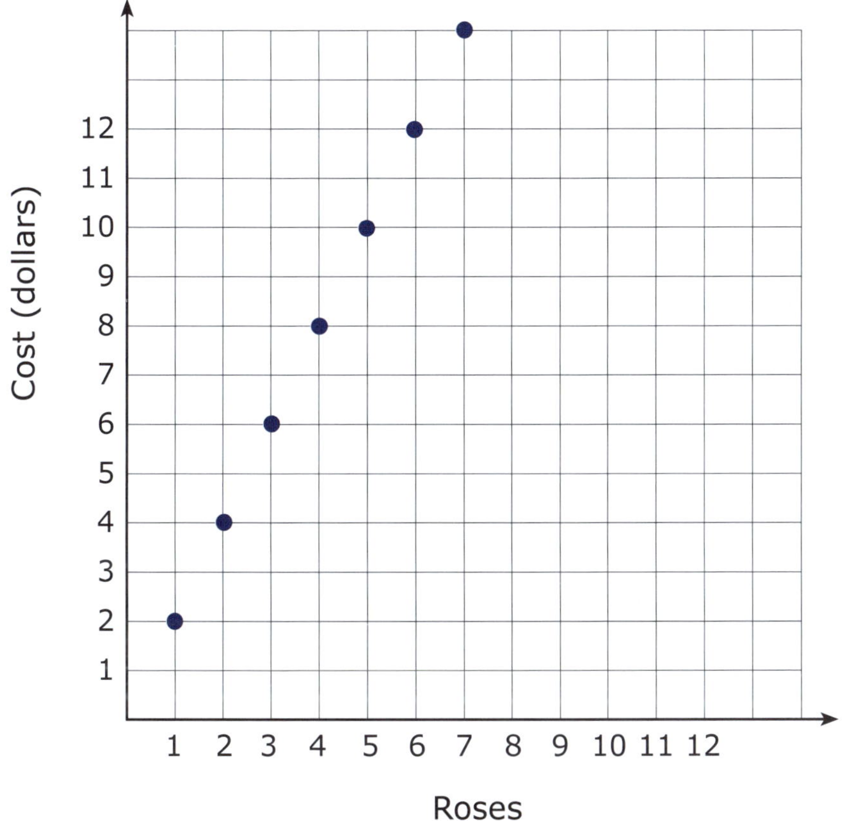

The graph is a "straight line" that goes through (0,0).

The points are not connected because you cannot buy part of a rose.

The equation is $c = 2r$. The constant of proportionality is 2 (the slope). If you divide $\frac{c}{r}$ or $\frac{y}{x}$, you get the constant of proportionality.

Example 2: Using the equation $c = 2r$ from the graph above, how much would you pay for 24 roses? How many roses would $72 buy?

$c = 2r$	$c = 2r$
$c = 2(24)$	$72 = 2r$
$c = \$48$	$36 = r$ (divide by 2)
You would pay $48 for 24 roses.	With $72 you can buy 36 roses.

Practice

Answer the following.

1. A can of three tennis balls is on sale for $2.50. Finish the table below.

No. of Cans	0	1	2	4	6	10	12
Price ($)		2.50					

   a. Is this a proportional relationship? Why or why not? Explain your thinking.

   ____

   ____

   b. Write the equation using c for cans and p for price. ____________

   c. What is the constant of proportionality? ____________

2. Last year for a school trip 190 students paid $1,567.50. This year 200 students have to pay a total of $1,650. Is this a proportional relationship? Explain your thinking.

   ____

   ____

   If so, what is the constant of proportionality? ____________

3. Which of these tables show a proportional relationship?

a.

x	y
2	5
4	9
10	21
12	25

b.

x	y
0	0
3	9
4	12
6	18

c.

x	y
0	2
1	5
2	8
3	11

d.

x	y
2	9
3	11
4	13
5	15

e.

x	y
2	2
3	3
4	4
5	5

f.

x	y
5	2
6	3
7	4
20	17

Explain your thinking. ______________________________

____

4. Write the equations for Table a ___________ ,Table b ___________ , and Table e ___________.

5. Look at Table c. Can you see that the rate of change is 3? ($2 + 3 = 5$, $5 + 3 = 8$, $8 + 3 = 11$). If $x = 0$ then y is 2. Write the equation that is shown by the Table c). ___________

6. What is the equation for Table d? Hint: Find the rate of change and the y-intercept. Remember the y-intercept is found when $x = 0$. ___________

7. What is the equation for Table f ? ___________

8. Look at the table at the right.

x	y
1	2.5
2	3
3	3.5
4	4

   a. What is the rate of change? ____ Explain your thinking.

   ____

   b. When $x = 0$, find y ____. Explain your thinking.

   ____

   c. Write the equation ___________. Is it a proportional relationship?

   d. Why or why not? Explain your thinking. ______________________

   ____

9. Club Fitness One charges \$60 a month for a regular membership. Island Gym charges a one time fee of \$200 and \$20 a month for a regular membership. Let m = month and c = cost.

   a. Write an equation for Club Fitness One. ___________

   b. Write an equation for Island Gym. ___________

   c. Which of the two clubs has a proportional relationship between cost and months of membership? Explain your thinking.

   ____

   ____

10. On the grid provided below graph both equations to problem 9.

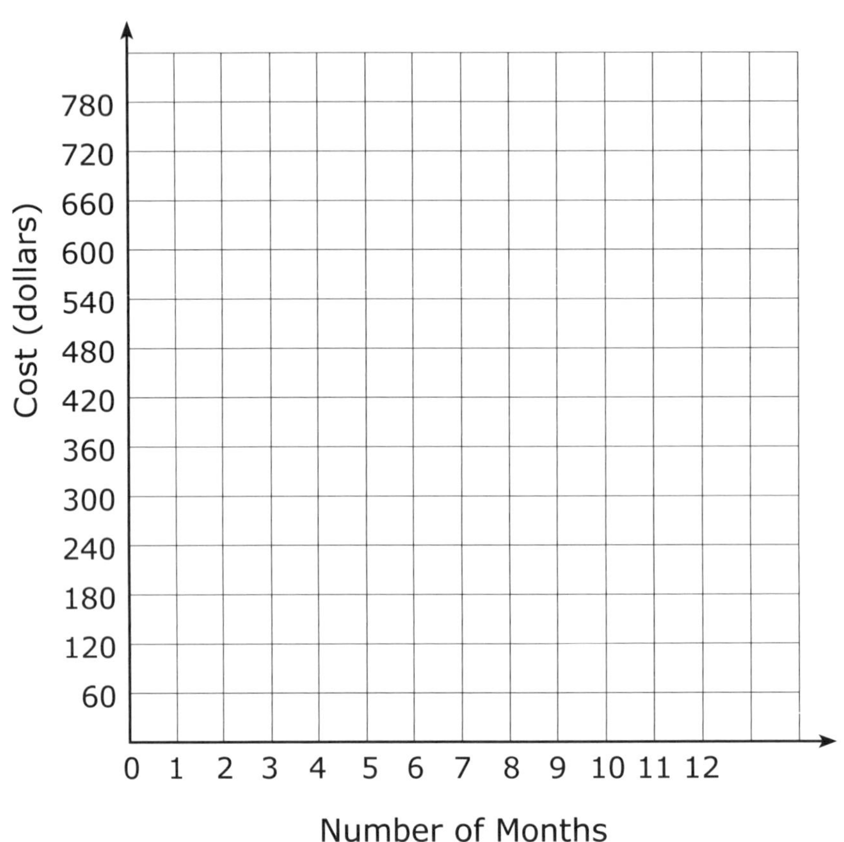

a. Which membership is cheaper if a person wants to join for only 3 months? Explain your thinking.

____

b. What is the cost of each membership at month 5? ____________

c. After month 5, which membership is the better deal, assuming both gyms are of equal quality? Explain your thinking.

____

d. What is the difference in cost at one year of membership? Show your work.

____

Systems of Equations

A system of equations is one or more equations that are solved together.

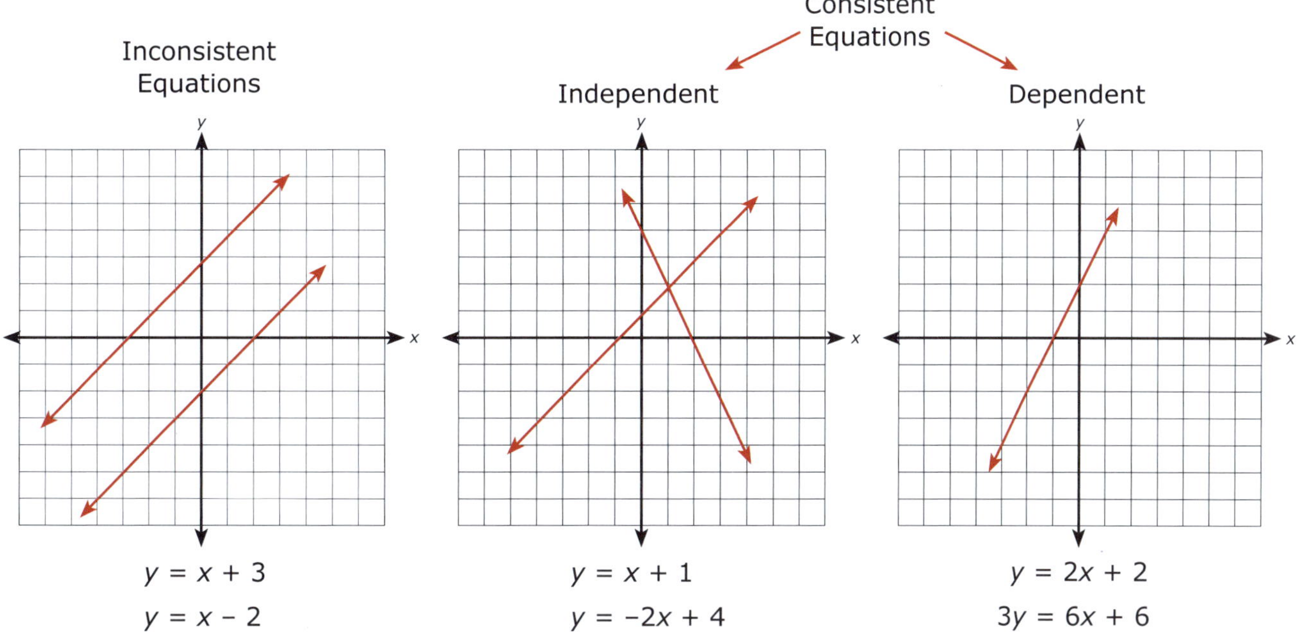

Practice

1. What do you notice about the slopes of the inconsistent equations shown above? Explain your thinking.

___

___

2. What is the solution to the lines $y = x + 1$ and $y = -2x + 4$? Look at the middle graph and show why your answer is correct.

___

___

3. Why are $y = 2x + 2$ and $3y = 6x + 6$ the same equation? Explain your thinking.

___

___

Graph the following systems of equations to find a solution, if any.

4. $2x + y = 6$

$x + y = 1$

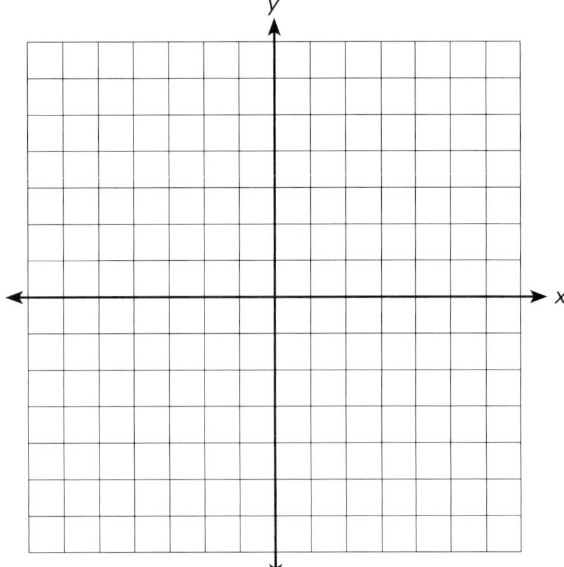

6. $x + y = -1$

$2x + y = -2$

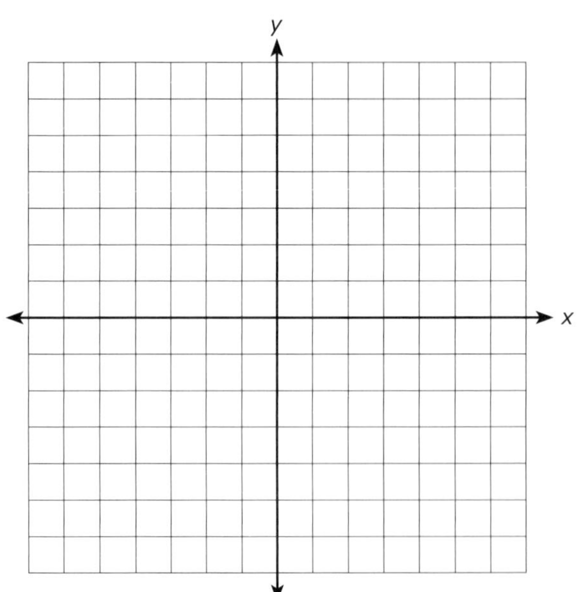

5. $2x + y = 5$

$3x - y = 5$

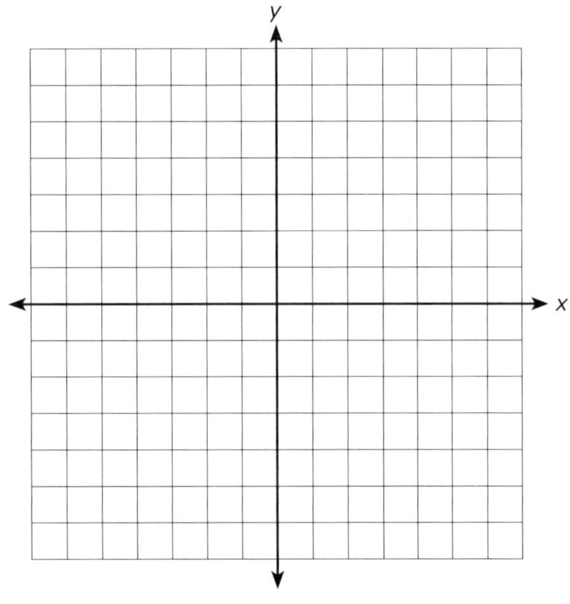

7. $y = x - 3$

$y = -2x - 3$

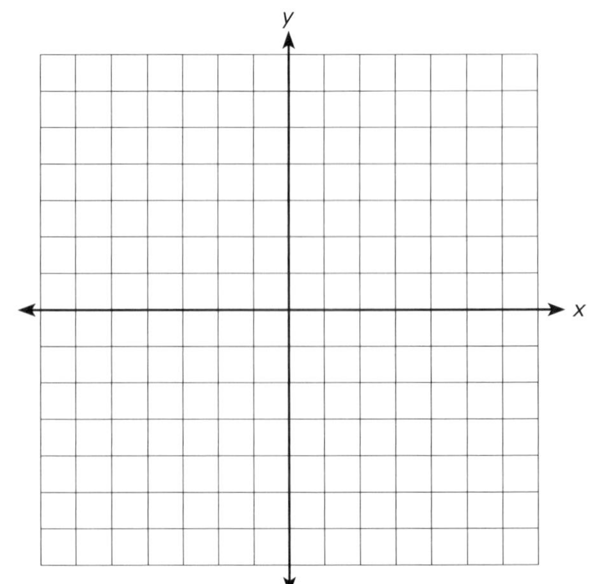

8. $2x + y = -6$

$x - y = 3$

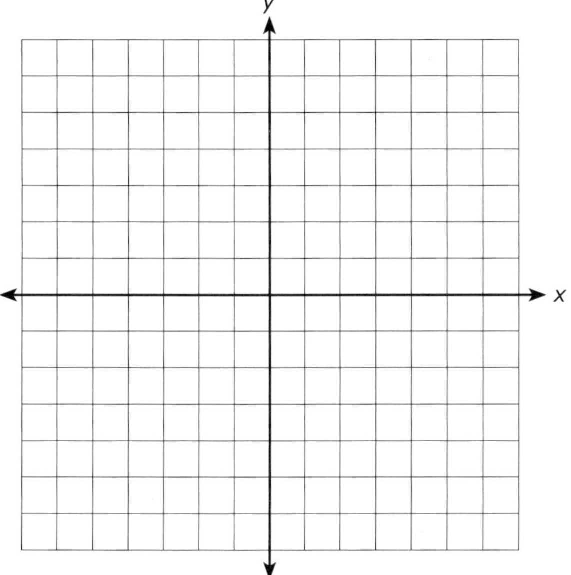

10. $y = 3x - 1$

$2y - 6x = -2$

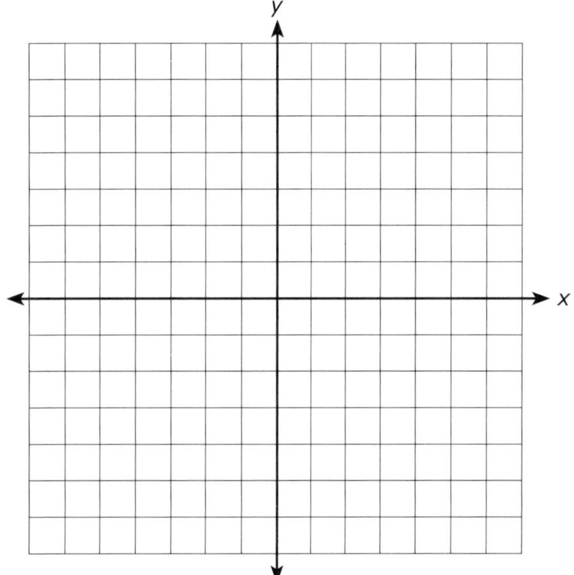

9. $-x + y = 5$

$y - x = 1$

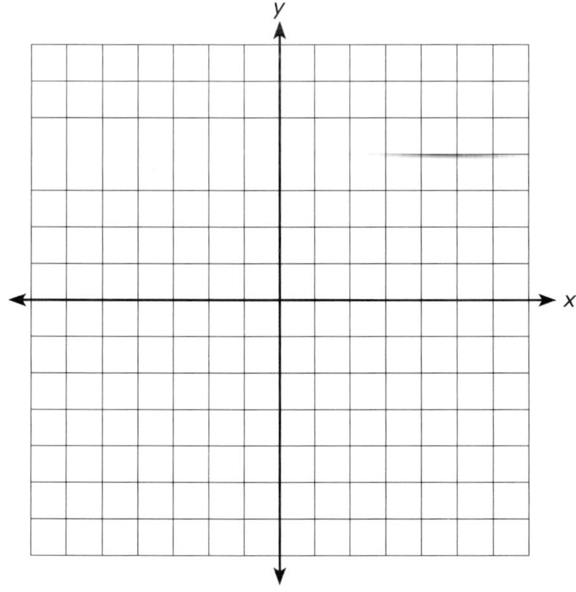

11. Is (−2.5, −3) the solution to this system of equations? ___________

$x - y = .5$

$2x + 2y = -11$

Show your work:

Chapter 12 Review

Tell in which quadrant or axes each of these points are found?

1. (−3, 4) __________
2. (5, −6) __________
3. (−10, −2) __________
4. (0, 14) __________
5. (−12, 0) __________
6. (5, 15) __________

Graph the following equations using the given tables.

7. $y = 2x - 3$

x	y
−2	
−1	
0	
1	
2	
3	

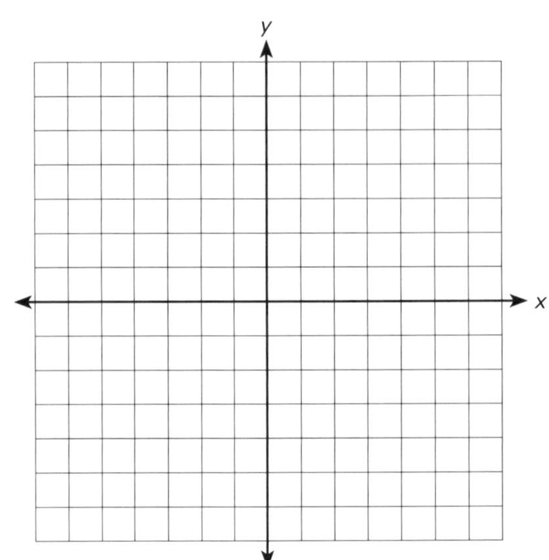

8. $y = -\frac{1}{4}x + 1$

x	y
−4	
−2	
0	
2	
4	
3	

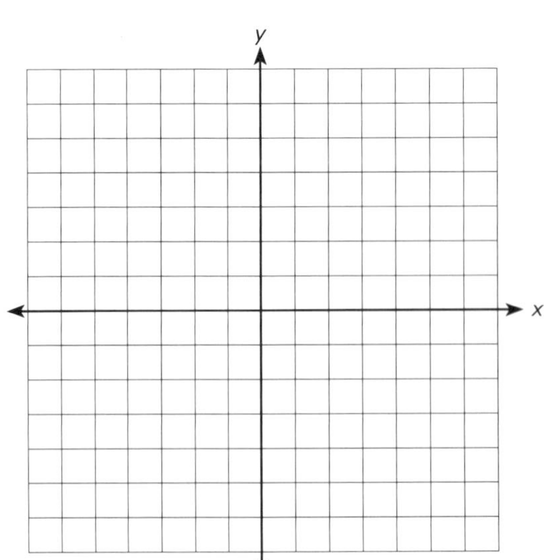

Solve for y:

9. $3x - y = 6$
10. $4x + 8y = 4$
11. $-y = 6 + 2x$
12. $4x - y = 6$
13. $-5y = 10x - 15$
14. $8 + 2x - y = 0$

Graph the following. Use your own graph paper.

15. $y = 5$

16. $x = -3.5$

17. $y = 0$

18. $2x - y = 4$

19. $y = \frac{3}{4}x - 1$

20. $y = -\frac{4}{3}x - 1$

21. What can you say about the graphs of #19 and#20?

____

Find the slope of the line that passes by these points.

22. (−5, 6) and (0, 7)

23. (3, 5) and (−2, −5)

24. (2, 3) and (2, 6)

25. (−4, 5) and (2, 5)

Write the equation of the line given the information below.

26. $m = 5$ and $b = -2$

27. $m = -2$ and passes through (4, 8)

28. Line passes through (5, 6) and (5, −3)

29. Line has these points shown on this table.

x	y
1	3
2	6
3	9
4	12
5	15

30. Why is the relationship shown in problem #29 a proportional relationship? What is the constant of proportionality?

____

31. Lucia earns $8.00 an hour babysitting. Her cousin Miriam gets $10 as a flat fee and $6.00 an hour after that. Graph their earnings and then answer the questions.

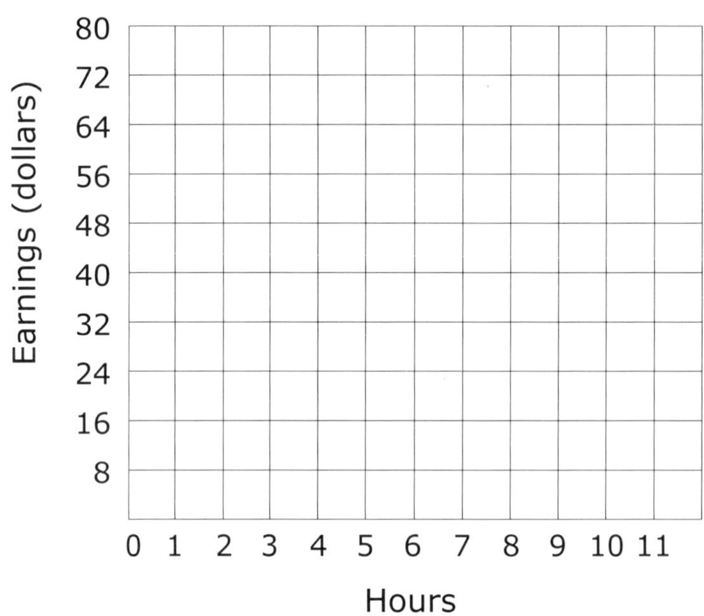

a. Which graph represents a proportional relationship? Explain your thinking.

____

b. Which variable is the independent variable? __________ Why?

____

c. Write an equation to represent their earnings.

Lucia: __________ Miriam: __________

d. How much does Lucia and Miriam make in 5 hours of babysitting?

____________________.

e. If Miriam made $70 babysitting, how many hours did she work?

____________________.

Find the solution (if possible) to these systems of equations by graphing.

32. $2x - y = 4$

$x - y = 1$

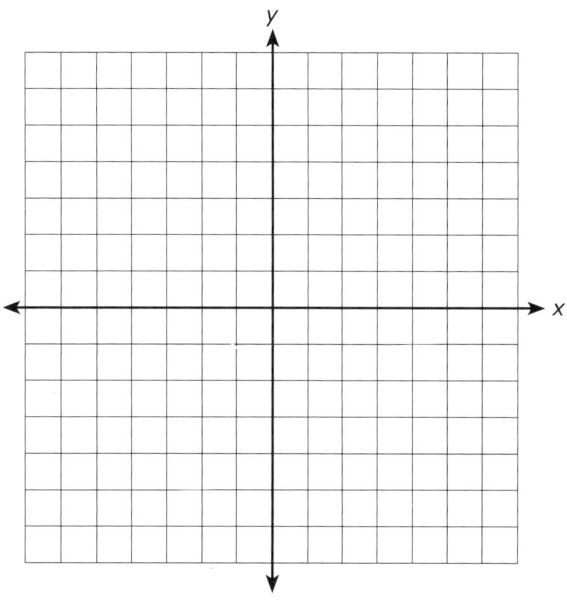

The above equation is classified as consistent and ________________ because it has ________________ solution (s).

33. $y - 3x = 0$

$y = 3x - 4$

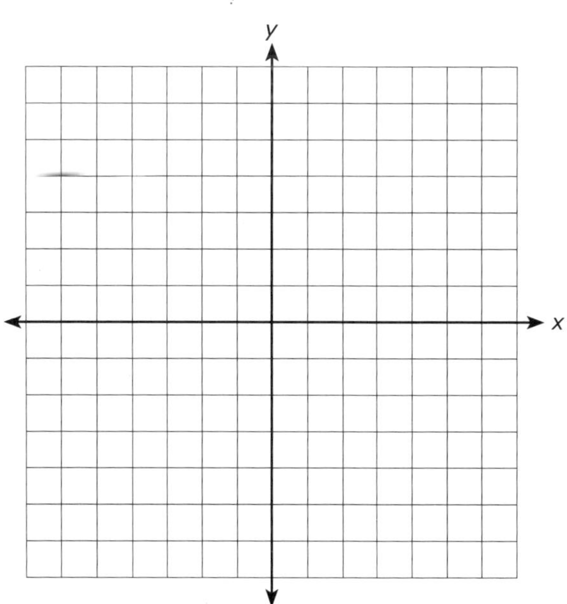

The above equation is classified as ________________ because it has ________________ solution (s).

Chapter 13

Transformations and Congruency

In this chapter, you will be learning the different ways you can move or transform figures on a plane. There are four types of transformations: translation (a slide), reflection (a flip), rotation (turning a figure about fixed point), and dilation (shrinking or enlarging in proportion).

Rigid transformations (translation, reflections, and rotations) do not change the original image. The figure remains congruent (having the same size and shape). Non-rigid transformations (dilations) can change the size of the original shape as long as the result is in proportion to the original shape.

The figure you start with is called the "preimage" and the result is called the "image."

Translations

To slide or translate a figure, every point is moved the same distance in the same direction. Sometimes a vector is used to perform a translation. A vector looks like a ray with an endpoint and an arrowhead. A vector indicates direction and distance.

Example 1: Translate ΔABC using vector $\overrightarrow{DE}$.

Translate (or slide) the triangle in the direction of the vector and only for the length of the vector (from point D to E).

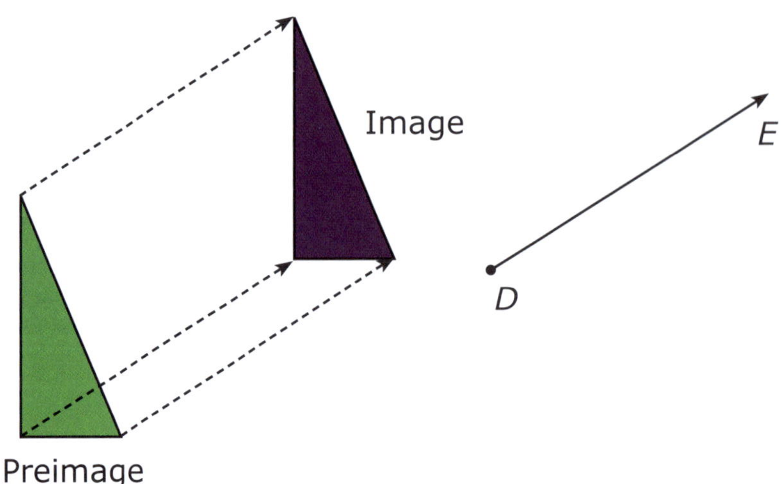

Can you see that the resulting image is congruent to its preimage?

When you translate on a coordinate plane, another notation is often used. $T_{a,b}$ (x, y). You add a to the x value and b to the y value to get the new image $(x + a, y + b)$.

Example 2: Translate ΔABC by using this translation $T_{5,\,-3}$.

Each vertex moves 5 units to the right and 3 units down.

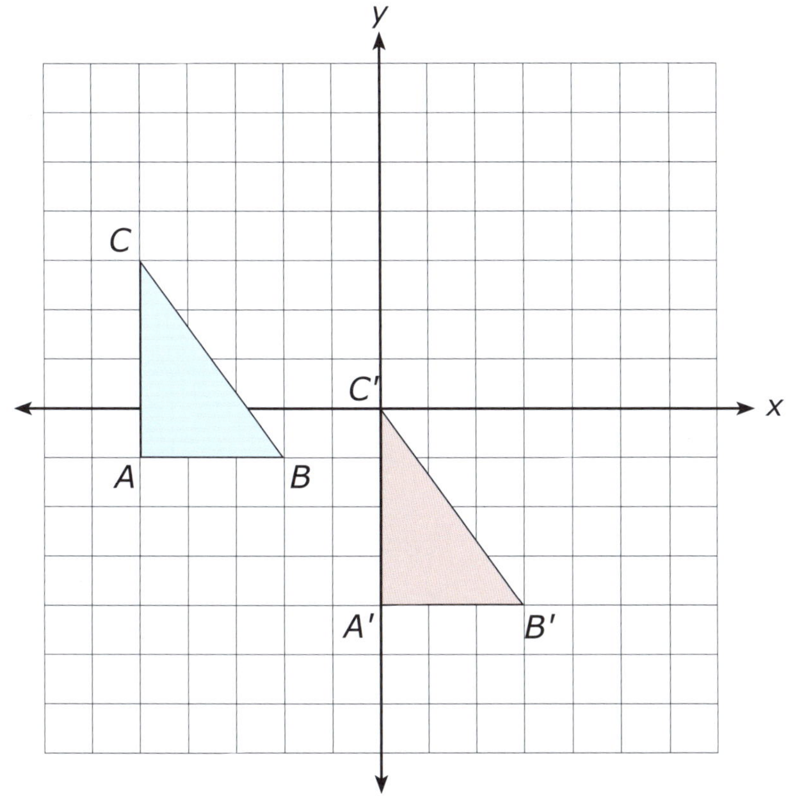

The image is now called $A'B'C'$. This is read as A prime, B prime, C prime.

Practice

1. Is the distance from A to B the same as from A' to B'? How about from A to C as compared from A' to C'? Explain your thinking.

____

2. What is the distance from B to C? ________ How does it compare to the distance from B' to C'? Explain your thinking.

____

3. Does every translation preserve congruency? ________ How do you know?

____

4. Translate point D and E using vector $\overrightarrow{AB}$. Label your images D' and E'.

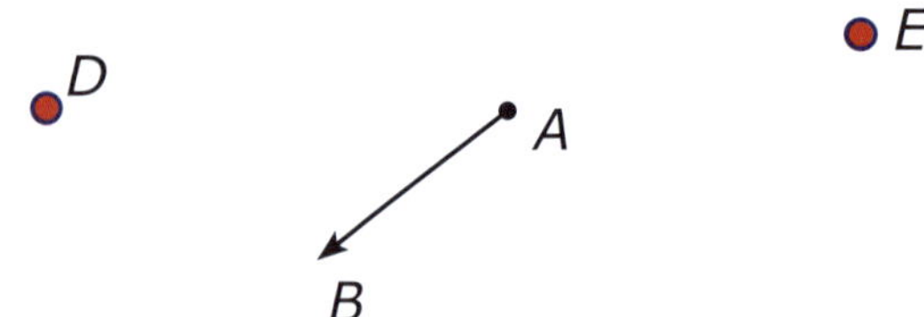

5. Translate ΔFTQ using vector $\overrightarrow{PR}$. Label your image $\Delta F'T'Q'$.

6. Translate rectangle $ABCD$ using the translation $T_{-2,\,-7}$. Label your image $A'B'C'D'$.

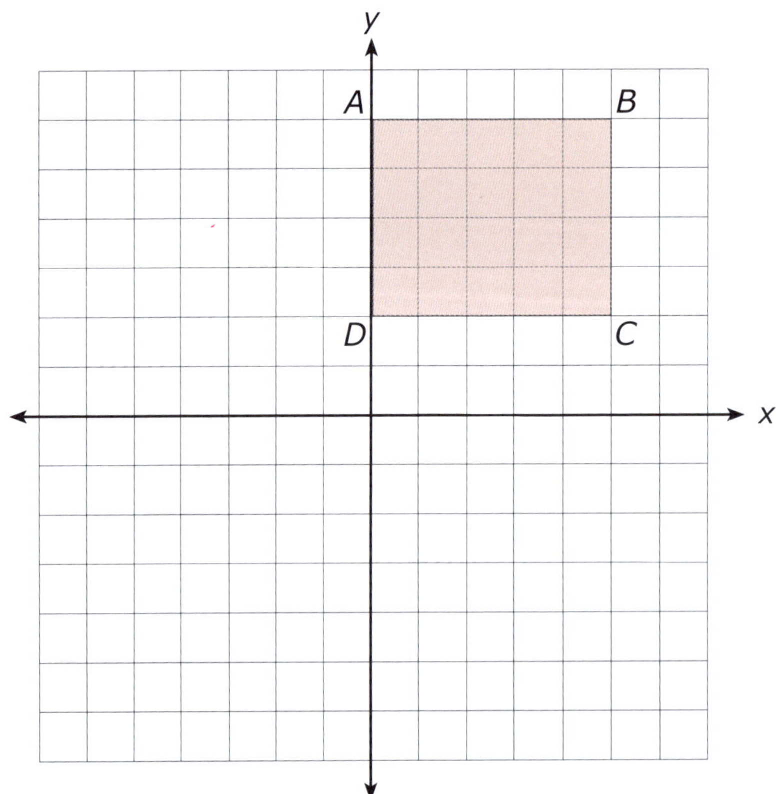

Is your image congruent to your preimage? How do you know?

____

7. Translate ΔRET using the translation $T_{4,-2}$. Label your image $\Delta R'E'T'$.

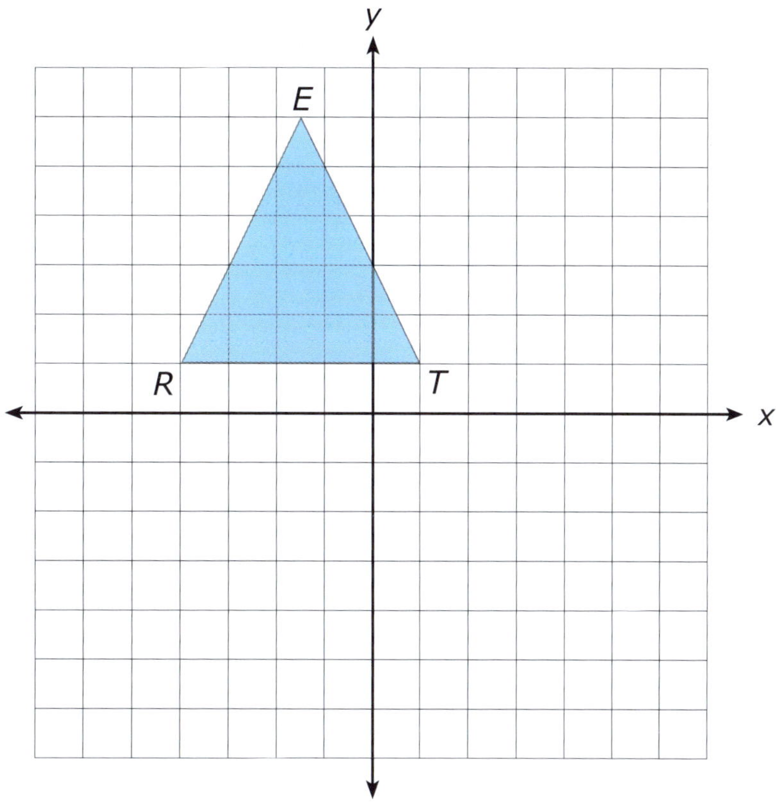

a. Is it possible for two triangles to have the same area and not be congruent? Explain your thinking with an example.

____

____

b. When two triangles have three corresponding sides congruent, are their corresponding angles also congruent (identical in size and shape)? Explain your thinking.

____

____

8. Which vector was used to translate $\angle A$ to $\angle A'$?

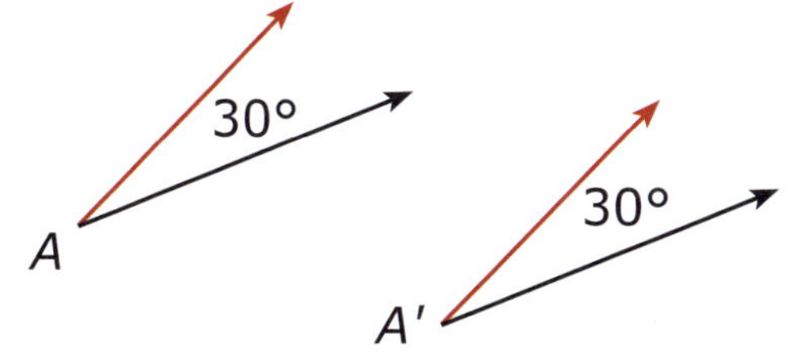

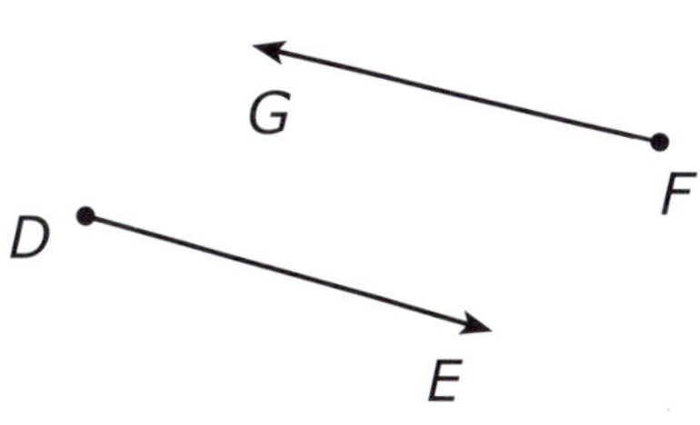

Reflections

A reflection is another rigid transformation where a figure is flipped or reflected about a given line of symmetry or about a point.

Example 1: Reflect ΔABC about the y-axis. Label your image.

Another way to say this is to say $r_{y\text{-axis}}$.

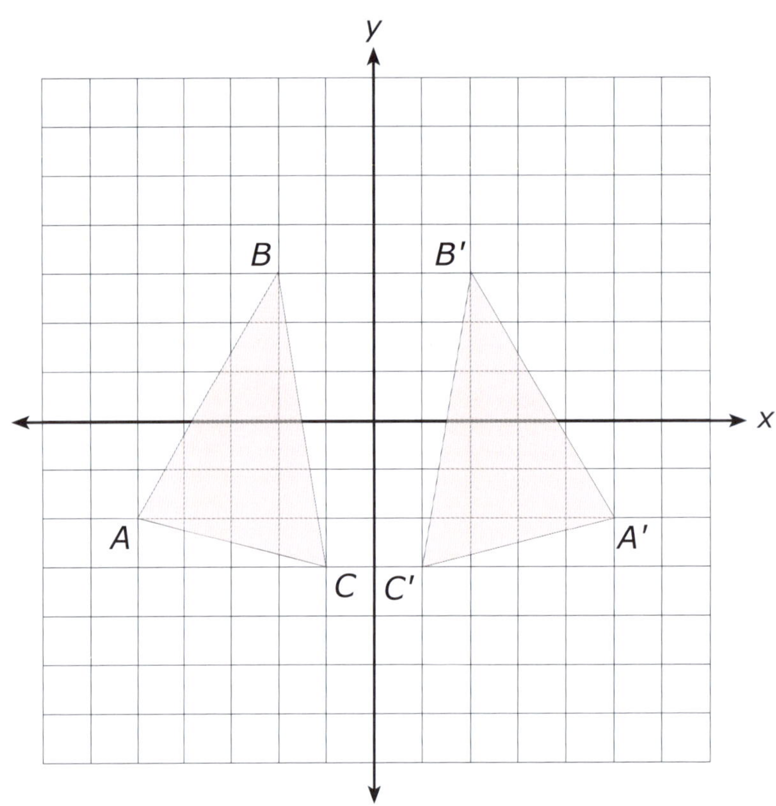

Practice

Answer the following questions based on Example 1.

1. List the ordered pairs of ΔABC and those of $\Delta A'B'C'$.

   A _________ A' _________ B _________ B' _________

   C _________ C' _________

2. Which value in the ordered pair changed, the *x* or the *y* value? ____________.

3. If you had reflected ΔABC about the *x*-axis, which value would you expect would change? ____________. Why? Explain your thinking.

   ____

   ____

Example 2: Reflect ΔTRS about the origin.

Remember that the origin is the point (0, 0). When you reflect about the origin, (x, y) will become $(-x, -y)$.

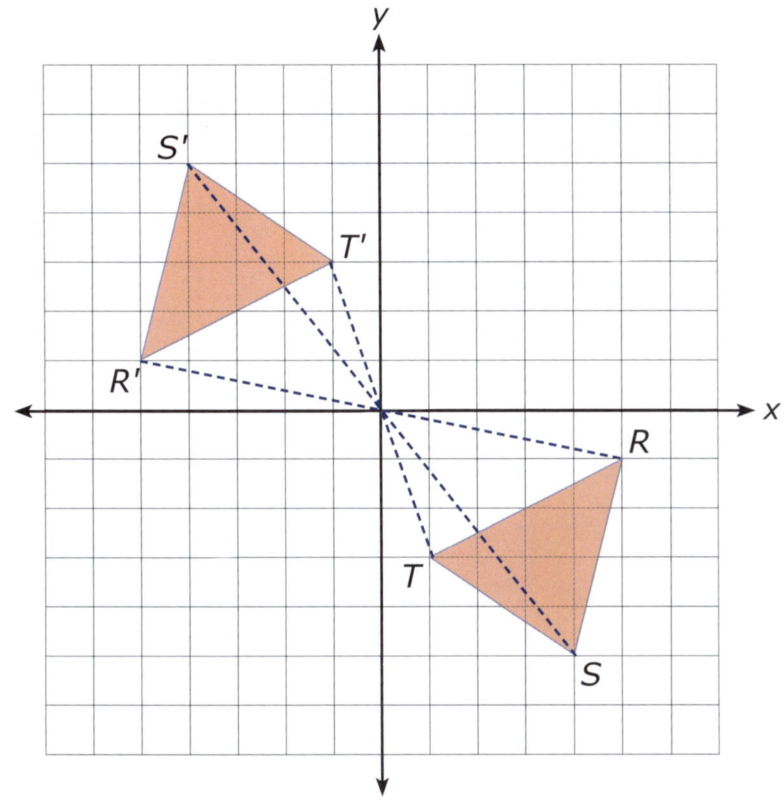

$T(1, -3) \dashrightarrow T'(-1, 3)$

$R(5, -1) \dashrightarrow R'(-5, 1)$

$S(4, -5) \dashrightarrow S'(-4, 5)$

Practice

1. In the example above, which point is the midpoint (halfway point) between R and R'? ________? How about between T and T'? ________ , and between S and S'? ________?

2. If point (3, −2) is reflected about the origin, what is its image? ________.

3. Reflect the point A (3, −2) about the x-axis and label it A' ________. Now reflect A' about the y-axis and label it A'' (a double prime) ________.

4. Compare your final answer to #3 to your answer to #2. What do you notice? Explain your thinking. ____

____

5. Reflect each of the following according to this rule, $r_{y\text{-axis}}$.

   a. (3, 4) ____________ b. (−5, −6) ____________

   c. (−2, 5) ____________ d. (0, 10) ____________

Example 3: Reflect the following about the line $y = x$.

Remember the line $y = x$ from the last chapter? When you reflect about the line $y = x$, the point (x, y) becomes (y, x).

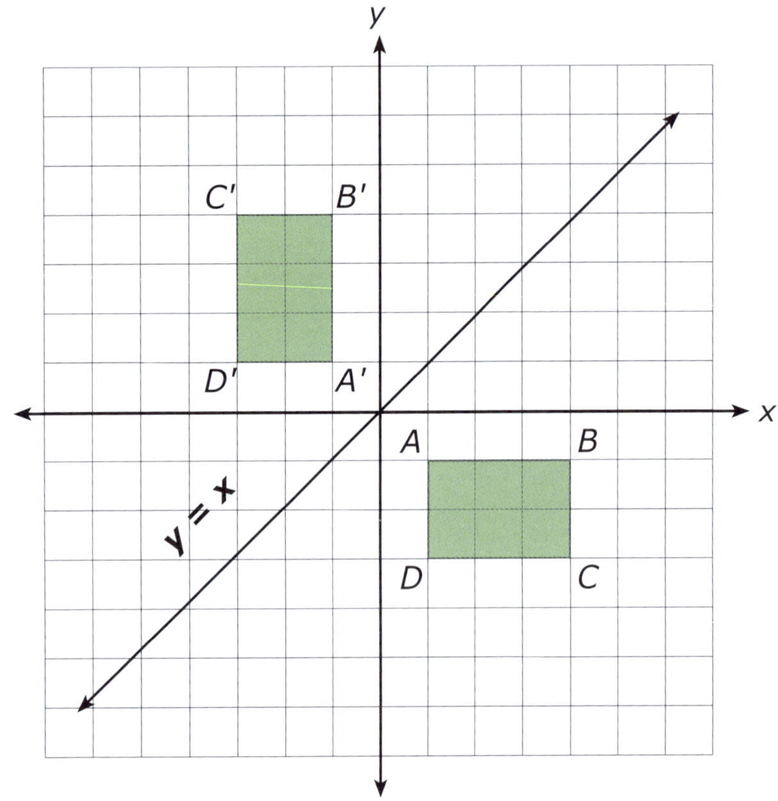

A (1, −1) --➔ A' (−1, 1)

B (4, −1) --➔ B' (−1, 4)

C (4, −3) --➔ C' (−3, 4)

D (1, −3) --➔ D' (−3, 1)

Practice

1. Using tracing paper, trace rectangle $ABCD$ and using the line $y = x$ as your line of symmetry, show how the image shown above is the correct reflection.

2. What would be the reflection of these points across the line $y = x$?

   a. (−2, 3) ____________ b. (0, 5) ____________

   c. (3, −5) ____________ d. (20, 30) ____________

3. Reflect A'B'C'D' about the line $x = 1$. List the ordered pairs of your new image.

   a. A'' ________ , b. B'' ________ , c. C'' ________ , d. D'' ________

4. Does a reflection guarantee congruency? How do you know? Explain your thinking. ____

   ____

Rotations

A rotation is the third rigid transformation where a figure on a plane is rotated about a fixed point at a given number of degrees. The most common angles of rotation are 90º, 180º, and 270º. You can rotate either clockwise or counterclockwise. However, when you see R_d an (*R* for rotation and d for degree), you always turn counterclockwise if *d* is positive.

You can use tracing paper for any of these rotations marking the fixed point with your pencil to verify your results.

Example 1: Rotate Δ*DEF* using R_{90° about the origin.

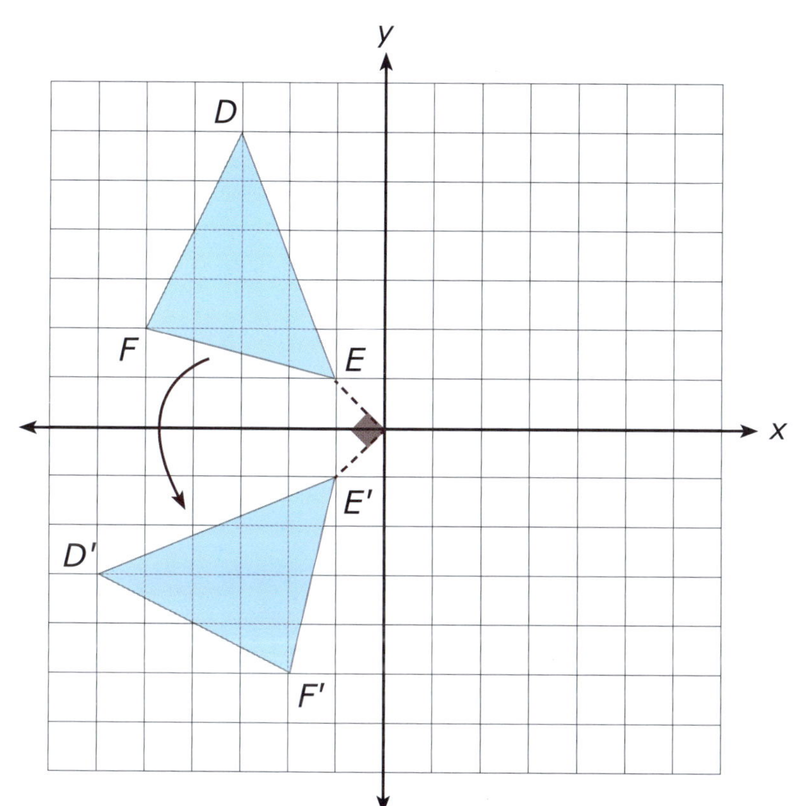

D (–3, 6) --→ *D'* (–6, –3)

E (–1, 1) --→ *E'* (–1, –1)

F (–5, 2) --→ *F'* (–2, –5)

It is easy to do this with tracing paper as long as you put your pencil on the origin and fix that point as you rotate. The *x* and the *y* values change places, and the signs of the image's ordered pairs match which quadrant the triangle ends up at. In quadrant III both signs are (–, –).

Once again, the image is congruent to the preimage.

Example 2: Rotate ΔABC using R_{180° about the origin. Label your image $A'B'C'$.

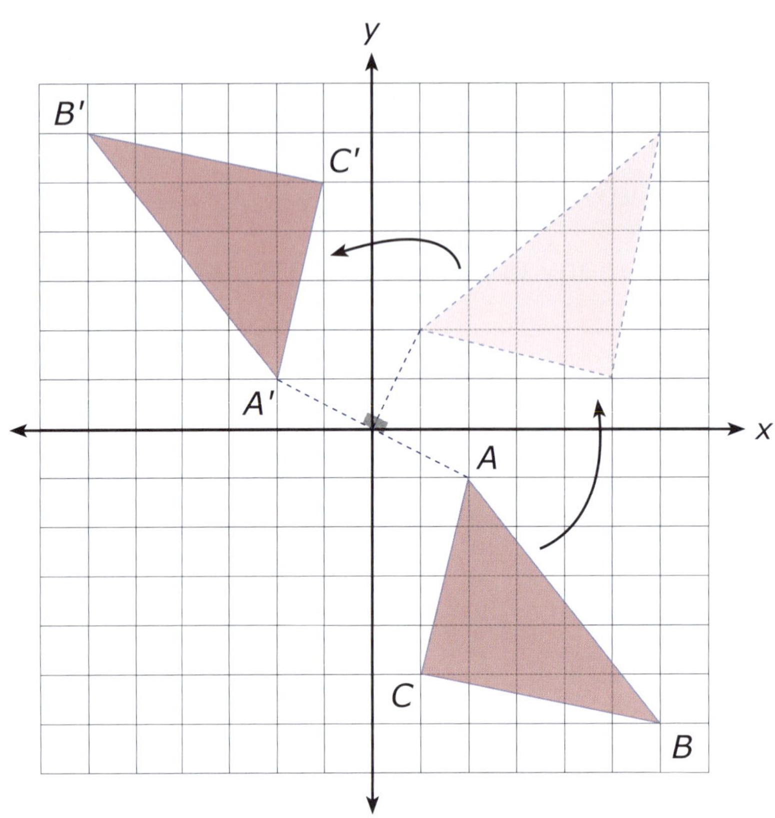

		After 90º Rotation		After Another 90º Rotation (180º)
A (2, −1)	--→	(1, 2)	--→	A' (−2, 1)
B (6, −6)	--→	(6, 6)	--→	B' (−6, 6)
C (1, −5)	--→	(5, 1)	--→	C' (−1, 5)

Practice

1. Compare the ordered pairs from the preimage ΔABC with the ordered pairs of the image $\Delta A'B'C'$. What happens to the x and y values under a 180º rotation? Explain your thinking.

____

____

2. If you now rotate $A'B'C'$ 90º counterclockwise one more time around the origin, what are the new coordinates of $A''B''C''$? Use tracing paper if you wish.

a. A'' __________ b. B'' __________ c. C'' __________

You can use tracing paper to help you do the following problems.

3. Translate the following objects using vector $\overrightarrow{RQ}$ shown.

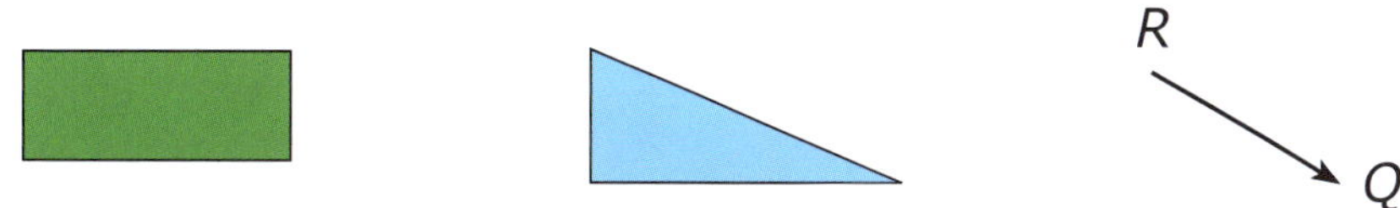

4. Triangle *ABC* has these coordinates: *A* (−3, 5), *B* (0, 2) and *C* (−6, −2). Translate ΔABC using this translation $T_{2,-2}$. Use your own graph paper. State the coordinates of *A′B′C′*.

A′ ________________ *B′* ________________ *C′* ________________

5. Using the figure below, perform the following transformations.

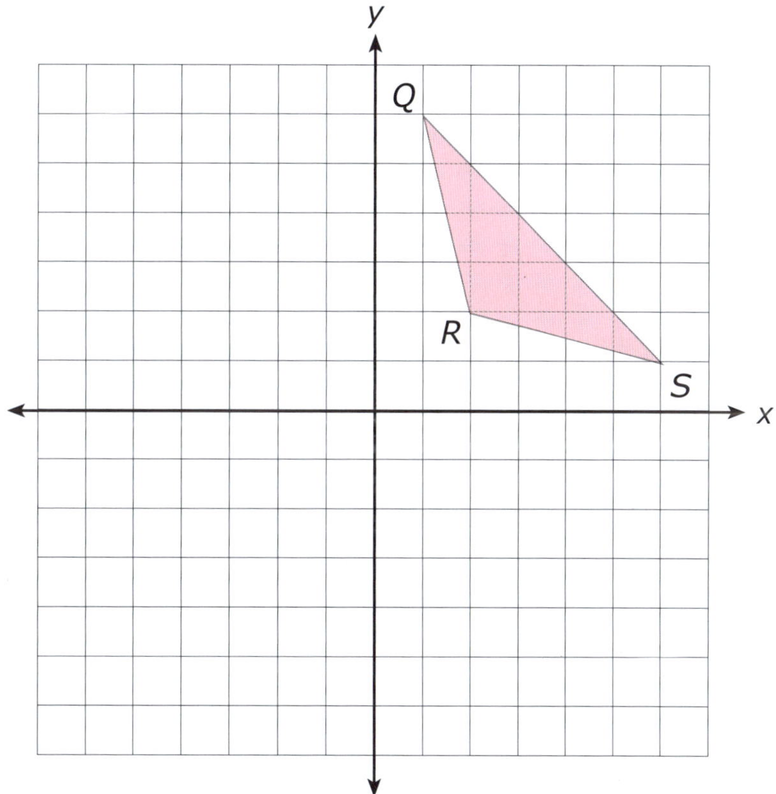

a. Reflect ΔQRS about the *y*-axis. *Q′* ________, *R′* ________, *S′* ________

b. Reflect ΔQRS about the origin. *Q′* ________, *R′* ________, *S′* ________

c. Rotate ΔQRS 270º counterclockwise about the origin.

Q′ ________, *R′* ________, *S′* ________

Understanding Triangle Congruency

You've seen how the rigid transformations, translation, reflection, and rotation, do not change the size and shape of the preimage. The symbol ≅ is used to indicate congruency. When two figures are congruent they are identical in size and shape. One is an exact copy of the other.

When you work with triangles, you can assure congruency if certain parts of the triangle remain identical. The first way to assure congruency between two triangles is SSS (Side, Side, Side).

SSS means that if the sides of two triangles are identical, then the triangles will be congruent.

Example: Are these triangles congruent?

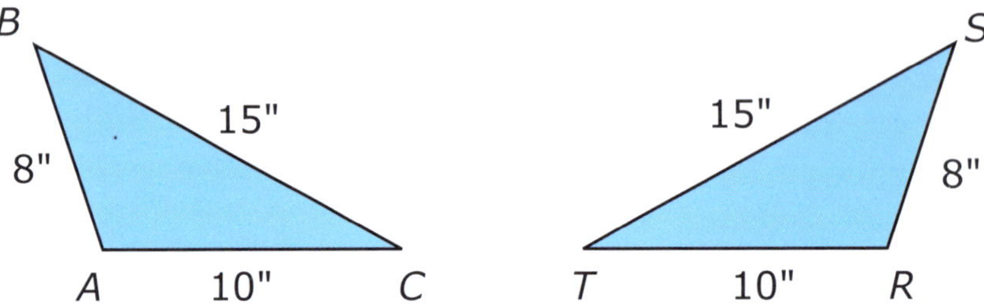

Yes! The corresponding sides are congruent to each other; $\Delta ABC \cong \Delta RST$ (make sure you state the corresponding vertices in order).

If two triangles are congruent by SSS, their corresponding angles will automatically be congruent to each other. This is because corresponding parts of congruent triangles are congruent (cpctc). Now that the triangles are congruent by SSS, you can state any of the following:

$$\angle A \cong \angle R$$
$$\angle B \cong \angle S$$
$$\angle C \cong \angle T$$

Now, take a look at this drawing. You only know two sides are congruent.

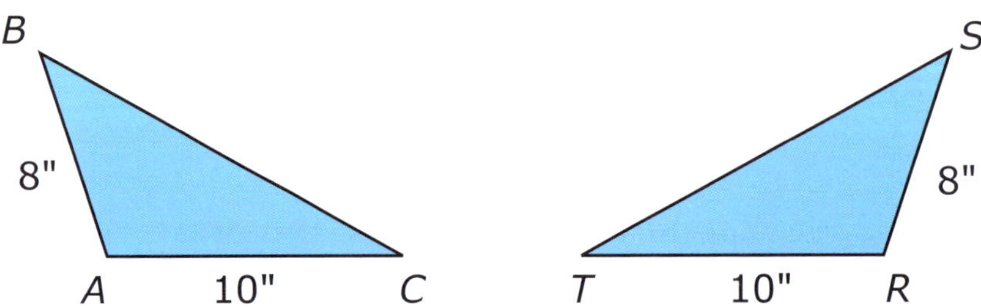

You have no information about segments $\overline{BC}$ and $\overline{ST}$. Could this happen?

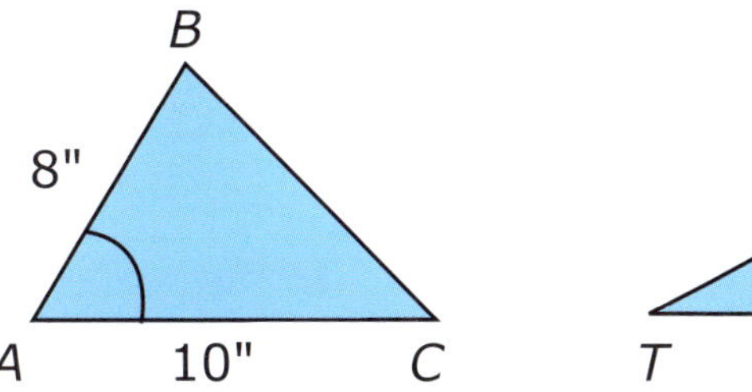

$\angle A$ and $\angle R$ can be different and now the triangles are no longer congruent!

Practice

1. Given two sides are congruent (as shown above), would making $\angle A$ congruent to $\angle R$ (angles that are in between the two congruent sides) guarantee that the triangles would return to being congruent? Explain your thinking.

____

____

2. Use the congruent angles shown and a ruler to extend one side 2" and the other side adjacent to the angle 3". Then close them to make a triangles. Are your triangles congruent? Trace and compare them.

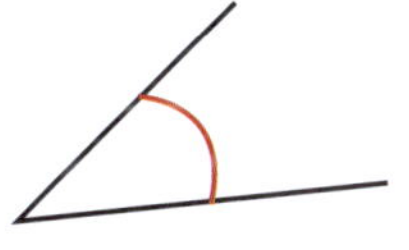

What conclusion can you make from the above experiment?

____

____

____

The above experiment should have led you to conclude that SAS (Side, Angle, Side) guarantees congruency between two triangles. In other words, if you know two sides are congruent, and the angle between those two sides is also congruent to those of another triangle in that order, then the two triangles are congruent.

Rely on the information given, not the shapes, to answer these questions.

3. Are these triangles congruent? Why or why not?

The "tick" marks shown indicate which sides are congruent.

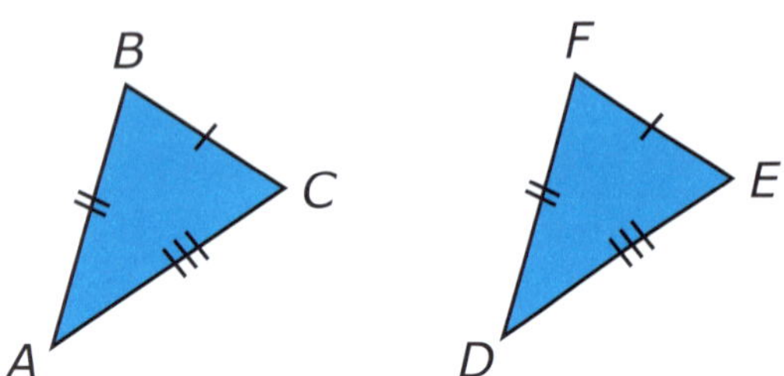

____

____

____

4. Are these triangles congruent? Why or why not?

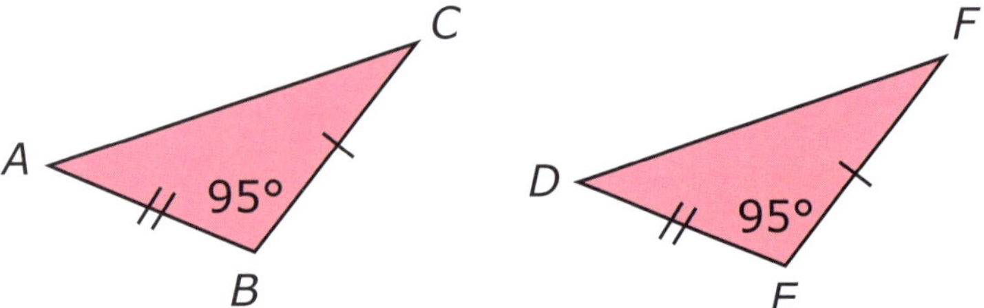

____

____

____

5. If $\Delta ABC \cong \Delta RST$ by SSS, then why is $\angle A \cong \angle R$?

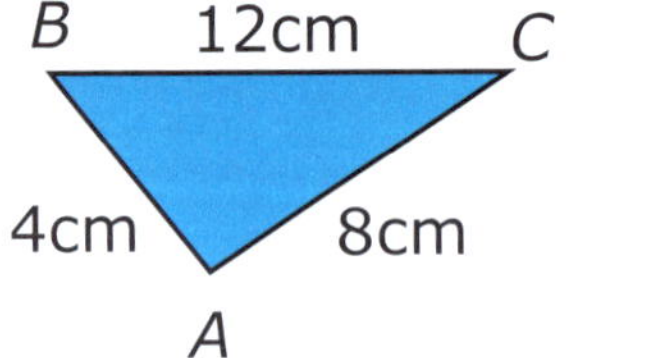

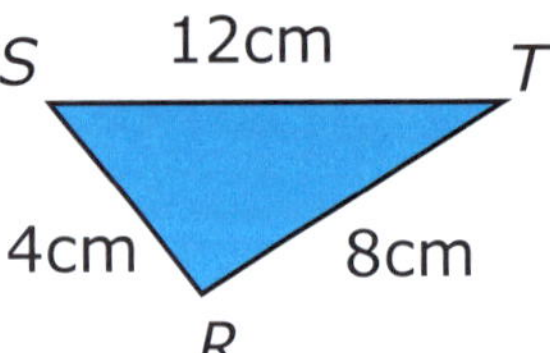

____

____

____

6. Are these triangles congruent? Why or why not?

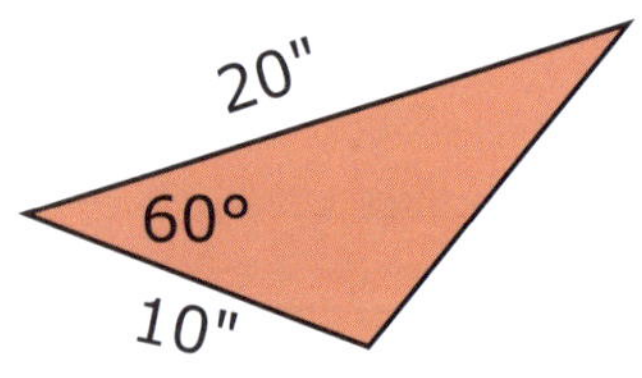

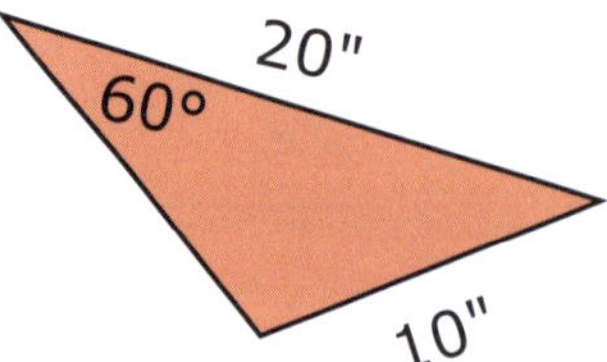

____

____

____

7. Given $\overline{AB} \cong \overline{DE}$, $\angle A \cong \angle D$ and $\angle B \cong \angle E$, finish both triangles with the given restrictions. Label the top vertex of the first triangle C and the top vertex of the second triangle F. Answer the questions below.

a. Is $\Delta ABC \cong \Delta DEF$? Explain your thinking. ______________________

____

b. The above reason is not SSS, or SAS. What abbreviation would you use? Why?

____

____

> If you answered Angle, Side, Angle (ASA) to the above, remember that the corresponding congruent side of each triangle must be in-between the two corresponding congruent angles of the triangles. Otherwise, you cannot use ASA.

How to Prove Trianges Are Congruent

The three ways of proving triangles are congruent are SSS, SAS, and ASA. You must be sure you are looking at the corresponding parts of the triangle. Rigid motions guaranteed congruency, but if you're given two triangles and need to determine if they are congruent or not, study the information given about their sides and angles and the above three postulates (statements that are true based on experiments) to help you determine congruency.

Look at problem 6 on page 288.

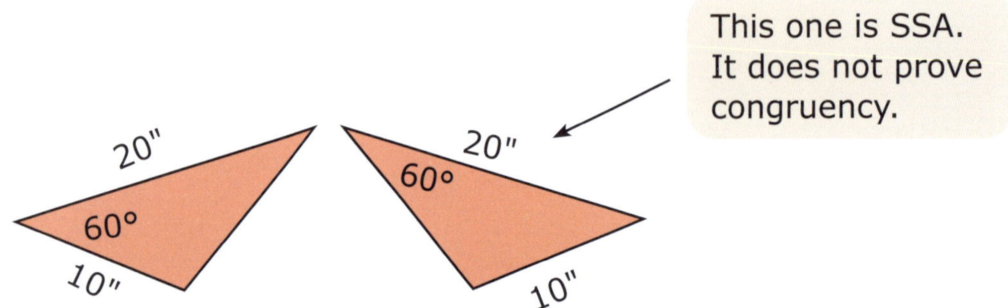

You can see that in the second triangle, the 60° angle is not in-between the two sides. Yet, it seems the two triangles should be congruent. Look at the picture below. Another triangle NOT congruent to the original can be created with the same given information.

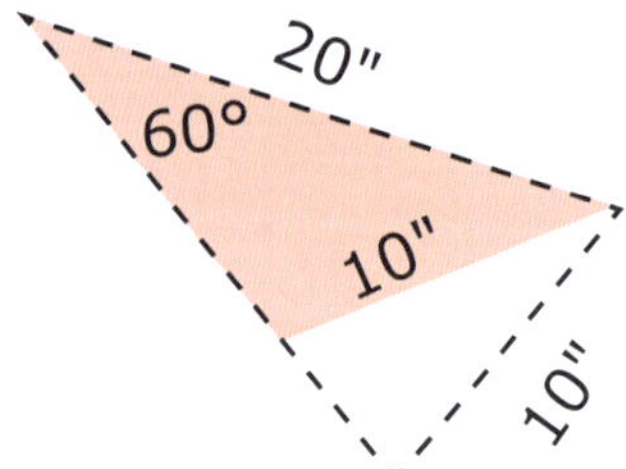

How about SAA? If you know two angles of a triangle would you know the third angle? Why? So SAA is the same as ASA.

State if these pairs of triangles are congruent based on the given information. If congruent, state if by SSS, SAS, or ASA. If not congruent, write "not congruent."

1. 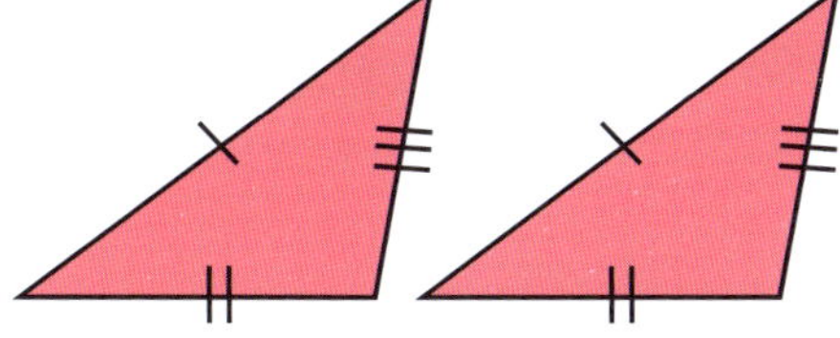

____

2. 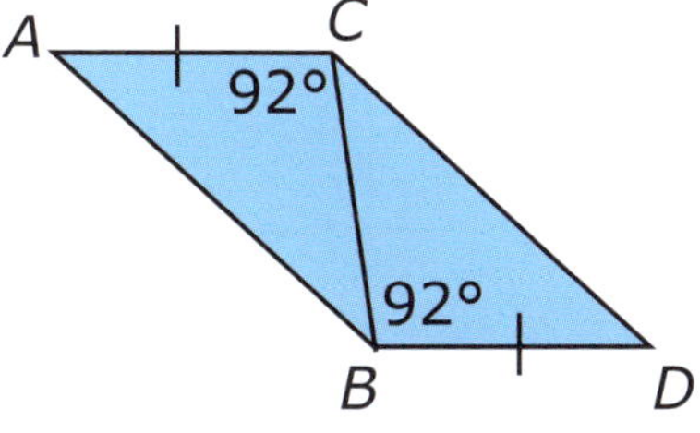

ΔABC and ΔCBD share side $\overline{BC}$.

____

3. 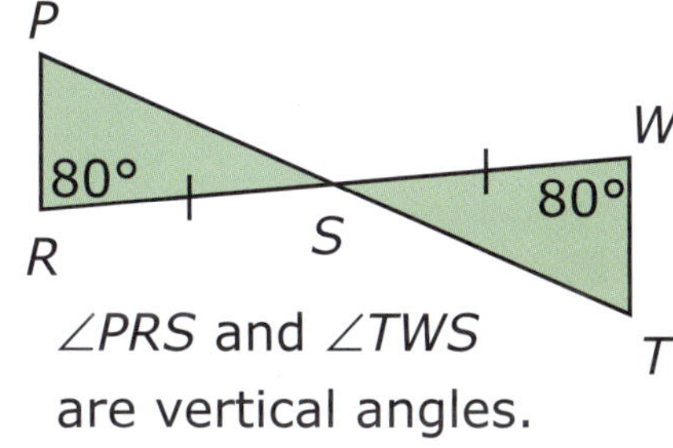

$\angle PRS$ and $\angle TWS$ are vertical angles.

____

4. 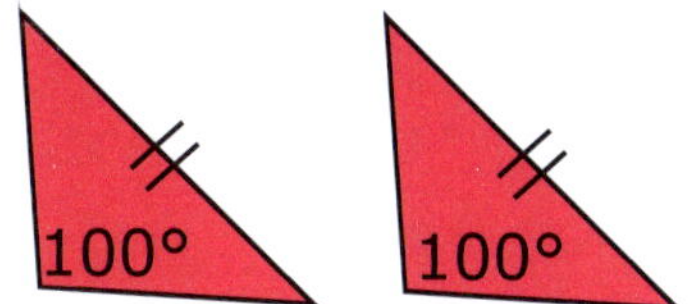

____

5. 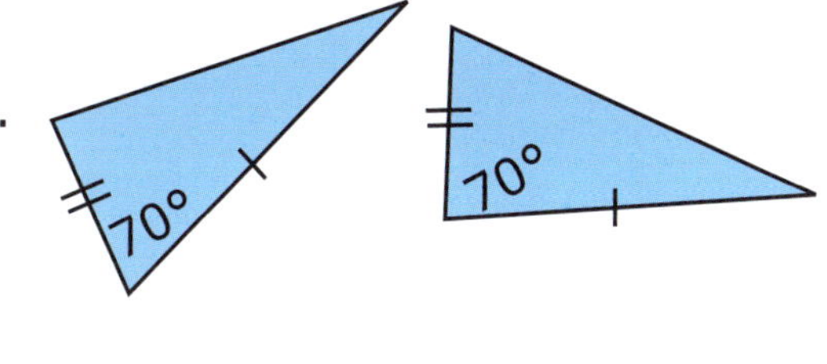

____

6. 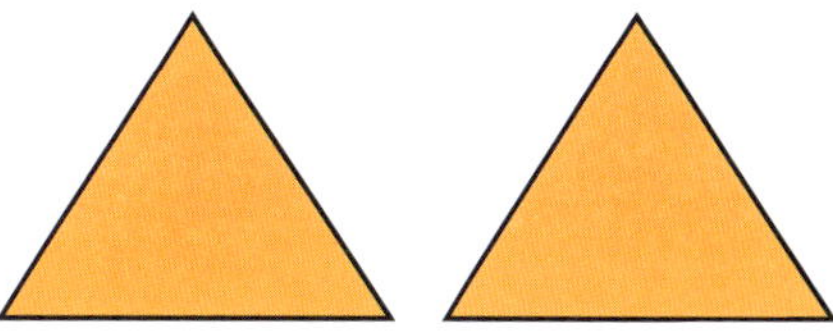

Two Equilateral Triangles.

____

7. 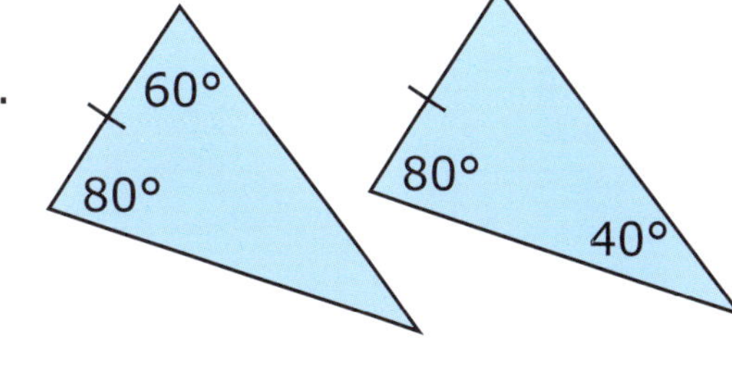

____

8. 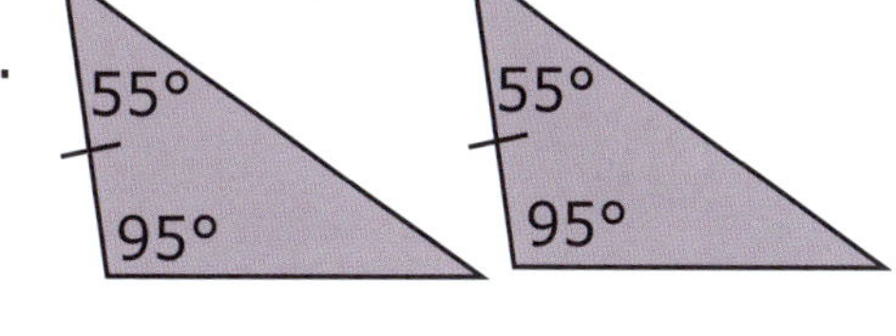

____

9. 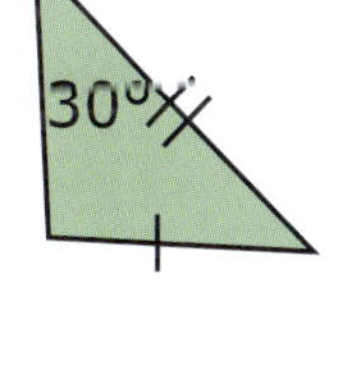

____

10. 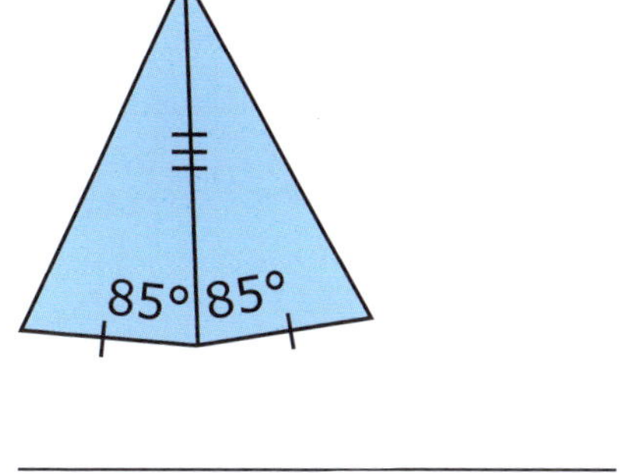

____

Dilations

Unlike translation, reflection, and rotation, dilations are non-rigid transformations. This means that the figures can enlarge or shrink by a given factor called *r*, but they do so in proportion. A dilation from the origin with a scale factor *r* will move a point (*x*, *y*) to (*rx*, *ry*).

Example 1: Dilate the ΔABC from the origin by a scale factor of 2. Label your results $\Delta A'B'C'$. You may see this notation: D_2.

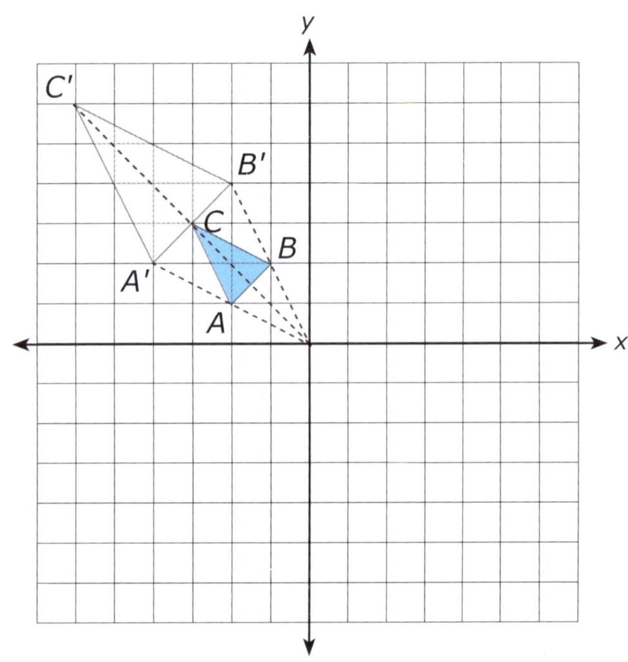

$A\ (-2, 1) \dashrightarrow A'\ (-4, 2)$

$B\ (-1, 2) \dashrightarrow B'\ (-2, 4)$

$C\ (-3, 3) \dashrightarrow C'\ (-6, 6)$

Example 2: Dilate from the origin the following circle *P* by a factor of $\frac{1}{2}$.

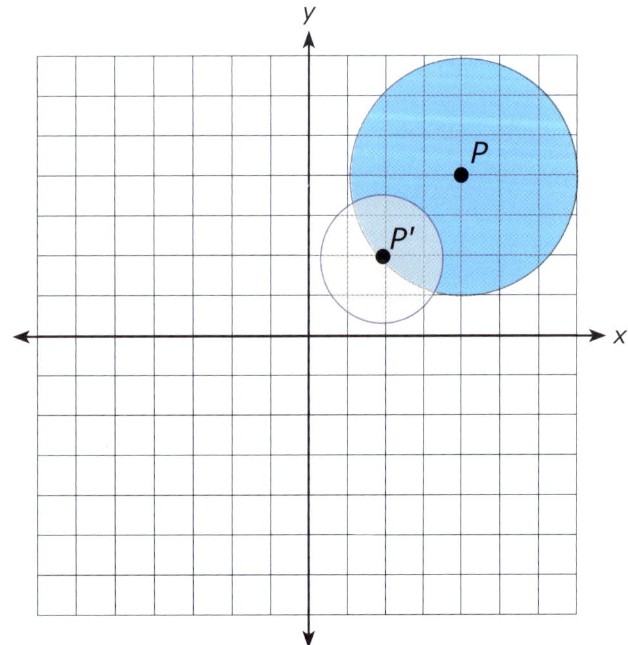

The center of the circle is at (4, 4) with a radius of 3. The image, circle *P'* has a center at (2, 2) and a radius of 1.5.

Practice

1. A triangle has the following ordered pairs, *A* (−6, 6), *B* (−12, 8) and *C* (0, 4). After a dilation from the origin the image has the following ordered pairs, *A′* (−9, 9), *B′* (−18, 12), and *C′* (0, 6). What is the scale factor? ______

2. If you dilate rectangle *DEFG* below from the origin by a scale factor of 2, what are the coordinates of *D′E′F′G′*?

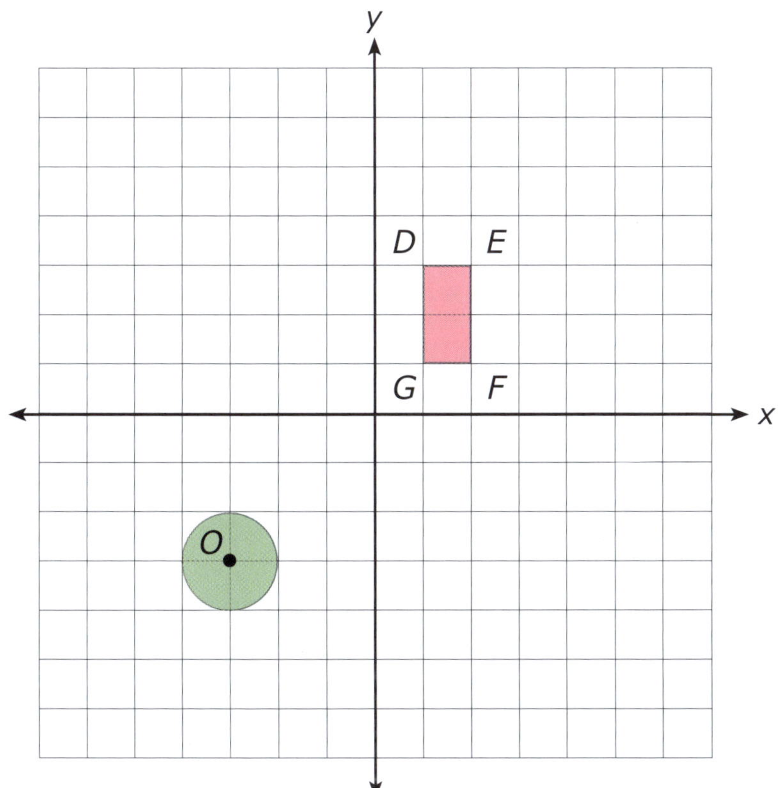

G′ __________

F′ __________

E′ __________

D′ __________

3. On the coordinate plane above, dilate circle *O* from the origin by a scale factor of 1.5.

    a. What are the coordinates of the center of your new circle? ___________

    b. How long is the new radius and the new diameter? ___________

4. Triangle *QRS* has these ordered pairs, *Q* (−3, 6), *R* (9, 12), and *S* (21, 18). If you dilate it from the origin by a factor of $\frac{2}{3}$, state the new coordinates of *Q′R′S′*.

    Q′ ___________ *R′* ___________ *S′* ___________

5. To get *Q′R′S′* from problem #4 back to the size of *QRS*, what scale factor would you use? ___________

You can also dilate a figure from a point other than the origin. Dilate the small circle about its center point *P* by a scale factor of 3. The new circle would have a radius 3 times the original radius.

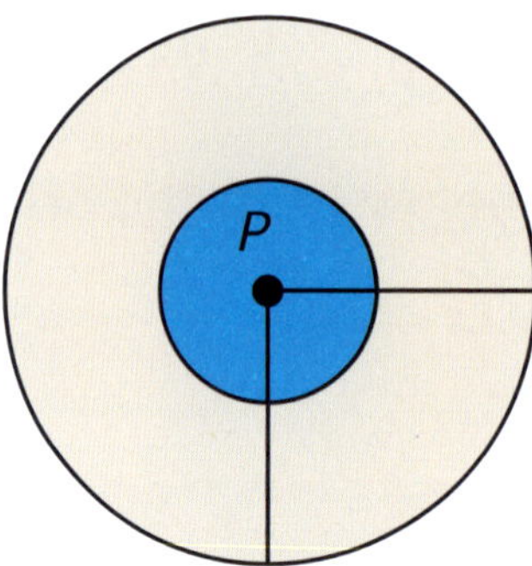

6. Look at the drawing above and answer the questions.
   a. What is the ratio of the new radius to the original radius? __________
   b. What is the ratio of the old diameter to the new diameter? __________
   c. What is the ratio of the circumference of the image to the circumference of the preimage? __________
   d. What is the ratio of the area of the image to the area of the preimage?

      ____

7. Dilate ΔBEH by a factor of $\frac{1}{4}$ from *P*. Label *B'E'H'*.

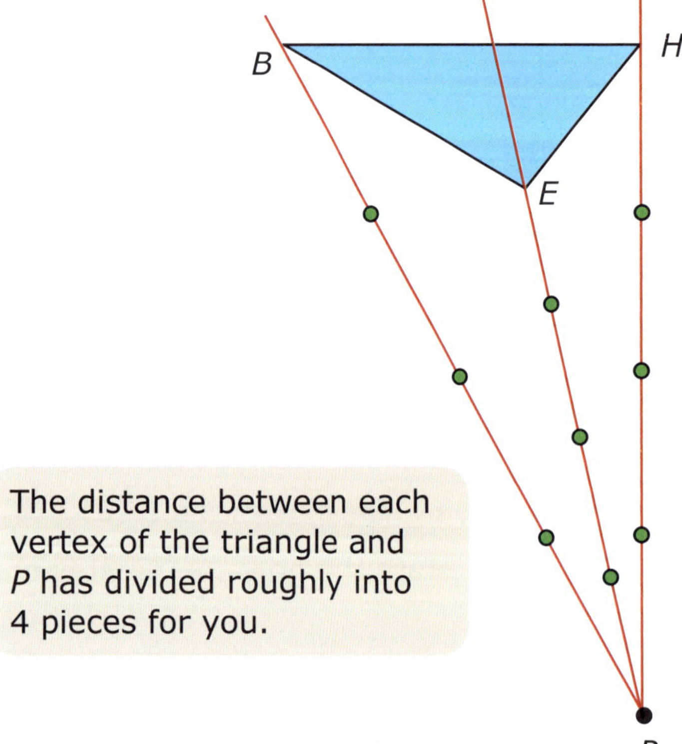

The distance between each vertex of the triangle and *P* has divided roughly into 4 pieces for you.

Similarity

Figures dilated in proportion are called similar figures. For two figures to be similar, their corresponding sides must be in proportion AND their corresponding angles must be congruent.

Two equilateral triangles are always similar.

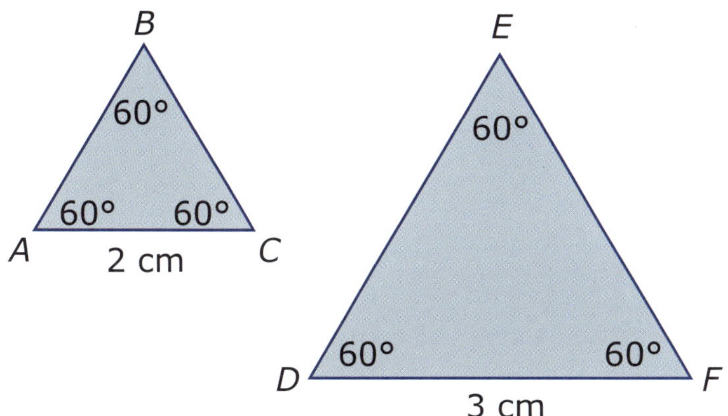

Their corresponding angles have equal measures, and the sides are in proportion. The ratio of the small triangle to the bigger one is 2:3.

The symbol used for similarity is ~. You can say $\Delta ABC \sim \Delta DEF$.

If two triangles have congruent corresponding angles, then the two triangles will be similar (and their corresponding sides will be in proportion). The converse is also true. This is called AA (Angle Angle) similarity.

Practice

1. Why AA and not AAA? Why does having only two corresponding angles congruent become sufficient for two triangles to be similar? Explain your thinking.

____

____

2. Which of the following statements is true? Explain your thinking.

   Statement 1: Congruent triangles are always similar.

   Statement 2: Similar triangles are always congruent.

____

____

3. These triangles are similar. Find the missing side. ______________

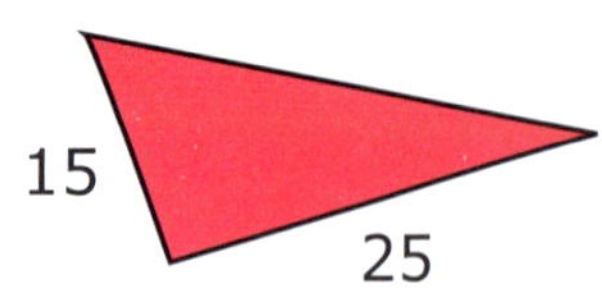

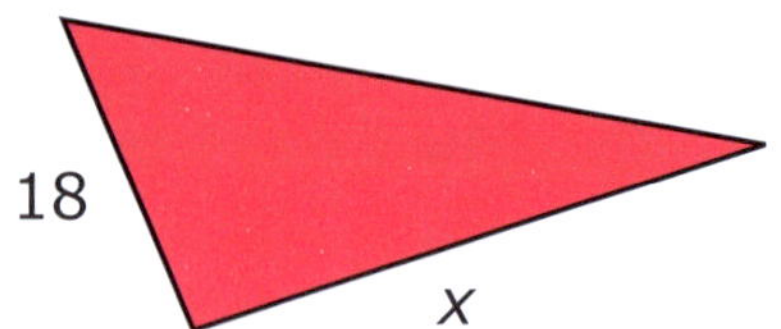

4. Which of the following shows the dilation of rectangle *ABCD* by a scale factor of $1\frac{1}{2}$? Why is the rectangle you chose similar to *ABCD*? ______________

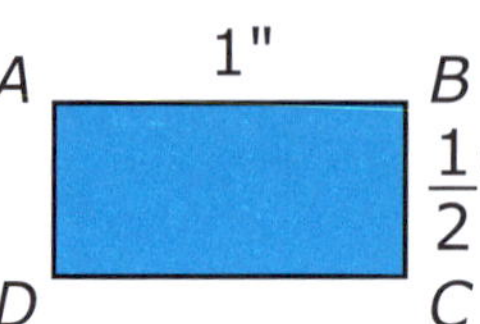

a. 1"

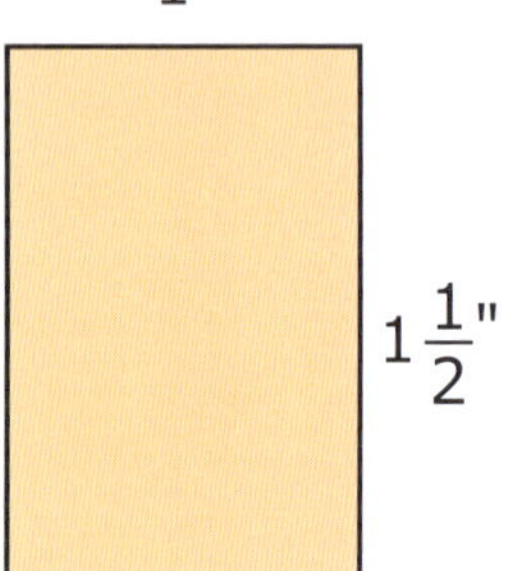

b.

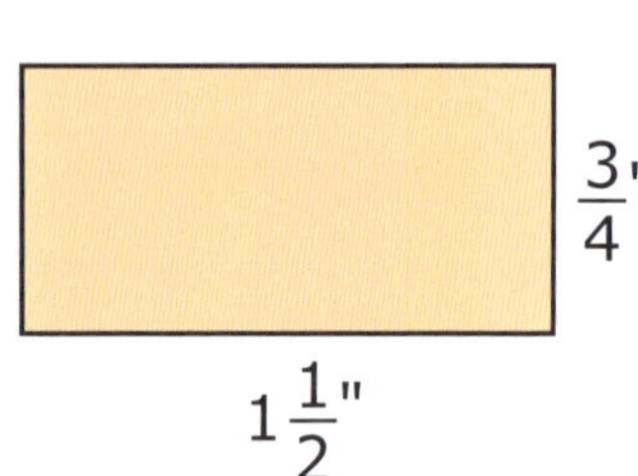

c. $\frac{1}{2}$"

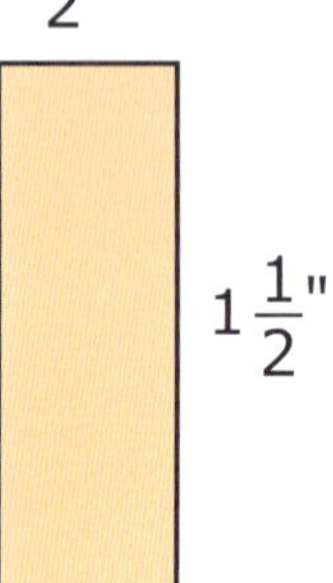

Explain your thinking ______________

____

5. Are these triangles similar? Explain your thinking.

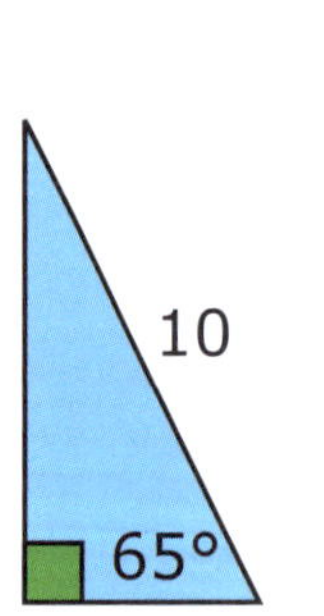

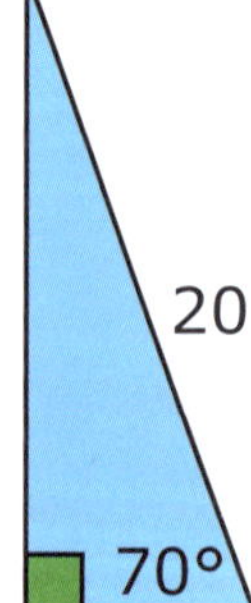

____

6. Why are the following triangles similar? Explain your thinking.

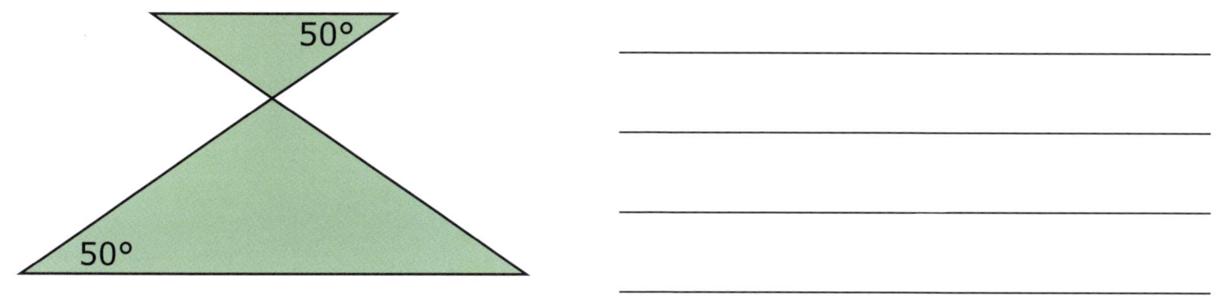

7. In the figure below, if $\overline{AC}$ and $\overline{DG}$ are parallel segments, why is $\Delta DEG \sim \Delta AEC$?

Explain your thinking. ______________________________

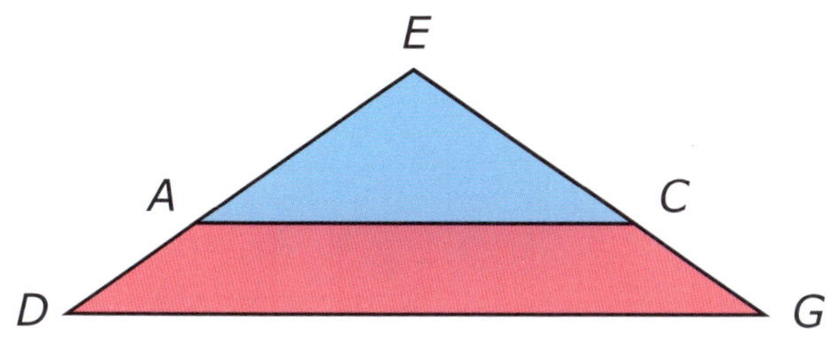

8. In the figure above $DE = 18$, and $AE = 6$. If $AC = 10$, find DG. ____________

9. Find the measure of $\angle x$ and $\angle y$ if the triangles are similar. ____________

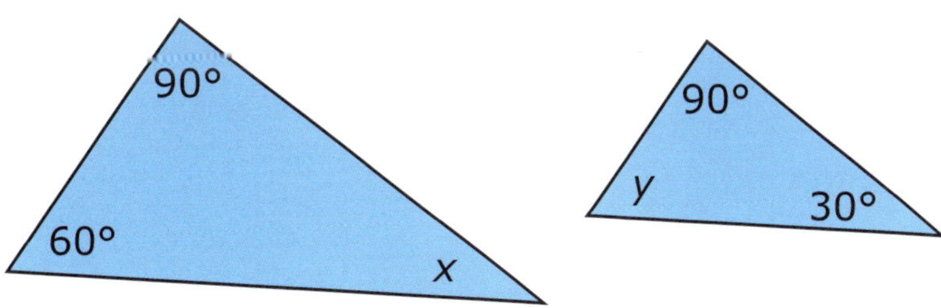

10. Are two right triangles always similar? Draw your own pictures and explain your thinking.

Chapter 13 Review

1. Translate the following square using vector $\overrightarrow{AB}$.

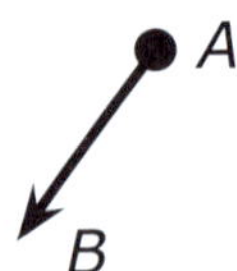

2. Translate ΔABC by using the translation $T_{-10,\ 5}$ if its coordinates are A (–3, 4), B (0, 9), C (–11, –12). State the coordinates of $A'B'C'$.

   A' __________ , B' __________ , C' __________

3. On the coordinate below, reflect ΔQRS about the y-axis. Label your image $Q'R'S'$. State the coordinates of your image below.

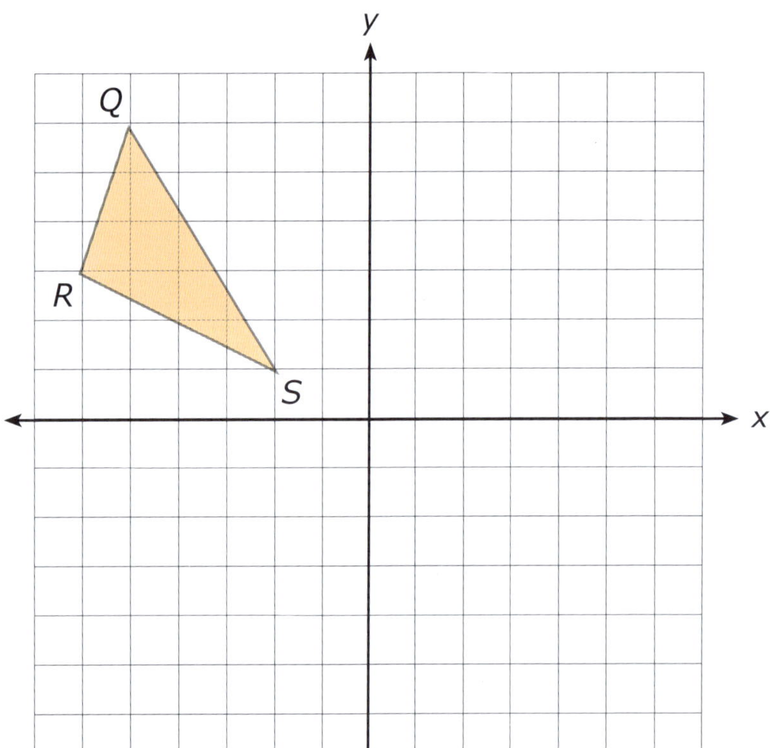

   Q' __________

   R' __________

   S' __________

4. On the coordinate plane above, take $Q'R'S'$ and now reflect it about the x-axis. Label your image $Q''R''S''$.

   Q'' __________ , R'' __________ , S'' __________

5. On the coordinate plane below, reflect ΔRST about the origin. Label your image $R'S'T'$. State the coordinates of the image below.

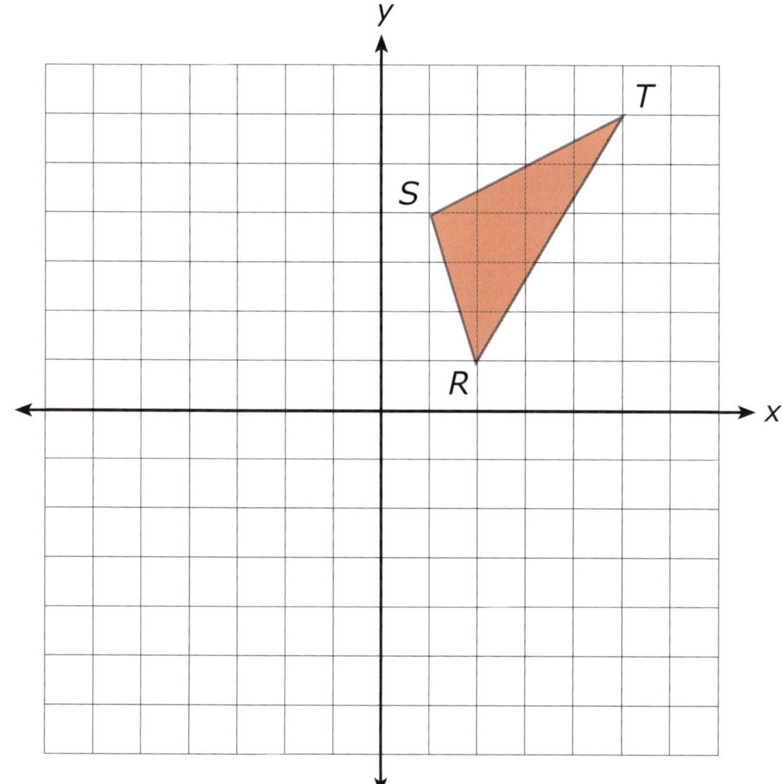

R' ____________

S' ____________

T' ____________

6. Rotate ΔABC using $R_{180°}$. Label your image $A'B'C'$. State the coordinates of the image below.

A' ____________

B' ____________

C' ____________

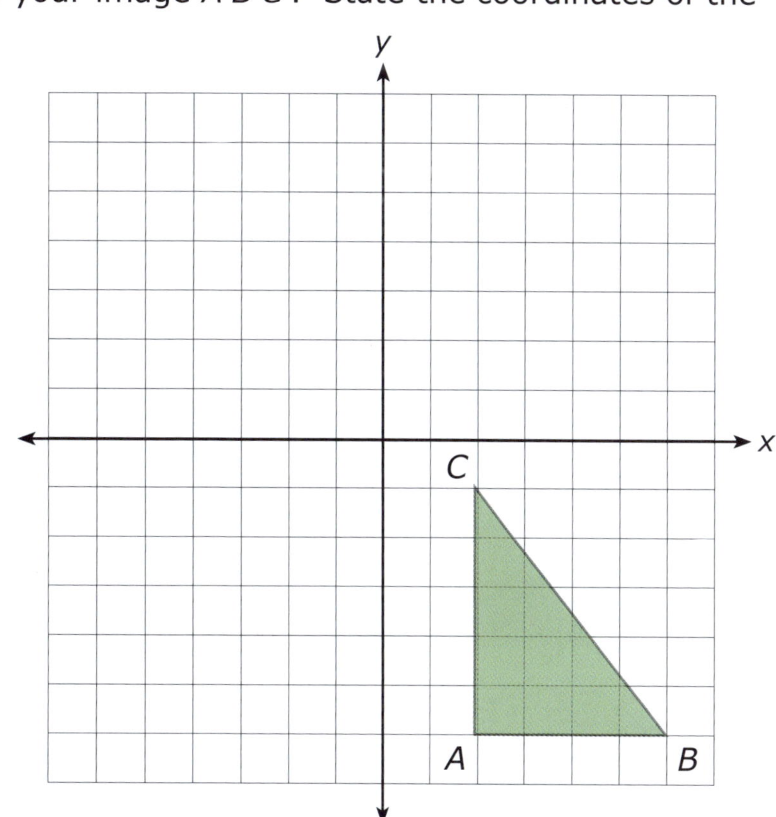

Given the following pairs of triangles and the information provided, state if these triangles are congruent and by what reason (SSS, SAS, ASA). If not congruent, write "not congruent."

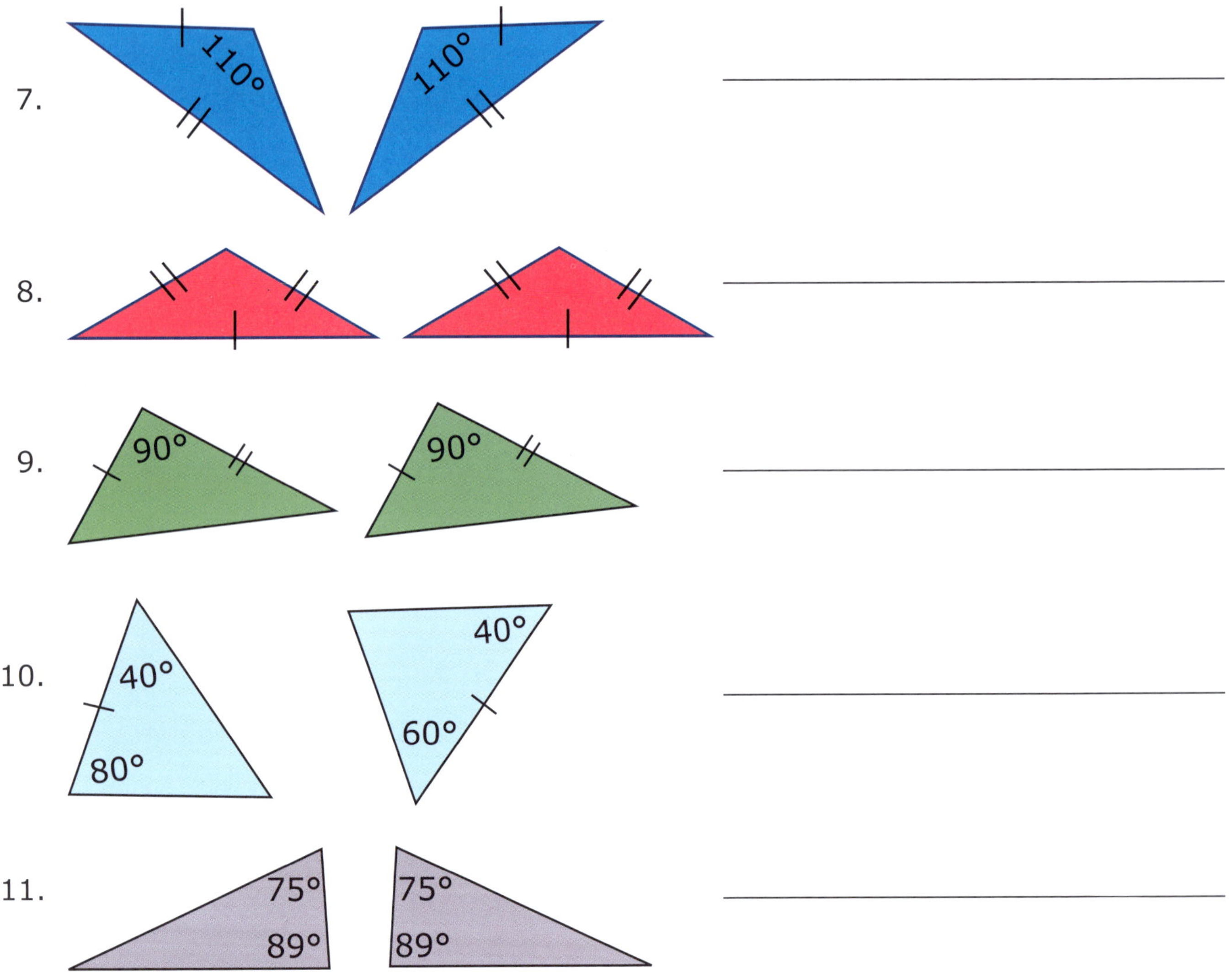

Answer true or false.

______ 12. A dilation does not guarantee congruency.

______ 13. To dilate a figure means only to enlarge it.

______ 14. Two triangles that are similar have corresponding angles congruent.

______ 15. The point (−3, 4) when reflected about the line $y = x$ becomes (4, −3).

______ 16. Congruent triangles are always similar.

Do the following problems.

17. The following triangles are similar. Find the missing side. ________________

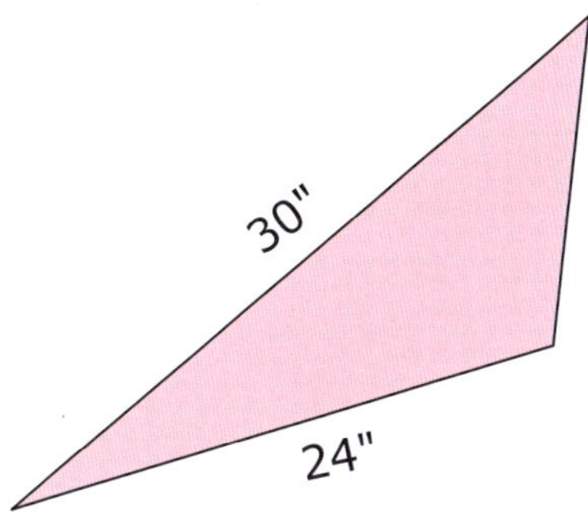

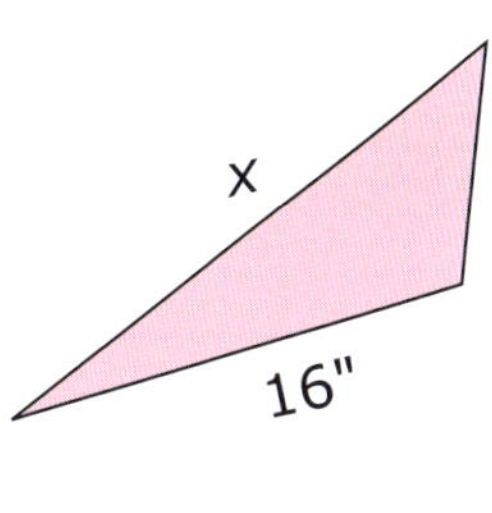

18. Dilate the right ΔWVZ from the origin by a scale factor of $\frac{1}{2}$. Label $\Delta W'V'Z'$. State the coordinates of $W'V'Z'$.

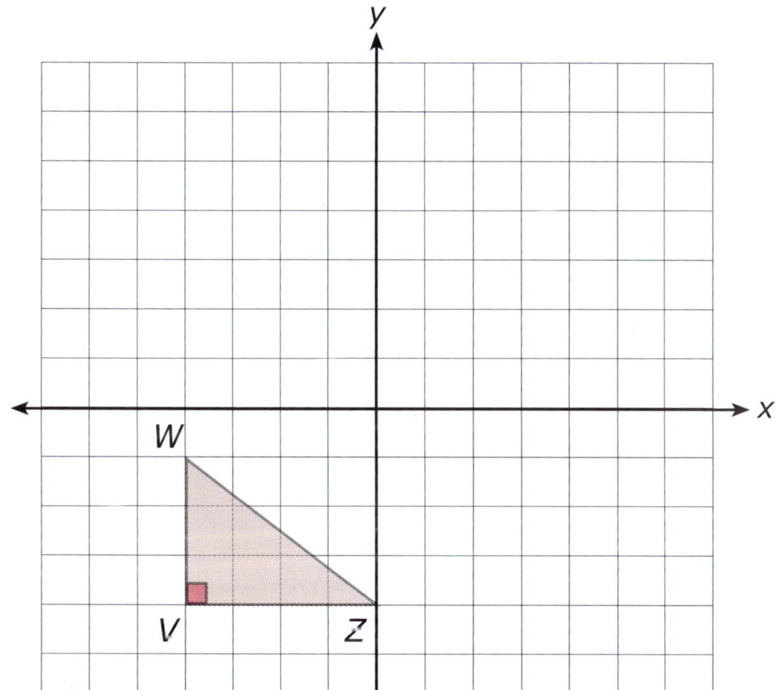

W' __________

V' __________

Z' __________

19. Why is the image of $\Delta W'V'Z'$ similar to ΔWVZ? Explain your thinking.

____

____

20. Compare the perimeter and the area of $\Delta W'V'Z'$ with the perimeter and the area of ΔWVZ. Then compare their ratios.

a. Perimeter of ΔWVZ ___________ Perimeter of $\Delta W'V'Z'$ ___________

b. Ratio of the perimeter $\Delta W'V'Z'$: perimeter of ΔWVZ ___________

c. Area of ΔWVZ ___________ Area of $W'V'Z'$ ___________

d. Ratio of the area of $\Delta W'V'Z'$: area of ΔWVZ ___________

e. State any conclusions from your findings.

____

____

____

____

Chapter 14

Understanding Functions

In this chapter, you will study the concept of functions in mathematics. You have been working with ordered pairs in many chapters of this book. A function is a special relationship between two sets of numbers. The following example is a fun and clear way to understand the definition of a function.

Suppose you have a "function machine." You put in several values (input), the machine processes a given rule and then spits out the results (output).

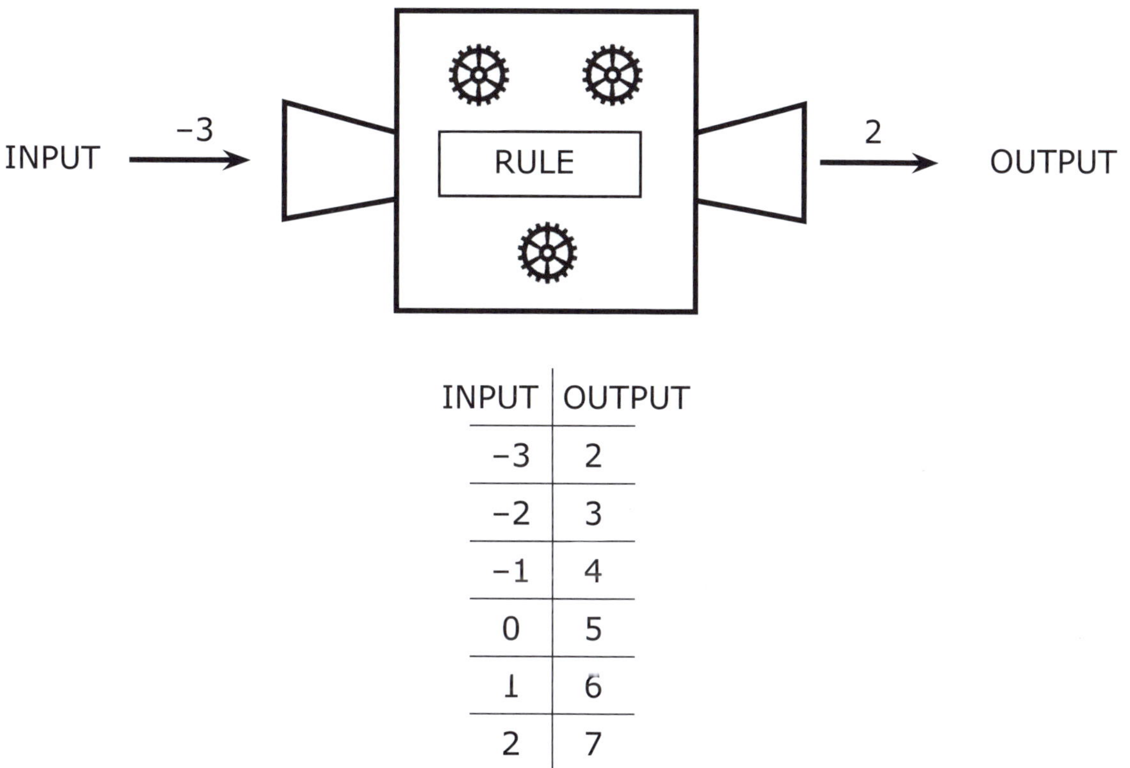

INPUT	OUTPUT
−3	2
−2	3
−1	4
0	5
1	6
2	7

Can you see that the "rule" or "function" is "add 5" to each input? The input is called the "domain," and the output is called the "range" of the function. What makes this a function is that for every input, you will get a unique output that corresponds to that input. In other words, if the next time you put in −3 with the rule of "add 5," you get something other than 2, then it's no longer a function.

A function is a special relation where given an input you will get the same output for that given input <u>every</u> time.

Now that you know the rule is a function, you can write it as $f(x) = x + 5$ instead of $y = x + 5$. $f(x)$ is read as "f of x." It means the value of y depends on the value you give x.

The following is not a function. Can you see why?

$$(-3, 5), (-2, -2), (-1, -1), (-3, -3), (1, 1), (2, 3)$$

The input −3 has two different outputs. Therefore, this relation is not a function.

One of the ways you can tell if you have a function or not is to graph it and use what is called the "vertical line" test. If you graph the points above you will see that two points are right on top of each other on a vertical line. When two points are above each other on a vertical line, then you no longer have a function.

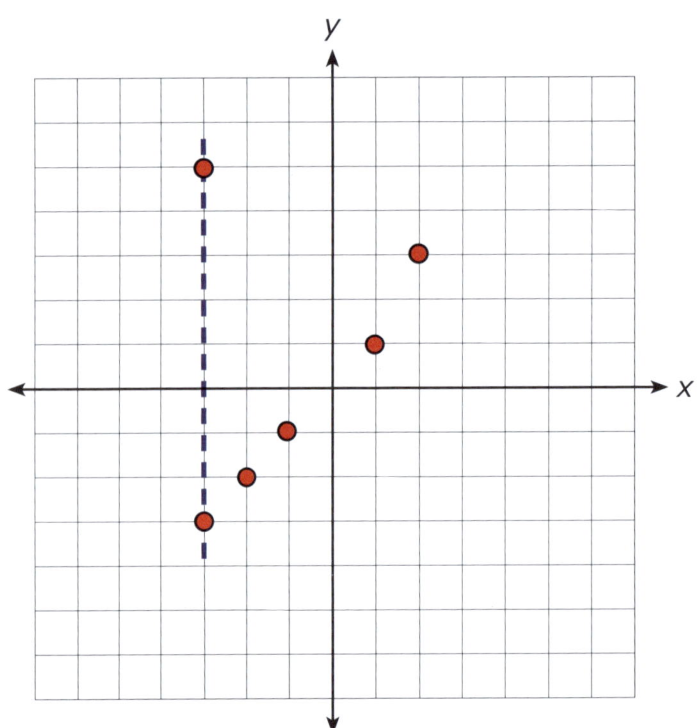

The following set of ordered pairs is a function, although it may not seem so. Why?

$$(-3, 4), (-2, 4), (-1, 4), (0, 4), (1, 4), (2, 4)$$

If you graph it you will get the horizontal line $y = 4$ or $f(x) = 4$. Again, every input will give you a unique output for that input. It's no different that this example with birthdays. Suppose your birthday is March 30th. Can other people have the same birthday as you? Yes, however, your birthday answer is always the same for you.

Practice

1. The following is a mapping between two sets of numbers. Is this relation a function? Explain your thinking.

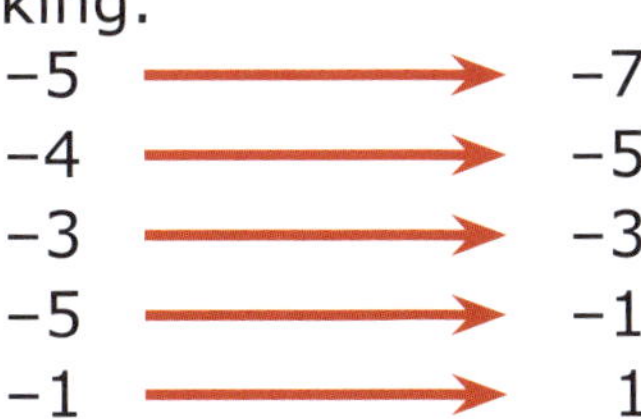

____

____

2. Answer the questions for these ordered pairs: (−2, −4), (−1, −3), (0, −2), (1, −1), (2, 0).

   a. What is the domain? ____________ b. What is the range? ____________

3. Using function notation, write the equation to problem 2. ________________

4. Which of the following graphs represents a function? Explain your thinking.

a. 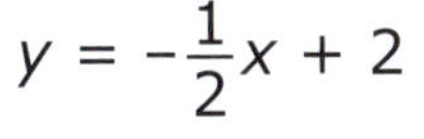

$y = -\frac{1}{2}x + 2$

b. $x = 2$

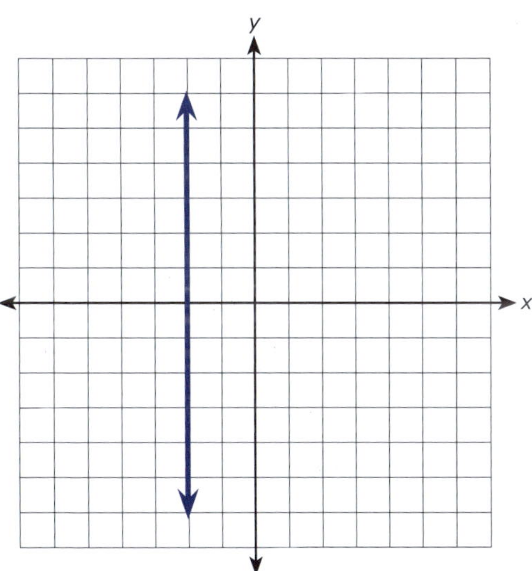

____

____

5. Thomas defined a function this way: "Every input has a unique output that matches that input, but you can have the same output from different inputs. Is he correct? Explain your thinking.

____

____

Quadratic Functions

Below is a table and graph for $y = x^2$ or $f(x) = x^2$.

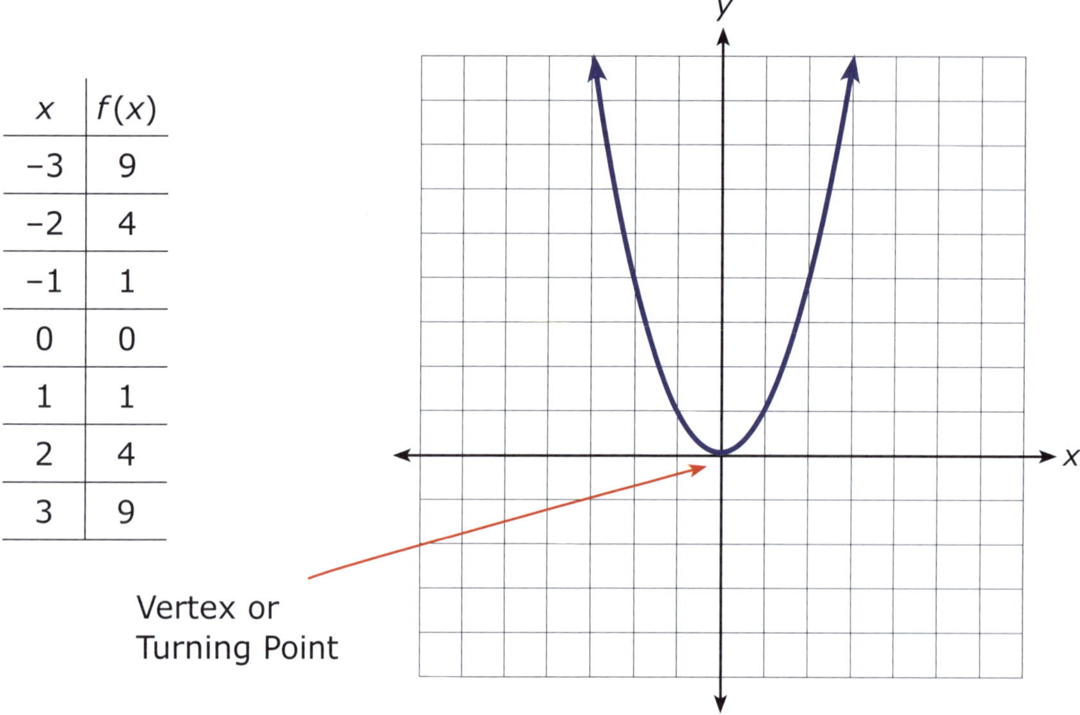

x	$f(x)$
−3	9
−2	4
−1	1
0	0
1	1
2	4
3	9

The exponent "2" makes the graph NOT linear. This graph is called a <u>parabola</u>. Parabolas are common in optical lenses. The path of a ball after it's thrown follows a parabolic path. Next time you get a drink of water at a water fountain, look at the path made by the water.

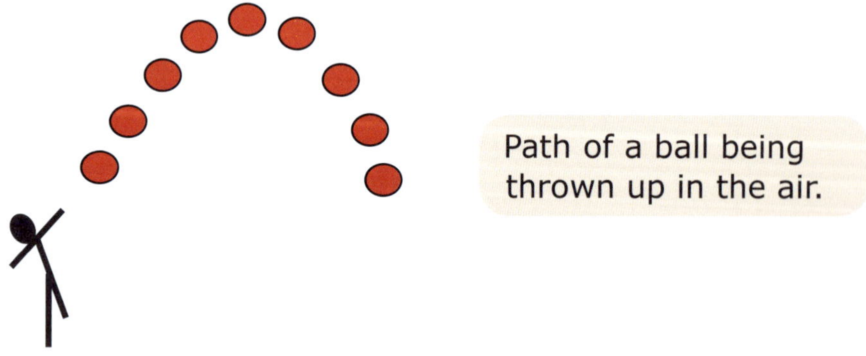

A parabola has perfect symmetry. You can reflect both sides of the parabola about the axis of symmetry (which in the case above is the line $x = 0$). The vertex or turning point is the minimum (or maximum point) before the parabola makes a turn.

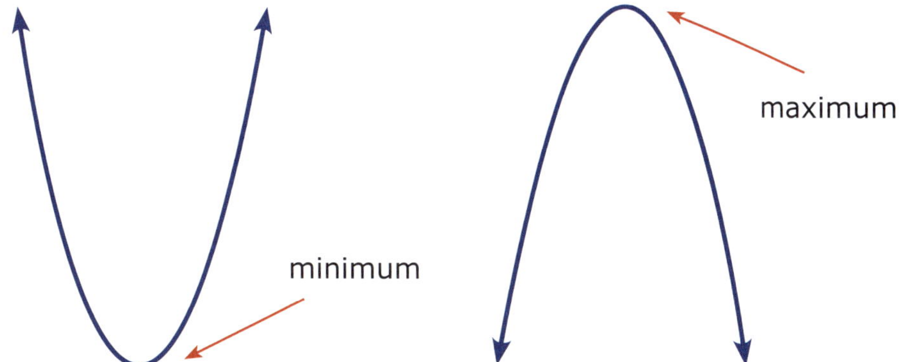

The general formula for any quadratic equation is $y = ax^2 + bx + c$, as long as the coefficient a does not equal 0. The quadratic equation graphed, $y = x^2$ or $f(x) = x^2$, is the most basic of all parabolas. When you see $f(x)$, think y.

Practice

Use your own graph paper when asked to graph.

1. In a quadratic equation why must the coefficient a in $f(x) = ax^2 + bx + c$ never be zero? Explain your thinking.

____

____

2. How would the graph of $f(x) = -x^2$ look different from the graph on the previous page? Predict what the parabola would look like. Graph it to check your prediction.

____

____

3. Graph $f(x) = 2x^2$.

4. Graph $f(x) = \frac{1}{2}x^2$.

5. How does the coefficient in equations #3 and #4 affect the graphs of the two quadratic equations? Explain your thinking.

____

____

6. Graph $f(x) = x^2 + 4$.

7. Graph $f(x) = x^2 - 4$.

8. How does the constant in equations 6 and 7 affect the graphs of the two quadratic equations? Explain your thinking.

____

____

9. This is the graph of a parabola. Explain why this one is not a function.

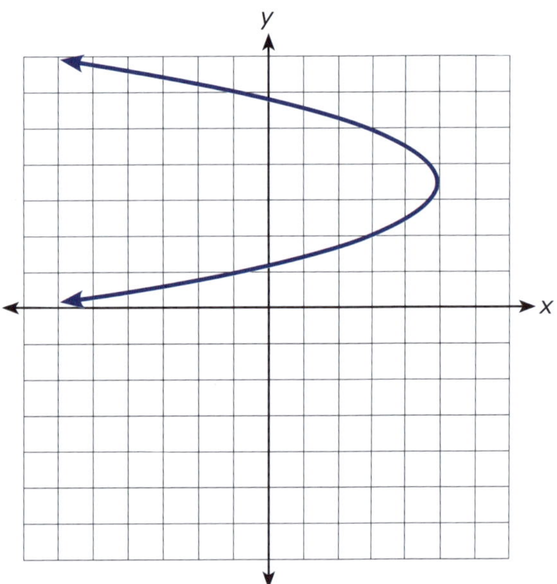

____

____

____

10. What is the axis of symmetry of the parabola shown in #9? ________________

Understanding Exponential Functions

An exponential function is a function that has the form $y = ab^x$ or $f(x) = ab^x$ where $a \neq 0$, $b > 0$, but $b \neq 1$. This time the variable is the exponent. Exponential functions grow or get small very quickly. This is the most basic exponential function, $y = 2^x$.

x	$f(x)$
−2	$\frac{1}{4}$
−1	$\frac{1}{2}$
0	1
1	2
2	4
3	8

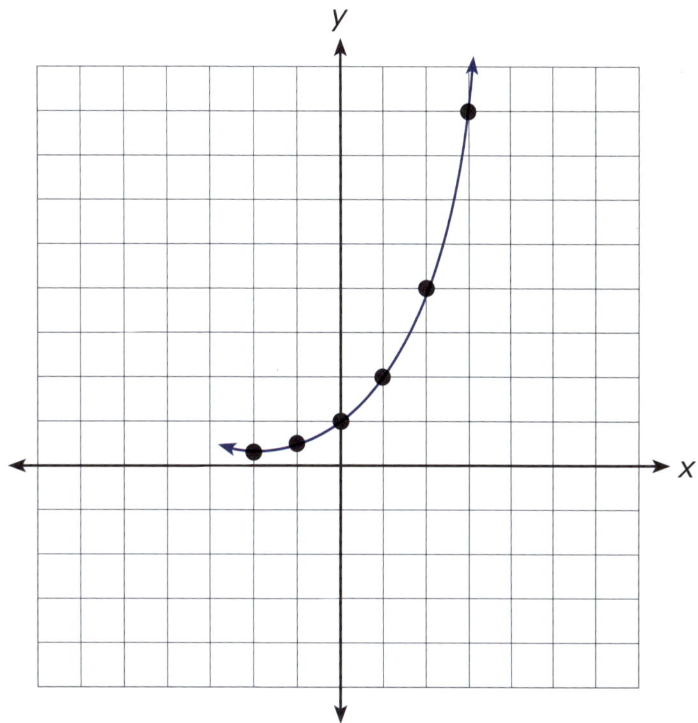

Notice how fast the curve rises as the exponent gets larger. In fact, when $x = 5$, the y value will be 2^5 or 32. Also as the exponent gets smaller and smaller, the y values will become smaller and smaller fractions, so this curve will never touch or cross the x-axis. For example, when $x = -5$, the y-value will be 2^{-5} or $\frac{1}{32}$.

Exponential functions exist in many situations in real life: the growth of bacteria, population growth and decline, the decay of certain radioactive compounds, and the growth or decrease in a bank account.

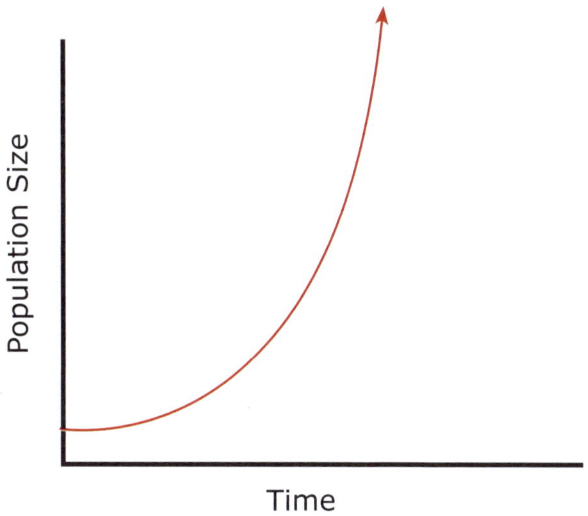

Practice

1. The equation form of an exponential function is $y = ab^x$, where $a \neq 0$, $b > 0$, but $b \neq 1$. Explain the following.

   a. $a \neq 0$ ____________________

   b. $b \neq 1$ ____________________

2. Which of the following equations represents an exponential relationship?

   a. $y = 5x$ b. $y = 2x^2$ c. $y = 4^x$ d. $y = 4x + 5$

3. Complete the table for each of these exponential functions.

   a. $f(x) = 3^x$

x	−3	−2	−1	0	1	2	3
$f(x)$							

   b. $f(x) = 4^x$

x	−3	−2	−1	0	1	2	3
$f(x)$							

   c. $f(x) = (\frac{1}{2})^x$

x	−3	−2	−1	0	1	2	3
$f(x)$							

4. Make a rough drawing of problem 3c.

   $f(x) = (\frac{1}{2})^x$

y

x

5. Suppose that there are 6 bacteria on a desk. The number of bacteria doubles every hour if the desk does not get cleaned. Finish the table.

a.

Time (Hours)	1	2	3	4	5	6	7
Bacteria	6	12	24				

b. Does this equation model the above table? $y = 3 \bullet 2^x$ where x is the number of hours, and y is the number of bacteria? Show a few examples from the table to justify your answer.

____

____

c. How many bacteria are there after 10 hours? Show your work.

____

Exponential Growth and Decay

In Chapter 5, you studied the difference between simple interest and compound interest. Look at this example from page 82.

> Jon charged his new $500 stereo on his credit card. His credit card charges 12% a year on any balance not paid. If Jon were to not pay his credit card monthly, what would he owe after 3 years?

This problem was solved using a table, but it would be too hard to solve the same problem if you had a greater number of years. This is a formula that will help you find the answer with a scientific calculator.

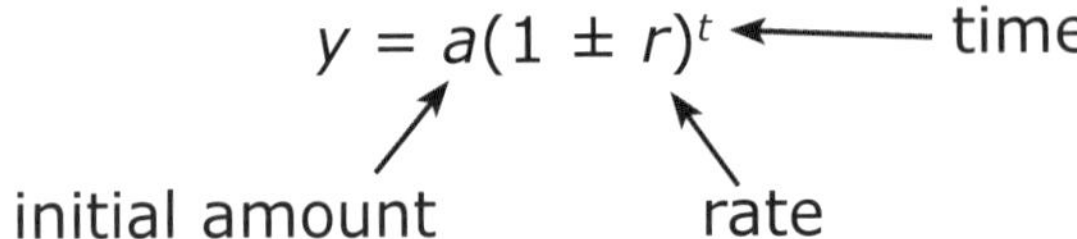

The problem above reflects exponential growth, so use (1 + rate). When a problem reflects exponential decay or decrease, use (1 – rate).

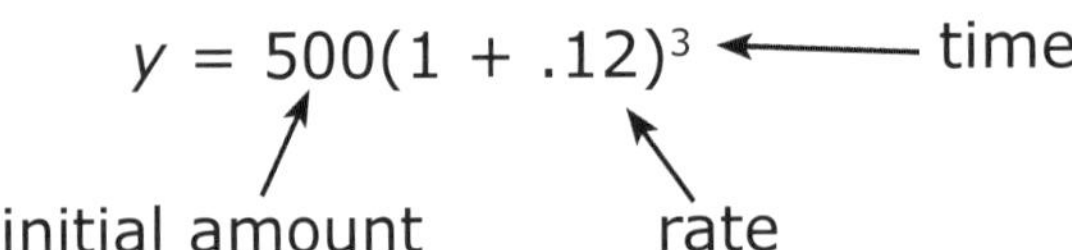

It's very important that the rate (per year) matches the time (years). If the rate is per month, the time is in months.

Computing the answer in the calculator, type 500(1 +.12)^3. You should get the same answer, which is $702.46. The calculator will follow the order of operations by taking value in the parenthesis to the third power and then multiplying by 500.

Practice

1. Why is 1 added each time? Explain your thinking.

____

____

2. Figure out the same problem above if Jon did not pay his credit card for 5 years. What would he owe then? Round your answer to the nearest cent.

____

3. Figure out the same problem if Jon did not pay his credit card for 30 months. Round your answer to the nearest cent.

____

Look at this exponential decay (or decrease) problem.

A radioactive substance decays at the rate of 7% per month. It originally weighed 600 grams. How much is left after one year? Round your answer to the nearest tenth of a gram.

Use (1 – rate), as this problem will show an exponential decrease.

$$y = a(1 - r)^t$$
$$y = 600(1 - .07)^{12}$$

Since the rate is per month, you must change one year to months. The answer is 251.2 grams left.

Use your calculator.

4. Chris deposits $500 into an investment account at his bank. His account earns 3.5% per year. If he has no deposits or withdrawals, and the rate stays the same, how much will Chris have after 15 years? Round your answer to the nearest cent. ____

5. Grace bought an antique car for $43,000. It increases in value 5% every year. What is Grace's car worth after 12 years? Round your answer to the nearest cent.

____

6. A brand new car that cost $30,000 decreases in value 2% per year. What is its value after 2 years?

____

7. Michael bought a new computer worth $1,800. The value of his computer decreases at a rate of 50% per year. How much is his computer worth after 9 months? Round your answer to the nearest cent.

____

8. The NCAA Basketball Championship, which is known as March Madness, starts with 64 teams. Teams play against each other, and the winning team moves on. Each round has half of the previous teams playing.

   a. Fill out how many teams are left after each round.

Round 1	Round 2	Round 3	Round 4	Round 5
32				

   b. Use the formula for exponential decrease to find the answer after round 5. Hint: Initial amount: 64 teams. Rate: 50% decrease per round. Time: 5 rounds.

   ____

   c. Suppose there were 512 teams in March Madness, how many rounds would it take to narrow it down to 2 teams? Hint: Make a chart or keep trying the formula.

   ____

Absolute Value Functions

You learned in Chapter 2 that the absolute value of a number is always positive. The absolute value function, $f(x) = |x|$, is an interesting function. Look at the table and its graph.

x	$f(x)$
−3	3
−2	2
−1	1
0	0
1	1
2	2
3	3

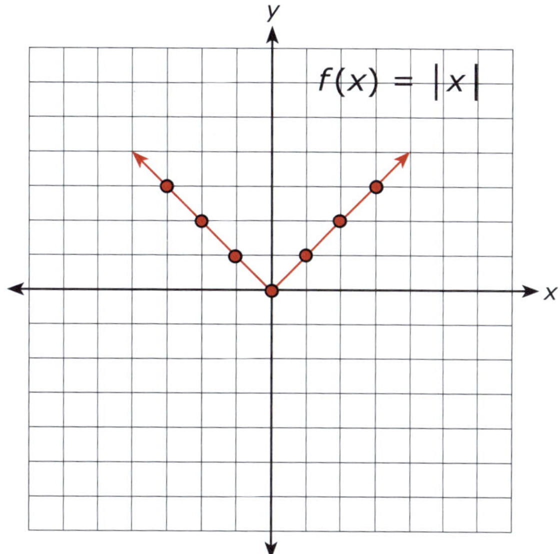

The graph resembles the letter "V." It is not a curve like the parabola. The graph also has symmetry.

Practice

1. In the above graph, what is the axis of symmetry? ________________

2. Graph the following absolute value functions and then answer the questions that follow. Create your own table of values.

   a. $f(x) = -|x|$

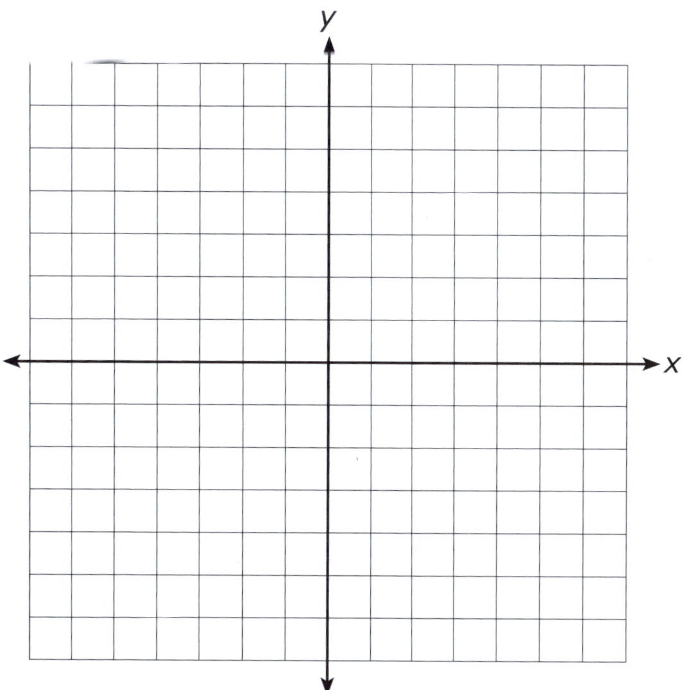

b. $f(x) = |x| - 3$

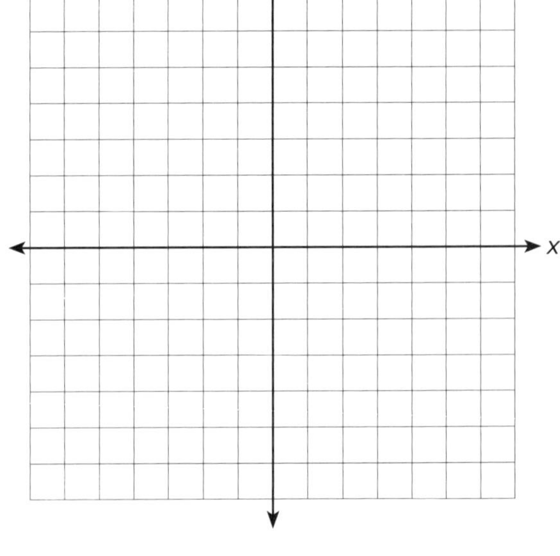

c. $f(x) = |x| + 2$

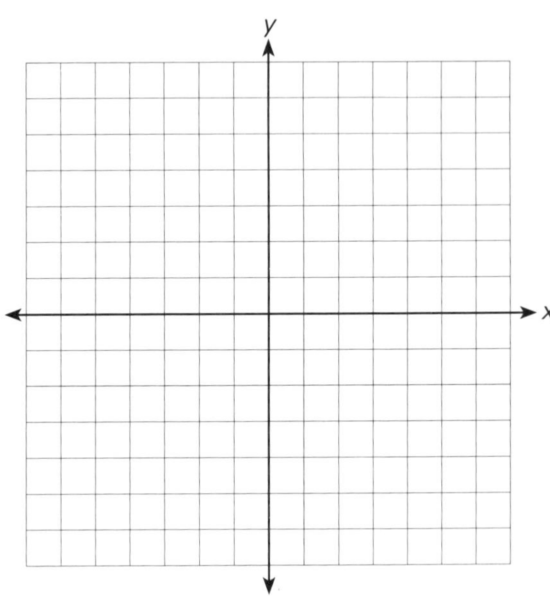

d. $f(x) = |x + 2|$

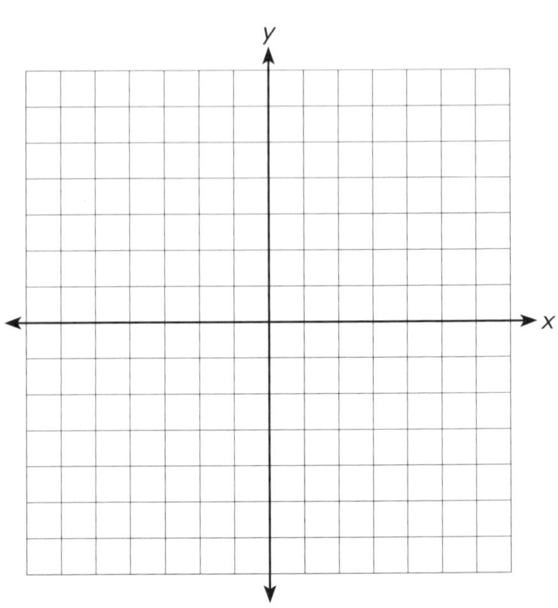

Answer the following.

3. Compare the graph for 2a with the graph of $f(x) = |x|$. What transformation (Chapter 13) would move one function onto the other?

4. Compare the graph of 2b with the graph $f(x) = |x|$. What transformation (Chapter 13) would move one function onto the other?

5. Without graphing the function $f(x) = |x| - 20$, can you describe how it compares with the graph $f(x) = |x|$.

6. Fill in the chart, then graph $f(x) = 2\ |x - 4|\ - 5$.

x	y
−2	
0	
2	
4	
6	
8	

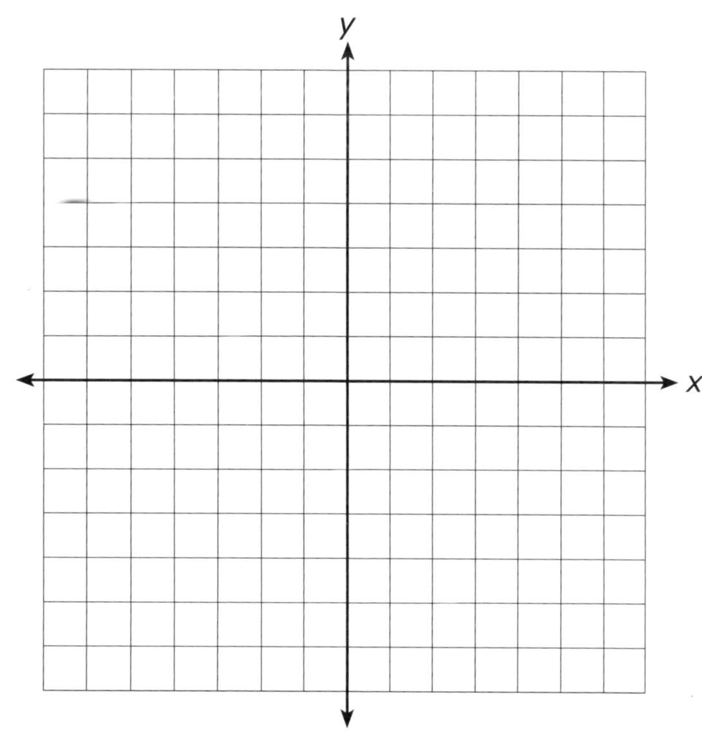

Linear, Exponential, and Quadratic Functions Review

Linear Functions - The difference between successive outputs is a constant. This is called the "rate of change" or "slope."

x	1	2	3	4	5
y	7	10	13	16	19

Example: $y = 3x + 4$

Rate of change: 3 (slope)

Note: $10 - 3 = 13 - 10$, etc.

Exponential Functions - The ratio between successive outputs is a constant.

x	1	2	3	4	5
y	2	4	8	16	32

Example: $y = 2^x$

Ratio: 2

Note: $8/4 = 16/8$, etc.

Quadratic Functions - The second difference is a constant.

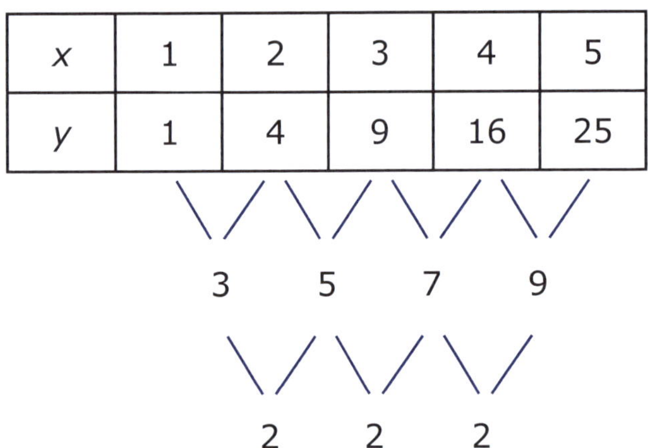

x	1	2	3	4	5
y	1	4	9	16	25

Example: $y = x^2$

When presented with a table of values, you can use this information as another way to help you determine if a function is linear, exponential, or quadratic.

Chapter 14 Review

1. Which of the following sets does not represent a function? Explain your thinking.

   a. (−3, −9), (−2, −6), (−1, −3), (0, 0)

   b. (−4, 16), (−3, 12), (−2, 8), (−1, 4)

   c. (−4, −1), (−3, 0), (−2, 1), (−4, 0)

   ____

2. Given this set of ordered pairs that belong to a given function, answer these questions.

   (−3, 9), (−2, 4), (−1, 1), (0, 0), (1, 1), (2, 4), (3, 9), (4, 16)

   a. What is the domain listed above? ______________________

   b. What is the range listed above? ______________________

   c. What is the function? ________

   d. Can any value from the set of Real numbers be used for the domain?

   ____

   e. Given the function you found, are ALL members of the Real numbers in the range of this function? Explain your thinking.

   ____

   ____

3. Why is the following NOT a function?

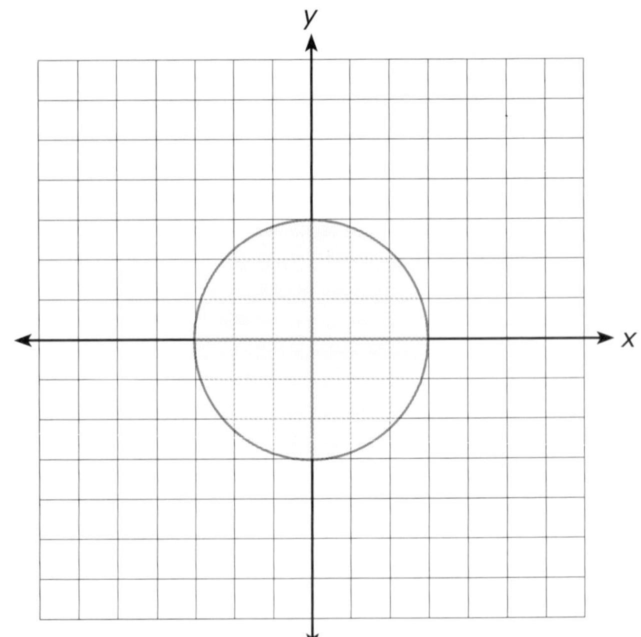

4. Which of the following is a quadratic equation?

a. $y = 5x + 2$ b. $y = 3^x$ c. $y = x$ d. $y = 2x^2 - 5$

5. Which of the following is an exponential equation?

a. $y = 3(5)^x$ b. $x = 0$ c. $y = 2x + 6$ d. $y = |x|$

Graph the following functions using the given domains.

6. $f(x) = x^2 - 4$

x	$f(x)$
−3	
−2	
−1	
0	
1	
2	
3	
4	

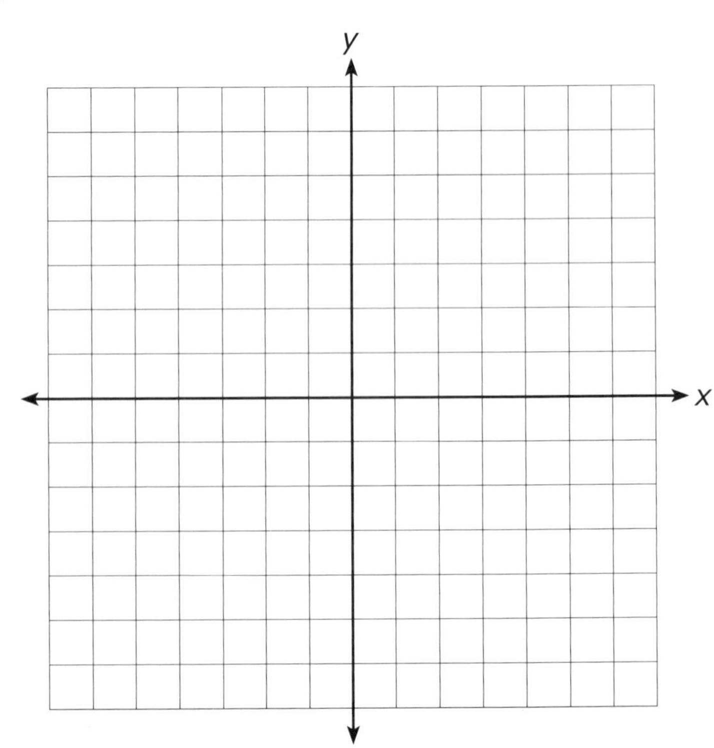

7. $f(x) = 2^x + 1$

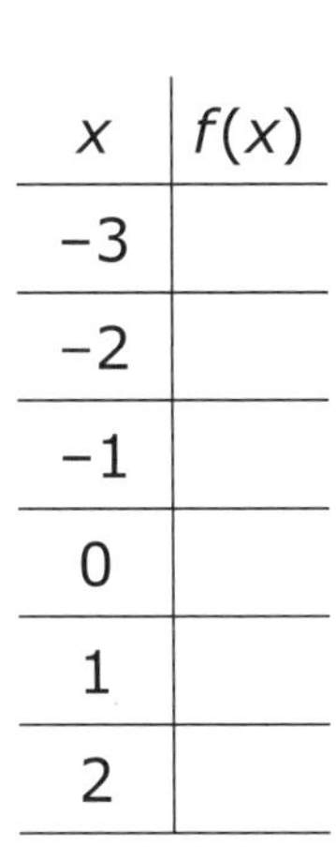

x	$f(x)$
−3	
−2	
−1	
0	
1	
2	

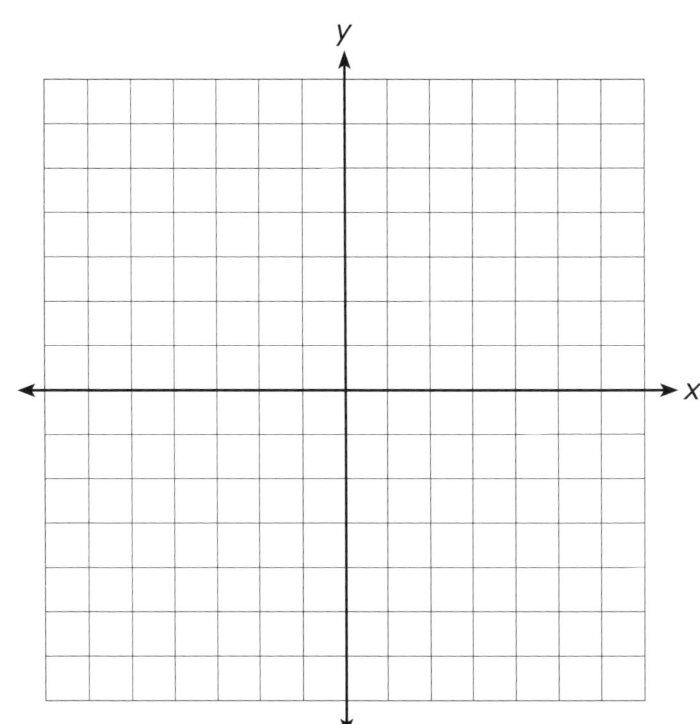

Fill out the rest of this table for this exponential function $f(x) = (\frac{1}{3})^x$

8.

x	−2	−1	0	1	2	3
$f(x)$						

Looking at the following tables, determine if these functions are linear, quadratic, exponential, or linear. Then write the function.

9.

x	−3	−2	−1	0	1	2
$f(x)$	−14	−9	−4	1	6	11

Type: ______________ Function: ______________

10.

x	2	3	4	5	6	7
$f(x)$	8	18	32	50	72	98

Type: ______________ Function: ______________

11.

x	−1	0	1	2	3	4
$f(x)$	$\frac{1}{3}$	1	3	9	27	81

Type: ______________ Function: ______________

12.

x	−3	−2	−1	0	1	2
$f(x)$	9	−6	3	0	−3	−6

Type: ______________ Function: ______________

13. Fill in the chart, then graph this absolute value function: $y = |x| - 4$.

x	$f(x)$
−4	
−2	
0	
2	
4	

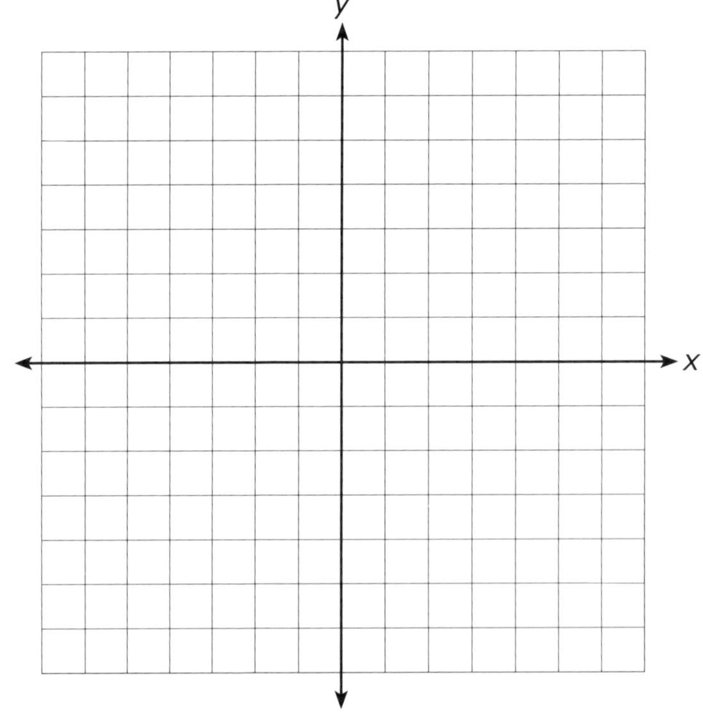

14. Compare the graph for problem #13 with the graph of $y = |x|$. What transformation would move one function into the other?

____

____

Chapter 15

Probability and Statistics

There are many concepts in the field of probability and statistics that incorporate algebra. Probability is the study of how likely or unlikely it is that an event will happen.

When you hear that the probability of rain is 80%, you have an understanding that it's likely to rain. The odds of an event can be written as a percent or as a fraction from 0-1. A probability of 0 means an event has no chance of occurring, and a probability of 1 means the event will certainly happen. The probability of an event is defined as:

$$P(\text{event}) = \frac{\text{total outcomes desired}}{\text{total outcomes possible}}$$

The sample space is a list of all the possible outcomes. You can write your sample space using a set.

Example 1: a. What is the sample space when you throw a fair six-sided die?

Answer: The sample space is $\{1, 2, 3, 4, 5, 6\}$.

b. What is the probability that when you throw a six-sided fair die you will get a prime number?

The prime numbers on a die are 2, 3, and 5. Remember 1 is not a prime. You have 3 primes out of a total of 6 possible outcomes.

Answer: $P(\text{prime number}) = \frac{3}{6}$ or $\frac{1}{2}$

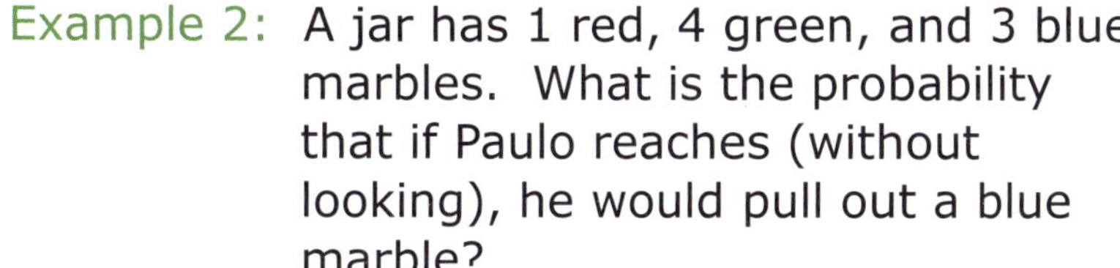

Example 2: A jar has 1 red, 4 green, and 3 blue marbles. What is the probability that if Paulo reaches (without looking), he would pull out a blue marble?

Answer: $P(\text{blue}) = \frac{3}{8}$

Example 3: What is the sample space when two dice are thrown?

You can get (1, 1), (1, 2), (1, 3), (1, 4), (1, 5), (1, 6), (2, 1), (2, 2), etc. Here's a way to show the sample space.

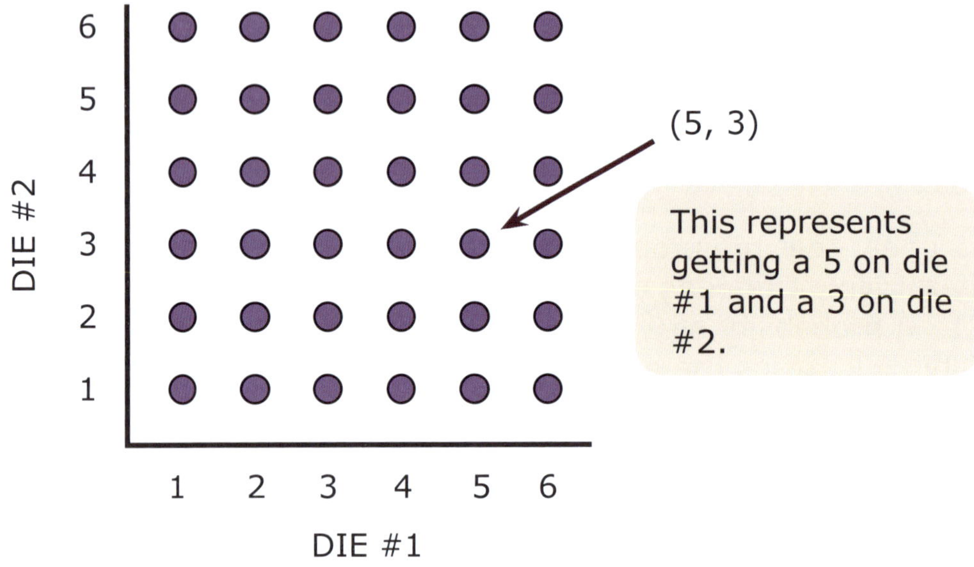

Answer: There are 36 possible outcomes.

Practice

For questions 4-7 refer to the sample space above.

1. What is the probability that when you toss a coin you will get tails? ____________

2. If you toss a coin three times and get tails three times in a row, what is the probability you will get tails a fourth time? ____________ Explain your thinking.

____

____

____

3. Looking back at Example 2, what is the probability that if you reach into the jar (without looking), you will get ...

   a. a red marble? ____________ b. a green marble? ____________

   c. a black marble? ____________

4. What is the probability that when you roll two, dice you get (5, 3)? ___________.

   Explain your thinking. ____

   ____

   ____

5. What is the probability that when you roll two dice each die will show the same number? ___________ Show your work.

6. What is the probability that when you roll two dice you will get a sum of 7? ___________ Show your work.

7. What is the probability that when you roll two dice you will get a sum of 13? ___________ Explain your thinking.

   ____

Understanding OR and AND

There are many probability problems that ask you to find the probability of more than one event happening at the same time (AND), as well as the probability of one event or another event happening (OR).

Example 1: What is the probability that when you throw a fair 6-sided die, you get a 3 OR a number greater than 4?

The probability of getting a 3 is $\frac{1}{6}$. The probability of getting a number greater than 4 is $\frac{2}{6}$ (the numbers 5 or 6).

With OR, you add the probabilities. Answer: $\frac{3}{6}$ or $\frac{1}{2}$.

Example 2: You have the numbers 1-10 in a box. What is the probability that if you reach without looking, you will get a number divisible by 2 and divisible by 3?

The probability of getting a number divisible by 2 is $\frac{1}{2}$ (the numbers 2, 4, 6, 8, 10). Divisible by 3 is $\frac{2}{10}$ (3, 6, and 9, but you cannot count 6 since it's been counted already).

Multiplying both you get $\frac{1}{10}$ ($\frac{1}{2} \bullet \frac{2}{10}$).

6 is the only number divisible by both 2 and 3 from our sample space, so the probability is 1 out of 10.

Practice

1. Looking at the spinner on the right, what is the probability that it will land on ...
   a. a number greater than 0?
   b. a number less than 8?
   c. a number divisible by 3?
   d. an even number or a prime number?
   e. a multiple of 4 or a multiple of 5?
   f. an even number and a prime number?

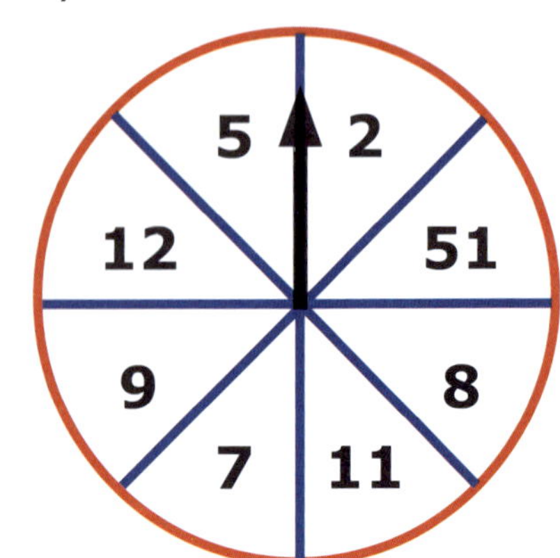

In a standard deck of cards there are 13 spades (black), 13 clubs (black), 13 hearts (red), and 13 diamonds (red). Included in each suit are three face cards: jack, queen, and king.

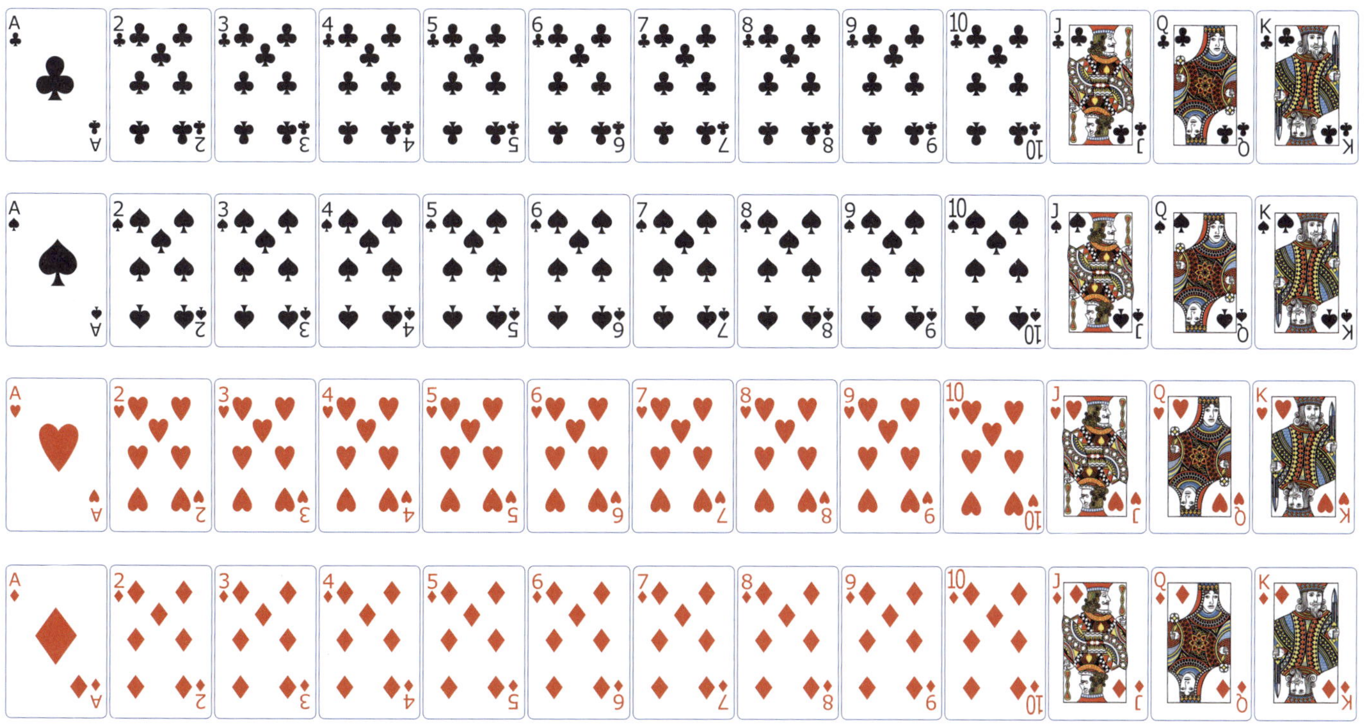

2. What is the probability that if you shuffle all the cards and you reach for one card, you will get ...

   a. the queen of hearts? _____

   b. a red card? _____

   c. a black card or the 3 of diamonds? _____

   d. a black card or a 2? _____

   e. a black card and a 3? _____

Understanding Many-Stage Experiments

In a one-stage experiment the sample space can be a list of all the possible outcomes for that experiment. In a many-stage experiment, for example, tossing a coin and then rolling a die, it's useful to make a probability tree as your sample space. The tree diagram will visually help you find the answers you need.

Example 1: What is the probability that if Maria rolls a die and then tosses a coin, she will get a even number and then tails?

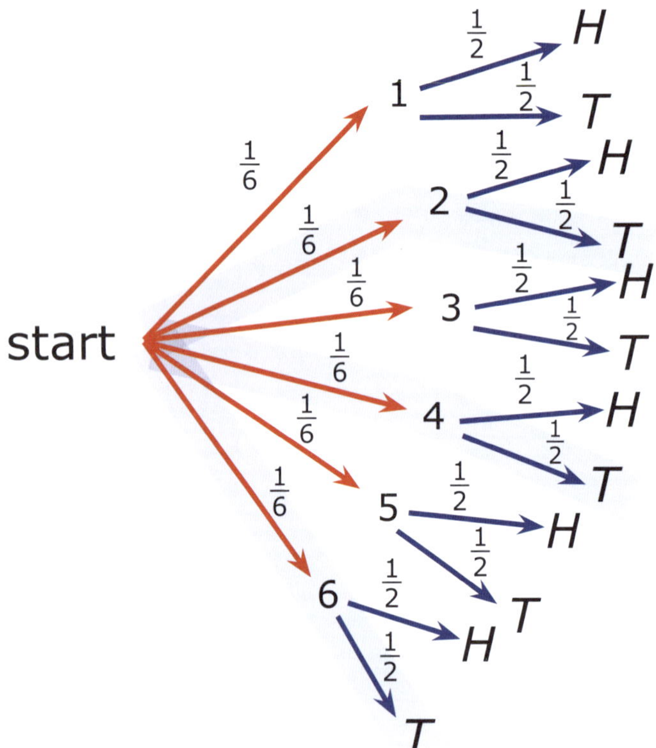

Highlight the paths that lead to *P*(Even and Tails).

P(2 and *T*) is $\frac{1}{6} \bullet \frac{1}{2} = \frac{1}{12}$.

$P(4 \text{ and } T) = \frac{1}{12}$,

$P(6 \text{ and } T) = \frac{1}{12}$.

Multiply across the branches, then add, because *P*(2 and *T*) or *P*(4 and *T*) or *P*(6 and *T*) would meet what is being asked.

$$\frac{1}{12} + \frac{1}{12} + \frac{1}{12} = \frac{3}{12} = \frac{1}{4}.$$

Example 2: Mr. Huckle has a jar with 6 red jelly beans and 3 purple jelly beans. He takes one out without looking, puts it back, then reaches again for another one. What is the probability that he got a purple one first and then another purple?

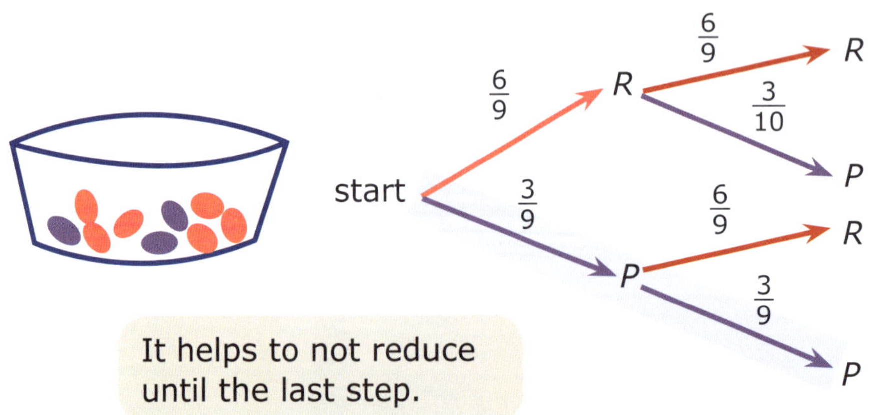

To find P(purple and purple), you multiply across the branch, $\frac{3}{9} \bullet \frac{3}{9} = \frac{9}{81}$ or $\frac{1}{9}$.

Example 2 was With Replacement. Mr. Huckle put the first object back. The following is an example called Without Replacement.

Example 3: Suppose Mr. Huckle reaches in the same bowl but this time he eats the first jelly bean he gets. What is the probability that he will get purple first and then purple again?

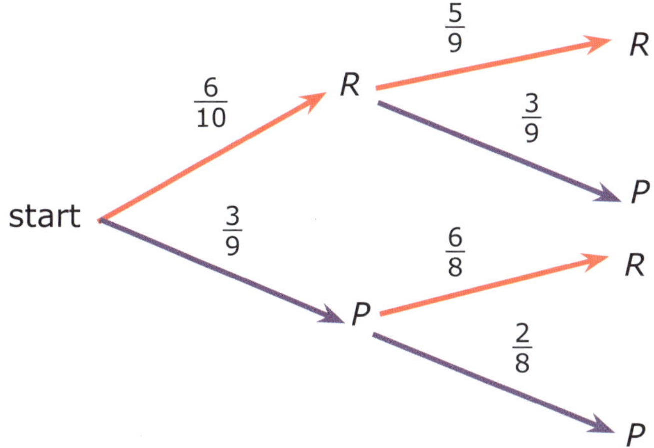

The probability of getting purple first is $\frac{3}{9}$. But if he gets purple first, there will be one less jelly bean in the bowl for the next event, and 2 instead of 3 purple ones left. So his probability of getting purple now is $\frac{2}{8}$, so the P(purple and purple) is $\frac{3}{9} \bullet \frac{2}{8} = \frac{6}{72}$ or $\frac{1}{12}$.

In Examples 1 and 2, the second event was independent from the first event, but in Example 3, the second event is dependent on the first event.

Practice

1. Using Example 3, find the following probabilities:

   a. P(red and red) __________

   b. P(red and purple) __________

   c. P(purple and red) __________

   d. P(same colors) __________

   e. P(different colors) __________

2. In Example 2, why is P(different colors) the same as $1 - P$(same colors)? Explain your thinking.

   ____

   ____

3. Paulo has 6 ties in a drawer. Three are green, 2 are yellow, and 1 is black. Paulo reaches into his drawer without looking and pulls out one tie. He puts it back and then draws another one. Find the following probabilities. Draw a tree diagram for your sample space.

a. P(green and yellow) = ________

b. P(green and black) = ________

c. P(same color) = ________

d. P(black and black) = ________

4. Now Paulo decides to pick one tie without looking and NOT put it back. Find the following probabilities. Make a tree diagram to show your sample space.

a. P(green and black) = ________

b. P(yellow and yellow) = ________

c. P(black and black) = ________

d. P(same colors) = ________

5. Lucia wants to make a necklace using some beads that her mother has in a box. The box has 12 beads. Five of the beads are red, 4 are blue, and 3 are white. Lucia reaches without looking and picks one bead and places it on a string (without replacement). Then she reaches without looking and draws another bead. Draw a tree diagram and find the following probability for her first two beads.

a. *P*(red and red) = ________

b. *P*(blue and blue) = ________

c. *P*(white and white) = ________

d. *P*(red and blue or blue and red) = ________

e. *P*(different colors) = ________

6. Show a shortcut for finding the probability of different colors based on your results above.

____

____

____

____

The complement of an event is always 1 - *P*(event). When you're asked to find the complement of an event you're being asked to find the probability that the event won't happen.

The Counting Principle

When a many-stage experiment has a large number of outcomes, tree diagrams can become too cumbersome. You can find the total number of outcomes of a many-stage experiment by multiplying the outcomes for each stage of an experiment. This is called the counting principle.

Example 1: In New York State, there are 4 main routes to get from Ithaca to Syracuse. From Syracuse to Rochester there are 3 main routes, and from Rochester to Buffalo, there are 2 main routes. How many different routes can Alexis take to get from Ithaca to Buffalo?

Using the Counting Principle, multiply 4 • 3 • 2 = 24. There are 24 possible routes.

Example 2: How many ways can the letters PAL be arranged without repeating any letters?

There are three choices for the first letter: **3** • ____ • ____

Once a letter is chosen, there are two choices left:
3 • **2** • ____

Then there is only one choice left: 3 • 2 • **1** = 6

The 6 possibilities are: PAL, PLA, APL, ALP, LAP, LPA

Example 3: Using the following digits: 3, 5, 6, 9, how many 3-digit numbers can you create that are greater than 700? How many 3-digit numbers can you create that are odd?

Choices: 1 • 3 • 2 Answer: 6 numbers are greater than 700.

The only choice to create a number greater than 700 is to choose the number 9, so you have one choice.

This leaves 3 choices, then 2 choices.

For an odd number, start with the last digit and work backward.

Choices: 1 • 2 • 3 Answer: 6 numbers that are odd.

Then 2 choices for the middle digit, and then 1 choices for the first.

Three choices for the last digit (either 3, 5, or 9).

Permutations

Each of the arrangements shown on the previous page is called a permutation. A permutation is an arrangement where the order matters, so "ALP" is considered different from "PAL."

Example 1: You have five books on a shelf. How many ways can you arrange them on the shelf if the order matters?

You have 5 choices for the first book, then once you pick a book, you have 4 choices, then 3 choices, then 2, then 1. This is written as 5, which is read as "5 factorial."
$5! = 5 \bullet 4 \bullet 3 \bullet 2 \bullet 1.$

> The number of permutations of n elements if you shuffle all n elements is $n!$

Practice

1. At a brunch, you have the choice of a main dish: eggs, pancakes or french toast. You have a choice of meats: bacon or sausage. For dessert, you have the choice of two cakes: cheese cake or chocolate cake. You can only choose one from each category.

   a. If you choose one from each category, how many choices do you have?

   ____

   b. If you're a vegetarian (you do not eat bacon or sausage), how many choices do you have?

   ____

   c. List one possible meal here if you do choose one from each category.

   ____

2. A gift store wants to name their store with the four initials of their four owners: T, H, A, S. How many permutations of the four letters are there if you're not allowed to repeat any letters?

Answer the following questions using only the digits: 1, 5, 6, 7, 8.

3. How many different 5-digit numbers can you make if repetition is not allowed?

____

4. How many different 5-digit numbers can you make if repetition is allowed?

____

5. How many different 3-digit numbers can you make if repetition is not allowed?

____

6. How many different 3-digit numbers can you make if your number must be greater than 700 and if repetition is not allowed

____

7. How many different 3-digit numbers can you make that are odd if repetition is not allowed?

____

8. How many different 3-digit numbers can you make that are divisible by 5 if repetition is not allowed?

____

9. How many different 2-digit numbers can you make that are even if repetition is not allowed?

____

10. List the 2-digit numbers that you can make (problem 9).

____

Understanding Permutations and Combinations

Suppose you have 9 students trying out for three parts in a musical. If those three parts were ranked differently such as major lead, minor lead, and chorus, you would be working with a permutation (where the order matters within the chosen group).

Example 1: How many permutations of 9 people choosing 3 at a time, would you have in the scenario above?

You would write this as nPr where n is the total and r is how many you're taking out at a time.

nPr is defined as $\frac{n!}{(n-r)!}$ so $9P3 = \frac{9!}{(9-3)!} = \frac{9!}{6!}$

$$\frac{9 \bullet 8 \bullet 7 \bullet \cancel{6} \bullet \cancel{5} \bullet \cancel{4} \bullet \cancel{3} \bullet \cancel{2} \bullet \cancel{1}}{\cancel{6} \bullet \cancel{5} \bullet \cancel{4} \bullet \cancel{3} \bullet \cancel{2} \bullet \cancel{1}} = 9 \bullet 8 \bullet 7 = 504 \text{ permutations}$$

Now if you were choosing a group (r) out of a total (n) where within the chosen group there was no difference (no rank) you'd be working with a combination and not a permutation.

Example 2: Choose 3 students out of 9 where those 3 positions were the same (had no rank). How many combinations would you have? The formula for a combination is nCr.

nCr is defined as $\frac{n!}{r!(n-r)!}$ so $9C3 = \frac{9!}{3!(9-3)!} = \frac{9!}{3! \bullet 6!}$

$$\frac{\overset{3}{\cancel{9}} \bullet \overset{4}{\cancel{8}} \bullet 7 \bullet \cancel{6} \bullet \cancel{5} \bullet \cancel{4} \bullet \cancel{3} \bullet \cancel{2} \bullet \cancel{1}}{\cancel{3} \bullet \cancel{2} \bullet 1 \bullet \cancel{6} \bullet \cancel{5} \bullet \cancel{4} \bullet \cancel{3} \bullet \cancel{2} \bullet \cancel{1}} = 3 \bullet 4 \bullet 7 = 84 \text{ combinations}$$

You can find nPr and nCr in a scientific calculator. What is most important is that you know when a problem is a permutation and when it's a combination.

Practice

State if these problems involve a permutation or a combination. Then find the answer.

1. A social studies teacher wants to use 4 students to form a debate team out of a group of 8 volunteers. How many different teams can she make?

____

2. Eight students are running for president, vice president, and treasurer. How many possible outcomes can there be?

____

3. A company wants to choose 2 letters for their logo out of 5 different letters. If *OA* is the same as *AO*, how many possible logos could there be?

____

4. If you choose 3 letters from the word THOMAS where repetition is not allowed, show that the counting principle is the same as 6*P*3.

   Counting Principle - Choices: ______ • ______ • ______

   6*P*3 = ________________

5. Five boys and three girls are running for president, vice president and secretary. Assume no one can hold more than one office.

   a. How many ways can a slate of officers be chosen? ________________

   b. What is the probability that out of those the three positions all will be filled by females? ____________________

6. List the 2-letter permutations you can form from the letters in the word BEES (remember you cannot tell the difference between the "E's" and repetition is not allowed.) List them.

____

____

____

Empirical vs Theoretical Probability

Practice

Perform the following experiment and answer the questions below.

1. Toss a coin 30 times and record your outcomes. Record your results here.

______ ______ ______ ______ ______ ______ ______ ______ ______ ______

______ ______ ______ ______ ______ ______ ______ ______ ______ ______

______ ______ ______ ______ ______ ______ ______ ______ ______ ______

   a. How many times did you get tails? _______ Fraction: $\frac{\quad}{30}$

   b. How many times did you get heads? _______ Fraction: $\frac{\quad}{30}$

2. If you had tossed the coin 10,000 times would you expect the results to be different? Explain your thinking.

____

____

____

In theory, tails should show up 50% of the time, and heads should show up 50% of the time. Empirically (based on an experiment), this does not always happen, but if your experiment is done a larger number of times, your results will approach the theoretical probability for that event. So, to summarize in theory...

The probability of an event E happening is defined by the compound inequality $0 \leq E \leq 1$.

The complement of E is defined as $1 - P(E)$.

Understanding Statistics

Knowing how to conduct research and knowing how to analyze data and trends are all tools employed in many fields of study including medicine, politics, sports, the environment, etc. As a consumer, you will enhance your critical thinking skills and make better decisions by knowing how to gather information, read and interpret graphs, and analyze results.

Measures of Central Tendency

When you're given a set of data, you can analyze it in different ways. One way is to find the mean (average), median, mode, and range of your data. The mean, mode, and median are the three main measures of central tendency.

To find the mean or average, add your data and divide by the number of numbers in your data.

To find the median (think middle of the road), organize your data from smallest to largest (it could be from largest to smallest) and find the middle number. If your data has an even number of numbers, then find the mean of the two numbers in the middle.

To find the **mo**de (**mo**st often), find the number that appears most often.

To find the range or the spread of the data, find the smallest number and the largest number and show them with a dash, or subtract the two to show how far the smallest number is from the largest number.

Example 1: At the Museum of Play in Rochester, NY, these are the ages of the people who entered the museum during the first fifteen minutes: 5, 31, 7, 25, 32, 38, 65, 65, 5, 42, 48, 27, 5, 30, 5. Find the mean, median, mode, and range of this data.

The mean is 430 ÷ 15 = 28.7 (rounded to the nearest tenth).

To find the median, make sure the data is in order:

5, 5, 5, 5, 7, 25, 27, **30**, 31, 32, 38, 42, 48, 65, 65

The median is 30. This tells you that, in those first fifteen minutes, there were as many people under 30 who came to the museum as there were people who were more than 30. Think of it as 50% were more than 30 and 50% were less than 30 years old.

The mode is 5 which is the most frequent number in the data.
The range is 5-65. There's a range of 60 years.

Example 2: A university pays these salaries to six professors in the English Department: \$35,000, \$40,000, \$30,000, \$29,500, \$32,600, and \$100,000. Find the mean and the median.

The mean is 267,100 ÷ 6 or \$44,516.67 (rounded).
The data in order is \$29,500, \$30,000, \$32,600, \$35,000, \$40,000, \$100,000.
So the median is (\$32,600 + 35,000) ÷ 2 or \$33,800.

Practice

1. Which measure of central tendency best informs a new English professor entering the university above as to what salary she would estimate making? Why? Explain your thinking.

____

____

2. Find the mode and range in Example 2.

Mode: ______________ , Range: ______________.

3. The low temperatures in Barrow, Alaska, during one week in April, were −1, 1, 2, 2, 2, 3, 12 degrees Fahrenheit. Find the mean, median, mode and range.

Mean: ______________ , Median: ______________ , Mode: ______________,

Range: ______________

4. Alice has these grades in math class: 42, 88, 100, 80, 42. Her mean is 70.4. Her mode is 42, and her median is 80. Which measure of central tendency is more fair for Alice's final grade? Explain your thinking.

____

____

5. When 30 students were asked if they liked the new school lunches, 25 said NO and 5 said YES. Which measure of central tendency is more useful to report results? Explain your thinking.

____

____

6. Find the mean and median for the following data. Round your answers to the nearest thousandths.

   0.95, 0.88, 1.24, 0.03, 0.222, 0.09

   Mean: ______________ Median: ______________

7. Construct a set of data with five numbers where the mean is $10\frac{3}{4}$.

   ____

8. Construct a set of data with 6 numbers where the median is 56.

   ____

9. Find the missing grade x if a student has a mean grade of 90 and these are his test scores: 88, 89, 92, x, and 95. Solve by using algebra.

   ____

10. Find the missing temperature x if a city has a mean average temperature of 66 degrees Fahrenheit and the temperatures for those six days are: 70, 55, 60, x, 65, 70. Solve by using algebra.

    ____

Answer true or false.

______ 11. The mean is affected by numbers that are unusually high or low when compared to the other numbers in the data.

______ 12. The mean and the median can never be the same.

______ 13. The mode can be very useful when our data is not numerical.

______ 14. The median of this data: 2, 5, 10, 11, 6 is the number 10.

Quartiles and Percentiles

When the data is large, it's often separated in <u>quartiles</u>. Look at this data which has already been organized from smallest to largest.

30 30 32 35 39 42 45 48 56 67 88 89 91 91 94 95

50% **median** 50%

The median is: $\frac{48 + 56}{2} = 52$. You can now separate the data into groups containing 25% of the scores.

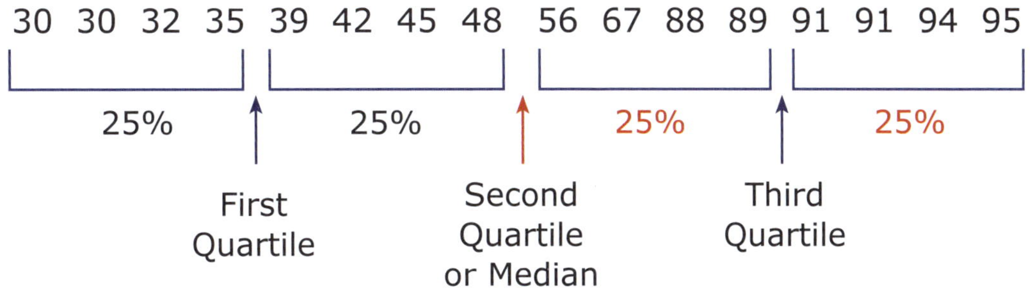

To find the first quartile: $\frac{35 + 39}{2} = 37$

The second quartile or median is 52.

To find the third quartile: $\frac{89 + 91}{2} = 90$.

Sometimes the first quartile is called the lower quartile and the third quartile is called the upper quartile.

Quartile 1 is the 25th percentile. Quartile 2 is the 50th percentile or the median. Quartile 3 is the 75th percentile.

<u>Percentiles</u> are often used to compare students after they've taken a standardized test. The data is divided into groups of 100. When a student gets in the 90th percentile, it means that the student did better than 90% of the rest of the group that took the same exam.

Do not confuse the words percentage and percentile. A percentage is the ratio of the actual points earned to total possible points changed to a percent. A percentile tells you what percent of other scores are less than your score.

Example: Rosa got 18 problems right out of 20. What is her score as a percent? Which of the scores below is Rosa's? What is her percentile when compared to the other students in the class?

Class Scores (in order):

49%, 50%, 52%, 60%, 65%, 70%, 75%, 80%, 88%, 90%, 99%, 100%

Rosa got a 90% on her test. Divide 18 by 20 and change to a percent.

To find her percentile, use this formula: Divide the number of scores below her score by the total number of scores and multiply by 100.

$\frac{9 \text{ (students who scored less than Rosa)}}{12 \text{ (total students in the class)}} = .75$ And .75(100) = 75th percentile

Rosa did better than 75% of her class. Notice how her percent score and her percentile are different.

Solve the following problems. You may use a calculator.

Practice

1. If Rosa's teacher chooses to award a student at random and places the names of the students who got above the 75% percentile, what is the probability that she would choose Rosa? ______________________________

2. These are the minutes that Julian worked out at the gym last week. Find the median, the lower quartile, and the upper quartile.

   40 45 60 45 60 65 35

   Median ______________

   Lower quartile ______________

   Upper quartile ______________

3. The following 18 students scored these points out of 40 possible points on a social studies test.

Sally	24
Danielle	39
Gustavo	40
Miguel	37
Sam	37
Kelly	35

Luisa	40
Nathan	37
Udi	40
Latarsha	39
Odin	39
Leo	34

Alyssa	38
Amanda	39
Javier	39
Courtney	32
Logan	33
Madison	36

a. Organize your data. ____________________

b. Find the median score or second quartile. ____________________

c. Find the lower or first quartile. ____________________

d. Find the upper or third quartile. ____________________

e. If the students got their scores as a percent, what percent score did Kelly get? Show your work. ____________________

f. In which quartile does Kelly fall in? Explain your thinking.

____

____

g. What is the mean of the data? Approximate the mean as a percent.

____

h. What is the mode? ____________________

i. A score that is outside of the majority of the scores is called an <u>outlier</u>. Which score is an outlier? ____________________

Frequency Tables and Histograms

A frequency table is great way to organize your data and the frequency of your data. The intervals below are of equal sizes. You can determine how many intervals you need or you'll be given the intervals. Here's the data from problem 3 from the previous page from smallest to largest.

24 32 33 34 35 36 37 37 37 38 39 39 39 39 39 40 40 40

Intervals	Tally	Frequency
24-26	|	1
27-29		0
30-32	|	1
33-35	|||	3
36-38	~~||||~~	5
39-40	~~||||~~ |||	8

This organized information can be made into a histogram. A histogram is a special bar graph where you graph the frequency of an event. Remember, your intervals must be of equal size. The bars must also touch each other. Make sure you label both axes.

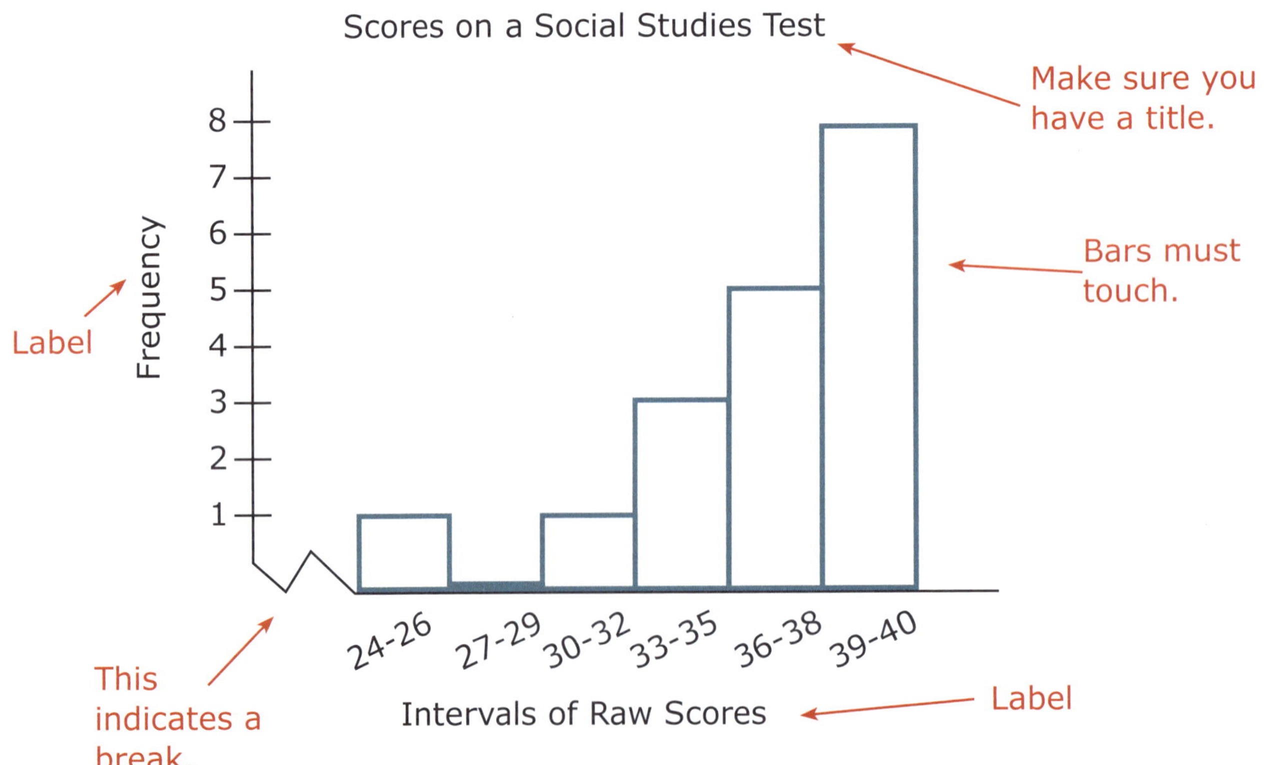

Often you will see what is called a <u>frequency polygon</u>, which is a dotted line connected to the midpoints of the bars. It starts on the horizontal axis and drops back down. The frequency polygon just gives you a visual picture of how the graph behaves.

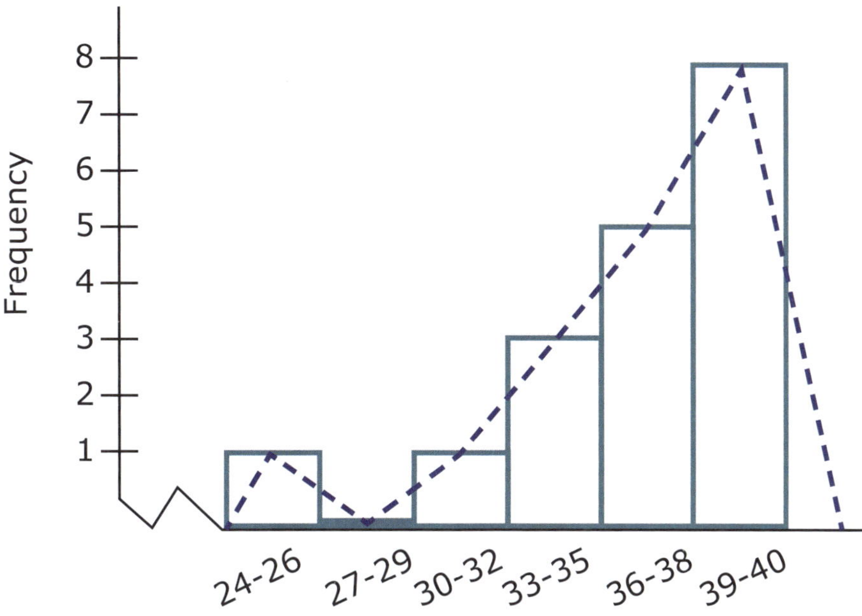

Another important histogram is the <u>cumulative frequency histogram</u>. It yields more information. Start with the same frequency table, just add a column called cumulative frequency and remove the tally column.

Intervals	Frequency	Cumulative Frequency
24-26	1	1
27-29	0	1
30-32	1	2
33-35	3	5
36-38	5	10
39-40	8	18

The cumulative column keeps adding each row down to the total 18.

Let's look at the cumulative frequency histogram below. Notice how the interval labels have changed.

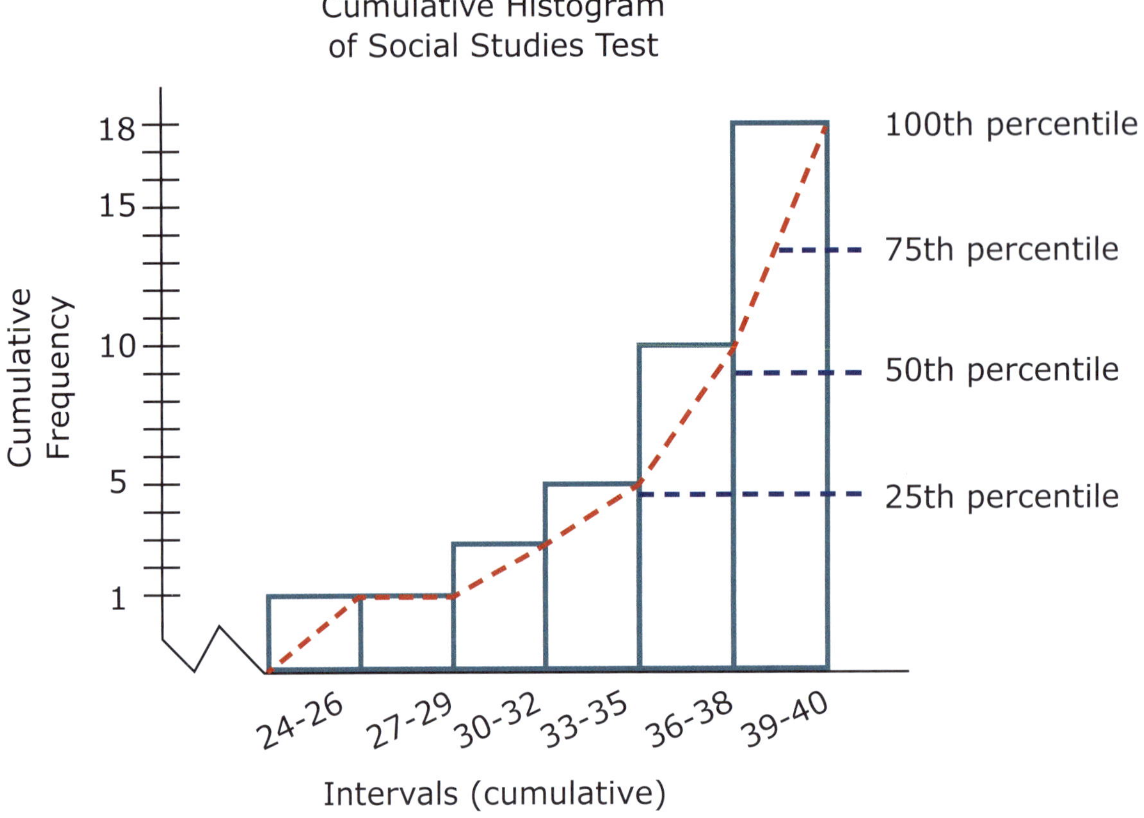

The cumulative frequency polygon is drawn to each right hand corner of each bar and does not drop down as in the frequency polygon. The importance of the cumulative frequency histogram and its polygon is that is shows us where the percentiles are located.

A dotted line is drawn from the percentiles to where this dotted line touches the cumulative frequency polygon. The 100th percentile is 18. Can you see that the 50th percentile or the median points to the bar that is marked 24-38? The median is then in the 36-38 interval (since 24-38 is too general). Remember the median is 9. The 25th percentile which is 4.5 can be found in the 33-35 interval and the 75th percentile which is 13.5 can be found in the 39-40 interval. So you use the cumulative frequency polygon to find percentiles, but use the intervals of your original frequency table to be more specific when you name the intervals.

Practice

1. Twenty middle schoolers were asked how many hours they spend playing video games on a given weekend. These are the number of hours they answered.

   3, 6, 8, 3, 3, 0, 1, 4, 3, 4, 4, 5, 6, 0, 1, 2, 2, 3, 3, 4

Intervals	Tally	Frequency	Cumulative Frequency
0-1			
2-3			
4-5			
6-7			
8-9			

   a. Organize your list from smallest to largest.

   ____

   b. Find the mean, median, mode, and range of your data. If needed, round to the nearest tenth.

   Mean: ______ Median: ______ Mode: ______ Range: ______

   c. Fill out the table above.

   d. On your own graph paper, construct a frequency histogram. Don't forget the title and labels. Draw the frequency polygon.

   e. On your own graph paper, construct a cumulative histogram. Don't forget the title and labels. Draw a cumulative frequency polygon.

   f. Using the cumulative histogram and its cumulative frequency polygon, find which interval contains the median. How do you know you're correct? Explain your thinking. ______________________________

   ____

   ____

   g. Using the cumulative histogram and its cumulative frequency polygon, find which interval contains the 75th percentile.

   ____

2. Twenty-four students entering graduate school were asked their ages. Below are their ages.

22 23 23 22 22 22 23 23 22 37 38 30

26 30 35 40 43 35 21 24 27 25 28 25

Intervals	Tally	Frequency	Cumulative Frequency
20-23			
24-27			
28-31			
32-35			
36-39			
40-43			

a. Organize your list from smallest to largest.

____

b. Find the mean, median, mode, and range of your data. If needed round to the nearest tenth.

Mean: ______ Median: ______ Mode: ______ Range: ______

c. Fill out the table above.

d. On your own graph paper, construct a frequency histogram. Don't forget the title and labels. Draw the frequency polygon.

e. On your own graph paper, construct a cumulative histogram. Don't forget the title and labels. Draw a cumulative frequency polygon.

f. Using the cumulative histogram and its cumulative frequency polygon, find which interval contains the median. How do you know you're correct? Explain your thinking. ______________________________

____

____

Stem and Leaf Plots

While histograms give you a lot of information, a stem and leaf plot actually shows you a pictorial look at the numbers in your data. It's a way to graph your data when the data is not too big.

Example 1: At a theater, twenty customers were asked their ages to determine their entry fee. These are their ages in order: 10, 11, 15, 20, 23, 27, 31, 33, 33, 35, 36, 36, 40, 43, 49, 61, 63, 65, 67, 68. Make a stem and leaf plot of this data. Define a key first. 1|0 means 10.

Ages

Stem	Leaf
1	0 1 5
2	0 3 7
3	1 3 3 5 6 6
4	0 3 9
5	
6	1 3 5 7 8

Example 2: Make a stem and leaf plot of the following data.

16.2, 16.4, 17, 18.2, 18.5, 18.6, 18.9, 19.4, 20.4, 21.8, 29.4, 30.2, 30.4

Define a key first. 16|2 means 16.2

Stem	Leaf
16	2 4
17	
18	2 5 6 9
19	4
20	4
21	8
29	4
30	2 4

Box and Whisker Plots

Another way that statisticians graph data, especially a large data set, is to use a box and whisker plot, also known as a box plot.

Box and Whisker plots use 5 pieces of information to create a graph. You need the median, first quartile, third quartile, lower extreme (smallest number in the data), and upper extreme (largest number in the data). While the graph will not show you as much detail as in a stem and leaf plot or a histogram, it will show whether your data is skewed and if you have outliers (unusual data that is way out of what you expected). Box and whisker plots are mostly useful for comparing two sets of data.

Example: Use a box and whisker plot to graph the following scores from Ms. Stein's social studies class. Here's the data in order:

40, 60, 60, 70, 70, 72, 74, 85, 85, 85, 85, 90, 93, 98, 100, 100

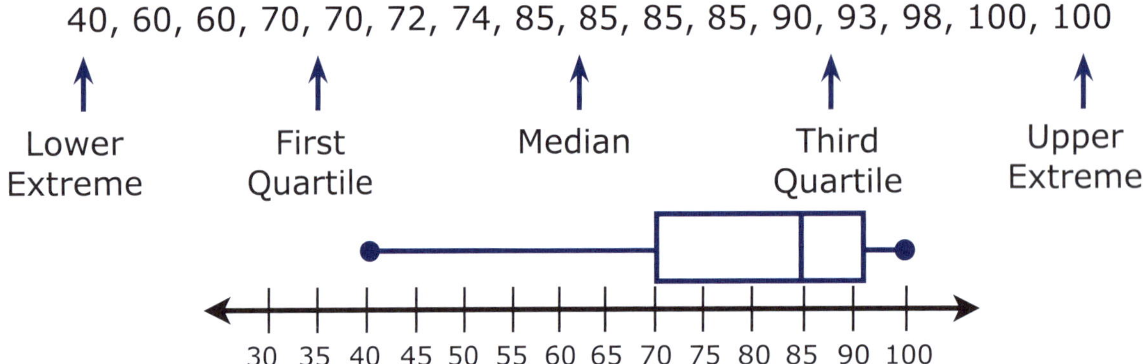

The first mark is the lower extreme (40). The box starts at the first quartile (70) and ends at the third quartile (92) with the median (85) marked with a vertical line inside the box. The upper extreme (100) ends the graph. The "whiskers" are the lines connecting the box to each extreme.

Practice

1. Mr. Roberts' social studies class had the following results on the same test.

   25, 60, 70, 76, 80, 85, 88, 88, 90, 90, 90, 91, 95, 95, 100, 100

   a. What is the lower extreme? _____

   b. What is the upper extreme? _____

   c. What is the first quartile? _____

   d. What is the third quartile? _____

   e. What is the median? _____

   f. Make a box and whisker plot.

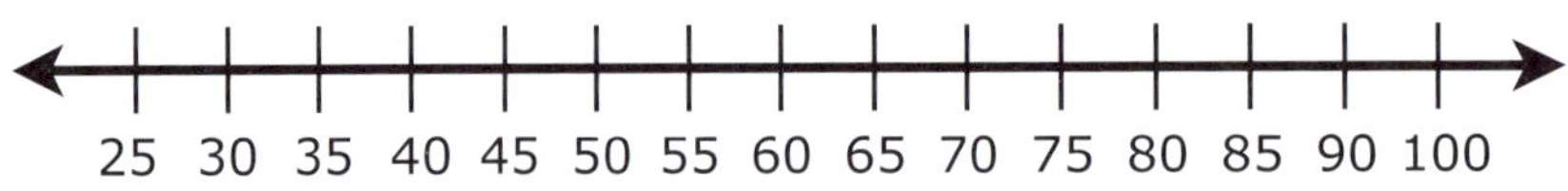

g. Compare Ms. Stein's and Mr. Roberts' box and whisker plots. Which class did better? Explain your thinking.

h. Find the mean score for both classes. Round to the nearest tenth. Do you still agree with your answer to 1g?

i. Which score in Mr. Roberts' class would you consider an "outlier?" Explain your thinking.

2. Make a stem and leaf plot of Ms. Stein's class scores.

3. Make a stem and leaf plot of Mr. Roberts' class scores.

4. What are the advantages and disadvantages of using a stem and leaf plot vs a box and whisker plot to compare Ms. Stein and Mr. Roberts' class scores? Explain your thinking.

____

____

____

____

5. Another teacher posted this box and whisker plot of her class scores. Answer the questions below.

30 35 40 45 50 55 60 65 70 75 80 85 90 100

a. What is the lower extreme? ______

b. What is the upper extreme? ______

c. What is the first quartile? ______

d. What is the third quartile? ______

e. What is the median? ______

6. Create a set of 11 scores that match the box and whisker plot above.

____

7. Is it possible for another set of 11 scores to have the same lower extreme, same upper extreme, same first quartile, and same third quartile as problem #5 and have a different median? Explain your thinking.

____

____

8. Is a box and whisker plot the best choice for a graph if the first quartile and the third quartile are the same? What would that tell you about the median? Explain your thinking.

____

____

Understanding Surveys

In this chapter you have learned how to determine the probability of events and how events are often displayed by tables and graphs. It's important to end the chapter by discussing the importance of accurate surveys and accurate graphs. It's not hard to make a graph that can distort real facts. Sometimes data is not obtained fairly. Also, a poor survey won't yield accurate results.

A good survey has to have a defined goal. It must contain vocabulary that is easily understood. A good survey does not ask more than one question at a time, and it must not lead the person into answering one way or another. It must also choose a population that will represent a fair representation of the goal. Remember, you want truthful answers.

A survey must represent a large sample of the population you're testing. The sample you choose must be random and not just target a group of people that may answer in one particular way. It's always a good idea to test your survey to find out ways to improve it!

Example: A company wants to open up a dance club in a neighborhood where more than half of its population are in nursing homes. Which survey would be more representative of what its citizens want?

a. Survey taken at the local gym.

b. Survey taken at the nursing home and at the mall.

c. Survey taken at the most popular restaurant.

d. Survey taken at a hospital.

Choice b might yield more accurate information. There may be senior citizens who want to attend a dance if they had transportation to the dance club, also, those shopping at the mall represent a large number of active people who may or may not want a dance club.

Practice

1. What is wrong with this survey question? Explain your thinking. "How many times a year do you get acute viral rhinopharyngitis?

___

___

2. What's wrong with this survey question? "How old were you when you lost your first tooth and did you get money from the tooth fairy?"

____

____

3. Maria wants to find out where the 8th grade students want to hold their prom dance. Which survey would yield the most representative answer?

   a. A survey taken on a Monday morning before school starts.
   b. A survey given to the entire school.
   c. A survey mailed home to parents of the 8th graders.
   d. A survey given to all 8th graders during school hours.

4. What's wrong with this survey question? "Good students go to bed no later than 8:30 p.m. What time do you go to bed?"

____

____

____

5. Improve this survey question: "How many times last year did you get up before 6 a.m.?"

____

____

6. What's wrong with this survey question? "Do you always eat a good breakfast?"

____

____

7. How could you improve the survey question in problem 6?

____

____

____

Chapter 15 Review

1. Maddy had these cards in a box. **3** **5** **2** **7**

   a. If she reaches without looking, what is the probability she will get the "2" card? __________

   b. If she reaches without looking, what is the probability she will get a prime number? __________

   c. In how many ways can Maddy rearrange the cards if repetition of the numbers is not allowed? __________

   d. How many three digit numbers greater than 400 can you make with Maddy's numbers, if repetition is not allowed? __________

2. Bobby has 6 marbles in a can. He has 3 red marbles, 1 blue marble and 2 green marbles. Bobby reaches without looking and chooses one marble. He gives the marble to his friend (without replacement) and then reaches to choose another marble. Show the sample space and find the following probabilities.

   Sample Space

   a. *P*(red, red) = ________

   b. *P*(red, blue) = ________

   c. *P*(green, red) = ________

   d. *P*(blue, blue) = ________

3. For the "Wizard of Oz" musical, there are 10 students trying out for the parts of Dorothy, the Scarecrow, the Lion, and the Tin Man. How many different outcomes are possible?

   ____

4. Eight students are trying out for a jazz chorus. Only three will be chosen. How many outcomes are possible if all three chosen will have the same parts?

   ____

5. There are four hiking paths from Park A to Park B. There are two hiking paths from Park B to Park C and only one from Park C to Park D. In how many ways can Fiona hike from Park A to Park D? Show your work.

____

6. At the Smart Tool Company, the following 5 employees with the same responsibilities, make these salaries: \$35,000, \$23,000, \$48,000, \$66,000, and \$130,000. Use your own thinking to explain why Kathy believes that if she gets a job at the Smart Tool Company, she will make at least \$60,000. Is she correct?

____

____

____

7. The following is a list of the number of calories found in one serving of chocolate ice cream from seven popular brands. Round to the nearest calorie.

285, 140, 130, 173, 230, 285, 235.

a. Find the mode. ________ c. Find the median. ________

b. Find the mean. ________ d. Find the range. ________

8. Twenty random elementary students' backpacks were weighed and these are the results in pounds: 8, 13, 16, 1, 2, 5, 16, 10, 8, 11, 3, 1, 2, 5, 9, 4, 6, 3, 5, 5.

a. Fill out the following frequency and cumulative frequency table.

Intervals (pounds)	Tally	Frequency	Cumulative Frequency
0-2			
3-5			
6-8			
9-11			
12-14			
15-17			

b. Make a frequency histogram and polygon of the data on the previous page. Use your own graph paper. Don't forget the title and labels.

c. Make a cumulative histogram and cumulative polygon of the data. Use your own graph paper. Don't forget the title and labels.

d. Which interval contains the 25th percentile? ________

e. Which interval contains the median? ________

f. Which interval contains the 75th percentile? ________

9. The nurse who weighed the students' backpacks in problem 8 sent out a letter to parents and teachers saying that no student should be carrying a backpack that weighs 10% more than the student's weight. Amy, who is in the second grade, was carrying the 13 pound backpack. She weighs 52 pounds.

   a. How much weight over the recommended weight is she carrying? Explain your thinking.

   ____

   ____

   b. Amir, who is in first grade, was carrying all his books and his backpack weighed 10 pounds. What is the least Amir should weigh to carry such a load? Explain your thinking.

   ____

   ____

10. In another school, the nurse only weighed fifth grade students and their backpacks. She found the weight of their backpacks was no more than 10% of the students' weight. Why is this not a good survey as to the weight of backpacks in elementary school? Explain your thinking.

____

____

11. John wanted to know approximately how much water (in ounces) people drink each day. He asked 16 athletes as they were leaving the local gym: "Approximately, how much water do you drink per day?" These are his results.

    80, 70, 80, 82, 32, 130, 70, 72, 89, 88, 55, 56, 64, 135, 92, 95

    Make a stem and leaf plot of the data.

12. Make a box and whisker plot of the data from problem 11.

    a. Find the lower extreme ________

    b. The first quartile ________

    c. The median ________

    d. The third quartile ________

    e. The upper extreme ________

    f. Do you think that John's sample is a good sample? Is he choosing the right population for his question? Why or why not? Explain your thinking.

    ____

    ____

    ____

    ____

Final Examination

Part I - 2 points each

1. Which of the following numbers is a prime number?

   a. 0 b. 51 c. 2 d. 111

2. What is true about any irrational number?

   a. It's a number that never ends.
   b. It's a decimal that repeats.
   c. It cannot be a negative number.
   d. It's a number that cannot be written as a fraction of the form $\frac{p}{q}$, q cannot be equal 0.

3. Which of the following fractions is undefined?

   a. $\frac{1}{0}$ b. $\frac{0}{5}$ c. $\frac{\sqrt{5}}{4}$ d. $\frac{-5}{5}$

4. Which of the following is the answer to $1 - 4 \bullet 5 \div -10$

   a. 3 b. 1.5 c. −3 d. −1.5

5. Simplify: $-5 - (2 + 5)^2 + 10$

   a. −95 b. 28 c. −44 d. −9

6. Simplify: $-8\frac{1}{8} - 10\frac{3}{4}$

   a. $2\frac{5}{8}$ b. $-18\frac{7}{8}$ c. $-2\frac{5}{8}$ d. $18\frac{7}{8}$

7. In a school there are 2 teachers for every 15 students. If the school has 240 students, how many teachers are there in the school?

   a. 12 b. 17 c. 30 d. 32

8. A bread recipe calls for 6 cups of flour for every $2\frac{1}{4}$ cups warm water. The chef wants to use 8 cups of flour, how much warm water should the chef use?

   a. 3 cups b. 2 cups c. 5 cups d. $3\frac{1}{4}$ cups

9. On a map 1.5 cm = 500 miles. How far apart in miles are two towns that on the same map are 9 cm apart?

   a. 600 b. 550 c. 3,000 d. 2,700

10. What percent of 8 is 5?

    a. 40% b. .625% c. 62.5% d. 87.5%

11. Change $\frac{1}{4}$% to a decimal?

    a. .25 b. .0025 c. .025 d. .14

12. 125% of what number is 20?

    a. 16 b. 45 c. 80 d. 25

13. Dalia bought a $58.50 jacket at the mall. She paid 8% tax on that amount. How much tax did she pay?

    a. $4.68 b. $63.18 c. $66.50 d. $46.80

14. Jonah spent $132.50 on a video game. This included a 6% tax. How much was the video game before the tax was added?

    a. $126.50 b. $175.00 c. $140.40 d. $125

15. A bicycle shop has a bike for sale at $250. The original price was $400. What is the percent of discount?

    a. 60% b. 20% c. 37.5% d. 62.5%

16. What is the simple interest you would pay if you borrowed $2,500 from your aunt at a yearly rate of 4.5% yearly for 3 years.

    a. $337.50 b. $112.50 c. $3,375 d. $2,837.50

17. If $a = 2$, $b = -5$, and $c = 10$, evaluate $-ab^2 + c$

    a. 110 b. 90 c. 60 d. –40

18. Which of the following expressions is undefined if $x = 5$?

    a. $\frac{1}{x}$ b. $\frac{1}{x + 5}$ c. $\frac{-5 + x}{5}$ d. $\frac{1}{x - 5}$

19. Translate the expression: Twice a number y less than eight.

a. $2y - 8$ b. $8 - 2y$ c. $2(y - 8)$ d. $2(8 - y)$

20. Translate the expression: Three times the sum of w plus five.

a. $3w + 5$ b. $3w - 5$ c. $3(w + 5)$ d. $3 \bullet 5 + w$

21. Simplify the following: $-4w + 5 + 4w^2 - 10$

a. $8w^2 - 5$ b. -5 c. 5 d. $4w^2 - 4w - 5$

22. Simplify: From $3a^3$ subtract $-2a^3 - 1$.

a. $5a^3 + 1$ b. $a^3 - 1$ c. $-5a^3 - 1$ d. $a^3 + 1$

23. What is the product of $-5r$ with $-6r^6$.

a. $30r^6$ b. $30r^7$ c. $-11r$ d. $11r^7$

24. What is the missing term: $10yw^4 \bullet$ __________ $= -100yw^{12}$

a. $-10w^8$ b. $-10yw^8$ c. $10w^3$ d. $-10yw^3$

25. What is the quotient when $-90y^5$ is divided by $90y^7$.

a. $-y^2$ b. 0 c. $-y^{-2}$ d. y^2

26. Write 86,000,000 in scientific notation.

a. $8.6 \text{ X } 10^{-6}$ b. $86 \text{ X } 10^6$ c. $8.6 \text{ X } 10^7$ d. $8.6 \text{ X } 10^{-7}$

27. Another way to write $(3.5 \text{ X } 10^6) \text{ X } (2 \text{ X } 10^3)$ is to write

a. $7 \text{ X } 10^{18}$ b. $7 \text{ X } 10^9$ c. $7 \text{ X } 10^0$ d. $7 \text{ X } 10^3$

28. Which property of numbers is shown: $3(4y + 20) = 12y + 60$?

a. Associative property for addition
b. Commutative property for addition
c. Distributive property of multiplication over addition
d. Identity property

29. What is the multiplicative inverse of −5?

a. $-\frac{1}{5}$ b. 5 c. −5 d. $\frac{1}{5}$

30. If $n + 1$ is an even integer, what is the next even integer after $n + 1$?

a. $n + 3$ b. n c. $n + 4$ d. $n + 2$

31. Which of these is the correct equation for this problem?

"The sum of three consecutive odd integers is 75."

a. $3(n + 1) = 75$
b. $n + (n + 1) + (n + 3) = 75$
c. $n + (n + 2) + (n + 4) = 75$
d. $3n + 5 = 75$

32. Which of the following is the inequality that matches this graph?

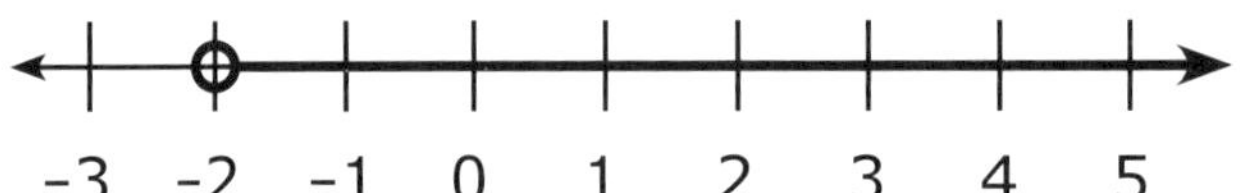

a. $x < -2$ b. $x \geq -2$ c. $x > -3$ d. $x > -2$

33. What is the solution to this inequality? $-(w - 5) > -15$

a. $w < 20$ b. $w < 10$ c. $w > -10$ d. $w < -20$

34. Which of the following is the compound inequality that matches this graph?

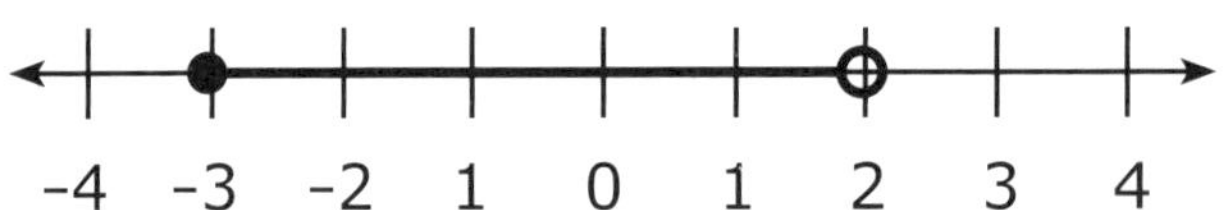

a. $-3 > x > -2$ b. $-3 \geq x < 2$ c. $-3 < x < 2$ d. $-3 \leq x < 2$

35. In a rectangle the width is half the length. If the perimeter must be less than 60 yards, what is the greatest <u>whole</u> number possible for the width?

a. 10 yds b. 9 yds c. 18 yds d. 19 yds

36. Which of the following fractions is the same as the decimal $5.\overline{6}$.

a. $\frac{56}{10}$ b. $5\frac{2}{3}$ c. $5\frac{1}{6}$ d. $5\frac{1}{3}$

37. Which of the following is NOT a perfect square?

a. 25 b. 441 c. 400 d. 1,000

38. Simplify the following: $\sqrt{48}$

a. $3\sqrt{4}$ b. $4\sqrt{3}$ c. 24 d. $2\sqrt{12}$

39. Simplify the following expression: $-5\sqrt{81} + \sqrt{25} - \sqrt{3}$

a. $-40\sqrt{3}$ b. $-9 + \sqrt{5}$ c. $40 - \sqrt{3}$ d. $-40 - \sqrt{3}$

40. Which of the following CANNOT be the sides of a right triangle?

a. 1, 1, 2 b. 3, 4, 5 c. 8, 6, 10 d. 5, 12, 13

41. Find the measure of $\angle x$ and $\angle y$.

a. $m\angle x = 20°$, $m\angle y = 160°$

b. $m\angle x = 200°$, $m\angle y = 20°$

c. $m\angle x = 160°$, $m\angle y = 20°$

d. $m\angle x = 160°$, $m\angle y = 80°$

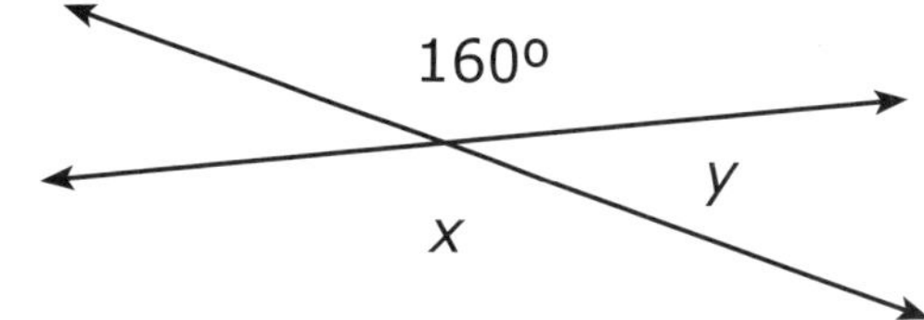

42. What expression represents the perimeter of a regular hexagon whose side is $n + 5$?

a. $5n + 25$ b. $6n + 30$ c. $7n + 35$ d. $8n + 40$

43. In a scalene triangle, the largest angle is five times the smallest angle and the middle angle is three times the smallest angle. Find the largest angle of the triangle?

a. 100° b. 20° c. 60° d. 120°

44. Which of the following is a true statement?

a. A square is a rhombus.

b. A trapezoid is a type of parallelogram.

c. A parallelogram always has congruent diagonals.

d. An octagon is a polygon with 9 sides.

45. What is the area of the following triangle.

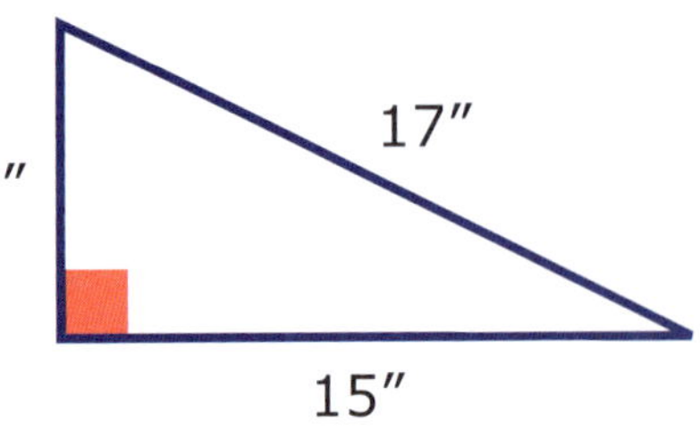

a. 120 in.^{2} c. 68 in.^{2}

b. 60 in.^{2} d. 240 in.^{2}

46. What is the radius of a circle whose circumference is 20π inches.

a. 5″   b. 40″   c. 10″   d. 20″

47. What is the area of the trapezoid whose perimeter is 54′.

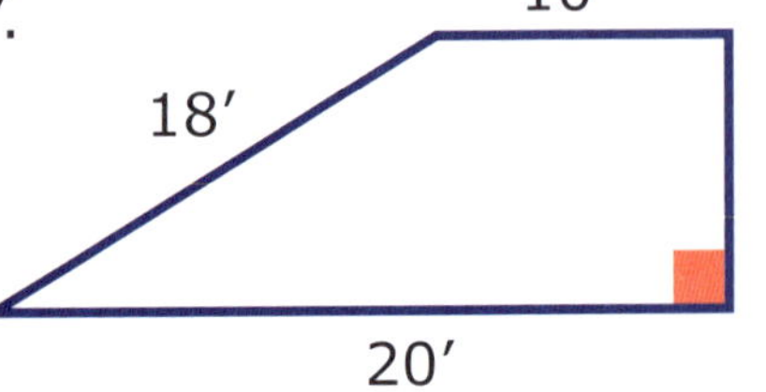

a. 600 ft^2 c. 300 ft^2

b. 270 ft^2 d. 90 ft^2

48. What is the volume of a pyramid with a base of 72 in.^{2} and a height of 10 inches.

a. 720 in.^{3} b. 360 in.^{3} c. 90 in.^{3} d. 240 in.^{3}

49. What is the volume of the cylinder. Leave your answer in terms of π.

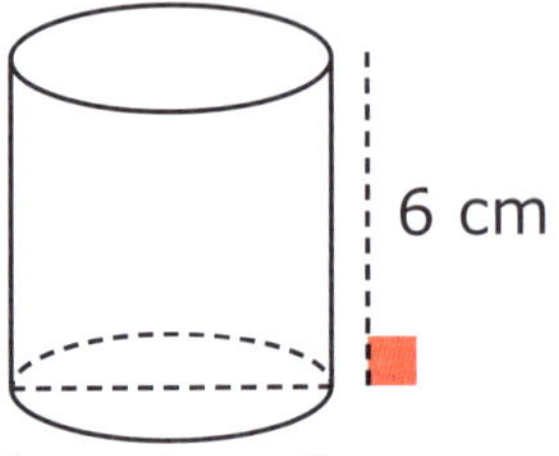

Diameter: 6 cm

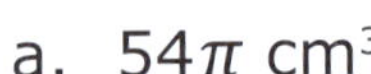

a. 54π cm^3 c. 216π cm^3

b. 36π cm^3 d. 18π cm^3

50. A cylinder and a cone have the same base area and the same height. What is the ratio of the cone to the cylinder?

a. 3   b. $\frac{1}{3}$ c. $\frac{1}{2}$ d. 2

51. What is the surface area of cube whose side is 1.5 cm.

a. 9 cm^2 b. 13.5 cm^2 c. 20.25 cm^2 d. 3.375 cm^2

52. What is the slope (m) and y-intercept (b) of this equation? $-2y = 6x - 8$

a. $m = 6$, $b = -8$ b. $m = -3$, $b = -4$ c. $m = -3$, $b = 4$ d. $m = 3$, $b = -4$

53. Which of these equations represents a horizontal line?

a. $x = 0$ b. $y = 2x$ c. $y = -3$ d. $y = -x$

54. What is the slope of the line that passes by (−6, −4) and (0 , 2).

a. 1 b. −1 c. 12 d. 0

55. Which of the following sets shows a proportional relationship?

a. (2, 5), (3, 7), (4, 9), (5, 11)
b. (−2, −5), (−1, −2), (0, 1), (1, 4)
c. (0, 2), (1, 5), (2, 8), (3, 11)
d. (−2, −10), (−1, −5), (0, 0), (1, 5), (2, 10)

56. Which of the following points is the solution to this system of equations?
$2x - y = 4$ $x + y = 5$

a. (−3, 2) b. (3, 2) c. (4, 1) d. (2, 3)

57. Which of the following transformations does not guarantee congruency?

a. Dilation b. Rotation c. Translation d. Reflection

58. By what reason are these triangles congruent?

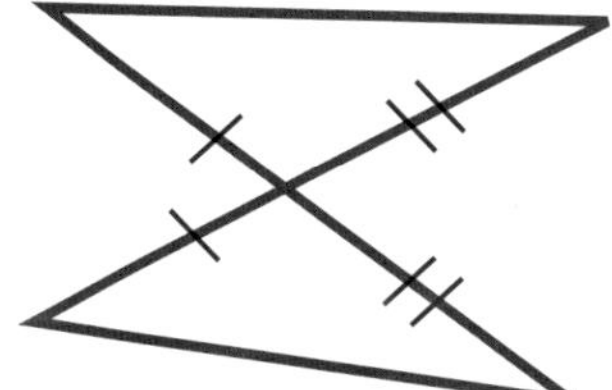

a. SSS c. ASA

b. SAS d. SS

59. Which of the following sets does NOT represent a function?

a. (−1, 0), (0, 0), (1, 0), (2, 0)
b. (−1, 1), (0, 0), (1, 1), (2, 4)
c. (5, 6), (5, −6), (4, 0), (5, 3)
d. (−1, −1), (0, 0), (1, 1), (2, 8)

60. Which of the following represents an exponential function?

a. $y = x^2$
b. $y = |x|$
c. $y = 3x - 5$
d. $y = 2^x$

61. Compare the graph of $y = |x + 2|$ with the parent function $y = |x|$.

a. $y = |x + 2|$ is a translation two units up.
b. $y = |x + 2|$ is translation two units down.
c. $y = |x + 2|$ is a translation two units to the left.
d. $y = |x + 2|$ is a translation two units to the right.

62. In how many ways can you rearrange the letters in the word MATH, if repetition is not allowed?

a. 24 b. 12 c. 256 d. 6

63. Find the minimum score Jon needs to get on his next test to have a mean (average) grade of 90. His current grades are 89, 85, 99, 85.

a. 87 b. 88 c. 91 d. 92

64. What is NOT true about this set of data? {3, 5, 3, 9, 12}.

a. The mean is greater than the median.
b. The mode is 3.
c. The median is greater than the mean.
d. The range is 3-12.

65. What is a reason for making a cumulative histogram and a cumulative polygon?

a. It helps to find the quartiles.
b. It helps to find the interval that contains the median.
c. It helps to find percentiles.
d. All of the above.

Part II - 5 points each

Use your own paper if needed.

1. Solve for w.

   $-3(w - 1) + 5 = 2(w + 5)$

2. Find $m\angle ABC$ if line $m \parallel n$. ______________________

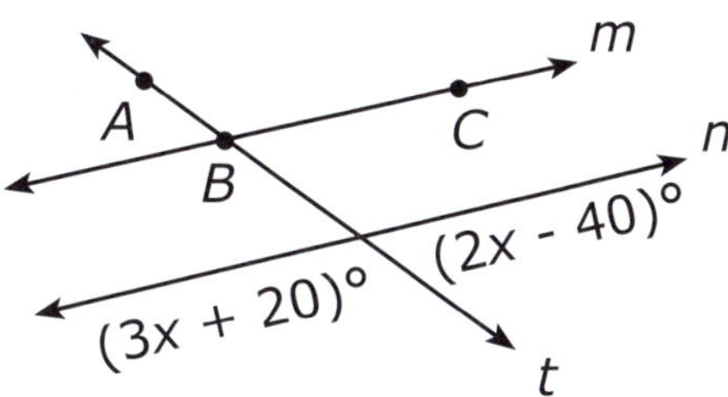

3. Find the missing side of this triangle. ______________________

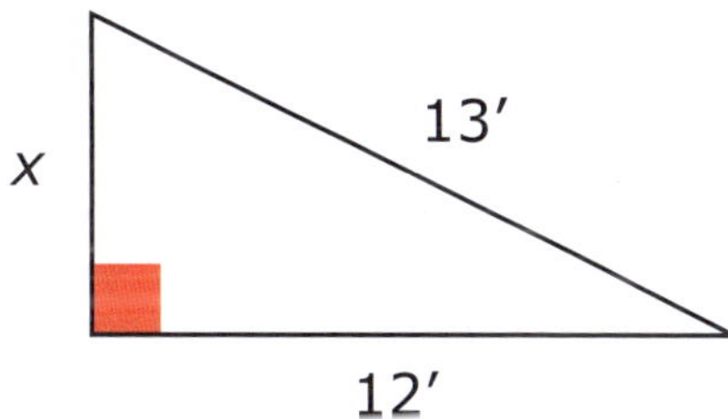

4. A jar has 3 red beads and 4 blue beads. You reach without looking and pull out one bead and don't put it back. Then you reach again without looking. What's the probability you will get blue first and then red. Show the sample space.

   ____

Total Points: ________ /150 = ________%

Glossary

absolute value The distance a number is away from zero. Absolute value is always positive.

additive inverse The opposite of a number; additive inverse of −10 is 10.

adjacent angles Angles on the same plane that have a common vertex and side

area The number of unit squares in a 2 dimensional shape

base The number or variable that sits under an exponent

binomial A polynomial with two terms

braces The symbols { } which are used to indicate a set, or inclusion

brackets The inclusion symbols [ ] often used in addition to parenthesis

circumference The perimeter of a circle. $C = \pi d$

circumscribe To place a shape outside another so that their boundaries touch but do not go through each other's boundaries.

coefficient A number that sits in front of a variable term. In $10n$, the coefficient is 10

combination An arrangement where inside a chosen group the arrangement does not matter

complementary Two angles whose sum is 90 degrees

composite Any whole number greater than 1 that is not prime

congruent Identical in size and shape

consecutive To go in order. Example: consecutive integers: 67, 68, 69; consecutive even integers: 20, 22, 24, 26, etc.

converse The converse of an "If Then" statement such as "If p then q" would be "If q then p." For example: the converse of "If it rains then in pours" would be "If it pours then it rains."

counting The set of whole numbers {1, 2, 3, 4, 5, ...}, sometimes called the natural numbers.

cubed To multiply a number by itself three times. Example: 2 cubed is 8.

denominator The bottom number in a fraction

dependent variable y is the dependent variable since y depends on what you let x be

diagonal A line segment joining one vertex of a polygon to a non-adjacent vertex

difference The answer to a subtraction problem

divisible A number is divisible by another number when you divide and there is no remainder

domain The set of x-values, or independent values, in a set of points

element of a set A member of a set

empty set A set with no solution

equation A mathematical sentence with an equal sign.

evaluate To evaluate means to substitute a value for a variable and then simplify the answer

even The set of whole numbers {0, 2, 4, 6, 8, 10...} divisible by 2. Remember 0 is even.

exponent or power A number that tells you how many times a base is to be multiplied by itself

expression A mathematical statement with no equal or inequality symbol. Example: $5x + 3$ and 15 are expressions.

factor A number that goes into another number evenly

finite A set that ends

hypotenuse The longest side of a right triangle

improper fraction A fraction with a numerator larger than a denominator.

independent variable *x* is the independent variable because you have the freedom to let *x* be any value

inequality A mathematical sentence with an inequality symbol (>, <, ≥ or ≤, ≠)

infinite A set that does not end

inscribe To place a shape inside another so that their boundaries touch but do not go through each other's boundaries.

integers The set {...–4, –3, –2, –1, 0, 1, 2, 3, ...}

intersect Intersect means to meet

irrational Any number that is not rational. A decimal that does not terminate AND does not repeat.

let statement Identifies what the variable stands for in a word problem

like terms Like terms are polynomial units that share the same ending. The coefficient can be different, but the variable components must be identical.

means vs extremes In a proportion $a/b = c/d$, a and d are called the extremes, and b and c are called the means

monomial A polynomial with one term

multiple A number obtained by multiplying an original number by an integer. Example: Multiples of 6: {6, 12, 18, 24, 30, 36, ...}

multiplicative inverse Another word for reciprocal. Multiplicative inverses always multiply to 1.

natural Another word for a counting number {1, 2, 3, 4, 5, ...}

numerator The top number in a fraction

odd The set of numbers {1, 3, 5, 7, 9, ...}

outlier A piece of data that lies "far away" from the majority of the data

perfect squares The set of numbers {1, 4, 9, 16, 25, 36, etc.}

perimeter The distance around a shape

permutation An arrangement where the order matters

perpendicular Two lines or segments that intersect to make a right angle

polynomial Another word for an expression that usually has variables and numbers. Any expression that has more than 3 terms.

prime Any number greater than 1 that has only two factors, 1 and itself. Remember 1 is NOT a prime. The first prime is 2.

prime factorization A number rewritten with its prime factors

product The answer to a multiplication problem

proportion Two ratios that are equal. In a proportion, the product of the means equals the product of the extremes.

quotient The answer to a division problem

range The set of all y-values, or dependent values, in a set of points

rate A special ratio that compares measurements

ratio The relationship between two amounts. Another word for fraction.

rational Any number that can be written as a fraction with an integer numerator and an integer denominator as long as the denominator is not 0

reals The set of rational and irrational numbers

reciprocal Also called the multiplicative inverse. In the fraction 3/4, the reciprocal is 4/3. When you multiply reciprocals you always get 1.

remote interior angles In a triangle, the remote interior angles are the interior angles that are not adjacent to a given exterior angle. In any triangle, an exterior angle is the sum of its two remote interior angles.

right triangle A triangle with a 90 degree angle

root The word root means "answer." In a parabola, the roots are where the parabola touches the x-axis.

roster Another word for a list

sample space A list of all the possible outcomes in a probability problem

satisfy When a value makes an equation or inequality a true statement, the value satisfies the equation or inequality.

set A collection of numbers or objects

simplify To write your answer in simplest form. With fractions, reduce as much as possible and never leave fractions in improper form.

squared To square a number means to multiply it by itself

subset A subset of a set is a set where every element or member can be found in another set

sum The answer to an addition problem

supplementary Two angles whose sum is 180 degrees

term A unit with either numbers or variables that is separated by either addition (+) subtraction (–)

terminate Another word for "end"

theorem A mathematical statement that can be proven to be true

transversal A line that intersects two or more lines

trinomial A polynomial with three terms

twin primes Prime numbers that are two units apart
Example: 3 and 5, 17 and 19

undefined An expression that has NO answer or has the empty set for an answer

unit rate A rate with a denominator of 1

variable A symbol or letter that stands for a number

vector A directed line segment. The length of vector is the distance between its endpoint and the tip of the arrowhead.

vertical angles Vertical angles are opposite each other when two lines intersect and are always congruent

volume The number of cubic units in a 3 dimensional shape

whole numbers The set of numbers: $\{0, 1, 2, 3, 4, 5, \ldots\}$

Reference Sheet

List of Formulas

Perimeter of Polygons: Add all around the outside of a polygon.

Circumference of Circles: $C = \pi d$

Area

Triangle: $A = \frac{1}{2}bh$

Parallelogram: $A = bh$

Trapezoids: $\frac{1}{2}(b + B)h$

Circles: $A = \pi r^2$

Volume

Prisms: $V = Bh$, where B is the entire area of the base.

Cylinders: $V = \pi r^2 H$, where H is the height of the figure.

Spheres: $V = \frac{4}{3}\pi r^3$

Cones: $V = \frac{1}{3}\pi r^2 H$

Pyramids: $V = \frac{1}{3}BH$

Surface Area

Prisms: Find the sum of the area of every face.

Cylinders: $2\pi rh + 2\pi r^2$

Cone: $\pi rs + \pi r^2$

Sphere: $4\pi r^2$

Pythagorean Theorem $a^2 + b^2 = c^2$

Exponential Growth/Decay $y = a(1 \pm r)^t$

a = initial amount
r = rate
t = time

Slope $\frac{(y_2 - y_1)}{(x_2 - x_1)}$

Probability

Permutation nPr $\frac{n!}{(n - r)!}$

Combination nCr $\frac{n!}{r!(n - r)!}$

Table of Square Roots 1-120

No.	Square	Sq. Root	No.	Square	Sq. Root	No.	Square	Sq. Root
1	1	1.000	41	1,681	6.403	81	6,561	9.000
2	4	1.414	42	1,764	6.481	82	6,724	9.055
3	9	1.732	43	1,849	6.557	83	6,889	9.110
4	16	2.000	44	1,936	6.633	84	7,056	9.165
5	25	2.236	45	2,025	6.708	85	7,225	9.220
6	36	2.449	46	2,116	6.782	86	7,396	9.274
7	49	2.646	47	2,209	6.856	87	7,569	9.327
8	64	2.828	48	2,304	6.928	88	7,744	9.381
9	81	3.000	49	2,401	7.000	89	7,921	9.434
10	100	3.162	50	2,500	7.071	90	8,100	9.487
11	121	3.317	51	2,601	7.141	91	8,281	9.539
12	144	3.464	52	2,704	7.211	92	8,464	9.592
13	169	3.606	53	2,809	7.280	93	8,649	9.644
14	196	3.742	54	2,916	7.348	94	8,836	9.695
15	225	3.873	55	3,025	7.416	95	9,025	9.747
16	256	4.000	56	3,136	7.483	96	9,216	9.798
17	289	4.123	57	3,249	7.550	97	9,409	9.849
18	324	4.243	58	3,364	7.616	98	9,604	9.899
19	361	4.359	59	3,481	7.681	99	9,801	9.950
20	400	4.472	60	3,600	7.746	100	10,000	10.000
21	441	4.583	61	3,721	7.810	101	10,201	10.050
22	484	4.690	62	3,844	7.874	102	10,404	10.100
23	529	4.796	63	3,969	7.937	103	10,609	10.149
24	576	4.899	64	4,096	8.000	104	10,816	10.198
25	625	5.000	65	4,225	8.062	105	11,025	10.247
26	676	5.099	66	4,356	8.124	106	11,236	10.296
27	729	5.196	67	4,489	8.185	107	11,449	10.344
28	784	5.292	68	4,624	8.246	108	11,664	10.392
29	841	5.385	69	4,761	8.307	109	11,881	10.440
30	900	5.477	70	4,900	8.367	110	12,100	10.488
31	961	5.568	71	5,041	8.426	111	12,321	10.536
32	1,024	5.657	72	5,184	8.485	112	12,544	10.583
33	1,089	5.745	73	5,329	8.544	113	12,769	10.630
34	1,156	5.831	74	5,476	8.602	114	12,996	10.677
35	1,225	5.916	75	5,625	8.660	115	13,225	10.724
36	1,296	6.000	76	5,776	8.718	116	13,456	10.770
37	1,369	6.083	77	5,929	8.775	117	13,689	10.817
38	1,444	6.164	78	6,084	8.832	118	13,924	10.863
39	1,521	6.245	79	6,241	8.888	119	14,161	10.909
40	1,600	6.325	80	6,400	8.944	120	14,400	10.954

Answers

Pages 3-5

1. $\begin{array}{r|l} & 0 \\ \hline 2 & 0 \\ & -0 \\ \hline & 0 \end{array}$ Zero is even because when divided by 2 there's no remainder.

2. Yes, every even integer is also an element or member of the set of Integers.

3. a. −10; b. 100
   c. x and $-x$ are additive inverses.

4. a. T; b. T; c. T; d. F; e. T

5. Both 51 and 57 are divisible by 3. The number 51 divided by 3 is 17 and 57 divided by 3 is 19.

6. The set of Primes is infinite but you cannot use "..." because there's no pattern to what prime number comes next.

7. a. 300 is divisible by 2, 3, 4, 5, and 10.
   b. 1,824 is divisible by 2, 3, and 4.
   c. 97 is prime.
   d. 5,925 is divisible by 3 and 5.
   e. 10,911 is divisible by 3.

8. No, 27 can be divided by 2. The answer is $13\frac{1}{2}$. However, 27 is not <u>divisible</u> by 2.

9. a. $2 \bullet 2 \bullet 2 \bullet 3 \bullet 3 \bullet 5$ or $2^3 \bullet 3^2 \bullet 5$
   b. $2 \bullet 2 \bullet 2 \bullet 5 \bullet 5 \bullet 5$ or $2^3 \bullet 5^3$

10. (Answer may vary.) 29, 31; 41, 43; 101, 103

Pages 7-9

1. 81, 100, 121, 144

2. $\sqrt{7}$ is not rational because you cannot write it as a fraction with an integer numerator and integer denominator. The answer to $\sqrt{7}$ is a decimal that does not repeat and does not terminate.

3. $3\frac{1}{2}$ can be written as $\frac{7}{2}$ and that fits the definition of rational.

4. 8 can be written as $\frac{8}{1}$.

5. b. The bar on the number line represents all numbers are graphed and included.

6. While $\frac{22}{7}$ is a good approximation of PI, it is rational because it is a fraction and all fractions when changed to a decimal either terminate or repeat.

7. The number 0 is Even, Whole, Integer, Rational, and Real.

8.

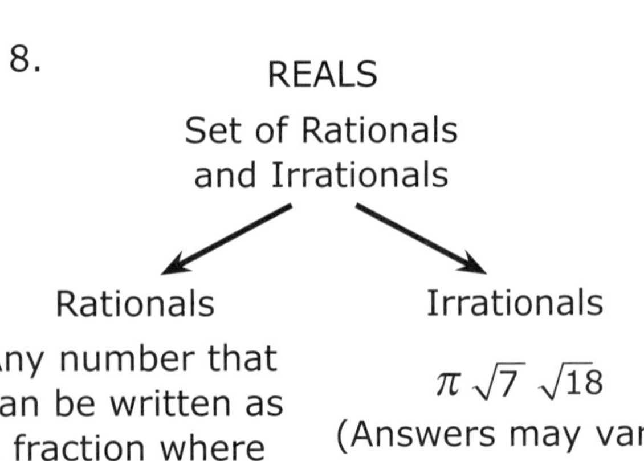

Any number that can be written as a fraction where the denominator is not 0.

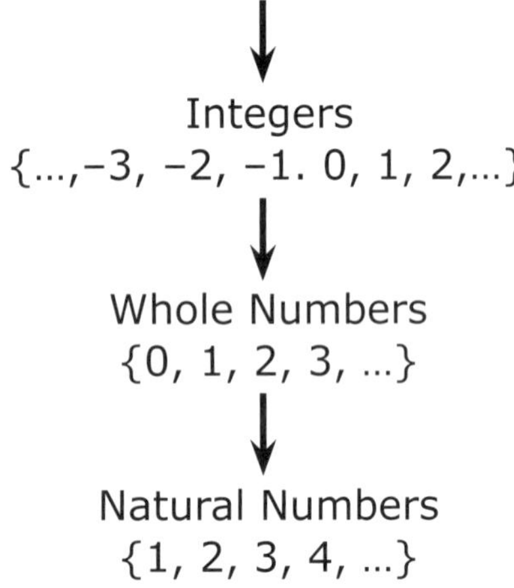

Pages 13-14 Chapter 1 Review

1. e
2. c
3. a
4. b
5. d
6. (Answers may vary.)
   π is irrational, so it is real.
   −3 is an integer, so it it real.
   6.5 is a rational, so it is real.
7. The numbers are all perfect squares. (13 • 13 = 169, 15 • 15 = 169, and 17 • 17 = 289)
8. a. 5 • 5 • 5 or 5^3

   b. 2 • 2 • 2 • 3 • 3 or $2^3 \bullet 3^2$

   c. 2 • 2 • 23 or $2^2 \bullet 23$

   d. 2 • 2 • 2 • 2 • 2 • 2 • 3 • 5 or $2^6 \bullet 3 \bullet 5$
9. a. F; b. T; c. F; d. F; e. F; f. T; g. T
10. a. No. 75 is divisible by 5 and 25.

    b. No. 91 is divisible by 7 and 13.

    c. Yes. 97 is prime. Its only factors are 1 and 97.

    d. No. 111 is divisible by 3 and 37.

    e. (Answers may vary.) No. 120 is divisible by 2 and 10.
11. a. RAT; b. RAT; c. RAT; d. RAT; e. RAT; f. IRRAT
12. (Answers may vary.) The number 36 is divisible by 2 and 3 and it is therefore divisible by 6.

Pages 18-19

1. 0
2. 0
3. −24
4. −50
5. 2
6. −23
7. −9
8. 80
9. −80
10. 17
11. 3
12. −45
13. −10
14. 0
15. 17
16. 2
17. 18
18. −2
19. c; −7 feet
20. −20 + (−5); −25 yards
21. −22°F
22. −5
23. −3
24. −3
25. −4
26. 7
27. −11
28. −5

Pages 22-23

1. 1
2. −17
3. 19
4. −7
5. −39
6. −98
7. −15
8. −15
9. −10
10. −23
11. −6
12. 9
13. −23
14. 24
15. 13
16. −14
17. 9
18. −44
19. −100
20. −68
21. You won 100 gold coins!

Pages 24-25

1. They both got a sum of −10, so Robert and Paulo are tied.
2. c; 57°F
3. c; 23 blocks
4. a. 0; b. 5; c. 40; d. 0; e. −199

   The strategy is to read the problem completely before starting in order to cancel any groups of additive inverses.
5. −9
6. 17
7. −63
8. 0

9. –34
10. –7
11. 34
12. –10
13. –6
14. –11
15. 21
16. –160
17. 29
18. 0

Page 29

1. –60
2. 45
3. –500
4. –27
5. 81
6. –39
7. 19
8. 0
9. –1
10. 19
11. 2
12. 27
13. 256
14. Ø No answer.
15. –4
16. –1
17. –18
18. 10,000
19. 100,000
20. –3
21. Nadia could say $\frac{0}{0} = 0$ (or any number), since the quotient times the denominator (0) will equal the numerator (0). Because there are infinite answers, there is NO answer or ø.
22. –28°F

Page 30 Chapter 2 Review

1. –1
2. –2
3. –38
4. –13
5. –19
6. 23
7. 9
8. 9
9. 78

10. 78

11. –4

12. 4

13. –980

14. –8

15. 16

16. 0

17. 0

18. Ø No answer.

19. 2

20. 91,000

21. 144

22. 169

23. 0

24. 52

25. 1,000,000

26. 1

27. $(-3)^5$

28. –3 • 5 or 5 • (–3)

29. –678; Cancel the additive inverses pairs.

30. 0; Read the problem before starting and remember that any number times 0 will give you 0.

Pages 34-35

1. –5.96

2. –1.02

3. –1.567

4. –16.59

5. –58.89

6. –1

7. $-\frac{1}{2}$

8. $-\frac{2}{5}$

9. $-3\frac{5}{6}$

10. $21\frac{1}{2}$

11. $-16\frac{1}{2}$

12. $9\frac{1}{12}$

13. $4\frac{3}{4}$

14. $-8\frac{3}{5}$

15. GCF: 1; LCM: 24

16. GCF: 1; LCM: 45

17. GCF: 7; LCM: 28

18. GCF: 6; LCM: 72

19. GCF: 12; LCM: 36

20. GCF: 5; LCM: 105

Page 37

1. $9\frac{2}{9}$
2. $-\frac{1}{6}$
3. $-9\frac{19}{20}$
4. $-\frac{1}{8}$
5. $-\frac{7}{24}$
6. $-3\frac{1}{12}$
7. $4\frac{13}{16}$
8. $4\frac{1}{42}$
9. $13\frac{1}{4}$ feet
10. The larger absolute value needs to be written on top. The correct work is:

$$\begin{array}{r} \not{2}\not{0}\frac{1}{8} \\ -\ 16\frac{3}{8} \\ \hline \end{array} \quad \begin{array}{r} 19\frac{9}{8} \\ 16\frac{3}{8} \\ \hline 3\frac{6}{8} = 3\frac{3}{4} \end{array}$$

The answer is $3\frac{3}{4}$.

Pages 40-41

1. −12
2. −20.25
3. −0.512
4. 200
5. 0.5
6. $\frac{4}{9}$
7. −1
8. $-\frac{2}{5}$
9. $-4\frac{3}{8}$
10. $\frac{2}{3}$
11. $\frac{1}{5}$
12. 3
13. $-\frac{20}{41}$
14. −1
15. −17.5°F
16. b
17. 16 pieces
18. The student dropped the negative sign in Step 2. Then in Step 3 the student added across instead of multiplying across.

Page 44

1. −3

2. −3

3. 0

4. 60

5. −67.4

6. 7

7. −300

8. $\frac{2}{3}$

9. −5

10. −48

11. 441

12. 0

Pages 45-46

1. 5 • 3 + 2 • 5 or 25 miles

2. 3($20) + 2($15) – 2 ($3.50) or 3($20) + 2($11.50) or $83

3. b; $14.67 rounded

4. (Answers may vary.) −3 • −2 • (1 + 2) • (−1 + 0)

5. −2 • 3 • 4 – 5 • 1

6. There is no dollar missing. Follow the order of operations. The cost of the car is $25 divided by 3, or $8\frac{1}{3}$ dollars for each. In addition, they each paid $\frac{2}{3}$ dollar for the tip for a total of $9.00 each. In all, the women paid $27 including the tip. The $3.00 that would have made $30 was returned and split between them.

Pages 47-48 Chapter 3 Review

1. $-\frac{3}{5}$

2. $-\frac{5}{8}$

3. $1\frac{3}{4}$

4. −15

5. −8.92

6. $-15\frac{7}{8}$

7. $-\frac{2}{7}$

8. −0.195

9. 2

10. 1

11. 2,000

12. 20.25

13. −50

14. 4

15. d

16. Heidi is correct. You need to go left to right. −80 ÷ 2 = −40. And −40 • 4 = −160.

17. 20 – (6 • $.35 + 3 • $.20 + 2 • $1)

Neese spent \$4.70, and she has \$15.30 left.

18. a. She needs $6\frac{1}{2} \div 3 = 2\frac{1}{6}$ cups.

    b. Emilia will be using $4\frac{1}{3}$ less flour than the original recipe.

Page 50

Bottom of page: $\frac{2}{5} = .4$; $\frac{3}{5} = .6$; $\frac{4}{5} = .8$

Since $\frac{1}{5} = .2$, then $\frac{2}{5}$ is twice $\frac{1}{5}$, $\frac{3}{5}$ is three times $\frac{1}{5}$, and $\frac{4}{5}$ is four times $\frac{1}{5}$.

Pages 51-52

1. $\frac{2}{25}$
2. $\frac{1}{250}$
3. $-5\frac{1}{40}$
4. $\frac{3}{8}$
5. $-9\frac{7}{8}$
6. $\frac{1}{6{,}250}$
7. $-6\frac{1}{125}$
8. $26\frac{3}{4}$
9. $-9\frac{31}{125}$
10. $\frac{13}{20{,}000}$
11. .07
12. .125
13. .4
14. .625
15. –8.0003
16. .1875
17. $-10.\overline{3}$
18. –9.375
19. 1.25
20. .75
21. –.15625
22. $3.\overline{142857}$
23. a. $.\overline{1}$ (this is point 1 repeating)

    b. $.\overline{2}$ (this is point 2 repeating)

    c. $.\overline{3}$, $.\overline{4}$, $.\overline{5}$, $.\overline{6}$, $.\overline{7}$, $.\overline{8}$

    d. 1. If you follow the pattern, $.\overline{9}$ is another representation of 1.

Page 53

1. The reason is that 2 and 5 both go into 10 so the fraction can be changed to a terminating decimal since decimal place value is determined by a power of 10.

2. a. T; b. T; c. R; d. T; e. R; f. R

Pages 55-58

1. $\frac{1}{4}$

2. $\frac{2}{5}$

3. $\frac{1}{3}$

4. $\frac{5}{8}$

5. $\frac{5}{13}$

6. 40 triangles since 5 out of 13 shapes are triangles, so $\frac{5}{13} \bullet 104 = 40$.

7.

Vehicle	Rate	Unit Rate
	$\frac{250\ mi}{10\ gal} = \frac{25\ mi}{1\ gal}$	25 mpg
	$\frac{300\ mi}{20\ gal} = \frac{15\ mi}{1\ gal}$	15 mpg
	$\frac{120\ mi}{3\ gal} = \frac{40\ mi}{1\ gal}$	40 mpg

8. a. Dan's trip: $23.00
   b. Elsie's trip: $46.00
   c. DJ's trip: $6.90

9.

Flour (Cups)	Sugar(Cups	Flour and Sugar (Cups)
2	1	3
3	$1\frac{1}{2}$	$4\frac{1}{2}$
6	3	9
8	4	12
10	5	15
11	$5\frac{1}{2}$	$16\frac{1}{2}$

10. 12c of flour. The recipe was multiplied by 6 since $\frac{1}{4} \bullet 6 = 1\frac{1}{2}$.

11. a. 3 mi/1 hr
    b. 6 mi/1 hr
    c. 100 m/1 min
    d. 35 mi/1 hr
    e. 27.5 mi/1 hr
    f. 70 mi/1 hr

12.

Number of Pizza Pies	Cost
1	$10.95
2	$21.90
3	$32.85
16	$175.20

13. You're free to choose the number of pizzas you want (independent variable) and the cost (the dependent variable) "depends" on how many pizzas you ordered.

Pages 61–62

Recipe	Eggs	Flour	Brown Sugar	Unsalted Butter
1	4	$4\frac{1}{2}$c	$1\frac{1}{2}$c	1c
2	$2\frac{2}{3}$	3c	1 cup	$\frac{2}{3}$c

1. 4 tsp vanilla extract (The recipe was multiplied by 4)
2. 3 tsp baking soda ($\frac{3}{4} \bullet 4$)
3. $\frac{2}{3}$ c unsalted butter. The recipe was changed by multiplying by $\frac{4}{3}$, so $\frac{4}{3} \bullet \frac{1}{2} = \frac{2}{3}$
4. a. 42 mi/gal
   b. 8 gallons
   c. 499.8 miles
5. 216 words; $\frac{90}{75} = \frac{n}{180}$
6. a. 557 lbs Eva Dad $\frac{100\ Earth}{236\ Jupiter} = \frac{236\ Earth}{n}$
   b. 90 lbs Eva Dad $\frac{100\ Earth}{38\ Mars} = \frac{236\ Earth}{n}$
   c. 90 lbs Eva Sister $\frac{100\ Earth}{236\ Jupiter} = \frac{38\ Earth}{n}$
7. 144 apples $\frac{4.50}{12} = \frac{54}{n}$
8. 500 pages $\frac{24}{20} = \frac{600}{n}$

Pages 64-66

1. 25″ X 37.5″; divide by 8
2. 628.6 miles; $\frac{1.4}{400} = \frac{2.2}{n}$
3. 1 cm = 3 meters; $\frac{72}{24} = \frac{3}{1}$
4. Drawings will vary.
5. 90 inches $\frac{10cm}{60in} = \frac{15cm}{n}$;
   5,400 sq in. (area) or 37.5 sq ft
6. 2.5 inches $\frac{\frac{1}{4}}{20mi} = \frac{n}{200mi}$
7. 2 m X 1.9 m X 1.68 m (200 cm X 190 cm X 168 cm); Volume: 6.384 cubic meters
8. 48.75 inches or 4′ 9″ $\frac{1.5''}{n} = \frac{2''}{65''}$
9. a. 1:3
   b. Figure A: 14″, Figure B: 42″
   c. 1:3 (14:42)
   d. Figure A: 10 sq in., Figure B: 90 sq in.
   e. 1:9 (10:90)

Page 69

1. $\frac{1}{4}$
2. $\frac{2}{1}$ or 2
3. $\frac{2.5}{100} = .025$
4. 12.5%

5. $66\frac{2}{3}\%$

6. 1.25

7. .15

8. $\frac{62.5}{100} = .625 = \frac{5}{8}$

9. 9%

10. 8.5%

11. $\frac{1}{400}$

12. 2.4% $(\frac{3}{125} = \frac{n}{100})$

Page 73

1. 2

2. $14

3. $0.51

4. $48.75

5. 30

6. 150

7. 21.33

8. 27

9. 400

10. 32

11. 50%

12. 20%

13. 25%

14. 17.5%

15. 9

16. 135

Pages 74–76 Chapter 4 Review

1.

Fraction	Decimal	Percent
$\frac{3}{20}$	.15	15%
$\frac{2}{25}$	.08	8%
$3\frac{24}{25}$	3.96	396%
$\frac{7}{8}$	.875	87.5%
$\frac{7}{5}$	1.4	140%

2. a. 22:14, or 11:7

   b. 14:22 or 7:11

   c. 6:36 or 1:6

   d. 6:14 or 3:7

3. There should be 30 teachers. The ratio of teachers to students is 6 to 36, so $\frac{1}{6}$ of 180 are teachers.

4. a. T; b. R; c. R; d. R; e. T

5. Rate: $\frac{200\ mi}{5.5\ gal}$ Unit Rate: $\frac{36.4\ mi}{1\ gal}$

6. $\frac{\$0.45}{1\ lb}$

7. The recipe was multiplied by 4.

   yeast: 5 tsp $(\frac{5}{4} \bullet 4)$

warm water: 12 T

sugar: 8 tsp

warm milk: $2\frac{2}{3}$c ($\frac{2}{3} \bullet 4$)

8. $n = 5$

9. $n = 12.5$

10. $n = 12$

11. $n = 1$

12. $n = 74.25$

13. $n = 20.8\overline{3}$

14. 175 words ($\frac{140}{1} = \frac{n}{1.25}$)

15. 345 miles $\frac{2}{150} = \frac{4.6}{n}$, the scale ratio is 1 cm= 75 miles

16. The ratio of their perimeters is 1:4 (same as the ratio of their sides) and the ratio of their areas is 1:16 (the ratio of the sides squared).

17. 17

18. 30

19. $0.85

20. 7.5

21. $1.50

22. 16

23. 64

24. 40

25. 400

26. 48

27. $33.\overline{3}\%$

28. 80%

29. 125%

30. .5%

Pages 79–80

1. $1.50

2. $262.50

3. $4,302.40 ($4,000 + $302.40)

4. $324 ($300 X 1.08)

5. 6% ($\frac{50}{100} = \frac{53}{n}$, $n = 106$ so 6%)

6. $210,000 ($\frac{1}{8} \bullet$ $240,000 = $30,000 so $240,000 – $30,000 = $210,000)

7. Hanna set the problem correctly because the new price is 140% (100% which is the old price plus 40%). The correct proportion is $\frac{250}{100} = \frac{n}{140}$; $350

8. It is the same. If you take $24.00 • .075 = $1.80. Adding $1.80 to $24.00 is $25.80. Taking $25.80 • .70 = $18.06.

   On the other hand if you take $24.00 • .70 you get $16.80. Taking $16.80 • .075 = $1.26 and adding $1.26 to $16.80 = $18.06.

9. 110% ($\frac{550}{500} = \frac{n}{100}$)

10. No, $650 • 1.05 = $682.50

and $682.50 • .95 = $648.38 (rounded)

Pages 83–84

1. 250% ($\frac{3,000}{1,200} = \frac{n}{100}$)
2. 25% ($\frac{60}{240} = \frac{n}{100}$)
3. 37.5% ($\frac{3}{8} = \frac{n}{100}$)
4. Inflation created a rise in the price of gluten-free bread. Now people who need to buy gluten-free bread have less buying power because their money cannot buy as much bread as before.

   $33\frac{1}{3}$% increase ($\frac{1.50}{4.50} = \frac{n}{100}$)
5. No, he was hoping for 105% of $50,000 = $52,500 but he only got $52,000. He got a 4% raise. ($\frac{2,000}{50,000} = \frac{n}{100}$)
6. a. $360 ($3,000 • .03 • 4)

   b. $3,360
7. a. $1,500 ($5,000 • .06 • 5)
   Total: $6,500

   b.

Year	Principal	Interest	Principal + Interest
1	$5,000	$300	$5,300
2	$5,300	$318	$5,618
3	$5,618	$337.08	$5,955.08
4	$5,955.08	$357.30	$6,312.38
5	$6,312.38	$378.74	**$6,691.12**

8. No, it depreciated about 22%. ($\frac{8,000}{36,000} = \frac{n}{100}$)

Pages 85–86 Chapter 5 Review

1. $31.73 (30 • 1.0575)
2. 10% increase ($\frac{5,000}{50,000} = \frac{n}{100}$)
3. Nathan is correct. 62.5% ($\frac{50}{80} = \frac{n}{100}$)
4. $40.00 ($\frac{42.80}{n} = \frac{107}{100}$)
5. 93% ($\frac{14}{15} = \frac{n}{100}$)
6. 200 questions ($\frac{150}{n} = \frac{75}{100}$)
7. 6 male nurses

   $\frac{2}{3}$ of n = 12, n =18 total nurses.

   So 6 are male nurses.
8. $562.50 ($\frac{450}{80} = \frac{n}{100}$)
9. $2,000 (10,000 • .05 • 4);
   $12,000 ($10,000 + $2,000)
10. $240 (500 • .02 • 24)
11.

Year	Principal	Rate	Interest	Principal + Interest
1	$10,000	.05	$500	$10,500

2	$10,500	.05	$525	$11,025
3	$11,025	.05	$551.25	$11.576.25
4	$11,576.25	.05	$578.81	$12,155.06

12. In problem 11, the compound interest is being compounded or added each time to make a new principal. So it results in a larger amount than in problem 9, even though the starting principal is the same and the interest rate is the same.

Pages 88–89

1. Nathan is mistaken. Any variable can stand for a positive number or a negative number. If n is a positive number, then $-n$ would become a negative number, but if n is a negative number, then $-n$ would become a positive number.
2. In Expression 1, you add the value of the x to the 3 then take that sum and cube it (multiply it by itself three times). In Expression 2, you would add the value of the x to 27 since $3^3 = 27$.
3. a. 27; 27

   b. 4^3 or 64; 28
4. a. $x \neq 0$, b. $x \neq -8$, c. $x \neq 9$, d. $x \neq 3$
5. −5
6. 10
7. −32
8. 945
9. -36
10. 35
11. 10,000
12. Ø
13. Ø
14. -6
15. 432
16. 18
17. 18
18. 0

Pages 91–93

1. $2n + 10$
2. $2 + 5n$ or $5n + 2$
3. $n - 20$
4. $\frac{n}{3}$
5. $n - 11$
6. $n^2 - 4$
7. $n - 17$
8. $2(n + 8)$
9. $2n + 8$
10. $\frac{1}{2}n$ or $\frac{n}{2}$
11. $\frac{1}{2}(n + 1)$ or $\frac{n + 1}{2}$

12. $100n$
13. $4(20 - n)$
14. $n^2 - 15$
15. $n - 18$
16. Twice the sum of a number plus nine.
17. Eighteen minus a number, or a number less than eighteen.
18. The quantity of a number less four squared, or the difference of a number less four squared.
19. The sum of twice a number plus three divided by five, or one-fifth the sum of twice a number plus three.
20. A number cubed less four, or four less than the cube of a number.
21. Twice a number less five or five less than twice a number.
22. Five less twice a number or twice a number less than five.
23. The cube of the product of three times a number.
24. A number divided by nine plus one.
25. d
26. k
27. m
28. p
29. l
30. i
31. a
32. f
33. n
34. b
35. j
36. g
37. h
38. o
39. e
40. c

Pages 96–98

1. $5a$ and $-6a$
2. $8n$ and $-8n$
3. $10n$ and $-4n$
4. $5xy$, $-10xy$, and xy
5. $3ab$, $-9ab$, and $8ab$
6. $-4x - 7$; binomial
7. 0; monomial
8. $-3n^3 + 9n^2 + 10n$; trinomial
9. $-5a + 15b - c$; trinomial
10. $17p + 8r$; binomial

11. $3n + 4$; binomial

12. $3x + 19$; binomial

13. n; monomial

14. $8abcd$; monomial

15. $-6w + 3$; binomial

16. $8 \bullet 3 + 2 \bullet 3 = 24 + 6 = 30$, which is the same as $10 \bullet 3 = 30$, while $10x^2$ is $10 \bullet 9 = 90$

17. Evaluating each side of the equation:
$$(5)(-2)(3) + (-2)(3) = (6)(-2)(3)$$
$$(-30) + (-6) = -36$$

18. If $x = 3$, then
$$5 \bullet 3 + 6 \bullet 3^2 \neq 11 \bullet 3^3$$
$$15 + 6 \bullet 9 \neq 11 \bullet 27$$
$$15 + 54 \neq 297$$
$$69 \neq 297$$

19. $-22a$

20. $-4x^2$

Page 100

1. $7x - 3$
2. $-n + 17$
3. $3ab$
4. $3Q + 1$
5. $n - 4$
6. $-b$
7. $10f - 9n - 15r + 5w$
8. $3xy - 1$
9. $-4x + 7y$
10. $3b - 2$
11. $2x + 37$
12. $3x + 3$
13. 0
14. $7x - 10y$

Pages 102–103

1. $4 + 4 + 4 + 4 + 4 + 4 = 6 \bullet 4 = 24$
2. $4 \bullet 4 \bullet 4 \bullet 4 \bullet 4 \bullet 4 = 4^6 = 4{,}096$, not $6 \bullet 4 = 24$.
3. h^{15}
4. $27x^4$
5. $30y^2$
6. $-48w^2$
7. $-34n^{11}$
8. $8x^6y^6$
9. $81w^{10}$
10. $-n^5$
11. $-121w^{13}y^6$
12. $54a^2b^2c^2$
13. $144m^3$
14. v^4

15. $17a^4$

16. $-3w^2$

17. $\frac{1}{2}x$

18. $18n^3y^7$

19. $18x^3$

20. $\frac{3}{4}$

21. $10x^5$

22. -1

Pages 104–105

1. $81x^2$
2. $16m^{12}$
3. $64w^6$
4. $8h^{18}$
5. $-1{,}000n^{15}$
6. $10{,}000n^{20}$
7. $81x^8$
8. $225x^2$
9. $225x^2$
10. $27a^3b^3$
11. Take 10 to the 7th power then multiply the powers by the outside power. Answer: $10{,}000{,}000n^{21}y^{42}$. In general the rule is $(cx^ny^w)^r = c^rx^{nr}y^{wr}$
12. In $10^3 \bullet 10^3$, 10 is the base, so the answer is 10^6. Put the base down and add the powers.
13.

	Number		Written Out		10 to a Power
a.	1,000,000	=	10 • 10 • 10 • 10 • 10 • 10	=	10^6
b.	100,000	=	10 • 10 • 10 • 10 • 10	=	10^5
c.	10,000	=	10 • 10• 10 • 10	=	10^4
d.	1,000	=	10 • 10 • 10	=	10^3
e.	100	=	10 • 10	=	10^2
f.	10	=	10	=	10^1
g.	1	=		=	10^0

Page 107

1. h^3
2. h^0 or 1
3. $-4n^4$
4. $28a^6$
5. $25a$
6. $29n^3$
7. $\frac{1}{2}w^4$ or $\frac{w^4}{2}$
8. $\frac{1}{12}$
9. 1
10. $\frac{1}{2}x$ or $\frac{x}{2}$

Page 109

1. 2
2. $\frac{20}{c^5}$ or $20c^{-5}$
3. $\frac{-2}{a}$ or $-2a^{-1}$

4. $\frac{1}{100a^2}$ or $\frac{a^{-2}}{100}$

5. $\frac{1}{x}$ or x^{-1}

6. $\frac{-2m^2}{n^7}$ or $-2m^2n^{-7}$

7. $\frac{8n^7}{m^8}$ or $8m^{-8}n^7$

8. $\frac{2}{3w^2}$ or $\frac{2w^{-2}}{3}$

9. $\frac{2}{w}$ or $2w^{-1}$

10. $\frac{1}{2x^8}$ or $\frac{1}{2}x^{-8}$ or $.5x^{-8}$

11. $\frac{-2}{x^9}$ or $-2x^{-9}$

12. $\frac{1}{3}$ or 3^{-1}

Page 111

1. 5.88; 8
2. −9
3. 10^9
4. −6
5. 3×10^{-6}
6. 1×10^{10}
7. 3.24×10^8
8. 1.3×10^{-7}
9. 1,387,000,000
10. .000000000025
11. 186,000
12. 238,900

Pages 112–113

1. 7.5×10^{12}
2. 9×10^{11}
3. 2×10^3
4. 1.408×10^{14}
5. 5×10^{-1}
6. 9×10^9
7. 1.95×10^{13}
8. 2×10^4
9. 6×10^{-7}
10. 2.5×10^{10}

Pages 114–116 Chapter 6 Review

1. d
2. c
3. a
4. c
5. c
6. d
7. a
8. b

9. a
10. a
11. d
12. d
13. b
14. a
15. d
16. $14n^3 - 5n + 13$
17. $-4a + 2b$
18. $-w - 6$
19. $-81a^2b^2$
20. $-27n^{18}$
21. $3n^4$
22. 1,000,000
23. $10^{-5} = \frac{1}{100,000} = .00001$
24. 1
25. $\frac{1}{2m^2} = \frac{m^{-2}}{2}$
26. 8.3×10^6
27. 6.8×10^{-5}
28. 1.2×10^{14}
29. 4×10^5
30. 2.1×10^8

Page 119

1. $-80 + 12 = -90 + 22$
   $-68 = -68$
2. $7 \bullet -40 = 140 \bullet -2$
   $-280 = -280$
3. $30 - 20 \neq 20 - 30$
   $10 \neq -10$
4. $-7 \neq -\frac{1}{7}$
5. $-10 - 8 = -4 - (-2)$?
   $-18 = -4 + 2$?
   $-18 = -2$? NO
6. Answers will vary.

Pages 121–123

1. 3; The additive inverse of −3 is 3 because $-3 + 3 = 0$.
2. $-\frac{1}{5}$; The multiplicative inverse of −5 is $-\frac{1}{5}$ because they both multiply to 1 (the identity for multiplication).
3. $-2a$; The additive inverse of $2a$ is $-2a$ because they both add to 0 (the identity for addition).
4. $\frac{6}{5}$; The multiplicative inverse of $\frac{5}{6}$ is $\frac{6}{5}$ because they both multiply to 1 (the identity for multiplication).
5. $-\frac{6}{5}$; The multiplicative inverse of $-\frac{5}{6}$ is $-\frac{6}{5}$ because they both

multiply to 1 (the identity for multiplication).

6. Zero has no reciprocal or multiplicative inverse because 0 in the denominator is undefined.

7. $20n$; The additive inverse of $-20n$ is $20n$ because $-20n + 20n = 0$ (the identity for addition).

8. The distributive property only works for multiplication over addition or subtraction.
   $40 \div (10 + 5)$ is not $4 + 8$.
   It's $40 \div 15$ which is $\frac{8}{3}$ or $2\frac{2}{3}$.

9. It illustrates the commutative property of multiplication.
   $6 \bullet -3 = -3 \bullet 6$.

10. a. $-56 - 14$
       -70

    b. $90 + 10y$

    c. $-2n + 2$

    d. $-27 + 15 - 12$
       -24

    e. $32x^2 - 16x - 4$

    f. $25 + 10$
       35

    g. $150 - 250$
       -100

    h. $-16 - 4$
       -20

    i. $4a + 4b + 4c$

    j. $-3a - 3b + 3c$

    k. $5x - 5y$

    l. $-k - w$

11. $-(3 + 5 - 7)$ simplifies to $-(1)$ which equals -1.
    $-1(3 + 5 - 7)$ simplifies to $-1(1)$ which also equals -1.

12. The student multiplied -2 times 8 which is incorrect because the 8 is outside the parenthesis. The answer should be $-2n - 12 + 8$ which equals $-2n - 4$.

Page 125

1. $40 - 20$

2. $12 \bullet 3$

3. $\frac{48}{4}$

4. The student subtracted on the left side and added on the right side which does not preserve the balance of the equation.

Page 127

1. The symmetric property of equality.

2. The additive inverse property.

3. The addition property of 0.

4. $n = -3$

5. $n = 16$

6. $n = 3.5$

7. $n = 10.5$

8. $n = 5\frac{1}{4}$

9. $n = -6$

10. $n = -10.5$

11. $n = -7$

12. $n = -49$

13. $n = 0$

Pages 129–130

1. Multiplication property of 1.

2. The multiplicative inverse of $-\frac{4}{3}$ is $-\frac{3}{4}$ because their product is 1 (the identity for multiplication).

3. The 4 should not be placed by the denominator. Multiplying each side by 4 means multiplying by $\frac{4}{1}$.

4. Joanna is right. You must undo $\frac{1}{6}$ by multiplying by 6 on each side.

5. Peter: $\frac{1}{6} \bullet 6 = 36$? No, because $1 \neq 36$; Joanna: $\frac{1}{6} \bullet 216 = 36$? Yes!

6. $n = -25$

7. $n = 130$

8. $n = 25$

9. $n = -3$

10. $n = 7$

11. $n = 192$

12. $n = -45$

13. $n = -15$

14. $n = -90$

15. $n = 9.2$

16. $n = 125$

17. $n = 28$

18. $n =-7$

19. $n = -125$

Pages 131–132

1. $0 = 9 - \frac{n}{6}$

   $0 = 9 - \frac{54}{6}$

   $0 = 9 - 9$? Yes!

2. $w = 2$

3. $x = -22$

4. $p = 12$

5. $n = -6$

6. $c = 54$

7. $k = -176$

8. $n = 107$

9. $x = 3$

10. $y = -90$

11. $x = \frac{1}{2}$ or .5

12. $n = -8$

13. $n = 700$

14. $y = 19.4$

15. $y = 1.5$

Page 134

1. Let n = a number; $\frac{1}{2}n + 8 = 11$; $n = 6$

2. Let n = a number; $3n = -300$; $n = -100$

3. Let n = a number; $\frac{1}{2}n + 50 = 100$; $n = 100$

4. Let n = a number; $-n = 3$; $n = -3$

5. Let n = a number; $0 = -4n - 8$; $n = -2$

Pages 135–136

1. $n = -4$

2. $y = 10$

3. $m = 3$

4. $w = -22.5$

5. $p = -19$

6. $m = 8$

7. $y = -2.75$

8. $n = 7.3$

9. Answers will vary.

10. No, if you solve the equation you get $9 = 10$ or $0 = 1$, which is impossible. No value for the variable will work.

Pages 138–139

1. $w = 6$

2. $y = -35$

3. $y = 18$

4. $x = 20$

5. $n = 12$

6. $n = 40$

7. $w = -\frac{1}{2}$

8. $y = -4$

9. Let n = Mary's age. Equation: $12 + n = 2n + 11$; $n = 1$. Mary is 1 year old.

10. Let n = Paulo's locker number. Equation: $0 = \frac{n}{5} - 113$; $n = 565$. Paulo's locker number is 565.

11. Let n = *a* number. Equation: $n + 2n + 8 = n$; $n = -4$.

12. Let n = *a* number. Equation: $3n - n = 9 + 5n$; $n = -3$.

Page 141

1. $n = -11$
2. $n = -64$
3. $w = -5$
4. $x = 3$
5. $x = -120$
6. $n = 4$
7. $y = -13$
8. $n = 7$
9. $x = -60$
10. $w = 4.5$
11. $n = 11$
12. $x = -45$
13. $x = 6$
14. $n = 0$
15. Ø
16. −8

Pages 144–145

1. 122, 123, 124, 125
2. 56, 57, 58
3. 22, 24, 26
4. 141, 143, 145
5. −10, −9, −8
6. −3, −1
7. 12, 14, 16, 18
8. 15, 16, 17; $n + n + 2 = 32$
9. 20, 21, 22; $2n + n + 2 = 62$
10. 9, 11, 13; $3n + 2(n + 2) + n + 3 = 62$
11. 15 + 17 = 32? Yes
12. 2(20) + 22 = 62?
40 + 22 = 62? Yes
13. 3(9) + 2(11) + 13 = 62?
27 + 22 + 13 = 62? Yes
14. Answers will vary.
15. $n + 3$; If $n + 2$ is odd, then the next even integer is $n + 2 + 1$ which is $n + 3$.

Pages 148–152 Chapter 7 Review

1. e
2. f
3. d
4. c
5. b
6. a
7. The symmetric property of equality allows you to reverse the two sides of an equation. In this

problem both equations have an answer of 5.

8. $-\frac{7}{8}$ and $-\frac{8}{7}$ are multiplicative inverses because their product is 1 (the identity for multiplication).

9. $6a$; The terms $-6a$ and $6a$ add to 0 (the identity for addition).

10. The reciprocal (or multiplicative inverse) of $\frac{0}{1}$ cannot be $\frac{1}{0}$ because you cannot have a 0 in the denominator.

11. The student forgot to distribute the 3 times the −1. The correct answer should be $3n^2 + 6n - 3$.

12. $n = 13$

13. $w = -5$

14. $y = 90$

15. $x = -8$

16. $r = -40\frac{1}{3}$

17. $n = -19$

18. $x = -18$

19. $x = 18$

20. $w = 100$

21. $a = -6\frac{1}{4}$

22. $n = -4$

23. $x = -10$

24. $w = 0$

25. $y = -3$

26. $n = 1$

27. $x = 3$

28. All real numbers. Identity Equation.

29. Ø

30. a

31. c

32. b

33. a

34. d

35. Let n = hours taking care of pets; Equation: $40 + 2n = 52$; $n = 6$. Lucia spent 6 hours taking care of her aunt's pets.

36. Let n = the missing number; Equation: $2(n - 10) = n + 20$; $n = 40$.

37. Let $n = a$ number; Equation: $n + 3(-n) = 10$; $n = -5$.

38. Let n = today's date. Equation: $n + n + 7 = 23$. $n = 8$. Tomorrow's date is the 9th.

39. Let n = 1st consecutive integer, $n + 1$= 2nd consecutive integer, $n + 2$ = 3rd consecutive integer; Equation: $n + n + 1 + n + 2 = 87$; $n = 28$. Answers: 28, 29, 30.

40. Let n = 1st consecutive integer,

$n + 2$ = 2nd consecutive integer; Equation: $n + n + 2 = -280$. $n = -141$. Answers: -141, -139.

41. $$\frac{10(y-2)}{10} + \frac{20}{10} = \frac{30}{10}$$
$$y - 2 + 2 = 3$$
$$y = 3$$

42. $10(y - 2) + 20 = 30$
$10(3 - 2) + 20 = 30?$
$10 \cdot 1 + 20 = 30?$
$10 + 20 = 30$; Yes

43. Yes, Luke's steps are legal. He chose to move the variable terms to the right side and the constants to the left side.

44. $-n + 20 = 3n - 40$
$-15 + 20 = 3(15) - 40?$
$5 = 45 - 40?$ Yes

45. The transitive property of equality

Pages 154–156

1. It reads: "the set of all x's such that x is an element or member of the set of reals." This means the values you can use for your variable must come from the set of real numbers.

2. $\{n \mid n \in \text{Integers}\}$

3. b

4. d

5. e

6. c

7. a

8.

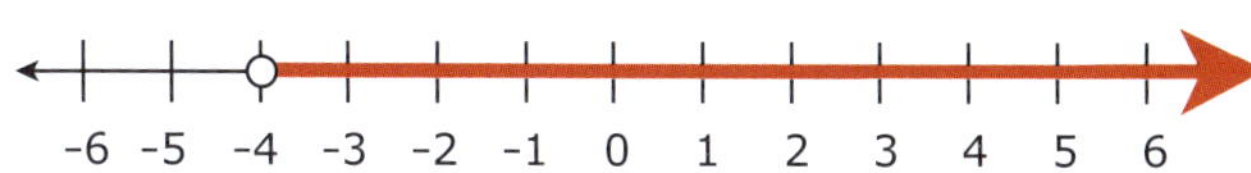

9.

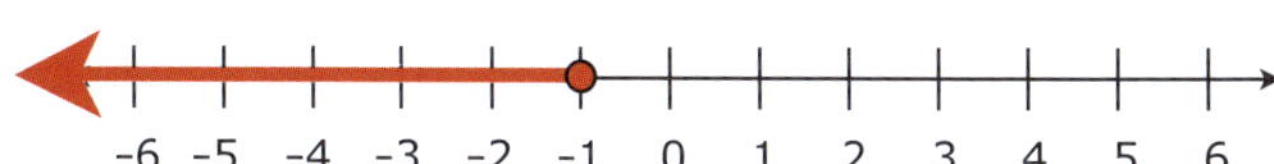

10.

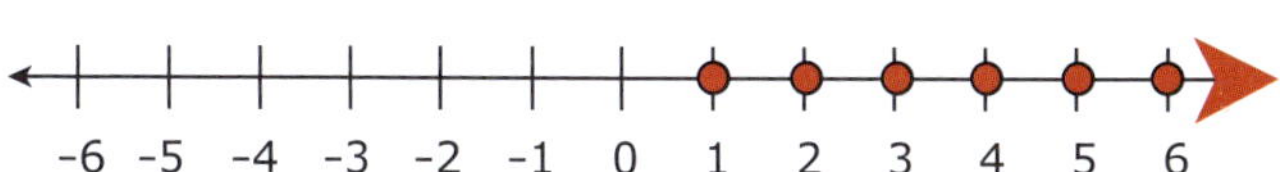

11.

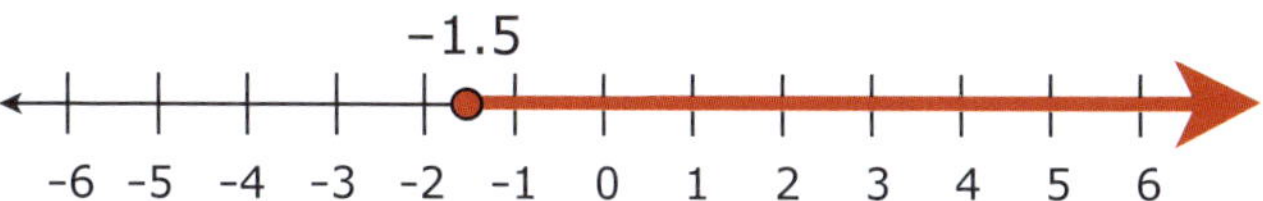

12.

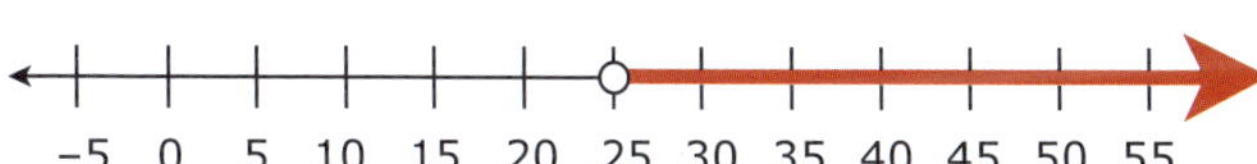

13. $n > 5$

14. $n \leq -6$

15. $-3n < 0$

16. $3n + 18 < 0$

Pages 159–160

1. $n > -11$

2. $n < 12$

3. $y \leq -7$

4. $w > 5$

5. $n \geq 3$

6. $n < -300$

7. $x < -160$

8. $y < 160$

9. $n < -6$

10. $0 > 3n + 18$, let's test -7 since it's less than -6.

    $0 > 3(-7) + 18$?

    $0 > -21 + 18$?

    $0 > -3$? Yes!

11. $n < -1$

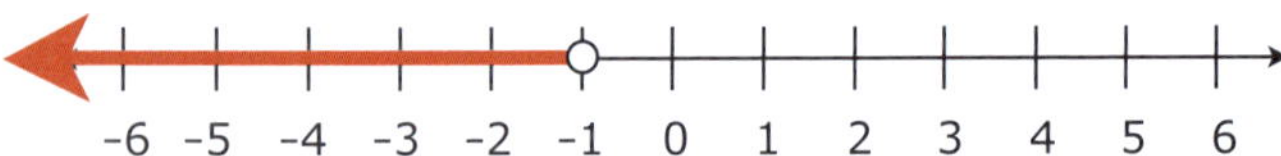

12. $n \geq 0$

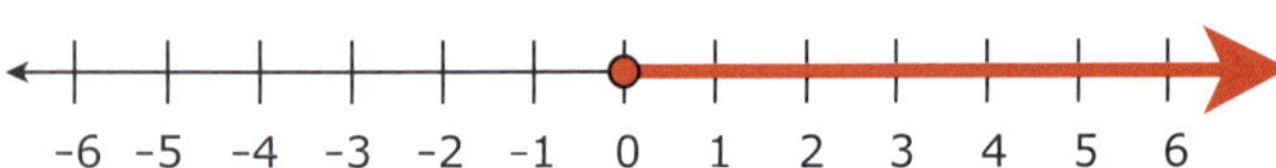

Pages 162–164

1. $20 - n = 3n$

2. $n + n + 1 + n + 2 \leq 60$

3. $10 + 5n > -50$

4. $n \geq 125$

5. $3(n - 4) < 40$

6. $\frac{n}{10} \leq 5$

7. $n \geq 4$

8. $n + 100 < 500$

9. $n \leq 2$

10. $11 + 2n = n - 5$

11. $n \geq 13$

12. $n \leq 2$

13. $n + n + 2 + n + 4 \leq 75$

14. $n > 1000$

15. $4n + 15 < 39$

16. Let n = number of baked goods; Inequality: $.75n \geq 225$. $n \geq 300$. The school needs to sell at least 300 baked goods.

17. Let n = cost of one notebook. Inequality: $10 + 5n \leq 40$. $n \leq 6$. Each notebook must be less than or equal to \$6.00

18. Let n = 1st consecutive integer, $n + 1$ = 2nd consecutive integer, and $n + 2$ = 3rd consecutive integer. Inequality: $n + n + 1 + n + 2 < 57$. $n < 18$. So the answers must be 16, 17, and 18.

19. Let n = number of hours renting a row boat; Inequality: $8 + 12n < 45$. $n < 3.08$. You can only rent the row boat for 3 hours.

20. Let n = number of overtime hours worked. Inequality: $80(5) + 12n \geq 520$. $n \geq 10$. Robert worked at least 10 hours of overtime.

Pages 167–168

1. $90 \le x < 120$
2. $x < 50$ or $x > 80$
3. $72 < x < 78$
4. $1 < x < 6$
5. $x \le -4$ or $x > 10$
6. $x \le 32$ or $x \ge 212$
7. $1 < x < 4$
8. $x \le -3$ or $x > 1$
9. $x < -1$ or $x \ge 4.5$
10. $-1 \le x < 6$

Pages 169–171 Chapter 8 Review

1.

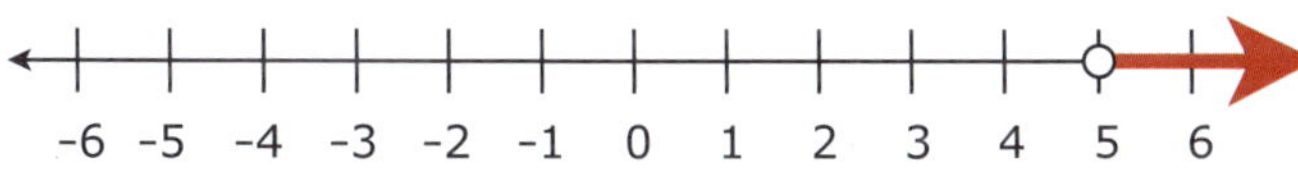

2.

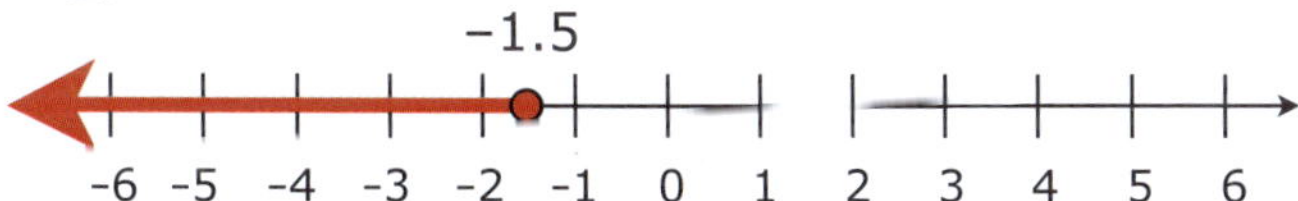

3.

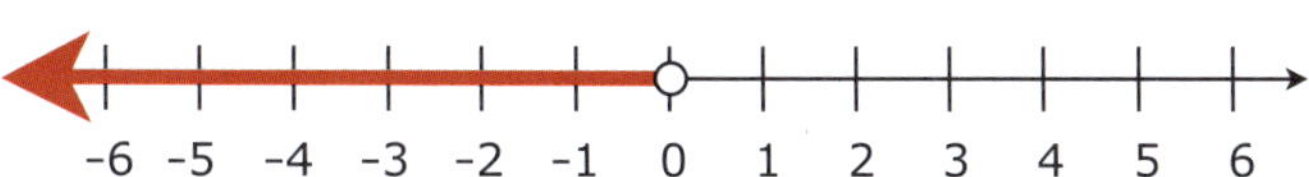

4.

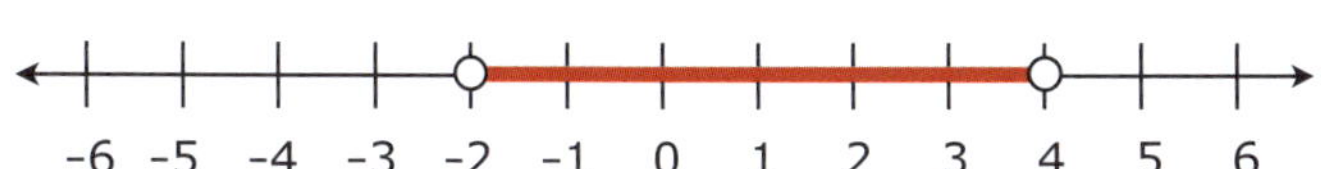

5.

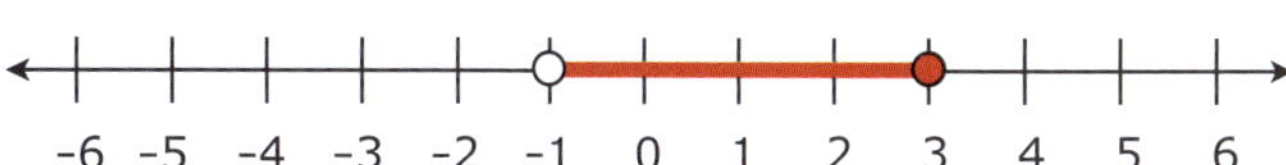

6.

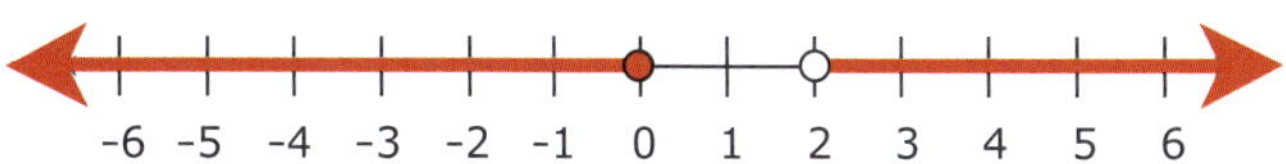

7. Let n = number of hours of overtime. Equation: $400 + 15n = 520$. José worked 8 hours of overtime.

8. Let n = 1st consecutive even integer, $n + 2$ = 2nd consecutive even integer, $n + 4$ = 3rd consecutive even integer. Inequality: $n + n + 2 + n + 4 < 102$. $n < 32$.

   So the answer must be 30, 32, and 34. (30 is the first even integer that is less than 32).

9. Let n = number of months. Inequality: $120 + 40n > 500$. $n > 9.5$ Marta has to save for at least 9.5 months.

10. Let n = number of chocolate bars. Inequality: $2.50n \ge 180$. $n \ge 72$. Andrew needs to sell at least 72 chocolate bars.

11. Let n = a number. Equation: $n - 11 = 24$. $n = 35$. The missing number is 35.

12. Let w = width, $2w$ = length. Equation: $w + 2w + w + 2w = 120$. This is the same as $6w = 120$. $w = 20$. The width is 20' and the length is 40'.

13. Let w = width, $2w$ = length. Inequality: $w + 2w + w + 2w < 120$. This is the same as $6w < 120$. $w < 20$. So the width is 19' and the length is 38'.

14. Let n = number of cookies Tom ate, $3n$ = number of cookies Maria ate. Equation: $n + 3n + 5 = 21$. $n = 4$. Tom ate 4 cookies and Maria ate 12.

15. Let n = a number. Inequality: $\frac{1}{2}n + 3n > 14$. $n > 4$.

    So the smallest integer that fits this situation is 5.

Page 173

1. $\frac{1}{3}$
2. $\frac{1}{9}$
3. $\frac{4}{9}$
4. $\frac{1}{11}$
5. $\frac{5}{11}$
6. $\frac{14}{111}$
7. $\frac{34}{999}$
8. Let $n = .\overline{9}$, $10n = 9.\overline{9}$

$$\begin{aligned} 10n &= 9.\overline{9} \\ n &= .\overline{9} \\ 9n &= 9 \\ \hline n &= 1 \end{aligned}$$

Pages 174-175

1. 144
2. 12
3. –7
4. 400
5. 9
6. 20
7. 625
8. 169
9. 19
10. 10
11. 1,600
12. 10,000
13. 11
14. 15
15. –17
16. 23
17. 361
18. 4,900
19. 1

20. 121

21. 289

22. 13

23. 40

24. 100

Pages 175–176

1. 2.236
2. 3.162
3. 8.888
4. 1.414
5. 7.937
6. 4.472
7. 1.732
8. 5.099
9. 10.050
10. –3.317
11. –2.828
12. –6.245
13. 7.746
14. –4.899
15. –2.646
16. 3.873
17. 7.071
18. 5.916
19. Since $\sqrt{49} = 7$ and the $\sqrt{64} = 8$, then $\sqrt{50}$ is just a little larger than 7. A good estimate is 7.1.
20. a. Estimate: Answers will vary; Correct answer: 5.9.

    b. Estimate: Answers will vary; Correct answer: 10.1.

    c. Estimate: Answers will vary; Correct answer: 10.9

Pages 177–178

1. 4
2. 32
3. 2
4. 1,000
5. 10
6. 64
7. 4
8. The reason is that no two same numbers can multiply to a –1. $-1 \bullet -1 = 1$ and $1 \bullet 1 = 1$, so there is no real answer to $\sqrt{-1}$.
9. The cube root of 64 is 4 and the cube root of 1,000 is 10, so the cube root of 64,000 is $4 \bullet 10$ or 40.
10. a. The square root of 961 is 31. So one side of the square is 31 units.

b. The cube root of 1,000 is 10 so one side of the cube is 10 units.

Pages 180–181

1. April is not done simplifying. She needs to continue to simplify $\sqrt{8}$. There is a perfect square (4) as a factor of 8. Maddy simplified completely.
2. b is correct. $\sqrt{4 \bullet 9} = \sqrt{36} = 4$. Whereas $\sqrt{4 + 9} = \sqrt{13}$ so the answer cannot be 5.
3. $10\sqrt{5}$
4. 16
5. −81
6. 5
7. $2\sqrt{3}$
8. $5\sqrt{3}$
9. −88
10. $7\sqrt{2}$
11. 200
12. −200
13. $4\sqrt{3}$
14. $5\sqrt{5}$
15. 25
16. 36

Page 184

1. $\frac{22}{7} = 3.\overline{142857}$ so it has the same two decimals places like PI after the 3.
2. $\frac{355}{113} = 3.1415929203...$ which is a better approximation of PI as it has the same 6 decimal places as PI after the 3. Remember this fraction will eventually repeat, but it can take as many as 112 digits before it repeats!
3. They are both fractions and all fractions terminate or repeat. All fractions are rational numbers.

Pages 187–189

1. Yes, $8^2 + 15^2 = 17^2$, $64 + 225 = 289$? Yes! So it is a right triangle.
2. Yes, it is a Pythagorean triple. $12^2 + 35^2 = 37^2$, $144 + 1{,}225 = 1{,}369$? Yes!
3. $x = 25''$ Equation: $7^2 + 24^2 = x^2$, $49 + 576 = x^2$, $625 = x^2$.
4. $x = \sqrt{61}$ feet
Equation: $5^2 + 6^2 = x^2$, $25 + 36 = x^2$, $61 = x^2$.
5. $x = 16$ cm
Equation: $12^2 + x^2 = 20^2$, $144 + x^2 = 400$, $x^2 = 256$.
6. $x = 4\sqrt{2}$ m
Equation: $4^2 + 4^2 = x^2$, $16 + 16 = x^2$, $32 = x^2$.

7. $x = \sqrt{31}$ units
Equation: $x^2 + 15^2 = 16^2$, $x^2 + 225 = 256$, $x^2 = 31$.

8. $3\sqrt{3}$ ft Equation: $x^2 + 3^2 = 6^2$, $x^2 + 9 = 36$, $x^2 = 27$.

9. 14.8′ Equation: $6^2 + x^2 = 16^2$, $36 + x^2 = 256$, $x^2 = 220$.

10. 127.3′ Equation: $90^2 + 90^2 = x^2$, $8{,}100 + 8{,}100 = x^2$, $16{,}200 = x^2$.

Page 190

1. c^2
2. a^2
3. b^2
4. $c^2 = a^2 + b^2$

Pages 191–195 Chapter 9 Review

1. $\frac{7}{9}$
2. $\frac{6}{11}$
3. $\frac{55}{999}$
4. 324
5. 10,000
6. 13
7. −7
8. 6.403
9. 8.185
10. −9.592
11. 5
12. 9 or −9; $\sqrt{81} = 9$, $-\sqrt{81} = -9$.
13. 100; 10
14. 64; 4
15. Answers may vary. For example: $\sqrt{9} = 3$, $\sqrt{121} = 11$, $\sqrt{169} = 13$, and $\sqrt{12}$ is about 3.5, $\sqrt{26}$ is about 5.1. So square roots of odd numbers can be rational or irrational. Square roots of even numbers can be rational or irrational.
16. $2\sqrt{2}$
17. $8\sqrt{2}$
18. $10\sqrt{2}$
19. $3\sqrt{5}$
20. 25
21. 35
22. $-11\sqrt{2}$
23. 16
24. −15
25. 4
26. 15 units; Equation: $9^2 + 12^2 = x^2$, $81 + 144 = x^2$, $225 = x^2$.
27. $\sqrt{65}$ units; Equation: $1^2 + 8^2 = x^2$, $1 + 64 = x^2$, $65 = x^2$.

28. $6\sqrt{2}$ m, Equation: $6^2 + 6^2 = x^2$, $36 + 36 = x^2$, $72 = x^2$.

29. 9″; Equation: $40^2 + x^2 = 41^2$, $1{,}600 + x^2 = 1{,}681$, $x^2 = 81$.

30. $8\sqrt{6}$ inches; Equation: $x^2 + 4^2 = 20^2$, $x^2 + 16 = 400$, $x^2 = 384$. $(x = \sqrt{64 \bullet 6})$

31. 5 units; Equation: $x^2 + 12^2 = 13^2$, $x^2 + 144 = 169$, $x^2 = 25$.

32. 10 miles; Equation: $8^2 + 6^2 = x^2$, $64 + 36 = x^2$, $100 = x^2$.

33. 29 feet; Equation: $20^2 + 21^2 = x^2$, $400 + 441 = x^2$, $841 = x^2$.

34. 11 feet; Equation: $5^2 + x^2 = 12^2$, $25 + x^2 = 144$, $x^2 = 119$. $x = 10.9'$

Pages 198-199

1. a. 70°
   b. 45°
   c. 5°
2. 35
3. 30
4. 18
5. 40
6. 11
7. 22.5
8. 15
9. 10
10. a. 45
    b. $m\angle AQR = 160°$
    c. $m\angle AQB = 20°$

Page 201

1. a. corresponding angles
   b. vertical angles
   c. adjacent supplementary angles
2. a. $m\angle 70°$, supplementary with 110°; $m\angle y = 70°$, vertical with $\angle x$ and supplementary with $\angle y$.
   b. $m\angle x = 80°$, corresponding with 80°; $m\angle y = 100°$, supplementary with $\angle x$.
   c. $m\angle x = 85°$, vertical with 85°; $m\angle y = 85°$, corresponding with $\angle x$.
3. $m\angle 1 = 120°$; $m\angle 2 = 120°$; $m\angle 3 = 60°$; $m\angle 4 = 60°$; $m\angle 5 = 60°$; $m\angle 6 = 60°$; $m\angle 7 = 120°$

Pages 202–204

1. Yes, because each alternate exterior angle is congruent to its opposite vertical angle and those vertical angles are congruent since the lines are parallel.
2. We can conclude that line m is parallel to *n* but lines *m* and *n* are not parallel to *p*. Looking at lines *n* and *p*, their corresponding angles are not congruent.

3. $m\angle x = 130°$; $m\angle y = 130°$, $m\angle z = 130°$

4. $m\angle x = 92°$

5. $m\angle x = 90°$; $m\angle y = 90°$

6. $m\angle x = 75°$; $m\angle y = 105°$

7. $m\angle x = 30°$; $m\angle y = 30°$

8. $m\angle x = 160°$; $m\angle y = 20°$; $m\angle z = 160°$

9. a. $x = 40$. The angles are corresponding and since the lines are parallel the angle measures must be equal.

10. a. $x = 18$

    b. $m\angle ABC = 78°$

    c. $m\angle BDE = 102°$

    $\angle ABC$ and $\angle BDE$ are not congruent because they are not corresponding or alternate interior, so they must be supplementary.

Pages 207–209

1. It is not a polygon because one side is a curve. In a polygon the sides must be straight and the polygon must be a closed figure.

2. pentagon; 90cm

3. heptagon; 17.5 cm

4. square; 100"

5. hexagon; 22.8 cm

6. triangle; 12.75 km

7. octagon; 6 units

8. $w = 25$ m; $l = 50$ m

9. a. $40n$

   b. $n = 4$

10. $x = 5$. The sides are 20 and 15 units.

11. $x = 4$

12. $17x$

Pages 210–211

1. heptagon; 900°

2. octagon; 1,080°

3. nonagon; 1,260°

4. decagon; 1,440°

5. 60°

6. 65°

7. 64°

8. 61°

9. 78°

10. 60°

11. $m\angle A = 90°$; $m\angle B = 60°$; $m\angle C = 30°$

12. $m\angle D = 22.5°$; $m\angle E = 45°$; $m\angle F = 112.5°$

13. $m\angle Q = 35°$; $m\angle R = 35°$

Pages 213–215

1. A right triangle can be isosceles (90°, 45°, 45°) or scalene. A right triangle cannot be equilateral because equilateral triangles have three 60° angles.
2. It's isosceles because it has two congruent angles.
3. They're not congruent. However, they both have 3-60° angles.
4. $m\angle x = 150°$. Yes, there's a connection because the exterior angle adds to the two remote interior angles. $30° + 120° = 150°$.
5. $m\angle x = 115°$
6. $m\angle x = 150°$
7. $m\angle x = 150°$
8. $m\angle x = 45°$
9. a. $m\angle 1 = 110°$
   b. $m\angle 2 = 30°$
   c. $m\angle 3 = 40°$
   d. $m\angle 4 = 140°$
   e. $m\angle 5 = 40°$

Page 217

1. F
2. T
3. T
4. F
5. T
6. T
7. T
8. F
9. F
10. T
11. T
12. F

Page 218

1. 20 in.^{2}
2. 100 ft^2
3. 169 m^2
4. 20.4 cm^2
5. 30 in.^{2}
6. 81 in.^{2}

Page 219

1. 75 in.^{2}
2. 13.5 ft^2
3. 15.75 cm^2
4. 2 ft^2

5. 3,400 ft^2

6. 10.3125 $units^2$

7. 37.5 ft^2

8. 150 $in.^2$

Page 221

1. 36 ft^2

2. 93.5 ft^2

3. 176 ft^2

4. 190.625 $units^2$

5. 19.5 $units^2$

6. 21.84 cm^2

7. a. 340 cm^2
   b. 100 m^2
   c. 240 m^2

8. An easier way is to just find the area of the parallelogram. The base is 12 (22 – 10) and the height is 20. So its area is 240 m^2.

Pages 222–223

1. $h = 4$ m $\frac{1}{2} \bullet 300 \bullet h = 600$

2. $b = 5"$ $\frac{1}{2} \bullet b \bullet 4 = 10$

3. $h = 4$ cm $\frac{(5 + 12) \bullet h}{2} = 34$

4. $b = 600'$

   $\frac{(b + 400) \bullet 250}{2} = 125{,}000$

Pages 224–225

1. 62.8'

2. 15.7"

3. 314'

4. 3.14 cm

5. 25 units

6. 12.5 units

Pages 225–227

1. 100π ft^2

2. 64π $in.^2$

3. 225π cm^2

4. $.25\pi$ m^2

5. 4.84π km^2

6. 121π $units^2$

7. radius = 7 meters, diameter = 14 meters

8. a. 7'
   b. 3.5'
   c. 38.465 ft^2
   d. 10.535 ft^2

9. a. 10 m
   b. 5 m
   c. 5 m
   d. 25 m^2
   e. 39.25 m^2
   f. 14.25 m^2

10. a. 14.13 ft^2
    b. 12.56 ft^2
    c. 1.57 ft^2

Pages 228–235 Chapter 10 Review

1. $m\angle ABC = 20°$
2. $m\angle ABC = 110°$
3. $m\angle ABC = 61°$
4. a. adjacent; complementary
   b. adjacent; supplementary
5. $m\angle x = 130°$
6. $x = 20$
7. $x = 70$
8. $m\angle x = 120°$
9. $x = 26$
10. $x = 90$ (Set both angles equal to 180°.)
11. d
12. b
13. e
14. c
15. f
16. a
17. 45°; It's an isosceles right triangle. It has two congruent angles which also means it has two congruent sides.
18. 60°; It's an equilateral triangle. Every angle is 60° which makes all the sides congruent.
19. $m\angle x = 50°$, $m\angle A = 80°$; It is an isosceles triangle. It has two congruent angles and two congruent sides.
20. $w = 13$ meters; $l = 26$ meters Area = 338 m^2.
21. a. octagon
    b. 1,080°
    c. 135°
    d. $x = 27$
22. a. $x = 40°$
    b. exterior, remote
23. $P = 61'$; $A = 205$ ft^2
24. $P = 24"$; $A = 24$ $in.^2$
25. $P = 29$ cm; $A = 42$ cm^2
26. $P = 40'$; $A = 80$ ft^2
27. $C = 14\pi$ in.; $A = 49\pi$ $in.^2$
28. $C = 11\pi$ ft; $A = 30.25\pi$ ft^2
29. 17.5 m^2
30. 53.5 $in.^2$ (Area of the circle: 78.5 – Area of the triangle: 25)
31. All three angles should line up on the line which proves that the angle measures add up to 180°.
32. b. 360°
    c. pentagon

d. 6
e. heptagon, 900°
f. 8
g. $(n - 2) \bullet 180°$

33. c. 5
d. 9
e. 14
f. 7
g. 4
h. $n - 3$
i. $n(n - 3)$
j. When you draw a diagonal from one vertex to another, for example, vertex *A* to *B*, you've already drawn the diagonal from *B* to *A*. Therefore, you need to divide the expression by 2.

Pages 237–238

1. 30 in.^{3}
2. 512 cm^3
3. 200 ft^3
4. 192 ft^3
5. 1,080 cm^3
6. 3,000 ft^3
7. 483 ft^3 $[(10 \bullet 3)\div 2] + [(10+8) \bullet 6 \div 2] \bullet 7$
8. $\frac{1}{2}$ in.
9. 6 ft
10. 8.6 cm

Page 240

1. 100 in.^{3}
2. 40 ft^3
3. 800 ft^3
4. 800 ft^3
5. 117.776 ft^3
6. 147 meters $(230 \bullet 230) \bullet x \div 3 = 2{,}592{,}100$

Pages 242–243

1. 720π ft^3
2. 64π in.^{3}
3. 200π ft^3
4. $60{,}000\pi$ in.^{3}
5. 96π cm^3
6. 108π ft^3
7. 31.25π ft^3

Page 245-246

1. 486 ft^2
2. 252 cm^2
3. 408 in.^{2}
4. 62.4 units^2

5. 274 mm^2
   175 (2 trapezoids) + 45 (bottom) + 30 (top) + 24 (sides)

6. 210π $in.^2$

7. 175 m^2

Page 247

1. 18π ft^2

2. 39π $units^2$

3. 96π ft^2

4. 5π $units^2$

5. 96π ft^2

6. 224π $units^2$

Page 248

1. $V = 288\pi$ ft^3
   $SA = 144\pi$ ft^2

2. $V = 972\pi$ cm^3
   $SA = 324\pi$ cm^2

3. $V = 166.\overline{6}\pi$ in^3
   $SA = 100\pi$ in^2

4. $V = 448.7\pi$ in^3
   $SA = 283.4\pi$ in^2

5. 288π $units^3$

Pages 249–251 Chapter 11 Review

1. $V = 650$ ft^3
   $SA = 525$ ft^2

2. $V = 144$ $units^3$
   $SA = 216$ $units^2$

3. 96 ft^3

4. 640π cm^3

5. 192π ft^3

6. 34π $units^3$

7. $4{,}500\pi$ cm^3

8. 972π mm^3

9. 270π mm^2

10. 22π ft^2

11. a. Trapezoidal prism. The base is an isosceles trapezoid. It's a prism because it has two parallel bases and polygon sides.
    b. Volume: 1,040 ft^3
    c. Surface Area: 708 ft^2

12. 813.92 ft^3 $(1{,}040 - 72\pi)$

13. a. 48π ft^3
    b. 324π ft^3
    c. 144π ft^3
    d. 516π ft^3

Page 252

2. (0, 6)

3. (−2, 1)

4. (−5, 0)

5. (−1, −5)

6. (6, 0)

7. (0, −2)

8. (−4, −2)

Page 253

1.

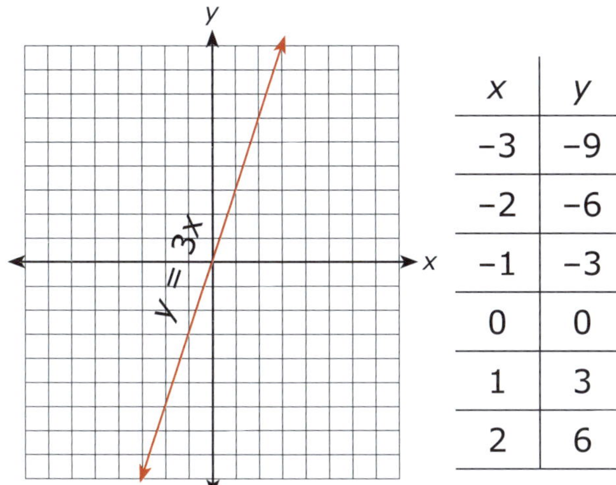

x	y
−3	−9
−2	−6
−1	−3
0	0
1	3
2	6

2.

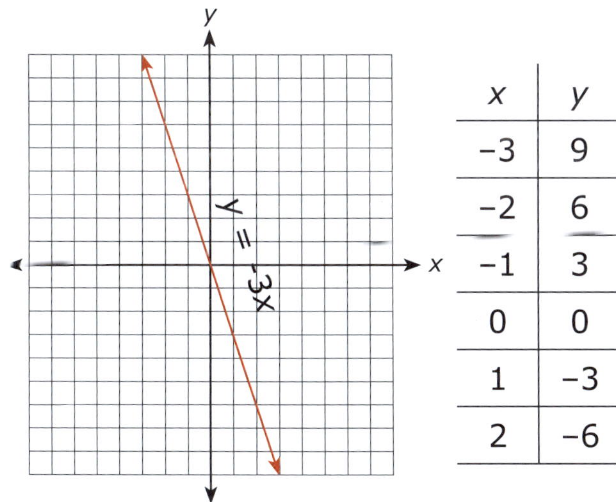

x	y
−3	9
−2	6
−1	3
0	0
1	−3
2	−6

3.

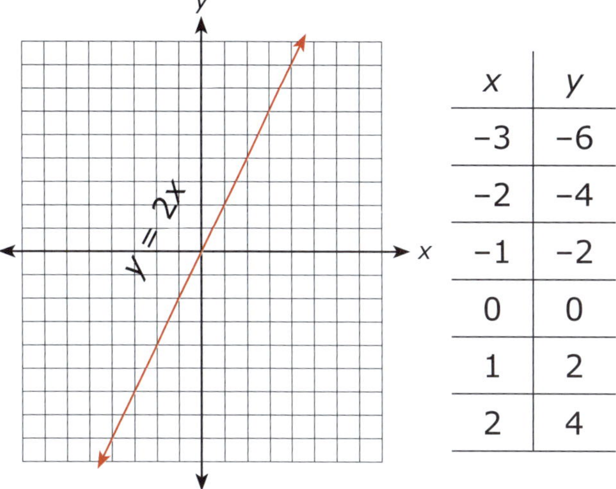

x	y
−3	−6
−2	−4
−1	−2
0	0
1	2
2	4

4.

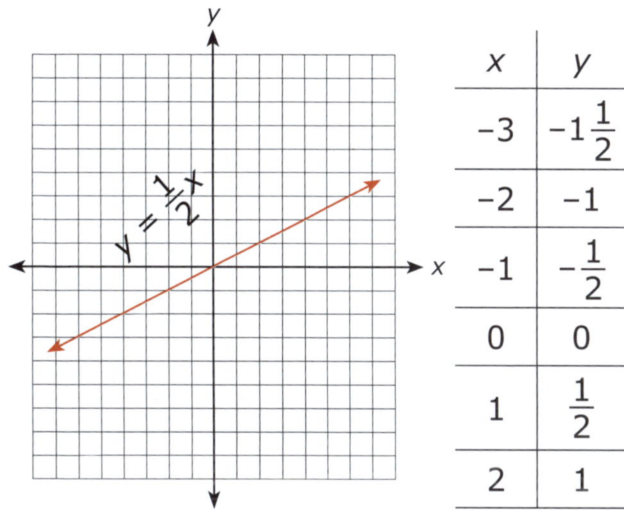

x	y
−3	$-1\frac{1}{2}$
−2	−1
−1	$-\frac{1}{2}$
0	0
1	$\frac{1}{2}$
2	1

5.

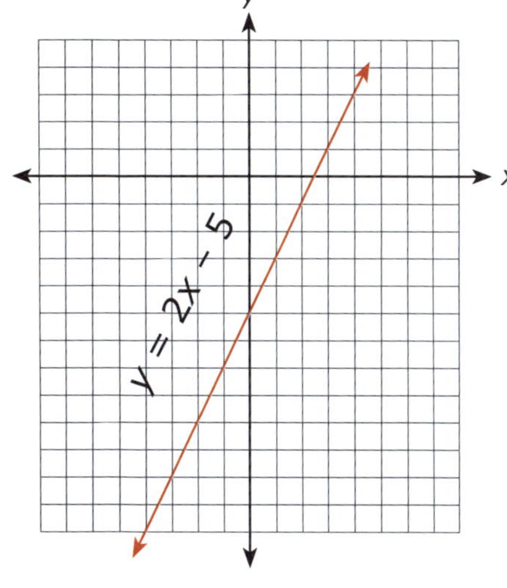

x	y
−3	−11
−2	−9
−1	−7
0	−5
1	−3
2	−1

6.

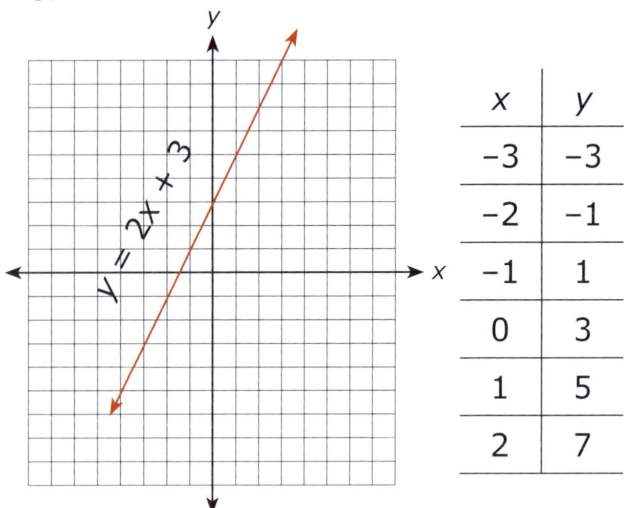

x	y
−3	−3
−2	−1
−1	1
0	3
1	5
2	7

7.

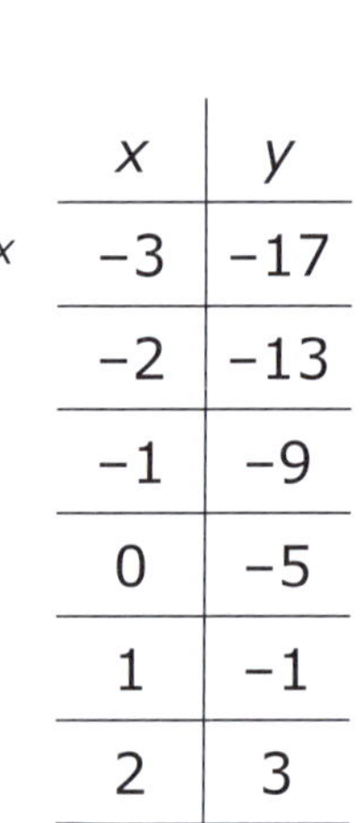

x	y
−3	−17
−2	−13
−1	−9
0	−5
1	−1
2	3

8.

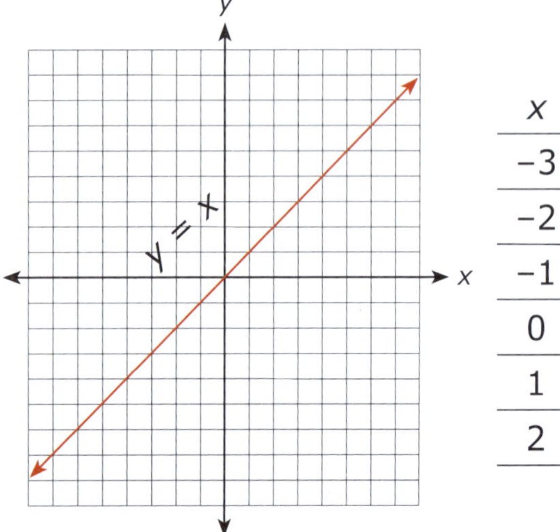

x	y
−3	−3
−2	−2
−1	−1
0	0
1	1
2	2

9.

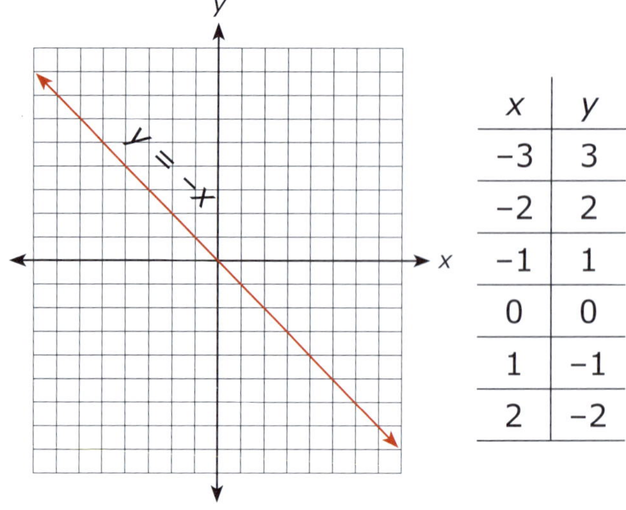

x	y
−3	3
−2	2
−1	1
0	0
1	−1
2	−2

Page 255

1. F
2. E
3. A
4. D (the y-axis)
5. B (the x-axis)
6. C

Pages 258–260

1. B; It's up 3 units from the x-axis crossing (0, 3).
2. D; It's 3 units to the left from the y-axis going through (3, 0).
3. A; It has a y-intercept of 5 and the slope is up 5, and to the right 3.
4. C; It has a y-intercept of 4 and the slope is down 4, and to the right 3.

5. $y = 0x + 3$.

6. $\frac{5}{0}$ is the slope that would indicate a vertical line. The slope is undefined.

7. $y = 2x - 2$; $m = 2$, $b = -2$

8. $y = -3x + 2$; $m = -3$, $b = 2$

9. $y = -3$; $m = 0$, $b = -3$

10. $y = x + 2$; $m = 1$, $b = 2$

11. $y = -2x - 3$; $m = -2$, $b = -3$

12. $y = -6x$; $m = -6$; $b = 0$

13. $y = 3x + 7$; $m = 3$; $b = 7$

14. $y = -\frac{4}{5}x + 4$; $m = -\frac{4}{5}$; $b = 4$

15. $y = \frac{1}{5}x + 4$; $m = \frac{1}{5}$; $b = 4$

16. $y = -30$; $m = 0$; $b = -30$

Graphs 17 and 22

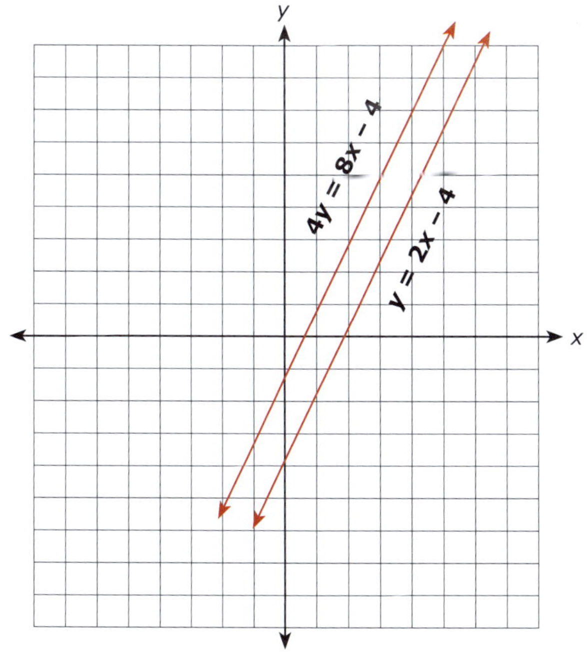

Graph 18 and 20

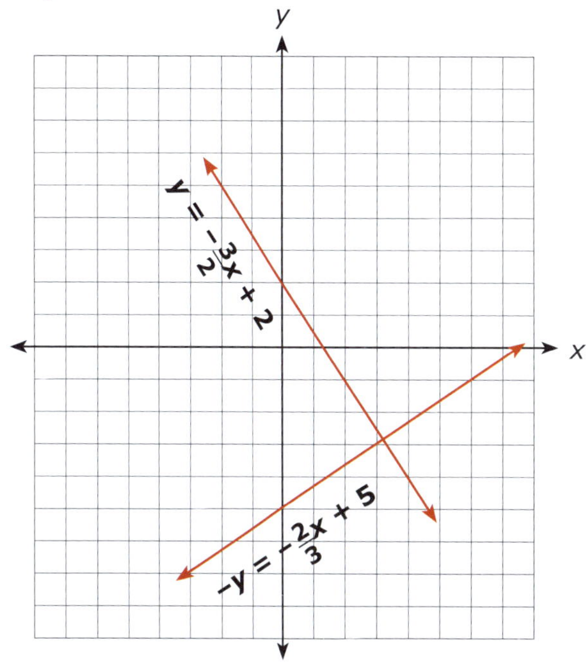

Graph 19

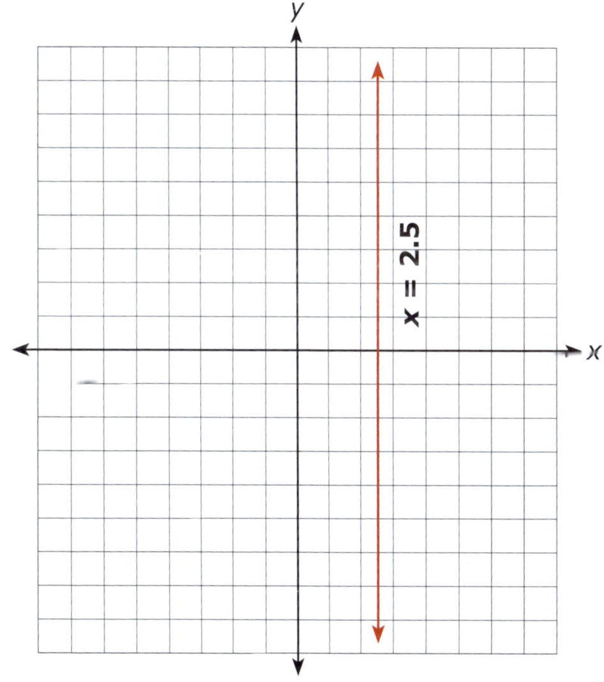

Graph 21

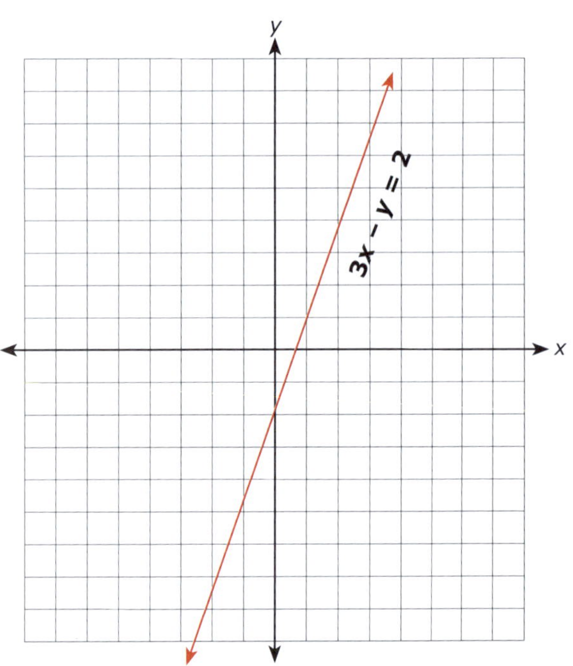

Graph 23

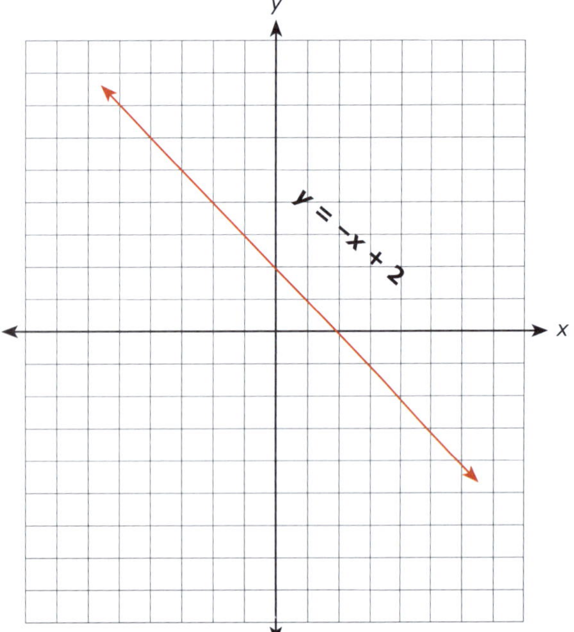

Graph 24

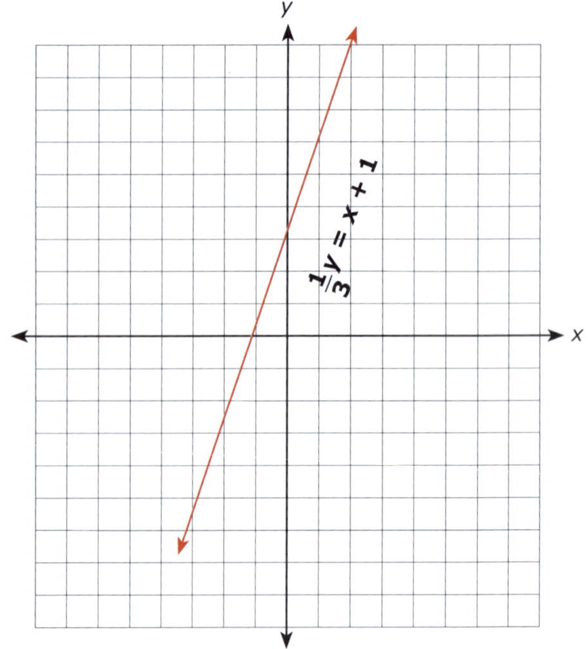

Graph 25

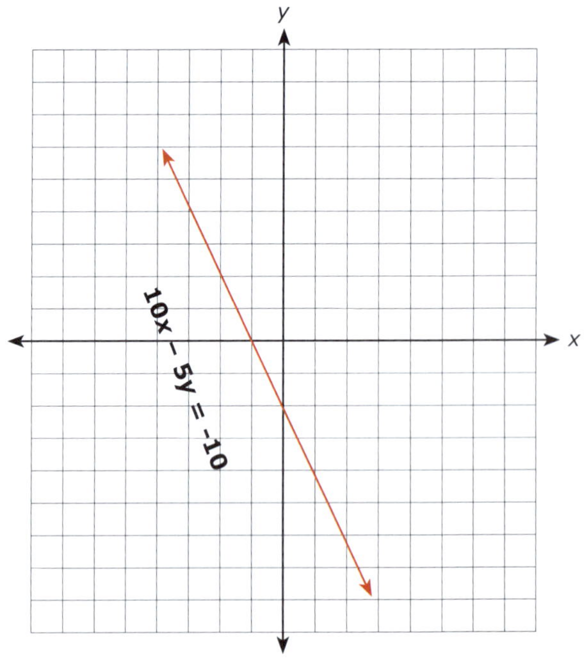

26. The equations have the same slope. The lines are parallel.

27. parallel.

28. The equations have negative reciprocal slopes. The lines are perpendicular.

29. perpendicular.

30. They are parallel because the equations have the same slope.

Page 262

1. $-\frac{3}{4}$
2. 3
3. $\frac{4}{3}$
4. 0
5. undefined
6. $-\frac{1}{5}$
7. $-\frac{1}{7}$
8. $\frac{3}{4}$
9. 5
10. 1

Pages 263–264

1. $y = 4x - 5$
2. $y = -3x$
3. $y = -2.5$
4. $y = -2x + 3$
5. $y = 3x - 1$
6. $y = 2x + 11$
7. $y = -2x + 4$
8. $y = 5$
9. Graph 4

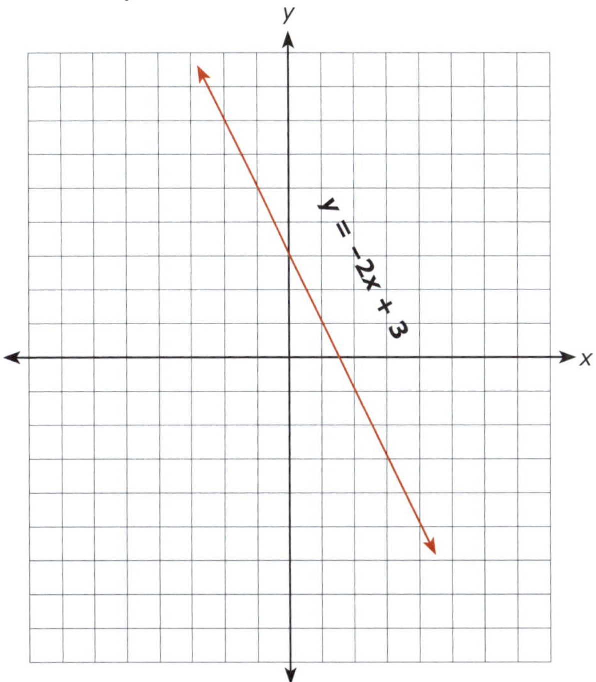

10. Graph 8

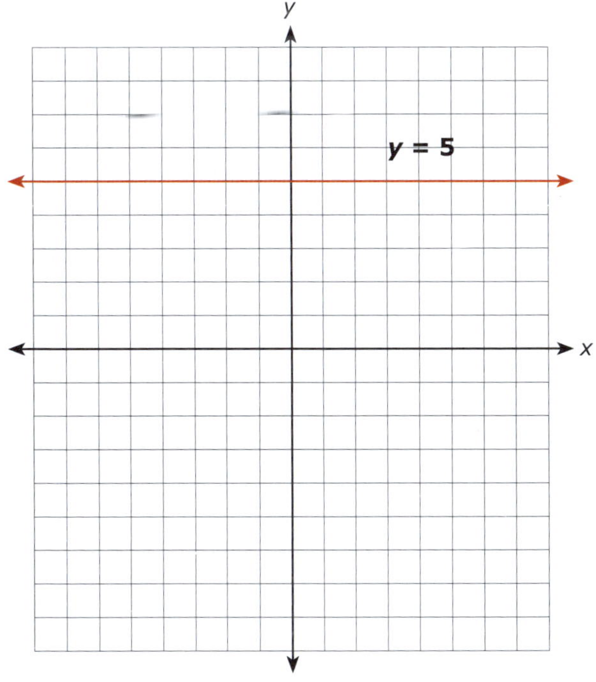

Pages 266–267

1.

No. of Cans	0	1	2	4	6	10	12
Price ($)	0	$2.50	$5.00	$10	$15	$25.00	$30

b. Yes, it is a proportional relationship. The number of cans is proportional to the price.

c. $p = 2.50c$

d. 2.5

2. Yes, it is a proportional relationship. It costs $8.25 per student for each year. The constant of proportionality is 8.25.

3. b and e. Both of those tables show a proportional relationship. Both have the point (0, 0). The constant of proportionality for table b is 3 and the constant of proportionality for Table e is 1.

4. Table a: $y = 2x + 1$; Table b: $y = 3x$; Table e: $y = x$.

5. Table c: $y = 3x + 2$

6. Table d: $y = 2x + 5$

7. Table f: $y = x - 3$

8. a. The rate of change or the slope is $\frac{1}{2}$. The change in y is $\frac{1}{2}$ divided by the change in x which is 1.

b. When $x = 0$, $y = 2$. As the x values are decreased by 1 the y values are decreasing by $\frac{1}{2}$.

c. $y = \frac{1}{2}x + 2$.

No, it's not a proportional relationship as it's not in the form $y = kx$.

9. a. $c = 60m$

b. $c = 200 + 20m$

c. Club Fitness One. The equation $c = 60m$ is of the form $y = kx$.

10.

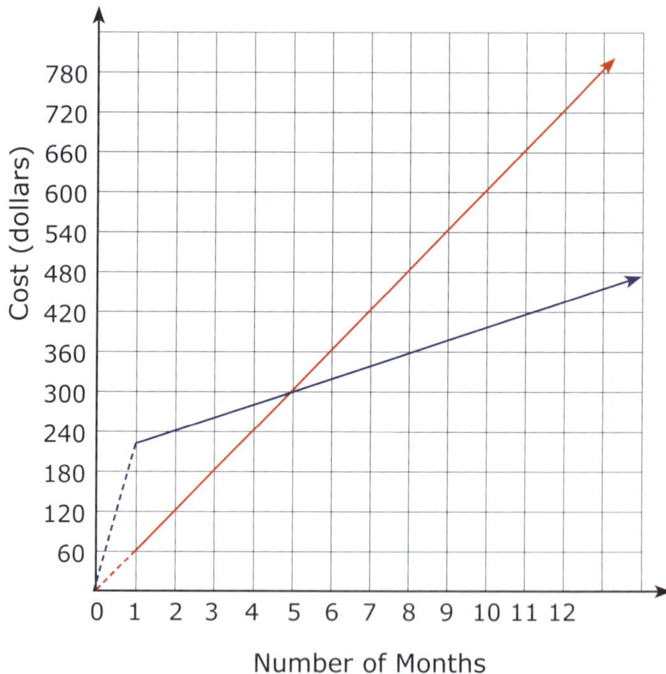

a. Club Fitness One is cheaper for the first 3 months as you can see from the graph. It's cheaper up to month 5.

b. $300

c. Island Gym after month 5 is cheaper as you can see from the graph.

d. At month 12 (1 year) Club Fitness One costs $720 and Island Gym is $440, so the difference is $280.

Pages 269–271

1. They have the same slope. The lines are parallel.

2. The solution is (1, 2) which is where the lines intersect. Substituting (1, 2) into $y = x + 1$ gives you $2 = 1 + 1$ which is true. Substituting (1, 2) into $y = -2x + 4$ gives you $2 = -2(1) + 4$ which is true. So (1, 2) satisfies both equations.

3. If you take $3y = 6x + 6$ and solve for y, you get $y = 2x + 2$.

4.

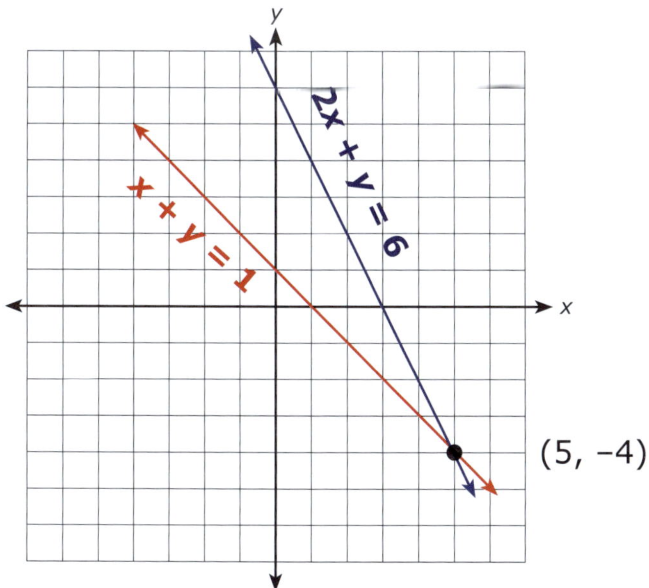

5.

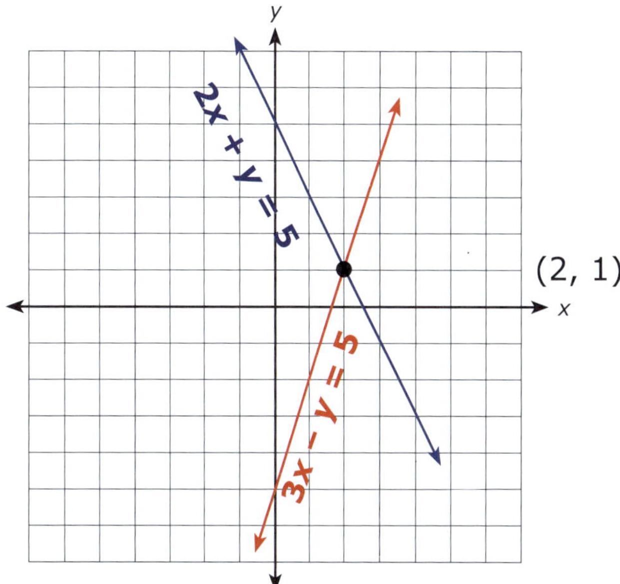

6.

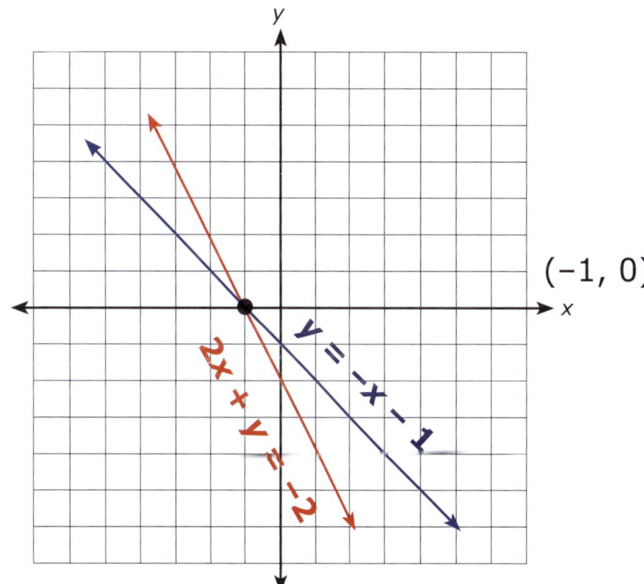

7.

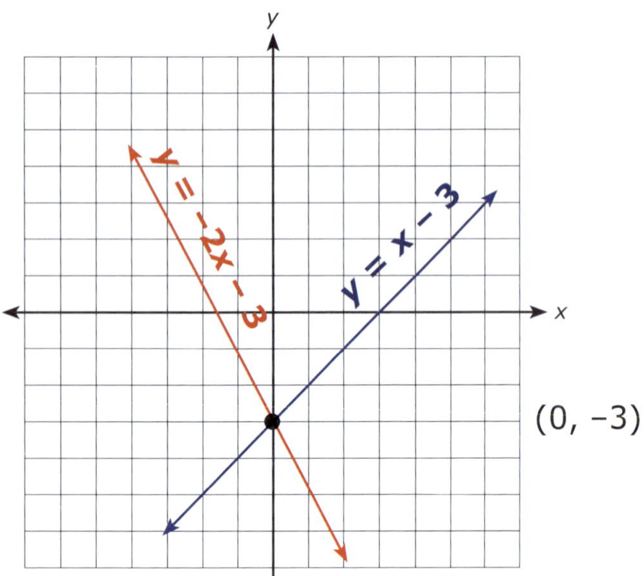

(0, −3)

8.

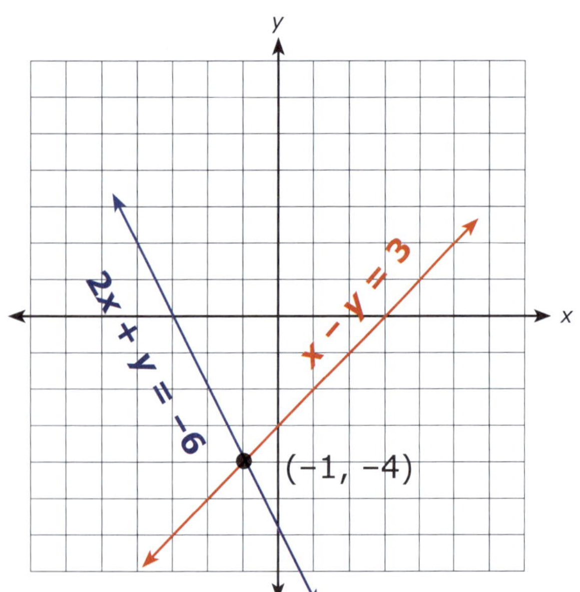

9.

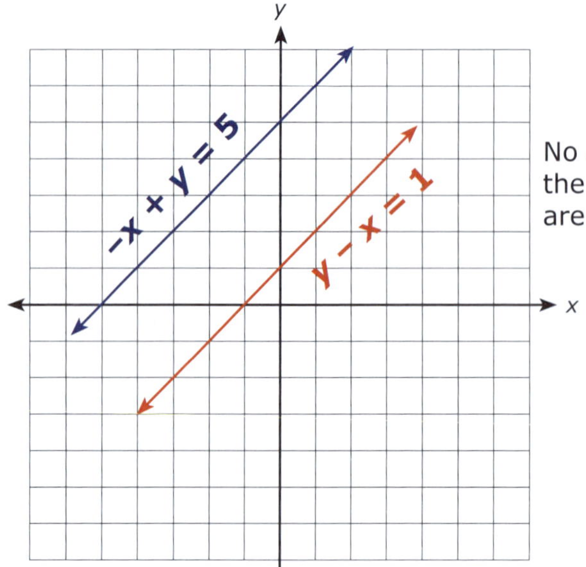

No answer, the lines are parallel.

10. $y = 3x - 1$

$2y - 6x = -2$

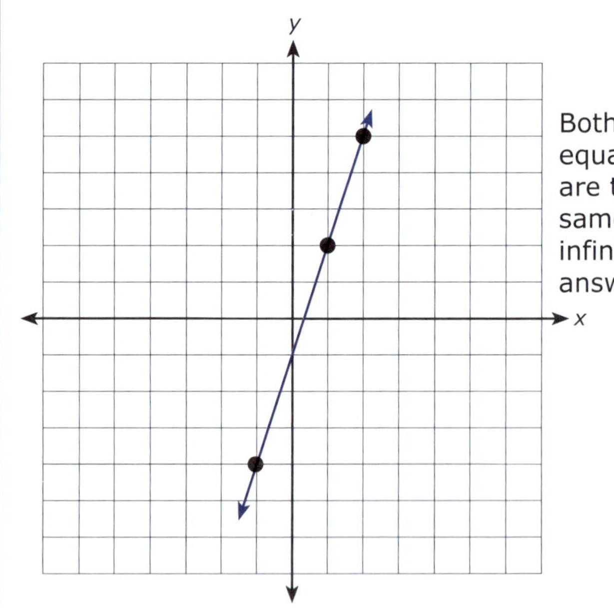

Both equations are the same line, infinite answers.

11. Yes, (−2.5, −3) is a solution.

$x - y = .5$

$-2.5 - (-3) = .5$? Yes!

$2x + 2y = -11$

$2(-2.5) + 2(-3) = -11$?

$-5 + -6 = -11$? Yes!

Pages 272–275 Chapter 12 Review

1. II
2. IV
3. III
4. y-axis
5. x-axis
6. I
7.

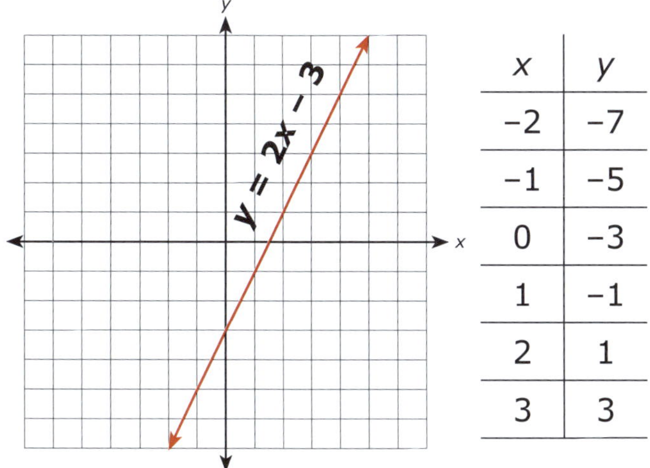

x	y
–2	–7
–1	–5
0	–3
1	–1
2	1
3	3

8.

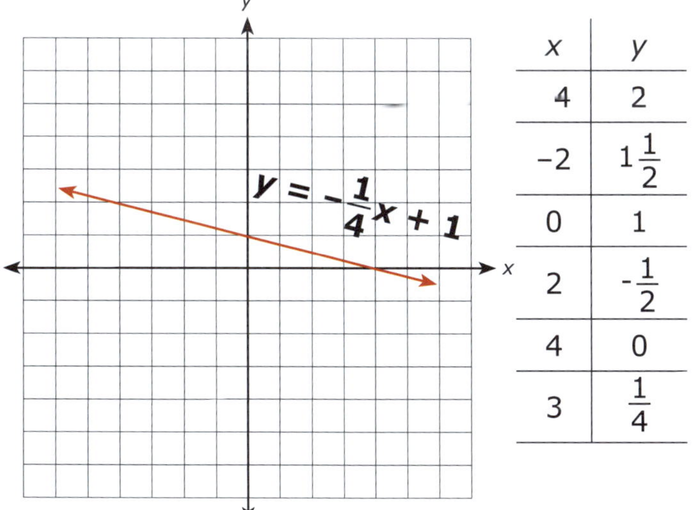

x	y
4	2
–2	$1\frac{1}{2}$
0	1
2	$-\frac{1}{2}$
4	0
3	$\frac{1}{4}$

9. $y = 3x - 6$
10. $y = -\frac{1}{2}x + \frac{1}{2}$
11. $y = -2x - 6$
12. $y = 4x - 6$
13. $y = -2x + 3$
14. $y = 2x + 8$
15.

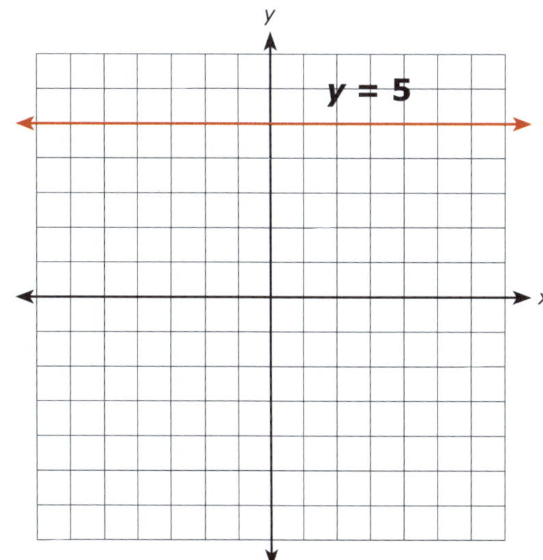

16.

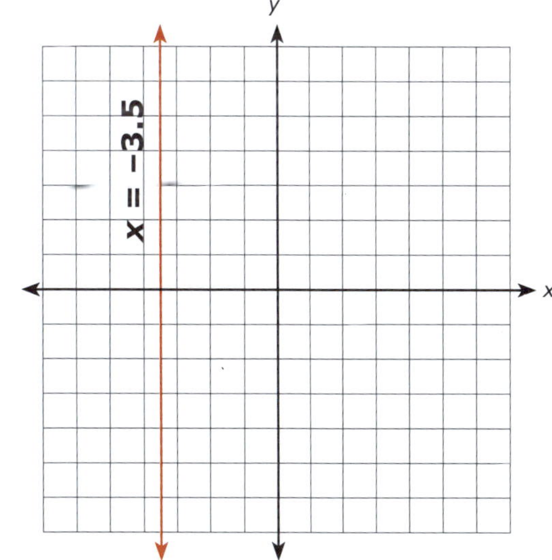

17.

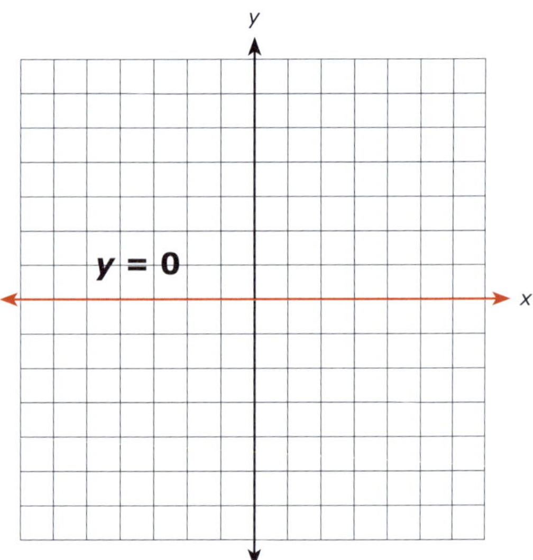

18.

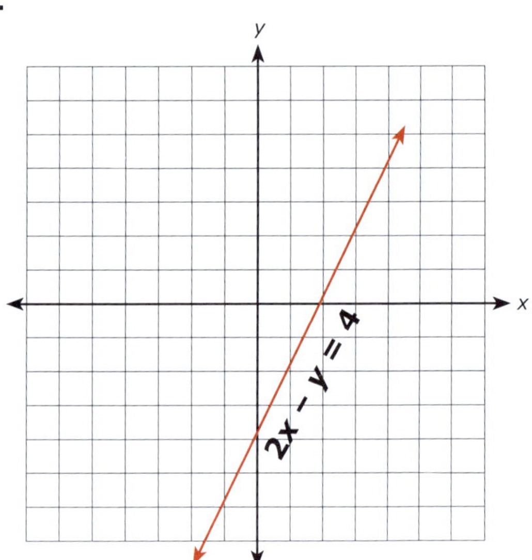

19.

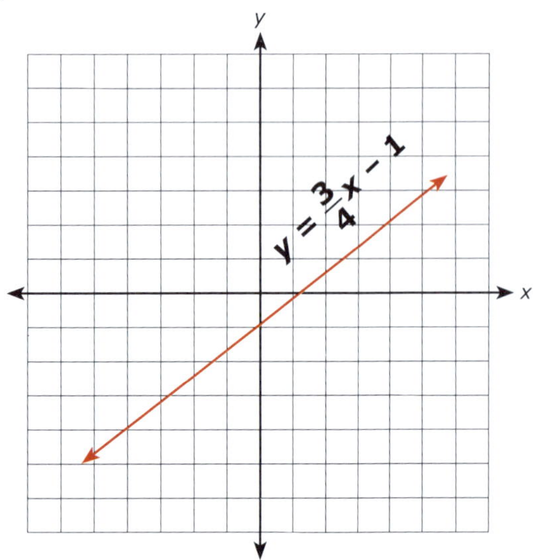

20.

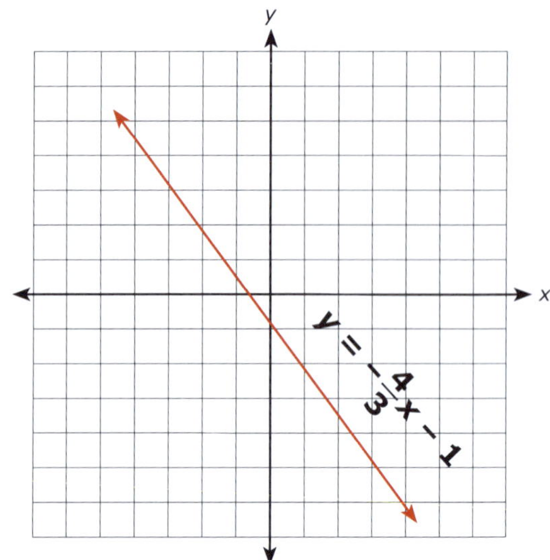

21. The equations have negative reciprocal slopes, so the lines are perpendicular.

22. $\frac{1}{5}$

23. 2

24. undefined

25. 0

26. $y = 5x - 2$

27. $y = -2x + 16$

28. $x = 5$

29. $y = 3x$

30. It is a proportional relationship since its equation is of the form $y = kx$. The constant of proportionality is 3.

31.

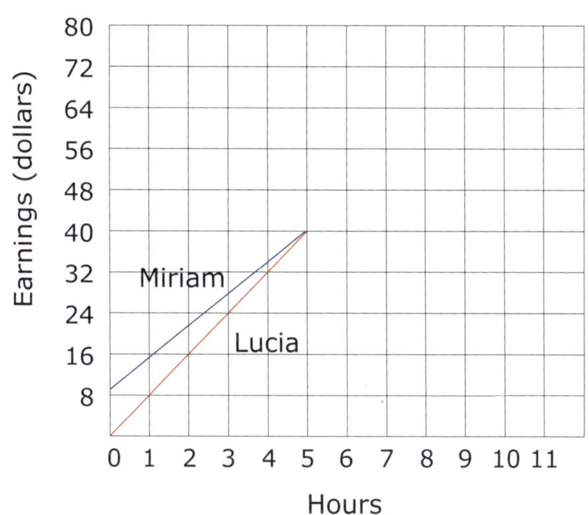

a. Lucia; the constant of proportionality is 8

b. Hours; Hours determine the money earned

c. Lucia: d = 8h; Miriam: d = 6h + 10

d. $40 (8 • 5), $40 (10 + 6 • 5)

e. 10 hours; 70 = 10 + 6h

32.

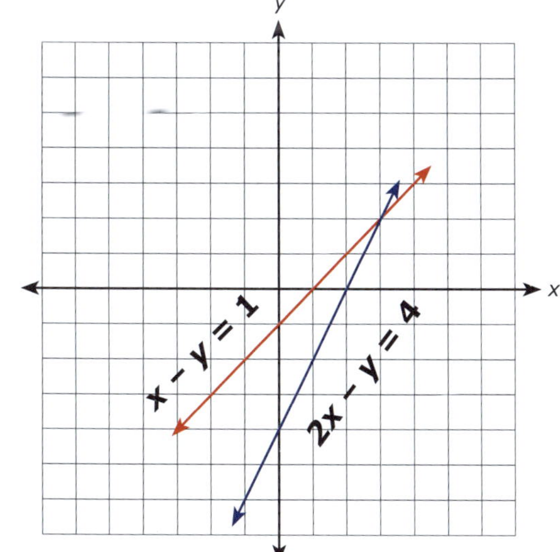

independent; one

33.

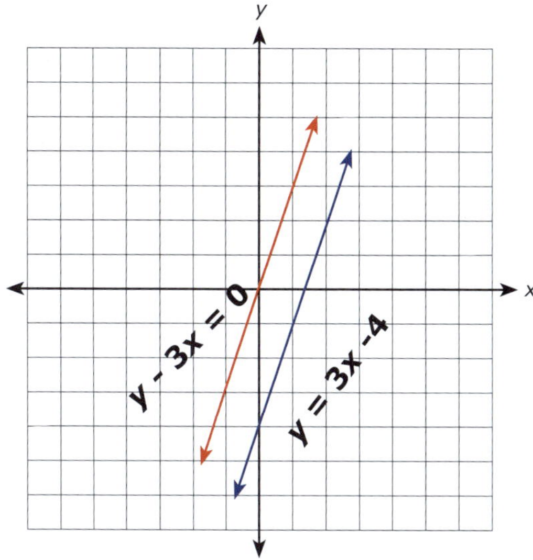

inconsistent (lines are parallel); no or 0 (zero)

Pages 277–279

1. Yes, the distance remains equal. From *A* to *B* is 3 units, and from *A*' to *B*' is also 3 units. From *A* to *C* is 4 units, and from *A*' to *C*' is also 4 units.

2. 5 units. It is the same. From *B* to *C* is 5 units (it's a 3-4-5 right triangle), and from *B*' to *C*' is also 5 units.

3. Yes. The corresponding sides of the preimage are congruent to the corresponding sides of the image. All the corresponding angles are also congruent.

4.

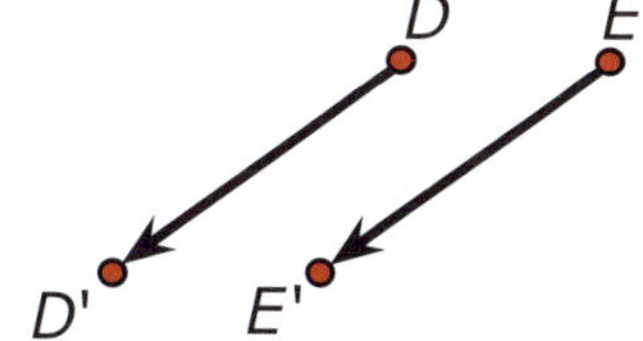

5. 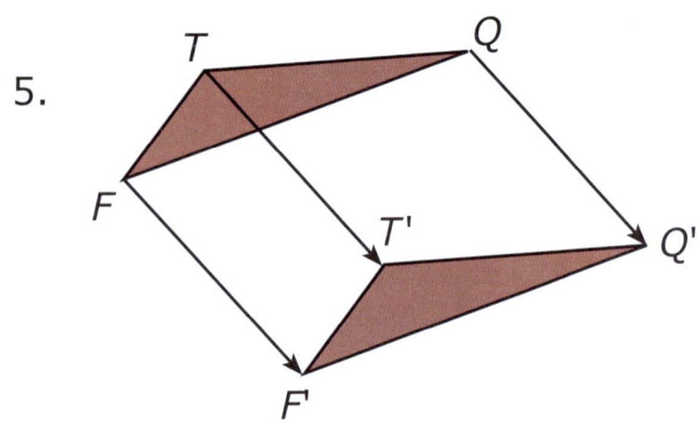

6. 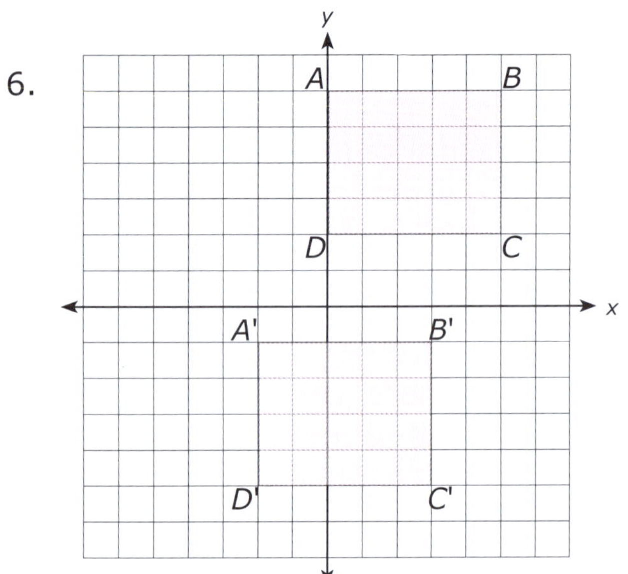

Yes, the corresponding sides are congruent and corresponding angles are still congruent. Both are rectangles with four 90° angles.

7. 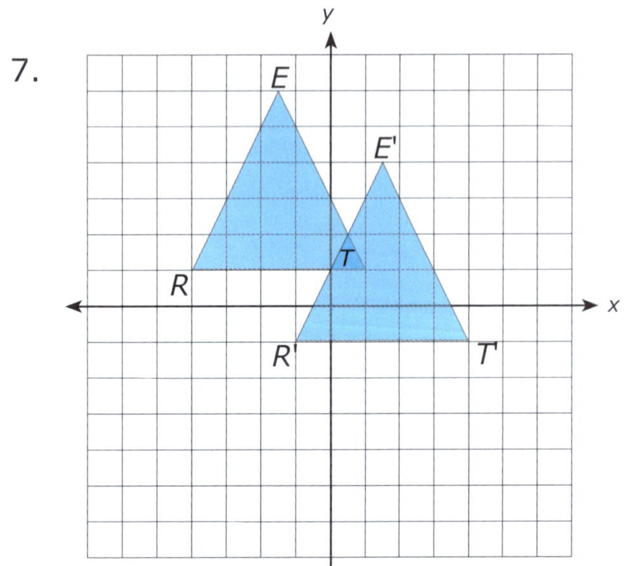

a. Yes, answers will vary. For example, these two triangles have the same area but are not congruent.

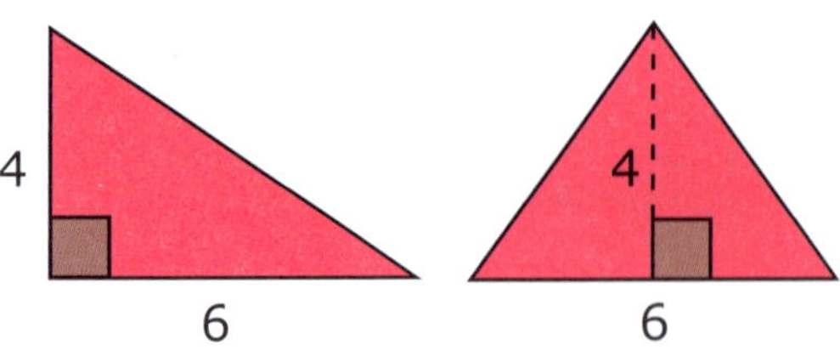

b. Yes, the triangles would automatically have corresponding congruent angles.

8. $\overrightarrow{DE}$

Page 280

1. A (−5, −2); A' (5, −2)

   B (−2, 3); B' (2, 3)

   C (−1, −3); C' (1, −3)

2. The x-value.

3. y. If you reflect about the y-axis, the figure moves to the other side of the y-axis which means the y value remains the same and the x value will change. If you reflect about the x-axis, the figure moves to the other side of the x-axis which means the x value remains the same and the y value will change.

Page 281

1. (0, 0); (0, 0); (0, 0)

2. (−3, 2)

3. (3, 2); (−3, 2)

4. They both have the same coordinates. Reflecting about the origin is the same as reflecting about one axis and then about the other axis.

5. a. (−3, 4)

   b. (5, −6)

   c. (2, 5)

   d. (0, 10)

Page 282

1. Answers will vary.

2. a. (3, −2); b. (5, 0); c. (−5, 3); d. (30, 20)

3. a. (3, 1); b. (3, 4) c. (5, 4); d. (5, 1)

4. Yes, the corresponding sides remain congruent and the corresponding angles are also congruent.

Pages 284–285

1. The *x* and *y* values changed signs.

2. a. (−1, −2); b. (−6, −6); c. (−5, −1)

3. 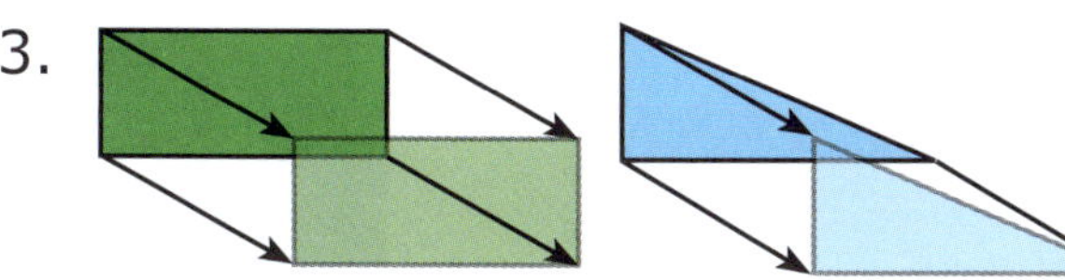

4. *A*' (−1, 3); *B*' (2, 0); *C*' (−4, −4)

5. a. *Q*' (-1, 6); *R*' (−2, 2); *S*' (−6, 1)

   b. *Q*' (−1, −6); *R*' (−2, −2); *S*' (−6, −1)

   c. *Q*' (1, −6); *R*' (2, −2); *S*' (6, −1)

Pages 287–289

1. Yes, fixing the angle between the corresponding congruent sides will guarantee congruency.

2. Both triangles are congruent.

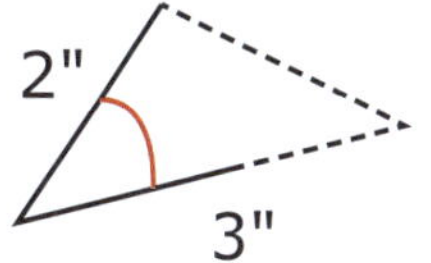

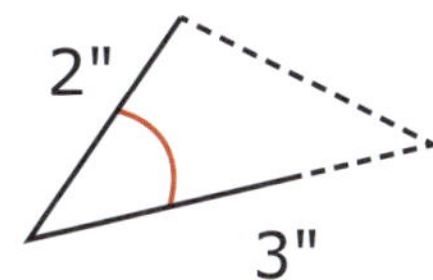

When two sides are congruent to the two corresponding sides of another triangle and the angle between those two sides is also congruent in both triangles then the two triangles are congruent.

3. Yes, SSS

4. Yes, SAS

5. cpctc; Corresponding parts of congruent triangles are congruent.

6. No, the triangle on the left is SAS, and the one on the right is SSA.

7. Triangles sides are extended to meet at one point.

   b. Yes, if you extend the sides you create two congruent triangles. Both triangles have two corresponding angles congruent with the side between those angles also congruent.

b. ASA; Two corresponding angles congruent with the side between those two same angles congruent.

Page 291

1. Yes, SSS
2. Yes, SAS (sharing a side)
3. Yes, ASA
4. Not congruent
5. Yes, SAS
6. Not necessarily congruent. They are similar (same shape but not necessarily same size).
7. Not congruent
8. Yes, ASA
9. Not congruent
10. Yes, SAS (sharing a side)

Pages 293–294

1. $\frac{3}{2}$
2. *G*' (2, 2); *F*' (4, 2); *E*' (4, 6); *D*' (2, 6)
3. a. (–4.5, –4.5)

   b. new radius: 1.5 units, new diameter: 3 units
4. *Q*' (–2, 4); *R*' (6, 8); *S*' (14, 12)
5. $\frac{3}{2}$
6. a. $\frac{3}{1}$

   b. $\frac{1}{3}$

   c. $\frac{D\pi}{d\pi} = \frac{6\pi}{2\pi} = \frac{3}{1}$

   d. $\frac{\pi R^2}{\pi r^2} = \frac{\pi \bullet 3^2}{\pi \bullet 1^2} = \frac{9}{1}$
7. 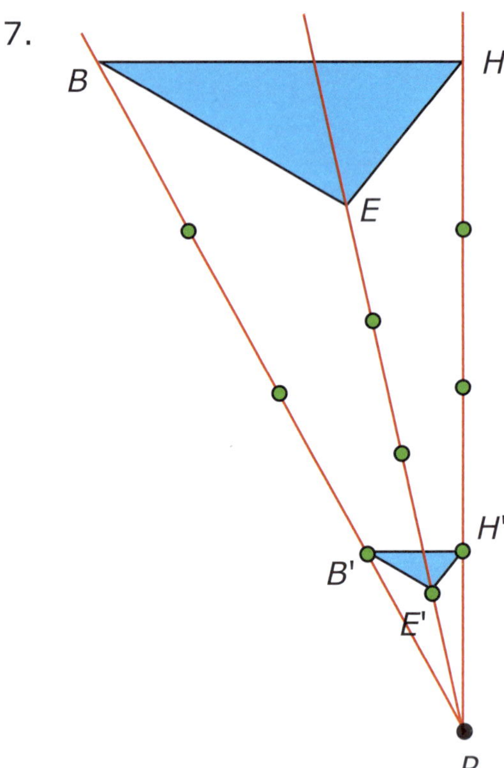

Pages 295–297

1. Since the measures of the angles in a triangle add up to 180° if two angles are congruent to two angles of another triangle, then their third angles will be congruent.

2. Statement 1 is true. Congruent triangles will have sides in proportion (1:1) and all corresponding angles congruent.

3. $x = 30$; Set up a proportion.

$$\frac{15}{18} = \frac{25}{x}$$

4. b. The scale is $1\frac{1}{2}$.

So $1 \bullet 1\frac{1}{2} = 1\frac{1}{2}$ and $\frac{1}{2} \bullet 1\frac{1}{2} = \frac{3}{4}$.

5. No. The third angle of the triangle on the left has a measure of 25°. The third angle of the triangle on the right has a measure of 20°. Therefore, the corresponding angles are not congruent and the triangles are not similar to each other.

6. Since the vertical angles are also congruent, the triangles are congruent by AA.

7. Since the segments are parallel, the corresponding angles would also be congruent.

8. $DG = 30$. Set up a proportion.

9. $m < x = 30°$ and $m < y = 60°$.

10. No, two right triangles are not always similar. For example, one could be 90°-30°-60°, and one could be 90°-45°-45°, or 90°-20°-70°.

Pages 298–302 Chapter 13 Review

1. 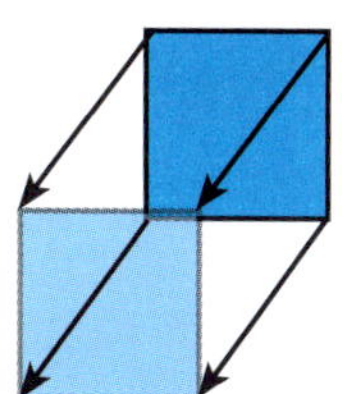

2. A (−13, 9), B (−10, 14), C (−21, −7)

3. 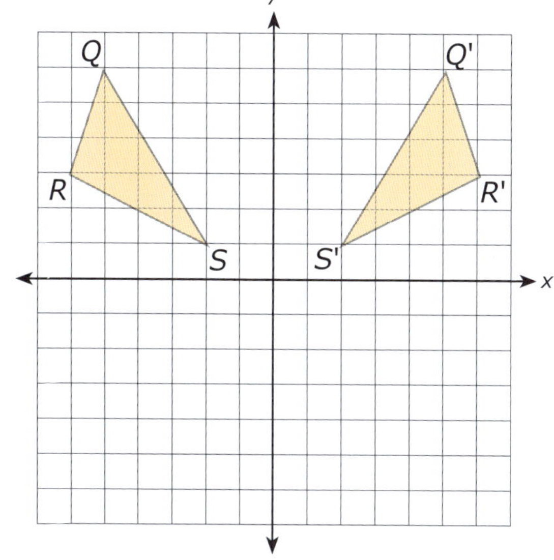

Q' (5, 6), R' (6, 3), S' (2, 1)

4. Q'' (5, −6), R'' (6, −3), S'' (2, −1)

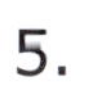

5. 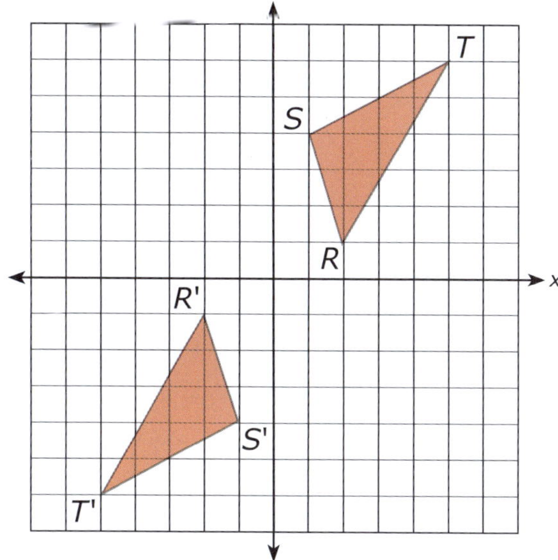

R' (−2, −1); S' (−1, −4); T' (−5, −6)

6.

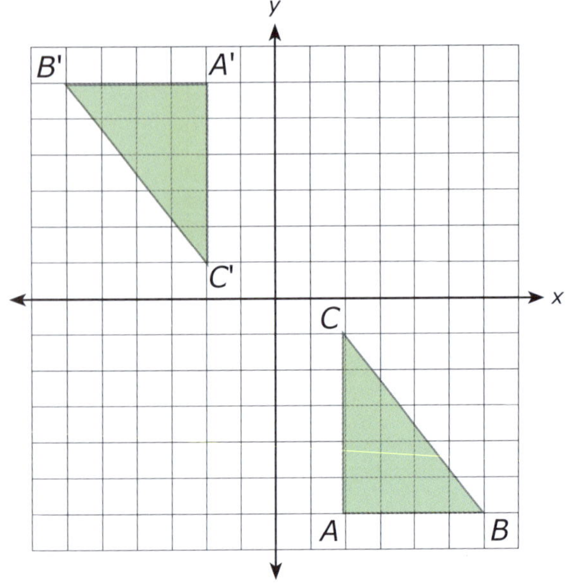

A' (–2, 6); B' (–6, 6); C' (–2, 1)

7. Not congruent

8. Yes, SSS

9. Yes, SAS

10. Yes, ASA

11. Not congruent (similar)

12. T

13. F

14. T

15. T

16. T

17. $x = 20$"

18.

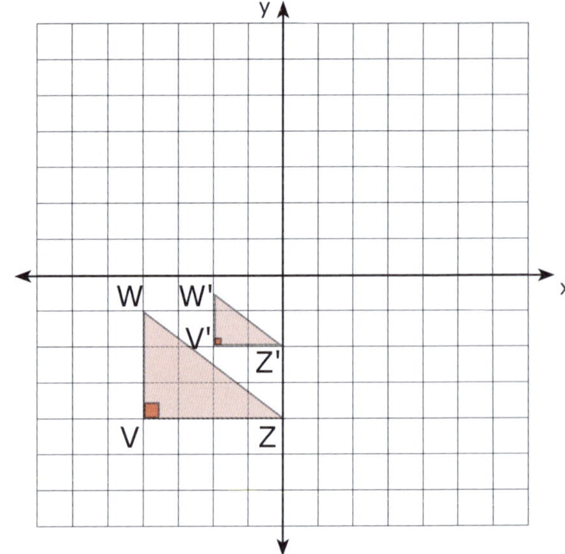

$W'\ (-2, \frac{1}{2}), V'\ (-2, -2), Z'\ (0, -2)$

19. The corresponding sides are in proportion and the corresponding angles are congruent.

20. a. 12 units, 6 units

b. $\frac{1}{2}$

c. 6 units, 1.5 units

d. $\frac{1}{4}$

e. The ratio of their perimeters is the same the ratio of their sides. The ratio of their areas is the square of the ratio of their sides.

Page 305

1. No, the input "–5" has two different outputs. (–5, –7) and (–5, –1).

2. a. {–2, –1, 0, 1, 2}

b. { –4, –3, –2, –1, 0}

3. $f(x) = x - 2$

4. Graph "a" represents a function. Every input (x) has a unique output (y) that corresponds to that input.

   Graph "b" does not meet the vertical test. Every input in graph "b" has multiple outputs.

5. Yes, Thomas is saying, for example, that (−3, 5) and (−3, 4) would not be a function, but (−3, 5) and (−5, 5) would be a function.

Pages 307–308

1. The equation would become linear as the term x^2 would disappear.
2. It would turn the parabola upside down.
3. $f(x) = 2x^2$

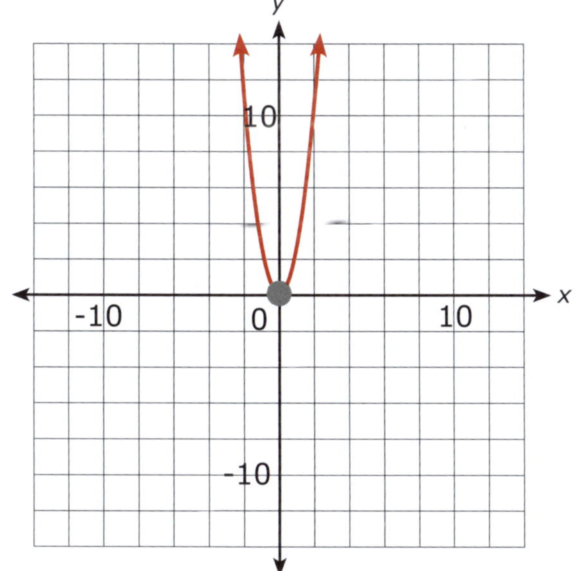

4. $f(x) = \frac{1}{2}x^2$

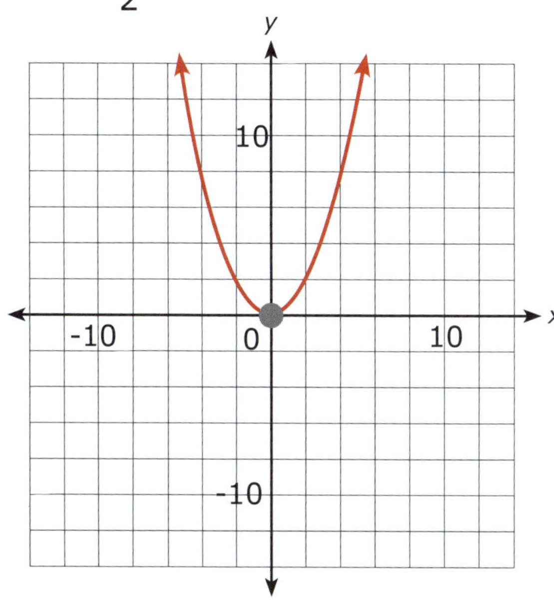

5. Graph 3 rises faster and Graph 4 is wider and growing slower.
6. Graph $f(x) = x^2 + 4$

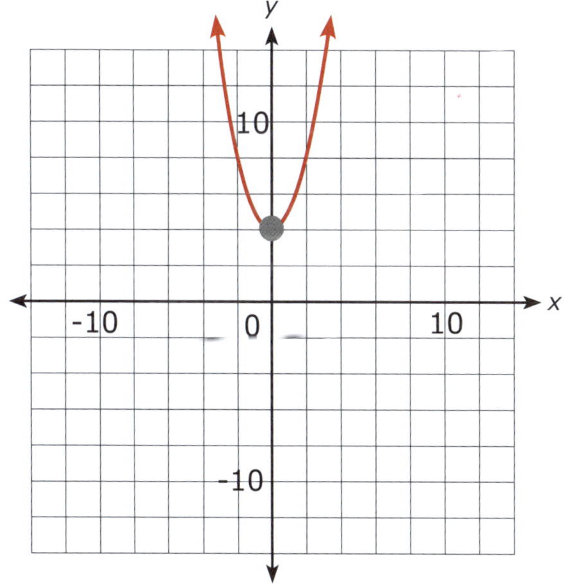

7. Graph $f(x) = x^2 - 4$

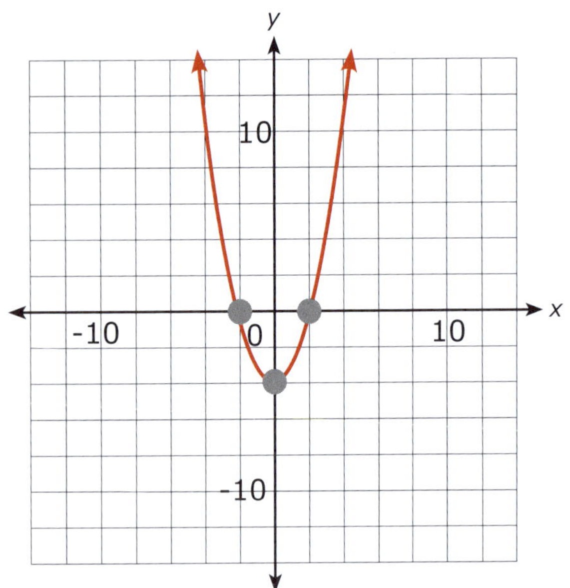

8. It moves the vertex up 4 units in Graph 6. It moves the vertex down 4 units in Graph 7.

9. It does not meet the vertical line test. (–6,1) and (–1, 6) demonstrate that the input –1 has two different outputs.

10. y = 3.5

Pages 310–311

1. a. If $a = 0$, the equation would be $y = 0$.

   b. If $b = 1$, the equation would be y = a constant.

2. c

3. a. Ordered pairs from table:

   $(-3, \frac{1}{27})$; $(-2, \frac{1}{9})$; $(-1, \frac{1}{3})$, (0, 1); (1, 3); (2, 9); (3, 27)

   b. Ordered pairs from table:

   $(-3, \frac{1}{64})$; $(-2, \frac{1}{16})$; $(-1, \frac{1}{4})$; (0, 1); (1, 4); (2, 16); (3, 64)

   c. Ordered pairs from table:

   (–3, 8); (–2, 4); (–1, 2); (0, 1); $(1, \frac{1}{2})$; $(2, \frac{1}{4})$; $(3, \frac{1}{8})$

4.

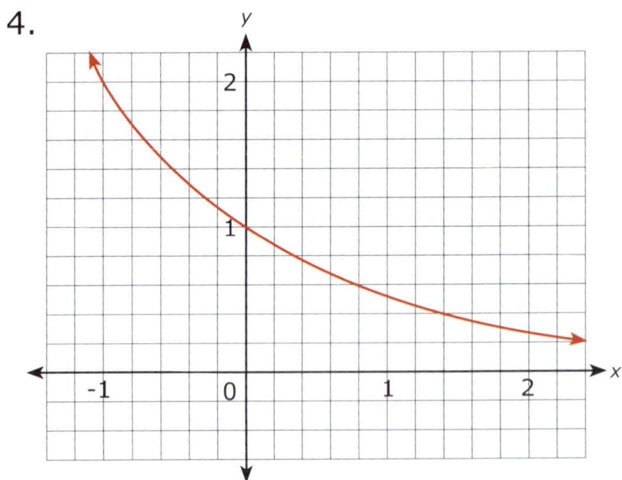

5. a.

Time (Hours)	1	2	3	4	5	6	7
Bacteria	6	12	24	48	96	192	384

   b. Answers may vary.

   $3 \bullet 2^3 = 24$?

   $3 \bullet 8 = 24$? yes

   $3 \bullet 2^5 = 96$?

   $3 \bullet 32 = 96$? yes

   c. $3 \bullet 2^{10}$= bacteria

   $3 \bullet 1{,}024 = 3{,}072$ bacteria

Pages 313–314

1. By adding 1 we are including the previous amount each time and adding interest to that new amount.

2. $500(1+.12)^5$ = $881.17

3. $500(1+.12)^{2.5}$ = $663.77

4. $500(1+.035)^{15}$ = $837.67

5. $43,000(1+.05)^{12}$ = $77,221.82

6. $30,000(1 -.02)^2$ = $28,812

7. $1,800(1 - .5)^{.75}$ = $1,070.29

8. a.

Round 1	Round 2	Round 3	Round 4	Round 5
32	16	8	4	2

b. $64(1 -.5)^5 = 2$

c. 8 rounds (64 • 2 = 128, 128 • 2 = 356, 256 • 2 = 512) or $[512 (1 - .5)^8 = 2]$

Pages 315–317

1. $x = 0$

2. a.

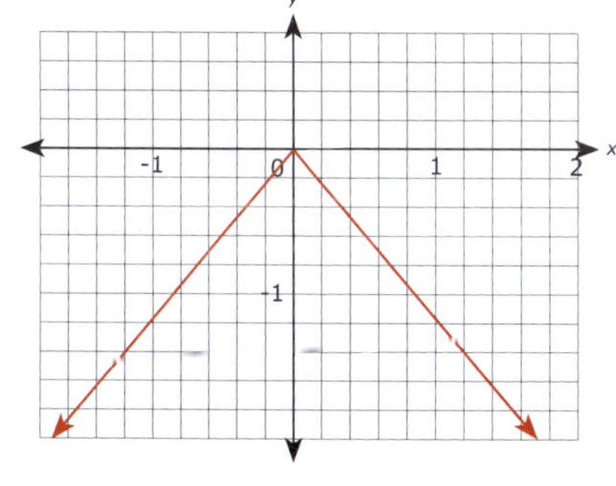

x	y
-4	-4
-3	-3
-2	-2
-1	-1
0	0
1	-1
2	-2
3	-3

b.

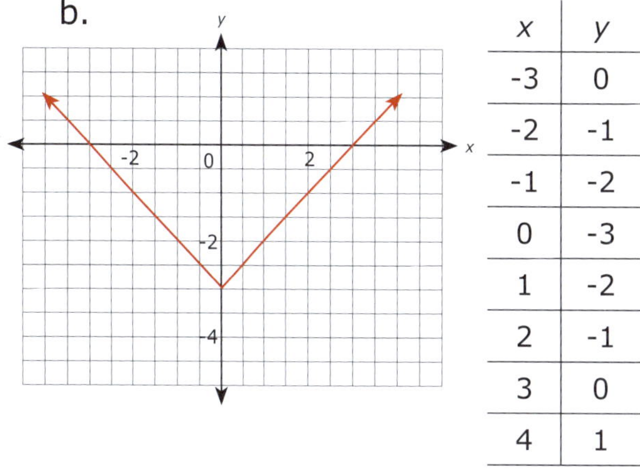

x	y
-3	0
-2	-1
-1	-2
0	-3
1	-2
2	-1
3	0
4	1

c.

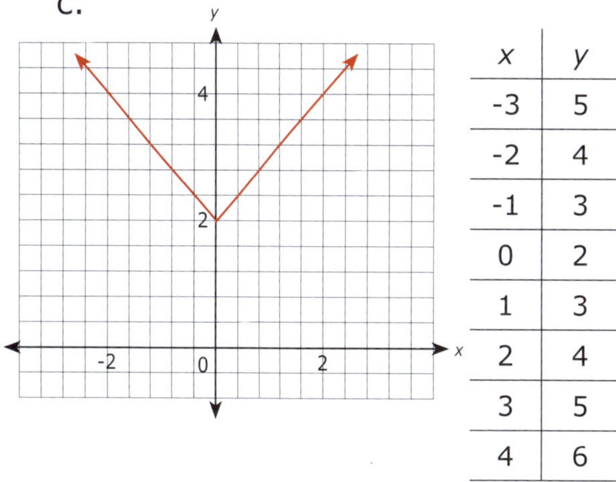

x	y
-3	5
-2	4
-1	3
0	2
1	3
2	4
3	5
4	6

d.

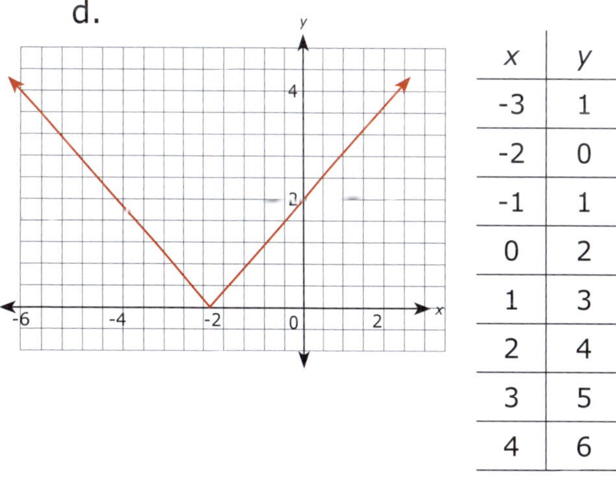

x	y
-3	1
-2	0
-1	1
0	2
1	3
2	4
3	5
4	6

3. It's the reflection over the x-axis of the basic absolute value function $y = |x|$.

4. Graph 2b is 3 units down and a translation of -3 ($T_{0,-3}$) compared the the basic absolute value function.

5. It will be down 20 units from the basic absolute value function.

6.

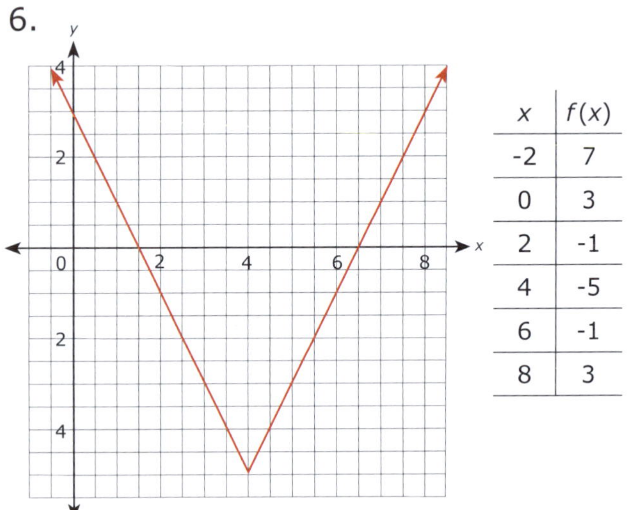

x	$f(x)$
-2	7
0	3
2	-1
4	-5
6	-1
8	3

Pages 319–322 Chapter 14 Review

1. c; The input −4 has two different outputs.

2. a. {−3, −2, −1, 0, 1, 2, 3, 4)

   b. {9, 4, 1, 0, 1, 4, 9, 16}

   c. $y = x^2$ or $f(x) = x^2$

   d. Yes, any real number can be substituted for x.

   e. The range will consist of positive real numbers greater than or equal to 0.

3. It does not meet the vertical test. Example: (0, 3) and (0, −3).

4. d

5. a

6.

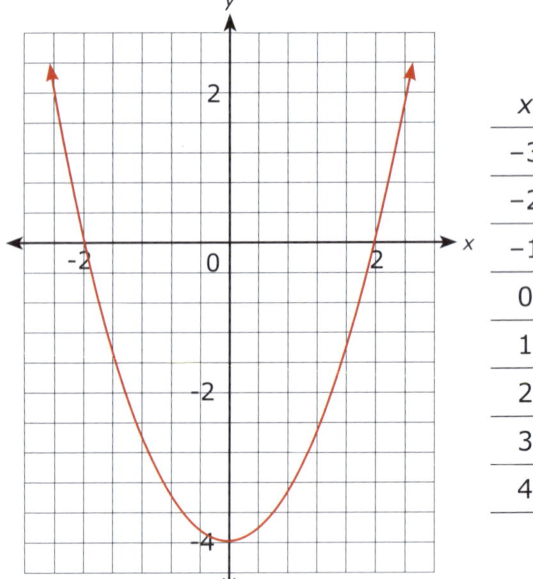

x	$f(x)$
−3	5
−2	0
−1	−3
0	−4
1	−3
2	0
3	5
4	12

7.

x	$f(x)$
−3	1.125
−2	1.25
−1	1.5
0	2
1	3
2	5

8. Ordered pairs from the table:

   $(-2, 9)$; $(-1, 3)$; $(0, 1)$; $(1, \frac{1}{3})$; $(2, \frac{1}{3})$; $(3, \frac{1}{27})$

9. Linear, $y = 5x + 1$

10. Quadratic, $y = 2x^2$

11. Exponential, $y = 3^x$

12. Linear, $y = -3x$

13. Ordered pairs from the table:

    (−3,−1), (−2, −2), (−1, −3), (0,−4), (1,−3), (2, −2), (3, −1).

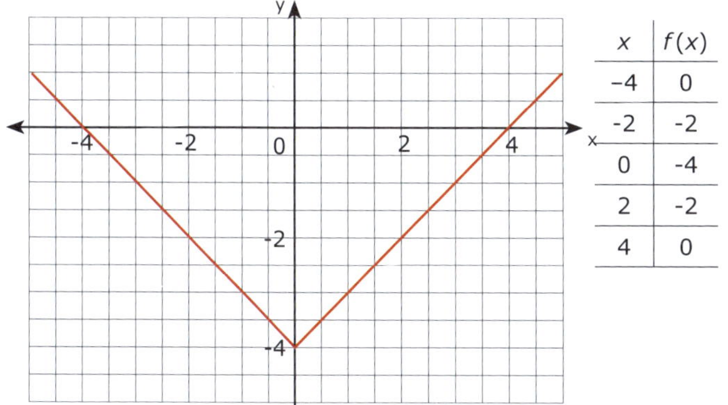

x	$f(x)$
−4	0
-2	-2
0	-4
2	-2
4	0

14. It's a translation 4 units down from the basic absolute value function.

Pages 324–325

1. $\frac{1}{2}$ or 50%

2. $\frac{1}{2}$ or 50%; The probability does not change just because you get tails 3 times.

3. a. $\frac{1}{8}$

   b. $\frac{4}{8}$ or $\frac{1}{2}$

   c. 0; There are no black marbles.

4. $\frac{1}{36}$; You have $\frac{1}{36}$ chances of rolling a 5 first and then a 3.

5. $\frac{6}{36} = \frac{1}{6}$ (1, 1); (2, 2); (3, 3); (4, 4); (5, 5); (6, 6)

6. $\frac{6}{36} = \frac{1}{6}$ sum of 7 (1, 6); (6, 1); (2, 5); (5, 2); (3, 4); (4, 3)

7. 0; There's no possible way of getting a sum of 13.

Pages 326–327

1. a. $\frac{8}{8} = 1$

   b. $\frac{3}{8}$

   c. $\frac{3}{8}$; remember 51 is divisible by 3.

   d. $\frac{6}{8} = \frac{3}{4}$; Evens: 2, 8, 12 or

      Primes: 2, 11, 7, 5 - do not

      count "2" twice.

   e. $\frac{3}{8}$; Multiples of 4: 8, 12.

      Multiples of 5: 5.

   f. $\frac{1}{8}$; Two is the only even prime.

2. a. $\frac{1}{52}$

   b. $\frac{26}{52}$ or $\frac{1}{2}$

   c. $\frac{27}{52}$

   Black: $\frac{26}{52}$ + 3 of diamond: $\frac{1}{52}$

   d. $\frac{28}{52} = \frac{7}{13}$

   Black: $\frac{26}{52} + \frac{2}{52}$

   (Remember the 2 of clubs and 2 of spades have been counted already.)

e. $\frac{2}{52} = \frac{1}{26}$

The 3 of spades and 3 of clubs.

Pages 329–331

1. a. $\frac{30}{90} = \frac{1}{3}$ $(\frac{6}{10} \bullet \frac{5}{9})$

   b. $\frac{18}{90} = \frac{1}{5}$ $(\frac{6}{10} \bullet \frac{3}{9})$

   c. $\frac{18}{72} = \frac{1}{4}$ $(\frac{3}{9} \bullet \frac{6}{8})$

   d. $\frac{5}{12}$

   RR: $\frac{6}{10} \bullet \frac{5}{9} = \frac{30}{90}$

   PP: $\frac{3}{9} \bullet \frac{2}{8} = \frac{6}{72}$

   $\frac{1}{3} + \frac{1}{12} = \frac{5}{12}$

   e. $\frac{7}{12}$ $(1 - \frac{5}{12})$

2. "Same colors" and "different colors" covers the entire sample space so together the probability is 1.

3. Sample Space:

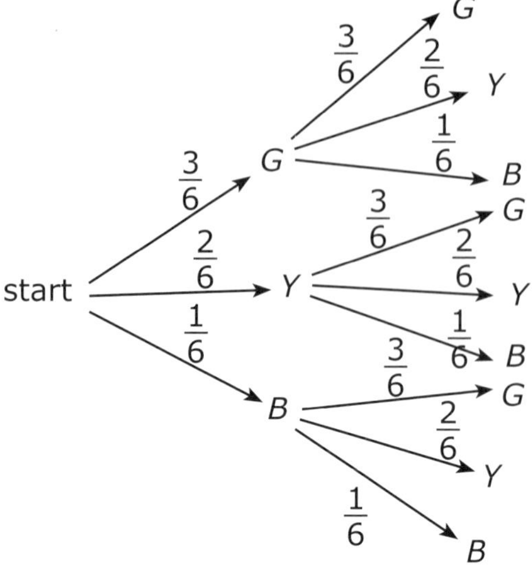

   a. $\frac{6}{36} = \frac{1}{6}$ $(\frac{3}{6} \bullet \frac{2}{6})$

   b. $\frac{3}{36} = \frac{1}{12}$ $(\frac{3}{6} \bullet \frac{1}{6})$

   c. $\frac{14}{36} = \frac{7}{18}$

   GG: $\frac{3}{6} \bullet \frac{3}{6} = \frac{9}{36}$

   YY: $\frac{2}{6} \bullet \frac{2}{6} = \frac{4}{36}$

   BB: $\frac{1}{6} \bullet \frac{1}{6} = \frac{1}{36}$

   d. $\frac{1}{36}$ $(\frac{1}{6} \bullet \frac{1}{6})$

4. Sample space:

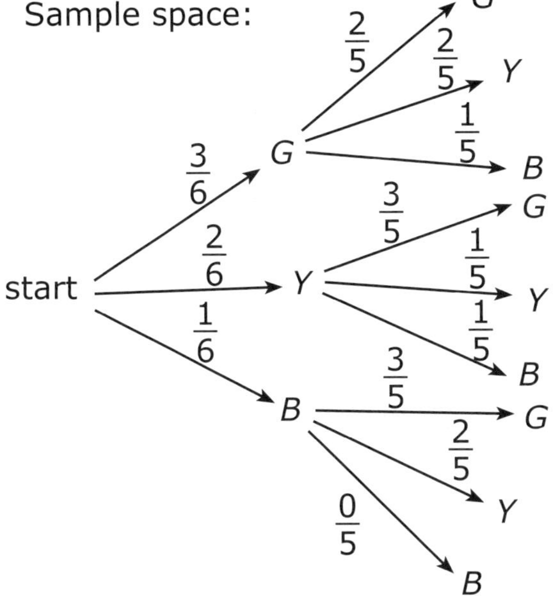

a. $\frac{3}{30} = \frac{1}{10}$ $(\frac{3}{6} \bullet \frac{1}{5})$

b. $\frac{2}{30} = \frac{1}{15}$ $(\frac{2}{6} \bullet \frac{1}{5})$

c. 0

d. $\frac{8}{30} = \frac{4}{15}$

GG: $\frac{3}{6} \bullet \frac{2}{5} = \frac{6}{30}$

YY: $\frac{2}{6} \bullet \frac{1}{5} = \frac{2}{30}$

BB: $\frac{1}{6} \bullet 0 = 0$

5. Sample space:

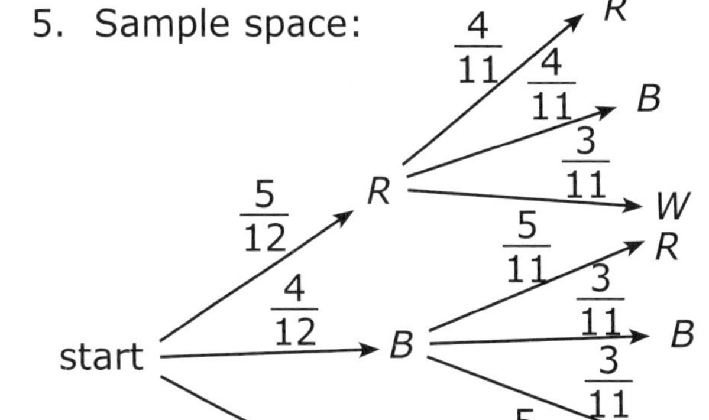

a. $\frac{20}{132} = \frac{5}{33}$ $(\frac{5}{12} \bullet \frac{4}{11})$

b. $\frac{12}{132} = \frac{1}{11}$ $(\frac{4}{12} \bullet \frac{3}{11})$

c. $\frac{6}{132} = \frac{1}{22}$ $(\frac{3}{12} \bullet \frac{2}{11})$

d. $\frac{40}{132} = \frac{10}{33}$

RB: $\frac{5}{12} \bullet \frac{4}{11} = \frac{20}{132}$

BR: $\frac{4}{12} \bullet \frac{5}{11} = \frac{20}{132}$

e. $\frac{94}{132} = \frac{47}{66}$

RB: $\frac{20}{132}$; RW: $\frac{15}{132}$; BR: $\frac{20}{132}$;
BW: $\frac{12}{132}$; WR: $\frac{15}{132}$; WB: $\frac{12}{132}$

6. Subtract the probability of "same color" from 1.

$1 - (RR + BB + WW)$ or

$1 - (\frac{20}{132} + \frac{12}{132} + \frac{6}{132})$,

so $1 - \frac{38}{132} = \frac{94}{132}$.

Pages 333–334

1. a. 12 (3 • 2 • 2)
   b. 6 (3 • 2)
   c. Answers will vary.
2. 24 (4 • 3 • 2 • 1)
3. 120 (5! = 5 • 4 • 3 • 2 • 1)
4. 3,125 (5^5)
5. 60 (5 • 4 • 3)
6. 24 (**2** • 4 • 3) Only two choices to get a number greater than 700.
7. 36 (3 • 4 • **3**) Only three choices for the last digit to be odd.
8. 12 (3 • 4 • **1**) Only one choice for the last digit to create a number divisible by 5.
9. 8 (4 • **2**) Only two choices to create an even number.
10. 16, 18, 56, 58, 68, 76, 78, 86

Pages 335–336

1. Combination 8*C*4 = 70 teams.
2. Permutation 8*P*3 = 336 outcomes.
3. Combination 5*C*2 = 10 logos.
4. 120 (6*P*3 = 6 • 5 • 4)
5. a. 336 (8*P*3)
   b. $\frac{6}{336} = \frac{1}{112}$; Three female positions: 3 • 2 • 1 = 6
6. 6 (4 • 3 ÷ 2) *BE, EB, ES, SE, BS, SB*

Page 337

1. Answers will vary.
2. The probability will approach $\frac{1}{2}$ or 50% the more times you do the experiment.

Pages 339–340

1. The median. The $100,000 salary is much higher when compared to the other salaries, so the mean misrepresented what she's most likely to earn.
2. Mode: none
   Range: $29,500-$100,000
   Range: $70,500
3. Mean: 3; Median: 2; Mode: 2; Range: −1 to 12 or −13 degrees.
4. The mean is more representative of her overall grade.
5. The mode since most students said No.
6. Mean: .569 (In order: 0.03, 0.09, 0.222, 0.88, 0.95, 1.24)

   Median: .551 (.222 + .88) ÷ 2
7. Answers will vary.
8. Answers will vary.
9. 86
   Solve: (88 + 89 + 92 + x + 95) ÷ 5 = 90)

10. 76
    Solve: (70 + 55 + 60 + x + 65 + 70) ÷ 6 = 66)

11. T

12. F

13. T

14. F

Pages 342–343

1. $\frac{1}{3}$

2. Median: 45; Lower quartile: 40; Upper quartile: 60

3. a. 24, 32, 33, 34, 35, 36, 37, 37, 37, 38, 39, 39, 39, 39, 39, 40, 40, 40

   b. 37.5

   c. 35

   d. 39

   e. 87.5%

   f. Q1; She falls in the first quartile.

   g. 36.6 (rounded); 92%

   h. 39

   i. 24

Pages 347–348

1. a. 0, 0, 1, 1, 2, 2, 3, 3, 3, 3, 3, 3, 4, 4, 4, 4, 5, 6, 6, 8

   b. Mean: 3.3; Median: 3; Mode: 3; Range 0-8 or 8

   c.

Interval	Tally	Frequency	Cum. Freq.
0-1	||||	4	4
2-3	~~||||~~ |||	8	12
4-5	~~||||~~	5	17
6-7	||	2	19
8-9	|	1	20

   d.

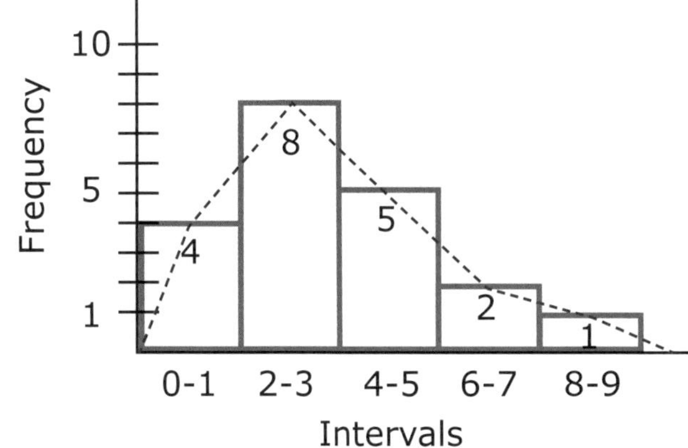

   e.

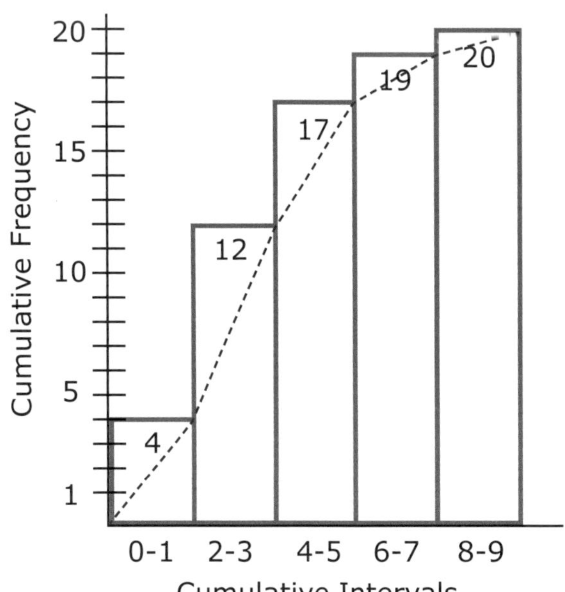

f. The median is in the 2-3 interval. Draw a line from the 50th percentile until it hits the cumulative frequency polygon. You can also look at the data and find the median which is 3.

g. Interval 4-5

2. a. 21, 22, 22, 22, 22, 22, 23, 23, 23, 23, 24, 25, 25, 26, 27, 28, 30, 30, 35, 35, 37, 38, 40, 43

b. Mean: 27.8; Median: 25; Mode: 22; Range 21-43 or 22

c.

Intervals	Tally	Frequency	Cum. Freq.
20-23	卌 卌	10	10
24-27	卌	5	15
28-31	|||	3	18
32-35	||	2	20
36-39	||	2	22
40-43	||	2	24

d.

Frequency of 24 Students' Ages Entering Graduate School

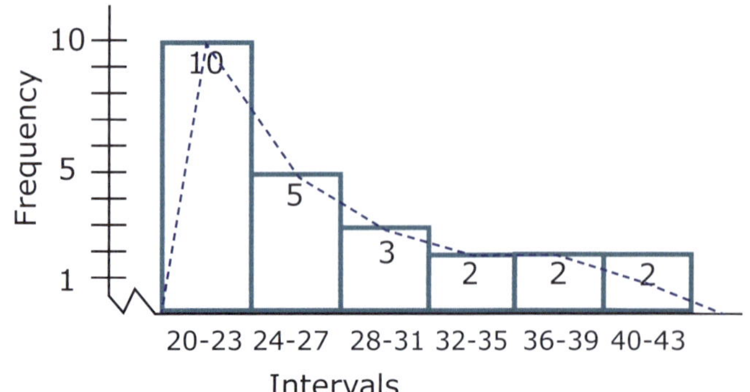

e.

Cumulative Frequency of the Ages of Students Entering Graduate School

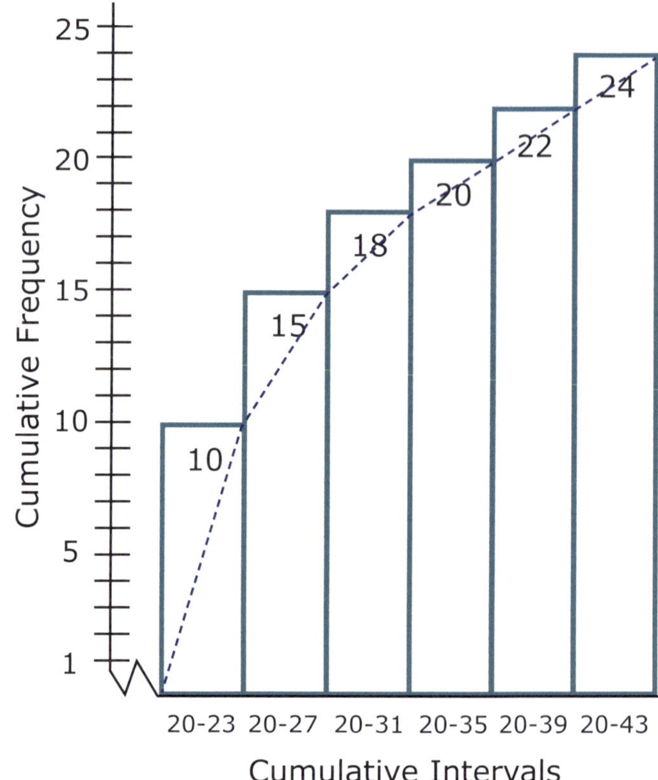

f. The 50th percentile line touches the cumulative frequency polygon at the 20-27 interval, so looking back at the frequency table the median is in the 24-27 interval. The median is 25 which is in the 24-27 interval.

Pages 350–352

1. a. 25

b. 100

c. 78

d. 93

e. 89

f.

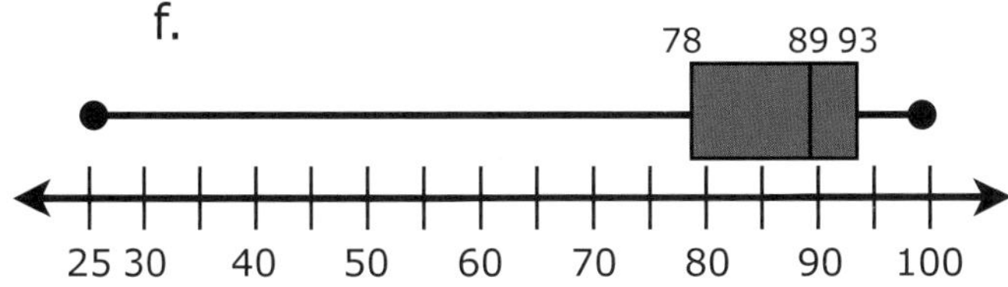

g. Mr. Roberts' class has more students between the 1st and 3rd quartile. Their mean was higher.

h. Ms. Stein's class mean: 79.2, Mr. Roberts' class mean: 82.7

Yes, Mr. Roberts' class has a higher mean despite the low score of 25.

i. The 25 score is an outlier. It's out of the range where most scores are clustered.

2. Ms. Stein's Social Studies Stem and Leaf - Key 4 | 0 = 40

4	0
6	0 0
7	0 0 2 4
8	5 5 5 5
9	0 3 8
10	0 0

3. Mr. Roberts' Social Studies Stem and Leaf - Key 2 | 5 = 25

2	5
6	0
7	0 6
8	0 5 8 8
9	0 0 0 1 5 5
10	0 0

4. The stem and leaf plot shows all the data. However, it doesn't readily give you the median or quartiles as the box and whisker plot. The box and whisker plot also shows you where most of the scores are clustered.

5. a. 50
   b. 100
   c. 70
   d. 85
   e. 80

6. Answers may vary. Example: 50, 55, 68, 72, 80, 80, 82, 83, 85, 90, 100

7. Yes, it is possible. Example: 50, 51, 70, 72, 73, 73, 82, 83, 85, 90, 100

8. No, not possible to create a box and whisker plot. The median would be the same as the 1st and 3rd quartile.

Pages 353–354

1. The vocabulary is too hard for the majority of the people surveyed. "Rhinopharyngitis" is the medical term for the common cold.

2. Most people probably don't remember when they lost their first tooth and not everyone believes in the "tooth fairy!"

3. d

4. It's a leading question making students feel that if they answer "later than 8:30" they're not good students.

5. Better: About how many times last week did you get up before 6 A.M.?

6. Too general. Avoid using the word "always."

7. How many times a week do you eat breakfast? Answers will vary.

Pages 355–358 Chapter 15 Review

1. a. $\frac{1}{4}$ or 25%

   b. 1 or 100% (They are all prime numbers.)

   c. 24 ways (4! or 4 • 3 • 2 • 1)

   d. 12 numbers (**2** • 3 • 2)

2. Sample Space

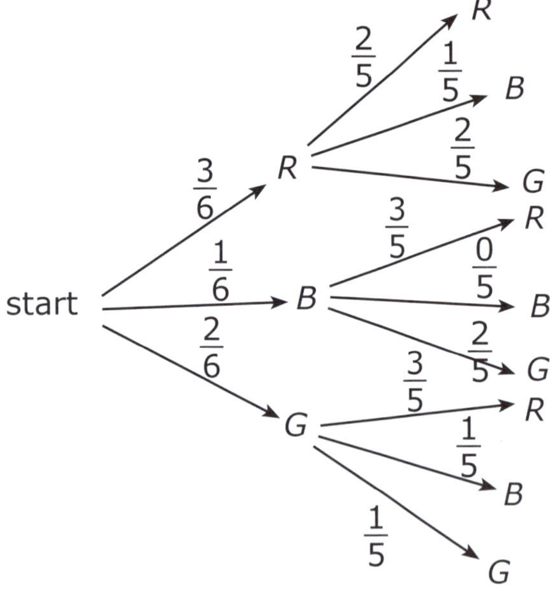

   a. *RR*: $\frac{6}{30}$ or $\frac{1}{5}$

   b. *RB*: $\frac{3}{30}$ or $\frac{1}{10}$

   c. *GR*: $\frac{6}{30}$ or $\frac{1}{5}$

   d. *BB*: 0

3. 720 outcomes (10*P*3)

4. 56 outcomes (8*C*3)

5. 8 ways (4 • 2 • 1)

6. If she finds the mean she may conclude that since the mean is $60,400. However, the median is $48,000.

7. a. Mode: 285

   b. Mean: 211

   c. Median: 230

   d. Range: 130-285 or 155

8. a.

Intervals	Tally	Frequency	Cum. Frequency
0-2	||||	4	4
3-5	~~||||~~ ||	7	11
6-8	|||	3	14
9-11	|||	3	17
12-14	|	1	18
15-17	||	2	20

   b.

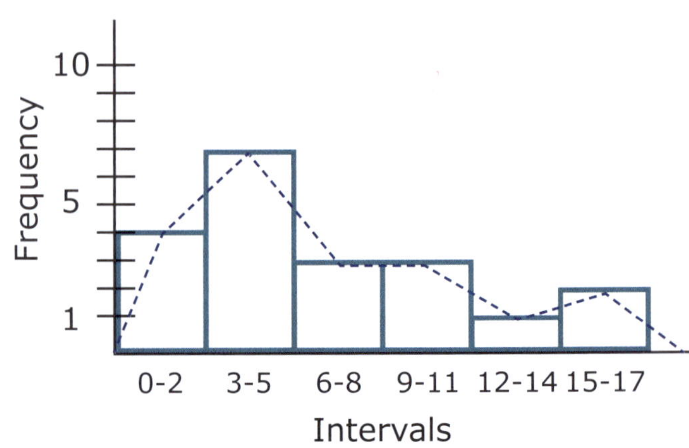

c.

Cumulative Frequency Histogram of Backpack Weights

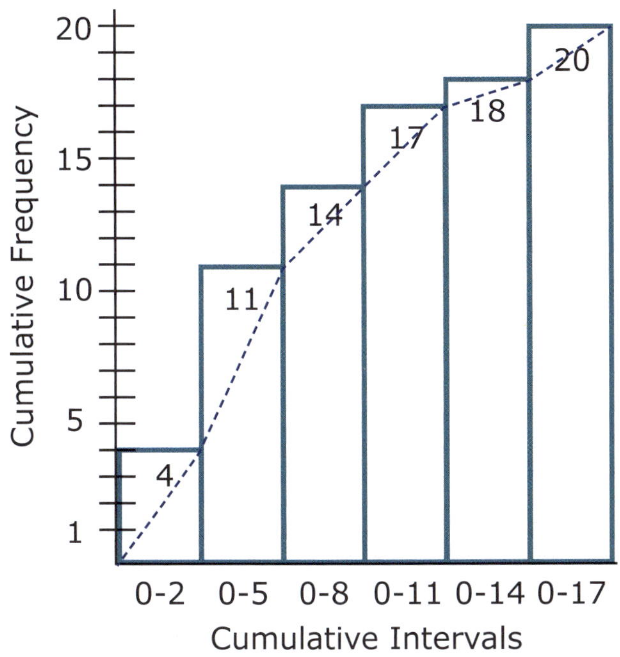

d. 3-5

e. 3-5

f. 9-11

9. a. She is carrying 7.8 lbs over what is recommended. Amy's backback should be at most 5.2 lbs (13-5.2 = 7.8).

b. He should weigh no less than 100 lbs. (10% of 100 = 10)

10. The school nurse only targeted one grade and she/he should have checked the weight of the backpacks of younger students as well as older students.

11. Stem and Leaf - Water Intake (Ounces) - Key 5|5 mean 55

Stem	Leaf
3	2
5	5 6
6	4
7	0 0 2
8	0 0 2 8 9
9	2 5
10	
11	
12	
13	0 5

12. a. Lower extreme: 32

b. First quartile: 67

c. Median: 80

d. Third quartile: 90.5

e. Upper extreme: 135

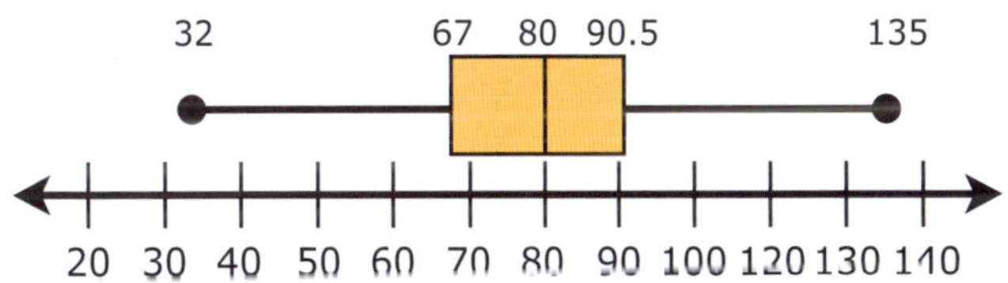

f. No, John should not have limited his survey to only athletes. Some athletes tend to hydrate more than the general population.

Pages 359–367 Final Examination

Part I (2 points each)

1. c	11. b	21. d	31. c	41. c	51. b	61. c
2. d	12. a	22. a	32. d	42. b	52. c	62. a
3. a	13. a	23. b	33. a	43. a	53. c	63. d
4. a	14. d	24. a	34. d	44. a	54. a	64. c
5. c	15. c	25. c	35. b	45. b	55. d	65. d
6. b	16. a	26. c	36. b	46. c	56. b	
7. d	17. d	27. b	37. d	47. d	57. a	
8. a	18. d	28. c	38. b	48. d	58. b	
9. c	19. b	29. a	39. d	49. a	59. c	
10. c	20. c	30. a	40. a	50. b	60. d	

Part II (5 points each)

1. $-3(w - 1) + 5 = 2(w + 5)$

$-3w + 3 + 5 = 2w + 10$ (1 pt)

$-3w + 8 = 2w + 10$ (1 pt)

$-5w + 8 = 10$ (1 pt)

$-5w = 2$ (1 pt)

$w = -\frac{2}{5}$ or $-.40$ (1 pt)

3.

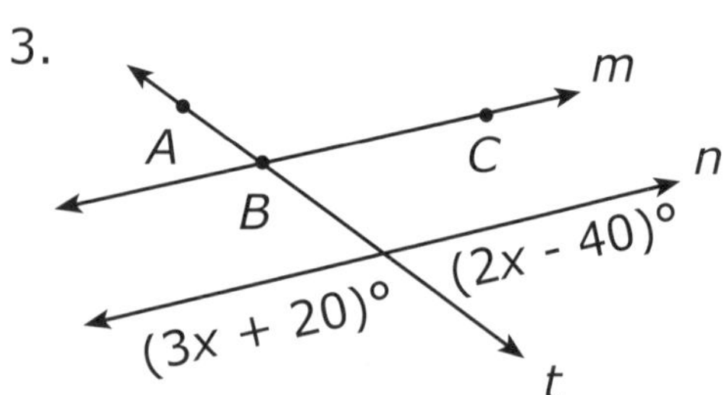

$3x + 20 + 2x - 40 = 180$ (2 pts)

$5x - 20 = 180$

$5x = 200$

$x = 40$ (1 pt)

$\angle ABC$ is the same as $(3x + 20)$

$3(40) + 20 = 140°$ (2 pt)

3.

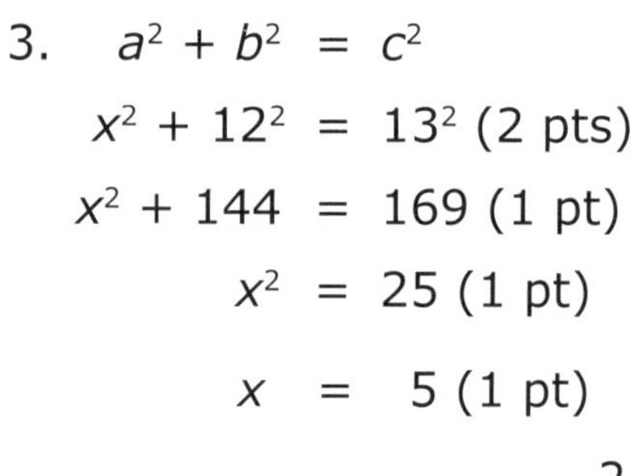

$a^2 + b^2 = c^2$

$x^2 + 12^2 = 13^2$ (2 pts)

$x^2 + 144 = 169$ (1 pt)

$x^2 = 25$ (1 pt)

$x = 5$ (1 pt)

4.

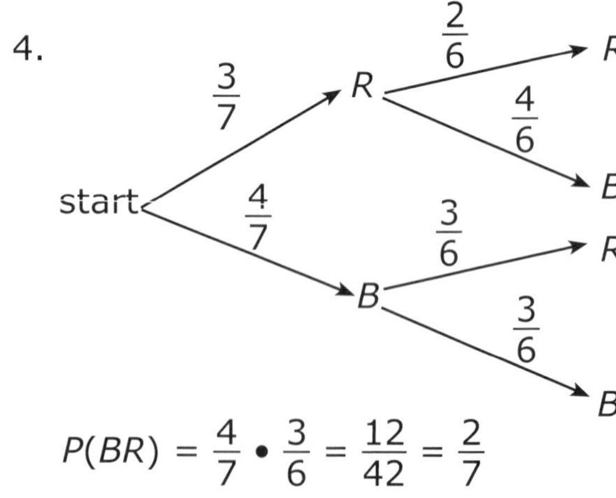

$P(BR) = \frac{4}{7} \bullet \frac{3}{6} = \frac{12}{42} = \frac{2}{7}$